Poetry as a Way of Life

Poetry as a Way of Life

Aesthetics and Askesis in the German Eighteenth Century

Gabriel Trop

NORTHWESTERN UNIVERSITY PRESS
EVANSTON, ILLINOIS

Northwestern University Press
www.nupress.northwestern.edu

Printed in the United States of America

ISBN 978-0-8101-3436-2

The Library of Congress has cataloged the original, hardcover edition as follows:

Trop, Gabriel, author.
Poetry as a way of life : aesthetics and askesis in the German eighteenth century / Gabriel Trop.
pages cm
Includes bibliographical references and index.
ISBN 978-0-8101-3009-8 (cloth : alk. paper) — ISBN 978-0-8101-6792-6 (ebook)
1. German poetry—18th century—History and criticism. 2. Aesthetics in literature. 3. Germany—Intellectual life—18th century. I. Title.
PT535.T67 2014
831.609—dc23

2014038244

In memory of Kim Brigati Wang

CONTENTS

ACKNOWLEDGMENTS

This book would not have been written were it not for the dedication of the friends, colleagues, family members, and mentors who guided me, helped me, and inspired me over the years. This book took shape largely through formative encounters with my dissertation advisor, Winfried Kudszus, with whom I had the pleasure of sharing many moving and intense intellectual exchanges. I also owe a debt of gratitude to the entire faculty and larger community in the Department of German at the University of California, Berkeley, during my time there as a graduate student.

I also would like to thank my colleagues, both the faculty and the graduate students, at the University of North Carolina at Chapel Hill and Duke University, without whose support and intellectual stimulation this book would not exist in its current form. I also have been the beneficiary of generous financial and institutional support from UC Berkeley, UNC-Chapel Hill, the Eberhard Karls University of Tübingen, the Humboldt University in Berlin, and the DAAD. I especially would like to thank the University Research Council for its generous financial assistance. I developed many of the ideas in this book while participating in the Ph.D. Net "Literatur des Wissens" at the Humboldt Graduate School, an experience made possible by a DAAD grant. My understanding of Hölderlin in particular benefited greatly from the graciousness and expertise of the staff at the Hölderlin-Archiv in Stuttgart.

I particularly would like to thank the following friends, colleagues, and mentors, each of whom contributed in different ways to this book: Frauke Berndt, Jeremy Brett, Eric Downing, Jocelyn Holland, Tony Kaes, Leslie Kurke, Niklaus Largier, Richard Langston, Sebastian Meixner, Alexandra Niskios, Thomas Pfau, Irmengard Rauch, Kaja Silverman, Elaine Tennant, Joseph Vogl, and W. Daniel Wilson. I give my deepest thanks to the entire editorial staff at Northwestern University Press, above all to Henry Carrigan and Nathan MacBrien. Special thanks also go to the anonymous readers whose invaluable input greatly aided me in the revision of the original manuscript.

I would also like to thank Professor Kenneth Weisinger, whom I never had the fortune of knowing personally, but who generously left the bulk of his library to a graduate student at Berkeley working on eighteenth-century German literature. I feel fortunate and grateful that I happened to be that graduate student, and I hope that this book honors his memory.

A portion of chapter 2 was previously published in the *Interdisciplinary Journal for Germanic Linguistics and Semiotic Analysis* 14, no. 1 (Spring

2009): 55–83, and I thank Irmengard Rauch for permission to present that material here in slightly revised form. I also, since writing this book, have expanded and developed the concept of aesthetic askesis in *Das achtzehnte Jahrhundert* 37, no. 1 (Summer 2013): 56–73, and I have explored in greater detail Hölderlin's modal poetics, which I briefly touch upon here in chapter 3 and the conclusion to part 1, in *MLN* 128, no. 3 (April 2013): 580–610.

The members of my family—my mother and stepfather, my father and my stepmother, and my grandparents—are such a part of my identity that I am unable to distinguish what comes from them and what comes from myself. I thank them for their support and their encouragement throughout the years. And finally, I thank my wife, Sonja Bertucci, whose presence, personality, intelligence, and passion have been a constant source of wonder and inspiration.

ABBREVIATIONS AND TRANSLATIONS

AA	Immanuel Kant, *Kant's gesammelte Schriften*, ed. Königlich Preussische Akademie der Wissenschaften (Berlin: de Gruyter, 1922–).
AGB	Alexander Baumgarten, *Handschrift der Ästhetik*, in *Alexander Gottlieb Baumgarten*, ed. Bernhard Poppe (Leipzig: Robert Noske, 1908).
BA	Alexander Baumgarten, *Ästhetik*, trans. Dagmar Mirbach (Hamburg: Meiner, 2007).
CD	Johann Jakob Breitinger, *Critische Dichtkunst: Schriften zur Literatur*, ed. Volker Meid (Stuttgart: Reclam, 1980).
FA	Friedrich Hölderlin, *Sämtliche Werke*, 20 vols., ed. D. E. Sattler (Frankfurt am Main: Stroemfeld, 1975–2006).
GMA	Johann Wolfgang von Goethe, *Sämtliche Werke nach Epochen seines Schaffens: Münchner Ausgabe*, 21 vols., ed. Karl Richter et al. (Munich: Hanser, 1985–98).
GS	Georg Friedrich Meier, *Gedancken von Schertzen* (Halle: Carl Hermann Hemmerde, 1754).
KSA	Friedrich Schlegel, *Kritische Friedrich-Schlegel-Ausgabe*, 28 vols. to date, ed. Ernst Behler et al. (Paderborn: Schöningh, 1958–).
MA	Friedrich Hölderlin, *Sämtliche Werke und Briefe*, Münchner Ausgabe, 3 vols., ed. Michael Knaupp (Munich: Hanser 1992).
NA	Friedrich Schiller, *Schillers Werke: Nationalausgabe*, 41 vols. to date, ed. Julius Petersen et al. (Weimar: Hermann Böhlaus Nachfolger, 1943–).
NS	Novalis [Friedrich von Hardenberg], *Novalis Schriften: Historisch-kritische Ausgabe in vier Bänden, einem Materialienband und einem Ergänzungsband in Vier Teilbänden*, 6.2 vols., ed. Richard Samuel, Hans-Joachim Mähl, and Gerhard Schulz et al. (Stuttgart: Kohlhammer, 1960–).
PF	Friedrich Hölderlin, *Poems and Fragments*, trans. Michael Hamburger (London: Anvil, 2004).
SL	Johann Wilhelm Ludwig Gleim, *Versuch in Scherzhaften Liedern und Lieder*, ed. Alfred Anger (Tübingen: Niemeyer, 1964).
VCD	Johann Christoph Gottsched, *Versuch einer critischen Dichtkunst*, vols. 6.1 and 6.2 of *Ausgewahlte Werke*, ed. Joachim Birke and Brigitte Birke (Berlin: de Gruyter, 1973).

A note on translations: All translations of foreign material are my own, unless otherwise noted or cited. I have reproduced the German in most cases where the original text is either linguistically obscure or not able to be easily located in libraries or online; otherwise, I have defaulted to English translations out of concern for space and consideration for a more general readership.

Poetry as a Way of Life

Introduction

✦

Attraction and Critique

There are words that, when spoken, simply fall from the lips, dying almost as soon as they are born. Perhaps registered and acknowledged by others in the world at the moment of their enunciation, they cause a minor vibration, a temporary provocation, a small but significant excitement of the mind or movement between souls, and then they are gone, having already passed into the inaudible and imperceptible totality of irretrievable worlds. No extended or tangible trace remains that they ever entered the space of the living.

And then there are words that, when spoken or written, they remain, they become extended things that permeate our most intensive and personal spaces, they curl about the mind, drawing thought into their magnetic sphere of influence. The force of these words will remain at least as long as the mind keeps coming back to them, if not longer through the works and deeds into whose essential fabric they might one day be woven. These words too one day might die, but for a certain amount of time, they have an extensive and intensive property that, for whatever reason, has endowed them with duration, expansion, and power. Such words, even when physically absent, enter into reality vicariously, through a thought, an impulse, a spontaneous or subterranean pattern of the body, the mind, the person.

Words do not exercise a monopoly over this power of infiltration, which may travel along any sensuous channel in any medium, but it is chiefly to words, and more specifically to those words that seem to be endowed with this magical property of attraction—a power that compels the mind to return to them and relate itself to them—to which this work owes its existence. Perhaps not all such instances of language may be called poetic, but without the impulse to continually return and relate to these words, to absorb them into patterns of existence and thereby to confer upon them a limited form of duration, there can be no poetry.

The subject of the following study approaches poetic texts from the following perspective: what would it mean to make a work of art the focal point of one's practices of life, what forms of perception would such a movement provoke, what patterns of thought and behavior would it imply, what sort of deviation from one's own tendencies would it entail, and what sort of value, if any at all, would such an exercise hold for the person who undertakes it? The question is intended as an experiment in thought and language, an attempt to generate the imaginative play of points of contact and divergence across permeable boundaries between self and work, to erode and perhaps reposition these boundaries. Such a critical practice seeks to increase the intensity of aesthetic experience, to unlock the magnetic potential of the work of art, to transform everything in it, around it, touched by it, into an *attraction*, to make our mind continually revisit it, question it, and be filled by it.

Such a perspective understands art not as an object of investigation whose essence might one day be found, nor as a set of formal properties or generic qualities that one day might be defined, but rather, as a way of life endowed with its own patterns and tendencies, rewards and risks, ecstasies and anxieties. This critical activity understands the engagement with art as a form of *askesis*, which in its more archaic sense denotes simply a form of exercise that continually modifies, often imperceptibly, the manifold patterns of being—whether they are perceptual, behavioral, or affective—of the person who undertakes it.

The conception of art as an exercise for the self, one that sets in motion a system of interaction between aesthetic praxis, cognitive performance, and social activity, may be found as early as in antiquity, for example, in the Hellenistic rhetorical manuals known as the *Progymnasmata*. In the eighteenth century, artists and theorists reaffirmed their interest in the exercise value of art by showing how aesthetic activity actively trains perception. In Gottsched's *Critical Poetics* (*Versuch einer critischen Dichtkunst*, 1730), for example, the aesthetic ideal of imitation does not merely presuppose the order of the external world as the main source of its legitimacy—as if the point were simply to reproduce poetic forms for the sake of pleasure, verisimilitude, or beauty—but rather, the mimetic act feeds back into the development of perceptual capabilities:

> Whoever wants to copy a sketch that lies before one's eyes must pay exact attention to all straight and crooked lines, relationships, sizes, positions, distances, emphases, shadings and strokes, indeed to the most tiny points. Through such exercise and effort one achieves a high degree of attentiveness to every thing that appears. (*VCD* 153)

The aesthetic subject, in the act of giving form and plasticity to the world, simultaneously molds its own perceptual capacities: the ability to judge distance, relation, and nuance, to move from a macroscopic picture of the world to a microscopic focus on the smallest of possible perceptual points. What begins as *mimesis*, or the drive to imitate the world—Gottsched uses the term *nachmalen*—culminates in a form of perceptual and cognitive *askesis*.

The conjunction between imitation and the exercise of cognition, a discursive phenomenon whose outlines become clearer in the early eighteenth century, nevertheless leads us to posit a bolder hypothesis, namely that within the Western tradition of art as a whole, beginning from its earliest manifestations in antiquity, one may uncover a latent and operative ascetic content that runs through poetic creation as a subtle but persistent thread. If this hypothesis—whose verification lies far beyond the scope of the present work—were in fact to yield critical insights, it would necessitate rethinking one of the central organizing terms of Western art, namely *mimesis*, in order to construct in its place a history of aesthetic *askesis*.

To a certain extent, to practice art as a vocation, as a craft requiring a set of skills and a certain *technē*, necessarily presupposes exercises that generate a specific way of being in the world. To become an artist—to bring some tangible thing into the world that previously did not exist and to make it a potential point of attraction for others, drawing others' attention to it and allowing them to respond, either to reject it or to embrace it—represents the most direct path into the life of art, into life as art.

At the same time, there are other pathways into art as a way of life, roads that may be taken not by those who produce tangible objects, but by those who have dedicated their lives to the preservation of art, or rather, to the maintenance and intensification of art's sway over the life of the imagination. From this perspective, criticism depends upon the increase of the attraction potential of works of art. Its goal is not to generate knowledge about the work—or not *only* to generate knowledge—but to tangibly and intensively increase its pull over the mind and body.

Such a goal does not seem to require anything methodologically revolutionary. This particular study—which investigates poetry's effect on ways of perceiving the world and associating ideas, words, forms, and affects—draws upon the traditional gestures that have ingrained themselves in the practice of criticism. Linguistic analysis, historical contextualization, speculative intertextuality—no technique is off limits in the attempt to recast the work of art as an entity that can draw sentience into its orbit, interacting with, perturbing, reconfiguring, or otherwise exerting its influence over patterns of action and experience.

However, a critic who has set for himself or herself the goal of making the work of art into such an exercise for thought walks a fine line between the poles of validity and intensity. One may understand intensity as the phenomenological measure of an affective engagement with the work that increases interest in the work. The philosopher Edmund Husserl defines interest as a power "that encourages our capacity to notice" (eine *das Bemerken fördernde Kraft*).[1] For Husserl, interest presupposes something out of the ordinary, indeed something extra-ordinary, whose novelty in turn generates stimulation: "The stimulation of novelty consists in a heightening of intensity [*Intensitätssteigerung*] that gives a stronger weight of interest to the intention relating to this stimulus."[2] The maintenance of intensity produces a continual process of *renewal* through which an object retains its hold over interest.

Interest, in turn, presupposes and maintains an attraction to the object, and it is in this sense of serving interest as something that "encourages our capacity to notice" that I refer to intensity and attraction as the goal of criticism.

The two spheres of intensity and validity—or that which increases an attraction to the work on the one hand, and that which draws us to formulate opinions about the work that will be recognized by an intersubjective interpretive community on the other—do not always harmonize.[3] The irreducible difference between these two spheres, far from being parasitic to the critical enterprise, in fact constitutes the condition of possibility of criticism as such. Seen from the perspective of increasing the exercise-intensity of the work of art, the worst possible outcome of the critic's investigation would consist in universal assent. Perfect consensus would hasten the death of the work's attraction. If everything has already been said about Goethe's *Faust*, why write about it, why make it into a continual object for thought and critical activity? And yet, we return again and again to the work. It is not necessarily because we want to *know* more about it (although such knowledge is undoubtedly important), but because we believe in its ability to continually open new vistas for experience, affect, and action. And when we do want to know more about a work, this is often because knowledge itself can function as a stimulus, as a force that draws us into the work's domain. In certain cases, one must adopt a conscious strategy of provocation—one that challenges the hegemony of the claims of knowledge over the work of art's power—in order to restore to the work of art its ability to attract.

The second worst possible outcome for the critic, however, would consist in universal dismissal and ridicule. To provoke overwhelming repulsion or remain utterly incomprehensible to others would seem to contribute little—at least in one's activity as a critic—to the work of art's ability to graft itself onto mental and bodily practices or become a focal point for patterns and styles of life.

This form of absorption—a state that holds pre-reflective, embodied action and critical reflection in tension—understands the artwork as an aesthetic exercise. To call the work of art an exercise does not intend to denigrate it or reduce it to a mere function in the optimization of an organism's self-regulation. The aesthetic exercise, unlike other forms of training or subject formation, oscillates between activity and passivity, operating in a space that is paradoxically saturated both by discipline and openness. It is an exercise that may or may not make individuals morally better, it may or may not make them more attuned to the world around them, and what precisely this exercise achieves depends upon how the critic—or the critical individual—approaches the phenomenon. To view art as an exercise of life coheres with Pierre Macherey's insistence that criticism align itself with "what can be said of the work" rather than illustrate "what the work is saying."[4]

The aesthetic exercise must therefore be strictly differentiated from an exercise that aims only at optimization and functionalization. Peter Sloterdijk formulates such a conception of exercise as follows: "I define as an exercise every operation through which the qualification of the agent is maintained or improved for the following execution of the same operation, whether it is declared as an exercise or not."[5] For Sloterdijk, exercise constitutes a critical element in the maintenance of the organism, in its optimization, in its ability to secure itself from the threats of its surroundings and in its expansive power over its environment. Exercise serves a primarily immunological function.

The aesthetic exercise, however, does not necessarily fit into such a schema. As the maintenance of an attraction, it does not have to be integrated into any economy of productivity or immunological functionality as such, neither for the organism nor for the world. To construe the work of art as an exercise in the optimization of an organism channels the energy unleashed by the work into a system of self-preservation, into a network of repeated and increasingly efficient actions, reducing the chances that the work will provoke in this organism a thought, a state, or an affect of unexpected novelty.

The reduction of exercise solely to optimization appears particularly problematic in the domain of art, above all because art often ends in questions rather than in imperatives. The difficulties involved in making a work of art speak as an étude or as mere disciplinary training become clear in Sloterdijk's attempt to see all exercise as "anthropotechnical" streamlining, thereby prioritizing the immunological system before all other competing frameworks. According to Sloterdijk's reading of Rilke's poem "Archaic Torso of Apollo," the poetic act lays bare the power of authority as such: the final imperative—"You must change your life"—stands in for "the absolute imperative—the metanoetic command as such,"[6] ultimately compelling its viewer to direct himself toward a hyperathleticized masculine ideal. Seen from the perspective of a properly aesthetic exercise, Sloterdijk does in fact correctly draw attention to the inner dynamic of Rilke's lines as an attraction to authority. However, the poem frames authority not as a solution to an inner deficiency in the viewer of the statue of Apollo or in the reader of the poem nor as an injunction to a specific way of being or form of training, but rather, as a *problem* for poetic consciousness.

The fact that Rilke's poem may function as an aesthetic exercise emerges precisely from the convergence of the question of discipline with the indeterminacy and openness of poetic form. If Rilke's archaic torso tells you, "You must change your life," it does not tell you *how* or *why*. The formal structure of the poem itself provokes the dispersal of authority into a series of questions rather than demanding acquiescence to the command. Indeed, the poem itself specifies neither the identity of the "you," nor of the voice that commands, and hence, cannot truly *interpellate*: is it the poet addressing the reader or perhaps even himself, is the torso addressing the poet, is the torso addressing the reader—or is perhaps the god, whose "unheard-of head" we do not know, addressing the poet or the reader? Moreover, the authority *of* the poem differentiates itself from the authority of the statue *in* the poem: does the authority of the command derive from the power of the torso or from the poem's own linguistic utterance?

Unlike the power of the statue itself, whose authority originates from its dispersed gaze, the poetic utterance loses its attractive force if it specifies anything about itself other than the basic form of the command. Indeed, it must turn upon the source of its own authority and fail to designate precisely what "you" must do; it must refuse to localize the origin of the command and remain held in a space between the absence of the object and the presence of the word. The command is so formal and empty that, in its generalizability, it misfires as a command, since no criteria could possibly be found to decide whether or not one has fulfilled it. Neither the statue nor the poem says: "you must become better," nor "you must become optimal," and certainly not, "you must become like me (whoever this 'me' happens to be): the god, the poet, or the fragmented masculine body that nevertheless lays claim to a totalizing power." Unlike the statue itself, the poem reveals authority to originate not from some invisible or dispersed panoptical power—"For there is no spot,/That does not see you"—but precisely from the poem's second-order interrogation of this visibility, in the *difference* opened up between language and stone, poetic act and visual stimulus—or for Rilke, the gap that opens up between word and thing. Depending on one's point of view, the command given by the statue might or might not be identical to the command given by the poem. The fundamental indeterminacy surrounding the origin of the command banishes its authority into a state of limbo.

The aesthetic exercise can therefore lead precisely not to optimization, but to a breakdown or crisis in intelligibility and in orientation, to a situation in which optimization appears impossible and desired pathways retreat into obscurity. If there were a work of art associated with breakdown in a system, if it were to attract the mind to *failure*, if it were to see in this failure not a deviation from the goal, but the very challenge and calling of the human being, would one exclude this work from the sphere of those who exercise? Hölderlin's poetry stands as a testament to the possibility of collapse as a world for the mind, to the *importance* of failure as an attraction for thought, an organization of sound and text that short-circuits the attempt to fashion the human being as an organism who exercises only for maintenance and optimization. Rather, the exercise value of a work permits it to become an inextricable part of one's identity, or on the contrary, to disrupt the self-sufficiency of one's identity, to occasion a brief respite from the ceaseless claims of self and community. Foucault, in *The Uses of Pleasure*, hints at this notion of askesis as perturbation when he discusses what motivates him in his critical and intellectual endeavors: "As for what motivated me, it is quite simple; I would hope that in the eyes of some people it might be sufficient in itself. It was curiosity—the only kind of curiosity, in any case, that is worth acting upon with a degree of obstinacy: not the curiosity that seeks to assimilate what it is proper for one to know, but that which enables one to get free of oneself."[7]

The concept of the aesthetic exercise refers to that process by which a sensually oriented activity in the world attempts to form, influence, perturb, or otherwise generate patterns of thought, perception, and action. The exercise therefore shares much in common with Bourdieu's habitus and its logic has, to a certain extent, already been explored from the perspective of theories of social and linguistic performativity. According to Judith Butler, "The social life of the body is produced through an interpellation that is at once linguistic and productive. The way in which that interpellative call continues to call, to take form in a bodily stylistics that, in turn, performs its own social magic constitutes the tacit and corporeal operation of performativity."[8]

While practices of reading, thinking, and imagining are inextricably bound up with the realm of the social, there remains an irreducibly *non-iterative* component to the aesthetic exercise inasmuch as the imagination is continually exploring a new landscape or returning to an old landscape with new eyes. The practice of the mind-body action implied in the aesthetic exercise, while conditioned by social practices, cannot be used, for example, to simply produce a subject. As such, aesthetic askesis differentiates itself from social performativity or "self-fashioning," which orients itself toward normative codes of selfhood rather than toward the sensuous apparatus as that which generates irreducibly idiosyncratic patterns of being.[9] As Foucault suggests, askesis may also free a subject from a given habitus rather than insert a subject into a pre-formed mold. Thinkers in the eighteenth century—for example, Baumgarten in his *Aesthetica*—draw attention to how reading technologies associated with art may introduce novelty on the microscopic level in acts of perception or sensuous cognition. Aesthetic askesis, as the stimulation of a way of being, creates and practices patterns in the mind-body nexus and in the perceptual imagination. It provokes acts that seek to bind and unbind the world of phenomena, that rehearse memory and hone prognostication, make present that which is absent and foreground absence in that which is present, create coherence out of contingent events, or make contingent a chain of events that otherwise appears necessary.

The aesthetic exercise therefore refers not solely to bodily activity, but to a way of being, a way of coping within, reacting to, and acting upon the world, a way of expressing a "view" on the world through action—in short, a concept more akin to the Greek conception of askesis. Foucault, influenced by Pierre Hadot's analysis of spiritual exercises, draws attention to the way in which ancient practices aimed to produce certain patterns of thought and action. Through the examination of alternative ways of being—and more specifically the sexual practices of ancient Greece and Rome—Foucault seeks to rethink and intensify counter-practices to those of his own historical-cultural moment, understanding philosophy as an exercise of the self:

> The "essay"—which should be understood as the assay or test by which, in the game of truth, one undergoes changes, and not as the simplistic appropriation of others for the purpose of communication—is the living substance of philosophy, at least if we assume that philosophy is still what it was in times past, i.e., an "ascesis," *askēsis*, an exercise of oneself in the activity of thought.[10]

According to Foucault, philosophy may open or suggest alternative practices for the self through the activity of *thought*. The specific movements of thought associated with philosophy as a discipline do not, however, exert a monopoly over the exercise of the self. Other forms of receptivity irreducible to the operations of reflective thought or critical examination may in their own way contribute to practices of selfhood.

This particular study focuses on aesthetic exercises. The aesthetic exercise fuses two conceptual spheres: ἄσκησις and αἴσθησις, exercise and sense perception. Exercises that function aesthetically are not only associated with the specific domain of "art"—but designate a material presence that enters through the senses and interacts with perceptual capacities. These exercises can only be tested within a particular sensuous or embodied experience in the world.

The aesthetic exercise ought to be carefully distinguished from spiritual or philosophical exercises. Unlike most philosophical or spiritual exercises, the work of art does not have to give an account of its own exercise value, nor does it dictate how it ought to be taken up into the practices of those who receive it. It does not make an explicit claim to ground or develop patterns that would ultimately prescribe the way a life ought to be led or the way the mind ought to be trained. Poetry can be didactic, but didacticism is neither a necessary nor a sufficient condition for poetry. The aesthetic exercise is therefore not intrinsically coupled with normativity and may at any moment detach itself from discursive claims of validity.

In contrast to an obsessive reliance on discursive validity—a central feature of most philosophical discourse—the work of art can exercise its influence almost magnetically, drawing people into its world with its particular gifts and its promises—of beauty, honor, elevation, humor, immortalization, edification, critical reflection, stimulation, release, or whatever else it purports to offer. Its influence depends completely on the interpretive practices of the individual or community within its orbit, and these practices can be open or closed to its claims.[11] For one community, poets may function as sages and sources of wisdom, as a vital part of a cultural background that articulates and holds up shared values and norms; for another, poets are entertainers, marginally important producers of cultural objects: harmless at best, nothing more and nothing less; and for yet another community, certain poets may be dangerous, their goals ideologically suspect and the means to achieve these goals dubious, in which case works of art provide a context through which one may hone one's capacity for critical reflection.

Whereas spiritual exercises often advance a claim to universal validity and generate an exercise value through the practices associated with philosophical thought—reading, repeating, meditating—aesthetic exercises make no such similar claim, nor do they make a pretension to transparency or univocity of purpose. The response to art and any particular exercise value it harbors is both culturally conditioned and particularized by any given individual.

In the following study, the aesthetic exercise designates less a poetic form—although form constitutes a necessary condition of the exercise—than a way of reading, an absorptive and attentive focus that probes, analyzes, gathers, and associates in order to uncover the latent and potential exercise value harbored in each work, a tentative and provisional response to the question: what sort of self does this text call into being, what practices of life does it invoke? To be sure, there are numerous examples of texts that could be considered exercises in the strict sense of the term. Rhetorical manuals, poetic imitations, and sketches or drafts are written to function as études, as instruments used to develop one's own skills, rather than as products intended for display and reception. Even these derivative works, exercises in the strict sense, may produce an aesthetic askesis in the larger sense.

In 1750, the aesthetic exercise emerges explicitly not merely as a form of aesthetic production, nor merely as a reading technology associated with the hermeneutic attempt to interpret a text in order to assess its value or meaning, but as a technology of the self. Alexander Baumgarten develops the concept of aesthetic exercises to designate the way in which the work of art and the practices associated with making and receiving art can train cognition and produce the "happy aesthete," the *felix aestheticus*. This aesthetic technology is quite different than the one implied by the text as étude. From the aesthetic exercise as Baumgarten develops it, one does not merely learn this or that particular skill—to fashion words "well" or to rhetorically manipulate your audience—but rather, to exercise perception and cognition in the world. Baumgarten correlates the act of producing, receiving, and imitating poetry and the cognitive acts stimulated by this process as an induction into an entire way of being.

To be sure, certain texts have been more successful at producing meaningful social practices and generating patterns of human cognition and action than others. The intensity of aesthetic askesis travels along a spectrum of cultural objects and their corresponding textual communities. At the limit point of one end of the spectrum one may find sacred and religious texts and texts that throw a culture's implicit or explicit values and norms into relief: the Bible, the Homeric epics, Dante's *Divine Comedy*. In the *Stanze of Raphael* in the Vatican, Dante appears in both secular and sacred frescoes, in the *Parnassus* and in the *Disputation of the Holy Sacrament*. The numerous commentaries that were written in the wake of the *Divine Comedy* testify to the force it exerted over the imagination of its time, to its status as a work that presents in earthly form the order and the pull of the divine. Heidegger claims that the work of art makes clear to a culture how beings appear as that which they are: the Greek tragedy, for example, differentiates and reveals to its audience "what is holy and what is unholy, what is great and what is small, what is courageous and what is cowardly, what is noble and what is transient, what is master and what is slave."[12] Works that do not perform this revelatory function are not considered works of art. And because the sacred appears as one of the most important ways in which art "lets beings be," Heidegger is drawn to Hölderlin's poems inasmuch as they open the possibility of an alternative form of sacrality—one that is not yet realized, but latent as a cultural possibility.

On the other end of the spectrum, one may encounter texts that are not as readily associated with establishing practices or producing human types, texts such as bagatelles, humoristic texts, or even products that make no explicit claim to being art: inscriptions, road signs, anything that can *signify*. These texts too, however, can become the subject of an aesthetic exercise. The aesthetic exercise is generated not from the object itself or its intrinsic properties, but from the attempt to weave it into our identities, our actions, and our commitments. Against Heidegger's conception of art—according to which art is only alive if it holds up to a culture an entire way of being—the aesthetic exercise maintains the life of the work within the microscopic facets of cognition, perception, ideality, emotion, or corporeal focus. The work of art lives on in the aesthetic exercise even long after its specific cultural moment has passed; it may still be active in the life of the individual that relates himself or herself to it and continually returns to it—as a poem learned by heart, an image meticulously studied and reproduced in the imagination, a musical phrase that accompanies the listener through all stages of life.

The notion that art—all forms of poiesis—can alter, influence, enhance, or even shape one's way of being in the world infuses poetic practices long before Baumgarten articulates this idea in his *Aesthetica*. Poetry as a form of language that is tightly coupled with exceptional or altered physiological and perceptual states may be found in diverse literary traditions throughout the history of Western literature. In Horace's Ode 4.11, it is written: "black cares are diminished by song" (*minuentur atrae/carmine curae*),[13] and the ode performatively confirms its own representation of itself as a measured activity driving away melancholy, regulating and reducing the black bile circulating in the body. In Wolfram's *Parzival*, Parzival falls into a trance-like state when three drops of blood in the snow conjure the cheeks of his beloved: "thus he began to fall into thought/until he stood there unconscious" (*sus begunder sich verdenken,/unz daz er unversunnen hielt*).[14] An imaginative association takes hold of the knight: he loses his capacity to reason, and, captivated by a vision of his beloved, held fast in the clutches of desire, he affirms in a state of absorption the beauty of divine creation. Although Wolfram turns this spiritual and erotic scene of mystical transcendence into a burlesque comedy—a scene in which the sacred and the secular orders physically collide when Gawan charges at Parzival only to be deflected by Parzival's lance at the last second—the text nevertheless reveals an awareness of the way in which sensuous input may suddenly take hold of the mind, seize the body, and transport the human being into a mode of perception qualitatively different than that of quotidian reality.

To fully illuminate the history of art as a history of aesthetic exercises, as an investigation into the way in which art and its formal particularities produce certain cognitive states correlated with specific intensities of being, would require a horizon much more vast than can be offered by this study. It would require, above all, going backwards and forwards in time as well as sideways into other languages and other cultural spaces.

Moreover, although poetry forms the central focus of this book, the scope of the aesthetic exercise is not limited to language. The statue of Laocoön became an exercise and a challenge for the interpretation of antiquity in eighteenth-century Germany.[15] In eighteenth-century France, Fragonard's paintings play with the gaze, making the work an attraction for the eye and an incitement for the viewer to discover hidden provocations that often remain unseen.[16] Of all possible mediated forms, it is perhaps music that may integrate itself most intimately into our patterns of behavior and into the very space of our mental organization, coordinating affect and phenomenon in ways that often evade our direct awareness. However, music can also become an aesthetic exercise, an attempt to shape a certain way of perceiving, interpreting, or otherwise relating to phenomena. The compositions of John Cage show how sound can become transformed into music through a redirection of intentional consciousness and an act of concentration.

In this study, however, I focus on language, and more specifically on poetic language. The self-imposed limitations on this horizon of inquiry arise not merely from pragmatic concerns and personal inclinations, but from historical considerations as well: Baumgarten himself, despite his desire to incorporate all the arts in his account of sensuous knowledge, nevertheless uses poetry as the primary medium for the aesthetic exercise.[17] If the goal of criticism, as I have envisioned it, consists in restoring to works their ability to attract, or, as the case may be, to repel (which would have to be construed here not as the opposite of attraction but as a variant of a more fundamental aesthetic momentum of the mind in relation to the work), and through this attraction or repulsion to exercise the mind, history appears as an indispensable tool to aid in this task. However, the work does not serve history, but on the contrary, history serves the work; the critical project cannot come to an end when one has discovered the historical frameworks within which aesthetic objects emerge or the discursive networks that constitute the specific conditions of their appearance. Rather, if such historical frameworks are to have a heuristic value, they constitute the point of departure rather than the end of inquiry. The historical point of view can form a horizon within which works that have lost their attractive power can once again become an aesthetic exercise. The Anacreontic poets of eighteenth-century Germany are almost unreadable for a modern audience. Their poems eschew the normative tendencies of modern aesthetics: genius, originality, depth, lexical variation, affective intensity, rhythmic complexity—almost everything of value according to the normative criteria of that which today would tend to bestow aesthetic worth is absent from this poetry. And yet, when one considers Gleim's *Attempt in Jocular Songs* (*Versuch in Scherzhaften Liedern*) from the perspective of how it interacts with ways of making sense of the world in its localized time and place—it cannot but appear as a masterpiece in its specific exercise of sensuous cognition.

History therefore constitutes an important strategic horizon for a reconsideration of the exercise value of any aesthetic object. In Borges's "Pierre Menard, Author of the Quixote," the narrator, partially inspired by an idea he finds in Novalis about the possibility of *total identification* with an author, imagines that a twentieth-century French writer has rewritten Cervantes's *Don Quixote* word for word. He compares the two versions of the same text, one written by Cervantes and the other by Menard, and discovers several important differences. The style of the text, for example, must be evaluated differently depending upon authorship: "Menard's archaizing style—who is after all a foreigner—suffers from some affectation. This is not the case with the style of his precursor, who handles the Spanish of his time with ease."[18] The same semantic content, produced at different times by different people, provokes a difference in the way a text is read and interpreted. That is why a translation, or an imitation, or any supposedly derivative form of art, in fact may function as its own exercise for any given community. From the perspective of the aesthetic exercise, no object can be—in the strict sense—a merely derivative work, since even the most unoriginal work can nevertheless produce or provoke novelty. Hence the translation of Anacreon's songs (most of which were not, in fact, written by Anacreon but by Hellenistic poets writing in the Anacreontic style) by Götz and Uz in the early eighteenth century does not merely intend to communicate a tradition or a legacy, but interacts with, appeals to, and reconfigures its own time and place.

Although history has been chosen as one point of entry in order to intensify the power of certain texts to attract and exercise the total sensuous apparatus, it too has its limits. A certain irreducible degree of anachronism—a form of temporality derived from the Greek *anachronizein*, the inevitable presence of an "other" time in all presence, or the lateness that characterizes textuality as such—can be productively channeled into the work of art as an aesthetic exercise. For all texts that are *read*, are, strictly speaking, late: even when a contemporary reader reads a text—or even when the writer writes words on a piece of paper—the reception or intellectualization of this text necessarily appears only after its supposed moment of origin. The lateness of the reception of a work of art is therefore a necessary part of its structure; such temporal difference is not a liability, but the necessary condition of a work's duration over time.

Speculation, the exploration of possibilities rather than facts, also appears as a necessary precondition for an attempt to enhance the specifically *aesthetic* qualities of a work of art. Formal elements—rhythm, tempo, diction, structure, or whatever particularities happen to manifest themselves in the act of reading—may intensify the aesthetic exercise, and any time we speak of the role these formal elements play in producing meaning and provoking cognitive states, more often than not, we are speculating. The aesthetic exercise therefore moves in a space of possibilities rather than facts.

To be sure, an understanding of genre can help one evaluate the meaning of form. However, the rules of genre, although helpful for delineating the horizon of an aesthetic exercise and drawing out its specific attractive force, do not exhaust the particular interface between form and consciousness. In addition to considerations of genre, the movement of concentration should be counterbalanced by an oppositional, nominalistic pull, namely to read a poetic artifact as it presents itself immediately to the senses. One of the best models for this countermovement could be described as a sort of phenomenological *epochē*, a bracketing of everything outside of the experience of the text. Such a technique would not intend to reveal the essence of the object or structures of consciousness, but to examine and intensify the states of the mind-body-text system in potential acts of aesthetic reception.

To read texts as aesthetic exercises requires a movement toward the intensity of form, not merely as something bound to genre, nor as the manifestation of a poetic rule, nor as something that can be or ought to be completely historicized, but as experience, as point of attraction, a quantum of energy that, sometimes imperceptibly, introduces a new thread into the texture of work and consciousness.

Because the attempt to consider a work of art as an aesthetic exercise both historicizes and dehistoricizes at one and the same time, invariably including a certain amount of anachronism and speculation in its movements of thought, it may also appear to some readers as unacceptably arbitrary. Critical practices that do not reduce the speculative, the anachronistic, and the arbitrary to a minimum generally encounter a hostile environment in discourses geared toward consensus. However, in the attempt to reconstruct a work's value as an aesthetic exercise, the speculative, the anachronistic, and the arbitrary constitute, at the very least in their capacity as limit-points, integral components, indeed structural necessities, of critical activity. The question is not how to suppress or avoid these potentially parasitic qualities inherent to the genre of criticism, but rather, how to place them in relation to the counterbalancing tendencies toward knowledge, historical accuracy, and coherence also claimed as the domain of the critic.

In the attempt to negotiate these tendencies, I have limited my investigation to the specific time and cultural space in which the aesthetic, as a discipline and as a way of conceptualizing sensuous knowledge, becomes explicitly formulated as a potentiality for thought. In 1735, Alexander Baumgarten wrote a treatise entitled *Philosophical Meditations on Certain Matters Pertaining to Poems* (*Meditationes philosophicae de nonnullis ad poema pertinentibus*). This treatise examined the relation between cognition and poetry, the forms of knowledge presupposed by and generated by poetry, and the normative poetics that such an undertaking implies. In this treatise, he coined the term "aesthetics" (*aestheticae*) as the analysis of "inferior cognition," which includes knowledge generated both by immediate sensory perception and by the imagination, whereby the latter is understood as the ability to make present in the mind something that is absent to the senses.

Gleim and Uz, both of whom were writers of Anacreontic poetry, were students at Halle, and they were not only familiar with Baumgarten as a professor at the university, but they continually referred to Baumgarten's treatise in their correspondence. It is unclear to what degree the ideas in this treatise informed their poetic activity, and it does not seem that Gleim and Uz sought "aesthetic knowledge" in their Anacreontic poems. And yet, one may read their poetry as a certain form of exercising the mind, as a stimulation of poetic thoughts (*cogitationes poeticae*), even though Baumgarten does not use the term "aesthetic exercises" until 1750. However, whereas Baumgarten sees "inferior" aesthetic cognition and the so-called higher forms of cognition—mathematics, logic, geometry—as analogical forms of truth and reason, therefore coupling sensuality and rationality in one overarching logos, Gleim's *Attempt in Jocular Songs* is dissociative: he uncouples his own poetic activity from metaphysical truth, religious piety, ethical universality, social and economic productivity, indeed, from any movement toward transcendence.

One of the implicit presuppositions of this study is that certain forms of eighteenth-century literature are responding to a problem articulated in Baumgarten's *Aesthetica*—even in cases where poets or thinkers may be ignorant of Baumgarten—namely, how art influences patterns of cognition and ways of perceiving the world. If aesthetic exercises consist not merely in the imitation of works of art, but rather in ways of interpreting, observing, and acting in the world, Baumgarten ought to be seen as a groundbreaking figure who makes possible an understanding of the specific poetic practices that unfold throughout the eighteenth century—indeed, as a figure whose conception of aesthetics as exercise extends far into the poetic projects of modernity. However, it must be stressed that Baumgarten does not exert an overt influence over the poets and artists of his generation and beyond, but rather, that he fashions a response to the problem: how does one resignify the contingency of sensuous experience, redeem its inherent fragility, and draw from this vulnerability one of humankind's greatest intellectual resources? The organization of signs, sounds, and meanings that occurs in subsequent poetic projects also responds to this problem, allowing such texts to function as exercises of sensuous cognition through the microscopic textures, relations, and patterns inherent in the poetic object.

In this study, I examine three regimes of aesthetic exercises, each invoking the sensuousness of the poetic object in its own way to shape patterns of perception and to provoke ways of associating and dissociating words, things, and bodily-mental states. These regimes crystallize around Hölderlin's late hymns and sketches, Novalis's philosophical and poetic texts, and Anacreontic and rococo lyric. In certain cases, the text often points to its own sensuous formal activity and its own lyrical voice as the specific type of being that it seeks to produce, a being that one may often simply call "the poet." Baumgarten calls this being the "happy aesthete" (*felix aestheticus*), and it describes a person for whom the production and reception of poetry appears an integral part of the ideal human life.

The history of aesthetic exercises in the eighteenth century is in fact much larger and more complex than the focal points that form the central nodes of this study. Focusing merely on the German tradition, alternative genealogies drawing on other authors could be made, and there are other works by Hölderlin, Novalis, and early eighteenth-century poets than those in this study that bear self-conscious traces of the aesthetic exercise as a textual practice. Many such works that one might expect to appear in this study find scant mention. These blind spots—one of the most prominent being Novalis's *Heinrich von Ofterdingen*, for example—occur not because these works are unimportant for the phenomenon under investigation; rather, these omissions are due mainly to constraints of time, space, and paper. To provide a hint of how broadly the textual practice of aesthetic askesis in the eighteenth century extends, one would have to include early literature influenced by Pietism, such as, for example, the literature of sentimentality. It is not a coincidence that Sophie von la Roche ends her sentimental novel *Geschichte des Fräuleins von Sternheim* with the concept of exercise as the central affirmative category of human existence. In the final sentence of the novel, Mylord Rich, a character exhibiting Stoic characteristics, binds together the truth of happiness, the contingency of happenstance, and the text itself as exercise, culminating in the blessing of those who prove "that these exercises [*Übungen*] do not disrupt the joys of life, but rather, ennoble and confirm them, and that they are our true happiness amidst all contingencies [*Zufällen*] of life!"[19]

In addition to Sophie von la Roche's sentimentalist—and thoroughly sensuous—asceticism, one would have to include Wieland's poetry of the Graces, Klopstock's religious poetry as the sensuous movements of transcendence, Blanckenburg's theory of the novel, Schiller's theory of play, and a large part of Goethe's body of work—scientific and fictional—as instances of aesthetic regimes of practice. Even Lessing's theory of the fable—which is a form of pedagogical training via sensuous experience in production and reception, through which, as producer, one moves from general moral propositions to particular sensuous instantiations, and as receiver, one moves from this sensuous particular back to the general idea—understands sensibility as such as an opening onto a new form of cognitive exercise.[20] Such a project would be impossible to undertake in this book, above all because the central interface of the aesthetic exercise takes place in the interaction between the strenuousness of the reading consciousness and the thickness of textual detail. I have thus chosen to concentrate on three specific regimes of aesthetic exercises in different historical times and places rather than to become dispersed in an attempt to generate an overarching or exhaustive historical narrative.

Part 1, after an introduction to the concept of the aesthetic exercise in the philosophy of Alexander Baumgarten, focuses on the work of Friedrich Hölderlin. For Hölderlin, the harmony of the natural and historical world is not something given, but something that one has to be trained to perceive amidst the facticity of suffering and violence. The deliberate confusion of Hölderlin's poetry, triggered by complex syntactical structures and a dense semantic texture, challenges the human mind to find evidence of the divine in its own mental self-organization. Poetry becomes an exercise in tension, stretching human cognitive capacities to the point of breaking such that they may better perceive the latent divine order. In Hölderlin's case, disjunction and chaos eventually triumph over organization, leading to a form of aesthetic exercise that undermines rather than bolsters a conception of nature and history as self-organizing, harmonious systems.

In part 2, turning to the work of Novalis, I argue that Novalis rejects a philosophical conception of the absolute in favor of a "physiological absolute," redefining the absolute as an intensification of stimulation rather than a realm of pure identity. For Novalis, poetry exercises the mind by generating imaginative multiplicities and differences, continually overturning orders of representation, and creating magnetically attractive signs and permeable poetic spaces. Novalis's aesthetic exercises often posit inaccessible realms that continually disorganize spaces of discursive organization. The disorganization and perturbation of discursive order entails drawing, negotiating, and effacing boundaries—between life and death, pagan and Christian, self and other. This repositioning of boundaries in turn develops alternatives to regimes of disciplinary normalization in the late eighteenth and early nineteenth centuries. In *The Novices of Sais* (*Die Lehrlinge zu Saïs*), the poetic space of the fairy tale organizes language, nature, and knowledge differently than the institutionalized regimes of bodily and mental exercise characteristic of the school at Sais. The aesthetic exercise of the fairy tale, in this case, perturbs disciplinary regimes that attempt to produce normatively stable subjects, seeing *disorganization* as an integral part of a process of self-overcoming. Like *The Novices of Sais, The Hymns to the Night* (*Die Hymnen an die Nacht*) attempt to clear a space where perturbation and difference become possible, pushing the mind into novel imaginative spaces.

Finally, stepping back in time, I examine the work of Anacreontic and rococo poets in the middle of the eighteenth century. Some Anacreontic poets—above all Gleim in his *Attempt in Jocular Songs*—develop their aesthetic activity not in relation to any absolute ideal, but rather, as a complete disavowal of all normalizing structuring schemas as such. Their poetry embraces pure immanence through the pleasure of repeated vocalic, thematic, and syntactic patterns. By replacing all stabilizing and organizing codes—God, virtue, economic productivity—with a seemingly derivative poetry of imitation and repetition, they develop a form of aesthetic exercise detaching human beings from their own culture's way of organizing and making sense of phenomena. The Anacreontic form represents a lost poetic exercise in pleasure, one that would soon be overcome by competing poetic paradigms: the attempt to link poetry to religious experience (Klopstock), poetry as education into ethical autonomy (Schiller), the cult of genius and personalized expression (Herder and Goethe), or the fantastic as a source of novelty (romanticism). Pleasure itself, however, generates its own forms of novelty, its own way of loosening the hold of social and cultural norms and laying bare the contingency of these norms.

Chronological, and even logical order would seem to dictate that I move in the opposite direction, from the Anacreontic poets to Hölderlin's hymns. However, I have opted for a movement toward increasing lightness. If this study, which analyzes aesthetic exercises, also intends to *be* one, albeit in a modest and limited form, the exercise that I have chosen is one toward immanence rather than transcendence. In an age that seems fixated on trauma, melancholy, and violence, it seems to me a necessary corrective to hold open the possibility for joy, lightness, and play.

Lightness, joy, and play are not the opposite of askesis; rather, they can be a product of it. Lightness, the dissociation of phenomena from higher orders of intelligibility or meaningfulness, appears to be one of the more difficult styles of life for a human being to adopt. Even the immanence of Anacreontic poetry requires the movement of concentration and exercise.

One of the most important cognitive attitudes, without which the aesthetic exercise cannot be an exercise, consists in the movement of concentration. Johannes de Silentio, in Kierkegaard's *Fear and Trembling*, describes a knight as one who can make the movement of affective and temporal concentration, gathering the intensity of a whole being into a single mental desire and a single moment of consciousness:

> For the knight will then, in the first place, have the strength to concentrate the whole of his life's content and the meaning of reality in a single wish. If a person lacks this concentration, this focus, his soul is disintegrated from the start, and then he will never come to make the movement, he will act prudently in life like those capitalists who invest their capital in every kind of security so as to gain on the one what they lose on the other—in short, he is not a knight. Secondly,

> the knight will have the strength to concentrate the whole of the result of his reflection into one act of consciousness. If he lacks this focus his soul is disintegrated from the start and he will then never have time to make the movement, he will be forever running errands in life, never enter the eternal.[21]

Such is the way that Johannes de Silentio envisions the commitment to a single phenomenon in the world, to a person, a task, a desire. The movement described by Johannes consists in a thought experiment, a cognitive act, and a conscious decision to make this experiment permeate every moment of one's existence. This wish enters into one's very identity such that one cannot be *the same person* if one were to give up this wish. It requires a threefold concentration: a single object that attracts greater than all other objects, a single desire that overcomes all other desires, and a single act of consciousness that places its stamp on every act of consciousness.

If a critic were to make a text into an aesthetic exercise, such a movement of concentration—as an active form of receptivity through which consciousness enters text and text enters consciousness—would represent an ascetic limit point. Indeed, an absolute commitment would seem almost impossible—and, for the most part, undesirable—for critical activity as a form of askesis. It seems impossible for the simple reason that, to borrow a concept from Baumgarten, art is *heterocosmic*, disclosing worlds whose logic, coherence, and frames of reference are different than our own. Although Baumgarten designates heterocosmic truth as the ability to imagine contingent appearances—in an imagined or literary world—as "possible elements of another universe" (*BA* 419), thereby conforming to the metaphysical truth of sufficient reason, it may also stand as a reminder to the critic that he or she makes the movement of concentration in multiple and often incommensurable literary worlds. In the realm of art, one may cross heterogeneous imaginative spaces without making any one of them into the absolute. The same critic can engage equally intensively with Hölderlin's hymns and Anacreontic odes despite the almost opposed attractions they generate. The critic's ability to feel multiple attractions—contrary to Johannes de Silentio's claim—may actually *enhance* the intensity of experience. More importantly, the attraction to multiple aesthetic worlds impedes the dogmatic identification with only one world, one style of life, one imaginative landscape.

Part of the critical task consists in making space for the unfamiliar and often destabilizing appearance of difference and novelty. As an example of the contrast between truth in the strict sense of the term (logical truth) and heterocosmic truth (the truth of fictional worlds), Baumgarten cites two lines from the *Panegyricus Messallae* in which the narrator, after having described the wanderings of Odysseus, describes two diverging accounts of these wanderings. The representation of these diverging accounts articulates the truth of the difference between the logos as such and the space of the work of art:

Whether these events happen in our lands
Or whether the story gives to these wanderings a new world. . . .

Atque haec seu nostras intersunt cognita terras
Fabula sive novum dedit his erroribus orbem. . . . (*BA* 422)

Part One

✦

Organization, Bifurcation, Instability

Chapter 1

The Improbable Coherence of Contingent Things

Aesthetic Exercises in the Work of Alexander Baumgarten

The Birth of Aesthetics and *Homo Exercitans*

If it belongs to one of the possibilities of human beings to exercise not merely their bodies, but also their minds, and through this exercise to modify their outlook on the world and their way of being in the world, it follows that the human organism is endowed with a plasticity that continually reveals its own existence as an open project. To regard the human being as one who practices, as *homo exercitans*, gives to the human being the perpetual status of being unfinished.

In classical antiquity, the malleability of the human was the *conditio sine qua non* of philosophy. According to Pierre Hadot, philosophy in classical antiquity consisted not merely in a set of doctrines about the world, but rather, in regimes of spiritual exercises that "correspond to a transformation of our vision of the world and a metamorphosis of our personality."[1] The spiritual exercises associated with Hellenistic and Roman philosophy seek to arrive not merely at a correct account of reality or a description of the good life; rather, the primary purpose of a spiritual exercise is transformative, and it culminates in the production of a total way of being: a way of seeing, a way of thinking, and a way of acting in the world.

A spiritual exercise is not reducible to a mere textual genre, and the reader's work is not finished when he or she finally recognizes the generic features of a text or explains the effects of a specific textual form. Rather, the spiritual exercise must insert itself into an idiosyncratic psychic and cognitive space and thereby produce the subject that in turn animates the text in its everyday life. The success or failure of the exercise therefore depends upon a permeability and interdependence in the relationship between words, the individual that receives them, and the individual's environment in the broadest sense of the term.

The exercise therefore gives rise to its own particular philosophy of language: language does not merely store information, it does not communicate mental contents, it does not express interiority, nor is its central function performative in the sense of transforming social reality, but rather, language—as a practice rather than as a structure—becomes imbued with the potential of shaping the spatiotemporal patterns of one's cognitive landscape.[2] The insight to be drawn from the effect of spiritual exercises is that language itself, whether implicitly or explicitly, contains an exercise value. To speak is to practice, to *exercise* thought, to generate rhythm in behavior, consciousness, and body. All linguistic acts therefore harbor an exercise value ranging from a relative minimum to a relative maximum, from the seeming self-evidence of phatic communication to the challenge of poetic form, from the utterance that negligibly and imperceptibly acts on one's total organism to the word that irrevocably and decisively alters patterns of being.

Propagandists, behaviorists, and psychoanalysts have, to a certain extent, always been aware of the exercise value of linguistic acts.[3] However, the exercise value of language cannot be reduced to a vulgar form of psychic manipulation and self-deception. The exercise value of artistic practices in particular—and here one would have to include all sensuously mediated forms in this rubric and not merely the reception and production of language—makes possible a conception of art not as performative but as *transformative*, that is, as a specific manner in which any concrete life integrates ways of producing and receiving the sensible world into its mental and bodily activity.

Art as a form of askesis constitutes such a basic presupposition of the meaningfulness of artistic endeavor that one might, in all likelihood, if one were to look hard enough, find this notion in almost every literary tradition and in every epoch—and to each tradition and each epoch would correspond a particular form of exercise, a particular nexus of sensuous forms and practices that constitute and are constituted by the self in a state of transformation.

The sustained interrogation of art as an exercise of the individual's cognitive and perceptual apparatus appears in an explicit and concentrated form at the origin of aesthetics as a discipline in the eighteenth century. Alexander Baumgarten, in his *Aesthetica* (1750/58), theorizes a new form of practice to this end—the *aesthetic exercise*—that explicitly draws upon art, its production and reception, to produce habits of sensuous perception and patterns of selfhood.[4] The aesthetic exercise differs from didactic normativity and projects of self-fashioning: whereas normative art seeks to "fill" a subject with information or content—for example, with correct moral beliefs—aesthetic askesis modifies the very structures of perception and cognition of the self. And whereas self-fashioning tends to orient behavior around the problems and tensions of exemplarity—the process of seeking concrete models of selfhood and perhaps embodying these models or producing new ones—aesthetics examines the interface between perception and art in order to generate character in the process of tarrying with the sensuous world. Rather than beginning with the givenness of the social world, as complex and problematic as this givenness might be, aesthetic askesis takes its point of departure from the production and reception of sensuous form.

The discipline of aesthetics—*as* an autonomous discipline with its own horizon of inquiry—begins with an epistemological proposition. Baumgarten defines aesthetics as follows: "AESTHETICS (theory of the liberal arts, inferior gnoseology, the art of beautiful cognition, the art of an analogy of reason) is the science of sensuous cognition" (*BA* 10). Epistemologically, Baumgarten's aesthetics revises Descartes's and Leibniz's prioritization of clear and distinct ideas—which are properties of the mind and not of sense experience—as the only ground for true and certain knowledge.[5] According to Leibniz, unlike geometric shapes or logical propositions, sense perception is "confused" because it cannot be analyzed into its constituent parts. That which is recognized as beautiful, for example, triggers a striking incapacity to localize the source of one's own pleasure, let alone analyze this impression; the beautiful represents a paradigmatic case of the indefinable "je ne sçay quoi" inherent in all sense perception.[6] Baumgarten, following Leibniz, considers the very upsurge of indeterminacy that makes itself so strongly felt in poetic works—the incapacity of sensory cognition to analyze the complexity of the object into distinct properties—as constitutive of its beauty.

Beauty—in Baumgarten's formulation, "the perfection of sensuous cognition as such [*perfectio cognitionis sensitivae, qua talis*]" (*BA* 20)—in fact conceals a bifurcation into two distinct spheres that overlap: the ontological and the functional.[7] Ontologically, the beautiful expresses the perfection of cosmic order and generates processes that bind together potentially contingent or incommensurable multiplicities: it mediates between things in the world and cognitive states (*pulcritudo rerum et cogitationum*), between signs that interrelate with one another and the subjects that express them and perceive them (*pulcritudo significationis*), and finally between the microscopic organization of phenomena and the macroscopic organization of nature (*pulcritudo ordinis*).[8] Beauty facilitates connectivity across heterogeneous orders: the order of mind, the order of phenomenal appearances, the order of signification, and the order of the total system of the creation.

For Baumgarten, the harmonious unity of contingent multiples—the cosmos as a beautiful and coherent totality—exists as an ontological given. However, this ontological conception of beauty does not preclude its deployment as an impetus for patterns of thought and action. Beauty transcends its status as a purely metaphysical category inasmuch as it is absorbed into an anthropological drive toward perfection, thus orienting sensuous cognition toward certain objects or goals.[9] As orientation and as drive, the metaphysics of beauty is channeled into the dynamics of the self through the "vital powers" (*viribus vivis*) of one who thinks beautifully.[10] The ontological order of beauty is integrated into the overarching characterological dynamic of the aesthetic self, a process whereby the beauty of the self unfolds according to a similar logic that governs the order of sensuous objects in the world.[11]

This alternative conception of beauty as orientation toward perfection makes all art into a potential exercise in thought and an exercise of thought. Within the framework of the *ars pulcre cogitandi*, beauty designates both the presupposed harmony of the cosmos as well as the structure of transcendence at the center of the being of the aesthete.[12]

Aesthetic philosophy therefore does not merely signal a shift in the theory of knowledge from purely logical or mathematical truths to an affirmation of the epistemological value of clear yet confused sensuous perceptions, but rather, marks a more fundamental shift toward poiesis as an integral and incontrovertible feature of cognition, even in supposedly pure theoretical acts of consciousness. Within the framework of aesthetics, every theoretical insight is simultaneously endowed with an exercise value that feeds back into the sensuous capacity of the aesthetic subject.

It is perhaps not a coincidence that aesthetics came into being at a historical moment of intensified disciplinary transformation, at a time when, as Foucault notes, bodies became docile, subject to "meticulous, often minute, techniques . . . [that] defined a certain mode of detailed political investment of the body, a 'new micro-physics' of power."[13] Although the aesthetic exercise does in fact presuppose the sensuous and perceptual apparatus as malleable, its particular askesis is designed not to render bodies docile, but to produce an openness within the realm of sensibility itself. If one may speak of character formation in the aesthetic exercise, such a character emerges from an indeterminate and indeterminable set of perceptual givens. Aesthetics therefore operates under the guise of an "open disciplinarity." Discipline, in this sense, has a paradoxical effect: it does not constrain subjects and thereby equalize them, but produces a horizon of possibilities whose particular form depends upon the particular realization of an aesthetic project. This realization can be—and of course is—shaped and informed by the order that exists beyond the self, but it must necessarily travel through the idiosyncrasy of the mind and body of the aesthete.

An aesthetic exercise must therefore be distinguished from a rigidly technological conception of exercise, one that would attempt to fashion the human being as a carpenter fashions a house. The aesthetic exercise does not prescribe a pre-given characterological end point, but rather, initiates a process of emergence that may take many different and divergent pathways and that opens up onto unexpected vistas of possibility. The reductive and distorted notion of exercise as a teleological concept may perhaps be traced to its association with a philosophy of the will and the *homo faber*, with a vigorous and repeated activity that intrudes upon and shapes human life with a view to some specific preconceived end.[14] On the contrary, an aesthetic exercise, for Baumgarten at least, does not necessarily presuppose an act of willful intervention. To be sure, a form of activity is involved, an act of concentration and engagement, the presence of thought or judgment that accompanies the aesthetic act—but not necessarily an act of will as the attempt to bend reality, the body, or the imagination to a prefabricated image or model of normativity. He says, "when I read beautiful texts, when I see beautiful paintings, and thereby think convincingly: this is beautiful, that gives pleasure—I am already exercising myself" (*AGB* 102). The pleasure of the work of art provides a sensual springboard to higher-order cognitive acts of questioning—for example, *why is this beautiful?*—that form a minimum threshold for the concept of exercise. The aesthetic exercise thus implies the interrogation of the given rather than the fabrication of a predetermined subject or object.

Nevertheless, for Baumgarten, the ability to generate rules for art or to construct a theory of art does constitute one of the central activities through which an aesthetic exercise comes into being. However, the irreducible presence of the contingency of sense experience in aesthetic cognition opens up a space of indeterminacy that saturates the field of the exercise. As we shall see, the space of the aesthetic exercise is not rigidly determined by social institutions, nor are such exercises a result of individual decision-making strategies—which would represent a decidedly subject-centered mode of exercise—but the energy of the exercise travels through an openness and attunement to heterogeneous ways of associating phenomena, to the alterity of imaginary worlds.

The aesthetic exercise is therefore always associated with risk and vulnerability. The indeterminacy inherent in perceptual and poetic self-organization—an indeterminacy that will later manifest itself in Hölderlin's poetry, for example—may generate a form of anxiety that sets the human being adrift amidst the confusion and the complexity of the sensuous world. On the other hand, this very openness and indeterminacy constitutes the condition of possibility of inspiration, of a sacred entry point through which the divine might travel in order to touch the realm of mortals with its palpable and ineffable presence.

Fields of Sensibility

From a philosophical perspective, Baumgarten appears as one of the heroes of rationalist philosophy, as the champion of an epistemological rehabilitation of sensuous experience.[15] More important, he simultaneously opens a new zone of interaction between the exercise of cognition and patterns of selfhood.[16] Philosophical aesthetics cannot be separated out from its actualization in human practices, which in turn produces a new type of human being that Baumgarten calls the "happy aesthete":

> As beauty of knowledge is brought about by the beautifully thinking being and is neither greater nor more noble than this person's living powers, above all else we will sketch the emergence and the idea of the beautifully thinking being, the CHARACTER OF THE HAPPY AESTHETE, as well as an enumeration of those things that are the more germane causes of beautiful thinking in the soul. (*BA* 27)

Baumgarten's aesthetics does not merely rehabilitate sensuous knowledge, but rather, constructs the type of human being—one capable of beautiful thinking—for whom the knowledge and practice of the senses become a way of life.[17] However, the capacity to think beautifully is only open to thought that immerses itself in the organization and disorganization of the sensible world. If, as Descartes and Leibniz claimed, knowledge must be apodictic, and as such can be generated only through rational, higher-order cognitive operations such as those associated with logic or geometry, then it cannot change, it remains eternal and immutable in a space of validity beyond the domain of the senses. If, however, knowledge includes that which one may derive from sense experience, this knowledge, in accordance with the givenness of the world, is exposed just as much to ugliness as it is to beauty, to error as to truth, to monstrosity as to harmony, to disorder as to order.

Baumgarten calls the particular self that exercises its own sensuous capacities the "happy aesthete," a figure whose central characteristic consists in blurring the boundaries between nature and art, *physis* and *technē*: to the character of the happy aesthete belongs therefore a "natural disposition" (*dispositio naturalis*, *BA* 26), as well as "aesthetic exercises" (*exercitia aesthetica*, *BA* 38). Nature requires techniques in order to produce a viable and self-sustaining way of life: only the aesthetic exercise releases, maintains, and augments the full potentiality of the human being, the *felix aestheticus*, whose natural dispositions would otherwise remain stagnant, or worse, fall prey to corruption.

It is only through the "inferior" cognitive capacities that aesthetics may become a way of life and provide for human beings an induction into thinking beautifully. The aesthete's cognitive dispositions are ultimately extra-moral capacities, since all sensuous "modes" of the soul are essentially mutable: "All modes in my soul are variable [*veränderlich*] and I can give my soul modes that are good or evil" (*AGB* 98). And yet, each of these inferior capacities, and each in its own way, gives way to an ethos; each indexes a way of being in the world that takes a potential weakness or limitation of human sensuous cognition and resignifies it as a potential source of strength. Baumgarten's enumeration of innate cognitive tendencies therefore elucidates the specific contours of poetic cognition, and more specifically provides a blueprint for how poetic activity might expand or deepen the dispositions, tendencies, and potentialities that are present in everyday perception and cognition.

The operations of sensuous cognition generate zones that are particularly open to exercise, each of which forms a field of attraction for the character of the "beautiful spirit" (*der schöne Geist*). It is largely within this field of malleable dispositions that numerous poetic projects of the eighteenth century—among which one may count the works of artists as diverse as Wieland, Hölderlin, Schiller, Goethe, or the Jena romantics—unfold their exercise potential. These dispositions are enumerated as follows.

Inner Sensibility

The aesthete is endowed with "the ability to experience acutely so that the soul not only achieves the primary goal of thinking beautifully with the external senses, but also can experience the changes and effects of all of the other faculties in order to steer them better by means of an inner sense and an inward conscience" (*BA* 28). Heightened sensitivity to the realm of the sensible not only furnishes the aesthete with concrete matter that may then be shaped through aesthetic activity; more importantly, this sensitivity is channeled into a feedback mechanism that allows the aesthete to survey his or her processes of cognition as a whole. The aesthete deploys inward sensation—an attentiveness to his or her own cognitive processes—to unify and harness the exteriority that threatens to overwhelm the sensuous apparatus. Such a disposition allows the aesthete to take control of his or her multiple and potentially conflicting mental operations: discipline mediates between outer and inner perception.

The disciplinary potential of the inner sense, however, does not take control over the exterior senses in a way that standardizes or automatizes their movements. Instead, this control differentiates the human from the machine: "In [the beautiful soul] an especially strong feeling and inner consciousness of what is happening inside of him must dominate, otherwise he will simply stand in a machine-like movement" (*AGB* 86). The control of the inner sense over the input given by the outer senses ultimately sets perception into a dynamic motion, animating rather than standardizing the operations of the soul. "Feeling" along with "inner consciousness" produces irregularity rather than predictability. Disciplinary control and surveillance of the self, far from constituting the other of creative spontaneity, operate as its necessary precondition.

The ability to perceive the operations of all other faculties, or the surveying gaze of second-order acts of cognition from within the cognitive apparatus, presupposes a subject for whom such faculties are in fact dispersed and multiple. However, rather than constituting a weakness of the soul, the capacity to intensify sensation makes possible one of the central technologies of aesthetic selfhood: the gathering of multiplicity in sensuous experience. Each of the dispositions of the aesthetic spirit must not only be developed as an isolated capacity, but rather, must be coordinated with other dispositions if the redemption of the entire sensuous system is to be guaranteed.

What will later become a transcendental a priori condition of cognition as such for Kant—the transcendental unity of apperception—for Baumgarten appears as a fluid and inward dynamic process, one that is exposed to differing degrees of coherence and control for different subjects. In other words, the unity of apperception is not merely *presupposed*, nor does it belong to the transcendental conditions of possibility of experience, but it constitutes a part of concrete sensuous access to the world whose unifying activity can be harnessed, redirected, and potentialized. It is *empirical* in the fullest sense of the term, and therefore open to exercise and formation.

Imagination and Temporality

Of each of the sensuous cognitive capacities, the imagination, or the *dispositio naturalis ad imaginandum*, possesses the highest degree of negative potentiality: the capacity to diverge from that which is sensuously present and to linger in that which is absent, either in the mode of having already passed, having not yet occurred, or in a temporally unspecified irreality.

Even the commonplace definition of the imagination as a power that makes present that which is absent to the senses—a definition adopted by Christian Wolff—foregrounds its essential negativity.[18] The negativity of the imagination—always taking its point of departure from absence rather than from presence—is in turn always linked to the temporality of human cognition: as an exercise of the capacity to make present that which is absent, the imagination presupposes the finite and temporal position of the human subject. The imagining subject does not surrender to time, but can use the imagination to explore the cognitive possibilities inherent in temporality itself.

Every movement of imaginative aesthetic cognition emphasizes in its own particular way the temporal modalities of past, present, and future.[19] The temporality and finitude of the human being are thereby resignified; rather than indexing the fallen state of the human being, the negativity of human temporality makes possible the aesthete's processes of transcendence and the act of thinking beautifully within time. If the negativity of the imagination turns to the past, it can foster the development of historical consciousness; as Baumgarten says, it is only through the imagination that "things of the past must be recalled" (*BA* 28). If the imagination turns to the present, it permits not only an abstraction from one's own sensuous givenness, but also the preservation of phenomena that are continually passing away, since "things that are present often disappear before beautiful thought about them has been completed" (*BA* 28). The imagination therefore extends the fragile life of objects and thoughts that are continually subject to oblivion, an oblivion that progresses with every passing moment. Finally, the imagination makes possible projection into the future: "not only from things that are present, but also from things that are past, future things are discovered" (*BA* 28). The aesthete is capable of seeing into the future inasmuch as his or her cognitive acts—the examination of and reflection upon the past, an attunement to the conditions of the present, and the exercise of hypothetical thought—may be directed toward that which is to come. The imagination as an aesthetic disposition therefore not only foregrounds a fundamental negativity at the heart of human temporality, but draws upon this nothingness as the condition of possibility of a form of selfhood that can preserve the past, manage the unpredictability of the present, and interpret the void of the future.

Noticing and Proportionality

Essential for the aesthetic spirit is the disposition toward sharpness of insight, *dispositio naturalis ad perspicaciam* (*BA* 30). This faculty drives the aesthete to focus on the proportionality of the world of appearances, which in turn designates the architectonic and dynamic order of mental operations: "Through this faculty, both the beauty of cognition, inasmuch as it demands phenomena that are proportional and refuses phenomena that are disproportional, as well as the beautiful proportionality of the spirit in a larger sense is achieved" (*BA* 30).

Proportionality refers not simply to the formal characteristics of beautiful objects, but to a set of relations inherent to the total system of being, both mental and physical. Perspicacity, as that which is exercised in the cognition of harmonious proportions, presupposes an engagement with a system of differences from which the aesthete constructs relations. Eighteenth-century poetics located the ability to perceive differences and to generate resemblances from these differences as part of the respective operations of *Scharfsinnigkeit* (acumen) and *Witz* (wit). Gottsched, drawing on Wolff's definition of acumen and wit in the *Psychologia empirica*, situates these operations between identity and difference, unity and multiplicity: "Wit is a power of the mind that easily perceives the similarity of things and therefore can make a comparison between these things. It presupposes acumen as its ground, which designates a capability of souls to perceive many facets in one thing" (*VCD* 152). For Baumgarten, these two faculties—which are in fact inverted operations of one another, whereby one begins with similarity to arrive at difference, and the other begins with difference to arrive at similarity—are often mistaken for one another, since the difference of *acumen* (*Scharfsinnigkeit*) often conceals itself in the resemblances of *ingenium* (*Witz*): "Since acumen often conceals itself under the name of wit (*ingenium*), all beautiful cognition is sometimes ascribed to wit" (*BA* 30). In his reflections on perspicacity, Baumgarten resignifies the logical categories of identity and difference as poetic practices. The capability to perceive as many differences as possible as quickly as possible, to construct comparisons and relations, to draw the latency of differentiation into the openness of conscious awareness—each of these phenomenological operations is more critical to the aesthete than the metaphysics of identity and difference that supposedly makes these operations possible. Identity and difference therefore appear not as ontological categories, but as perceptual and poetic challenges, as tools for the exercise of cognition.

Proportionality, as a category of organization applicable both to mind (in the interplay between wit and acumen, resemblance and differentiation) and to external appearances (in the architectonic structure of phenomena), resignifies ontological givens as cognitive tasks for the aesthete. According to the metaphysics of proportion that features so prominently in Leibniz's ontology, proportionality can be understood primarily as an axiomatic feature of reason, more a geometric postulate than a property of the sensible realm: "Every relation, proportion, analogy, proportionality derives not from the will, but from the nature of God, or, what is equivalent, from the idea of the things."[20] However, Baumgarten considers proportionality not merely from an ontological or mathematical point of view, but as an integral feature of aesthetic practices and sensuous cognition: the aesthetics of proportionality and the exercise of perspicacity suture the conceptual divide between mathematical knowledge (*mathesis*) and sensuous perception (*aisthesis*), or between an ontology based primarily on number, axiom, and rule, and one linked to the organization of non-quantifiable sensuous experience. Perspicacity therefore denotes the cognitive process through which numerological *ratio* (as quantity) is transformed into aesthetic *cognitio* (as quality).

As Baumgarten emphasizes, when perspicacity and proportionality become products of the aesthetic self and can be set in relation to the sensible world, harmony is confronted with its other, namely, disorder and disproportionality. These elements of experience appear as forms of organization that must be excluded from the exercise of the sensible realm, and perspicacity, as a cognitive function, takes up this critical protective role: "disproportional phenomena are not admitted [*disproportiones phaenomena non admittit*]" (*BA* 30) in beautiful thought. Aesthetic technologies of being therefore implicitly recognize the potential disorder of the world of appearances as a threat to be held at bay. Proportion and coherence no longer appear to the aesthete as given—or rather, not as *merely* given—but as that which must be wrested from the world, transforming the very concept of harmony from ontological presupposition to aesthetic injunction.

Recognition and Remembrance

One of Baumgarten's most important philosophical-rhetorical strategies consists in recontextualizing, resignifying, and transforming mythological concepts of antiquity into cognitive categories of aesthetic philosophy, inaugurating a movement from *mythos* to *aisthesis*. The permeability between the categories of mythological thought and those of aesthetic philosophy comes to the foreground in the disposition of the aesthete to recognize and to remember, the *dispositio naturalis ad recognoscendum et memoria*. Baumgarten notes, "Mnemosyne was called the mother of the muses by the ancients, who saw the recollection of the imagination as part of the process of memory" (*BA* 30). According to Baumgarten, mnemotechnology belongs to aesthetic action as an integral part of the production of the beautiful. Memory does not merely refer to the ability to recall that which happens or has happened, but also describes the means through which the mind generates order in its expressiveness.

Memory, as an aesthetic disposition, consists less in the recollection of the past than in the coherence-generating action of a cognitive operation that guards the mind from dissonance within any chain of events or narrative sequentiality. The exercise of memory assures that present or future events in any fictional work do not contradict that which precedes them, thereby sensuously embodying the law of non-contradiction in narrative form; logical truth becomes narratological truth.[21] At the same time, the notion of a "future" that follows from the past without break or rupture—as if diachronic time could be flattened and seen from the perspective of a coherent and total picture—constitutes a central feature in the temporality of theodicy, according to whose logic time unfolds as a preestablished harmonious whole. The very organization of narrative action—the basic operation of which consists in generating coherence among multiple events—is to secure a non-contradictory and well-ordered temporality. Narrative sequentiality provokes cognitive processes that maintain sensuous analogs of metaphysical truth. The faculty of remembering therefore serves not merely the recollection of past deeds, immortalized for their preservation or glorification, but more importantly, generates coherence and order in a system of contingent multiplicities.

Binding and Separating

Baumgarten singles out the poet as a particular type of aesthetic self. The poets are endowed with the ability to bring another world into being, a world that may be—indeed must be—organized differently than our own. Baumgarten invents a new form of truth that governs the contingent singularities of invented worlds (as opposed to the contingent singularities of the objective world): *heterocosmic* truth, or truth that governs alternative worlds.[22] Heterocosmic truth presupposes the binding and separating of contingent multiples, and it produces forms that cohere with metaphysical truth but differentiate themselves from the order of the real. As such, poetic action can appear at one and the same time metaphysically true and objectively false. The harmonious organization of parts within a whole characteristic of a fictional work has no external referent that points beyond itself, but nevertheless functions as a mirror of metaphysical order.

Heterocosmic truth at the same time makes possible a conception of novelty as a difference from that which exists and that which has habitually existed. The central thrust of poetic action includes bringing something new into the world, or adding the new to the existence of the old: "since [the poet] now is supposed to create something new, he must not only reveal old sensations again, but rather bind the old sensations with imagination and put them together with new ones" (*AGB* 89). The differential event of novelty is then made harmonious by using the imagination—the capacity to make present an absence—to link the new world to a familiar world, either by attaching the new fictional world to the (objective) order of the real or to the (heterocosmic) order of other poetic artifacts.

For Baumgarten, the world-generating capacity of the poetic aesthete presupposes the "binding and separating of imaginative phenomena [*combinando praescindendoque phantasmata*]" (*BA* 30). Binding and separating occurs not merely in the mind of the aesthete, in the association and dissociation of mental images, but has its correlate as part of the semiotic structure of poetic works, for example in the syntagmatic chain of signifiers or in the episodic and sequential organization of narrative events. Without the binding and separating capacity of aesthetic cognition, the invented world—and perhaps the phenomenal world—would lose its intelligibility. The centrality of binding and separating as aesthetic capacities continues far into the eighteenth century: poets such as Hölderlin continue to see the intelligibility of the world—not merely the poetically created world, but the world of the real in which the aesthete lives and works—as dependent upon the binding and separating power of aesthetic cognition.

Judgment

The problem of judgment exists as a marginal concern of Baumgarten's aesthetic theory. It will later be made central by Kant, who builds his aesthetics around an interrogation of the conditions of possibility of synthetic a priori judgments. For Baumgarten, however, the cognitive operation of judgment constitutes merely one disposition among others that can be found in the patterns of the aesthetic self. The aesthete does not concern himself or herself with the conditions of valid judgments, but rather, with judgment as a disposition that contributes to the art of thinking beautifully. Aesthetic judgment can function autonomously from the operation of higher-order logical faculties: "The form of taste [related to judgment] is a judge in matters for which the intellect [*der Verstand*] does not wish to decide" (*AGB* 89). In other words, judgment does not *embody* the intellect as much as make possible an alternative pathway of thought—one not linked to higher-order cognitive operations—that nevertheless results in normatively valid propositions.

Taste operates in the absence of clear and distinct knowledge of why something is beautiful, and even so, arrives at a correct judgment: "[The aesthete] will not always know why [something is beautiful] and yet he will have judged the matter correctly" (*AGB* 89). Being correct is not equivalent to being able to articulate reasons; unlike the philosopher, the aesthete does not need to justify him- or herself with reasons in order to make a judgment that seems correct to others. The grounding of judgment is thereby confronted with its own groundlessness, coming into play at moments when reason itself falls inarticulate.

Aesthetic judgment, which takes as its central object phenomena whose totalities cannot be broken down into constituent parts, forms one of the exemplary operations of the aesthetic self. Judgment itself signifies a decision-making process when faced with sensuous matter that is resistant to analysis. Inasmuch as the reasons for a judgment may or may not be apparent to the person making the judgment, cognitive action necessarily references an opacity of the self to itself—a concept of selfhood that differentiates the aesthete from the Cartesian ideal of self-transparent subjectivity.[23]

Hypothetical Cognition

We have previously discussed how Baumgarten aestheticizes the mythological categories of antiquity, transforming archaic *mythos* into cognitive *aisthesis*. The poet as a seer, as one who has privileged insight into the future, constitutes one such archaic myth that reveals itself as part of the structure of aesthetic cognition. The science of aesthetics desacralizes and demythologizes the cult of poets as prophets, translating the poetic capacity of foresight into the aesthetic-cognitive capacity of expectation. The aesthetic ability to see into the future is not tantamount to the ability to *predict* the future, but rather, refers to the way in which the aesthete holds open the future as a field of possibilities: "[The poet] must always see certain worlds that would be true if certain hypotheses were true. So intensely must he create poetry and practice the capacity of foresight [*Vorhersehungsvermögen*]" (*AGB* 90). The aesthete tends toward mental operations that invoke what Musil would later call the sense of possibility, *Möglichkeitssinn*, albeit here in a way that still remains bound to the order of the real and the exercise of hypothetical cognition.[24]

In addition to foresight, the poet must, in a certain sense, downplay his or her own particularized emotional life in order to establish a wider affective sphere of future possibility: "[The poet] cannot stir [*rühren*] the affects if he does not excite desire, and he cannot excite desire if the object of desire is not awakened in the future. Indeed, if he wants to create a particularly beautiful object, he must be able to suppress all of his sentiments and let the insight into the future alone dominate and prioritize itself above all else" (*AGB* 90). The aesthetic disposition of foresight resignifies the ancient figure of the poet, or one endowed with a privileged access to the future, as the modern poet whose central gift is a rhetorical and affective one, culminating in the ability to excite future passions in others while suppressing the present passions of the poetic and productive individual.

The disposition to foresight links the futurity of poetic creation with the capability to generate desire in the members of an ideal reading community. However, aesthetic cognition is ultimately irreducible to the desires of the community.[25] Aesthetic foresight—as the maintenance and generation of desire for the aesthetic act—unfolds in a relationship of tension between individual inclination and communal expectation. Desire for the aesthete is therefore amorphous and unlocalizable: it belongs neither to the individual subject nor to the norms of a concrete community, but orients itself toward a projected ideal community of the aesthete's own imagination.

The centrality of foresight to the aesthetic act draws upon an aesthetic limitation—the unavailability of future time, closed to direct sensory perception although open to a horizon of expectation—to make possible the affirmation of the sensible realm. The temporal finitude of the human being, the incapacity to know determinately what will happen in the future and the anxiety surrounding this future, is channeled into the work of art as a strategy to generate affective states in those who will later come into contact with the work. It is in this sense that the poet must be a visionary: the poet must not only remain mired in his or her own emotional world, but extend his or her activity to an indeterminate sphere of possible affects.

Thought, Expression, Signification

The aesthete exhibits a "disposition to make perceptions into signs" (*BA* 38). This disposition presupposes an affinity between the sensible world of phenomena, sensuous cognition, and signifying systems. In his lecture notes to the *Aesthetica*, Baumgarten shifts the emphasis from expressivity to communication, whereby communication extends over all forms of intelligibility: "The beautiful spirit must have a natural disposition to communicate his thoughts to others. We do not merely understand language here. One can also explain oneself to others through other signs" (*AGB* 90). The implicit value of communicability for the aesthetic self suggests that sensuous thought seeks out a world of others, and it does so in forms other than language; the inclination to expressivity or communicability does not restrict itself to one specific medium over another. Rather, the inclination to expression and communication points to a larger and more inclusive form of aesthetic selfhood, one that does not understand its own semiosis as part of a struggle in which one mediated form—for example, painting, writing, or music—exists in perpetual combat with other forms in a contest for supremacy.[26]

Unlike the Cartesian philosopher, the aesthete, rather than gravitating toward introspective or meditative cognitive states, exists in perceptual motion, moving from exteriority to interiority and from interiority to exteriority.[27] This movement from the interiority of perception to the exteriority of signification does not merely refer to a specific ability to generate utterances, but constitutes part of the aesthete's habitus. For the aesthete, signification moves quickly from natural disposition to technological exercise, one that consists in binding signifiers with concrete individual and communal instances of perception. Signification as aesthetic exercise follows the law of intensification latent in a natural disposition toward greater semiotic productivity: the more signifiers the aesthete binds to more conceptual contexts of significance, which in turn are bound to collective forms of perception, the greater is the faculty of signification.[28]

The Redemption of the Sensible World

The inclinations and dispositions of aesthetic cognition bear within themselves the incipient traces of a redemptive project, one that emerges from sensuous perception itself, from its finitude and its uncertainty. Baumgarten himself stresses not the imperfection of sense perception, but rather, the aesthetic as that which opens the human being to perfectibility as a continual and open-ended process. The fallibility, contingency, and resistance to analysis characteristic of aesthetic cognition, or sensuous perception in general, had given the rationalistic philosophical tradition good reasons to designate the sensible realm as "inferior" to the purity of human reason. Baumgarten, however, discovers the potential lying dormant in these supposedly inferior capacities. Aesthetics draws upon art to reveal how sensuous knowledge itself produces the human being as a malleable entity—an unstable being, to be sure, but one whose very instability appears as a prerequisite for reconfiguring the self. From this perspective, the primary function of beauty as the perfection of sensuous cognition is not to glorify the order of the creation, nor to produce pleasure through mimetic activity, but to generate the motor through which the human being takes up the strenuous task of self-modification.

For Baumgarten, each natural disposition harbors its own potential corruptibility, and nature alone cannot prevent the aesthete from becoming enmeshed in a realm of negative appearances: one recalls Baumgarten's statement that all modes of the soul are changeable and can be modified for better or for worse (*AGB* 98). To prevent the corruption of the dispositions and desires of the aesthete, Baumgarten recommends a regime of aesthetic exercises, channeling the attraction of art into a concentration of performative power. The aesthetic exercise consists in a carefully regimented pedagogy of the soul through which the repetition of actions and thoughts produces the character of the happy aesthete (*felix aestheticus*):

> The character of the happy aesthete demands *askesis* and aesthetic exercises, the more frequent repetition of similar actions, so that there is an agreement between one's mental power and the character [of the "natural" happy aesthete] described in §§ 28–46 . . . and indeed, in reference to one object that is to be thought, to one thing, so that he might gradually acquire the habit of thinking beautifully. (*BA* 38)

Baumgarten's use of the term "askesis" refers to the genre of the spiritual exercise inherited from Hellenistic philosophy, a term that was virtually synonymous with the training of the mind through the careful coordination of semiotic practices (above all speaking, reading, and writing) with patterns of thought and bodily activity. The aesthetic is therefore an *ascetic*, but only in the more archaic sense of the term as one who exercises.

The aesthetic exercise does not castigate the flesh, but rather, develops patterns of thought, cognition, and behavior precisely by means of the flesh. Aesthetic activity could be designated, in the largest sense of the term, as a provocation of the flesh—not as a disciplinary structure that submits the flesh to regimes of self-negation, nor as an attempt to encumber the subject and merely constrain action through norms and rules, but as a form of subjectivization whose experience of the world has been intensified by concentrated acts of sensible cognition.

The goal of the aesthetic exercise is to produce a unity between mental states and natural dispositions in the concentration of the mind on one thing (*in unum cogitandem, in rem unam*). The aesthetic exercise therefore modifies the self not by turning the self toward its own consciousness—that is, precisely not through Cartesian introspection—but rather, by focusing its activity on an object, by redirecting psychic energy toward sensuous phenomena. The act of concentration draws the subject away from its own consciousness and into the world of things, and in doing so, maintains, shapes, and refines its dispositions.

The continual maintenance and exercise of beautiful thought is necessary because the natural dispositions of the happy aesthete are constantly in danger of falling into torpor and inactivity: "Nature . . . if its dispositions or capabilities are not augmented by means of continual exercises . . . grows quite a bit weaker and degenerates, regardless of the extent to which it is endowed" (*BA* 38). Although Baumgarten claims that an act of reflection in aesthetic cognition is sufficient to generate an aesthetic exercise, he nevertheless recommends daily regimes of practicing oneself in beautiful thought depending upon the specific realm or medium of the beautiful toward which one directs oneself. The intrinsic temporality of the exercise consists in continual repetition. The form of the exercise simply demands a medium, be it painting, writing, or the body itself. A painter practices with the brush, a writer practices with the pen, and a woman, whose medium, for Baumgarten, is her own body, decorates and embellishes herself through artifice: "a woman who grooms herself daily in order to give pleasure and be beautiful" also partakes in aesthetic exercises (*AGB* 98).[29] The basic condition of the aesthetic exercise is that it be directed to the world of the senses and the world of appearances.

In addition to repetition, the aesthetic exercise requires imitation. If, according to Baumgarten—who shared the Aristotelian prejudices of his day—works of art are primarily mimetic, then the exercise in fact exults in its own derivative status as a second-order imitation: the imitation of an imitation. The task of imitation itself nevertheless presupposes an authority, an *Anführer*, or one who has made judgments about the beautiful and who pre-selects the material: "These exercises . . . must be determined according to a very good choice on the part of those who should first educate the beautiful spirit. . . . However, one must also turn the exercise away from ugliness and prevent such an exercise by drawing attention to that which is better" (*AGB* 98).

The aesthetic exercise therefore unfolds within the intersecting demands of repetition, imitation, and authority. Moreover, the exercise harnesses and directs the cognitive powers of the aesthete in such a way that both the works generated by aesthetic activity as well as the self that produces these works become subject to a process of constant revision: "The exercises must be continued, but in such a way, that one always corrects the mistakes" (*AGB* 99). The authority figure that guides the exercise—a shadowy presence that is felt more than explicitly thematized throughout Baumgarten's writings on aesthetic exercises—in fact becomes responsible for a fully saturated training of perception, from the most minute and microscopic detail of attentiveness to the most extravagant and explicit rule-based products of theoretical rationality. Baumgarten constructs an ascetic ladder, one that begins with perception and the simple enumeration and recognition of particular details, continues through passive exercises of reading and understanding, moves onward to active exercises of imitation, until it finally culminates in "discipline" (in the sense of a learned doctrine), or the capacity to generate a *theory* of art, which itself feeds back into the construction of the self. Baumgarten describes "aesthetic discipline [*Disziplin*]" as "the epitome of all theories of the beautiful that show me how I can bring it about, how I can think more richly, more nobly, more truthfully, without the input of which, to a certain extent, I would not have been able to achieve such a lofty goal" (*AGB* 106).

The purpose of the aesthetic exercise is not to maintain the human being in a state of equilibrium with nature, but rather, to stimulate and spur the drive toward transcendence and maintain it in a state of continual excitation.[30] If aesthetic cognition shapes its own dispositions through a regime of successful aesthetic exercises, it nevertheless produces a being whose activity is characterized by perpetual restlessness. The aesthete does not have a fixed personality with a given set of traits, even though Baumgarten believes to have isolated certain innate inclinations that tend to be associated with the aesthetic character. The openness of the aesthete is in fact constitutive of his or her existence, although this openness is drawn instinctively toward expansiveness inasmuch as it consists in an innate magnitude of the heart (*magnitudinem pectoris connatam*), or "the instinct most driven toward greatness, above all in those who attend to how easy is the transition from great things to the greatest things" (*BA* 36). Greatness of heart is predicated on an impetus toward perfection, a movement toward that which is most noble, and as such, must necessarily remain indefinite; it describes not the property of a static entity, but the drive of a dynamic being.

The happy aesthete has been endowed with qualities as well as a set of practices that both structurally prohibit inertia and become emblematic for the capacity to transcend, that is, to progress beyond his or her initial situation. Moreover, although Baumgarten fashions the exercise as a ladder that leads eventually to a system of reciprocal interaction between producing beautiful works, producing theories about beautiful works, and producing a beautiful self, he nevertheless comprehends that certain regimes of aesthetic training cannot travel through channels of explicit, rule-guided action. Indeed, rather than banishing contingency and danger from the sphere of the exercise, Baumgarten concedes that certain aesthetic practices may corrupt the flesh, but claims that such risks in no way invalidate the overall existence of aesthetic askesis. The aesthetic exercise is peculiar because it does not seek to diminish the inherent contingency of sense perception; rather, it draws upon this very contingency as part of the order of nature itself.

Just as sensuous experience—which falls under the rubric of clear yet indistinct cognition—is incapable of being analyzed into its constituent parts, so too are some forms of aesthetic exercise incapable of being articulated in a system of rules. One may properly call such exercises "aesthetic" not only because they exercise capacities of human cognition, but also because these exercises themselves are rich, overdetermined, and resistant to explication. Certain aesthetic *exercises* (as exercises of the senses) may themselves become *aesthetic* exercises (as exercises that cannot be "analyzed" into a predetermined set of properties) inasmuch as they draw upon the unpredictability of spontaneity rather than the explicit guidance of preestablished authority. Baumgarten not only legitimizes properly "aesthetic" (irreducibly sensuous and non-theoretical) exercises, but sees such exercises as the point of entry into aesthetics as a character-generating practice. He calls these exercises "αὐτοσχεδιάσματα," or "improvisations without the direction of the learned arts by which the exercising person is strengthened" (*BA* 42). The term αὐτοσχεδιάσματα is borrowed from Aristotle, who describes the birth of poetry—or more precisely, the origin of poetic activity—as a result of non-theoretical and immediate action: those gifted with poetry "brought poetry into being from improvisations [ἐγέννησαν τὴν ποίησιν ἐκ τῶν αὐτοσχεδιασμάτων]" (*Poetics* 1448b).[31] For Aristotle, improvisation plays an important role not only in his account of how human beings create works of art, but of how art as a distinct mode of human activity came into being. The aesthetic exercise anthropologizes Aristotle's insight, construing spontaneous and unexpected activity not merely as a part of artistic creation, but as an irreducible part of the aesthete's interaction with the sensuous world in general.[32]

Through the figure of the aesthetic exercise, Baumgarten—perhaps unintentionally—aestheticizes the figure of the aesthete: some part of the aesthete's very way of maintaining his or her identity will remain forever obscure and impenetrable to all attempts at clear and distinct apprehension. He compares the nature of such aesthetic exercises to a child who learns but does not know exactly what he or she is learning nor how he or she is learning it—nor even perhaps *that* they are learning: "The naturally beautiful mind will be exercised and strengthened and obviously exercises itself, even when it does not know what it is doing" (*BA* 44).[33] In this instance, the exercise happens not merely as the result of a conscious choice or an act of will, but in a state that confounds the categories of activity and passivity, fitting itself into a chain of spontaneous actions and reactions. The aesthetic exercise functions even when its mechanism is not transparent to the agent who acts.

Despite an attraction to the complexity and richness of sensuous perception, the need for constant stimulation, the spontaneity of self-organization, and the non-transparency of the aesthete's actions to his or her own conscious activity, Baumgarten's aesthetics nevertheless operates explicitly within the rationalist framework established by Descartes and Leibniz. As we have previously mentioned, he believes strongly in the inherent correctness of rule-guided cognition, and believes that one of the characteristics of the happy aesthete consists in the ability to "theorize," that is, the ability to develop normative rules for beautiful art: "For the general character of the happy aesthete, *learning* [μάθησις] and aesthetic education [*disciplina aesthetica*] is necessary, a theory about what influences the form and content of beautiful cognition that is more perfect than that which may be achieved through nature alone" (*BA* 48). However, in the aesthetic exercise, what matters is not merely the inherent truth of such rules, but more importantly, the transformative capacity that rules bring to the human mind, the way in which they insert the human being into the dynamic of transcendence that is the central feature of beautiful thought.

The domain of aesthetics as a whole, however, cannot be reduced to rules precisely because of the "confused" nature of sensuous experience, its impossibility of ever being broken down into constituent parts. From the perspective of the happy aesthete, rules can only take on a heuristic value; they function as steering mechanisms, as controls over the development of the self that immerses itself in the organization and disorganization of the sensible world. Rules appear as formal reservoirs of potentiality, neither intrinsically good nor bad: hence, "a false rule is always worse than no rule" (*BA* 56). Within the parameters set by the aesthetic exercise, rules are not mere constraints to action, but discursive forms that actively and productively contribute both to the formation of the sensible world and the expansion of the self that inhabits it.

If rules have their place in the aesthetic exercise, such rules do not preclude the maintenance of a horizon of openness, an attunement to a space in which the validity of rules is suspended and unpredictable affects intrude on the otherwise tightly controlled practices of aesthetic askesis. Such is the space of inspiration: a total state of being that, following the model offered by Plato's *Ion*, is incapable of giving an account of itself or codifying its activity such that it could be reduced to rule-guided cognition. Inspiration represents the limit horizon of askesis since it points to a way of being that cannot be made part of an exercise. The inspired self exists outside the central organizing characteristics of aesthetic askesis, namely, repetition, imitation, and disciplinary control.

Inspired cognition transgresses the law of probability, creating a space in which the improbable becomes actual: in inspiration, "a certain strength expresses itself and the soul manages to do something that—without this *furor*—it would not have been able to achieve" (*AGB* 114). Inspiration is made possible by an excess of potential energy through which the soul overcomes its own apparent limits. However, Baumgarten's concept of inspiration is not theologically inflected; it is not predicated upon divine intervention, nor does it come about by a miracle or a deviation from the order of nature, but rather, it results from a purely immanent operation conditioned by the fluidity and indeterminacy of the sensible world, of the physiological state of the body and the happenstance of situation. As such, inspiration is very much part of the world rather than outside it; it is temporally and spatially anchored in sensuous reality. Baumgarten describes inspiration as follows:

> [The creative act in inspiration] does not take place through a miracle, but rather, it is achieved according to the position of the body in its exterior circumstances, through its present and past condition. In this way, one is endowed with the capacity to achieve something that, in hindsight, one realizes one would not be able to achieve again and about which another person would have to confess that he would not have been able to achieve this act in similar circumstances. (*AGB* 115)

Inspiration takes place from within the interwoven system of subject, body, and environment as something that appears to the aesthete as a form of exteriority. The aesthete may be prepared and trained to make this state into an aesthetically productive one, but inspiration itself cannot be conjured up actively by the will of the aesthete alone. Phenomenologically, however, the inspired aesthete in fact amplifies the very cognitive states that had been produced in aesthetic askesis. Specifically, inspiration shares characteristics with an ascetic ecstasy: "The beautiful spirit meditates with such strong powers on his theme that he cannot at this time pay attention to other objects. This is the degree of consciousness that one calls ecstasy [*Ekstasis*]" (*AGB* 114). The aesthetic exercise aims at this very state, namely, the concentration of attentive powers onto one thing such that distraction becomes impossible. Whereas askesis reconciles this state of heightened concentration with controlled techniques of self-formation, inspiration comes from the outside and occasions a sudden perturbation of the ascetic system. Rather than training the self, inspiration provokes a phenomenological dispossession of the self: a state of transport irreducible to the self-produced ecstasy of the aesthetic exercise.

Inspiration that is channeled into a work of art must embody itself and must thus move from ecstatic cognition to the organization of signs, becoming legible precisely as that which escapes the mimetic order, as that which cannot be imitated:

> If one wishes to investigate whether inspiration was present in an author, one must read him precisely. It will often appear to us that we could very well imitate it; and yet, when we try it afterwards, we are everywhere lacking, and we feel that we are unsuccessful. When we perceive this phenomenon, then we can certainly deduce that the author was in a sort of inspiration [*Begeisterung*]. (*AGB* 115)

Inspiration, although it escapes the control of the aesthete, nevertheless can be fed back into an aesthetic exercise as regulative stimulation, as a state at which the exercise aims, but which remains ultimately just beyond its reach. That is why, at its core, the aesthetic exercise can never claim complete sovereignty in its attempt to produce the happy aesthete. Intrinsic to the aesthetic exercise is therefore an attunement to that which comes from outside of the exercise itself. Some aspect of aesthetic cognition will continually and irreducibly remain sensitized to the unconscious, opaque, and ultimately, unknowable presence of an exteriority inherent within one's own aesthetic-perceptual capacities, the possibility that at any instant, one might be carried away by powers beyond the limits of conscious control to improbably perform that which, as inimitable, breaks the chain of mimetic reproduction.

Although inspiration can neither be provoked nor controlled, it nevertheless presupposes a nature that has already been "awakened" through improvisational exercises.[34] Moreover, the openness to inspiration must be balanced by the aesthetic exercise of the learned arts, or the *ars erudita*. The learned arts prepare the aesthetic individual for developing a theory of art, that is, the ability to intuit and select rules that guide not only aesthetic activity, but the dispositions of the sensuous self. These dispositions include an openness to all situations in which inspiration might suddenly, and perhaps unexpectedly, grab hold of the aesthete. The acquisition of knowledge through erudition facilitates an open attunement to the exteriority of the event of inspiration. The *felix aestheticus* therefore forms a bridge between contradictory tendencies, between the health of spontaneity and the need for agency, between the features of sensuous perception that are impossible to analyze and those that can lead to a theory—in the sense of an ability to formulate rules—of the beautiful.

Baumgarten's aesthetics, from its inception, moves in a space that is at once philosophical and anthropological, one that modifies the rationalist devaluation of the senses in order to produce a new type of human being.[35] However, if aesthetics seeks to produce a subject, this production can in no way be seen as "anthropotechnical," or as a system of exercises that aims at the immunological optimization of the human being faced with life-threatening risks. Above all, the aesthete does not represent a finished product corresponding to a given normative or ethical ideal. In order to conceptualize the formation of the human being in a way consistent with its inherent finitude and openness, as a being sensitive to the indeterminate and overdetermined complexity and unpredictability of sensuous reality, Baumgarten invents a new type of exercise. He situates the aesthetic exercise in a region located between spontaneity and order, between opacity and transparency of action. Above all, these exercises produce a subject who is never complete, but continually thirsts for beautiful thought, a form of mental activity that represents the desire for perfection of sensible knowledge rather than its attainment.

Whereas Leibniz saw the necessity of a well-ordered cosmos in the timeless, mathematical structures of the human mind, Baumgarten, by modeling the happy human being on sensuous experience, opened not merely knowledge, but also the order of the cosmos itself to the contingency of human perception. At the same time he understood that only by opening oneself to sensuous experience does one have the ability to attune oneself—or to fail to attune oneself—to an ordering of the world that exists merely in potentiality and not as a metaphysical or ontological given.

Baumgarten therefore found it necessary to theorize a new type of truth—namely, aesthetic truth—as a discursive form produced by the practices particular to the aesthetic self. As a form of truth derived from sensuous being in the world, aesthetic truth moves in a horizon that is permeated with risk: it acknowledges the possibility of progress and improvement, but may at any time fall victim to the temptation of error. As an analogy of reason (*analogon rationis*) rather than reason itself, aesthetic truth makes sensuous the unchanging realm of metaphysical truth; but *as* sensuous, aesthetic truth unfolds in a horizon of contingency. Its validity can only be made manifest in the modality of probability rather than certainty. For Baumgarten, art exercises what one might call a *Wahrscheinlichkeitssinn*. It is also for this reason that he adopted the Aristotelian conception of truth as probability; aesthetic truth is determined by what is "believable" or "relevant" in a work of art. He cites Terence's dictum in *Heautontimorumenos* as an example of aesthetic truth: "You seem to speak truth and how the matter stands [*Videre verum, atque ita, uti res est, dicere*]" (*BA* 404). Aesthetic truth, or the truth of sense experience, stands continually under the sign of appearances, and as such, differentiates itself from purely logical truth by the integration of unpredictability—the "seeming" of the sensuous world rather than the "being" of the logos—into its operative horizon of meaningfulness.

The principle of aesthetic truth as probability, all appearances to the contrary, does not merely reformulate the Aristotelian principle of mimesis in a derivative manner. Probability as a feature of poetics for Aristotle and probability as aesthetic truth for Baumgarten refer to two entirely different conceptions of probability. For Aristotle, the probability of a work of art was linked to its mimetic efficacy; works of art were effective when they gave not an exact, but a probable or necessary representation of a series of events (*Poetics* 1451a). Far from diminishing poetry's importance for Aristotle, the "law of probability" increases the gravity and the philosophical value of poetry, for poetry thereby concerns itself, above all, with universals of exemplarity, or with "what such or such a kind of man will probably say or do" (*Poetics* 1451b) and not with singular events that did happen. For Baumgarten, aesthetic truth as probability does not refer merely to truth as exemplarity—what such a man might have or might not have done given his character—but foregrounds the human being as one who can produce alternative worlds precisely *from* contingent singularities.[36]

Aesthetic truth can therefore never be separated from contingency, or in the philosophical language of rationalism, contingent things (*contingentia*). According to Baumgarten, contingent things require relations to other contingent things in order to become intelligible: "contingent things cannot be represented as singular things unless they are possibilities of some total universe" (*BA* 418). Aesthetic truth therefore designates precisely that which "is" and "is not" the case, that which refers to an order of coherence that holds contingent things together in one and the same space. And this striving for aesthetic truth foregrounds yet another singularly sensuous capability, namely, the ability to invent worlds that diverge from that which is given. The aesthete introduces novelty into the sensuous world in such a way that this novelty, this "difference" between the real and the fictional, aligns itself with metaphysical paradigms of order and organization. Baumgarten calls the form of truth peculiar to the aesthetic coherence of contingent things "heterocosmic" truth (*veritas heterocosmica*), or the truth of other worlds. Heterocosmic truth belongs to the work of art as its inherent principle of organization and to the activity of the happy aesthete as a way of making contingent phenomena hang together.

Aesthetic truth as probability therefore does not merely reconfigure the mimetic theory of art as it had been articulated in antiquity, subordinating action to what a specific type of person would or would not have done. Rather, aesthetic mimesis as the creation of *probable* worlds—as the creation of a world that differs from that which exists—expands the imagination such that its only constraint consists in its conformity to the laws of cosmic order as a whole. The conformity to such laws describes how the work can simultaneously be "fictional" and "true." Moreover, this criterion for aesthetic truth—as the coherence of contingent multiples in a way that is analogous to the binding forms of ontological order—demarcates the line that Baumgarten dares not cross, and it is here that he reveals himself as the intellectual heir of Leibniz and Wolff: the creation of other worlds, although irreducibly different than the real, must nevertheless cohere with the principle of sufficient reason, with the notion that all appearances—even those that are invented by the human mind—have a reason for being the way they are.

Baumgarten's aesthetics therefore lays the groundwork for a conception of literature and art as a realm burdened by the weight of a metaphysical, transcendent ontology, a realm that functions as both test and guarantor of the well-ordered organization of phenomena. The coupling of aesthetic form with ontological order opens up not only a new horizon for the role of art—one that undergirds eighteenth-century poetic practices and whose traces can be found in the works of Klopstock, Goethe, Schiller, Hölderlin, and Novalis—but also conditions the emergence of modern aesthetics. This paradigm of art shifts the burden of sacrality from the axis of content onto the axis of form: it is the self-organization of aesthetic semiosis itself that clears a pathway into the realm of transcendent divinity. In this way, even "profane" poetry becomes sacred by virtue of its inscription in a system of coherent and cohesive probabilities that are governed by the metaphysics of the principle of sufficient reason. Baumgarten therefore redefines the terms of mimesis in a way that has decisive conceptual ramifications for modern aesthetics. Adorno's aesthetic theory, for example, may be understood as an inversion of Baumgarten's most significant gesture, investing form with the ability to bear witness not to the truth of ontology, but to its essential falsehood.

In the wake of Baumgarten's aesthetics, however, poetic form becomes not simply a mirror of ontological order, but its testing ground. To make art the central sensuous medium through which aesthetic consciousness generates and verifies metaphysical order invests artistic production and reception with a high degree of risk, and indeed, amplifies this risk.[37] Aesthetic truth therefore appears almost parasitic to the stability of the metaphysics of truth as such; a form of truth that was formerly confined to the pure realm of a priori rationality, as soon as it becomes part of sensuous reality, is at that moment susceptible to deviation, negation, and the stress of continual testing.

The logic to which this conception of art tends could be expressed as follows: the grand metaphysical truths—the principle of sufficient reason, the unity of the manifold, the law of non-contradiction, or the correspondence of thought with matter—are no longer simply self-evident, ontological givens, but must be actively *produced* in aesthetic cognition if their *aesthetic* truth is to be guaranteed. Such an aesthetic exercise demands effort and generates a certain way of being in the world, one that is attracted to cognitive processes that bind the world of phenomena: the harmony of form must be drawn out of the confusion of sensuous matter. *Aisthesis* therefore becomes an exercise in probability, in a way of relating contingent particulars that might—or might not—hang together. If the truth of the work of art is an exercise in probability, it makes possible a conception of art as an exercise that tests the human capacity to create order amidst a world that may at any point lapse into disorder. More than forty years after the appearance of Baumgarten's *Aesthetica*, one may find precisely such a conception of art in the work of the poet Friedrich Hölderlin.

Chapter 2

✦

The Persistence of the Fragile World

The Self-Organization of the Poetic Mind

Rivers hold a special significance in the works of Hölderlin. One can imagine why he was drawn to them. On the one hand, as figures of flow and turbulence, of movement and flux, there is something about rivers that remains unbound: an excess of energy that must be restrained, harnessed, or sublimated. On the other hand, rivers create natural and, in certain cases, political boundaries, zones of delimitation and difference that are often utilized to mark—or bind—distinct geographical areas. In Hölderlin's words, the spirit of a river makes "passage and border, with violence, on the originally pathless and outwardly expanding earth" (*MA* 2:384). In a concrete sense, the river gestures toward a metabolism of nature with itself that separates and links human populations, an energetic flow that traces the emergence of geopolitical lines of demarcation and coupling. Indeed, the two rivers that feature prominently in Hölderlin's poetry—the Rhine and the Danube—do not merely articulate geographical boundaries, but move through regions whose political boundaries were at the time themselves fiercely contested.

The attraction to rivers may therefore be linked to an overriding fascination with boundaries. As a thread that runs throughout his work, Hölderlin rarely ceases to interrogate the forms of power that emerge from the generation or breakdown of boundaries, be they physical, geographical, political, ethical, poetic, cognitive, or even ontological: how do boundaries emerge, what holds them in place and what perturbs their integrity, when ought one to stay within bounds and when ought one to transcend them, what renders the lines between heterogeneous spheres strict or porous, stable or chaotic, oppositional or harmonious?

Hölderlin's attempt to question the forms of activity linked to the positing or questioning of boundaries is something that he shares with the predominant philosophical tendencies of his age, an age for which a boundary was not merely something to be crossed in a geographical or political sense, but very much part of the internal dynamic of the landscape of the mind. In the forty years since the publication of Baumgarten's *Aesthetica*, the central philosophical revolution in Germany, after all, occurs through a revaluation, redeployment, and repositioning of the figure of the boundary, a movement whereby reason becomes resignified as that power that regulates what boundaries may be crossed in what particular way. Such is the fundamental gesture of the Kantian conception of *Kritik*. In its negative capacity, Kantian critique generates a boundary, guaranteeing that we "never dare to go beyond the limit of experience" (*AA* 3:16). And yet, this prescribed limitation of theoretical reason is counterbalanced by another form of reason—practical reason—as that which invokes the very space of noumenality that lies beyond the world of appearances: the suprasensible freedom of the human will. Critique, as both a negative limitation of speculative reason and a positive expansion of practical reason, therefore constrains and liberates at one and the same time: it holds knowledge within the boundaries of the sensible and secures the freedom of moral autonomy by placing it beyond these very boundaries.

Despite Kant's attempt to hold speculative reason within the strictly delineated boundaries of sensibility, the drive of speculative reason toward transcendence—toward an overcoming of the limits prescribed to it—proved to be too strong to contain. Hölderlin belonged to a generation of thinkers and poets that sought precisely that which Kant wanted to mark as forbidden: a sensuous sign, a legible text, or some form of physical manifestation that would reveal the concrete presence of freedom, of order, of coherence, of the divine as *part* of the world and not as that which lies beyond it. All those who had attempted to make this move—such as Schiller, for example, who in *On Grace and Dignity* (1793) claimed that beauty could harmonize the realms of transcendent reason and sensuous phenomenality—did not go far enough for Hölderlin. In a letter to Christian Ludwig Neuffer, Hölderlin writes that Schiller "had dared one step fewer over the Kantian borderline than he in my opinion should have dared" (*MA* 2:551).

At the same time, Hölderlin's poetry is driven by the withdrawal of this very object of desire, or that which would fully and unproblematically manifest and guarantee ontological order—be it a sign, a text, or an object—from the order of poetic discourse. Poetry does not give all at once, in a moment of perfect plenitude, to sensuous cognition that which reason denies it, namely, an opening onto the transcendent embodied in a singular, sensible sign; it does not come to an end with an "intellectual intuition,"[1] or a direct vision that opens onto a realm of noumena otherwise closed to human cognition; and its primary function is not to uncritically affirm a religious, moral, or cosmological order whose viability is so palpably called into question by the facticity of violence and suffering everywhere visible in the world. Rather, Hölderlin's later hymnic poetry derives its point of enunciation from the proposition that order as such—the order of sensibility, of nature, of history—has become problematic, that the world and our role within it are in need of clarification, if not transfiguration.

Poetry therefore does not provide an answer to the problem of order, but stimulates the mind to seek and produce the order that seems to have withdrawn from the world of appearances. The poetic spirit ("der poetische Geist") writes poetry in order to promote operations of connectivity amidst the facticity of dissolution, to find the "means of binding between spirit and sign" (*MA* 2:85). In doing so, poetry aims at a recurring movement that continually posits or generates a poetic-sensuous order only to undermine it, and then undermines it only in order to rebuild this order from the ashes of ruin. The movement of poetry is therefore non-dialectical inasmuch as it cannot progress unimpeded to its goal; in Hölderlin's words, poetry as a "standstill of movement" culminates in a privileged cognitive attunement, the "*infinitely beautiful* reflection" (*MA* 2:100), rather than in the direct and immediate intuition of transcendent harmony.

Although Hölderlin's poetic activity has often been examined as a response to Kantian aesthetics—and Kantian aesthetics does provide the central vocabulary and the central framework for understanding his poetics—one has less often seen the importance of Baumgarten as a thinker that, to a certain extent, makes Hölderlin's poetry possible.[2] To be sure, any positivistic evidence for a link between these two figures is scant. And yet, they both respond to similar problems: for both Baumgarten and Hölderlin, the process of producing and receiving poetry feeds back into the generation and verification of order, be it metaphysical-sensuous (for Baumgarten), or natural, historical, and political (for Hölderlin). Moreover, like Baumgarten's aesthete, Hölderlin's poetry concretizes the link between poetic cognition and the linguistic form-content matrices of the poems themselves. It is only in the living perception of the poem, with its irreducibly sensuous characteristics, that the problem of order can properly be raised for both poet and reader. For Hölderlin, although the concept of the aesthetic exercise was almost certainly foreign to him, the function of poetry nevertheless comes to light as a problem for sensuous cognition, the dynamic structure of which had been articulated by Baumgarten: as an exercise of the fields of sensibility, of remembrance, of binding and dissolving, of prognostication, of judgment, of measure, proportionality, and harmony. For Hölderlin, however, the ability to separate and bind attunes the human being not merely to his or her own personal capacities, but to the forces of binding and dissolution that inhere in both nature and history, in time itself as natural and historical temporality.

The exercise value of Hölderlin's poetry responds to the specific challenges posed by Kantian aesthetics and subjectivity. It is not merely that Hölderlin links poetry—the structure of the strophes, their moods, their articulations, and the process of poetic production itself—to specific configurations between subject, object, and a realm of identity that precedes the differentiation of subject and object, thereby suturing these differences into a more expansive totality. Rather, as we shall see in the next section in detail, poetry triggers an attunement to organization, one which attempts to recast moments of discontinuity as the necessary condition for the organic emergence of novelty. Hölderlin's contribution to the conception of art as an aesthetic exercise consists in the insight that properly "beautiful" art must stimulate cognition and binding procedures, and hence generates textual forms that are difficult, strenuous, and obscure. The formal difficulty of Hölderlin's later poetry should therefore not be seen as a psycho-pathological manifestation of mental collapse as much as the conscious provocation of cognitive performance: to increase the productivity of the exercise, one must push cognition to the limits of its capabilities. It is in this sense that Hölderlin dared to attempt one step further over the Kantian limits of reason.

Figures of disjunction in Hölderlin's poetry therefore signify both the condition for the generation of novelty—novel patterns of cognition, novel relations to a transcendental reality, novel political structures—and the danger and threat of collapse. Hölderlin's later poetics can therefore be described as an agonistic poetics, or a poetics of bifurcation: poetry becomes that linguistic act revealing points of discontinuity as an absolute potentiality poised between the emergence of the new and the threat of chaotic dissolution.[3]

Hölderlin initially saturates his poetry with disjunction in order to provoke a unifying cognitive act from the reader; the rhetorical strategies for which he is famous, be it parataxis, hyperbaton, or hard articulation (*harte Fügung*), do not reflect a conscious attempt to mirror the disorganization of experience, but rather, provoke and stimulate the human ability to find or generate coherence.[4] And yet, in certain poetic objects, the formal emphasis on discontinuity overtakes its supposed poetological goal of integration into a higher-order unity. In Hölderlin's later odes—for example, in his revisions of "Patmos"—gaps in poetic form correspond to lacunae in schemas of transcendental organization, in signifying systems attempting to guarantee coherence—in God, in nature, in the purposiveness of history.[5] The willful exaggeration of disjunction as an aesthetic exercise thus eventually undermines its own purported cognitive efficacy.

In the context of eighteenth-century aesthetics, one may therefore understand Hölderlin's formal complexity as a hermeneutic-cognitive response to the crumbling belief in traditional theological conceptions of natural and historical order.[6] In the *Enquiry Concerning Human Understanding* (1748), Hume had called into question the notion that one could, by analogy, infer the attributes of a divine being from a conception of nature operating as a harmonious, purposive system. As a response to Hume, in the *Critique of Judgment*, Kant grants that human cognition is ultimately incapable of intuiting the totality of nature, but nevertheless insists on nature's teleological purposiveness as an a priori idea.[7] More decisively for Hölderlin's poetics, in the essay "Idea for a Universal History from a Cosmopolitan Point of View,"

Kant links the purposiveness of nature to the historical emergence of a cosmopolitan political order:

> One may regard the history of the human race as a whole as the realization of a hidden plan of nature in order to bring to fruition an internally—and for this purpose as well externally—perfect political constitution as the only state in which all natural human capacities can be fully developed. (*AA* 8:27)

Kant invokes the self-organization of nature in order to bolster an idea of historical development toward a self-sustaining political order in which all citizens of the world can actualize their self-determination in a manner compatible with the self-determination of others. Kant portrays such a political order as an *idea* of reason, one that might never be actualized, but that nevertheless functions in a regulative sense. The validity of this political and historical idea shares the same teleological structure as the idea of nature as a well-ordered system. There is no longer any philosophical justification possible of a strictly metaphysical ontology of divine order; in its stead, Kant places the a priori regulative principle of natural purposiveness, a principle that, translated into the domain of human activity, posits the world-historical development toward a civic republican order as part of the dynamic of its unfolding.

Hölderlin's poetic response to the problem of order foregrounds dissatisfactions with Kant's postulates of reason—dissatisfactions that were all the more palpable for someone who clung with such intensity to the promises and dangers of revolutionary action in the attainment of this republican ideal. Kant, as Hannah Arendt has noted, was left in the peculiar position of having to deny the moral legitimacy of revolutionary violence while simultaneously affirming this violence inasmuch as it seemingly played a role in a collective movement toward a more just cosmopolitan order.[8] Hölderlin, however, was a revolutionary poet in every possible sense of the word, and sought not to justify revolutionary violence as much as to reinterpret the conditions under which such violence could be seen as redemptive rather than transgressive.[9] For Hölderlin, the conviction that natural or historical order could simply be posited as a regulative idea—especially when the revolutionary energy and violence required to achieve this cosmopolitan order (above all in the French Revolution) appeared ever more suspect—was not a sufficient principle of action; a revolution, as an intensification of contingency in which the old laws are suspended in order to make possible a new political order, may very well end in tragedy and catastrophe, that is, in a state in which this new order never materializes. To simply postulate an ideal order as an impetus for action does not take account of the difficulty of the suspension of order that this regulative ideal requires.

Poetry intercedes in the revolutionary space of modal transition, from possibility to reality to a historically intelligible necessity. Hölderlin remarks in his poetological essay "The Declining Fatherland" that poetry consists in "the explanation and unification of the gap and the contrast that takes place between that which has newly emerged and that which has ceased to be [*zwischen dem Neuen und dem Vergangenen*]" (*MA* 2:73–74). In this space between past and future, Hölderlin uses poetry to generate an "ideal recollection," or a form of cognition in which "the extant real, real nothingness appears, and that which is dissolving in the state between Being and Non-Being is grasped as necessary [*im Nothwendigen begriffen*]" (*MA* 2:73). Because the very existence of revolutionary disruption suspends the continuity of lawfulness and hence belies the sensuous manifestation of order—either as metaphysically harmonious or as teleological—the central task of poetry consists in the resignification of such disruption precisely not as contingent, but as the embodiment of a higher-order necessity.

Hölderlin draws on Kant's attempt to ground natural and historical teleology in the same faculty of practical reason by developing a form of poetry in which the reading of natural signs—as filtered through poetry—trains the mind for the reading of historical signs. If thinkers or poets could invent a new way of reading nature, they might find evidence to suggest whether the contingency of politically revolutionary action fits into a conception of nature as a purposive system. Poetic processes held between dissolution and emergence therefore attune the mind to perceive the disorganized organization inherent in natural and historical processes, thereby simultaneously foregrounding and stabilizing the contingency of revolutionary acts.[10] For Hölderlin, the dynamic of natural order—and hence of political order—cannot exist merely in a realm of utter transcendence, nor can it be invoked as a regulative idea, but it must be capable of being *felt*. It is through poetic semiosis, or through the sensitization of the mind to coherence amidst an intensification of contingency, that such a feeling becomes possible.[11]

The challenge to the poetic voice—for both poet and listener—therefore becomes to discern order amidst the chaos of suffering and thereby to justify the pain that accompanies unstable points of transition.[12] The cognitive state triggered by the fragmented and dissonant flows of poetic language tests both the poet's and listener's ability to discern the thread of organization amidst confusion. This cognitive state of organized confusion, or confused order, is in turn politicized. If consciousness can find and secure the thread of poetic language, then destabilizing revolutionary activity, which might otherwise appear as chaotic, meaningless terror, can be reinterpreted as the birth pangs of a new political order and reinscribed into a system of natural self-organization. The poetological and philosophical works in which Hölderlin articulates these intersecting semiotic operations of poetry, nature, politics, and consciousness are complex, and it is to these works and their particular metaphysical presuppositions we now turn.

Retention and Oscillation as Aesthetic Exercises

Within the framework of Baumgarten's aesthetics, the sensuous organization of the work of art becomes an analog for metaphysical truth inasmuch as it generates procedures of binding: that which is multiple, dispersed, and contingent is gathered together and made coherent. Such was the basic definition of metaphysical truth: the "order of multiples in unity" (*ordo plurium in uno*).[13] The work of art, as the sensuous analog of metaphysical truth, does not merely presuppose and manifest the coherence of an inherently differentiated cosmos, but calls into being a subject imbued with a form of cognition that would be adequate to this task.

Hölderlin's early philosophical and poetological reflections also aim to incite procedures of binding and connectivity in the actions undertaken by the poetic spirit. Although his reflections are often couched in the vocabulary of Fichtean philosophy, they are concerned with the problematization of the metaphysical definition of truth that the rationalist tradition took as an ontological presupposition: the relation between identity and difference, or that which makes a system of differences into a coherent and legible unity. There is nevertheless a critical distinction between metaphysical truth as the "order of multiples in unity" and Hölderlin's reflections on difference and identity. Whereas the metaphysics of unity includes internal differentiation as a precondition of divine order, Hölderlin attempts to conceptualize Being as a realm that consists not in the harmony or unification of multiples, but as a form of absolute identity that, although incapable of being represented discursively in a direct manner, nevertheless grounds and moves through differences.

Hölderlin takes up precisely this problem of relating difference to identity in an early philosophical fragment that has come to be known as "Being, Judgment." Written in 1795 on a single piece of paper torn from a book, this fragment demarcates two ontologically originary spheres, one for each side of the page: "Judgment" (*Urtheil*) and "Being" (*Seyn*). The fragment underscores an aporia—indeed, one of the central aporias of Western metaphysics beginning with the pre-Socratics—that results from the attempt to think identity and difference as ontologically primordial givens. The central problem is that the intuition and cognition of these two spheres—identity and difference, Being and Judgment (*Urtheil*)—presuppose and simultaneously exclude one another:

> Judgment [*Urtheil*] is in the highest and strictest sense the primordial separation of object and subject which are intensively unified in intellectual intuition, that separation through which object and subject first become possible, the "originary separation" [*Ur-Theilung*]. In the concept of separation there already lies the concept of the reciprocal relationship between object and subject and the necessary presupposition of a whole of which object and subject are the parts.

> . . .
>
> Being [*Seyn*]—expresses the connection between subject and object. Where subject and object as such are not only partially united, but so united that no separation can be undertaken without wounding the essence of that which is to be separated, there and nowhere else can *Being as such* [*Seyn schlechthin*] be spoken of, as is the case in an intellectual intuition. (*MA* 1:49–50)

Hölderlin links judgment to differentiation since *Urtheil*—both as concept and as signifier—can be broken down and analyzed into separate parts: the prefix "Ur" (originary) and the root "Theil" (part) designate an originary splitting. Originary differentiation is in turn related to reflective cognition: the act of judgment in reflection, traditionally articulating the relationship between particulars and generals, is anchored in the primordial splitting or differentiation that takes place between subject and object. Fichte—Hölderlin's central interlocutor in this document—had noted that this split takes place *within* the subject itself as a foundational act of reflective consciousness; according to Fichte, in the formulation "I am I" (*ich bin ich*), the subject posits itself as an object and only then can it reflect upon itself, becoming an object for itself as subject.[14] Judgment, for Hölderlin, therefore designates the split at the center of the subject that makes possible a form of reflective thought separating the self from the world, or rather, self as subject and self as object.

Being, on the other hand, designates *absolute* identity, a concept of identity that is quite different from the identity of two entities as *the same* or the harmony of singular multiples (what the rationalist tradition calls *contingentia*) in a coherent whole. The access to absolute Being does not occur via reflection or discursive thought—which tends to analyze and synthesize, differentiate and unify—but via "intellectual intuition." Intellectual intuition designates a pre-reflective sensitivity to the *ground* of differentiation.[15] The ground of differentiation and identity is localizable neither in the subject nor in the object, but rather, designates that domain of identity by virtue of which subject and object appear *as* subject and object. Hölderlin agrees with Kant that the totality of this ground is not available to experience in a single act of cognition.

Strictly speaking, there can be no relation between Being and Judgment. The conceptual paradox of the fragment thus consists in the—necessarily abortive—attempt to articulate relationlessness. If primordial differentiation relates itself to primordial identity, then one may not speak of identity at all, since the very category of relation presupposes difference. The two realms can only be conceptualized as non-relatable modalities. From the perspective of Being, differentiation exists as a form of violence; it cannot take place without "wounding" (*verletzen*) the being that is thus separated out from primordial identity. Being is not available to a subject as subject, but only to a cognitive operation—intellectual intuition—that bypasses subjectification and differentiation as such. From the perspective of Judgment, however, Being appears as precisely that which its own cognitive operations logically presuppose, and yet, that which must be excluded from appearing as that which it actually is (absolute Being) in the reflective cognition of a subject. One may therefore not speak of a return to Being through art or poetry as the "healing" of a wound inflicted by reflective thought, since the means whereby a subject might return—in and through the world of differences—would continue to hold open the primordial wound of separation.[16]

In what sense, then, could this document be understood not merely as a philosophical document, but as a poetological one? Poetry, as a movement among differences—Hölderlin will later describe this movement as an alternation of tones (*Wechsel der Töne*)—cannot be reduced to an intellectual intuition, or a mode of cognition that by definition excludes difference. If poetry is to remain confined within a field of pure differences, thereby condemning the subject to remain eternally damaged—separated from that which grounds it and binds it with all other phenomena—it must open up a zone of permeability between the seemingly mutually exclusive domains of Being and Judgment. The function of poetic activity would therefore consist not simply in provoking an "intellectual intuition" (whatever that particular act might be), nor in constructing Being as that which never appears in the world and therefore is banished absolutely from poetic representation, but rather, in generating an awareness that Being and Judgment do not simply constitute mutually exclusive ontologies by showing that they are in some even more primordial manner reversible with one another. Hölderlin's poetry will aim to generate a cognitive operation that is reducible neither to reflection nor to intuition—one that both binds together and separates Being and Judgment—as an oscillation between the identity of intellectual intuition as *felt* in poetic *aisthesis* and the differentiation of reflective consciousness as realized in poetic semiosis.[17] As we shall see, the poetic text, as well as the poetic consciousness called forth by this text, both makes visible this reversibility between Being and Judgment and seeks to train the human being to perceive this reversibility in the act of poetic cognition.[18]

The materiality of the object, the paper upon which Hölderlin writes the text "Being, Judgment" (or "Judgment, Being"), already suggests a novel approach to the problem of bringing together these cognitive modalities. The text itself—written on a sheet torn from a book, in effect sundered from its place of origin—embodies the operation of reversibility: on one side appears "Judgment," on the other side, "Being." The sheet of paper itself—like the leaf that stands for a form of poetic subjectivity that Goethe would later thematize in his poem "Gingo biloba"—becomes the emblem for that which is simultaneously identical and differentiated. In Goethe's words, "Do you not feel through my songs/That I am one and doubled?" (*GMA* 11.1.2:71). The composition of Hölderlin's fragment—its recto-verso structure, such that Being is part of Judgment and Judgment part of Being, both forming not mere "opposites" of one another, but each embodying the condition of possibility of appearance of its other—enacts an ontology that Hölderlin cannot fully capture conceptually.[19] The movement between these mutually exclusive modalities demands an embodied oscillation. In a letter to Christian Ludwig Neuffer, Hölderlin claims precisely to advance through an alternation between two different positions: "With my speculative pro and contra I believe to be coming ever closer to my goal" (*MA* 2:597). Being cannot appear (as appearance) without identity and difference, just as identity and difference only exist because of something that makes them recognizable *as* identity and difference. The flip of the paper, the turn of the page, represents a passage from one mode to the other—and it *shows* the Being that cannot be conceptually articulated, as articulation itself would seem to enter into the play of differences, and hence, be confined to the domain of Judgment, never to wager that step beyond the limits of reflective consciousness and symbolic representation.

One may approach the permeability of these two domains phenomenologically in a concrete and embodied manner reminiscent of Husserl's analysis of perception: while these two domains will never come to occupy the same spatial form of presence (one term remains obscured to the degree that the other is visible, e.g., as one turns the page), this difference is nevertheless sutured in the experience of the observer, one for whom the absent trace of the invisible domain remains as a ghostly presence of its other even after it has withdrawn from immediate perception. These supposedly mutually exclusive operations therefore come to occupy the same virtual space (rather than actual space) through binding procedures generated in an act of reading that consists primarily in an act of retention. It is perhaps for this reason that the operation of remembrance (*Erinnerung*) saturates this zone of permeability in Hölderlin's later poetological writings—a point to which we will return.[20]

Although the system formed by reader and text operates in excess of conceptual articulation, language itself forms the axis around which the whole exercise turns. In his later poetry and poetological writings, Hölderlin attempts to show—through continually thematizing the process of poetic production, *die Verfahrungsweise*—how Being also manifests itself *through* language, thereby dismantling the illusion that a supposedly conceptual medium presupposing differentiation is necessarily confined to the sphere of Judgment. According to Hölderlin, the poetic spirit aims for success at the most important moment (*Hauptmoment*) of representation, an act in which identity suffuses the realm of differentiation, "when [the poet] has understood . . . during the alternation of the spiritual form, *the form of the subject matter remains identical in all of its parts*" (*MA* 2:78). The purpose of Hölderlin's alternation of tones (*Wechsel der Töne*), a doctrine that he articulates in later poetological essays—in which constellations of objectivity, subjectivity, or the synthesis of both enter into second-order constellations with one another, each with a different set of cognitive intensities depending on the tone (lyric, epic, or tragic)—can best be understood within this larger framework of an originary identity that emerges from the dynamic of alternation itself.[21] The attunement to an originary identity moving through a system of differences prepares the poet for a cognitive receptivity to an internal logic of semiotic organization, one which illuminates the space of poetic expression "between the expression (the representation) and the free idealistic treatment [*Behandlung*]" (*MA* 2:81). The choice of material and the form of the poem, inasmuch as the poem alternates between modalities of language and thought that are both self-differentiating and yet part of the same poetic process, reveal the realms of Being and Judgment to be chiasmatically imbricated in one another.

Critical to this project's success is the activation of remembrance (*Erinnerung*), which designates the capacity to hold multiple—contradictory and complementary—tones in one and the same cognitive space.[22] In this context, Hölderlin's conception of remembrance resembles neither Platonic anamnesis, nor an elegiac remembrance of a lost relation to nature, nor does it even invoke a concrete memory associated with a specific intentional object. Although each of these forms of memory is present in Hölderlin's poetic work, remembrance as a poetological concept shares more in common with Husserlian retention than with either Platonic anamnesis, elegiac remembrance, or a memory preserved from past experience. Rather, Hölderlin describes as essential the activation of memory itself as a power that binds disparate temporal moments and links events that would otherwise appear as contingent multiples. In effect, he refers to remembrance somewhat as Baumgarten did in his *Aesthetica*, as an example of a binding procedure that brings the representational appearance of contingent multiples closer to the ontological ground that subtends their poetic organization, above all by framing these multiples as parts of a larger whole to which one has no overarching perceptual access. In Hölderlin's case, poetic consciousness presupposes a process whereby a seemingly incoherent chain of events—events that foreground the facticity of dissolution—is recollected, and in the process of making this dissolution present in the representation of recollection, "gaps" are filled out, thereby rendering the order of events intelligible. Hölderlin uses the term "ideal recollection" to designate the poetic conversion of contingent dissolution into necessary dissolution, that is, a movement whereby decline becomes the precondition of novelty:

> From the perspective of ideal recollection, dissolution as a necessity becomes the ideal object of the newly developed life, a glance back upon the path that had to be taken, from the beginning of the dissolution up until the point when, in the new life, there can occur a recollection of that which has been dissolved, and thus, as explanation and union of the gap [*Lüke*] and the contrast occurring between present and past, there can occur the recollection of dissolution. (*MA* 2:73–74)

The idealistic recollection functions as a differentiated temporalization of that which was formerly reserved for the intellectual intuition, replacing the absolute unifying function of Being with a differentiated and more relative proxy: the cognitive—and poetic—power of memory.

One ought to recall that for Baumgarten, the ability to "bind and separate" constituted one of the central capabilities of the *felix aestheticus*. For Hölderlin, it is this cognitive faculty itself, not the particular object to which this faculty attaches itself—although the poet does require an object that nevertheless must be appropriate to remembrance as the act of temporal binding—that guarantees the stability of Being as a primordial domain of ontological identity suffusing the system of differences.[23]

The cognitive excitation provoked by the poetic spirit is that of an exercise in generating coherence amidst the difficulty of any such operation. This feature, integral to Hölderlin's poetological writings, reaches a limit point in the form of the writings themselves, in their long and complex syntax, in the piling up of conditional phrases, in a confusion of words that stretch the limits of retention at the same moment in which they proclaim its centrality. These works are also examples of poiesis, indeed, perhaps the most extreme of poetic experiments with cognitive retention. Hölderlin says of the poetic spirit:

> It is its final task to have a memory [*Erinnerung*] in the midst of harmonic alternation so that the spirit remains present to itself not in the individual moment, but in one moment as in another in a state of progression and in the different moods [*Stimmungen*], just as it is wholly present to itself in the infinite unity which is the point of separation for the unified as a unity, but also the point of unity of the unified as oppositional, and then finally both at the same time, so that in it [in *ihr*, the *memory*] the harmonically opposed neither opposes as something unified, nor unifies as something opposed, but rather both in One are felt as inseparably unified opposed, and as something felt, it is brought into being [*als gefühltes erfunden wird*]. (*MA* 2:87)

Memory is less a relationship to the past than a focusing of the present, a concatenation of multiplicity and unity—in fact, of oppositional terms that, by logical definition, would seem to exclude one another—in one and the same cognitive landscape. The poetic process unfolds not merely in order to unify oppositions, but in order to establish a higher-order coherence of oppositionality and identity. Difference must efface itself as difference, just as identity must disperse itself across difference and thereby become something "felt." It is the thread created by memory as something felt amidst the alternation of tones that restores an awareness of poetry, consciousness, and history as a self-organizing totality.

Hölderlin explicitly says that this originary unity-difference imbrication is invented or found (*erfunden*). *Erfinden* signifies both to invent and, in a more archaic sense, to find.[24] To invent through language, at least according to Hölderlin's elaboration of the procedure of grasping the poetic spirit, is indeed to find a form of differentiated coherence that is always already there, one that is called forth through the faculty of remembrance. Hölderlin's phrase from the poem "Remembrance" ("Andenken"—which here carries elegiac undertones that are not present in the concept of *Erinnerung*) comes to mind: "But what remains, the poets provide" (*Was bleibet aber, stiften die Dichter, MA* 1:475). The phrase, seen in the context of Hölderlin's poetological writings, does not merely repeat the hackneyed claim of poetry to immortality, its ability to eternalize as handed down from Pindar and Horace, but rather, foregrounds the traces of the cognitive process by means of which the poet has phenomenologically provided himself with the evidence of originary being, that which "remains." The act of creativity and the foundation of "that which remains" are therefore reversed: it is not that the poets create something that remains, but rather, that which remains, the poets bring into being. The creative process (*stiften*), one that is also a grounding or a foundational gesture, emerges from something remaining that predates this process. This form of remembrance minimizes the importance of intentionality in the production of coherence: poetry does not produce the "remembrance of" an original unity existing in the past, but remembrance itself—as cognitive act—reveals identity as the thread that binds the alternation of contingent and often distressing forms of differentiation.

Hölderlin's *Hyperion* and the Askesis of Narrative Enunciation

In Hölderlin's only novel, *Hyperion*, remembrance itself—the narration of the past as that which binds disparate events to one another and reveals their latent principle of organization—constitutes the primary channel through which, in the words of the narrator, the "dissonances" of the eponymous character are resolved.[25] The novel begins at what seems like a catastrophic end point: the point at which all normative and intersubjective means of binding—Hyperion's friendships, political ambitions, kinship ties, possibilities for erotic fulfillment, links to the nation as spatiotemporal landscape and as historically conditioned culture—have been effectively reduced to a zero point; all outward manifestations of order have been suspended. Hyperion returns from a period of exile in Germany to his native Greece to establish his life in separation from others as a hermit. Although the novel begins with the completion of a homecoming, a *nostos*, Hyperion nevertheless remains in exile, displaced in his own land, and thus fully under the thrall of Judgment as *Urtheilung*: isolated, detached from the world, dispossessed, with the permanence of nature as his only consolation. His only human attachment is to the German Bellarmin, the figure to whom Hyperion addresses his letters as well as the figure who prompts Hyperion to retell his story.

The story Hyperion narrates thus begins as the story of an inverted order, of a potentiality that has seemingly culminated in a nothingness: the loss of friendship (Alabanda), the failed revolution (the abortive liberation of Greece from the Turks), a doomed erotic relationship (Diotima), and the self-evidence of a historically fallen world in which new forms of natural sacrality and renewal are routinely dismissed and mocked. Hyperion begins his narrative with the incapacity to represent that which he has lost, a double negativity inasmuch as he has lost not only his friends, but their voices, the traces that would make them present: "dead and gone are my beloved friends, and I hear nothing more through no voice of theirs [*ich vernehme durch keine Stimme von ihnen nichts mehr*]" (*MA* 1:614). The nothingness of this "nothing more" (*nichts mehr*) at the beginning of the novel becomes, through the process of narrating the past, an openness to a latent possibility inherent in the world of appearances at the very end of the novel, one suggested by the novel's final words: "more to follow," or *nächstens mehr* (*MA* 1:760). To summarize: the narrative describes the process through which "nothing more" (*nichts mehr*) is converted into "something more" (*nächstens mehr*).

A close examination of the structure of *Hyperion* reveals inversion as its main—even if irregular and complex—narrative principle, an oppositional relationship between the enunciation of the narrative act (in narratological terms, something belonging to *discours*) and the content of the narrative act (*histoire*).[26] At the beginning of the novel, Hyperion's narrative voice has already reached the nadir of despair, whereas the narrative content of Hyperion's story at this point—that which he tells to Bellarmin in his letters—begins with an opposed state of almost edenic bliss: his experiences as a child, exploring nature with the father figure Adamas, soon to be followed by a politically idealistic friendship with Alabanda and an erotic relationship to Diotima. As every one of these relationships disappears or disintegrates, the narrating voice gains in coherence and confidence, becoming paradoxically more *empowered* just as that which it narrates declines and the bonds that hold together the world founder.[27]

The recollection of the catastrophic past therefore serves the strengthening of the present, and the act of narration itself becomes a form of askesis: "I want to try my breast on the joys of the past until it becomes like steel, I want to exercise myself through them [*ich will mich üben an ihnen*] until I become invincible" (*MA* 1:673). The basic gesture of the narrative therefore moves in a direction opposed to that which is narrated: the narrative content that is most full of hope and possibility (childhood) is related at the most closed and dispossessed point of narration. The more catastrophic the narrative itself becomes, the more hopeful becomes the position of the narrator, until he finally tells his entire life story, returning to the moment of his exile from which the story begins. This return to the beginning of the story in fact constitutes the true *nostos*: a narrative homecoming of the mind to its point of departure.

This return to the present through the narration of the past occasions a radical resignification whereby each of the contingent forms of loss have been revivified and reappropriated by virtue of the power of recollection. Ultimately, in the novel's final pages, Hyperion recovers the unrecoverable, conjuring and animating the ghostly voices of those that had been lost: "It was as if I heard Diotima's voice, the voice that once exhilarated me in the days of joy" (*MA* 1:759). The narrative of catastrophic decline is converted through its very means of narration into an emergent renewal of being, an ecstatic monologue (or perhaps even a dialogue with this ghostly voice) that rises, phoenix-like, "like the crackle of fire when it flies up and leaves the ashes behind" (*MA* 1:760). As others have pointed out, the narrative culminates not in the full resolution of internal dissonances, but in yet another ontologically ambiguous act of speech: the narration of a present moment of reconciliation still saturated with its conflict-ridden past that nevertheless—and this is its most important feature—produces an openness to a future: "More to follow" (*MA* 1:760).[28]

Such is the dynamic that is central for an understanding of Hölderlin's work: poetry takes the raw material of dissonance, contingency, and confusion and, through the organization of this material in poetic form, seeks to convert the detritus of its own history into an exercise for the affirmation of the self and the totality of being in which this self is embedded. This ruse of narrative logic—whereby a negative can be, in an almost alchemical fashion, converted into a positive—is often difficult to perceive, since it always still bears the traces of its traumatic origin.

Let us take an example: Hyperion's "Song of Destiny." The song begins with a transposition of the meaning of Hyperion's own name, "he who wanders above," to the realm of the gods, "you wander above in the light" (*Ihr wandelt droben im Licht*, *MA* 1:744). Hyperion thus appears alienated at first from the redemptive content of his own name; he emphatically belongs among those who do not "wander above in the light." The poem seems to mirror the narrative logic of his own life story, culminating in a series of contingent events and stochastic processes that have no necessary link to one another. The final strophe appears as follows:

> To us it is given
> Never to rest,
> The suffering mortals
> Disappear, fall
> Blindly from one
> Hour to the other,
> Like water thrown
> From cliff to cliff,
> All year long down into uncertainty.

Doch uns ist gegeben,
Auf keiner Stätte zu ruhn
Es schwinden, es fallen
Die leidenden Menschen
Blindlings von einer
Stunde zur andern
Wie wasser von Klippe
Zu Klippe geworfen,
Jahr lang ins Ungewisse hinab. (*MA* 1:745)

The final lines of the song reveal the logic that seems to characterize Hyperion's own narrative. And yet the poem itself, in the context of the novel, performatively provokes the opposite cognitive response from Hyperion: in the moment before singing the song, Hyperion remarks, "I wanted to strengthen myself, I took my long-forgotten lute in order to sing a song of fate that I had learned from speaking after Adamas in happy, unknowing youth [*das ich einst in glücklicher unverständiger Jugend Adamas nachgesprochen*]" (*MA* 1:745). Hyperion's "Song of Destiny" does indeed function as a microcosm of the novel of the whole, but not because it reveals this narrative to be one of merely contingent events thrown together, but precisely because it resignifies and recontextualizes the narration of contingency as something that performatively "strengthens" the person who narrates.

The blindness of fate is resignified at its moment of enunciation as a form of connectivity in a meaningful web of associations and memories, joining the verbalization of adult despair to the openness of the child: a linguistic gesture that animates, appropriates, and revitalizes the words of an absent, beloved father-figure (Adamas). Contingency and necessity, fate and uncertainty, become inextricably bound with one another. The narrative of the fall is told with the breath of paradise, just as paradise contains within it the story of the fall.

The formal organization and disorganization of Hölderlin's poetry is therefore not mimetic—or at least not merely mimetic—but ascetic inasmuch as it aims to produce forms of cognition that, precisely in narrating dissonance and contingency, stimulate higher operations of connectivity. The misrecognition of poetic form solely as mimetic leads Adorno, for example, to portray fragmentation and poetic dissonance as the reflection of a problematic reality. For Adorno, the form of Hölderlin's poetry enacts a "paratactic revolt against synthesis."[29] On the contrary, if one takes Hölderlin's poetological remarks into account, the complexity of poetic form does not mirror a problematic reality, but produces cognitive work in poets, readers, and listeners—work that binds together potentially incommensurable events and modalities.

Unlike Baumgarten and the rationalist philosophical tradition, metaphysical unity—the *ordo plurium in uno*—is not posited as part of the given ontological structure of reality, but is thematized as an unknown to be guaranteed or refuted by the exercise of poetic cognition. The fragility of aesthetic truth—its "analogical" relation to rationality that holds sensible experience poised between transcendent order and pernicious error—was already present as a latent possibility, albeit one not explicitly problematized as such by Baumgarten, of the discourse of aesthetics. For Hölderlin, this fragility becomes concretized, integrated into the patterns and flows of the poetic spirit. Poetic form therefore aims at the stimulation of retention, or that which permits human beings to generate coherence in the midst of dissolution. It cannot ever guarantee this order perfectly (because to do so successfully would lead to the superfluity of the aesthetic act itself), but it can open the possibility of this order at the moment of its supposed foreclosure.

Hölderlin's poetry may thus be regarded as the stimulation of acts of binding in the representation of the seeming failures of historical, political, and personal realities. Parataxis, although Adorno emphasizes this formal property of Hölderlin's poetry in particular, does not constitute the only—nor even the central—rhetorical figure through which poetic form triggers and exercises capacities of binding. When Hölderlin advocates the "inversions of periods" in poetic organization, Adorno understands such techniques to bolster his thesis concerning the primarily disruptive value of parataxis:

> The inversion of the periods itself therefore must become greater and more effective. The logical position of periods in which the ground or reason (the grounding period) [*dem Grunde (der Grundperiode)*] is followed by becoming, becoming is followed by the goal, the goal is followed by the purpose, and where the subordinate clauses are simply attached at the end of the main clauses to which they refer—is only very rarely useful for the poet. (*MA* 2:57–58)

Hölderlin argues that syntax should not simply reflect teleological order, that a sentence should not simply unfold in an unproblematic and direct manner from ground to purpose. He also calls into question all forms of hypotactical arrangement that streamline cognitive work. And yet, through this critique of unproblematic syntactical subordination, one should not be tempted to elevate parataxis to a position of paramount importance for Hölderlin's poetry. Indeed, the indeterminacy brought about by Hölderlin's negation of a certain form of hypotaxis makes it questionable to pinpoint a precise rhetorical structure as an element of disruption in Hölderlin's poetics. Furthermore, Hölderlin often uses parataxis not as a figure of disruption, but on the contrary, as a foil for complex syntactical structures—in effect, as cognitive relief. Parataxis, far from resisting synthetic acts, provokes cognitive states that imply or demand a binding function from the receptive activity of the reader as a precondition for the generation of meaning. Disjunction and inversion intensify the demand for and power of synthesis.

For Hölderlin, poetry activates a process of recollection and retention, testing the human capacity to "hold" a memory or to maintain its presence in the face of rapid alternation or at a moment of danger in which the connective tissue joining different temporal moments threatens to dissolve. Inversions must be "greater and more effective" (*MA* 2:57) in order to intensify the stimulation of reading technologies that gather and retain fragmentary multiples. Hölderlin's use of the "period" in fact already invokes an act of binding, since this concept in eighteenth-century poetics refers to any phrase that elicits the hermeneutic process of understanding: the presentation of parts whose comprehensibility emerges from a process of self-organization, taking on its final contours only when the passage itself has come to an end. According to the contemporary encyclopedist Sulzer—whose definition may also be found in other eighteenth-century manuals of poetics—a period consists in "a speech, or if you will, a comprehensible proposition that is determined by itself and composed of many other sentences in such a way that the complete meaning of the speech is not fully available until the last word."[30] Hölderlin's attempt to increase the intensity of "inversions" in the period seeks to prolong the process of incomprehensibility, to stretch the boundaries of the intellect and defer the moment of totality that would organize parts into a coherent whole.

Hölderlin's deployment of poetic form does not therefore maintain the integrity of the particular against its subsumption in the general—as Adorno would have it—as much as poetically stimulate processes of retention, something that any rhetorical gesture of interruption or inversion could perform. Moreover, Hölderlin's use of poetic form does not "mirror" social or cosmic order—neither positively nor negatively—and therefore must be differentiated from Baumgarten's aesthetics, whose central semiotic function consisted in linking the particularized artifact with a transcendent, metaphysical ontology. Rather, form acts as a catalyst for the strenuous deployment of cognitive attentiveness whose central medium is the flux of poetry itself: it is an aesthetic exercise for which the self-evident givenness of the transcendent order has been suspended.

And yet, some concept of order—which is both sensuous and sacred, natural and political—nevertheless posits the attractive point toward which the poetic act tends, a point that, regardless of the extent to which it recedes or eludes capture, cannot fully disappear from the horizon of poetic cognition. Paradoxically, it is only through a semiotic-cognitive increase in tension through the *deferral* of final meaning that poetic language can forge a pathway into the reversibility of Being and Judgment. Incommensurable modalities and alternating tones (as instances of differentiation, *Ur-Theilung*) are shown to be part of a larger self-identical system (as a manifestation of absolute identity, *Seyn*) in one and the same cognitive act. For Hölderlin, the formal complexity of poetry does not index the weight of a fallen world—or at least does not succumb to this weight—but on the contrary, attunes the poetic spirit to the self-organization of oppositional multiplicities through a regime of perceptual training.

On Falling Apart and Coming into Being

The following section will not attempt to interpret Hölderlin's poem "The Rhine" in its entirety—an undertaking that would be impractical and quixotic in this context—but will instead focus on the final third of the poem as the culmination of an attempt to think the co-presence of conflicting modes of poetic cognition (Judgment and Being, cognitive differentiation and non-cognitive indifferentiation). Taken as a whole, "The Rhine" offers a view onto a potentially threatening but ultimately harmonious self-organization of nature, or the way in which overwhelming natural forces (the Rhine's origin as an overabundance of energetic autonomy) are eventually tamed, creating the conditions whereby human cultures may grow and flourish. Human development is embedded within natural processes that foreground, harness, and redirect the revolutionary capacity of dissolution as an inherent dynamic of life itself. The production of an energetic equilibrium through a form of sublimation—a river whose tempestuous origin threatens to overflow its boundaries—generates the conditions that govern the reconfiguration of a political and social order.

In light of the seeming equilibrium established at the end of the poem, "The Rhine" has been interpreted by scholars as a poetic meditation on the conditions of possibility of cultural renewal, a renewal whose terms include a critique of the autonomous subject that strives for mastery over the world; a critique of proximity to, or overdependence on, the gods; the poetic mediation of a divine or transcendent order; and the instantiation of an interiorized poetic language and the knowledge of its limits (as exemplified by the figure of Rousseau).[31] My own reading approaches the poem as an exercise in poetic cognition that realizes itself in the flow of poetic temporality, in a space that is simultaneously chaotic and indifferentiated, as well as highly structured and linked to a system of differences. It is only in a state of cognition that can alternate between differentiation and indifferentiation (or between Judgment and Being) that the world can reveal itself as well-ordered. However, as we shall see, this justification of the order of the world is anything but a traditional metaphysical ontology that posits an order to all that is and thus seeks to maintain the status quo; rather, the specific form of order that the poem explores is one that includes the possibility, and perhaps the necessity, of upheaval and revolution as one of its essential characteristics.

One of the most striking characteristics of "The Rhine" (both as the poem itself and as a sign within the poem)—which is confirmed by the diversity of critical opinions about the poem—consists in its irreducibly enigmatic quality. In the poem, this enigmatic quality is marked by the phrase: "Ein Räthsel ist Reinentsprungenes" (*MA* 1:343), which may be translated as "a riddle originates from purity" or "that which originates in purity is a riddle" or, as the *rein/Rhein* wordplay indicates, "a riddle springs from the Rhine" or "whatever originates from the Rhine is a riddle." The gnomic quality of the utterance makes it a prime example of its own metalinguistic proposition: it is both the representation of and the performance of a riddle. The phrase suggests that the world of appearances, including all figures that could and should function as mediators of the divine (the river, Rousseau, Socrates, Isaak von Sinclair), has become problematic, and that one must be trained to decode the grammar of mediation in order to dissolve the knot of the riddle. The following investigation is based upon the premise that the poem is attempting to teach its readers what cognitive and aesthetic movements are necessary for the reception and interpretation of its own enigmatic logic of appearances. To read this poem as an aesthetic exercise is to ask the question: what movements of the mind is this object demanding from those that enter into the flow of its sounds and meanings?

The final third of the poem addresses this very issue. That Hölderlin understood the end of the poem to represent something like an idealized form of cognition is evident from what he described as the structural law of the poem. "The Rhine" was composed concomitantly with the doctrine of the alternation of tones.[32] Hölderlin had noted the "law" (*Gesez*) of the poem in the margins of the manuscript as follows: a chiasmatic, triadic structure whereby the first two parts alternate between equalization and opposition in the relation between form and content and the third part signals a reconciliation of oppositions.[33] The scenes of harmonious equilibrium characteristic of the third section of the poem are accompanied by a rigorous cognitive training implicit in the poetic representation of this reconciliation. The current analysis will turn its attention to the specific exercise value invoked in the course of the poetic act.

In the poem's final strophes, the concept of remembrance shifts from a recollection of origins to a form of memory as cognitive retention in the midst of poetic flux. The phenomenological complexity of poetic retention may be illustrated in one of the culminating scenes of the poem, a "bridal feast" in the thirteenth strophe in which humans and gods are supposedly reconciled:

> . . . those unreconciled
> Are changed and hurry now
> To hold out their hands to the other
> Before the benevolent light
> Goes down, and night comes.
>
> For some, however,
> This quickly passes, others
> Retain it longer.
> The eternal gods are full
> Of life at all times; but until death
> A mortal too can retain
> And bear in mind what is best

And then is supremely favoured.
Yet each of us has his measure.
For hard to bear
Is misfortune, but good fortune harder.
A wise man, though, was able
From noon to midnight, and on
Till morning lit up the sky
To keep wide awake at the banquet.

To you in the heat of a path under fir trees or
Within the oak forest's half-light, wrapped
In steel, my Sinclair, God may appear, or
In clouds, you'll know him, since, youthfully, you know
The good God's power, and never from you
The smile of the Ruler is hidden
By day, when all
That lives seems febrile
And fettered, or also
By night, when all is mingled
Chaotically and back again comes
Primaeval confusion. (*PF* 511)

. . . aber die Unversöhnten
Sind umgewandelt und eilen
Die Hände sich ehe zu reichen
Bevor das freundliche Licht
Hinuntergeht und die Nacht kommt.

Doch einigen eilt
Diß schnell vorüber, andere
Behalten es länger.
Die ewigen Götter sind
Voll lebens allzeit; bis in den Tod
Kann aber ein Mensch auch
Im Gedächtniß doch das Beste behalten,
Und dann erlebt er das Höchste.
Nur hat ein jeder sein Maas.
Denn schwer ist zu tragen
Das Unglük, aber schwerer das Glük.
Ein Weiser aber vermocht es
Vom Mittag bis in die Mitternacht,
Und bis der Morgen erglänzte
Beim Gastmahl helle zu bleiben.

Dir mag auf heißem Pfade unter Tannen oder
Im Dunkel des Eichwalds gehüllt
In Stahl, mein Sinklair! Gott erscheinen oder
In Wolken, du kennst ihn, da du kennest
Des Guten Kraft, und nimmer ist dir
Verborgen das Lächeln des Herrschers
Bei Tage, wenn
Es fieberhaft und angekettet das
Lebendige scheinet oder auch
Bei Nacht, wenn alles gemischt
Ist ordnungslos und wiederkehrt
Uralte Verwirrung. (*MA* 1:347–48)

An apparent moment of reconciliation at the bridal feast—in which those who are unreconciled hurry to embrace their enemies before the setting of the sun—emerges from the background of an intersubjective and transcendent disharmony, a dissonance that appears both between human beings themselves and between the divine and the human. A typical approach to such dissonances would, one might think, consist in the attempt to concretely represent a scene of reconciliation. However, the crux of the poem consists less in the *representation* of reconciliation as such than in the *retention* of that which is only reconciled in a space of non-representation. The space of reconciliation is concentrated in the figure of a gap. Hölderlin himself defined the "ideal recollection" as an attempt to fill the gaps of the past in order to reinterpret contingent events as the emergence of a higher-order necessity.[34] The bridal feast foregrounds this process directly inasmuch as the locus of reconciliation in fact occurs in the space of a problematic temporality: a pause generated by a scene situated between stasis and acceleration. Hence, the passing of time is both frozen and rushing by: at the banquet, those who are not reconciled (*die Unversöhnten*) hurry to offer one another their hands at a liminal time and space, a marriage feast in the twilight of a setting sun. And yet, those who are "unreconciled" appear fixed in a gesture of reaching that ultimately never arrives. If there is a space of reconciliation, it occurs precisely in the transition *between* periods, at the end of one strophe and the beginning of the next. The beginning of the fourteenth strophe hints at this unrepresented reconciliation: "For some however/*This* [my emphasis] quickly passes." The deictic "this" projects the moment of reconciliation back into a space between strophic turns, ultimately leaving this moment imaginatively indeterminate. The moment of fulfillment therefore occurs at what is simultaneously a moment of poetic transition.

The representation of this space in which both gods and mortals commingle does not appear *in* language, but *through* language, in the gaps of the poetic space itself as the space of remembrance (*Erinnerung*). It becomes the task of the reader to retain *this*—not only the moment of reconciliation that has not been represented, but also, and more importantly, the specific cognitive state that accompanies this non-representation, an in-between cognitive poiesis: if, "for some, however/*This* quickly passes," others, however, "retain *it* longer" (my emphasis). The poetic space unfolds in a tension between "this" and "it"—introducing yet another layer of indeterminacy into the order of deictic reference—which in turn points not only to the imagined moment of reconciliation, but also self-reflectively to the poem itself: the poetic stream passes too quickly for some, whereas others retain it longer. When the poet foregrounds the retention of "this," he moves the domain of reconciliation into the space of poetic self-reflection. The desire to "retain" the stream of poetry, to hold something into place that is rushing by, places the figure of the river itself, "The Rhine," the half-god figure of mediation between the divine and the human, in the place of the poetic stream of semantic content. Mediation becomes integrated into the immediacy of the poetic flow, itself fixed by the continual presence of the fleeting moment. The memory of the rush of poetry in which the germs of reconciliation lie dormant holds the key to keeping that which "is best" amidst the perpetual facticity of instability, indeed of misery and suffering: "but until death/A mortal too can retain/And bear in mind what is best/And then is supremely favoured."

To give an idea of the tenuousness of this image: the poem does not represent reconciliation as such, but rather, initiates a *potential* retention of a *temporary* state of *imagined* reconciliation between figures of unreconciled opposition. Yet it is precisely this tenuous and imagined reconciliation that seeks preservation. Ironically, it is this imagined and potential fortune, the improbable happiness (*Glük*) of poetic retention—rather than the mere experience of negativity and trauma—that triggers the desire for permanence and stability: "For hard to bear/Is misfortune, but good fortune harder." Unhappiness does not abhor transience; indeed, misery wishes that the moment might pass. Only the fortune of happiness truly seeks eternity. As Diotima says in *The Symposium*, the principal text to which these lines allude, "love loves the good to be one's own forever" (206a).[35] The Socratic hero, both drunk (inspirationally and non-cognitively attuned) and sober (conceptually and semantically reflective) at one and the same time, dwells not merely in an erotic affirmation of the transient moment as it opens onto eternity, but in a state of poetic balance: "Yet each of us has his measure [*Maas*]," where "measure" refers to poetic meter, moderation, and self-limitation.[36] A wise man (*ein Weiser*), embodying the Socratic doctrine of eros, can *retain* the oscillation between immediacy and reflection, poetic intoxication and sober contemplation—or what would later, in Nietzsche's terms, be framed as Dionysian dissolution and Apollonian form (here embodied by Socrates, who for Nietzsche was an emblem of the rationalistic decline of Dionysian tragedy). The capacity to differentiate and unify, to conceptualize and inspire, belongs inherently to the poetic state in which limitation and delimitation, *Maas*, fuse with a sense of infinite expansion, or where Judgment meets Being. Only

Socrates drinks as much as everyone else and nevertheless retains full control over himself, remaining "wide awake at the banquet" (*beim Gastmahl helle zu bleiben*).

For the Socratic hero of the penultimate strophe, the reconciliation of inspiration and reflection, immediacy and mediation, no longer occurs in a fleeting liminal state of non-representation, but unfolds along a temporal continuum from "midday" to "midnight" to "morning." The reconciliation of oppositions would seem to have reached its zenith at this point. And yet: the one temporal modality omitted here is that of the dawn, the dusk, the *Dämmerung*—afternoon jumps discontinuously from midday to midnight and morning without a twilight—that time of transition during which, in the immediately preceding strophe, the gesture of frustrated reconciliation had been frozen. Even in the supposed representation of permanent plenitude through the figure of Socratic drunken sobriety, the poet foregrounds a temporal gap that the listener must fill in—and the content of this gap (twilight) refers this very process, as if in a hermeneutic loop, to the moment of the bridal feast in which the representation of reconciliation was first refused in its concreteness, admitted only as a projection in a space of retentive consciousness. At the very moment of supposed plenitude, the poet, via an absence in the temporal continuum, sends the listener back to the space of twilight liminality between the thirteenth and fourteenth strophes. The structure of the poem itself attracts the listening consciousness to these gaps and involves the participation of consciousness in the lines' own poetic self-referentiality. It is this process of "filling in" gaps that poetic retention is meant to activate.

The final strophe, building upon this exercise of retention, thematically brings together individual perception, a conception of the divine, and as we shall see, the disruptive event of revolutionary politics. The choice of Sinclair as the hero of the poem's final strophe is, in this respect, carefully chosen (although Hölderlin first meant to dedicate the poem to Wilhelm Heinse, author of *Ardinghello*). Sinclair cannot be merely understood as "the other," as Heidegger, for example, would claim,[37] but refers back to the nexus of ideas that Hölderlin was exploring with Sinclair when Hölderlin wrote "Being, Judgment." Isaak von Sinclair, in manuscripts that have come to be called "Philosophical Raisonnements" ("Philosophische Raisonnements"), claims that the unity of primordial identity and reflective differentiation, Being and Judgment, is only possible in aesthetic perception: "The binding of all points of view takes place in that of *Aeisthesis*."[38] Only aesthetic cognition can transcend the limitations of subject-centered thought and come to encompass the binding of all possible perspectives. In the Fichtean terms employed by Sinclair, *aeisthesis* does not designate merely the traditional conception of aesthetics as sensuous cognition in a particular relationship to the experience of art, but rather, refers to a positing that exceeds the positing of the subject, or rather, a form of positing outside of that which posits itself as a subject. Sinclair derives his account of "aeisthesis" etymologically from a reconstruction of the

Greek as "A Εις (εαυτον) Θεσιν," a "not-into-itself" positing that Sinclair calls "a higher positing" (*ein höheres Setzen*).[39] In later corrections to his manuscript, Sinclair wrote "athetic" above "aesthetic" in several instances, thereby moving the aesthetic closer to a non-posited, absolute realm—although he continued to regard the aesthetic not as a denial of self-reflective subjectivity, but as "something *appearing*, but not *being* and something what *should not be* [etwas *erscheinendes*, aber nichts *seiendes* und etwas was *nicht sein soll*] . . . . The principle (true *Principium*, beginning, as axiom) cannot be athetic, and must therefore be aesthetic, a totality for the imagination."[40] Although aesthetic consciousness implies a totalizing cognitive operation that nevertheless cannot "exist" as a thing (inasmuch as aesthetic cognition tends toward something *unbedingt* or un-thinged), it also exhibits certain features of sensuous cognition—akin to Baumgarten's conception of aesthetics—and hence appears irreducible to conceptual or discursive knowledge. Sinclair writes, "knowledge [*Das Wissen*] is always imperfect for the aesthetic, for inasmuch as it is a product of reflection, it presupposes originary differentiation [*die Urtheilung*], which makes it impossible to think unity as something concrete, impossible to think the aesthetic ideal."[41] For Sinclair, *aeisthesis* binds sensuous experience to the realm of the "unposited" that cannot enter reality as an entity, operating instead along cognitive channels distinct from discursive knowledge (*das Wissen*). Sinclair opens up the semantic potentiality in the very concept of the aesthetic itself, revealing a continuum stretching from sense perception (or for Hölderlin, the activation of poetic retention) to *aeisthesis* as the binding force of all disparate points, from lower aesthetic cognition (as that which escapes discursive analyzability) to ideal aesthetic cognition (as that which binds all particulars into a whole in a non-cognitive, non-discursive experience).[42]

As we have shown previously, Hölderlin's poetological reflections, which are in dialogue with Sinclair, do not frame poetry as an attempt to grasp the divine through an inexplicable, mystical form of intuitive cognition but rather, by linking the absolute identity of Being to the differential self-organization of acts of poetic receptivity and creativity. The unrepresentable identity of Being, although it conditions the appearance of individual differences, more importantly emerges negatively from these differences in the temporal succession of poetic organization. It is this process to which Hölderlin refers when he uses the term "poetic spirit." In "The Rhine," Hölderlin fashions Sinclair—along with Rousseau and Socrates as they had appeared in earlier strophes—as different models of a type of *felix aestheticus*, a human being (or perhaps a demigod) who can move fluidly between contingent phenomenality and the realm of the absolute that infiltrates appearances and binds them together. The aesthetic human being, through the particular cognition triggered by the work of art, generates the coherence of signs and things in a way that mitigates their fragmentary multiplicity and inherent contingency.

The poem frames the reversibility between the differentiation of Judgment and the non-differentiation of Being—both of which, without the other, appear as deficient and threatening forms of signification—as a relationship between light and dark. Sinclair, as the poem's final hero, inserts himself into this oppositional relation, remaining luminous in a way true to his proper name: as "Saint Clair" (saint of light, "Sinclair" pronounced in French), he dwells in brightness, even in the absence of visibility, "By night, when all is mingled/Chaotically and back again comes/Primaeval confusion." Hölderlin, through Sinclair, elucidates the relation between non-differentiation and differentiation as a perceptual chiaroscuro:

> And never from you
> The smile of the Ruler is hidden
> By day, when all
> That lives seems febrile
> And fettered, or also
> By night, when all is mingled
> Chaotically and back again comes
> Primaeval confusion. (*PF* 511)

The conceptions of daytime and nighttime seem negatively connotated in this passage, as if the divine smile—as the smile of the "ruler" of the gods—were somehow "shining through" a living force that is either feverishly connected (*fieberhaft* and *angekettet*) or chaotically undifferentiated (*gemischt* and *ordnungslos*). Both modes of appearance, which seem to refer respectively to a predominance of reflection or immediacy, mask the divine, since Isaak von Sinclair is singled out for his ability to know the divine *despite* the conditions brought about by day and night. In this respect, it would be incorrect to see "night" as simply identical to Being in the fragment "Judgment, Being," since Being, in the earlier fragment, seems to be endowed with hints of an idealized erotic fusion and wholeness, whereas night, as the darker side of that which is without differentiation, represents a parasitic form of absolute signification. Above all, these two modalities, day and night, are not mere allegories for cognitive functions; they also describe a poetic semiotics, language as "feverish" and "chained"—each word somehow connecting to every other word, even if syntactically they appear separated far from one another—and nevertheless chaotic and mingled.

In spite of the idealization of Sinclair's act of aesthetic mediation, one cannot speak of a "reconciliation" of conflicting modes of apprehending the world in the final strophe. The poem does not permit the facile resolution that one can intuit the divine in both conceptual density (mediated reflection) and the rush of the poetic experience (immediate intuition), in both the feverish "connection" of all things as discrete objects and the chaotic "mingling" of all things as belonging to absolute indifferentiation. A close examination of the grammar of Sinclair's mode of perception suffices to complicate the notion that some originary opposition between Judgment and Being is simply resolved in the final lines of the poem.

In the poem, it is written that the divine is never hidden from Isaak von Sinclair, "by day / . . . or also / by night" (*Bei Tage . . . / oder auch / Bei Nacht*). Let us reflect briefly on this formulation. The phrase used in the poem is "or also," *oder auch*. A paradoxical relation emerges from the revelation of the divine, for taken together one of these prepositions potentially designates exclusion ("oder" in the sense of "either/or"), the other inclusion ("auch"). Hölderlin infuses the word cluster "oder auch"—a normally rather common conjunction—with its literal strangeness, approximating what Deleuze would later call a "disjunctive synthesis."[43] At the very point of transition between night and day—precisely that realm of twilight that both mixes and separates two opposing modes of appearance—there emerges a disjunctive-conjunctive chiasm: the exclusionary force of the "or" (*oder*) is not merely negated, but rather, transformed by the inclusionary force of the "also" (*auch*). The "oder auch" structure therefore enacts poetically the turning of the double-sided page connecting and separating Judgment and Being. If both reflection and intuition appear negatively connotated in the final strophe as forms of cognition and semiotic modalities that obscure the divine rather than reveal it (presenting the world as either feverish or chaotic, overdetermined or undifferentiated), the hinge or the point of transition—the "or also"—appears precisely as that which participates in the revelation of the divine: a fulcrum linking two mutually exclusive domains, a moment of fusion at the instant of separation. For Hölderlin, retention amidst alternation fills out the gap between reflection and immediacy; poetic language does not simply describe this transition, but linguistically enacts it.

As far as I am aware, the phrase "or also" (*oder auch*) occurs in only one other instance in Hölderlin's poetic oeuvre: at the end of "Menon's Lament for Diotima" ("Menons Klagen um Diotima"), the poet apostrophizes multiple and differentiated sacred forms ("you divine ones," "you hours of consecration," "holy intimations," "you pious requests," "you inspirations," "you goodly spirits"), imploring each of these forms to remain until we—poet, beloved, reader, and these differentiated manifestations become inseparable in this "we"—meet again:

> Stay so long with us until we meet, on communal ground,
> There, where all the blessed souls stand ready to return,
> Where the eagles are, the planets, the messengers of the father,
> Where the Muses are, from whence come heroes and lovers,
> There, or also here, we meet, on dew-covered island . . .

> Bleibt so lange mit uns, bis wir auf gemeinsamem Boden
> Dort, wo die Seeligen all niederzukehren bereit,
> Dort, wo die Adler sind, die Gestirne, die Boten des Vaters,
> Dort, wo die Musen, woher Helden und Liebende sind.
> Dort uns, oder auch hier, auf thauender Insel begegnen . . . (*MA* 1:295)

In this poem as well, "or also" occurs at the precise moment of a deictic shift, from there to here, simultaneously linking and separating the transcendent and the immanent. The shift, as it swivels around the disjunctive-synthetic "or also," catapults the poetic voice into the beyond and the beyond into the fabric of the relation between first-, second-, and third-person plurals, between "we," "you," and "they," creating a common network of pluralities in which difference is simultaneously instituted and elided, generated and revoked.

The "or also" of Hölderlin's poetry therefore toggles between two different perspectives—one in which the experience of connection and separation appears, and one in which there is a ground outside of all subjectivity and outside of all objectivity, and yet interior to both, a poetic disjunction-conjunction that joins and separates originary indifferentiation and discursive reflexivity. In "The Rhine," it is not the description of these two perspectives that leads to an intuition of the divine, but rather, the poetic performance of these two perspectives in the condensation of meaning and the flow of rhythm that occurs at a moment of transition. Hölderlin's poetry in this instance attempts to linguistically disclose the inseparability of originary unity and reflective consciousness, between intuitive attunement and poetic semiosis, and it does so by provoking the paradoxical state of the "or also" in the consciousness of the reader. The "or also" therefore condenses the particular cognitive state for which Hölderlin's poem functions as an aesthetic exercise.

One may therefore regard Hölderlin's poem as a phenomenological poetic experiment. The successful poetic experiment, for Hölderlin, would secure an ontological interpretation of the world, one in which all supposedly disparate elements of life hang together. In his poetological writings, Hölderlin repeatedly refers to the concept of solidity (that which is solid or *vest*) as something that would guarantee the security of the human being amidst the instability of appearances. As Hölderlin's poetological comments make clear, however, the quest for solidity is itself fraught with uncertainty. Hölderlin's concern with securing, holding tight, verifying, bears witness to the lack of a solid ground at the center of existence. The poetic revelation of the reversibility of Being and Judgment, in their positive forms, or night and day, in their semiotically parasitic forms, is meant to secure what the intelligibility of myth gave to the ancient Greeks and what theology ought to provide for Christians in an age in which both of these relations to reality are either no longer viable (myth) or are becoming less so (Christianity).

The verification of the reversibility of Being and Judgment is not a simple semiotic operation that remains confined within the boundaries of poetic cognition, but one that opens up onto the order of all that exists, encompassing natural and historical phenomenality.[44] In Hölderlin's poetry, all is resonance. Language, nature, sacrality, consciousness, and sociopolitical organization—every layer of being sounds out the others through a dense web of interrelationships. This resonance model, as we have seen, is not unique to Hölderlin; even Kant had argued for an analogy between the purposiveness of nature and a teleological history of political development.[45] Kant, however, believed that the mysterious operations of nature—as well as the ever-changing configurations of history—were fully inaccessible to human cognition, thereby opening up a gap between natural and historical order on the one hand and human subjectivity on the other. Hölderlin, unlike Kant, understands poetic activity as a mode of cognition through which the organization of nature lays itself bare *through* human signifying practices; he thereby seeks to reveal the Kantian gap between nature and subjectivity as an illusion by making poetic cognition part of the same textual fabric of natural order. And if Hölderlin can poetically embed human cognition in nature, he can perform a similar operation—drawing on the Kantian logic of analogy—with respect to political organization.

The resonance model of semiotic layering thereby permits Hölderlin to politicize the mental state of the reader in the flow of poetic cognition, framing both text and perceptual consciousness as a cipher for an emergent nation.[46] Hölderlin's poetic form of the aesthetic exercise is unthinkable without this political subtext. In the poetological text "The Declining Fatherland," Hölderlin makes explicit the reciprocal relationship between the human being, nature, and sociopolitical order. The movement that poetry initiates with its conception of alternation, or *Wechsel*, mirrors the logic of nations: "This decline or transition [*Untergang oder Übergang*] of the fatherland (in this sense) is felt in the parts of the existing world in such a way that, at the very moment and to the very extent that the existing world dissolves, the newly entering, the youthful, and the possible is also felt" (*MA* 2:72). The affect generated by the alternation of tones, the feeling of continuity amidst chaotic fluctuation, reverberates with a hermeneutic procedure that Hölderlin applies to history and the potential development of a new state. The poetic procedure becomes the testing ground for this state's future validity.[47] The poet's attempt to secure the spirit—if successful—would interpret the birth of a republican state from revolutionary violence. The French Revolution, the violence of which had been disseminated and amplified in German-speaking principalities, becomes the testing ground for Hölderlin's poetic hermeneutics. Hölderlin's poetry, however, unlike Jacobin propaganda, concerns itself less with bringing the revolution into being than interpreting its consequences, its plausibility, and its legitimacy.[48]

In "The Rhine," Hölderlin once again uses a turning point to convey the reciprocity between human beings, nature, divine order, and finally, political revolution: "To you may . . . /wrapped/In steel, my Sinclair! God appear." The ambiguity brought about by the apposition purposefully blurs God and Sinclair—either God appears wrapped in steel to Sinclair, or God appears to Sinclair wrapped in steel—at a moment in which one or the other appears prepared for violence. Steel would seem to refer concretely to armor; but a god, hidden in steel, could just as easily metonymically stand for a blade, and more importantly, for the emblem of revolutionary violence as such: the guillotine.

The entire passage, however, is subordinated to the indeterminacy of the verb *mögen* (may), expressing possibility. The last strophe suggests that if Isaak von Sinclair—and the listener—can retain the thread of memory through the alternation of the ancient "confusion" of night and the "chained" (*angekettet*) feverishness of day, then God would also reveal himself in steel—just as he reveals himself in nature, in the forest, in the sky. The poetic process intends to describe the conditions of possibility whereby revolutionary violence and pantheism become compossibilities, where God reveals himself not merely in nature, but in the steel of the blade, in violent upheaval.

The specific form of poetic cognition ascribed to Sinclair—who, in addition to sharing Hölderlin's philosophy of aesthetic cognition, was also an engaged Jacobin—is therefore linked to a way of reading revolutionary signs. To successfully alternate between immediacy and reflection stimulates the process of retention—as an aesthetic exercise—in the poetic hermeneutic act, an act that, when applied to history, reinterprets radical change as the emergence of a more complete organic and political order. Such is the exercise given to the poet: to discern order at the point of dissolution. Hölderlin's poetry, however, reveals the tenuousness of this project; nature, the human being, and political organization, at points of transition between becoming (*Werden*) and dissolution (*Vergehen*), become concentrated in a tipping point between the birth of a new order and a descent into chaos.[49] Hölderlin restores to these transition points a sense of urgency; the longing for stability holds open the abyss at his feet.

Hölderlin therefore shows the world falling apart *or also* coming into being: a moment in which human cognition confronts a phenomenal world poised between dissolution and emergence. To attribute this operation to a crisis inscribed within an always already damaged world goes against the grain of Hölderlin's poetic project, namely to uncover the process whereby disorder might be revealed *as* latent order.

The node of concentration, this paradoxical space that appears as both dissolution and latent order, continually calls for its own repeated testing as evidence for the self-organization of natural, social, and cognitive systems. More provocatively, one could say that Hölderlin's form of poetic cognition, to the degree that it seeks to secure the operations of the poetic spirit and the natural world, continually tempts itself with its own destabilization. Such a practice opens itself onto the continual construction of the figure of the poet as a sort of self with its own peculiar way of reading signs: poetry does not merely attempt to verify a preexistent, dynamic order inhering in nature and history, but to strengthen the human being's ability to perceive this order. In order to strengthen this capability, however, Hölderlin must test and expand the limits of human cognition. Hölderlin's later poetic activity can therefore be seen as a provocation of the very breakdown against which poetry ought to secure the human being.

The figure of bifurcation, a figure for which the "or also" could stand as an emblem—in turn, an agonistic principle that inheres not only in aesthetic cognition, but in the order of nature and history as such—seeps into his poetic production, above all in his writings about tragedy. Alternative historical pathways, multiple forms of political organization, conflicting fields of sacrality torn between polytheism, pantheism, monotheism—each division multiplies, intensifies, reproduces itself until the attempt to unify these strands becomes more and more tenuous. The principle of bifurcation constitutes a latent figure motivating Hölderlin's own poetry; individual poems become confronted with their opposing tendencies—as with "The Rhine" and "The Ister," or "Andenken" and "Mnemosyne"—or themselves split into different versions, self-bifurcating, as is the case in "Patmos." Ultimately, Hölderlin seems to find himself confronted with a world in which multiple possibilities and incompatible trajectories threaten to overtake the attempt to integrate such possibilities into a revelation of a higher-order, transcendent unity. A cosmos in which no suffering goes unredeemed, one in which no act in the continuum of history is undertaken in vain, recedes further into improbability.

Chapter 3

✦

Resistance to Harmony and the Limits of Order

Hölderlin's Poetics of Bifurcation

Hölderlin's later poetic activity is sustained by a paradox that may be described as an intensification of the disjunction between the means and the ends of poetry, between what it actually does with its language and the desire that supposedly generates it. In Hölderlin's case, this disjunction seems to continually doom poetry to fall short of satisfying the demands placed upon it.

For Hölderlin, the ostensible goal of the poet is motivated by the desire for unity and coherence, an overcoming of the division of self and world, a mediation of the divine and the earthly. The poet therefore aims to illustrate the way in which all differences are inextricably bound together, positing a world in which all, even those who are most wretched and annihilated by fate, are still touched, incomprehensibly, by the secret of an emergent, sacred order. The desire of the poetic act is sustained, however, only to the degree that the fulfillment of the promise of poetry remains unrealized, in infinite approximation. Only then does the poet exist in a state of perpetual poiesis. Hölderlin's introduction to the second volume of *Hyperion* formulates the goal of the poet as follows:

> To end that eternal conflict between our self and the world, the peace of all peace, higher than all reason—to bring this back, to unite ourselves with nature in One infinite whole—that is the goal of all of our striving, whether or not we agree what this means.
>
> But neither our knowledge nor our action manages to arrive in any period of existence, where all conflict ceases, where everything is one; the definite trajectory unifies itself with the indefinite only in infinite approximation [*in unendlicher Annäherung*].
>
> We would also have no idea of that infinite peace, of that Being, in the only sense of the word, we would not even strive to unite ourselves with nature, we would not think and would not act, in fact there would be nothing at all, we would ourselves be nothing

> for ourselves, if that infinite unification, that Being, in the only sense of the word, were not nevertheless present. It is present—as beauty. (*MA* 1:558)

The story is a familiar one: there is an originary unity; the human being cannot intuit this order directly; and yet, such an order must exist; therefore, it manifests itself through beauty, in the self-organization of the natural world and in the poetic works of those who seek to draw this order out of its hidden latency. What is atypical in Hölderlin's poetic response to this rather traditional schema consists in the fact that poetry itself does not attempt to illustrate this unity—to *represent* it—on a formal or aesthetic level. Although Hölderlin speaks of beauty as an originary presence that bears witness to the existence of this order, the poetic act itself is not governed by an aesthetics of beauty—neither as "harmony" (the unproblematic and coherent unity of multiples for Leibniz and Baumgarten) nor as Kantian "disinterested pleasure." Instead of attempting to represent the unification of opposites, the poetic act intensifies oppositional poles of attraction: it thus widens the gap between the human and the divine, rendering the possibility of a higher-order unity difficult rather than inevitable, contingent rather than necessary. Stylistically, Hölderlin's later poetry (up to 1806) therefore throws down the gauntlet, challenging rather than comforting those who seek the divine: the poet, the reader, indeed nature itself, must find in the disorder of the sensuous world the resources to bear witness, to embody, and to reveal the presence of a possible higher-order unity.

Hölderlin's poetry invites this challenge precisely by multiplying the instances and intensities of unstable bifurcation points. Events are held in liminal states between anarchic chaos and emergent stability, and the road leading to salvation appears practically indistinguishable from the road to perdition. If Hölderlin's poetry is attracted to such figures of bifurcation, then the poetic act itself cannot be understood primarily as a pathway toward a higher-order unity, nor does it uncritically presuppose the existence of this unity—a presupposition that Hölderlin calls an "empty, easy play of shadows" (*leeres leichtes Schattenspiel*, *MA* 2:78). The increase in points of bifurcation and in their instability, the intensification in the generation of contingency concerning the outcome of any historical or natural process, trains and attunes the mind to the possibility of order when faced with the overwhelming evidence of disorder.

Perhaps more clearly than elsewhere, it is Hölderlin's theory of tragedy that dramatizes the attempt to read order into the contingency of radical change. The tragic work is characterized, above all, by strenuous cognitive labor. Sophocles's *Antigone* illustrates a culture at a point of transition in which the experience of contingency is intensified. The actors in the drama appear in the thrall of a process of revolution, "seized in infinite overturning, and shaken" (*von unendlicher Umkehr ergriffen, und erschüttert, MA* 2:375).

The tragedy captures this moment of transition as one in which time itself has betrayed the human being. Because time appears discontinuous rather than teleologically intelligible, characterized by uncertainty rather than stability, the logic of temporality itself can only appear to observers as inherently demonic rather than divine. It is the seeming necessity of revolutionary rupture (i.e., the necessity of a state of affairs in which the experience of contingency is intensified) through which the divine betrays the human. Tragic language therefore foregrounds disorder rather than order, although its central operation consists in making present the necessity of such a betrayal of time in order to ultimately redress and repair the fractured course of history: the tragedy is "language for a world, where, among plague and the confusion of the senses . . . god and human communicate in the all-forgetting form of betrayal, so that the course of the world has no gaps and *the memory of the heavenly ones doesn't disappear*" (*MA* 2:315–16). The tragedy must ultimately redeem its own moment of betrayal, or the fact that the coming into being of a new order manifests itself phenomenally as decay to those in its midst. Its own form of representation therefore tends toward oblivion inasmuch as the discontinuity, rupture, and incomprehensibility characterizing the tragic moment will ultimately be replaced by the intelligibility of a retrospectively constituted order.

The condition of possibility of such an operation—a redemption of tragic historicality—occurs by means of a pause that allows the "re-collection" of the past. Hölderlin gives to this break, which in fact restores intelligibility, the name of the caesura. The caesura designates the means by which the intelligibility of history becomes restored in a seeming moment of betrayal:

> In this way, in the rhythmic sequence in which the *transport* is represented [*sich darstellt*], *that which one calls caesura in poetic meter*, the pure word, a counter-rhythmic interruption becomes necessary, in order to meet the rapid alternation of representations [*Vorstellungen*] at its high point, so that no longer the alternation of representations, but the representation itself [*die Vorstellung selber*] appears. (*MA* 2:310)

The speeches of Tiresias mark both instances of the caesura in *Oedipus* and *Antigone*. Tiresias, as "custodian [*Aufseher*] over the power of nature" (*MA* 2:310), is the only agent capable of overseeing the totality of the order of nature amidst the normative and political suspension characteristic of revolutionary temporality. Tiresias's speeches prevent the horror of tragic suffering from achieving total domination over a culture's understanding of the moment of revolutionary upheaval, for this moment appears precisely as monstrous to the general populace. The tragic figure himself or herself functions as a cipher for this historical abomination, embodying "the monstrosity [*das Ungeheure*], how god and human mate" (*MA* 2:315). The god, however, in this moment, is "nothing but time" (*MA* 2:316), that is, the logic of time itself at the point of its turning from one regime of intelligibility (perceptual, cultural, political) to another. The monstrosity therefore appears when the human being becomes *pure time* in the process of revolution, concretely manifesting the becoming in dissolution (*das Werden im Vergehen*). At the moment of revolution, to embody pure time is to become the revolutionary moment; the tragic figure must be dragged into the sphere of the dead (or the negative realm of dissolution as *Vergehen*), but it is the function of the caesura to reveal this tragic downfall as the necessary precondition for organic growth, for novelty, for becoming (*Werden*).[1]

The tragic figure is incapable of seeing his or her own participation in the moment of radical change, since this figure *embodies* this moment and is perfectly identical with it. The fate of the tragic figure appears monstrous precisely because the god has stepped out of its sphere and into the sphere of the human as pure revolutionary time, an act that perturbs the human order and can only appear as rupture. The identity of the human with the god in this instant produces a *monstrum*, a violation of the order of nature. The moment of catharsis, however, purifies the tragic action by expelling the god from the human, a tragic action that "is grasped inasmuch as the unbounded becoming-one [*das gränzenlose Eineswerden*] is purified through unlimited separation" (*MA* 2:315). Only when the human and the god separate can one comprehend the actions of the divine; only when the human being does not embody time at the moment of pure potentiality, as one form changes into another ($t = 0$), can this being give an account of its own moment from the vantage point of another temporal framework, from the perspective of a moment that has already begun the process of *becoming* ($t > 0$).

If tragic temporality consists in a betrayal—revealing itself to human beings as disorder rather than order, as death rather than life—Tiresias, by interrupting time as betrayal, intimates the restoration of order, but only inasmuch as he foregrounds the necessity of death as part of the order of nature and history itself. Tiresias functions as "custodian over the power of nature," but it is this very power that "tragically tears the tragic figure from his sphere of life, displaces him from the midpoint of his inner life into another world, into the eccentric sphere of the dead" (*MA* 2:310–11). The caesura, however, renders this tearing into the eccentric sphere part of the order of intelligibility itself; it poetically creates a space that appears from outside the domain of its own sphere of immanence, slowing down time, interrupting a form of temporality that is itself an interruption, thereby permitting the mind, in a brief moment of respite, to grasp the order that otherwise eludes it. And so it is with the figure of the caesura in poetry: a break in the line that permits the mind to process, semantically and sonically, what is being said and how it is being presented.

The caesura is therefore not an absolute rupture, but a pause that joins two spheres, a break that heals the facticity of historical trauma. With the figure of Tiresias, revolutionary perturbation no longer appears *as* revolution, or "the alternation of representations," but the order of history appears as continuous, without gaps, as "the representation itself" (*MA* 2:310). In this latter sense, it is almost more appropriate to translate "representation" (*Vorstellung*) as "idea," since it is the Idea of History, its internal logic of self-organization, that is here made visible. The caesura, then, constitutes the locus of divine presence (as tragic absence) in a specific modal operation, namely when the contingency of possibility is poetically recast as the intelligibility of necessity. The caesura creates a bifurcation in the structure of the tragedy, but it is a bifurcation whose function is to reveal the organization of nature, or to resignify the perturbation and anxiety of revolution as the latent operation of order. Its function is less to disrupt the action than to generate balance amidst disequilibrium, and therefore, lend credence to the Kantian teleology of nature and history that had previously appeared defunct when confronted with the tragic state of the suffering human being.

The theory of tragedy, although it occurs in a different genre and in a different tonality, therefore reproduces the exercise value characteristic of Hölderlin's other poetic experiments. Only through honing the capacity of the mind to perceive order, to bind disparate phenomena, to construct unity out of difference and intelligibility out of complexity—a critical feature of Baumgarten's *felix aestheticus*—can evidence for an originary unity and order be made sensuously manifest. However, since such evidence can never be directly intuited, the exercise instigates an unending process of experimentation, one whose difficulty increases with every attempt to verify the order that it seeks to secure. Hölderlin's later poetic practices often seem to linger at points of indeterminacy, in turn producing a disequilibrium between disorder and order—in favor of disorder—whose differences then seem incapable of being recuperated into any coherent unity.

Another point of bifurcation emerges from Hölderlin's theory of tragedy that hints at such a dynamic. It is not the bifurcation *in* each respective tragedy, but between the two tragic instances themselves, *Oedipus* and *Antigone*. The figure used by Hölderlin to describe the relation of *Oedipus* to *Antigone* in its placement of the caesura, which must be strategically positioned so as to "protect" the tragic action against the overwhelming rapidity of representations and thus allow a space for the intelligibility of these events, is represented as follows: "_____/__ to _______" (*MA* 2:369). This figure enacts a pattern of intertextual and intratextual differentiation and opposition that surfaces frequently in Hölderlin's later poetic works. Each work balances the other; at the same time, each position of the caesura calls for its other, a process that can, in theory, continue multiplying and bifurcating ad infinitum for any discrete poetic instance. The balancing act of poetic works, in the permutation offered by Hölderlin, might therefore never end, for every work requires some configuration exterior to its own pattern of organization in order to redress its asymmetrical structure. Just as Tiresias provides the caesura to Oedipus's insatiable curiosity and monstrous becoming-one with the structure of time itself, so does *Antigone*, as a drama, provide a balance for *Oedipus*.

Inherent in Hölderlin's theory of tragedy, then, one may perceive the threat of continual bifurcation, an essential asymmetry—or in Hölderlin's language, *eccentricity*, a differential form that perturbs the unity of a closed system—that appears as a necessary condition for novelty, albeit a form of necessity whose instability continually demands its reinscription in the newly emergent paradigm of order. And that which demands endless verification approaches the very problem at the core of the tragic, namely, the desire to interpret and fully grasp the logos of the cosmos; such is in fact the main tragic problem of Oedipus. As Hölderlin says, "It is precisely this tendency to seek everything, to interpret everything, that pushes his mind to finally capitulate to the raw and simple language of his servants" (*MA* 2:315). The fall of Oedipus takes place not merely through a latent class conflict (master/slave), but in a clash between linguistic and hermeneutic registers. Poetry, as a complex form of language that seeks meaning and interprets the world of appearances, is defeated by the simplicity and roughness of everyday speech. It is Oedipus's search for meaning that occasions the breakdown in the stability of this meaning, revealing his own standpoint—that of the tyrant—as a false order. The solution proposed by the tragic form, or the continual search for a higher unity or symmetry that repairs a fundamental disorder or asymmetry in the world of the given, represents precisely the means through which Oedipus succumbs to the catastrophe of his own situation. The continual interpretation of fate, the search for an ultimate meaning through the opening of channels that seek to guarantee the stability of the natural, historical, and political system, leads to the destabilization of this very system. Oedipus falls victim to this process, and thereby comes to understand his own position *as* the very one that requires negation.

Because one's own position can at any moment be subject to negation, the "current situation" demands a continual poetic testing, a reproduction of experimental instances that may destabilize the order previously established as secure. Hölderlin's later poetic experiments therefore subject to rigorous examination the idea of a higher-order unity that would ground and justify the inherent breakdowns—the necessary injustices and betrayals—associated with the process of radical change. "The Rhine" suggests that such a unity can only be perceived by a "poetic" individual, a type of human being who is capable of holding conflicting cognitive states and signifying tendencies in harmonically opposed reciprocity at one and the same moment in time: a figure who can perceive coherence amidst the threat of chaos. Hölderlin's poetry, however, does not simply remain satisfied with this proposed solution to the problematic perception of order. The poem "Now come, Fire!"—often referred to as "The Ister," or the Greek name for the Danube, although the poem is not named as such in the manuscript—seems to form a companion piece to "The Rhine," and it introduces yet another system of divergences into Hölderlin's poetic corpus. The bifurcation occurs intertextually, in an intensification of the split between the Rhine and the Danube, not merely as rivers, but as poems. The split between the two poems posits a problem for thought, a break or discontinuity that cannot be bridged, or as one says in German: The Rhine and the Danube never meet (*Rhein und Donau fliessen nicht zusammen*).

Hölderlin's "The Ister" and Aporetic Consciousness

Now come, Fire!
We are impatient
To look upon Day,
And when the trial
Has passed through the knees
One may perceive the cries in the wood.
But, as for us, we sing from the Indus,
Arrived from afar, and
From the Alpheus, long we
Have sought what is fitting,
Not without wings may one
Reach out for that which is nearest
Directly
And get to the other side.
But here we wish to build.
For rivers make arable
The land. For when herbs are growing
And to the same in summer
The animals go to drink,
There too will humankind go.

This one, however, is called the Ister.
Beautifully he dwells. The pillar's foliage burns,
And stirs. Wildly they stand
Supporting one another; above,
A second measure, juts out
The roof of rocks. No wonder, therefore,
I say, this river
Invited Hercules,
Distantly gleaming, down by Olympus,
When he, to look for shadows,
Came up from the sultry isthmus,
For full of courage they were

In that place, but, because of the spirits,
There's need of coolness too. That is why that hero
Preferred to come here to the wellsprings and yellow banks,
Highly fragrant on top, and black
With fir woods, in whose depths
A huntsman loves to amble
At noon, and growth is audible
In resinous trees of the Ister,

Yet almost this river seems
To travel backwards and
I think it must come from
The East.
Much could
Be said about this. And why does
It cling to the mountains, straight? The other,
The Rhine, has gone away
Sideways. Not for nothing rivers flow
Through dry land. But how? A sign is needed,
Nothing else, plain and honest, so that
Sun and moon it may bear in mind, inseparable,
And go away, day and night no less, and
The Heavenly feel warm one beside the other.
That also is why these are
The joy of the Highest. For how
Would he get down? And like Hertha green
They are the children of Heaven. But all too patient
He seems to me, not
More free, and nearly derisive. For when

Day is due to begin
In youth, where it starts
To grow, another already there
Drives the high splendor, and like foals
He grinds the bit, and far off the breezes
Can hear the commotion,
If he is contented [my modified translation: That one is content]
But the rock needs incisions
And the earth needs furrows,
Would be desolate else, unabiding;
Yet what that one does, the river,
Nobody knows. (modified translation based on *PF* 581–85)

Jezt komme, Feuer!
Begierig sind wir
Zu schauen den Tag,
Und wenn die Prüfung
Ist durch die Knie gegangen,
Mag einer spüren das Waldgeschrei.
Wir singen aber vom Indus her
Fernangekommen und
Vom Alpheus, lange haben
Das Schikliche wir gesucht,
Nicht ohne Schwingen mag
Zum Nächsten einer greifen
Geradezu
Und kommen auf die andere Seite.
Hier aber wollen wir bauen.
Denn Ströme machen urbar
Das Land. Wenn nämlich Kräuter wachsen
Und an denselben gehn
Im Sommer zu trinken die Thiere,
So gehn auch Menschen daran.

Man nennet aber diesen den Ister.
Schön wohnt er. Es brennet der Säulen Laub,
Und reget sich. Wild stehn
Sie aufgerichtet, untereinander; darob
Ein zweites Maß, springt vor
Von Felsen das Dach. So wundert
Mich nicht, daß er
Den Herkules zu Gaste geladen,
Fernglänzend, am Olympos drunten,
Da der, sich Schatten zu suchen
Vom heißen Isthmos kam,
Denn voll des Muthes waren
Daselbst sie, es bedarf aber, der Geister wegen,
Der Kühlung auch. Darum zog jener lieber
An die Wasserquellen hieher und gelben Ufer,
Hoch duftend oben, und schwarz
Vom Fichtenwald, wo in den Tiefen
Ein Jäger gern lustwandelt
Mittags, und Wachstum hörbar ist
An harzigen Bäumen des Isters,

Der scheinet aber fast
Rükwärts zu gehen und
Ich mein, er müsse kommen
Von Osten.
Vieles wäre
Zu sagen davon. Und warum hängt er
An den Bergen gerad? Der andre
Der Rhein ist seitwärts
Hinweggegangen. Umsonst nicht gehn
Im Troknen die Ströme. Aber wie? Ein Zeichen braucht es
Nichts anderes, schlecht und recht, damit es Sonn
Und Mond trag' im Gemüth', untrennbar,
Und fortgeh, Tag und Nacht auch, und
Die Himmlischen warm sich fühlen aneinander.
Darum sind jene auch
Die Freude des Höchsten. Denn wie käm er
Herunter? Und wie Hertha grün,
Sind sie die Kinder des Himmels. Aber allzugedultig
Scheint der mir, nicht
Freier, und fast zu spotten. Nemlich wenn

Angehen soll der Tag
In der Jugend, wo er zu wachsen
Anfängt, es treibet ein anderer da
Hoch schon die Pracht, und Füllen gleich
In den Zaum knirscht er, und weithin hören
Das Treiben die Lüfte,
Zufrieden ist der;
Es brauchet aber Stiche der Fels
Und Furchen die Erd',
Unwirthbar wär es, ohne Weile;
Was aber jener thuet der Strom,
Weis niemand. (MA 1:475–77)

The poem narrates the course of a river that does not deliver that which it promises. It is, first and foremost, the story of a disappointment and an arrested development. The form of the poem itself appears truncated, cut short in such a way that many critics have labeled the poem incomplete: four strophes, three of twenty lines each, with the last strophe containing only twelve lines.[2] Whether the poem is incomplete or not is a matter of conjecture. However, if the poem is a fragment, its sudden rupture with its own form has a logic in and of itself, mirroring the problem of the river that it describes. This incompleteness is fully appropriate to the character of the Danube, or in Greek, the Ister, a river that is all too "patient" (*allzugedultig*), one that appears to travel in the wrong direction, one that is either too "content" (*zufrieden*) or "sorrowful" (*betrübt*)—both variants can be found in the manuscript. Like the river itself, the poem grows, declines, and ceases abruptly, dying before its time. The river promises evolution—"For rivers make arable/The land" (*PF* 581)—but ends in incertitude, doubt, aporia.

The integrity of the strophes becomes compromised as the poem progresses, just as the narration of the river charts the course of a disintegration. This movement can be followed precisely, the basic structure of which can be ascertained by close attention to the all-important points of transition. The first strophe appears complete and closed in itself. There is no enjambment from line to line and the end of the strophe coincides with the end of the rhetorical period. The poem begins with the promise of potentiality and wholeness, as if the object of desire—the sun and the blossoming form of a new culture—were close at hand. And yet, a test looms: "And when the trial/Has passed through the knees/One may perceive the cries in the wood" (*PF* 581). The test, however, appears enigmatic, not merely because of the semantic and sonic dissonance introduced by the "knees" (*Knie*), but because the conditions of the test are held poised between past and present, without any explicit indication of what would constitute success.[3] For one can "feel" the "cries in the wood" (*Waldgeschrei*) only as a sign that the moment of testing has come, not as a sign that the test has successfully been completed. Moreover, the test condenses semantically incompatible possibilities: *Waldgeschrei* may be associated not only with birdsong, as is normally assumed, but with the battle cry of the warrior, alluding to the corresponding passage in "The Rhine": "To you in the heat of a path under fir trees or/Within the oak forest's half-light, wrapped/In steel, my Sinclair, God may appear" (*PF* 511).[4] The forest is a space not of simple beauty, but of a looming violence. The poem, however, turns abruptly away from this possibility: "But here we wish to build" (*PF* 581). The strophe ends with a seemingly idyllic image of the human being drinking from the river, although this very gesture is something that the human shares in common with the animal ("For when herbs are growing/And to the same in summer/The animals go to drink/There too will humankind go" [*PF* 581]). Although the first strophe seems complete in and of itself, the poem conceals points of latent unrest, blurring the boundaries between human and animal, between the idyllic scene of a *locus amoenus* and the site of potentially violent forest screams (*Waldgeschrei*).

As the poem unfolds, it gives voice to a precarious instability, one that is realized in the surprising turns that constitute the main movement of the poetic flow. The second strophe, which begins and finishes with the naming of the river, ends at such a turning point, transitioning to an unexpected and almost impossible movement in the course of the river: "Yet almost this river seems/To travel backwards" (*PF* 583). After the naming of the river, the mark of its identity, there appears a sudden interruption and a regression, a regression that is enacted through a reversal in poetic momentum, or the shrinking of the dactylic rhythm (*An harzigen Bäumen des Isters*) to an iambic rhythm (*Der scheinet aber fast*), leading to a contamination of iamb and dactyl that then trails off into rhythmic irregularity (*Rükwärts zu gehen und/Ich mein, er müsse kommen/Von Osten*). The growth, which ought to be audible, or the link between *Wachstum* and *hörbar*—manifests itself as an audible slowness and distortion of the tempo of the poem itself.

Similar to the transition between the second and third strophes, the movement from the third to the fourth appears interrupted at the beginning of a temporal clause:

> . . . But all too patient
> He seems to me, not
> More free, and nearly derisive. For when
>
> Day is due to begin
> In youth, where it starts
> To grow, another already there
> Drives the high splendor, and like foals
> He grinds the bit, and far off the breezes
> Can hear the commotion,
> [That one is content;] (*PF* 583–85; modified translation)

Hölderlin is rarely considered an ironic poet. This poem, however, ironizes its principal object, the river itself, which appears to the poet in a gesture approaching mockery (*scheint der mir . . . / . . . fast zu spotten*, *MA* 1.477). Even the enjambment between strophes serves to break off a thought before it can even begin to develop. In the manuscript itself, the writing appears compressed, marking a transition from a *Reinschrift* to draft-like handwriting. One may add to these considerations the confusion generated by the use of demonstrative pronouns that make the differentiation of the two rivers, Rhine and Danube, quite difficult in this final strophe. Finally, the poem appears truncated at the end of the manuscript page, the twelve lines of the last strophe deviating from the pattern of twenty lines established by the other strophes.

Along the journey to this premature end, the flow of the poem itself is interrupted by the "other" river, the Rhine, whose excessive power—"another already there/Drives the high splendor"—overwhelms the languid flow of the Danube and separates the temporal phrase, which is forced into an extended hyperbaton, from its smooth completion. The phrase, which in fact is quite simple, can be reformulated as such: "For when/Day is due to begin/In youth,/ . . . /That river is content" (it ought to be remarked that an alternative reading for "content" as "sad" or *betrübt* is also available in the manuscript—a point to which I will return).[5] In comparison to the Rhine, the Ister—assuming the pronoun *der*, "that one," does indeed refer to the Danube—refuses to grow, and thus represents the danger of a failed formation, a *Bildung* gone awry.[6]

Just when the river should have reached its full potential, it appears to rest complacent (*zufrieden*)—or sorrowful (*betrübt*), almost melancholy—in itself. Whatever the case may be, the river does not provide the poet with the sensuous sign that he requires: "A sign is needed,/Nothing else, plain and honest [*schlecht und recht*], so that/Sun and moon it may bear in mind, inseparable" (*PF* 583). Day and night, as we have shown in "The Rhine," refer to two different semiotic and cognitive models, one signifying differentiation and binding, the other chaos and indifferentiation. Here too, what is sought is a model of representation that construes opposites as reversible and compatible modalities of being, a semiotic function in fact signaled by the idiomatic "plain and honest" (*schlecht und recht*). In the expression *schlecht und recht*, "schlecht," which normally signifies "bad" or "base," refers to its more archaic meaning, which is precisely the opposite of its habitual meaning. In the expression, according to Adelung, *schlecht* is equated with "honest, righteous, according to propriety and the law, in contrast to a crooked, impure disposition."[7] The expression itself straightens out the crooked sign in the movement from "schlecht" to "schlecht und recht." And each part of the line in fact expresses the same sentiment, that of holding opposites in harmonic tension with one another, albeit in different registers: "Nothing else" (*Nichts anderes*), "straight and pure" (*schlecht und recht*), "Sun and moon it may bear in mind" (*Sonn und Mond trag' im Gemüth*), "inseparable" (*untrennbar*). If the required sign ought to demonstrate the reversibility of day and night, Being and Judgment, identity and difference, presenting them as an indissoluble unity, the river does not fulfill this requirement.[8] Neither of the rivers in this particular instance, *as* poetic signs, adhere to the poem's own metalinguistic ideal of sign function; both rivers, Rhine and Danube, function as signs, but both signs misfire. Each river seems "schlecht" (bad), but precisely not in the sense of "schlecht und recht" (straight and honest); even the Rhine does not travel straight (it "has gone away/Sideways" [*PF* 583]). And as for the Danube—the presumed subject of the final line—"what that one does, the river,/Nobody knows" (*PF* 585).[9]

In the eighteenth century, the Danube was thought to practically disappear at the precise moment when it crosses over into the Swabian Jura. This precise moment of transition—from one boundary to another—is described in the third strophe, where the river "hangs" on the mountains. At this moment, the river moves not from dissolution to becoming, but on the contrary, from Being to Non-Being, or in Hölderlin's own terms: it manifests not the becoming in passing-away (*das Werden im Vergehen*), but rather, the passing-away in becoming (*das Vergehen im Werden*), and hence, an inversion of his poetological aspirations. And if, as Hölderlin wrote in the preface to *Hyperion*, poetry manifests the unconscious desire for the unity of Being, "The Ister" points to another possibility: that nothing will come to be. From the perspective of a perfect poetic teleology of nature, the development of "The Ister" can only be described as anomalous. The poem itself foregrounds both the possibility of a deviation that cannot be recovered into a history of Being and the impossibility of producing a representation of nature or history without gaps or ruptures.

Even the use of the Greek for the Danube—in previous poems, Hölderlin calls the river by its German name, *die Donau*—produces an ontological instability. The second strophe begins with this appellation: "This one, however, is called the Ister" (*Man nennet aber diesen den Ister, PF* 581). The very phrase produces a dissonance between what it claims and the language in which it makes this claim. The poem is written in German, and in German, *one* does not call the river "the Ister." The poet uses the impersonal pronoun "one" (*man*) to refer to a set of communal practices that do not actually exist from its own standpoint of enunciation. In the third strophe, the poetic voice will use the Germanic "Hertha" to refer to the earth, suggesting a lyrical voice that travels between mythological and cultural spaces, Greek and Germanic, or more precisely, a voice that occupies no determinate place in particular.[10]

In another sense, however, "Ister" is not merely a Greek word, but a concatenation of German words: the "Ist er," which can be translated as "is it"—as if the poem were questioning the ontological status of its own phenomenon. The phonemic resonance is eventually explicitly integrated into the poem itself. In the final strophe, one may read: "Zufrieden ist der" (it is content), a phrase that turns its gaze onto the complacent state of the river while transposing the Greek phoneme into German. In the manuscript, this particular line exhibits a noteworthy ambivalence. Hölderlin had apparently originally written "ist der betrübt" (it is sorrowful), with "zufrieden" (satisfied, content) appearing next to the line as a correction to "betrübt" (sorrowful [*FA* 7:465]). The variant is striking because it suggests an alternative that is not merely a stylistic improvement of what amounts to the same idea, but the introduction of a diametrically opposed concept into the cluster of associations surrounding the river. The replacement of "sorrowful" with "content" at first seems to positively reevaluate the movement of the Ister. However, it simultaneously thematizes the river as a site of contrary and conflicting meanings, flowing in a state of indeterminacy that the poet construes either as melancholic or content.

A similar ambiguity is produced syntactically by the marginal emendation, as the line hesitates between multiple possibilities: "ist der betrübt," "zufrieden ist der," or even, were one to replace "betrübt" with "zufrieden," the line would read "ist der zufrieden." As it stands in the manuscript, the river bifurcates on both the semantic and syntactical axes, generating oppositional movements radiating from one and the same point of concentration.

Sattler, the editor of the historical critical edition of Hölderlin's works, suggests that the word "betrübt" (sorrowful) is not crossed out, but underlined (*FA* 7:465). This proposition in fact opens up the Danube to its own problematic nature, constructing the river as a locus of potentialities that are simultaneously coexisting, and yet, mutually exclusive. If "betrübt" is underlined for emphasis, it functions even more intensively as a point of divergence from the overflowing energetics of the Rhine. "Betrübt" carries the implication, especially in reference to water, of murkiness, inasmuch as it contains the root *trüb* (cloudy, murky). The Danube, in direct opposition to the Rhine, presents the reader with a riddle, and far from being the riddle of that which emerges from purity (*Reinentsprungenes*), it alludes instead to the impure, *das Unreine*, occupying a space between being and non-being, contentment and despondency, clarity and contamination.

Both the poem and the river intensify contingency, or the possibility of divergent outcomes from one and the same narrative event, at foundational moments of cultural development. The poem begins with colonists who have come from India across Greece to Germany and choose a site situated along the Danube to establish a dwelling.[11] Their first desire is for fire, for heat, for the light of day. But the river, at least in Hölderlin's interpretation of Pindar's *Olympian 3*, offers shade and coolness, not heat, and therefore refuses the colonists' imperative, "Come now, Fire!" In *Olympian 3*, Hercules travels to the land of the Hyperboreans, beyond the boundaries of the known world, to bring the shade of the olive tree back to Greece as part of the founding of the Olympic Games. According to Hölderlin's translation of *Olympian 3*, Hercules finds at the origins of the Danube the olive tree, which "he brought [to Greece] from the Ister's shadowy sources/The son of Amphitryon" (*MA* 2:193). The space that existed beyond the boundaries of the Greek world, in the land of the Hyperboreans, is transferred to Hölderlin's own cultural sphere, marking the space of one's own as the other of the other.

These boundaries—between Germanic and Greek, self and other—are characterized by an inherent permeability. Just as Isaak von Sinclair provides a model of one who can hold opposing paradigms in states of perpetual reversibility in "The Rhine," so in "The Ister" does Hercules succeed in balancing the heat of Greece with the cool shade of the north, located across a boundary, beyond his own cultural space. He brings shade in the form of the olive tree back to Greece and founds a cultural institution, which in turn gives rise to what remains to us of Pindar's odes. Like Hercules, the colonists desire to cross a boundary and ground a culture, and they note that "not without wings may one/Reach out for that which is nearest/Directly/And get to the other side" (*PF* 581). One cannot travel to the other side effortlessly, and one who only grasps that which is closest (*Zum Nächsten . . . greifen*), who remains within the boundaries of one's own culturally circumscribed space, will not achieve the goal of cultural foundation. Hercules provides a model of one who, through strenuous exercise, in a movement so rapid that its poetic form manifests itself as swinging, *Schwingen*, crosses a boundary and breaks through to the other side: one who achieves, through the magnitude of heroic effort, transcendence.

The poem, however, sets up the initial conditions designed to secure a cultural foundation as doomed to failure; an imperfect fit between geography and national character introduces an irrevocable dissonance in the march of historical and cultural development. If the colonists in the first strophe of the poem desire fire and warmth, and they decide to establish their dwelling next to the Danube, it turns out that they profoundly misread the signs of nature.

One might speak, then, of a performative refusal by the river to grant that which the colonists desire, of a dislocation in time and space—they have arrived at the wrong river at the wrong point in time—that seems to thwart the colonists' goals. For above all, they desire duration, a culture that can exist over time, and for this they require furrows, soil, and water in order to sustain themselves. The river, however, does not seem to grant them this duration:

> But the rock needs incisions
> And the earth needs furrows,
> Would be desolate else, unabiding;
> Yet what that one does, the river,
> Nobody knows. (*PF* 585)

> Es brauchet aber Stiche der Fels
> Und Furchen die Erd',
> Unwirthbar wär es, ohne Weile;
> Was aber jener thuet der Strom,
> Weis niemand. (*MA* 1:477)

The Danube neither confirms nor rejects the success of founding a culture and establishing duration over time. The failure of the Danube operates more on a hermeneutic level than on a literal level: it presents the mind with an illegible, unreadable sign at a critical moment of cultural emergence.

In this poem, which is at first concerned with the conditions whereby cultural moments may acquire lasting meaningfulness, the poetic and semiotic stabilization of meaning itself misfires. The legibility of the river depends upon the ability to cognitively attune the human being to perceive difference as a higher-order unity: "A sign is needed/ . . . so that/Sun and moon it may bear in mind, inseparable,/And go away" (*PF* 583). Both rivers in the poem, however, do not function as signs that would facilitate—or even permit—the ability to read opposition in the light of any such higher-order intelligibility. Rivers form networks, complex prisms of bifurcation, and not neat linear patterns of progression. In addition to the organic non-linearity in the ecology of rivers, the poem itself holds open the bifurcation between the Rhine and the Danube, relativizing the normatively positive development of the Rhine from the perspective of the sick Ister, a point at which the possibility of a healthy development seems to disappear from the scene: "The other/The Rhine, has gone away/Sideways" (*PF* 583).

Indeed, both rivers represent a fluid imbalance couched in the terms of humoral-pathological physiology. The Rhine appears choleric and the Danube melancholic or phlegmatic: the Rhine "grinds" and the Danube is "sorrowful" or "content." Physiologically, the rivers do not fulfill their function, which is to stimulate the "joy" of the divine being: "That also is why these are/The joy of the Highest" (*PF* 583). The rivers, however, circulate in a humoral economy in which the sanguine, the desired humoral presence, appears precisely as lack. In this instance, the rivers seem to diverge not merely from their semiotic and cultural-foundational purposes for human beings, but misfire as a sign for the divine as well.[12]

In "The Rhine," the river achieves the sanguine state after its moment of breakthrough—a state that is never explicitly represented in "The Ister." There, the river's intensity, its transgression of boundaries, has been sublimated into cultural productivity:

> And it is good to see
> How then, after leaving the mountains,
> Content with German lands he calmly
> Moves on and stills his longing
> In useful industry, when he tills the land,
> Now Father Rhine, and supports dear children
> In cities which he has founded.

> Und schön ists, wie er drauf,
> Nachdem er die Berge verlassen,
> Stillwandelnd sich im deutschen Lande
> Begnüget und das Sehnen stillt
> Im guten Geschäffte, wenn er das Land baut
> Der Vater Rhein und liebe Kinder nährt
> In Städten, die er gegründet. (*MA* 1:344)

The river has progressed from its juvenile and adolescent state to that of adulthood, eventually embodying the law of the father that does not inhibit, but bestows life. "The Ister," however, portrays the Rhine at the moment just before its breakthrough, a point suffused at maximal intensity, in a conflict between chaotic dissolution and lawful constraint. The poem restores the river to a state of potentiality before its development to maturity as represented in "The Rhine," when it has subdued its drive to self-assertion and achieved a balance of opposing tendencies—activity and passivity, assertion of self and loss of self—or in other words, before it becomes *beautiful*, a balance one may hear in the harmonious alliterations of its state of culmination (*Stillwandelnd sich*; *das Sehnen stillt*; *Im guten Geschäffte*). In "The Ister," however, the sound of the Rhine bears no resemblance to its later, beautiful state. It is not "growth" (*Wachstum*) that becomes "audible" (*hörbar*), but dissonance and violence, marked by the collision of "n" and "z," "m" and "k," "k" and "n," *in den Zaum knirscht er* ("he grinds the bit"). The river struggles against containment, yearning to break free, and thereby biting *into* his bridle (rather than biting while being constrained by the bridle). The Rhine, the paradigmatic river for an idealized and beautiful cultural sublimation of energy, is thrown back to its state of potentiality at a point of bifurcation, when, not yet satisfied, it still clamors for release.[13]

In "The Ister," Hölderlin claims that acts of breakthrough—points of attack or penetration, the *Stiche* (incisions) that are turned against the cliff—are necessary for the development of a durable human community and economy. Such "incisions" refer, in all likelihood, to the moment at which a stream breaks through a chain of mountains and draws new boundaries, making possible agriculture, the development of human communities, and geopolitical markers. In one of the *Pindar Fragments* entitled "The Animating Power" ("Das Belebende"), Hölderlin portrays the moment of breakthrough as the order of life itself, as that which initiates a movement from the inorganic to the organic. He associates "stechen" (to stick or to penetrate) with the Greek κεντεῖν, in turn associated with centaurs (κεντεῖν and ταῦρος). Centaurs embody the spirit of the rivers themselves, inasmuch as they must, in an act of violence, break through the boundaries that constrain them and create new pathways, draw new points of connection, and institute new limits:

> The notion of centaurs must be that of the spirit of a river, inasmuch as it makes a course and limit, by force, on the originally pathless and upward growing earth.
>
> Their image, therefore, is at those places where the bank is rich in rocks and grottoes, especially at places where originally the river left the mountain ranges and had to sweep its way diagonally across their direction.
>
> Centaurs, therefore, in their origin are also the teachers of natural science, because from that perspective nature is best discovered.
>
> In such regions the river originally had to meander before it could sweep a course for itself. In that way wet meadows, like those by ponds, were formed, and caverns in the earth for mammals, and at that time the centaur was a wild herdsman, like the Odyssean cyclops; the waters, yearning, looked for their direction. (*PF* 721)

Centaurs perceive the dynamics of nature as a process of constraint, a buildup of tension, a moment of breakthrough and release, and finally the creation of a new order, the grounding of a new culture. Centaurs, who, like rivers, embody this process, are thus best able to observe the organization of nature as a cycle of revolutionary events requiring violence before new orders can be generated. The organization of nature coheres with humoral pathology in this case as well: the tension generated by the mountains' constraint of the river requires release just as the imbalance of humors in the body requires bloodletting in order to restore equilibrium. The geopolitical map is drawn according to an economy organized by the same logic as that governing the regulation of energy in the human body.

The bifurcation of the system of rivers, the Rhine and the Danube, foregrounds the possibility that the natural system will not, for whatever reason, be able to generate the movement of breakthrough and redraw the necessary boundaries for the grounding of new cultural forms. While the Rhine appears poised to perform this function—something that the river does succeed in doing in the hymn "The Rhine"—the Danube, on the other hand, in this particular manifestation, does not. Both rivers are portrayed poetically at moments of instability, when neither river's capacity to ground culture had yet become an inevitability. Inscrutable and unknowable, the river issues a challenge to the mind that would seek to guarantee the order of nature, suggesting that this task may ultimately end in aporia, if not in outright failure. Rather than a poetics of unification subsumed under an aesthetics of the beautiful, an unfurling of the order of nature along the lines of a teleologically guaranteed organization of sensuous matter, one sees in Hölderlin's later hymns a poetics of bifurcation: a movement from the promise of unity—having proved abortive—back into the dispersal of differentiation, a dispersal that in turn renders the desire for the order of the beautiful, precisely as that which refuses to show itself poetically, all the more palpable.

Hölderlin's "Patmos" and the Collapse of the Solid Letter

Of all Hölderlin's poems, it is perhaps "Patmos" that grapples most intensely with hermeneutics as a way of life, one in which exegesis itself—both in the narrower sense of biblical exegesis as well as in the wider sense of the interpretation of all that exists—becomes a divine injunction.[14] As the first lines of "Patmos" make clear, there can be no question of a simple intuition of a redemptive or divine principle. Difficulty, resistance, obscurity, and impenetrability constitute the conditions of possibility through which the "redemptive power" reveals itself: "Near is/And difficult to grasp, the God./But where danger threatens/That which saves from it also grows" (*PF* 551). The structural requirement for danger, for the abyss that yawns at the feet of those who wander on mountains linked by "bridges lightly built" (*PF* 551), conditions the basic task facing the poet: an attempt to bind differences in such a way that incommensurabilities become compossibilities. Hence the call, at the beginning of the poem, to link discrete spaces that are held apart at points of extremity, zones within which all phenomena have reached their maximum intensification. The "most dear ones" live on "most separated mountains," which triggers the call to "give us [wings], with minds most faithful [*treuesten Sinns*]/To cross over and to return" (*PF* 550–51). Poetry is construed as an art that draws together and gathers superlatives: the "most separated" mountains, the "most beloved" individuals, the "most faithful" sense (*Sinn*, which may mean "sense," "mind," or the "meaning" of a text).

The geographical and mythological nature of Patmos, the island to which the poet is transported, is constructed as a space of exception, the maintenance of a difference—"For not like Cyprus/the rich in well-springs,/Nor any one of the others,/Magnificently does Patmos live" (*PF* 553)—that itself generates a binding function, drawing in those who are most alone and despondent. Patmos is "hospitable nonetheless" (*PF* 555), and "when, after shipwreck or lamenting for/His homeland or else for/The friend departed from him,/A stranger draws near/To her, she is glad to hear it" (*PF* 555). Patmos, itself a holy island (and Hölderlin was fascinated by islands, or the discrete formation of solid ground surrounded by the turbulence of the sea), is a site of poetic production and reception. As the place where John the Apostle wrote the Book of Revelation, it represents above all a sanctuary where the rejected and cast-out figures of poetic mediation can find a space for their visions—visions that are at one and the same time redemptive and apocalyptic, revelatory and hidden, healing and destructive.

The island functions as an emblem for a form of textual production and reception that is both marked as "foreign" and "other"—and therefore in a state of tension with prevailing norms and modes of aesthetic activity—and yet, one that aims at producing its own readerly community.[15] Such a community seems at first to be associated with reading practices derived from Pietism. Hölderlin dedicates the poem to the Landgrave of Homburg, whose yearning for a form of biblical interpretation as an alternative to philological Enlightenment textual criticism seems to have furnished the main impetus for the work.[16] In an apparent nod to these Pietistic reading circles, the poet notes, "many timid eyes/Are waiting to see the light" (*PF* 561). And although they are held back from a direct intuition of the divine—"They are reluctant to flower/Beneath the searing beam" (*PF* 561–63)—they nevertheless constitute their own textual community through a form of aesthetic exercise:

> But when, as if
> By swelling eyebrows made
> Oblivious of the world,
> A quietly shining strength falls from holy scripture,
> Rejoicing in grace, they
> May practice on the quiet gaze. (*PF* 563)

> Wenn aber, als
> Von schwellenden Augenbraunen
> Der Welt vergessen

Stilleuchtende Kraft aus heiliger Schrift fällt, mögen
Der Gnade sich freuend, sie
Am stillen Blike sich üben. (*MA* 1:452)

This particular engagement with textuality aims to produce a way of seeing that differentiates itself from the dominant tendencies of the present: an automatic and almost effortless conception of exercise (*sich üben*) that reduces the traumatic intervention of the divine to a minimum and holds itself at a distance from the incomprehension of the world, a world in which "swelling eyebrows" can only seem strangely out of place.

Hölderlin immediately supplements this mode of reading with a different reading practice, a more heroic and pantheistic one in which "holy scripture" is equated with "lightning" as an exegetical object:

But all the heroes, his sons,
Have come, and holy scriptures
About him, and lightning is explained by
The deeds of the world until now,
A race that cannot be stopped. . . . (*PF* 563)

Es sind aber die Helden, seine Söhne
Gekommen all und heilige Schriften
Von ihm und den Bliz erklären
Die Thaten der Erde bis izt
Ein Wettlauf unaufhaltsam. . . . (*MA* 1:453)

In this passage, Hölderlin enlarges the surface of that which is read, an expansion that embeds the "holy scriptures" in the larger context of the manifold signs of nature and human history. Ultimately it is not merely sacred texts that anchor the exegetical act, but "the deeds of the world until now," a spatiotemporal widening of the horizon of textuality to include all possible historical moments considered up until the moment of poetic enunciation.

Moreover, the present moment seems to require violence and trauma as part of its own hermeneutic practices, or as the very means through which the invisibility of the divine enters into the world of the visible: "Too long, too long now/The honour of the Heavenly has been invisible./For almost they must guide/Our fingers, and shamefully/A power is wresting our hearts from us" (*PF* 563). The textual community of the present therefore reinforces the need for sacrifice that is the essence of Christian history: "For every one of the Heavenly wants sacrifices and/When one of these was omitted/No good ever came of it" (*PF* 563). In contrast to the effortless reception of the truth granted to timid eyes faced with scriptural textuality, Hölderlin ends the poem with a call to "cultivate the solid letter" (*daß gepfleget werde/Der veste Buchstab, MA* 1:453)—which in turn refers to a way of interpreting well the totality of existence (*bestehendes gut/Gedeutet, MA* 1:453).[17] The textual community of Pietist spirituality has undergone a radical transformation, ultimately encompassing practices of reading, interpreting, and active caring (*pflegen*) in a way that recognizes sacrifice, violence, and trauma as constitutive of these practices.

One may therefore regard "Patmos" as an attempt to generate a textual community whose mediation is predicated upon a structural moment of disruption. Indeed, Hölderlin seems himself to have turned against the textual integrity of "Patmos," continually revising the poem and increasing the prevalence of historical moments of traumatic suffering as a necessary precondition of the mediation of the divine.[18] As we have seen, one of Hölderlin's central poetological techniques consists not in the facilitation of textual interpretation, but in the construction of formal impediments that continually challenge the attempt to generate unity from multiplicity. This technique reaches a fever pitch in his revisions to "Patmos."

"Patmos" therefore internalizes Hölderlin's poetics of bifurcation, applying this pattern to its own textuality and its attempt to read the progression of history as a well-ordered system. Whereas other poems, such as "Remembrance" ("Andenken") and "Mnemosyne" or "The Rhine" and "The Ister," appear as bifurcations of one another, "Patmos" produces multiple self-bifurcations. The mutilation of the word itself, of the logos, corresponds to an interpretation of the Christian history of redemption that has become coextensive with violence.

The later reworkings of the poem, rife with decapitation, war, and destruction—vivid images associated with revolutionary violence, and more specifically with imaginative figures associated with the French Revolution—seem to call into question the very project of a redemptive vision implied by the first version of "Patmos."[19] On the other hand, perhaps the violence itself *constitutes* this redemptive vision. The later fragments exhibit such a temporal blending between Christian history and French revolutionary history that these versions of "Patmos" simultaneously rewrite the Christian narrative as a narrative of revolutionary violence (transposing the cultural situation of the eighteenth century onto scriptural history) while sacralizing the violence of the French Revolution by embedding it in an eschatological framework (transposing scriptural history onto the eighteenth century).

The goal of this section is not to investigate how the poetic work expresses Hölderlin's particular ideological stance—much less to discern whether Hölderlin was advocating or problematizing the French Revolution—but rather, to examine how these ideological resonances intensify, break up, rearticulate, de-articulate both the lyric word and the larger poetic project of cultural transformation in which this word is invested. The collision of different temporal and mythological systems—pagan, Christian, and revolutionary—gives rise to poetic formulations that do not seem to "cultivate" the solid letter in these later versions, but rather, to bear witness to its collapse. The later poetic formulations in turn problematize the Pietistic exercise of exegesis that the first version of the poem set out to explore.[20]

The collapse of the solid letter in "Patmos" results from an intensification of the exercise value of poetic form. In the poetic exercise, disorder and perturbation introduce novelty into the organization of the sensible world, which is then subsequently revealed as constitutive of divine order itself. However, the apparent poetic intensification that marks a shift from the first version to the later versions of "Patmos" gives rise to a more fractured poetic world, one in which revolutionary violence oscillates ambiguously between irredeemable destruction and potential salvation. The theological bulwark that supports the linking of disparate events—those "bridges lightly built," stretched over the abyss—are held in a state of suspension, and ultimately one is not sure if these bridges can bear the weight demanded of them by the course of history unfolding, a history whose tragic structure seems to demand the abrogation of the law in order to bring about its fulfillment.

The later versions of the poem intensify the presence of potentiality in narrative turning points by holding the interpretation of historical rupture (and of sacred textuality) in a state of undecidability. If the first version of "Patmos" exhausts its own exercise value in a hermeneutic act—the desire that "the existing/Be well interpreted" (*PF* 565)—the later versions of "Patmos" disavow a teleology that would otherwise facilitate integrative acts of interpretation, or the construction of an unproblematic whole from a series of violent events. The transition from the first version to the later versions of "Patmos" dramatizes a shift in the exercise value of each work, namely from a semantically stabilizing hermeneutic injunction to the formal instigation of cognitive acts of separation and binding that might not add up to any conclusive or redemptive recovery of meaning.

In the later versions of "Patmos," two historical frameworks—the French Revolution and the Christian history of salvation—become grafted together, mutually intermingling and contaminating one another with their various potentialities. The main interpretive difficulty lies in understanding how revolutionary violence, or the suspension and disruption of order, relates to the narrative of salvation. In the later fragments, it would seem that the poet uses revolutionary violence to problematize Christianity—and that in turn, this problematized Christianity then reflects back upon revolutionary violence as ultimately futile and senseless. The extent to which Hölderlin reformulates—indeed, inverts—the early formulations of "Patmos" becomes evident through comparing the first lines of the earlier poem with those of the later version:

> Near is,
> And difficult to grasp, the God (*PF* 551)

> Nah ist
> Und schwer zu fassen der Gott. (*MA* 1:447)

The reworking of this opening in later versions appears as follows:

> Most kind is; but no one by himself
> Can grasp God. (*PF* 567)

> Voll Güt ist. Keiner aber fasset
> Allein Gott. (*MA* 1:453)

The earlier version, "Near is/And difficult to grasp, the God," formulates succinctly a problem that finds its resolution in the doctrine of the solid letter: the divine is all-encompassing in the sense that it pervades culture, religious practice, and the production and reception of poetry itself. Hence the care of the solid letter—as hermeneutic activity that is attuned to the presence of the divine in the text of nature, the sacred scriptures, and the inspiration of song—does not necessarily "grasp" God, but revives points of mediation between the divine and the human in different ways.

The opening lines of the later version, in contrast, appear fragmentary, enigmatic, and almost pessimistic. This version does not merely restate the argument of the earlier version in a different form, but in a certain sense, works in opposition to it, as one might glean from examining the verses on a purely formal level, where a striking topographical inversion becomes evident.[21] One way of reading the rhythmic transformation is as follows:

> – ⏑
> ⏑ – ⏑ – ⏑ ⏑ –

to

> – ⏑ – / – ⏑ – ⏑ – ⏑
> ⏑ – –

Whereas the earlier formulation incorporates God into the momentum of the rhythm, the later version detaches God from any sense of inner rhythmic pulse. Here, God appears as an accented word at the end of the second line, and although the poem is composed in free verse, the line appears almost catalectic, as if the word "God" were being deployed abruptly to end the poetic thought, or conversely, as if the divine were to reveal itself only in the abruptness of this end. And yet, the rhythmic detachment of God from the metrical flow mirrors on a semantic level the excision of God from the opening sentence, "Most kind is" (*Voll Güt ist, PF* 567). God as the grammatical subject of the sentence drops out, becomes textually invisible as a feature of the poetic topography, whereas God as the object of the second sentence (*Keiner aber fasset/Allein*

Gott) must be read back into the first sentence in order to reconstruct its meaning.

The words "Most kind is" (*Voll Güt ist*) constitute a fractured theodicy that can only be repaired—if at all—in the act of reading.[22] Each word refers to one of the divine attributes presupposed by traditional ontology: totality, omnibenevolence, and existence. Yet without the active constitution of meaning on the part of the listener or reader, the first three words threaten to dissolve into three disparate elements, mere attributes without any term that would provide the ground for their unity. That which "holds together" the system is therefore located outside of that system: the opening words form a phrase in search of a subject. Indeed, the real subject of these first two lines is not even a human subject, but a negation of the human subject, a "no one": "no one by himself/Can grasp God" (*keiner aber fasset/allein Gott*). That no one can grasp God alone (*allein*) harbors a theological wordplay. Analyzing "allein" into its constituent parts produces "all" and "ein," articulating in microcosm the Heraclitan doctrine that the eighteenth century interpreted as the central tenet of pantheistic Spinozism: the *hen kai pan* or *die Alleinheit*.[23] And yet, the phonemes *all* and *ein*, the one and all, signaling divine perfection and totality, have become the concatenated emblem of a lonely God and an even lonelier creation, one cut off from the other: God as absent subject and unattainable object, the human being as negative presence unable to grasp God's perfection. In the opening lines, the figure of mediation appears precisely as linguistic *lack*; not only does "no one" grasp the divine alone, but the very grammar necessary to link the presence of God to the human being is conspicuously absent. The divine and the human are situated on the opposite sides of a gulf whose connecting elements lie outside the scope of the lines' discrete formal construction.

These lines pose the question, in a fragmentary and provisional manner, whether or not a response to the problem of theodicy can still be sought in the Judeo-Christian framework of salvation. Preoccupation with the redemption of history exists already in the earlier version of "Patmos" in the parable of the sower. There, the statement "And there's no harm if some of [the grain]/Is lost" (*PF* 561)—the notion that some part of history may ultimately remain unredeemed—is shown to be the *wrong* way of conceptualizing the presence of the divine in time. This thought leads the poet down a path of imitating the divine through representation (making a "picture" of God) at the end of which the poet becomes rejected by the anger of the gods.[24] In order for the divine to qualify *as* the divine, all events must be capable of redemption. In the earlier version, the possibility of suffering unredeemed, of human destinies gone lost, is addressed by the ideology of the solid letter and interpreting well the divine, namely in a way that would justify the violence and the sacrifice necessary to achieve the ends of history.[25]

The seemingly negative theology implicit in Hölderlin's opening lines of the later version do not merely show that—in a negative representation—the human cannot "grasp" the divine, but also that this very negativity throws the interpretation of history into a state of crisis. The revisions of "Patmos" integrate this negative theological gesture into a historical moment in which the possibility of suffering unredeemed—in a Christian sense—appears palpable on the stage of world history. The later manuscripts emphasize that Christ does not die for human beings, but rather, human beings must die for Christ:

> From Jordan far from Nazareth
> And far from the lake, at Capernaum, where they sought
> Him and Galilee the breezes, and from Canaan.
> A little while I shall stay, he said. So with drops holy
> He quenched the sighing of the light that was
> Like thirsty wild beasts
> Or like the scream of the cock, on that day, when for Syria, withered,
> Lamented the native grace in dying of
> Small children killed, speaking well while disappearing,
> And the Baptist's head fell, the golden, and lay like inedible and
>   unwitherable writing
> Visible on a dry platter. Like fire, in cities, deadly loving
> Are voices of God.[26]

> Vom Jordan fern von Nazareth
> Und fern vom See, an Capernaum, wo sie ihn
> Gesucht und Galiläa die Lüfte, und von Cana.
> Eine Weile bleib ich, sprach er. Also wie mit Tropfen heiligen
> Stillte er das Seufzen des Lichts, das durstigem Thier war oder
> Dem Schreien des Huhns ähnlich, jenes Tages, als um Syrien, verblüht,
> Gewimmert der getödteten Kindlein heimatliche
> Anmuth wohlredend im Verschwinden, und des Täuffers
> Sein Haupt stürzt und das goldene, lag uneßbarer und unverwelklicher
>   Schrift gleich
> Sichtbar auf trokener Schüssel. Wie Feuer, in Städten, tödlichliebend
> Sind Gottes Stimmen. (*MA* 1:464–65)

Instances of extreme suffering and points in the history of redemption are interwoven in this passage so as to become indistinguishable. For Hölderlin, the narrative of Christianity is in fact a narrative of trauma. The sacred itself can only appear damaged once the events of history begin to be recounted and recalled.

To affirm the miracles and baptisms performed by Christ—"So with drops holy/He quenched the sighing of the light"—requires that one be able to affirm the moments of anguish in Christian history: Herod's massacre of the children in Syria and the decapitation of John the Baptist. Such is precisely what Hölderlin sets out to do. When Christ "quenches" the sigh of the light with "drops"—which recall both the ritual of baptism as well as the blood of Christ, an emblem of his own suffering—his service is intended to address and redress the scream of outrage that accompanies the bloody sacrifices of history. The word *stillen* has multiple associations: it means to bring to silence, to calm raging emotions, but also to assuage or appease, in the sense that giving an infant the breast also "silences" the infant. And when Christ "quenches" with "drops," he thereby adopts the characteristics of the Madonna Lactans, an image that in turn is infused with a perversely macabre sense when one recalls that the passage being represented details the murder of babies. Above all, however, these moments of Christian history are emblems of revolutionary violence: the beheading of John the Baptist as well as the overturning of civic order, with cities in flames, unmistakably recalls images associated with the chaos of revolutionary upheaval.

The poem lingers on points of instability that accompany the overturning of order, gesturing on the one hand toward the ongoing hope for redemption, and on the other hand, giving voice to a palpable despair stemming from the undeniable facticity of creaturely violence. The decapitation of John the Baptist becomes symbolic of this unresolved struggle; his decapitated head inverts the Christian narrative of salvation through a negative representation of the Eucharist. In contrast to the body of Christ, the Word become flesh ingested during the sacrament of Communion, the head of John the Baptist is likened to "inedible writing" (*uneßbarer Schrift gleich*). Its appearance on a "dry" platter (*auf trokener Schüssel*) testifies to the absence of blood, and hence to the impossibility of transubstantiation when faced with the conspicuous lack of any embodied substance that would mediate the divine.[27]

Hegel would come to a similar conclusion in his interpretation of the French Revolution in the *Phenomenology of Spirit*: in this instance, widespread revolutionary violence annuls the redemptive potentiality of sacrifice. Those who die at the hands of revolutionary factions are cursed with a death "which has no inner significance or filling . . . . It is thus the coldest and meanest of all deaths, with no more significance than cutting off a head of cabbage or swallowing a mouthful of water."[28] The terror of the revolution renders martyrdom impossible and nullifies the very economy underlying the concept of sacrifice: revolutionary terror represents a moment in which Spirit would seem to have evacuated itself from history (although, as always, Hegel recovers this seeming evacuation dialectically). Hölderlin's formulation is even more radical inasmuch as death does not merely stand in cold indifference to the redemptive concept of sacrifice, but actively negates any and all figures of redemptive recuperation. In an earlier version, the allusion to the Eucharist is more explicitly emphasized through the use of the word "plucked" (*gepflükt*) to describe John the Baptist's head (*MA* 1:461)—a formulation evoking the production of wine and the miracle of transubstantiation. In the later version, all positive traces of transubstantiation, figures of aesthetic mediation between the transcendent and the sensuous, have been purged. For the announcer of Christ—the mediator of the mediator, and hence the poetic figure of mediation as such—transubstantiation, or the infusion of the divine in that which is irreducibly mortal and finite, remains only a negative possibility.

The characterization of John the Baptist's head as something akin to inedible writing reveals him to be incapable of embodying the immediacy of the divine as does Christ, traditionally the only true figure of mediation between the realm of the transcendent God and that of humanity. John the Baptist, a human mediator of the divine mediator, is *not* God, and the poetic word is not identical with the divine Word, the embodied logos. One may, of course, explain the negative Eucharistic imagery of John the Baptist's head according to the temporality of Christian history itself: when John the Baptist dies, the divine sacrifice has not yet taken place, and the transubstantiation of Christ has not yet filled the bread and the wine with the immanence of divine presence. Yet the presence of the negative Eucharist in relation to John the Baptist's decapitated head remains enigmatic inasmuch as there is an obvious denial of divine immanence in the death of he who announces the coming of Christ. The poet himself—as mediator figure—becomes formally associated with Eucharistic sacrality, but emptied out of redemptive potentiality.

If the head of John the Baptist paradoxically functions in the text itself as both an embodiment and a negation of divine immanence, the contemporaneous resonance of this scene with the violence of the French Revolution equally embodies and negates the immanence of the divine in human history. Because this decapitation represents an emblem of the ultimate machine of the Terror, the text of John the Baptist's head appears as a complex cipher for the interwoven narratives of early Christian history and eighteenth-century revolutionary violence.

The poet implies that revolutionary violence—whether or not such violence is justified for the creation of a future state—could be rendered intelligible by drawing upon the model in which sacred violence is redeemed in the Christian tradition. The problem of theodicy then becomes central for the poet's attempt to interpret contemporary political struggle, as both Christian theodicy and the violence of revolution share the same temporal structure of justification: an ultimate end suffices to redeem seemingly unjustifiable means to achieve this end. However, if the theological structure of justification loses ground, the poet will be incapable of sustaining his role in the overall project of "interpreting well" the phenomenon of revolution, or a historical moment whose redemptive status seems to have been placed under suspension.

It is in this sense that the aesthetic exercise of the poet—that which supposedly links the order of signs to the order of the divine—is confronted with an ontological rupture, a blockage between the sensible world and the various manifestations of the divine. Hence the poet "would like" to sing Christ, John the Apostle, and other figures from Christian history, only to find himself incapable of doing so:

> John. Christ. This one, a
> Bearer of burdens I would like to sing, like Hercules, or
> The island, which was banished, and flowered, full of meaning, refreshing
> The neighboring one with cool sea waters from the desert
> Of the flood, the vast, Peleus. But not
> Enough. A fate is different. More marvelous.
> More rich to sing. Immeasurable
> The fable ever since. And also I would like to sing
> The journey of the noblemen to
> Jerusalem, and like swans the motion of the ships and the suffering
> wandering in Canossa, burning hot
> And Heinrich. But from the very start
> Let my courage itself not expose me. We have to see, with conclusions,
> Of invention beforehand. For it is dear [*theuer*],
> The face of the most dear one.
> Namely suffering colors the purity of this one, purity that is
> Pure like a sword.[29]

> Johannes. Christus. Diesen, ein
> Lastträger möcht ich singen, gleich dem Herkules, oder
> Der Insel, welche gebannet, und angeblümt, sinnreich, erfrischend
> Die benachbarte mit kalten Meereswassern aus der Wüste
> Der Fluth, der weiten, Peleus. Aber nicht
> Genug. Anders ist ein Schiksaal. Wundervoller.
> Reicher, zu singen. Unabsehlich
> Seit dem die Fabel. Und auch möcht
> Ich die Fahrt der Edelleute nach
> Jerusalem, und wie Schwanen der Schiffe Gang und das Leiden irrend in
> Canossa, brennendheiß
> Und den Heinrich singen. Aber daß uranfangs
> Der Muth nicht selber mich aussezze. Schauen, müssen wir mit Schlüssen,
> Der Erfindung vorher. Denn theuer ists,
> Das Angesicht des Theuersten. Nemlich Leiden färbt
> Die Reinheit dieses, die rein
> Ist wie ein Schwerdt. (*MA* 1:465)

To sing "Christ" or "Johannes" entails that one must also sing the entire course of historical unfolding marked by these figures. The poet appears seduced by the blending of Christian and pagan history; and yet, it is not "enough" for him to compare Christ to Hercules, since Christian history institutes a redemptive economy of sacrifice unknown to pagan religiousness. And just as equally, the poet appears incapable of fully singing the bloody unfolding of history that ensues, violence undertaken in the name of Christianity: the Crusades and the denigration of Henry IV.[30] Not only does Henry IV's walk to Canossa iconographically put on display the triumph of sacred power over secular power, but the king himself was later deposed, a movement which intensified civil strife at the beginning of twelfth-century Germanic history. One wonders whether the poet would like to sing about the suffering of Henry in a way that valorizes his martyrdom—or perhaps to sing the king who was *deposed*. In any case, the suffering of the king is "erring" (*das Leiden irrend*)—not merely as one who wanders in suffering, but also, as a history of suffering, or the Christian "passion," that has strayed from the path.

The story of Henry cannot be integrated into an overarching historical narrative that would render his suffering intelligible. The poet thus expresses doubts not just about his own ability to sing, but about the content of that which he *wishes* to sing: "But from the very beginning/Let my courage itself not expose me" (*Der Muth nicht selber mich aussezze*). On the one hand, the poet seems to think that his courage, in the act of singing, could "expose" him to danger, either because of the song's revolutionary implications or because of the hubris of what the song is attempting to perform, namely, the wholesale redemption of the negativity of history; on the other hand, the phrase could refer to the "exclusion" of the poet from that which he sings, to the concern that the courage to sing would "put the poet outside" (*aussetzen*) of the historical order itself. Finally, the use of the verb *aussetzen* may equally designate the wish that courage would not "set the poet out" with the Crusaders, with those who take arms against the pagan world. The verb *aussetzen* condenses a multiplicity of meanings, each of which is present in the line: exposure, setting out, and exclusion. Or more succinctly put: the poet's courage demands an exposure to danger, a form of danger that places the poet both inside and outside the narrative of violence that he wishes to sing. In this space of poetic indeterminacy, none of the models of history seem to function in the poetic voice's attempt to render intelligible the suspension of order—the facticity of violence—as a precondition for the emergence of a new order.

The poet notes: "it is dear [*theuer*]/The face of the most dear one [*theuersten*]." The divine being is both beloved and costly, referring to the two senses of the word *theuer*. The violent order of sacred history implies that human beings must pay dearly to hold on to any given conception of the divine. The poet has not forgotten the Crusades; he desires to sing of religious wars, and yet he finds this undertaking almost impossible—or at least fraught with danger—"from the outset" (*uranfangs*). And although the history of religious strife and suffering for which the divine image is directly responsible "colors" the purity of Jesus, this purity nevertheless remains pure—as a sword.[31] Whether the blood spilled tarnishes the image of Christ or whether Christ ennobles the power of the blade constitutes the central dilemma of the work—a dilemma that can be traced back to Christ's phrase, "I did not come to bring peace, but a sword" (Matthew 10:34).

The poet suggests that the duplicity of vision necessitated by a hermeneutic confrontation with violent rupture—making that which is dissonant appear as a condition of harmony—appears to furnish the poet with a task that transcends his capabilities. In order to produce a song whose central content consists in sacred renewal, one must be able to "see" with the "ends" of "invention" beforehand, that is, to be able to read the ends of history that would justify violent conflict: "We have to see with ends [*mit Schlüssen*],/Of invention beforehand." The phrase "with ends" (*mit Schlüssen*)—alluding to the "ends" of history that would redeem the violence arising from the incommensurability of systems of belief—recalls the platter, or the *Schüssel*, upon which rests the head of John the Baptist.[32] Evoking this moment in the poem is tantamount to a reminder of the violence incurred in religious history and revolutionary violence: a violence that in fact evacuates all redemptive potentiality from purported signs whose function is to mediate the divine (e.g., the Eucharist). The resonance of these two moments in the poem—Jesus's sword-like purity and the head of John the Baptist—is effected linguistically by means of a shift in letters, a contamination of ends of invention (*Schlüsse*) with the bloodless platter (*Schüssel*). And here one sees clearly: the doctrine of the solid letter (*der veste Buchstab*)—along with the acceptability of the Christian eschatological history of redemption at the "end" of time—defeats itself ironically in the textual self-fragmentation of the later versions of "Patmos."

The defeat of the solid letter—which is, even in the first version of "Patmos" not quite so solid as it seems, as *vest* (solid) could be spelled either with a "v" or with an "f"[33]—erodes the theological foundations bolstering the attempt to read a well-ordered universe from a history of continual suffering. With this strophe, the intelligibility of Christian theodicy appears to become a problem rather than a solution for the lyrical voice. In the later versions of "Patmos," the Holy Spirit, sent to human beings as a consolation for the disappearance of earthly divine presence that occurs with the death of Jesus, does not function as a guarantor of divine order as much as hold open a space of potentiality in which new forms of sacrality can emerge:

> But those
> Did not want to let go
> Of the tears and the temples on the forehead [*Schläfen*] of the lord
> And the homeland. Inborn, glowing
> Red like fire that was, in iron. And harmful the face of God
> Really. For them

Like a plague went beside them the loved one's shadow.
Therefore he sent them
The Spirit, and mightily trembled
The house, and God's thunder-storms rolled,
Rumbling in the distance, creating men, as when dragon teeth, of glorious fate,[34]

. . . Aber jene nicht
Von Thränen und Schläfen des Herrn wollten
Lassen und der Heimath. Eingeboren, glühend
Wie Feuer roth war im Eisen das. Und schadend das Angesicht des Gottes wirklich. Denn ihnen
Wie eine Seuche gieng zur Seite der Schatte des Lieben.
Drum sandt er ihnen
Den Geist, und freilich bebte
Das Haus und die Wetter Gottes rollten
Ferndonnernd, Männer schaffend, wie wenn Drachenzähne, prächtigen Schiksaals (*MA* 1:466)

The scene culminates in an allusion to the founding of Thebes. Here, however, the teeth of the dragon, pregnant with a glorious fate, are themselves cut off in the poem—for the poem ends here—before they can develop into warriors and ground a new civic order. Moreover, the grounding of this state is founded on an autochthonic agonism, or warrior-brothers who spring from the earth only to cut down their siblings. The process leading to this climactic simile again merges Christian, pagan, and revolutionary narratives, holding the poetic idiom in a state of ambivalent and unresolved tension. The love of the divine is equated with the love of the homeland, a love that is inborn like "fire in iron" (*Feuer . . . in dem Eisen*), like a glowing and metallic weapon in the process of being forged. The shadow of the dear one, of the departed Christ, accompanies the disciples "like a plague." This shadow—the memory of the beloved and the yearning for his irrecoverable presence, as he is now "a shade"—contaminates everyone with whom it comes into contact. The Holy Spirit is sent in order to remedy this illness. The healing of the Holy Spirit, however, manifests itself in images that recall the Greek pantheon more than Christian redemption, above all in the thundering skies, functioning metonymically for Zeus. The thundering skies, supposedly part of the process of healing, nevertheless generate yet another problematic figure of regeneration: an oppositional and rebellious counter-figure, here Kadmos, who, like the Promethean titan of Goethe's poem, "creates men" (*Männer schaffend*). Christ, a sensuous cipher of divine presence, sets into motion a chain of violence, the redemption of which only serves to generate more violence. Sacred time unfolds as a history of catastrophe.

The final lines of the poem (fragmentary as they are, cut short by the end of the manuscript page) give rise to a poetic space in which the institution of the law and the suspension of the law appear indistinguishable. The autochthonous men who are born from the teeth of the dragon—springing from the ground of the homeland—are both founders of a new state as well as duplicitous bearers of civil strife. The passage in Ovid's *Metamorphoses* that describes this primordial scene, one in which a civic order emerges from violent struggle, emphasizes the duplicity in this moment of transition from anarchy to order:

> "Take not your arms," one of the earth-sprung brood cried out, "and take no part in our fratricidal [civil] strife." So saying, with his hard sword he clave one of his earth-born brothers, fighting hand-to-hand; and instantly he himself was felled by a javelin thrown from far.

> "ne cape," de populo, quem terra creaverat, unus
> exclamat "ne te civilius insere bellis."
> Atque ita terrigenis rigido de fratribus unum
> comminus ense ferit; iaculo cadit eminus ipse.[35]

The verb *insero* (graft, sow) that the warrior uses in order to urge his brothers to lay down their arms—just as he himself cuts down one of his companions and is in turn struck by a spear—continues the sowing metaphor through which Cadmus raises his army from the earth. The example of Thebes illustrates both the potential becoming in dissolution as well as the equally possible dissolution in becoming, since this foundational myth, one in which figures are cut down at a moment of emergence, embodies a model of tyrannical kingship in Sophoclean tragedy. Thebes, as the principal setting of Athenian tragedy, thus becomes the site for a continual series of struggles for power—conflicting obligations between the dictates of civic order secured by the sovereignty of kingship and the sanctity of local customs rooted in the power of the *demos*, or more simply, the struggle between monarchism and republicanism—foregrounding the political upheaval that may or may not culminate in a successful civic revolution. By portraying the moment of the birth of the new state in orgies of violence, Hölderlin, as in "The Ister," returns this foundational gesture to its state of incipient contingency: a revolution whose ends have not yet crystallized, whose event has not yet revealed itself as capable of generating the order that it holds out as a promise.

An interpretive poetic gesture that would secure a redemptive meaning for such violence in the later version of "Patmos" itself becomes truncated in the middle of its own simile. The poem leaves off at precisely the moment of potentiality in which a new civic order might emerge from a form of violence that is at first opposed to civic order. This is where, it would seem, Hölderlin's poetry seems to leave its readers: in a heightened state of cognitive intensity poised between potentiality and necessity, dissolution and becoming, negation and emergence. In the revisions of "Patmos," Hölderlin dedicates himself less to the cultivation of the solid letter than to the attempt to hold readers in a space of indeterminacy, a space in which the seemingly opposed paradigms of order and transgression become indistinguishable from one another. The very concept of order, a binding force that resignifies contingencies as necessities, continually withdraws from poetic discourse, leaving behind, if nothing else, the all-encompassing desire for something—a sign, a word, a feeling, whatever it might be—that might verify and secure the meaning of all that is given to the senses, and more importantly, of all that has ever appeared over the course of human history.

As long as Hölderlin's desire to cultivate the solid letter remained limited to the attempt to uncover the immanence of the divine in nature, in human relations, and in those elements of Christianity that unproblematically cohere with divine grace (Christ as God and man, Johannes as divine mediator through the word), the project—as manifest in the first version of "Patmos"—seems to have remained on relatively solid ground. As soon as Hölderlin began to explore history in a wider sense—in a way that brought together the catastrophes of Christian mythology with those of his own age—the solidity of this letter began to crumble.

Conclusion to Part One

✦

Poetic Modalities of Being

One of the most important ways in which poetry functions as an aesthetic exercise for Hölderlin consists in the capacity of poetic language to stimulate modal thought. In eighteenth-century philosophical discourses, modal thinking was typically understood to express a relation between three primary modalities: possibility, reality, and necessity.[1] Already in his early philosophical fragment "Being, Judgment," Hölderlin thinks the relationship (or non-relationship) between subjectless and objectless absolute identity (*Seyn*) and subject-centered differentiation (*Urtheil*) in terms of a theory of modality. Hölderlin notes that "reality" (*Wirklichkeit*) and "possibility" (*Möglichkeit*) can both appear in concrete acts of consciousness: "There is for us no thinkable possibility that was not reality" (*MA* 2:50). For Hölderlin, these two modalities are aligned inseparably with one another (and above all with the realm of Judgment) inasmuch as they presuppose a world conditioned by differentiation and separation.

The concept of necessity, on the other hand, is aligned with reason, or in Kantian terms, with postulates of practical reason. Necessity belongs not to the order of the real, but to how the real ought to be: "Hence the concept of possibility does not apply to objects of reason because they never appear in consciousness as that which they should be; only the concept of necessity [applies to the objects of reason]" (*MA* 2:50). For Hölderlin, necessity cannot appear concretely as a differentiated entity, nor can it appear as a determinate possibility in consciousness; indeed, necessity cannot manifest itself as an element in the system since it characterizes the organization of the system as a whole.[2] Human cognition cannot therefore *perceive* necessity—the harmonious and well-ordered organization of nature and history or the freedom that makes possible the moral law—in any sort of sensuously concrete manner. It would seem that, if one proceeds in a strictly Kantian manner, the limits of cognition demand that one can only approach such a realm of necessity (be it natural, historical, or moral) as a matter to be decided through postulates of practical reason.

To postulate necessity philosophically, as does Kant, constructs necessity as a regulative idea; no form of cognition, no human action can sensuously reveal the hidden order that is thus postulated. According to Hölderlin, the poet cannot accept the construction of mere "postulates" of reason as a cognitively satisfying relationship to the world as it ought to be. And yet, poetry can only operate through appearances in the world; it can only be conceptualized and produced as a reality and as a possibility, as a sequence of discrete temporal moments and sensuous signs. How, then, is the poet to proceed, if poetry aims to make present the realm of that which is necessary, that is, a form of perfect identity in which the differentiation of the modalities of reality and possibility would be subtended by some overarching ontological ground?

Hölderlin comes to the following conclusion: although poetry cannot make visible the realm of necessity in any one image, it can resignify the points of transition between orders of reality and possibility and thereby generate the affect of necessity. That which appears radically contingent to the evidence of the senses—as possible or as real—becomes felt as necessity in the poetic act. For Hölderlin, poetry can therefore produce a cognitive state wherein the modalities of possibility, reality, and necessity coalesce in one and the same cognitive space. As discussed in chapter 2, Hölderlin uses the notion of "idealistic recollection" to refer to this particular operation of modal conjunction: "The dissolution therefore as necessary, from the point of view of idealistic recollection, becomes as such the ideal object of the newly developed life" (*MA* 2:73). The order of necessity that makes itself felt can be applied to anything that can be narrated as a recollection of dissolution or change over time: a personal failure, an erotic relationship, indeed, the course of history itself, in which empires fall and new political regimes of organization emerge. Seen in this latter sense, the transition between radically different cultural and political orders—a transition that in certain instances appears to require violence, the suspension of order, and revolution (as we have seen in "The Rhine" and in "Patmos," for example)—makes manifest divine necessity through the poetic act. Hölderlin describes this poetic resignification of violence and trauma as a process in which "the dissolution of the infinitely new" is felt "not as destructive violence, but as love" (*MA* 2:76).

Hölderlin is aware of the ambivalence of this poetic operation, and in light of his revisions to "Patmos," one may ask whether or not the act of idealistic recollection is ultimately sustainable. This ambivalence seems to run far deeper than merely calling into question whether such a resignification of traumatic disruption is possible or desirable. If the central purpose of the idealistic recollection is to convert contingencies into necessities, to do so successfully, without any remainder, would eliminate the state in which human freedom itself dwells: "In the condition between Being and Non-Being, the possible becomes everywhere real, and the real becomes ideal, and this is in the free imitation of art a terrible, but divine dream [*ein furchtbarer, aber göttlicher Traum*]" (*MA* 2:73). If poetry resignifies the gaps between Being and Non-Being, making the possible real, and the real ideal, the one modality that recedes into the background is that of the possible. Hölderlin therefore sees the success of a process of "idealistic recollection" as both a terrifying, and yet, a divine dream (*ein furchtbarer, aber göttlicher Traum*). His poetic practice itself unfolds over time with an ever-greater awareness of the ambivalence of this goal, simultaneously desiring and fearing the full manifestation of the divine, which would in turn annihilate the realm of the human *as* a being who exists in the realm of the possible.

One may therefore detect a divergence in his poetic practices from that which his poetological texts often portray as the ideal to be actualized. In "The Ister," in "Patmos," in "Mnemosyne," in "Half of Life," indeed in countless other texts, Hölderlin's poetic utterance intensifies not the attraction to idealistic recollection, to divine necessity, but to its contrary, to the notion that not all dissolution can be reintegrated into the order of the beautiful. This deferral of the modality of necessity, or more precisely, this poetic inversion of idealistic recollection, amounts to a reopening of the space of possibility. If poetry consists in an exercise in modal cognition, the attempt to activate these modalities in one and the same poetic space, his later poems suggest that the order of modalities must lose their integrity: poetic cognition should be simultaneously encouraged to dis-integrate. The attempt to grasp the order of nature and history poetically, the dynamic of a phenomenal world situated between the contingent domain of possibility and the deterministic domain of necessity, veers toward the contingent precisely because it unfolds *between* these two modal intensities.

What remains in Hölderlin's poetry is a movement of transcendental concentration, or the requirement that language bear the burden of verifying the necessity of the real at the precise moment when the real appears only at a position of intensified possibility. In order to both preserve the divine dream of necessity and prevent the terrifying elimination of all possibility from human experience, he conceptualizes poetry as modal reversibility, or the representation of spaces in which necessity, reality, and possibility can coexist in the same affective and poetic texture. Such was, as we have seen, the central function of the tragic caesura: to bring these different modalities into contact with one another and facilitate operations of modal resignification.

In this space of modal indifferentiation—where possibility can become necessity, and necessity can open itself once again to an as-yet unperceived order—the mind is challenged to seek out not only its own integrity, but the integrity of the history and the world into which it has been born. To find this integrity, the force that binds all things and makes out of contingent events an intelligible whole, is the central task of aesthetic cognition. And yet, the world is so tragically and irrevocably infused with horror that any necessary or divine order can only be predicated upon the brutal facticity of the events that are to be bound together. The modal indifferentiation of aesthetic cognition ends up spreading into the realm of the divine in such a way that divinity itself can no longer claim something like transcendent purity. The resignification of the real as necessary entails that divine order become implicated in the trauma of the real, a conclusion that becomes increasingly visible in the revisions of "Patmos." Hegel seemed to believe that this movement, the reinscription of negativity into an overarching narrative that makes this negativity productive, was in fact intellectually possible (and indeed: necessary and constitutive of knowledge). Hölderlin, who approached this task as a matter for poetic spirit rather than for philosophical discourse, ultimately leaves his experiment in a state of undecided openness, at an intensified moment of danger. Poetry entails, as one might glean from the concept of *aussetzen* (to set out, to expose, to exclude) central to the later fragments of "Patmos," a necessary exposure to this indeterminacy, one that is also a setting forth or a poetic journey that may or may not lead to one's own exclusion from any given ontological order.

Hölderlin's later poetry often lingers in zones of possibility before any given order has had the chance to crystallize, for example, in the lawless and fratricidal slaughter of autochthonous soldiers as the precondition of the grounding of a civic order, which in turn, as Thebes, will become yet another site of tragic action, repeating, as it were, the original trauma and struggle that rise up from its own ground. He tarries with such scenes of becoming not merely to invest these turning points with a sense of emergent necessity, but also to amplify the equally evident facticity of contingent suffering inherent in the narrative of order itself. To view the violence of the world as necessary violence, the presence of holy terror in the form of earthly suffering, to see any such "riddle" (*Rätsel*) as "sprung from purity" (*Reinentsprungenes*)—"For suffering colors the purity of this one, purity that is/Pure like a sword" (*MA* 1:465)—raised a possibility that, it seems, neither Hölderlin nor perhaps the gods themselves could sustain.

Part Two

✦

Imagination, Perturbation, Stimulation

Chapter 4

✦

Disequilibrium and the Movement of Poetry

Poetry as a Way of Life

Poetry is not merely something that we do, a thing composed or enjoyed, one human activity among others. It is the atmosphere in which we live and breathe, or so it seemed to the romantic poet Friedrich von Hardenberg. In accordance with his own dictate to live poetically rather than merely to write poetry, I prefer to call him by his pseudonym: Novalis. Novalis writes in a letter to Caroline Schlegel, "One must construct a poetic world around oneself and live in poesy [*in der Poësie leben*]" (*NS* 4:275). For Novalis, the form-generating activity of the human being does not merely create things, objects in the world, but rather, new worlds in which objects themselves find their home. It is in this sense that romantic poetry could be said to be absolute—or in German, *unbedingt*, "unthinged"—for poetry is not a thing (*Ding*), but a world in which things appear.

Novalis is fully aware of the difficulty—the impossibility—of ever being able to *live* poetry in the manner he describes above. In the same letter, he writes, "Now I am living completely in *engineering* [*in der Technik*] because my apprenticeship years are coming to an end and bourgeois life, with its many demands, is coming ever closer" (*NS* 4:275). The impossibility of ever being able to fully live in a realm of poetic enchantment suggests that poetry represents a task for thought rather than a universal ontology. Despite the fact that Novalis believes that all cognition contains an irreducibly fictionalizing impulse, he often does not make a naive equation of life with poetic being, but rather, speaks in imperatives: "The world must be romanticized" (*NS* 2:545). Life does not begin as poetry, but it has the potential to become poetic. Every true romantic is simultaneously a failed romantic, as poetry must ultimately—or so it seems—cede to the demands of everyday life.

What, however, is poetry, according to Novalis, and from where does its claim over life originate? Although Novalis considers many different definitions of poetry, each of which illuminates certain facets of the poetic enterprise, one of his most striking statements about poetry culminates in a tautology: "Poetry is thoroughly personal and therefore indescribable and indefinable. Whoever does not immediately know and feel what poetry is cannot be taught what it is. Poetry is poetry. Worlds apart from rhetoric [*Rede(Sprach)kunst*]" (*NS* 3:685). In this instance, Novalis's definition of poetry would seem to be a non-definition, or a paradoxical one at best: the defining characteristic of poetry is that it does not have any such defining characteristic. Poetry makes a scandal of the question: "What is it?" And yet, this non-definition says more about Novalis's conception of poetry than any assertoric statement could hope to accomplish.[1]

Above all, the statement "poetry is poetry," despite what might seem to be the case, does not assert that the ineffability of poetry can only be "felt" or "experienced," and hence, can only be approached non-discursively, in some way that eludes articulation. In order to understand why this is so, one must differentiate between the semantic content of the utterance and its value as a task for thought.

The divergence between the semantic content and the exercise value of an utterance may be considered a form of irony, but it is an irony that emerges in a gap between what a statement *claims* and what a statement intends to *produce* as a movement of consciousness. The exercise value of the utterance can only be approached by examining closely the form of the utterance. To anticipate the main argument, which will only become clear after a certain amount of conceptual explication: Novalis is not saying that the essence of poetry escapes language, but rather, that poetry *emerges from the logical, cognitive, and creative movements implicit in the attempt to grasp a tautology.*

This interpretation of Novalis's conception of poetry explicitly diverges from the typical understanding of romantic poetry as centering primarily on inexpressibility, a mere variation on the topos of the unutterable (*Unsagbarkeitstopos*).[2] If Novalis were truly claiming that the essence of poetry is feeling and it therefore cannot be expressed, one would have to say with Wittgenstein, "Whereof one cannot speak, thereof must one be silent."[3] The work of art would close itself to language, to thought, and become an uninterpretable excess of sheer aesthetic experience.[4] And yet, Novalis does not remain silent about poetry. If there is something about poetry that escapes articulation, it nevertheless requires language to foreground its own transcendence within a system of differences. On the contrary, then: poetry is not that which escapes articulation, but that which *calls out for* articulation. Here is the enigma of poetry, its *explicandum*: in its very irreducibility to language, it beckons language.

In the same passage, when Novalis claims that poetry must be felt in its immediacy, he is neither relegating poetry to a matter of opinion nor construing poetry as a mere subjective feeling. If Novalis does claim that poetry can only be "felt," or known "immediately," one must distinguish between feeling as a subjective state, and feeling as a more primordial form of awareness. Much of this ground has already been covered in depth by other scholars (above all by Manfred Frank and Winfried Menninghaus), but it is worth rehearsing the general arguments.[5] In Novalis's notes on Fichte's philosophical texts, written in 1795–96 and now known to scholars as the *Fichte Studies* (*Fichte-Studien*), feeling, as a technical philosophical concept, does not refer to a mere subjective emotion, nor is it an affective state inherently opposed to rationality. For Novalis, feeling is nevertheless irreducible to cognitive acts of reflection, the specific form of consciousness in which an "I" conscious of itself as a subject examines its own consciousness as an object. At the same time, feeling, as an originary awareness or acquaintance with the self before the self (either as "subject" or as "object"), can become an object for thought, and therefore can become the (itself absent) content of a reflective act. There is a paradox at the center of subjective reflection: in order for the subject to recognize itself as an object, it must already know itself prior to its having become an object for itself. It is precisely this problem that motivates Fichte to claim that the I posits itself, so that one may speak of a "knowing" prior to the structure of subject-object reflection. According to Fichte, the self-positing I must be able to intuit its own act of positing, so that every intuition (*Anschauung*) is grounded in this primordial act of self-positing.

Novalis disagrees with Fichte's conception of a self-positing I as a solution to the problem of self-recognition in the act of reflection. The origin of self-recognition cannot be grounded in a subject that has an awareness of itself positing—an origin that merely reproduces the very problematic structure of subjectivity in which there is supposedly not yet a subject. Instead, Novalis derives philosophy from an originary *feeling*, not from an act of positing: "Philosophy is originally a feeling. The philosophical sciences conceptualize the intuitions [*Anschauungen*] of this feeling" (*NS* 2:113). Feeling, unlike the Fichtean concept of self-positing, designates a more originary form of awareness: states of being that are pre-discursive, pre-reflective, and above all, pre-subjective.

Feeling designates a primordial contact with pre-reflexive givenness, a form of awareness operating prior to any possibility of reflecting upon that which is given to consciousness in a higher-order act of cognition. Novalis notes, "There must be a feeling of inner, necessarily free relations. Philosophy therefore always needs *something given*" (*NS* 2:113). Feeling, as that which brings us into contact with our own awareness before it can become an object for reflective consciousness, escapes all attempts at representation: "It is impossible to represent the pure form of feeling. It is only singular [*Es ist nur eins*] and form and content, as composite concepts, are simply not applicable to it" (*NS* 2:116). Prior to representation, prior to reflection, however, there must be *something* to reflect upon. Only a pre-discursive, pre-reflexive feeling can access this originary something that then becomes an object for reflection.

Feeling therefore has the unique capacity to be present both in consciousness and as an unconscious ground of givenness. Manfred Frank conceptualizes Novalis's notion of "feeling" as a "relationless intimacy" with one's self, or a *beziehungslose Vertrautheit*.[6] One could expand this definition from a relationless intimacy with the self to one that is equally co-present with the totality of all that is given to the self, including the world and other human beings; for in this intimacy, there is presumably no "self" with which one could be intimate, but rather, mere non-differentiated presence. If Novalis later refers to poetry as accessible only to feeling, he is not claiming that poetry is accessible only to an inarticulate and inarticulable emotional state, but rather that poetry comes into contact with a pre-reflexive sphere of intimacy, a domain of originary, undifferentiated givenness.

Feeling as a form of intimacy cannot merely be understood as the absolute other of language or articulation. To be sure, if one considers language merely as a differential system of signs—as representation—then language as such must exclude feeling as "relationless intimacy." However, when Novalis claims that "poetry is poetry" and distinguishes it from rhetoric, or *Redekunst*, he is introducing another model for the operation of language at the basis of poetry, and it is from this model that we might perhaps be able to better understand not only what poetry is, but why it is important for life, why Novalis thinks it could become the very space in which we live.

In order to think of poetry *as* poetry, as a pre-reflective intimacy that permeates all contexts of being, Novalis gives an account of language that can neither be reduced to a mere play of differences, nor to a form of signification as mere representation. Whereas rhetoric, or *Redekunst*, implies a conception of language as stylistic manipulation, poetry illuminates that by virtue of which human beings have awareness in the first place, both of themselves and of the world of phenomena.[7] And yet, by opposing poetry to rhetoric, he is not claiming that poetry only inhabits a realm of truth, nature, or pure presence. Like acts of cognition that generate knowledge, poetry is made possible by its identity with itself, but at the same time, it must nevertheless enter the system of differences in order to appear at all. The essence of poetry consists not in its connection to this realm of absolute being, but rather, in the *movement* from absolute being to differentiation. Poetry therefore describes not an originary identity with truth or presence, but encompasses an attraction to deception, artifice, and impurity: a fall into appearances. It is only by virtue of these impure movements that poetry can become a way of life, a task for thought, an activity that pushes the human being toward an intensification of his or her own finitude rather than a formless and bloodless intuition of undifferentiated Being.

Originary Impurity and the Fiction of Truth

With this philosophical context in mind, let us return to Novalis's definition of poetry. "Poetry is poetry" (*NS* 3:685), says Novalis. The statement, written in 1800 shortly before Novalis's death, takes the appearance of a tautology,

A = A. In his studies of Fichte, Novalis draws attention to the fact that a tautology does not simply reproduce an innocent claim of self-identity. At the center of the tautological assertion, in the space of the copula—indeed at the supposed Archimedean point of equivalence—lies a fundamental deception. Novalis begins his *Fichte Studies* with the following statement:

> In the proposition *a is a* there is nothing except a positing, differentiation, and binding. It is a philosophical parallelism. In order to make *a* more distinct, *A* is divided. *Is* is proposed as a general content, and *a* as a determinate form. The essence of identity can only be expressed in an *illusory proposition* [*Scheinsatz*]. We take leave of the *identical* in order to represent it. (*NS* 2:104)

The attempt to linguistically represent Being, the realm of the absolutely identical, can only take place within the differentiated world of appearances. The formula "a is a," by virtue of its participation in an order of differential signs, reveals the duplicity of the formula vis-à-vis that which the formula intends to express, namely, an operation of equivalence; in the formula, there are, after all, two instances of the letter "a."[8] Moreover, the formula introduces differentiation not merely in number, but in an implicit oppositional force that any discrete element acquires relative to other elements: the variable "A" exists in what Novalis calls a "determinate form,"[9] and as such can be opposed to all forms that are "Not-A." No tautological formula—because formulas are always constructed using differential signs—can ever express a pure, perfect identity of Being, since "no modification, no concept clings to mere Being—one cannot oppose anything to it" (*NS* 2:106).

It would seem that only Non-Being (*Nichtseyn*) can be opposed to the realm of Being. And yet, the very action of opposition is only made possible by the conception of Being as a copula binding two particulars—or as Novalis says, "a little copulating hook [*ein copulirendes Häckchen*] that is only hanged on *pro forma*" (*NS* 2:106). Being as copula, as the joining of identicals, covers up its own dissimulation. A "copulating hook" that joins two identicals together, by entering into a system of differences, is incapable of expressing Being as an absolute (*Seyn*), as undifferentiated, pure identity. The sentence expressing the most self-evident truth, A = A, becomes an illusory sentence, a *Scheinsatz*—that is to say, a proposition that is both deceptive inasmuch as it expresses appearance instead of Being, *Schein* instead of *Seyn*, and apparitional inasmuch as it moves in the world of appearances. The tautological sentence does not therefore primarily express identity. Its primary function is rather to produce a plurality through the world of signs, two instances of A instead of the expressionless plenitude of pure indifference.[10] As we shall see, for Novalis, every use of language presupposes the dynamic of the tautological sentence as the simultaneous and paradoxical production of difference through the attempt to express non-differentiation.

Later in the *Fichte Studies*, Novalis calls the relationless realm of Being a necessary fiction: "Pure—what is neither related nor relatable [*weder bezogen noch beziehbar*] . . . everything pure is therefore a deception of the imagination—a *necessary* fiction" (*NS* 2:179). For Novalis, purity is a fiction, since it can only enter the world as difference, as impurity.[11] However, it is not merely that purity itself constitutes a *mere* lie, or a *mere* fiction, but rather, that fiction itself becomes the bearer of this false notion of purity. Fiction is endowed with the unique capacity not to purify the impure world—for according to Novalis's conception of Being, nothing that appears can be pure—but rather, and more radically, *to impurify* more intensively the world in its impurity. To impurify in this context means to move deeper into the world of appearances, to multiply differences rather than leading differences back to an originary unity.

The movement of Being as an intensification of impurity or differentiation appears already in the tautological statement "A = A," as the very statement itself moves *Seyn* into *Schein*—not merely as a movement into deception, but as a movement into *appearing*. Because the tautological statement cannot express Being in its fundamental non-relational indifferentiation—at best, it achieves "absolute or total form" (*NS* 2:172), which is to say the pure relationality of a relationship and nothing more—it nevertheless throws both the particular phenomenon *A* and the operation of the copula into relief. The tautological statement functions not as a logical proposition, but as a revelatory one; it does not merely issue an empty claim of identity, and hence represent what would otherwise be a wholly superfluous statement, but the very utterance brings phenomena into a higher degree of clarity, or more precisely, a higher degree of distinction: " 'A' is split in order to make 'a' *more distinct* [*deutlicher*]" (*NS* 2:104).

Only the revelatory character of a tautological statement can index non-differentiated Being as a cognitive or non-cognitive imaginative possibility. The copulative or relational tautology emerging from the identity of two particulars triggers the postulation of absolute Being as an irreal, or imaginary realm. The tautology, far from resting in itself as a static equation, sets into motion the dynamic operation of an infinite process. It makes possible the *imagination* of absolute Being, but only by foregrounding absolute Being itself as something impossible. The ontology of Being is incompatible not only with the symbolic system of signification, but also with the differentiation of perception. Absolute identity and difference both constitute and exclude one another in the tautological statement, and it is from this paradoxical space that poetry—*Poësie ist Poësie*—is born.

The tautology can be regarded as the most poetic of poetic statements, not because it expresses the inexpressibility of absolute being, but precisely because it forces the movement from absolute Being into the manifold world of appearances. From the tautology, one may derive an important feature of Novalis's aesthetic attraction: the central function of the (necessarily self-defeating) representation of Being, which cannot be thought without difference, does not *express* an inexpressible identity, but instead *produces* differences, a plurality of appearances.[12] The movement from Being to appearances dramatized in the formula of the tautology does not simply reveal the transcendental operation of language itself—namely that Being can only be made visible in a differentiated semiotic system outside of Being—but rather, invests language with a specific exercise value, leading to a conception of poetry as a practice, as an imaginative way of life.

Not all linguistic acts produce this translation from Being into appearance, from *Seyn* into *Schein*, in the same manner. Novalis discusses two different modes of representation through which this originary translation takes place:

> We take leave of the *identical* in order to represent it—either this happens only apparently—and we are brought by the imagination to believe it—what *happens*, already Is—naturally through imaginary separating and binding—Or we present it through non-being, through something non-identical—sign—a determined thing for an isomorphic determining thing—this isomorphic determining thing must actually determine the communicated sign in a thoroughly immediate manner, like the I—free and yet exactly like the I. Taste and genius. (*NS* 2:104)

Novalis contrasts two different procedures for approaching non-differentiated Being. In the first case, we represent Being through an imaginative movement, by moving from the supposed differentiation in the copula to an imagined sphere of non-differentiation. Novalis labels this operation taste, or *Geschmack*. For Kant, to exercise aesthetic judgment allows one to move from private, sensuous taste (*Sinnen-Geschmack*) to a more generalized form of validity (*Reflexions-Geschmack*) (*AA* 5:214). According to Kantian aesthetics, taste designates a movement from the particular to the universal through the use of reflective judgment. Novalis's designation of the imaginative projection of a realm of absolute identity from the givenness of particulars draws upon this conception of taste. Representing the unrepresentable in the imagination introduces both an appearance and a deception, since Being appears, but only through a construction of being as a composite, or as a unification of differences—hence as *artifice*.

The second pathway through which the presence of absolute Being makes itself felt occurs through genius. Novalis's understanding of genius departs from Kant's formulation of genius as "the inborn frame of mind (*ingenium*) *through which* nature gives the rule to art" (*AA* 5:307). Rather, genius is that power through which absolute, non-differentiated Being nevertheless touches the world of appearances and manifests itself in the world of signs. In this process, signs themselves are understood as elements that nevertheless exclude Being and hence belong, in a certain sense, to Non-Being and non-identity:

"we make present [the identical] through its non-being, through something non-identical—sign" (*NS* 2:104). The sign is a form of presence that stands in for something absent: "Being," as sign, cannot be identical to the realm of pure identity. From the perspective of such identity, signs as such exist only in the realm of non-Being, since they are determined and differential. However, this "determined" conception of Being, Being as a sign, whose sign character only becomes manifest as in the attempt to represent Being as undifferentiated identity, presupposes a *determining* power that exists isomorphically with the determined sign ("an isomorphic determining thing," *ein gleichförmig bestimmendes*, *NS* 2:104). Novalis conceives absolute Being not merely as a space of non-differentiation, but as a ground of all appearances, permeating all signs—and hence the copulative sign "to be" as well.

Novalis's revelation, or rather, non-revelation of absolute Being in aesthetic categories—namely through *Geschmack* or *Genius*—reveals less a conceptual distinction than an oscillation inherent in the very attempt to conceptualize the absolute. Taste and genius are not oppositions, but chiasmatic reversals of one another. Taste moves from the particular to absolute, undifferentiated generality, all the while seeking to sublate the particular in this imagined, and hence fictional, generality. Genius, on the other hand, moves from the absolute to the particular, a process through which this originary sphere of absolute non-differentiation contiguously permeates all differentiated phenomena. Taste seeks the absolute through exercising the imagination, whereas genius lets the absolute touch all particulars through the intimacy of language with itself. The power of the absolute, a non-determined and non-differentiated non-thing, filters into language and frees the realm of signs in the same way that the intangible freedom at the core of the subject realizes itself in acts of will and differentiated reflections; the system of signs, by virtue of its contact with the realm of absolute Being, is "free and yet exactly like the I" (*NS* 2:104). Genius appears not as nature giving itself rules through art, but rather, in the immediate intimacy between signs and absolute Being.

According to Novalis, the totality of the semiotic system exhibits the same structure as the absolute ego. Language, then, partakes in the very same "relationless intimacy" or *beziehungslose Vertrautheit* with itself, as does the human being. It is only when taste is united with genius, or when the imaginary and hence illusory nature of the absolute infiltrates all differences, that poetry, as the infinite exercise of the imagination, can in turn permeate every sphere of life. Novalis ends this thought by signaling that genius too can only appear in the realm of the imagination, thereby linking mediation and immediacy through a hybrid "genius taste" (*Genie Geschmack*) as opposed to "mere taste" (*bloßer Geschmack*, *NS* 2:104]). The poet as genius imaginatively posits the fictional realm of the absolute (*Geschmack*), and then lets this imagined absolute seep back into the world of concrete appearances (*Genie*).

Novalis famously claims in his "Monologue" that "precisely the peculiarity of language—that it is only concerned with itself—no one knows" (*NS*

2:672). It is the strange and wondrous property of language to exhibit the very structure of *self-feeling* characteristic of human sentience. As is the case with the human being, this relation of self-feeling or intimacy seems at first incommensurable with discursive knowledge or reflective acts. No one can "know" this intimacy; although the human being knows *in* language, human sentience does not *know* language. In the "Monologue," Novalis is not claiming that people do not know *that* language cares only about itself, but rather, that they do not *know* language caring about itself. This particular activity of language is not open to analytical or discursive knowledge, which moves in the realm of differences, but rather, reveals itself only to the more primordial sensitivity of intimacy. And precisely the genius of language, which acts analogously to the genius of the I, consists in letting absolute Being touch the realm of appearances through determinate signs.

It is in this sense that language is feeling: signs are made possible through a sphere of intimacy with themselves in the same way that human beings come to an awareness of themselves, namely in a pre-reflective identity with that which is given. Moreover, in the "Monologue," although the narrator claims that language partakes in an originary realm of intimacy with itself, in this very articulation the narrator excludes his own utterances from this intimacy: "If I thus believe to have expressed the essence and office of poetry in the most distinct manner, nonetheless I know that no person can understand it, and I said something utterly foolish—because I wanted to say it—and in this manner no poetry comes about" (*KSA* 2.672). The narrator cannot claim to represent the truth of language, its identity with itself, since, in the very attempt to grasp it reflectively in its self-identity, the intimacy of language with itself recedes.[13] Language thus operates in excess of the will, and poetic acts come into being inasmuch as they reveal all acts of reflection as partial, limited, and thus, in some sense, as missing the mark of the essence of language. Ultimately, the attempt to represent the relation of language to itself can only represent its own attempt to represent; language can speak only of its own desire for itself, its self-reproduction *in* differences, or a "language drive [*Sprachtrieb*]" (*NS* 2:672).

Novalis's doctrine of poetry rests upon the following claim: language exhibits the same structure vis-à-vis the realm of absolute Being as does human sentience. Like human beings, it is the particularity of signs to partake in both an intimacy with Being as well as in a system of differentiation and limitation. Absolute Being itself exists in a precarious and paradoxical state, as it *requires* the articulation that excludes its very essence—as relationless intimacy—in order for this essence to appear *as fiction*. The central problem of poetry therefore appears in a parallel form to the problematic relationship between reflection and feeling: how can poetry manifest itself in language, in a system of differences, and simultaneously claim to operate within the same sphere as feeling, as pre-reflexive, pre-discursive givenness?

The Inversion of Order and the Drive to Transcendence

For Novalis, the human being is capable both of discursive reflection and non-discursive feeling, but can never engage these two forms of cognition in one and the same act of consciousness; the presence of the one extinguishes the possibility of the other. From within the structure of subject-object cognition, feeling escapes from our field of view. As Novalis says: "[A feeling] may only be observed in reflection—the spirit of the feeling has then departed" (*NS* 2:114). However, it cannot be the case that when the subject begins to observe itself as an object via reflective cognition, feeling simply ceases to exist. Feeling, as a primordial awareness of givenness, is not something that can fully disappear: "The thread holding together [*Der Zusammenhang*] thinking and feeling must always exist—we must be able to find it everywhere in consciousness" (*NS* 2:117). The connection between thinking and feeling, as mutually exclusive modes of access to the world, is necessarily elusive, if not impossible; after all, feeling, as relationless intimacy, would then be brought into a relationship—with thought. There is only one conclusion left for Novalis: that same "relationless intimacy" characteristic of the human being's originary acquaintance with its self and its world must extend into the very faculty of reflection as well, and indeed the two acts must be in some sense identical to one another, albeit in a peculiar manner.

Novalis inscribes the mutually exclusive attitudes of thinking and feeling in a larger process, portraying them as parts of one and the same act. Drawing on Fichte, he refers to this primordial act as an *Urhandlung*. This originary act, however, can only be known in reflection. In reflection, however, one becomes aware of this originary act as precisely that which excludes feeling, its other, from its own reflective activity. Feeling is therefore present in reflection as the negative of reflection, as that which is unthinkable, unrepresentable, incommensurable, and unavailable to reflective thought. It is only through a hyper-reflection, or a reflection on the very limits of reflection, that reflection and feeling may come to be regarded as the same act merely seen from different points of view. If feeling is only available from within reflection as its own negative, as Manfred Frank and Gerhard Kurz have shown, feeling and reflection must constitute inverted images of one another.[14]

Within the framework of Novalis's thought, feeling is therefore assigned a function that draws less on its status as an "intuition" of some realm of absolute identity than as an element exterior to the system of subject-object reflection that then provokes or reconfigures this system. Because feeling is exterior to reflection, the attempt to approach this form of exteriority prompts a never-ending inversion of cognitive movements. This reversal, as Manfred Frank emphasizes, this *ordo inversus*, aims to fill in the total sphere of human sentience by making present the blind spot of reflection, namely, the originary givenness of feeling.[15] This process, which continually inverts acts of reflection that posit feeling as their original content, ought to reveal the hanging together of reflection and feeling, these supposedly mutually exclusive modalities: "*Back* and *forth* direction. Sphere exhausted—connection is there [Hin *und* her *Direction. Sfäre erschöpft—Zusammenhang da*]" (*NS* 2:117). Novalis calls this movement the "deduction of philosophy," in the sense of leading differentiated acts of reflection back to their origin in relationless feeling, which is at the same time the origin of philosophy as a discourse:

> Need for a philosophy in consciousness—apparent movement from limited to the non-limited—reflection about this—seeming movement from the non-limited to the limited—results of this reflection—results of the feeling of this reflection—reflection about these results after the other results—connection found or philosophy. (*NS* 2:117)

Let us reconstitute the operations Novalis calls a "deduction" of philosophy. The philosophical project begins by feeling the need for philosophy. It feels this drive in a mode of reflection, or in consciousness. In consciousness, when we attempt to conceptualize the originary givenness of the world, we seem to be moving from our limited sphere, the sphere in which we as subjects reflect on objects, to the sphere of the absolute, namely the sphere of feeling. Importantly, this is only a movement that appears in consciousness as a *seeming* progression, *ein scheinbares Schreiten*, for here we continue to operate in the realm of appearances in consciousness, in a reflective mode. From this moment on—indeed from the beginning of our first reflection, the first operation that could be labeled as knowing—all thinking as such occurs as a movement within appearances. However, when we reflect on this reflection, we understand that we are in fact seeing a movement toward the unlimited realm of feeling *from the limited perspective of reflection*. In order to see it from the perspective of feeling itself, which reflection excludes, we must reverse our reflection; in this second reflection, the activity of reflection interprets itself from an opposing point of view, namely as a movement not from reflection to feeling, but from feeling to reflection, from the absolute to the limited, *vom Unbeschränkten zum Beschränkten*. In the first pages of the *Fichte Studies*, it is this very act of oscillation that Novalis describes in the language of aesthetics as "genius taste."

If we appear to be moving toward the absolute, the absolute must appear to be moving toward us. Although each of these movements occurs only in reflection, the second, in which the absolute moves toward us, is a higher-order reflection, or a reflection upon a reflection from another point of view. This inverted reflection gives us a result for reflection, but it also gives a result *for the realm of feeling in reflection*, namely, as an inverted image of the first reflection. Philosophy, for Novalis, therefore consists in the reflection upon a reflection and an inverted reflection. In this reflection that reflects on two reflections—a still higher-order reflection—the identity of feeling and thought, which occurs only in thought, emerges from the oscillation of opposing reflective movements. The continual inversion of thought establishes a pattern through which a reflection becomes raised to a higher order by becoming the object of another reflection.

The attempt to retrieve the identity of feeling, something exterior to the system of reflection, only leads to a multiplication of reflective acts, each one inverting its precedent. If the production of multiplicity and differences appears as one important tendency of Novalis's philosophy, the positing of something outside the space of reflection (e.g., feeling) as a negative or non-element that then perturbs the system of differences—thereby triggering a continual overturning of orders of reflection rather than undertaking a continual "filling in" of the blind spots of reflection—may be considered as a second important contour of his thought. Being is thereby endowed with a function in the differential system of reflective representations that draws upon this realm of posited absolute exteriority as an impetus for reconfiguration. The function of Being does not lead to some mystical intuition of unity, nor to any "infinite approach" toward a more complete totality of consciousness, but rather, posits an otherness to thought that in turn produces acts of inversion and differentiation in cognition. For Novalis, Being is not simply a perfect identity with all that exists; rather, considered from within a system of differences, primordial Being is a void at the heart of all representational, reflective, or differential systems. Being is that which cannot be made into an element of the system. It can therefore only make its presence known within this system as perturbation.

The Physiological Absolute

At a certain point in the *Fichte Studies*, Novalis postulates that the continual inversion of acts of reflection does not bring the reflecting consciousness any closer to the absolute. In yet another inversion, the impossible attainment of the absolute itself becomes a new absolute:

> All philosophy must therefore end with an absolute ground [*bey einem absoluten Grunde*]. If this ground were not given, if this concept contained an impossibility—then the drive to philosophize would be an infinite activity . . . Through the voluntary renunciation of the absolute the infinite free activity emerges within us—the only possible absolute that can be given to us, and that we can only find through our incapacity to attain and to know anything absolute. (*NS* 2:270)

The passage represents a significant shift in Novalis's thinking, not because Novalis gives up the absolute and becomes a relativist, but more significantly, because he subtly redefines the absolute in terms of *drives*. Novalis defines a drive in the following manner: "A positing-forth in itself is a drive" (*Ein Fortsetzen in sich selbst ist ein Trieb*, *NS* 2:134). This drive, which Novalis expresses in Fichtean terminology as a type of positing—literally a positing-forth, or a *Fortsetzen*—ultimately becomes the new absolute.

The puzzle of the absolute, a realm that eludes predication, attribution, relation, and hence definition, shifts to an inquiry into the generation of life itself, into the enigma of the plurality of appearances. And it is here that philosophy merges with physiology, for both domains presuppose the structure of a drive that demands reproduction. In Novalis's unfinished novel of nature (*Naturroman*), *The Novices of Sais*, the fixation on the philosophical absolute of identity at the expense of the physiological absolute as a drive toward differentiation may easily lead to the misrecognition of this absolute at the end of the fairy tale of Hyacinth and Rosenblüthchen. The absolute does not announce itself when Hyacinth lifts the veil of Isis only to discover his beloved—or the eroticized other—as the origin and telos of his own inner subjective world. The absolute as a vision or an intuition of Being or identity appears conspicuously absent from the fairy tale. Rather, directly following this supposed act of union, the couple is blessed with innumerable grandchildren, "unzählige Enkel" (*NS* 1:95).[16] If there is an allusion to the absolute in the fairy tale, the location and localization of the absolute (itself a paradoxical venture) is to be found not in the lifting of the veil, but in the final celebration of an imagined infinite reproductivity. For, as we shall see, this reproductivity occurs not literally, but rather, as a reproductive capacity of the imagination; the countless grandchildren appear primarily as products of Hyacinth's dream life. The dynamic of the mind as a continual positing-forth, a *Fortsetzen*, announces the presence of this other form of the absolute, an absolute that consists more in movement than in image, more in differentiated serialization than in immediate intuition.

This alternative absolute unfolds by subordinating philosophical-logical paradoxes of self-reflection to patterns of physiological development. Already in the *Fichte Studies*, Novalis turns to the natural sciences, to chemical, magnetic, or electrical processes, which each in their turn translate the basic facticity of the reproductive drive into their respective discursive spaces.[17] The concept of drive, the realm of the absolute as it generates its own particularity, merges with the concept of attraction. When Novalis thinks about the exchange relationship characteristic of the general and the particular, he characterizes this relationship not as an opposition, but as a movement between differences: "Attraction of the general and the particular—the actually opposed—in one sense different, in one the same—of intuition and representation [*der Anschauung und Vorstellung*]—and sensibility and feeling [*des Empfindens und Fühlens*]—. About the power of attraction and drive" (*NS* 2:224). The relation between the general and the particular is modeled on a concept of attraction as a power governing the circulation of energy; hence, in the midst of the *Fichte Studies*, Novalis turns his interest to centripetal forces and to speed, to the relationship between bodies through attraction: "Centripetal force accrues through speed—is it in the body or is it attraction [*Anziehungskraft*]/Magnet. Electricity" (*NS* 2:192). The failure of philosophy to attain the absolute does not make Novalis a relativist, but a certain type of naturalist: a *poetic naturalist*, or a naturalist whose understanding of nature includes his or her own imaginative structure of interpretation as part of the dynamic of nature, and whose imagination in turn posits this dynamic—which is physiological inasmuch as it seeks the logos of *physis*—as a model for its own semiotic and cognitive acts.

Over the course of the *Fichte Studies*, one may therefore observe a shift from a philosophical absolute to a physiological one, a movement from the absolute as undifferentiated ground to one of infinite activity. The second absolute is no longer linked to feeling, but rather, to the principle of life as the production of continual stimulation, as an excitation whose only purpose is to continually generate its own multiplicity of particulars.[18] The absolute exists no longer outside time, but rather, designates the operation of time itself; it is no longer a realm outside of space, but movement itself; it is no longer the deathless realm of the infinite, but the mortal and vulnerable desires of finite beings; it is no longer an absence of differentiation, but the multiplication of reflective orders continually overturning themselves. The absolute can therefore be considered as a self-sustaining and self-generating process that is taken up into the horizon of the mind as a particular intensification of experience.

This second conception of the absolute, whose logic is dictated more by a notion of drive than by a pre-reflexive indifferentiation of being, nevertheless presupposes the first absolute—absolute identity available to humans through feeling—as a continual source of perturbation, as that which prevents any particular order from making itself the absolute. If for the philosopher Alain Badiou, an absolute unpredictability destabilizes the normal procedures for generating truth in given frameworks of action, or in his terms, the Event perturbs and reconfigures Being, for Novalis, Being *is* the Event.[19] And yet, for Novalis, the event-quality of being is not something that intrudes upon us, but something that human beings can excite within themselves as a source of stimulation: an active overturning of reflective orders. It is therefore not the case that the first absolute (the absolute of identity) becomes wholly supplanted by the second (the absolute of stimulation). Without the first absolute, the pristine and immobile realm of Being beyond beings, this second absolute as activity, as striving, as floating oscillation, would divest itself of its drive character. The motor of this new absolute—the temporal, spatial, finite absolute of drive—requires the impossibility of the first absolute *as* an impossibility: a basic incommensurability within the particularity of appearances, representations, discursive configurations, and discrete thoughts that keeps the system of differences in a state of flux.

All thinking of absolute identity requires a thinking of the simultaneous drive-character of the movement from identity to differentiation. The central horizon of philosophy—which in turn holds open the possibility of a physiological philosophy and a philosophical physiology—is constituted not by the enigma of Being, but rather, by the enigma of beings, of concrete, particular, individualized entities. Novalis notes this peculiarity of the absolute when he notes that there must be "the drive to be an I" (*Der Trieb Ich zu seyn, NS* 2:134), a drive primordially coextensive with the absolute itself. Freud would later say, "Where Id was, there Ego should be" (*Wo Es war, soll Ich werden*)[20] in order to articulate not only the task of psychoanalysis, but the formation of the ego as something poised between past (*war*) and future (*werden*), exhibiting a structure not unlike the movement from undifferentiated and impersonal chaos (*es*) to the bounded self (*ich*). Novalis's ontology gives rise to a similar dynamic, although he concentrates the movement of individuation in the present, seeing the human being as that sort of being that desires a self. His formula is: "What wants to be Ego, is that which I am" (*Was Ich seyn will, das bin ich, NS* 2:146). The formulation is nevertheless ambiguous. Cited out of context, it might easily be mistaken for the affirmative phrase: "What I want to be, I am." And yet, the more accurate translation (signaled above all by the capitalization of the "I," *Ich*), in the context of the *Fichte Studies*, would read: "That which wishes to be an I, that is the being I am," or rather, "I am that being that manifests Being as wanting to be an I." At the same time, in the ambiguity of the phrase, Novalis has nevertheless affirmed that he *is* what he wants to be; he construes individuation not merely as parasitical to an otherwise perfectly undifferentiated identity, but as the manifestation of an affirmative process of differentiation.

Does the first absolute, the realm of indifferent givenness, nevertheless exist—if indeed one can speak of the predicate of existence, which, in this case, is doubtful—for Novalis? After all, Novalis's poetics might be understood to advance the claim that the activity of the imagination in poetic intuition has access to the realm of the given in a manner that is impossible for reflective knowledge.[21] The claim that poetry somehow bypasses reflection associates art with a special mode of intuition, leading to a sort of cognitive exceptionalism in the case of aesthetics that has long been understood to constitute the hallmark of romanticism. Schelling will later argue something akin to this position in his *Philosophy of Art* (1804–05): art exists as a means of making present that which can never become present in acts of reflection.

Seen from within this framework, Novalis's poetic enterprise maintains the importance of the first absolute in two distinct manners. In philosophical thought, the absolute of undifferentiated givenness becomes a Kantian a priori regulative idea. We never achieve the absolute in thought, but we postulate it as a realm that we can approach through infinite approximation. In poetry, on the other hand, the unrepresentability of absolute being is itself represented; poetry has a privileged access to this absolute in a way that discursive thought does not. With respect to the absolute, two very different, and even contradictory images of Novalis come to the fore: philosophically, Novalis is a pragmatist (positing the absolute as a regulative idea); poetically, he is a mystic (positing art as the means to intuit a realm of primordial givenness).

Although there is evidence for both of these interpretations of Novalis, we will attempt to pursue a different path, another way of integrating these two conceptions of the absolute into Novalis's thought and poetic practice. In this alternative reading, feeling no longer constitutes a pathway into the absolute, but makes itself present as disruption, disorder, as a perturbation of the validity and the self-sustainability of reflective thought and its concomitant institutional and social contexts of hegemony.

The persistence of feeling fictionalizes not merely all mental operations—including the operation of reflection—but makes possible poetry as a way of life, as an askesis.[22] The absolute provides an impetus for a poetic exercise—an exercise that does not use poetry as a means of representing the unrepresentable, nor intuiting undifferentiated identity or primordial givenness, but rather, uses the very fictionality of the absolute as feeling as an attempt to undo the stranglehold of reflective knowledge's grip on reality from within its own domain.

We have seen that there are two conceptions of the absolute in Novalis's thought. One absolute is associated with feeling (*Gefühl*), the other with drive (*Trieb*). The second absolute reinterprets the first as a motor, as a pretext for the generation of differentiated reflections. The unrepresentability of feeling, or the *irreality* of the first absolute, leads to an awareness of the structure of all appearances as drive, movement, stimulation, excitement—thereby foregrounding the *reality* of the second absolute. The absolute of undifferentiated Being does not merely raise awareness about stimulation as a higher-order absolute; it also introduces, necessarily, the *fictional* as the central motor of the process of stimulation. All phenomenality is fictional inasmuch as it is differential. Poetic representation, which moves in the world of appearances, would thus seem to exclude feeling as pure intuition of Being, but in fact, it produces feeling as part of the domain of falsehood or appearances—as *Schein*. In acts of poetry, then, feeling and fictionality become concomitant, coextensive modes of cognition and representation.

We have already mentioned Novalis's claim that "everything pure is thus a deception of the imagination—a *necessary* fiction" (*NS* 2:179). He goes on to write:

> Truth—Fiction or appearance. The imagination has two sorts of products—the true and the apparent [*das Wahre und den Schein*]. One excludes the other—negates it. Both are identical—appearance is appearance—truth—truth. Truth is the form of appearance—appearance the form of truth. (*NS* 2:179)

For Novalis, truth can only exist as perfect identity. However, the necessary representation of identity in the form of the copula—its appearance within a system of differences as copula—guarantees that there can be no truth as perfect identity. There can only be truth as appearance. And yet, appearance negates truth as perfect identity. Truth and appearance thereby collapse into one another, condition one another, become so inextricably intertwined with one another that they cannot be thought separately: "Appearance is the primordial form of truth, of primordial matter. It is truth related to itself" (*NS* 2:181).

Ultimately, through this operation, it is not merely that truth becomes *fictionalized*—but more importantly, fiction, or *Schein*, becomes associated with the truth of the second absolute, namely, with drive as "a positing-forth in itself" (*NS* 2:134). This positing-forth of itself is the process whereby truth, in its absolute identity with itself, relates itself to itself—*die Wahrheit auf sich selbst bezogen*—and thereby enters the world of appearances and relations:

> The principle of identity is the principle of truth—reality. The principle of contradiction—principle of illusion—negation. The principle of sufficient reason lies in the two preceding [principles]—thesis—antithesis—synthesis.
>
> The principle of identity belongs to illusion and truth.
>
> The principle of contradiction expresses their relationship to one another.
>
> The principle of sufficient reason, or rather the principle of the excluded middle—the relationship of both to the imagination or their common sphere and opposing sphere. (*NS* 2:182)

Novalis formulates the relation between appearances and reality in three different logical propositions. Truth, as that which is identical with itself, applies universally to all phenomena, even to appearances or *Schein*, comprising the realm of the contradictory or the non-self identical. The principle of sufficient reason, or the notion that all individuals are grounded in a higher order—*der Satz des zureichenden Grundes*—was formulated by Leibniz to explain the movement from the realm of axiomatic, logical identity to the realm of nature, from the science of mechanics (mechanical causal explanation) to that of dynamics (self-organization, or the harmonious operation of the whole).[23] Novalis associates this proposition with the law of the excluded middle, which holds that in the relationship between A and Not-A, there can be no third term; A and Not-A exclude one another, and are not merely opposed to one another. Such is the relation between truth and fiction—which exclude one another—and yet, each of them makes the other what it is and cannot be thought without the other. In the imagination, then, the only reality open to human beings, the manifold differentiation of appearances and signs, is both identical and not-identical to itself.

Because both truth and appearance, identity and contradiction, mutually constitute and yet exclude one another, there is neither pure truth nor pure falsehood in our imaginative lives. All appearances are false truths and true fictions. The relationship between reality and appearance is therefore chiasmatic. The *ordo inversus* no longer functions as a philosophical technique to conceptualize the unrepresentable domain of feeling, but constitutes an internal dynamic of the fictional truth and true fictionality of all appearances. The particular cognitive act requiring the inversion of order is not the means whereby human beings attempt to reach truth, but the means whereby the essentially reproductive dynamic of the universe, its back-and-forth, self-generating movement of oscillation, its joy in its own stimulation, provides evidence for itself through continually overturning orders of reflection. The *ordo inversus* is the great exercise not of Being, but of beings; it is less a philosophical procedure than a physiological dynamic. The *ordo inversus* no longer functions as method to get closer *to* the absolute (which is the position that Novalis seemed to articulate in the earlier sections of *Fichte Studies*), but *becomes* the absolute itself: the absolute as the perpetual stimulation of an infinite oscillation.

We may now return to the question at the beginning of these reflections: what is poetry, or rather, how can poetry become that atmosphere in which we live? For Novalis, the omnipresent realm of fictionality, the inescapable logic of appearances built into human sentience, assures that we exist as poetic beings. The poetic nevertheless requires the non-poetic as a differential sphere against which it positions itself: only in this manner can it maintain its own system in motion and assure the existence of some exteriority to its own logic that will provoke dynamic and normative reconfiguration. Whatever poetry is, it must reproduce and intensify the chiasmatic dynamic of life itself.

When Novalis says that "poetry is poetry" (*NS* 3:685), he moves poetry into the domain of the tautological proposition of identity, whose main function, as we have seen, is not to express identity but to generate difference. The generation of difference nevertheless depends upon an identity that makes difference possible. In poetry, language exhibits the same relationless intimacy with itself as do human beings that use reflection to make present feeling—as a negative of its own system of organization. It is this openness to something outside of its own system of representation that differentiates poetry from rhetoric, or *Sprachkunst*. Rhetoric, as a linguistic practice that Novalis differentiates from poetic language, does not acknowledge its own participation in a relationless intimacy: the "feeling" that belongs, in this case, not to a subject, but to language itself, which in turn allows language to always exceed the willful control of the subject that attempts to master it discursively.

Being, as the making present of feeling, does not only generate a void in the order of representations that then becomes the impetus for inversions and perturbations of this order. It also makes possible what one might term *points of indifference*, spaces in which *a* can be said to be identical with *a* even though one can *count* them as two, as differentiated. This sort of indifference generates an *attraction* between signs and allows them to seep into one another, to move toward one another, to oscillate between heterogeneous and mutually exclusive domains.

Only the presupposition of a zone of indifference makes possible the *ordo inversus* as its own "order" (and not as simply formless chaos), for it is by virtue of this indifference that any reflection—*as* a discrete reflection that becomes other and yet remains the same—can be inverted. One must therefore qualify all attempts to characterize Novalis's theory of signs as a form of Derridean *différance*, as does Winfried Menninghaus, who notes: "Referring to Derrida one could describe the form of reflection [for Novalis] as a form of *différance* in the double meaning of difference and deferral."[24] For Derrida, *différance* functions as an intrinsic property of the system of signs, whereas Novalis sees *identity* as an equally necessary presupposition of differential systems. Without identity (which, to be sure, exists as a *difference* from difference itself), no system can account for coherence, resemblance, and attraction; only the mutual presupposition of identity and difference in all forms of semiosis prevents a collapse into a chaotic morass of sheer noise.

Novalis approaches the unthinkable figure of non-differentiated identity through the positing of localized "spheres" of indifference or "points" of indifference (a point to which we shall return later). Points and spheres of indifference are themselves parts of heterogeneous systems, and yet, they exhibit an internal coherence that allows them to present themselves as recognizably similar entities. Anton Brugmans, in his *Philosophical Essays on Magnetic Materials* (translated into German in 1784), notes that the poles of a magnet are both separated and joined by a plane of indifference, a term that Johann Wilhelm Ritter, a close friend and associate of Novalis, uses in his own galvanic and magnetic experiments.[25] Brugmans himself uses the term to describe the identity of two points along an iron bar, each of which appears imbued with an equal attractive force at any given distance from the end, and each of which thereby cancels the other out.[26] Schelling also refers to the possible communication between homogeneous spheres within a more global system of heterogeneity as a "point of indifference" (*Indifferenzpunkt*).[27] These points of indifference—which are at the same time negotiators and generators of difference—allow signs to communicate, to gravitate toward other signs, toward affective, imaginative, and linguistic patterns.

The existence of linguistic points of indifference therefore presupposes something akin to the relationless intimacy of language with itself, although these points only manifest themselves in the larger context of a drive to difference within the system of signs and phenomena, for example, as the + or – along the length of the magnet. The structure of language, which, as we have shown, is analogic with respect to the structure of human sentience, conditions the production of poetry: in both language and human sentience, one may observe the same structure of non-coincidence with self-coincidence, or the essential falsehood of the intimacy of identity once it enters the world of differences. Novalis condenses this dynamic in a poetic formula: poetry is poetry. The tautological proposition, simultaneously indifferential and differential, is nothing other than a paradoxical generator that generates its own paradoxes, stimulating a potentially unending oscillation, or an *ordo inversus* that recasts the poetic absolute as a physiological drive.

To recapitulate: the *ordo inversus*—the movement by which one reflects upon reflection as an attempt to make present the elusive identity of an originary self-feeling—does not bring the human being closer to truth or to an absolute, but rather, closer to the reproductive operativity of life. Poetry generates not the unity of being, but the multiplication of difference through a non-unified unity of non-identical identities. Language participates in a cosmos—one that Schelling describes in his *Ideas Toward a Philosophy of Nature* (1797)—that is born from its continually frustrated attempt to be identical with itself, imbued with an order that emerges from a primordial state of disequilibrium.

If there is an order to Being, it consists precisely in *provoking* its own difference from the world of beings, a process that in turn produces differences *in* the world of beings. Because these differences, however, are all generated in their common differentiation from a fictional realm of indifference that is required to sustain their identities *as* differences, they are nevertheless linked to one another, even if only fictionally. If pure indifference does not exist, neither does pure difference. That is why, even in fiction, the categories of identity and difference ultimately appear hopelessly inadequate to the movements of Novalis's poetry. There is no purity, and both identity and difference seem to demand purity in their conceptual spheres.

Instead of identity and difference, there are multiple identifications and inversions; there is attraction, separation, communication, permeability, disruption, reconfiguration, intensification among multiples. What begins as a philosophical approach to ontology ends by calling into question the terms established by ontology as such. It is not *Being* that defines poetry, but *movement*. The philosophy of movement, or of attraction, as an alternative to traditional ontology, appears as the proper domain of poetry. This is why, in Novalis's *Hymns to the Night*, if there is an absolute at all, it is not the night or the space of mysterious non-differentiation, but the womb—a womb that is equally the space of being and of non-being, both identical and oppositional with itself, the place from which we came into being, moving from nothingness into existence, and to where, when we die, we will move from being back into nothingness.

Chapter 5

Stimulation and Disorganization in Novalis's *Hymns to the Night*

Infinite Gaps and the Intensification of Making Present

Within the ontological framework established by Novalis, poetry, as a form of language made possible through a system of differences, cannot simply reflect Being, since Being consists precisely in the void of the differential system: that which is excluded from the set of its representational possibilities. However, the void of Being is nevertheless present in poetic acts as an exteriority that is resignified as a provocation. It is precisely through an attunement to this void—or a foregrounding of the fictionality of absolute identity, which in turn generates an oscillation among multiples rather than stasis in an ineffable domain of indifferentiation—that the specific linguistic form of poetry can function as an incitement for poetic consciousness. The perturbation of the system of differences is repurposed as an exercise for the aesthetic spirit.

There is perhaps no other poem by Novalis that reveals the exercise value of poetry as dramatically as the *Hymns to the Night*. A close examination of the background materials that inform the composition of this poem reveals that Novalis did indeed conceptualize something like an aesthetic spiritual exercise in relation to this specific work. In the time leading up to the *Hymns to the Night*, Novalis wrote passages in his journal that would eventually be integrated into the poem itself. The journal has therefore often been invoked as a source of biographical insight that provides a point of entry into the genesis of Novalis's poetic works.[1]

The story is familiar to scholars of German romanticism: Friedrich von Hardenberg and Sophie von Kühn are engaged on March 17, 1795. Sophie dies on March 19, 1797. It is at this time that Novalis begins conceptualizing the *Hymns to the Night*. The death of Sophie von Kühn, so the argument goes, furnishes Novalis with the experiential core of these hymns. The third hymn, after all, seems to recount a scene of mourning over the grave of the beloved, the poet's despair, and the ensuing rebirth of the poetic spirit—and in so doing, incorporates impressions that Novalis had recorded in his journal on May 12, 1797 (*NS* 4:35–36). For a long time in the history of German literature, the "Sophie experience" became a cipher for the immediacy of the pregnant moment that gives birth to a work whose intensity can only have sprung from an authentic experiential source.

Novalis's citation of his own journal may be considered, however, from another perspective. The journal as a genre in the eighteenth century did not merely provide a linguistic form in which experience could be recorded; indeed, the journal enabled the transformation of the self through the process of writing.[2] The form of writing particular to this genre—in which a self-relation becomes articulated in language—could at any moment be taken up in the attempt to expand or refine one's character and one's modes of sensuous cognition. In the various examples of the journal entry, one may often discover less biography than bio-transformation, or an askesis of life in words.

It is therefore not a biographical anchoring point that is to be sought in Novalis's journals, but rather, the use of writing as a transformational context for perceptual and cognitive capacities. In one journal entry, Novalis turns his gaze toward these capacities: memory (*Gedächtnis*), attentiveness (*Beobachtungsgabe*), expression (*Ausdruck*), and presence of mind (*Besonnenheit*). Each of these mental operations was touted by Baumgarten as particular faculties that were included in the scope of the aesthetic exercise.

The journal entries themselves present an image of Novalis's relationship to Sophie von Kühn that is much more complex than the hackneyed claims of an eternal erotic transfiguration. Nor is it that Novalis merely transposes the love of the transcendent divine onto that of the physical and immanent corporeality of the beloved. Rather, ever present in Novalis's diaries are technologies of autostimulation through writing. Sophie von Kühn—along with Christ—are invoked within a regime of exercises designed to intensify experience and shape the writer's modes of perception. His meditations on Sophie von Kühn appear linked to the singularly aesthetic (in Baumgarten's sense of the term) capability of the imagination: to make present that which is absent.

At the end of the journal entry from the 16th to the 29th of June 1797 appear the following words:

> Xstus and *Sophie* (*NS* 4:48)

Novalis seems at first to be establishing a relation between the transcendent and the immanent.[3] To relate to the divine through one's own erotic attachment has literary predecessors and successors: Dante's Beatrice, Werther's Lotte, Gerard de Nerval's Aurélia, and Kierkegaard's Regine—each relation, in its own way, either outlines a path to the divine or embodies and concentrates the divine in a living being. Similarly, Novalis places Christ and Sophie in relation to one another, although the terms of this relation remain indeterminate. Nevertheless, Sophie is typographically marked—underlined—with an intensified attraction, as if the divine were not merely setting one term in relation to another term, but rather, *moving* from one term to another, being displaced.

The absolute, if it is to announce itself at all in the world of appearances, must necessarily wander: it must continually be displaced because its very essence is not to have a place. Because the absolute is fully indeterminate, it escapes all attempts at reification. Schelling defines the absolute (*das Unbedingte*) as that which is un-thinged, that which "as such cannot be conceptualized as a thing."[4] Because it cannot become a thing—neither a subject, nor an object, nor anything that has properties at all—the absolute ought to be present everywhere, manifesting itself in all things. The absolute, for Novalis, however, does not simply dissolve into a pervasive pantheism, a religiousness in which the immanence of all phenomena becomes infused with divine presence. Nor does he prefer to approach the absolute—as Hegel would later criticize in the *Phenomenology of Spirit*—in a vague act of mystical intuition, as a night in which all cows are black. Novalis remains attached to the world of appearances, to individualized beings, to operations of language. In this world, the absolute can only appear negatively: not as a thing, but as a movement between things.

As we shall see in the *Hymns to the Night*, the absolute is continually displaced between different figures that become fictional and figural bearers of the seemingly inarticulable and non-conceptual operation of indifferentiation present in the ground of Being (Night, Death, the Beloved, Christ, the Womb). The poem neither represents a celebration of mystical intuition nor, conversely, a continually frustrated attempt to represent the absolute. Rather, the multiplicity that is generated in the proliferation of fictional signs that stand in for the absolute of indifferentiation (as a movement of displacement) is sustained by the productive power of a physiological absolute that is continually turning against the identity of its own concepts in order to internally differentiate itself.

The replication and multiplication of figures for the absolute reveal less the adherence to a specific poetic or philosophical doctrine than an almost compulsive addiction to autostimulation. Novalis's diaries themselves reveal a multiplicity of discursive spaces, each of them driven by the tendency toward increasingly intensified imaginative and physiological states. By turns, the journal entries drift in and out of generic forms: the self-relational confession, the daily admonitions of a hypochondriac, writing as a recording system, spiritual exercises characteristic of devotional writings—each of these discursive areas blends into the others in Novalis's journal, and more importantly, each feeds back into the multiplication of discourse itself.

The cryptic utterance "Xstus and Sophie" does not set out to make the transcendent immanent or the immanent transcendent, but signals an autostimulative tendency intrinsic to the very process of writing. For Novalis, Sophie is just as transcendent as Christ, since her death ultimately provides the impetus for Novalis to challenge himself aesthetically: to call into being that which has ostensibly disappeared from the world of sensuous givenness. Sophie, and the love of Sophie (*Philosophie*), posit an attractor outside the sensible world that sets the terms of an aesthetic exercise designed to push the mind to probe the limit points of its own representational capacities.

Sophie, or more precisely, the writing of Sophie, cannot be separated from askesis as a genre on full display in Novalis's journal. The journal entries are full of recordings, notes, observations, exhortations whose central goal is to develop a feedback loop between physical and imaginative capabilities and the system of writing. In the entries from the 16th to the 29th of June, Novalis begins with the following observation: "On Friday the 16th I felt horribly lazy and ill-tempered—the same thing for the morning of the 17th—then I suddenly woke up after a satisfaction of my fanciful pleasure, force and strength [*meiner fantastischen Lust, Vis et Robur*]. I decided upon frequent bodily exertions in the future and to be on my guard against indolence" (*NS* 4:46). Novalis correlates strenuous physical exercises with the satisfaction of "fanciful pleasure"—mental and bodily acts with strong erotic overtones. At the same time, this pleasure is linked to a self-diagnostic observation of the soul. This self-observation was no longer solely assigned to the order of religious discipline, but had become a general anthropological impulse within the eighteenth-century discipline of *Erfahrungsseelenkunde* (empirical psychology as the science of experience). However, in Novalis's case, self-observation serves not merely to record mental states, nor to compose an objectivistic description of the mechanism of his psyche. Rather, the process of writing itself seeks both to illustrate and incite the stimulation of psycho-physiological states by drawing upon sensuous and imaginative resources to upset the pull of inertia. Novalis's central goal in this journal entry is to remove impediments to flows, thereby enabling the coordination of psychic, bodily, and semiotic systems.

Alternative spiritual practices in the early eighteenth century paved the way for the development of introspection as a scientific technique of self-monitoring.[5] Moritz, for example, who was active in establishing *Erfahrungsseelenkunde* as an autonomous discipline, describes the simultaneously constraining and world-disclosive properties of Pietistic discipline in his novel *Anton Reiser*. Moritz's "soul dietetics" (*Seelendiätetik*) does not make a complete break with the disciplining of inwardness. Rather, he advocates work on the self in order to bring the soul into a harmonious balance with its inherently oppositional tendencies; the goal of *Seelendiätetik* consists in "maintaining all capacities of the soul *according to their relations to one another* in the most perfect possible condition."[6]

One may also see a form of *Seelendiätetik* in the journals of Novalis, but the dynamic structure of these dietetics differs from Moritz's attempt to eliminate the contradictions and tensions that arise between the different faculties of the mind. Like Moritz, however, Novalis analyzes and differentiates the mental faculties that he sees as essential to his development:

> My head was very clear tonight. I feel in general that I have progressed by many steps. Furthermore, my memory, my attentiveness, and my expressivity are getting better. *My presence of mind* [*Besonnenheit*] however must become much more intense. There are still infinite lacunae. (*NS* 4:48)

The cognitive faculties enumerated by Novalis—memory, attentiveness, expression, presence of mind—belong to the domain of sensuous cognition and therefore, as Baumgarten would have claimed, are open to modification. In the process of self-observation, writing opens up a technological space for surveying the operations of sensuous cognition.

The exercise of these powers of the mind—rather than the "experience" that supposedly lies at the origin of the poetic act—can push us to rethink the aesthetic purpose of Novalis's works. One of the basic impulses of artistic production, one that has grounded, justified, and legitimized works of art since antiquity, consists in making present that which is absent. Mnemosyne—as Hölderlin, who also understood poetry as an exercise of the power of retention and the generation of coherence, knew well—is the mother of the muses. The attempt to bring that which is gone back into the world of the living, or to make the world of the present live long after it has ceased to be—such are the basic impulses behind memory and memorialization—has long been one of the central functions of art, and it even describes one of the central capacities of Baumgarten's *felix aestheticus*.

Novalis also understands memory as an important faculty that can be exercised, but it is not this faculty in particular that he sees as most central to his own self-formation in this journal entry. To be sure, memory constitutes one cognitive capacity among others enlisted in the project of crafting an aesthetically autostimulating self. The ability to notice, *die Beobachtungsgabe*, which in a sense also makes present that which is latent or hidden, constitutes yet another such faculty. The ability to express (*der Ausdruck*) gives to that which is thought, remembered, or noticed a tangible form. It describes the means through which the absent not only becomes present, but becomes present for others as well: through sensible signs.

It is the presence of mind, or *Besonnenheit*, however, that occupies a special place in Novalis's journal entry. As a concept, it is connected to self-mastery, to control, to a self-organization of the mind whose analogical image would duplicate something like the organization of the solar system. *Besonnenheit* infuses the mind with the power of attraction and repulsion that holds the cosmos in balance, and as such, it can be equated with the drive to life, to a physiologically instigated propagation of forms. Novalis says in one of his fragments, "Light is the symbol of true presence of mind [*Besonnenheit*]. Light is therefore according to analogy—*Action*—the *self-touching* of matter. The day is therefore planetary consciousness [*das Bewußtseyn des Wandelsterns*]" (*NS* 2:619). The analogy between the order of appearances and the structure of the mind—an analogy that, already palpable in Kant's writings, blossoms into a fully fledged philosophical hermeneutics in Schelling's *Naturphilosophie*—establishes an imaginary isomorphism between the psychical and the physical realms that has significant consequences for aesthetic semiosis. The mind organizes itself through *Besonnenheit* just as the natural world organizes itself according to the transcendental laws of attraction and repulsion—a movement that is characterized by "wandering" rather than fixity. Novalis, by shifting the emphasis of this system from sun to planet, develops a model of consciousness that mirrors the movement from center to periphery, from singularity to multiplicity, from fixed point to eccentric path.

When Novalis claims that his presence of mind, his *Besonnenheit*, must grow more intense—drawing attention to the inexhaustible presence of lacunae that fuels this intensity—he correlates the drive toward self-organization in nature with the dynamic of an aesthetic exercise. He never declares outright that his poetic works are to be understood as such an exercise, one that seeks to model its own activity according to invisible cosmological forces; but Novalis's reflections do permit us to investigate the work of art as a formal experiment with signification that is invested with an implicit exercise value. A critical structure of such works therefore becomes the designation of operations that—like the forces of attraction and repulsion that can never "appear" as such but can only manifest themselves indexically through the movement of bodies—simultaneously organize phenomena and appear as transcendentally problematic. Often these domains manifest themselves in a center that attracts all other signs but nevertheless constitutes a void or an exteriority in a given representational, narrative, normative, or institutional framework (e.g., Heinrich von Ofterdingen's blue flower, the statue of Isis in *The Novices of Sais*, or death in the *Hymns to the Night*). Such signs then form the impetus for an unexpected aesthetic journey. The "lacunae"—blind spots that can never be fully integrated into experience—become critical for this process inasmuch as they generate a challenge for presence of mind. Without these gaps in cognition, presence of mind would remain fixed in a mere static image rather than unfold in a dynamic process. Novalis's self-monitoring foregrounds the lacunae fueling his presence of mind in a series of otherwise typical exhortations:

> Pay attention above all to compliant and careful behavior toward your father—be on your guard in your association with Schlegel—practice yourself constantly in sober-minded effectiveness—*have little Sophie always before your eyes*—do not forget the brevity of three months—don't burn the candle at both ends—*be moderate*—and don't give in to your tendency to tease and to amuse—it is now no longer appropriate for you—or at least only in extreme moderation.
>
> Xstus and Sophie (*NS* 4:48)

Nestled between banal, almost clichéd self-admonitions—obey your father, beware of the corrupting influence of your radical friend (Friedrich Schlegel), be productive, do not take on too much work, be moderate, be polite—one can find a different sort of exercise, namely an exercise of the imagination: have little Sophie always before your eyes (*habe Söffchen stets vor Augen*). This task, in its most basic form, aims at transforming that which is absent into a continual form of presence.

Novalis's demand to have Sophie continually before his eyes derives from the tradition of spiritual exercises through which the suffering of Christ was continually re-created before the inward eyes of the believer.[7] Both Christ and Sophie enter into relation with one another, but this relation is itself subordinated to the imaginative practice that both of them stimulate in aesthetic cognition. Characteristic of this practice is a displacement between multiple terms: in this case, from Christ to Sophie. Presence of mind, *Besonnenheit*, does not, then, simply designate the ability of the mind to monitor and control its own activity. If presence of mind refers to the ability to make present, it nevertheless foregrounds a more primordial lack that renders this activity an infinite project: "infinite lacunae" (*unendliche Lacunen*) impede self-mastery and the total apprehension of any realm of absolute transcendence.

Absence, however, does not remain mired in its own negativity as a perennial symbol of lack, but generates an alternative form of plenitude. For Novalis, a lack is not a moment of pure negation: if the presence of the beloved is not absolutely retrievable, the beloved is also not absolutely lost. The death of Sophie, her permanent absence, sets Novalis the impossible but never-ending task of making present: the forever abortive but forever productive attempt to bring that which has disappeared back into the domain of appearances.

The Disruption of the Aesthetico-Physiological Economy of Balance

For the purposes of this study, let us recall the most important features of Novalis's philosophical aesthetics: (1) for Novalis, the attempt to represent the absolute leads not to identity, but to the multiplication of plurality; (2) the absolute changes its function from grounding truth to generating reflections that continually invert previous reflective orders; (3) this philosophical or logical operation of the *inverted order*, orders that are linked with one another and made permeable by *points of indifference*, eventually becomes a theory of drives. Poetry, which continually overturns paradigms of organization and makes all differentiated forms permeable, lays bare and intensifies the auto-stimulative dynamic of life.

These aspects of Novalis's *Fichte Studies* are integrated into Novalis's poetry as attractions and tendencies of poetic form. The latent dynamic of life as the stimulation and multiplication of plurality and difference—a dynamic that announces itself in the very being of appearances, in the movement from *Seyn* to *Schein*—is woven into the texture of poetic utterance. So too, in the *Hymns to the Night*, does the poet's desire for death, the unrepresentable and unknowable other of life, in an analogous movement to that of the reflective subject's continually frustrated attempt to represent Being, ultimately produce differentiation, plurality, and expansive oscillation.

Let us now turn to the opening section of the *Hymns to the Night*. The hymns begin in a state of tension:

> Which living being, gifted with sense, does not love above all miraculous appearances of extended space around him the all-pleasing light—with its colors, its rays and waves, its mild omnipresence, as waking day. Like life's inmost soul the giant world of the restless orbs breathe it, and swims dancing in its blue glow—the scintillating, eternally resting stone, the thoughtful sucking plant and the savage burning, variously formed animal—yet above all the magnificent stranger with the meaningful eyes, the swaying gait, and the tenderly closed lips, rich in tones. Like a king of earthly nature it calls every force to innumerable transformations, binds and dissolves endless pacts, hangs its heavenly image around every earthly being.—Only its presence reveals the miraculous magnificence of the kingdoms of the world.
>
> Away I turn to the holy, inexpressible, mysterious night.

> Welcher Lebendige, Sinnbegabte, liebt nicht vor allen Wundererscheinungen des verbreiteten Raums um ihn, das allerfreuliche Licht—mit seinen Farben, seinen Stralen und Wogen, seiner milden Allgegenwart, als weckender Tag. Wie des Lebens innerste Seele atmet es der rastlosen Gestirne Riesenwelt, und schwimmt tanzend in seiner blauen Flut—atmet es der funkelnde, ewigruhende Stein, die sinnige saugende Pflanze und das wilde brennende, vielgestaltete Tier—vor allen aber der herrliche Fremdling mit den sinnvollen Augen, dem schwebenden Gange, und den zartgeschlossenen, tonreichen Lippen. Wie ein König der irdischen Natur ruft es jede Kraft zu zahllosen Verwandlungen, knüpft und löst unendliche Bündnisse, hängt sein himmlisches Bild jedem irdischen Wesen um.—Seine Gegenwart allein offenbart die Wunderherrlichkeit der Reiche der Welt.
>
> Abwärts wend ich mich zu der heiligen, unaussprechlichen, geheimnisvollen Nacht. (*NS* 1:131)

The title of the poem—the hymns to the night (Novalis originally intended to call the cycle of poems simply "Night" [*Nacht*])—tells us that they will direct their attention to the night as the god to which they call. The poem begins, however, with praise of the day. The question that launches the poem would at first appear merely a rhetorical gesture, phrased negatively so as to provoke a positive response. It would seem to suggest: there is no living being who does not love the light above all other things. The question, however, is not merely rhetorical. The poetic voice does, after all, say: I turn toward the night, therefore *I* do not love the light above all other things. If these hymns initiate an entrance into the lyric world by praising the light, they begin with an act that provokes its own overcoming. If all living beings, those gifted with sense, ought to love the light, the poetic voice exempts himself from this order, thus construing himself as one who does not merely belong to the living, but to the dead as well, as one who is not merely aesthetic (gifted with sense), but also *inaesthetic*, in a position of liminality with respect to the domain of sensuous differences. The initial gesture of the poem consists in the positing of a generalization that then finds its own exception.

Just as the *Hymns to the Night* begin in a field of tension, so might one see the poem as a series of movements that never resolve into an equilibrium that permits the consciousness of the reader to stand still. Such an interpretation of the *Hymns to the Night* might seem surprising to those familiar with the work. The poem closes with the famous sixth hymn, the desire for death (*Sehnsucht nach dem Tode*), the return to the resting place, the end of action, the becoming-inorganic of all dynamic forms of life. However, even when the poet finishes his poem with the seeming release of consciousness into a space of eternal rest, the poetic reworking of death initiates an exercise in finitude that contributes to the never-ending stimulative process of life—and therefore acts in a sense precisely opposed to what one might initially proleptically associate with a Freudian death drive.

The poem radically rethinks not merely what death means, but what semiotic function and exercise value ought to be assigned to death as a fictional sign, as the appearance of that which, strictly speaking, cannot appear, or can only appear as void. As we shall see, death will come to signify—as a form of askesis—precisely the opposite tendency to the set of associations that are normally conjured by the phenomenon itself. When death becomes poetized, its central function is to paradoxically contribute to an expansion of selfhood and the production of difference.

The attempt to approach death as an expansion of the possibilities of the self was already hinted at in the *Fichte Studies*. Novalis articulates this notion as follows: "Relinquishing of our selfhood [*Entäußerung unsrer Ichheit*]—Nonbeing through Being is our theoretical goal, expansion of our selfhood—or Being through Nonbeing—our practical goal./They must stand in contradiction to one another in order to exist in the I" (*NS* 2:145). The very form of the *Hymns to the Night* appears motivated by the idea that the negation of our selfhood, or the attempt to escape from the boundaries of subjectivity, give rise to conditions whereby selfhood itself becomes more expansive, integrating ever more differential possibilities into the horizon of its practices. Selfhood expands when the stasis of a perfect identity is perturbed and a self-multiplying process of differentiation is unleashed in its stead, generating movements of consciousness that otherwise would have remained merely latent and unrealized.

The sensitivity to the inversion of death as a sign therefore requires the activation of reading practices attuned to the way in which sense itself is subject to sudden differentiation. The *Hymns to the Night* dramatize the process of an inverted form of reading in which readers are allowed—or even provoked—to read the text as an attraction to oppositional spaces, spaces that ultimately overturn hierarchical or teleological conceptions of order.

Such is the function of death for Novalis: it signifies not the stasis of an end, but precisely a form of exteriority that in turn provokes alternative ways of organizing phenomena previously established as given. Death refers to the self-overturning dynamic that results from all mental confrontations with a primordial givenness that undermines the validity of specific reflective and representational acts, and must therefore be conceptualized as a physiological signifier, as an exteriority that regulates and perturbs the economy of a system and invests this system with the form of a drive.

In order to fully appreciate the extent to which death in the poem functions physiologically, it is necessary to examine Novalis's own interventions in this domain, above all his thoughts concerning the link between physiology and an aesthetics of life. In the eighteenth century, physiological discourses describing the mechanics of the body, in certain circles, come to be formulated in terms of theories of stimulation. Although the physiology of stimulation can be traced to antiquity, it acquired a new cultural relevance in the seventeenth century with Francis Glisson's *De Natura* (1672). In the middle of the eighteenth century, Albrecht von Haller developed an account of irritability describing the relationship of muscle contraction to the regulation of the nervous system, or what he called the relation between irritability (local muscular response, e.g., contraction upon contact with a foreign exteriority) and sensibility (the transmission of stimuli within the system itself).[8] For Haller, sensibility as a capacity transmits impressions from the body to the soul and vice versa, establishing physiology as a mediation between matter and spirit.[9] Irritability describes the reaction of a body to an exteriority, which in turn is processed by sensibility, or a regulatory physiological process that facilitates movement between differentiated domains. Haller's physiology posits a relation between exterior stimulus and internal transmission: such are the most basic terms of the physiology of irritability. In this model can be found not simply a description of the body as an object of a physiological discourse, but the germs of an incipient semiotic model that regards internal order as emergent from a relation between a system and its environment.

In 1795, as Novalis was writing the *Fichte Studies*, John Brown's treatise *Elements of Medicine* was published in German translation. Novalis's first written mention of Brown nevertheless appears only in 1798 in his *Notes for a Romantic Encyclopedia* (*Das allgemeine Brouillon*). If Novalis, in the *Fichte Studies*, perceives the drive-like character of Fichtean idealism, and therefore shows an increased sensitivity to philosophy as a physiological exercise, it is not until later that Novalis formulates thoughts explicitly marked by Brown's theory of medicine.[10]

In the *Notes for a Romantic Encyclopedia*, Novalis reconceptualizes the Fichtean absolute subject by blending transcendental philosophy and Brown's particular version of the physiology of stimulation. Both Brown and Fichte share an important basic tendency that characterizes their respective projects, namely, the desire to ground the plurality of appearances in the universality and simplicity of a single principle. For Fichte, the principle of identity presupposed by the self-positing subject makes the human cognition of reality possible; reality as such is unthinkable without the self-positing structure of the absolute ego, the I = I. For Brown, the absolute and single principle consists in his definition of life as a self-sustaining system.

Life, for Brown, is defined by the ability to be affected by both external stimuli and internal states such that an organism can maintain itself functionally; living creatures "can be affected by external agents, as well as by certain functions peculiar to themselves, in such a manner, that the phaenomena peculiar to their living state, that is their own functions, can be produced."[11] The living being is defined by a feedback loop between external stimulus and internal organization that guarantees the stability of functional mechanisms when faced with some form of perturbation. Both internal functionality and external stimuli contribute to the success—or breakdown—of self-reproductive processes. Brown calls the regulation of external and internal powers "excitability" or, in German translation, *Erregbarkeit*, while the powers themselves he calls "exciting powers" (in German, *Erregung* or *erregende Potenzen*): "The common effect produced by the exciting powers, is sense, motion, mental action, and the passions. . . . The effect of the exciting powers, acting upon the excitability, is to be denominated Excitement."[12]

Living beings begin their existence with a quantifiable and limited amount of excitability. The exciting powers decrease the quantity of excitability over the span of life. When the balance between the exciting powers and the excitability is perturbed, the body may fall into illness. When either the exciting powers or the excitability reaches a zero point, the body dies. Health consists in restoring the balance between stimuli and excitability, and although this balance itself can be restored, a certain quantity of lost excitability can never be recuperated.[13] Brown's conception of the body is of a functional system that is continually dispensing energy, one organized by a structurally determined economy circulating between excess and loss: what might appear as excess from the perspective of the dispensation of energy at any one moment in time appears as a gradual loss over time when considered from the trajectory of the system as a whole, up until the point when functional processes cease altogether.

Despite the structural disequilibrium characteristic of the economy of physiological energy, Brown still conceptualizes health as the—ultimately impossible and always frustrated—maintenance of equilibrium. Brown's description of the effect of the powers of excitability, although framed in physiological terms, therefore resonates with eighteenth-century theories of the work of art, specifically with the concept of grace.

Grace was seen as a movement that was not incompatible with the aesthetic stimulation of activity in the mind and the intensification of affective life in art. In German, the very concept—*Reiz*, which may signify "grace" or "stimulus" (one may still hear traces of this eighteenth-century inflection of gracefulness in the word *reizend*)—brings together these otherwise heterogeneous domains. The aesthetic conjunction of grace and stimulation, however, was not peculiar to German aesthetics. Hogarth, for example, conjoins the grace of painterly form with the motion of the eye itself, deriving the line of grace from the "love of pursuit . . . planted in our natures," one that leads the eye on a "wanton sort of chace [*sic*]."[14] For Hogarth as well, the line of grace triggers a response from the eye because of a disequilibrium in human nature, an originary form of energy drawing the eye to movement and pursuit rather than immobility and rest. This disequilibrium, which implies an attraction to motion rather than stasis, leads Lessing to conclude that "stimulation" or "grace" (*Reiz*) is easier to reproduce through poetry—an art of temporality as opposed to spatiality—rather than through the plastic arts: "Grace [*Reiz*] is beauty in movement, and precisely for this reason is it less suitable for the painter than for the poet."[15] For Lessing, grace, or *Reiz*, indexes a temporality—a before, during, and after—that can only be captured in media that structurally depend upon the arrow of time.

The ambiguity of the concept of *Reiz*—as both grace and stimulation—was later attenuated through the adoption of the concept of grace as such, or *Anmut*, in aesthetic contexts. Nevertheless, the German translator of Hogarth's *Analysis of Beauty* translates "line of grace" as *Linie des Reizes*, and this translation is not an error.[16] For Johann Georg Sulzer, *Reiz* is synonymous with *Grazie*.[17] However, whereas *Grazie* describes a way of being, a form of action that appears in and through the movement of bodies, *Reiz* nevertheless includes in its conceptual horizon the capacity of one phenomenon to produce excitation in someone or something else. Sulzer even misinterprets Winckelmann's philosophy of grace because of this ambiguity, claiming that Winckelmann uses *Grazie* "in order to express a particular mode, or perhaps only a certain property of the beautiful in visible form."[18] Winckelmann, however, does not see grace as a sensible quality of beauty as much as a form of mental attunement or a potentiality of being—indeed a result of an aesthetic askesis—explicitly stating, "Grace is a gift from heaven, but not like beauty: for it only designates a preparation for and capacity to create beauty. It is produced through education and deliberation, and it can become nature, which is created for this purpose."[19] For Winckelmann, grace is only produced through education and thought, uniting reason and pleasure, making a virtuoso out of the human subject who executes all tasks with lightness and ease. Grace makes artifice into a second nature, effectively bridging the gap between *technē* and *physis*.[20]

Winckelmann's aesthetics of grace is unthinkable from the perspective of *Reiz* as stimulation, whose physiological function is to act upon the living being rather than to express the potentiality of embodying the beautiful. However, even Brown's physiology shares certain features with the moral and aesthetic philosophy of grace. As a physiologist and as a doctor, Brown constructs his ideal of health around the notion of a balance between exciting powers and excitability. The generation of an equilibrium results from the interaction of all exciting powers—which can be internal or external, psychic or physical—with the fixed quantity of excitability granted to the organism at birth.

By assigning a function to both external and internal, physical and imaginary, stimulation in the self-regulation of excitability, Brown develops a framework for intensively relating psychic and physical processes: "The encrease [*sic*] of *the force of* the senses, of the motions, of the intellectual faculty, and of the passions, depends upon the increase of excitement in every one of their organs, among other actions, quickening the motion of the *blood* through them."[21] For Brown, mental and sensuous activity provides stimuli that maintain and restore the functional operativity of the organism. The mind and the senses are not merely passive receptacles for data, but active participants in processes of life: "The exercise of the senses, when it is agreeable, has a very great effect in exciting the whole body, and in producing emotions."[22] Regimes of aesthetic exercises in everyday life—not necessarily limited to the experience of works of art, but as pure sensory input—reconfigure the total system of the body.

Brown's physiology exerts a powerful attraction over Novalis, who sees both Brown and Fichte as thinkers that open up new possibilities for aesthetically driven autostimulation. Novalis rethinks Fichte's absolute ego—which, as we have seen, functions primarily as a generator of fictional propositions characterized by semiotic differentiation—from the perspective of Brown's physiology of stimulation when, in 1797, he says, "Fichte's Science of Knowledge is the *theory of excitation* [*Theorie der Erregung*]" (*NS* 3:383). The striving characteristic of Fichte's absolute ego, which is continually attempting to appropriate a self-posited exteriority that appears as an exteriority (a non-ego, or *Nicht-Ich*) to the empirical ego, construes this impulse (*Anstoß*) caused by something that appears foreign (but is in fact not foreign from the perspective of the absolute ego) as part of the structure of the absolute ego's own activity. The dynamic of the absolute ego is therefore in a current state of excitation.

Novalis nevertheless sees the limitations of both paradigms—Fichte's *Science of Knowledge* (*Wissenschaftslehre*) and Brown's physiology—as universal theories of the mind and the body. From a methodological perspective, Brown and Fichte make similar movements in thought. Just as Fichte seeks to lead the manifold and plural world of appearances back to the singular principle of the identity of the absolute ego, so does Brown attempt to integrate all acts of stimulation into the functionality of the closed system of excitability.[23] Brown thus subordinates the particular to the general, seeing in every individual manifestation of excitability merely a self-sustaining maintenance of excitability. It submits all mental and bodily phenomena to the law of *functionality*. The very definition of life as the maintenance of excitability therefore forecloses on the possibility of any excessive or expansive multiplication of particularity, any drive to differentiation within this closed system.

Novalis objects to Brown's system not merely because Brown, reacting against the prevailing chemical conceptions of physiology and humoral pathology, reduces life to the mechanistic regulation of excitability. To be sure, Novalis does claim, "The individual, *propter genesin*, and *falseness* of the Brunonian system is his inclination toward mechanics" (*NS* 3:407). The more significant error in Brown's system, however, results from the attempt to make its own theory into a closed absolute, or into a singularity rather than a duplicity. For Novalis, the operation of life must be dynamic, stretched between competing attractions:

> We must separate out this polemical relation [between the mechanistic and the chemical]—the oppositional part of Brown's system, from the general portion—his general, actual, instinct-like will from his private and temporal *intention*—We then obtain the *substantial* system—and the two accidental systems—and then from their *simultaneous* usage, we can achieve the true intermediate results (as in *differential calculus*). (*NS* 3:408)

Novalis, by positioning Brown's theory of stimulation in a higher-order systemic configuration, relativizes the theory itself and releases its own stimulative potential. Brown's theory cannot merely *describe* life, but it must also *participate* in it; it must, in the act of enunciation and articulation, embody and enact the processes that it otherwise attempts to describe. To manifest this process, and not merely describe it, requires a double movement, a "middle result" which does not rest in itself, but oscillates, like an infinite mathematical process, between differentiation and integration, between the attempt to break down and analyze differences and to recompose these differences in the larger system in which they are a function. His criticism of Brown follows closely his critique of Fichte: from the one, one must be able to generate a "two," or rather, from the seemingly univocal "substantial" system (substance was, at least in Spinozistic terms, considered as emblematic of the "one"), one must be able to generate the opposition of two contingent and accidental systems. The most important aspect of this critique therefore consists in the way the seeming one-sidedness of Brunonian physiology is used to generate a tension among multiples. Novalis invokes differential calculus at the end of this passage not merely as a formal procedure that produces mathematical knowledge, but as a process, a form of life, and an askesis: an oscillation between integration and differentiation.[24]

The core of Novalis's objection therefore cannot be construed simply as "anti-mechanistic," but as a criticism of a pure theory that bolsters its own identity and its univocal claim over a picture of the world: a disinterested and absolutizing point of view that hides from itself its own exercise value and its status *as* a practice of life that is invoked to navigate and intensify the cosmos of multiple phenomena. Ultimately, for Novalis, it is not the mechanical paradigm that renders Brown's theory incomplete or false, but rather, the fact that it universalizes its own formulas without taking into account the particularity of individual beings—particularities that are self-organizing differences rather than systems as a whole. Brown and his adherents, who "make general fundamental principles specific[,] . . . treat *a* and *b* as specific classes, and thereby classify their stock of illnesses, remedies and individuals accordingly. Thus, they fail to proceed *truly relatively*" (*NS* 3:378). Philosophy, in contrast to Brown's doctrines, makes possible an alternative physiological discourse, one that calls into question the positing of a general law and the subsumption of individuals under this law—a system that ultimately reduces the possibility of novelty and differentiation.

The task of philosophy consists in opening and relativizing the closed system of physiology: "Philosophy loosens everything [*macht alles los*]—relativizes the universe—like the Copernican system, it eliminates the fixed points—it makes something at rest into something that sways" (*NS* 3:378). Novalis's oft-cited claim for the "relativity" of philosophy is formulated in the context of a critique of Brown's system, as an alternative to the generalizing and absolutizing activity of medical and physiological discourse.[25] Philosophy functions as an antidote to forms of life that have become rigid, static, mired in a state of rest or inertia, self-totalizing rather than differential, governed by an aesthetics of *balance* rather than one of perturbation and relational *stimulation*. The relativism of philosophy does not merely follow from the impossibility of grasping the absolute, but rather, frames itself as an exercise for thought that redresses the deficiencies of universalizing physiological theories, theories that ultimately aim to keep the organism held in a state of maximum equilibrium.

Novalis ascribes a physiological function to philosophy itself. Philosophy negates any and all centripetal movements toward one anchored point of concentration, instead engendering *relations* between differences, contact points, and dynamic associations between multiplicities. The exercise of philosophy, or philosophy as askesis, generates *motion*; it should not be considered simply in relation to the truth or falsehood of propositions, but as a discourse that sets differences into variant dynamic configurations. A philosophical physiology would therefore not use general principles to eliminate differences or to lead all differences back to a more encompassing or originary identity, but rather, would intensify multiplicity, locality, and individuality. Novalis says, "All forces are without exception local powers" (*NS* 3:612).

Despite the seeming dogmatism and one-sidedness of Brown's theory, Novalis gravitates toward the physiology of excitability as a discourse that attunes the subject to the differentiation of stimuli and specificity of individual regimes of exercise. Just as Winckelmann sought a total way of life in the doctrine of grace, so too does Novalis believe that the physiological theory of stimulation produces life practices in which nature and art become indistinguishable from one another: "Medicine must become completely different. The doctrine of life as art and the doctrine of life as nature [*Lebenskunstlehre und Lebensnaturlehre*]" (*NS* 3:371). Brown's system, from a certain point of view, appears to Novalis too rigid and dogmatic to move from a description of life to a practice of life, from a dry conceptual theory that does violence to the individual to a dynamic discursive form that stimulates the reconfiguration of particulars. Novalis turns to that which negates the system as a whole in order to "loosen" Brunonian physiology: illness.

The primary function of illness consists in a negation of the healthy or normalized system of excitability. As the manifestation of a negative force, illness—the "other" of health that plunges the organism into a state of disequilibrium—may nevertheless play a critical role in the expansive dynamic of the individualized life. There is, then, an ambiguity in the phenomenon of illness, and when Novalis speaks of it, he does so at times positively and at times negatively. On the one hand, philosophy becomes sick when it believes in its own ability to articulate a total system of being, when it seeks completion and totality without comprehending the necessary and healthy presence of incompletion as integral to its own activity: "An absolute drive to perfection and completion is sickness as soon as it reveals itself to be destructive and disinclined against imperfection or incompletion" (*NS* 3:384).[26] On the other hand, sickness may also appear as a perturbation of the excitability, a foreign element that disrupts the equilibrium of the system and generates new forms of individuation. Brown's physiology allows no room for this conception of sickness; according to Novalis, "Brown utterly failed to explain *sickness*" (*NS* 3:453). Brown's holistic physiology understands sickness and health as part of the same system; sickness is nothing other than an imbalance in the relation between the exciting powers and the excitability.

Novalis resignifies sickness as an individualizing force, a form of exteriority that frustrates all attempts to reduce life itself to a single explanatory framework. Novalis writes, "Sickness belongs to *individualization*" (*NS* 3:681). Whereas Brown, whose physiology coheres with the aesthetic model of grace, sees illness as an imbalance that must be immediately redressed in order for the body to return to a state of equilibrium, Novalis emphasizes the potentiality of illness (as a disequilibrium) to stimulate the exercise of life and the formation of the mind: "illnesses, and particularly protracted ones, are apprenticeship years of the art of life [*Lehrjahre der Lebenskunst*] and the formation of the mind [*Gemüthsbildung*]" (*NS* 3:686). For Novalis, illness perturbs the physiology of equilibrium and particularizes the individual, thereby engendering a form of life that eludes the grasp of the totalizing framework of the excitability established by Brown.

Brown, following Hippocrates, does not understand health and sickness as ontologically distinct. Instead, the organism becomes sick under what he calls sthenic (characterized by an excess of stimulation) or asthenic (characterized by a lack of stimulation) conditions. Novalis, who, like Brown, believes that illness may be caused by too much or too little stimulation, nevertheless challenges the notion that illness is identical to excitation: "Illness in its actual meaning is a wondrous product of life—that admittedly can come about by too much or too little excitation (hunger and disgust)—but it is not excitation itself" (*NS* 3:602). From Brown's perspective, sickness can only appear as a deviation from order: the doctrine of excitability normalizes the state of health and sees sickness as something to be eliminated as quickly as possible. Novalis, however, portrays sickness—in effect, an overturning of order—as part of the very structure of the transcendence of life, as a novel form of positing-forth, *Fortsetzen*.

In the framework of the physiology of excitability, every particular input into a system can at various times appear either as overstimulation or understimulation, and it is precisely the relationality of this input that interests Novalis. "*Stimuli*," for Novalis, are "thoroughly relational [*durchaus relation*]" (*NS* 3:377). According to Novalis, stimulation, rather than leading human beings back to the identity of a single system of organization, is distinguished by its capacity to alter its essence, to become a positive or a negative, an overstimulation or a deprivation: "Should not every illness, every life be simultaneously—or successively—sthenic and asthenic—and should not the general Brunonian doctrines be principles of every sickness?" (*NS* 3:377). If sickness is already a particularizing force—a form of deviation as that which individualizes the organism—then the shape of this particular life itself is determined by the excesses and deficiencies of stimulation.

Moreover, it is not merely that deviant stimulation individualizes the self, but also that these very forms of stimulation are harnessed in order to enhance one's exterior and interior sensuous capacities: "Multiplication of the senses and education of the senses belong in my view to the main task of the improvement of the human race, the degree of elevation of humanity" (*NS* 3:318). The creation of a new type of human being depends upon a regime of aesthetic exercises, one that does not seek equilibrium as its goal, but a continual intensification in all spheres of sensuous and spiritual cognition. This intensification—defined as the constant return to a specific stimulus that incites differentiation—would not neglect the corporeal at the expense of the mental, but simultaneously develop exterior sensitivity and interior sensibility, *Reitzbarkeit* and *Sensibilität*: "everything depends above all on the multiplication and the formation of sensibility, and especially in such a way that sensitivity and the external stimulus [*Reitzbarkeit und der äußre Reitz*] do not suffer" (*NS* 3:318). Sensibility, which the physiologist Röschlaub uses to designate the activity of the brain and the nervous system, makes possible a field for the embodied exercise of the soul.

The soul, for Novalis, also has a sensible capacity; he speaks of "2 systems of senses. . . . one system is called body, the other, the soul" (*NS* 2:546)—and he envisions the expansion of the senses as a reconfiguration of the relation between this dual system of sensibility, mind and body.[27] Novalis seeks not equilibrium or balance between these two systems, but rather, the continual growth and intensification of both at the same time. Aesthetically, this change in the relation between the body and the soul signals a shift from a (classicist) aesthetics of balance to an aesthetics of perpetual transcendence. For Brown, according to Novalis, sickness is a mere anomaly, a perturbation of the vital condition of equilibrium: when "sickness has disappeared, so do excitability and sensibility [*Reitzbarkeit und Sensibilität*] exist once again in their usual static condition" (*NS* 3:477).

If health is physiologically characterized primarily by equilibrium, transcendence—as that which is non-self-identical and is always falling short of its desired object or subject—is, in comparison, pathological. Novalis analyzes the pathology of transcendence in his analysis of "magical idealism" and "magical realism" (*NS* 3:385). The magical realist and the magical idealist invent a pure object or a pure subject, transcendental matter or transcendental spirit, as the absolute ground of existence without any corresponding referent: philosophy as "magical idealism" occurs when "a pure thought—a pure image—a pure sensation—become thoughts, images, and sensations that are not awakened through a corresponding object etc., but exist outside the so-called mechanical laws" (*NS* 3:430). Magic, in this sense, designates the positing of a point that cannot be accounted for in a given semiotic or representational system along with the attempt to nevertheless attain this "other" outside its own limits: the psychic system evades mechanical and causal laws, just as fantasy (as a purely mental phenomenon) cannot contain or reproduce something that is materially substantial.

The transgressive modality of magic—when a seeming impossibility becomes a reality, when an outside suddenly becomes interiorized or vice versa—leads to an imaginative exercise that expands the power of the subject by continually repositioning the limits of the sayable and the thinkable; magic occurs through an act of differential positing rather than through a cognitive modality exterior to the structure of reflection. Novalis defines magic elsewhere as "the art of using the world of the senses according to one's will [*die Sinnenwelt willkührlich zu gebrauchen*]" (*NS* 2:546). Magic appears here, in its most simple formulation, as a variant of an aesthetic exercise, as the capacity to modify the world of the senses (rather than the capacity to "manipulate objects at will") that coheres with the larger forces of cosmic organization. However, whenever philosophical perspectives absolutize their own principles—when the magical idealist seeks a "miracle subject" and the magical realist seeks a "miracle object" to account for all phenomena, including those that supposedly elude and undermine the sovereignty of their respective domains—they become "logical sicknesses."[28]

However, the magical idealist and the magical realist are sick not only because their philosophical goals are impossible, but also in a more positive sense: they disrupt an economy of stimulation that seeks to maintain the physiological system in a state of equilibrium and stasis. Fantasy, as a cognitive act characteristic of magical idealism, becomes emblematic of a "force beyond mechanics [*außermechanische Kraft*]" (*NS* 3:430); it is situated outside the physical-mechanical system in such a way that it may nevertheless disrupt this system and may therefore become "pathological"—in a positive as well as in a negative sense.

The "outsider" status of fantasy ultimately becomes a critical element of Novalis's aesthetics. As a cognitive capacity, fantasy—like Heinrich von Ofterdingen's blue flower, the supposed primordial sign of romantic poetry, which first refers to a non-represented, preexistent element in a narrative told by "a foreigner" (*NS* 1:105) that Heinrich then recalls imaginatively—duplicates the logic of its own narrative manifestations in Novalis's texts, often coming from a point exterior to a specific bounded narrative space (e.g., in a fairy tale) in order to reconfigure the action inside the frame. Or more precisely, in order to anticipate the course of the argument, fantasy—here in the form of the blue flower—awakens a power of indifferentiation that is at the same time a perturbation of equilibrium: corporeal and imaginative states unfold in zones of permeability, spaces in which interiority and exteriority, one's ownmost self and that which is other, may pass into one another with more or less fluidity.

Novalis therefore permits a certain tendency toward absolutization when this tendency in turn functions as a stimulus. Some figure of the absolute may therefore appear as a sensuous sign (although precisely, because it is a differential figure, as deception, as something other than that which it is) in order to reconfigure any fixed system of relations. The self-absolutizing pathology of the magical idealist, for example—or, for that matter, of the magical realist—may provoke the individualization and transcendence necessary to make life into art, into a *Lebenskunstlehre*.[29]

Novalis carves out a space for pathological philosophy within the operations of the physiological absolute as moments within a process of transcendence and self-overcoming: "The act of springing over oneself is everywhere the highest—the primordial point—the *genesis of life*" (*NS* 2:556). For Novalis, unlike for Nietzsche, the act of self-overcoming does not declare morality and religion as the repository of the values of the weak. Instead, every sphere of life, including that of morality and religion, provides the human being with the possibility of developing its capacities. However, it is not that stimulation is inherently ethical, but rather, ethics becomes stimulation; all normative and normalizing frameworks thereby become subordinated to the higher-order movements of life, movements that demand the continual perturbation of all determinate forms of organization. Still, Novalis does not wish to *overturn* values, but rather, to make them into a source of excitement and incitement. Unlike Brown's physiology of grace in which the goal of health appears to consist in maintaining the equilibrium of a system, Novalis's physiology of stimulation seeks intensification, disorganization, a process of self-perturbation that displaces the functional concept of maintenance in favor of health as perpetual expansion.

Inverted Orders and Points of Indifference

In the *Hymns to the Night*, the dynamics of the physiological absolute unfold in poetic form itself, in the configuration of language as a proliferation and multiplication of differences predicated upon the continual overturning of order. Novalis's poetry in the *Hymns* is not "romantic" in the sense of something that provides immediate access to "feeling" (as a pre-cognitive intimacy with givenness) or something that produces an intellectual intuition of Being (as it would in Schelling's philosophy of art). For reflective cognition, which moves among a system of differences, feeling can appear only negatively, as an absence. So too in poetry does any conception of the absolute manifest itself negatively: as disruption, disorder, perturbation of the validity and the self-sustainability of any one reflective order.[30] The persistence of some idea of the absolute—its unrepresentable presence and palpable absence—becomes a stimulus, an impetus that pushes poetry to continually negate and re-create its own limited, concrete, and hence fictional points of attraction.

In the *Fichte Studies*, Novalis shows how the constant yet elusive presence of feeling, which is only present negatively in conscious reflection, fictionalizes all linguistic acts, turning all propositions into illusory propositions.[31] The absolute becomes a form of physiological exercise that does not use poetic language to represent the unrepresentable or intuit absolute identity, but rather, uses the very fictionality of the absolute of identity to disorganize any way of organizing the world that advances a claim to totality.[32] Poetry is power, but it is a very special type of power: a power not of discovering the unnamable, but of undoing the named.

The *Hymns to the Night* follow this pattern, illustrating the way in which figures that seem to stand in for the absolute relativize themselves once they enter into a system of representation and reflection. One of the most striking features of the *Hymns to the Night* consists in its continual provocation of strategies of reading that are associational and differential. The light does not merely represent light, that is, the purely physical phenomenon; it seems to point beyond itself, referring, for example, to the phenomenal, the sensual, the rational, or the economic (as a domain of productivity). The night follows this expansive symbolic structure: at turns, it invokes the noumenal, the holy oblivion of undifferentiated chaos, the fusion of eros and thanatos. If the poem contains any figures of multiplicity, heterogeneity, and plurality, they are to be found in these supposed signs that stand in for the absolute, namely, the light and the night. Signs that in other contexts could easily be read as representations of the ultimately unrepresentable absolute therefore become integrated into a reading process that can only read these signs as other than they are—as absolutely non-identical with themselves.

A simple conclusion follows from this observation: the *Hymns to the Night* do not attempt to represent the unrepresentability of the absolute. Instead, these poems put into practice how poetic signs portray *seeming* representations of the absolute in different forms (night, the beloved, death, Christ, the father's womb), thereby in fact generating multiplicity and plurality in the rhetorical fabric of the poem itself.

In any reading of the poem, one must therefore critically reflect upon the immediate impulse to see *through* the light and the night, to read them allegorically as other than they are. The light does not "represent" or "stand in for" the world of phenomena or intelligibility, nor does the night "represent" or "stand in for" the realm of the noumenal or unintelligible sacrality. Both the light and the night, as they unfold throughout the poem, enter into a chain of associations, and this flux of associations and relations supersedes any purported moment of intuition; the poetic act thus generates a patchwork of multiplicities from signs that are easily misread as allegories.

The signifying systems of "light" and "night" unfold along a movement of discursive expansiveness. In the first sentence, light becomes associated with Cartesian extension, *res extensa* (*des verbreiteten Raums*), with wondrous appearances that both constitute and exceed the order of nature (*Wundererscheinungen*), with aesthetic and natural-scientific discourses (*mit seinen Stralen und Wogen*), with the visible world (*seinen Farben*), and with omnipresence and idealized sovereignty (*seiner milden Allgegenwart*). What is striking about the light—and the night—is precisely the multiplicity of possible readings, each reading producing its own absolute, but each absolute being undermined by another possibility.

In the turn to the night, the poetic voice of the *Hymns to the Night* never completely disavows the light and everything the light represents, but merely undercuts the claim of the light to absolute sovereignty. Sovereignty, or the claim to universal domination, does indeed appear as one of the hallmarks of the light: "Like a king of earthly nature it calls every force to innumerable transformations, binds and dissolves endless pacts, hangs its heavenly image around every earthly being" (*NS* 1:131). The light acts as the sovereign of nature, the sun having long been associated with the figure of the monarch, an iconography that had been adopted and exploited by Louis XIV, *le Roi*

Soleil. One of its central powers—a capability that places the light in the orbit of Baumgarten's aesthetic exercises—consists in associating and dissociating, binding and separating, synthesizing and analyzing the world of phenomena. The light makes possible the very appearance of the sensuous world and the norms of social order that guarantee intelligibility. Like the monarch, the radiation of light transmits a call, and the world of earthly appearances is exhorted to obedience.

When the poet turns his back on the light—"Away I turn to the holy, inexpressible, mysterious night" (*NS* 1:131)—not only does he signal his refusal of total sovereignty as a regime of power, but he associates himself with an act of disobedience that could properly be called revolutionary.[33] On the level of poetic form, the gesture becomes more marked in print than in the manuscript. In the print version of the *Athenaeum* journal, there is a paragraph, or the equivalent of a strophic gesture in prose: the passage from the light to the night in the *Athenaeum* is thus marked by a difference. However, in Novalis's manuscript, there is no such graphic sign that signals the movement toward the undifferentiated space of holy, inexpressible night.[34] In the oscillation produced by different writing technologies and recorded forms, between the hand and the printing press, the transition from day to night is both continuous and discontinuous, it is both stream of language and strophic turn.

The temptation to see the night as an expression of the inexpressible absolute or as a space of pure indifferentiation may have some plausibility, but such a point of view only partially captures what is at stake in the representation of the night. Above all, the night does not refer to anything; it acts, or rather, it is a textual function. Its most important characteristic can be understood as a potentializing force, or that which poetically disorganizes schemas of intelligibility. The turn to the night directs itself against all accounts of natural organization modeled on a centripetal sovereign power. The fantasy domain of night therefore functions as a perturbation that lies outside of the physical, mechanical, economic, or political system that reveals these systems as inherently limited and relative. Novalis was drawn to this figure of perturbation in the order of nature; he writes in his comments on Schelling's *On the World-Soul* (*Von der Weltseele*, 1798): "The force of formation [*Bildungskraft*] becomes a *drive to formation* [*Bildungstrieb*] through perturbation from a foreign principle [*Störung eines fremden Princips*]" (*NS* 3:114).

Both the light and the night therefore function less as signifiers and more as attractors. They both are associated not with any one particular absolute (which is already a contradiction in terms), but a way of organizing phenomena, a way of gathering them and disorganizing them. In the *Athenaeum* version, light structures the world according to a great chain of being. Stages of life are grammatically organized, each noun bearing a certain number of parallel adjectives that increase in complexity as one moves up the chain: "the scintillating, eternally resting stone, the sensitive nursing plant [*sinnige saugende Pflanze*] and the savagely burning, variegated animal—yet above all the magnificent stranger with the meaningful eyes [*mit den sinnvollen Augen*], the swaying gait, and the tenderly closed lips, rich in tones" (*NS* 1:131). The poet progresses from the immobile stone to the sensuous plant to the savage animal, leading finally to the "magnificent stranger." The poetic voice, in describing the phenomena touched by the light, organizes, classifies, and hierarchizes forms of Being from the inanimate to the vegetative to the animal to the human.

At the same time, as one travels toward the human being as the seeming telos of an existential order, the movement of the poem fluctuates in both substance and rhythm. The stone shines and rests eternally, both part of the creation and yet, static. The plant, nursing and sucking (*saugend*), lives through the transaction of fluids and, as sensitive (in the sense of being endowed with sense: *sinnig*), it seems to incline already toward reason, indeed, functioning almost as a transitional stage between the vegetable and the human (much as it would later be portrayed by Shelley in "The Sensitive Plant"). The movement up the chain of being is therefore one that is saturated with ambiguities and points of indifferentiation; one may even discern fluctuations in tempo, a movement from the eternally resting stone, gaining momentum in the savagely burning animal, before slowing down again with the human being, a being whose nature is to float, not to rest anchored to one place. The turn to the night and the potentiality for a disorganization of the order of the light that governs appearances already constitute a latent dynamic of the light.

Moreover, the end toward which the system travels posits a point that is outside this system: the human being appears to the poetic voice as a "foreigner," a *Fremdling*. If the human being appears to this voice as foreign, it may signal not that the human being is ontologically simply alien, a creature whose essence is to be "strange," but that the one who is speaking—the poetic voice itself—does not fully belong to the order of beings that it describes. To call the human being a foreigner posits the speaking voice as both inside and outside the realm of the human. Furthermore, the human being's expressivity manifests itself only paradoxically, as both silent and speaking, a being endowed with tenderly closed lips, *zartgeschlossen*, that are nevertheless musical, *tonreich*. Since the poet himself speaks, with lips open rather than closed, his own poetic activity both associates himself with and distances himself from the figure he describes.

The poet approaches the realm of the light from the perspective of one who is at least partially outside its sphere of attraction. In the turn to the night, however, the poet does not merely become attracted to death, love, erotic fulfillment, and the ineffable realm of the noumenal. Rather, the turn to the night signals an alternative framework of organizing—or disorganizing—phenomena. Instead of the hierarchical chain of being, spaces are multiple, incompatible, metaphorical: the world is "sunk in a deep tomb"; in "strings of the breast blows deep melancholy"; the poet desires to sink into "dew drops" (*NS* 1:131). Interior and exterior states are thrown together, mixed, non-delineated. "In other spaces the light pitched joyous tents" (*NS* 1:131), says the poet. It is not merely that the light appears in "other spaces," but rather, that the spaces of the night become other than the order and organization characteristic of day. This disorganizing gesture is even present in the organization of sound and rhythm, with the light gravitating toward dactyls, the night more toward iambic patterns. Rhythmically, however, the poem appears "mixed" in each section, which is why one must speak of tendencies and attractions rather than structures. The presence of the night—which is "timeless and spaceless" (*NS* 1:133)—serves to undermine the claim to totality of the space of the day. It makes present an "other order" that disrupts the day's seemingly all-powerful tyranny, which the poet explicitly calls omnipotence, *Allmacht*.

The disorganization of phenomena that the night instigates, which in turn undermines all claims to a singular or central figure of omnipotence, spurs the mind in its flight toward self-overcoming. To the night, the poet says, "you lift up the heavy wings of the mind" (*NS* 1:131). The night, as a zone of indifferentiation, lifts the mind to a higher sphere by introducing difference into the poetic space: by interrupting the light's schema of organization. Poetic stimulation, as we have seen, consists in finding a point outside of a system capable of perturbing the system. The poet recasts the continual overturning of order through the power of the night as an intensification of mental life.

If night initiates the undoing of a way of organizing the world, it follows that it must in turn provoke its own moment of overcoming. It does not negate itself, but rather, constructs an attraction to the light and to life, to its other, in order to maintain the tension that sustains its own power. The presence of the light makes itself felt at a turning point in the third hymn. This hymn, referring to passages almost verbatim from Novalis's journals about his visit to Sophie's grave, is not striking because of the core of experiential content it may or may not represent. Rather, it lays bare the dynamics of presence of mind—*Besonnenheit*—that Novalis claims as the central cognitive faculty requiring exercise and stimulation.

Presence of mind, as we have seen, operates against a background in which there are infinite lacunae, gaps that prevent acts of cognition from achieving perfect, self-transparent mastery. One should recall that in Novalis's journal, the relation to Sophie, or the so-called experiential core of this third hymn, is framed as a problem for the imagination, or the making present of that which is absent. Poetry, as a form of making present, does not simply resuscitate that which has been lost: it transforms the being of appearances, unlocking a differential oscillation at the core of tautological identity. The third hymn is in fact structured around a seeming movement of identification, bracketed between two instances of crying: *Thränen* = *Thränen*. However, over the course of this hymn, these tears undergo a differential metamorphosis. The hymn begins, "Once as I wept bitter tears" (*NS* 1:135), and ends with tears that have been transfigured by the presence and contact of the beloved: "On her neck I wept delightful tears of new life" (*NS* 1:135). The tears have become polarized or magnetized, moving from bitter to sweet, from mourning the loss of death to celebrating the promise of a new existence.

The third hymn, which still stands under the aegis of the turn to the night, nevertheless appears to organize phenomena in a way reminiscent of the light's form of organization in the first hymn, namely, in the movement from stasis to movement, from the inert stone to the floating human being. The hymn begins with the poet in a state of paralysis, as if petrified: "As I looked around me for help, could not move forwards, not move backwards" (*NS* 1:135). An appearance interrupts this stasis, "then came from blue distances—from the heights of my old blessedness a storm of twilight [*Dämmerungsschauer*]" (*NS* 1:135). As the presence of a liminal figure between darkness and light, the twilight storm—which may refer both to the excitation of an interior bodily state (a shudder, *Schauer*) as well as to a quickly passing storm—introduces permeability between discrete domains, allowing a redemptive moment from the past to set the stasis of the present into motion. The poet becomes that floating being that was the principal characteristic of the human being in the first hymn: "above the area floated my released, newly born spirit" (*NS* 1:135). The inversion of the night, its overturning of the order of the day, passes through a sphere of indifferentiation—the *Dämmerungsschauer*—which appears as a necessary poetic precondition for the transition from inertia to dynamic movement, from a paralyzed and static being to a being whose essence is to float.

In his "Physical Fragments," which date from 1798, Novalis mentions the possibility of a chiasmatic movement between spheres of illness, each noted according to configurations of Brown's sthenic and asthenic, direct and indirect debilities. Although he crosses out a diagram of this schema, one may still observe that in the "sphere of health," there is a "saturation limit" (*Saturationsgrenze*), a "point of indifference" (*Indifferenzpunct*), or a "point of desire" (*Begehrungspunct, NS* 3:79). Novalis imbues spheres of indifference (*Indifferenzsfären*), however, with a physiological-aesthetic force, using indifference to link and blend mutually exclusive regions: body and mind, excitability and sensibility. He says, "synthesis of soul and body—and excitation and sensibility. Naturally they go through one another now through spheres of indifference—realization, filling out the *zero* is the difficult problem for the artist of immortality" (*NS* 3:318).[35] The "artist of immortality" must fill out the nullity of Being as absolute identity, using points of indifference to link differentiated domains. The twilight storm (*Dämmerungsschauer*) opens a zone of indifferentiation between the supposedly mutually exclusive codes of light and darkness, marking the transition between incommensurable regimes of organization.

The third hymn linguistically constructs an indifference point between light and dark, life and death, an indifference point that becomes intensified by the multiplicity of differential semantic possibilities concentrated along its grammatical plane of appearance. The manuscript version illustrates the indifference point more clearly than the printed version:

> . . .—there came from blue distances
> From the heights of my old blessedness a twilight storm
> And suddenly tore the bond of birth
> The light's fetter—away flew earthly splendor and
> My mourning with it.

> . . .—da kam aus blauen Fernen,
> Von den Höhen meiner alten Seligkeit ein Dämmrungs Schauer—
> Und mit einemmale riß das Band der Geburt, des
> Lichtes Fessel—Hin floh die irdische Herrlichkeit und
> meine Trauer mit ihr. (*NS* 1:134)

The word "tore" (*riß*) stands out at the midpoint of the line, almost lying at the midpoint of the third hymn as a whole. The act of tearing seems directed toward the bond of birth, or more concretely, the umbilical cord, bringing about a separation from the mother that will eventually be restored as a return to the "womb" of the father in the final lines of the hymns. In this context, it is difficult to determine whether the verb *reißen* is transitive or intransitive, and if transitive, it is difficult to decide which words form the subject and which the object. The sense of the passage lends itself to multiple possibilities: (1) "All of a sudden, the twilight storm tore the bond of birth, the light's fetter," or (2) "All of a sudden, the bond of birth, the fetter of the light, broke apart," or (3) "All of a sudden, the bond of birth tore the light's fetter." In the *Athenaeum* version, the passage is written thus: "and suddenly tore the bond of birth—the light's fetter" (*und mit einemmale riß das Band der Geburt—des Lichtes Fessel, NS* 1:135). Isolated from the previous phrase, the bond of birth seems to act as subject, to have torn the fetter of the light (option 3). And yet, if the verb is read intransitively—a possibility that, according to Adelung, exists for the verb *reißen*—the bond of birth and the fetter of the light become coextensive, almost identical expressions (option 2). The storm of twilight—or twilight as a perturbation, a momentary shudder—can also function as subject, which tears the bond of birth as well as the fetter of the light (option 1). In this case, it is the very figure of the point of indifference between light and dark, dawn or dusk, that de-structures the power of binding (the bond of birth), separates the poet from the world of light, from the world of the living—and thereby permits his entry into the exteriority of death, the space in which his beloved dwells. And yet, the point of indifference itself appears difficult to localize: it floats in possibilities, as a potential force that ruptures the fetters of the light.

When the poet reunites with the beloved, he seems to have crossed the boundary between life and death. And while this crossing is associated with the tearing of a bond (the bond of birth), or with the institution of a bond that frees the poet from the control of light, yet another bond is unquestionably put in its place, the bond of tears:

> I grasped her hands, and the tears became a scintillating, indestructible bond. Millennia flew off into the distance, like storms. On her neck I wept enraptured tears for the new life. It was the first, the only dream—and only since then do I feel the eternal, immutable belief in the heaven of night and its light, the beloved [*die Geliebte*]. (*NS* 1:135)

The passage travels through a series of state changes, culminating in a supposedly "immutable" (*unwandelbaren*) belief. The tears of the poet, which at the beginning of the hymn were pouring from the eyes in a liquid effusion of despair, have become matter: solid and scintillating like the stone of the first hymn. These tears invert the trajectory taken by the poet himself; if the tears have shifted states from dynamic to static (from "Once, when I poured out bitter tears, when my hope, dissolved in pain, melted away [*zerran*]" to "the tears became a scintillating, unbreakable bond"), the inverse holds true for the poet, namely, the static paralysis of the poet has brought about the acceleration of time itself (*Jahrtausende zogen abwärts in die Ferne*). Millennia travel across the sky like clouds.

The scene spreads outwards over the totality of all visionary moments; it represents the first and *only* dream (*der erste, einzige Traum*). The dream induces a form of presence of mind, a *Besonnenheit*, making present the beloved as a paradoxical figure of indifferentiation, the light of night: *den Himmel der Nacht und sein Licht, die Geliebte*. The figure of the beloved produces difference in a space of indifferentiation: the beloved illuminates the night, impurifying the purity of night by introducing its other, light, into its horizon. Night was itself previously characterized as a deviation, a "turning away" from self-evident norms. Here, light is integrated into night, thus provoking a movement whereby night turns against its own act of deviation; even the domain of night exists at a point of differentiated indifference with its opposite, with the light. Mutually exclusive spaces are made permeable through a membrane of indifferentiation—which Novalis had previously designated as a movement of health—in turn making possible the continual oscillation between domains that previously appeared homogeneous. There is no synthesis of opposing spheres into one and the same order of being, merely the co-presence of differences that communicate, come into contact, influence one another, and oscillate between separation and unity.

If the attraction to the night therefore becomes coextensive with an undoing of order that reorganizes experience, culminating in continual oscillation and inversion, one may see this attraction at work in the relation between the fifth and sixth hymn. The fifth hymn describes a historical progression of the spirit that supposedly culminates in the Christian synthesis of light and dark, life and death.[36] If, in the *Fichte Studies*, Novalis describes difference and multiplicity as part of a cognitive or logical philosophical consequence of the attempt to conceptualize identity, he transposes this procedure onto the movement of history in the fifth hymn, foregrounding the (negative) presence of the absolute as a stimulative principle driving cultural and historical change.

At every stage of historical order, some element outside the system of intelligibility perturbs this order, thereby provoking a cultural-historical paradigm shift. In the first historical stage, the organization of time was ruled by fate: "In times long since passed, an iron fate ruled with silent force over the far-flung clans of people" (*NS* 1:141). The "silent force"—which one might designate as a time before the word, before the logos—constructs fate as a relatively closed system. The romantic cliché of ancient Greece is certainly present in abundance: according to this historical schema, in the Greek world, human beings exist in supposed harmony with nature and with the divine, naive, like children: "an eternally colorful celebration of the children of heaven" (*NS* 1:143). However, less important than this makeshift order is the agent that initiates its undoing: death appears as that element outside the historical system which disrupts its equilibrium, therefore also overturning the "silent force" of fate. Death, as a figure of perturbation, manifests itself as a poetic disorganization of rhythm, in the *Athenaeum* version marked by a change from prose to poetry: "There was only one thought, a horrifying dream image,

> That horribly stepped to the festive tables
> And wrapped the mind in wild terrors.
> . . .
> It was death that interrupted this pleasure feast
> With fear and pain and tears. (*NS* 1:141)

Death disrupts the seemingly imperturbable organization of life in antiquity, setting the mind aflame with anxiety and marking the transition to what will become, for the poet, a godless and lonely rationalism: "Lonely and lifeless stood nature. The arid number and strict measurement bound her with iron chain" (*NS* 1:145). Where Enlightenment has rendered nature disenchanted, enchantment withdraws into an oppositional space, namely, the night: "No longer was the light the seat of the gods and a heavenly sign—they cast the veil of night over themselves. The night became the powerful womb of revelations" (*NS* 1:145). The night, normally associated with the negativity of death, carries within itself a latent redemptive power. By virtue of remaining "unresolved" (*unenträthselt*), the night becomes a source of heterocosmic thinking: a way of organizing the world that cannot be absorbed into the current historical moment, an inexplicable source of wonder that remains amidst all attempts to rob the world of its mystery.

The semiotic function of night—as the reserve of that which cannot be absorbed in a particular historical epoch—is carefully coordinated with death, whose "event" structure (rather than the more atmospheric and temporally extended "night") is always marked by an alteration, a sudden change, even if only in poetic form, usually from prose to meter and rhyme. Language marks the disorganization and reorganization of experience that death performs.[37] In the hymns, the power of death—as perturbation, as space of disorganization, and not merely as a sacred presence—is announced by a new era, namely, Christianity. The central event of Christianity—the birth of Christ—occurs poetically (in deviation from actual historical chronology) after the onset of rationalism and appears as its antidote.[38] However—and such an insight seems also to cohere with Novalis's maligned essay, "Christianity or Europe"—the Christian era is characterized by a fundamental resignification of death: whereas death previously marked an imbalance in other historical periods, an instance of negativity that could not be cognitively assimilated, Christianity seems to stabilize human history, leading to a higher synthesis of life in death as the basis of a new form of communal and cultural organization. The fifth hymn does indeed conclude in an image of perfect synthesis, suggesting a telos to the historical order:

> Only one night of bliss—
> An eternal poem—
> And the sun of all of us
> Is the face of God.

> Nur eine Nacht der Wonne—
> Ein ewiges Gedicht—
> Und unser aller Sonne
> Ist Gottes Angesicht. (*NS* 1:153)

The final lines of the fifth hymn form a trinity: Night (*eine Nacht der Wonne*), poetry (*ein ewiges Gedicht*), and the sun (*unser aller Sonne*) are brought together in an identity, made one with the divine countenance. All differentiation, all heterogeneity and oppositionality, merge in an act of concentration in the face of God. The culmination of the teleological narrative appears to have come to an end in the embodied synthesis of night, the sun, and poetry, binding all human subjects together in the light of the divine, *unser aller Sonne*.

If the fifth hymn were the end of the cycle, then this teleology would in fact stand as given. There is, however, a sixth hymn. In the *Athenaeum* version, the words "Longing for Death" (*Sehnsucht nach dem Tode*) are written above the hymn. Far from what might seem to be the case, the desire for death does not consist in a desire for stasis or rest, but rather, in a desire for death in its specific poetic manifestation, that is, a yearning for its specific sign-character. In the hymns up to this point, death has functioned both as perturbation leading to the overturning of orders as well as an index of points of indifference, spaces that both unite and separate conceptually homogeneous spheres, rendering them permeable.

The sixth hymn itself overturns and disorganizes the historical narrative developed in the fifth hymn, thereby undermining the validity of the teleological narrative leading to perfect synthesis in Christianity. Even "Christianity or Europe," which appears to synthesize the (potentially) heterogeneous spaces of church and state and articulate the desire for a universal, pan-European Catholicism, celebrates a fantasy of communal freedom, joy, and love of the multiplicity of religion as such: "the essence of the Church will become true freedom" (*NS* 3:524). Indeed, Novalis's idiosyncratic definition of Christianity is both specific and formal, multiple and one, since it signifies not merely the orthodox belief in Christ, but extends to the set of all possible religions, to an affirmation of "the element of fertility of religion, as joy in all religions" (*NS* 3:523). Christianity is therefore emptied out of its specificity and simply designates the structure of transcendence as such. However, if the fifth hymn prioritizes Christianity as a privileged form of religiousness, even if understood in its most basic, formal sense as the mere desire for transcendence, the sixth hymn disrupts this teleological schema.

In the sixth hymn, the poet describes an attachment to the "times gone by," a form of "pre-modern temporality" (*Vorzeit*), or those cultural-historical moments of the fifth hymn outside the sterile paradigm of positivistic rationalism. The representations of the moments of the *Vorzeit* occur in three strophes. The organization of these strophes, however, does not correspond to the teleological schema established in the fifth hymn. Instead, a remarkable thing happens. In the manuscript, the poet performs the recapitulation of these historical moments *backwards*. The historical narrative appears in the form of a countdown or an inversion. In writing the last hymn, it would seem that Novalis saw the historical framework of the fifth hymn as something to be inverted:

> O! lonely stands and deeply sad
> Whoever ardently and piously loves the times gone by.
> 3
> The times gone by, when in the glow of youth
> God himself announced his presence
> And dedicated his sweet life
> To early death in the courage of love
> And did not avoid fear and pain
> So that he would remain dear to us.

2
The times gone by, where, in full bloom,
Primeval races shone brightly,
And children, for the sake of the kingdom of heaven,
Yearned for death and suffering
And, even if pleasure and life spoke,
Many hearts from love still broke.
1
The times gone by where the senses' light
Burned in high flames,
Human beings still recognized
The Father's hand and face,
And with high sense, in simplicity
Still many a person resembled His original image.

O! einsam steht und tiefbetrübt
Wer heiß und fromm die Vorzeit liebt.
3
Die Vorzeit, wo in Jugendglut
Gott selbst sich kundgegeben
Und frühem Tod in Liebesmuth
Geweiht sein süßes Leben
Und Angst und Schmerz nicht von sich trieb
Damit er uns nur theuer blieb.
2
Die Vorzeit, wo noch blütenreich
Uralte Stämme prangten
Und Kinder für das Himmelreich
Nach Qual und Tod verlangten.
Und wenn auch Lust und Leben sprach,
Doch manches Herz für Liebe brach.
1
Die Vorzeit wo die Sinne licht
In hohen Flammen brannten,
Des Vaters Hand und Angesicht
Die Menschen noch erkannten,
Und hohen Sinns, einfältiglich
Noch mancher seinem Urbild glich. (*NS* 1:155)

Each of these strophes in the sixth hymn seems to correspond to a specific era in the historical narrative of the fifth hymn. The strophe labeled "3"—a strophe that is ultimately restored to its final position in the *Athenaeum* version—describes in broad strokes the passion of Christ, whereas the strophe labeled

"1," which precedes the others in the *Athenaeum*, describes the immanence of the divine in antiquity. The rationalist worldview, however, appears absent, having been replaced by a strophe that mixes multiple mythologies: the Greeks, the early Germanic tribes, the early Christians, and perhaps even the Jews. The historical teleology of the fifth hymn therefore represents an order that can be inverted, swiveled around a second strophe that functions as a zone of indifference. This zone of indifference permits the disorganization of the order that was previously established in the fifth hymn and makes possible the repeated inversion and impurification of homogeneous domains. The sixth hymn brings to light the *disorder* of history, or the way in which poetry can deviate from historical paradigms that have themselves been posited as organizing schemata.

In this sixth hymn, which seems on the surface to culminate in a desire for death, the poet introduces a difference between that which is enunciated and its mode of enunciation: if the semantic content of the hymn expresses a world-weary yearning for death as stasis, the way this desire is expressed inverts previously established orders of articulation, thereby contributing to the stimulative dynamics of perpetual inversion. The poem institutes a performative contradiction between what is being expressed—the desire for rest or a zero-degree of activity—and what this expression is actually doing poetically, namely disorganizing and inverting the order of phenomena and thereby intensifying stimulation. The final lines of the poem, far from revealing a desire for death as stasis or a return to nothingness, therefore reveal the desire for death *in its own literary manifestation*, that is, a desire for the potentializing and heterocosmic capacity of death that stimulates and urges onward the formal dynamic of the poem itself. The desire for death is therefore a desire for the exteriority of an event that disrupts intelligibility.

The final gesture of the poem appears reproductive in every possible sense, yielding figures of the divine that do not remain in one single image, but differentiate and multiply:

> Downward to the sweet bride,
> To Jesus, the beloved—
> Consoled, the evening twilight grays
> To those who love, to those who grieve.
> A dream breaks loose our bonds
> And sinks us in the father's womb.

> Hinunter zu der süßen Braut,
> Zu Jesus, dem Geliebten—
> Getrost, die Abenddämmerung graut
> Den Liebenden Betrübten.
> Ein Traum bricht unsre Banden los
> Und senkt uns in des Vaters Schooß. (*NS* 1:157)

Jesus, the beloved, the father, the womb: if any of these figures or spaces supposedly function as goal or telos of the poem, it is their multiplicity that remains the central point of astonishment. Each figure, each space becomes simultaneously differentiated from and identified with the other. The final stanza undermines any attempt to maintain divisions between supposedly exclusive orders: the secular and the religious, the general and the particular, the male and the female, the heteroerotic and the homoerotic. In this final stanza, the womb (no mere *lap*, which, although a valid translation of *Schooß*, would nullify the paradoxicality of the sign)—the father's womb, which is also the space of the beloved and of Jesus, of the beloved-Jesus—crosses over each of these lines of demarcation. The womb, or the *Schooß*, appears as the ultimate zone of indifferentiation. Even as a grapheme and phoneme, it is a near-palindrome, suggesting a form of reading that may be propelled both forwards and backwards.

We have seen that in the *Fichte Studies*, Novalis develops an account of the absolute that is physiological. This form of the absolute multiplies and develops drives that propagate—or posit forth (*ein Fortsetzen*)—life. The specific physiological absolute imagined by Novalis is a point outside of a coherent system that perturbs this system and pushes it into transcendence. The final image, the womb, the *Schooß*, reframes death, at least in poetic form, as the provocation of an inversion in the process of reading itself.

Novalis, an avid reader (and critic) of Schelling, appears at one point fascinated by "Schelling's individualization—or even better multiplication—drive of Nature" (*NS* 3:430). The differentiation and multiplication of nature constitute the very crux of Schelling's philosophical endeavors at this time, endeavors that are centered on a classic theological question framed in the language of idealism: why, if identity ultimately underlies all phenomena, does the absolute differentiate itself at all? There must be a drive toward differentiation that is coextensive with the phenomenality of life: the production of an inherent multiplicity of homogeneous spheres—the sun, the earth, gravity, warmth, material objects—in nature itself. These relatively homogeneous spheres are nevertheless differentiated, and therefore can only communicate by taking leave from an originary state of indifference. In the *First Outline of a System of a Philosophy of Nature* (*Erster Entwurf einer Philosophie der Natur*, 1799), Schelling notes, "Where the homogeneous touches its heterogeneity, it is displaced outside the point of indifference (the dynamical inertia is perturbed)."[39] Heterogeneous life emerges from the perturbation of an equilibrium. The world of differentiated phenomena, precisely because there are points of relative homogeneity and indifferentiation, or localizable zones in which specific differences cannot be disentangled, presupposes a primordial indifference and posits the continual striving to return to this state. Absolute indifference is both the origin and end of life; Schelling even refers to death as "absolute homogeneity," or an absolute of indifferentiation.[40] Light, on the other hand, cancels the state of indifference via the production of difference;

it is the exemplary medium of communication, making visible the transmission of homogeneous spheres—for example, sun and earth—and the ensuing transformation of these spheres, thereby initiating a movement from relative homogeneity to heterogeneity.

Because the subject of Novalis's hymn is purportedly a desire for death, such a desire may be expressed semiotically—and paradoxically—as a movement between multiple points of indifference. For "death," as it comes into the world of appearances—much like absolute Being (*Seyn*)—can only manifest itself as that which it is not: as perturbation, as a trigger of an inversion of given orders, and hence as the very system of communicative excitation that Schelling reserved for light in his *Naturphilosophie*. Death consists in a point of stimulation outside of the system of excitability that disrupts the economy of excitation.

The *Hymns to the Night* are characterized by a form of signification that appears highly paradoxical, concentrating in multiple signs (night, death, the womb) both the *irruption of difference*—the catastrophic impetus for a perceptual or historical shift in forms of organization—as well as a *point of indifference*, which is to say, a space that not only binds supposedly homogeneous spaces, but makes them permeable and communicable. The dynamic organization and disorganization of Novalis's *Hymns* may be described as a dance between aesthetic stimuli that provoke disorder and stimuli that link spheres previously considered homogeneous (light and dark, night and day, life and death, male and female, Christianity and antiquity), contaminated with one another via zones of indifference. Death, as a sign, ultimately inverts its own function of inversion, at times functioning as a perturbation that generates difference, and at other times functioning as a point of indifference that permits an intermingling of homogeneous-heterogeneous spheres.

The womb, more so even than death, operates as an indifference point whose importance grows organically throughout the poem, accruing a magnetic or transcendental charge, until it finally appears to alternate an electric current, forming the plus and minus sides of a galvanic chain in the sixth hymn.[41] Hence in the first line of the sixth hymn, the *Schooß* appears first as the grave, as the poet describes a journey "downward in the earth's womb (*NS* 1:153)." In the final line, which closes a circuit between beginning and end only by creating a collision of opposing meanings in the space of the *Schooß*, the poet resignifies this journey downward, which becomes an act of reverse birth, a dream that "sinks us in the father's womb" (*NS* 1:157). The sixth hymn is indeed a journey, but not merely to the grave, but to the origin of life, and the entire hymn becomes the invitation to a sexual act of inception. This inception leaves the poet in a matrix (here, not of the mother, but of the father, or the space of the father/beloved) of indifferentiated possibilities. If the end of the fifth hymn's teleological narrative unifies differentiated elements—night, poem, and light—in one image, a synthesis in the face of one God, the end of the sixth hymn reveals a divine being differentiated into incompatible, but permeable spaces. The identity of the *Schooß* functions as a channel for moving between these differences. Both female and male, inorganic and organic, become disjunctively conjoined, not synthesized, in the image of a sign whose very purpose is to reproduce itself in its own annihilation.[42] A synthesis unifies oppositions and brings a series to a close; an indifference point permits passages from homogeneous or discrete elements and leads thought and signification into states of further differentiation, inversion, or oscillation.

Ultimately, tension and release, the physiological motors of bodily stimulation, govern the dynamic of the poem up until the very end. It is the dream, however, that triggers release. As the poet stresses, there is only one dream, namely, the midpoint of the poem itself, the third hymn: "It was the first, only dream" (*NS* 1:135). "It" refers not merely to the vision of being reunited with the lover—which breaks the bond of birth only to restore another "scintillating, unbreakable bond" (*NS* 1:135) in a movement of release and tension—but to the poetic description of the vision itself, that is, to its figuration as text. "It was the first, the only dream": namely, the dream that the poet had just described poetically.[43] The text produces its own erotic stimulation, which it then satisfies in the final lines of the poem: "A dream breaks loose our bonds/And sinks us in the father's womb" (*NS* 1:157). The sexual destination of the poem, its telos, appears not in union with the erotic beloved, but rather, in the womb of the father, a space whose paradoxical nature clearly indifferentiates the domains of female and male, life and death.

In his physiological fragments, Novalis writes, "Every oversaturation of the muscles excites a violent desire for release [*Entladung*]—exercise of the strength of the muscles. In the erection—etc. this violent drive toward the movement of the muscles is most readily observed" (*NS* 3:180). The orgasm results not from a desire for the object itself, but from a desire to release tension in the body. This tension attracts human beings to the penetration of a boundary. Novalis writes, "The sexual organs are also the most supreme external organs that engender the transition from visible to invisible organs" (*NS* 3:264). For Novalis, the genitals are organs of indifference as such, and their excitation facilitates passage between the domains of the visible and the invisible, constructing a bridge between "aesthetic" and "inaesthetic" organs. The *Hymns to the Night* construct their own fantasy of something both visible and invisible, sensible and non-sensible—the first, the only dream of an absent-present beloved—that it uses to intensify and prolong the oscillation between tension and release, a movement between homogeneous-heterogeneous spheres: the emblem of an orgasm that never ends.

The womb (*Schooß*), as the quintessential zone of indifferentiation, appears as the beginning and ending, the alpha and omega of the sixth hymn. It may even form the central indifference point of the entire cycle, recurring ever more frequently and in ever more transcendentally saturated spaces. The word itself functions less like a sign and more like a force of attraction, or more precisely, it reveals the force of attraction as an intrinsic element in the system of signification itself. The womb first makes its appearance in the second hymn as an object of the night: the night hovers around "the tender girl's breasts" and makes her "womb into a heaven" (*NS* 1:135), rendering the sexual organs into a communion between visible sensuousness and invisible transcendence. From this point of erotic concentration, the womb becomes a figural matrix of possibilities, taking on different forms and moving between incommensurable spaces and times. As the space of the divine pagan immanence, "the sea's dark green depth was the womb of a goddess" (*NS* 1:141). Finally, it becomes the central indifference point between the grave of the earth and the fertile womb of birth in the sixth hymn.

As a mirror image of itself, the womb can be inverted ad infinitum between the poles of being and nothingness. Or in Novalis's words in the *Fichte Studies*: "Should there be a higher sphere, then it would be the one between Being and Non-Being—floating between both of them" (*NS* 2:106). Novalis's *Hymns to the Night* ends in an image that ultimately refuses all schemas of dialectical progress, choosing instead to abide in a movement of infinite oscillation between these poles.[44] It is not that the poem posits an absolute that it never attains and whose loss it must always mourn; rather, as exercise, the poem is always achieving what it set out to do, it is always beckoning the reader to come back to its pull of attraction. Such is the fantasy of an infinite poem, a poem that never ends, something to which one always comes back, an entity that, like every mortal, moves between life and death.

Chapter Six

✦

Difference/Indifference

Novalis's *The Novices of Sais*

Pedagogical Discipline and Monotheistic Obedience

The intensification of debates in the eighteenth century concerning the formation of subjects as complete human beings, useful citizens, and paragons of virtue reached a fever pitch with the publication of Rousseau's *Emile*.[1] Following *Emile*, there emerged in Germany a number of debates concerning the methods and limits of subject formation. The process of education, which must be initiated at the earliest stages of life, presupposes a conception of the human being as a potentiality that can be shaped and influenced through various pedagogical techniques.

According to Herder, the organic and cultural development of one's individual capacities—a process whose complexity appears condensed in flexible and negotiable patterns of formation (*Bildung*)—is subject to competing pulls: these capacities must be actualized in a space shared with others, depending on one's natural inclinations, according to the demands of civil society and differing national characters, and indeed within the trajectory of the human race considered as a species being.[2] The complexity surrounding conflicting ideals of *Bildung* was put on display in Goethe's *Wilhelm Meister's Apprenticeship Years* (*Wilhelm Meisters Lehrjahre*, 1795–96), which nowhere betrays a univocal conception of *Bildung* and thus ought not to be regarded as a *Bildungsroman* (novel of formation) in the traditional sense of the term, unless perhaps one designates novels of this sort as ones in which *Bildung* appears fraught with questions, contestations, contradictions, and divergences, as an open horizon under permanent investigation.

The novel, characterized by internal dissonances and collisions of ideals rather than a fixed and stable ideology of *Bildung*, was received by the Jena romantics at first with enthusiasm, and then with increasing skepticism. *Wilhelm Meister's Apprenticeship Years* eventually came to signify a pernicious and deficient aesthetic askesis, one in which the integrative and normalizing art of prose, rather than the differential and indifferential art of poetry, dominates the development of the human subject. Toward the end of 1799 (and after the bulk of his work on *The Novices of Sais*), Novalis, who at first appreciated the simple and yet variegated language of the novel as something suffused with a power of attraction (*NS* 568–69), noted with distress that Wilhelm Meister's reintegration into an ethic of diligent productivity belittled his artistic endeavors as juvenile poetic bohemianism. According to Novalis's later interpretation of *Wilhelm Meister*, the attraction to art in the novel constitutes a trajectory that is ultimately subordinated to becoming a functioning part of a social machine.[3] Especially *Heinrich von Ofterdingen* appears to offer an alternative conception of the way in which human subjects ought or ought not to be formed.[4]

Novalis's other novel, *The Novices of Sais*, left incomplete at his death, was intended not as a *Bildungsroman* (novel of formation), which at any rate did not yet exist as a generic or stylistic concept, but as a *Naturroman* (novel of nature). In the fragment that survives, however, it would be more apt to call the novel a novel of institutionalized education, or an *Erziehungsroman*. Although education—as *Erziehung* and not as *Bildung*—in pedagogical contexts concentrates more specifically on the education of children and on externally imposed discipline than the internal development of one's capacities, the line between *Bildung* and *Erziehung* is nevertheless difficult to draw in the discourses of the eighteenth century. Kant understands *Bildung* as part of *Erziehung* in *On Pedagogy*.[5] Nevertheless, just as *Heinrich von Ofterdingen* may be read as a response to *Wilhelm Meister's Apprenticeship Years*, so does one of the central problems thematized by *The Novices of Sais* concern the normalization of the human being through strictly regulated disciplinary institutions.

Novalis's *The Novices of Sais* was written at the end of the "pedagogical century," an age in which educational institutions were transforming to meet the demands of capitalistic bourgeois society.[6] The novel begins with a first-person narrative, a novice at the school of Sais in ancient Egypt, and then transitions into an exteriorized, third-person narrative, whose central term is nature (*die Natur*). Despite its polyphonic structure and its kaleidoscopic presentation of interpretations of nature, the novel ultimately provides just as much insight into institutional mechanisms of discipline as it does into the romantic philosophy of nature.

As an institution of subject formation, the school at Sais both coheres with and deviates from eighteenth-century forms of educational organization. It seems at first that the institution is characterized by a greater discursive variety, a greater freedom in mobility, and a notable lack of oversight. One of the most remarkable differences between the institution of Sais and the schools of the eighteenth century consists in the fact that there is only, as far as one can tell, *one* teacher at Sais. In 1777 Johann Bernhard Basedow, a leader of pedagogical reform, writes, "The number of the teachers must *at first* be equivalent to the number of students so that each one could be occupied only to the degree in which he must be exercised."[7] The singularity of the teacher is no mere insignificant textual detail in this instance; rather, it reveals the logic of an institutional order, one which, on the one hand, is emphatically non-hierarchical, and on the other hand, like a heliocentric system, revolves around the figure of the master as a sort of fixed point. In the novel, the teacher does not delegate authority or establish particularized regimes of practice, but construes his own form of exercise as a model to be imitated by the students, making himself the focus of a mimetic disciplinarity.

The structure of the school at Sais thus follows the pattern of a centripetal force of attraction, embodying the monotheistic tendencies that were associated with the school at Sais in the late eighteenth century. Sais, as one of the principal sites for the mystery cults of Isis, was presumed to be the birthplace of monotheism. At the center of the school stands the figure of the teacher, who has developed techniques to extend his authority over the discursive acts and over the very forms of perception of the children in the school. However, this authority does not exist by virtue of the organization of the school itself. Indeed, the authority of the teacher is secured less through direct observation and structured regimentation than through the manner in which he draws acts of speech into his orbit. He thereby inhabits the linguistic and mental space of the novices, much in line with Pestalozzi's representation of the ideal pedagogue: "Assure yourself control over the heart of your child, make yourself necessary to him. . . . He should trust you. . . . He should be obedient to the wise leader, the father who correctly warns of danger, but the leader must only command in cases of necessity."[8]

The teacher does allow, however, different forms of discourse to emerge from within the center of the institution, making possible not merely variations in orders of rhetoric, but in ways of organizing the world of appearances. His purported mastery over the space of the institution is at certain points undermined by acts of speech that surface in the walls of the school itself. In contrast to the organization of time, space, and perception in the school at Sais stands the fairy tale of Hyacinth and Rosenblüthchen, told from one novice to another, marking a form of speech that is not centripetal, but peripheral. The teacher's central position (which provokes centripetal responses among the novices) implies a certain way of exercising the senses, a regime of aesthetic exercise that depends on categorizing, ordering, and classifying the world, creating boundaries between objects. The space of the fairy tale, however, produces an alternative form of exercise, one no less important to the development of the child, but one that cannot be integrated into the attempt to create bounded and disciplined behavioral and perceptual patterns. Rather than organizing and categorizing nature, the fairy tale generates an entry point into the exercise of a poetic imagination sustained by mutual erotic attraction, and thus appears irreducible to the disciplinary patterns characteristic of the school at Sais.

As we have intimated above, when Novalis wrote *The Novices of Sais*, the reputation of the famed temple in Egypt was considered by some as the birthplace of a new form of religious sentiment, or more precisely, as the foundational site of the origin of monotheism. The veil of Isis, as a symbol of the separation between what can and cannot be known about nature, between the visible and the invisible, had long constituted a form of power equated with the capacity to draw and maintain lines of demarcation: under this veil was harbored the secret essence of the cosmos.[9] Sacred authority was defined by the maintenance of this limit. According to Schiller in *The Legation of Moses* (*Die Sendung Moses*), Moses, as a fiery political reformer, repurposes what he learns in the Egyptian mystery cults—above all, the immortality of the soul and a "scorn for polytheism" (*NA* 17:388)—and imparts these doctrines to the Israelites. More importantly, Schiller draws attention to the decline of the institution of Sais, and above all, the use of subterfuge in the constitution of religious authority; the power of relics, objects that make visible the distinction between the sacred and the profane, was used to consolidate the power of the priestly class:

> Among these [vessels] there was a sacred ark named the Coffin of Serapis, which, according to its origin, was supposed to be an emblem of hidden knowledge, and later, when the institute degenerated, was used as a plaything of mystical posturing and priestly fraud. . . . None of the priests were allowed to uncover this chest or even to lay a finger on it. (*NA* 17:384)

The priestly class maintains its power over the sacred through artifice; the continued belief in a transcendent reality and truth is held in place by a refined process of staging, and in this space of theatricality, the priests become custodians of truth.

Novalis makes his "novel of nature" (*Naturroman*) coincide with this origin story of monotheism—a story that, like Schiller's version, is situated in a field of tension between the authenticity of religious sentiment and the fraudulent theatricality of institutional and political power. In Novalis's text, the goddess Isis implicitly grounds the sacrality of the institution, and is thereby invested with a higher aesthetic and metaphysical significance. The transcendence of Isis, according to the various inscriptions found at Sais, was associated with the monotheistic god of the Israelites because it coincided with the Hebrew God's identity with Being itself. Schiller describes these inscriptions in *The Legation of Moses*: "Under an old column of Isis one could read the words 'I am, what is there' [*Ich bin, was da ist*], and on a pyramid at Sais one found the strange ancient inscription: 'I am everything that is, was, and will be, no mortal human being has lifted my veil' " (*NA* 17:385). Kant, in a footnote in the *Critique of the Power of Judgment*, claims that "nothing more sublime has ever been said, or any thought more sublimely expressed, than in the inscription over the temple of Isis" (*AA* 5:316). It is sublime because no determinate concept can possibly encompass the boundless infinity that the inscription seeks to imaginatively reproduce. Isis, in eighteenth-century aesthetic discourses, therefore came to be seen not merely as a symbol of a transcendent-immanent divinity, but also as a barrier beyond which the human mind could not penetrate: the opening of a horizon of thought that was at the same time a limit not to be transgressed.

In this sense, the veil of Isis does not symbolize the demarcation between acceptable and forbidden knowledge as much as foreground the human yearning for an impossible plenitude, or what would amount to a sensuous manifestation of pure Being. The goddess, who is both hidden and revealed—since if she is truly "all that is," she is not merely the statue, not merely the inscription that declares the truth of her own law, but also necessarily the veil and the observing subject at the same time—alludes to a process of indifferentiation that cannot be reduced to any concrete appearance, but moves through appearances. Novalis makes of this veil both a limit concept—between visible and invisible, sacred and profane, life and death—as well as a concatenation of desire that pushes the mind into further spheres of differentiation. The veil incites the desire to experience those realms marked as "other" than the subject: an exteriority beyond possible subjective experience. According to the novice of the first part of the novel, in order to intuit the sensuous manifestation of that which, by definition, refuses to manifest itself, the subject must become immortal: "if no mortal, according to the inscription there, can lift the veil, then we must attempt to become immortals; whoever does not wish to lift it is no true novice of Sais" (*NS* 1:82). The desire of the novice to become immortal, to leave behind the finitude of his own cognition, reveals an attraction to the subtext of the inscription (which remains unrepresented and implicit in Novalis's text): the plenitude of Being as the set of all things past, present, and future. To lift the veil is therefore to confront one's own identity with the immortal temporality of the goddess herself. That which is behind the veil must therefore simultaneously be outside possible experience, and yet, if the inscription is to be believed, it must be indifferentiated with experience, indeed, it must exist as the very essence of the perceiving subject, or more radically, of all possible subjects and all objects.

The fairy tale of Hyacinth and Rosenblüthchen in the second part of the text, which is recounted to the novice by one of his classmates and culminates in the lifting of the veil of Isis, implies that Hyacinth, the main character of this fairy tale, achieves that which is sought by the novice. The novice himself can only experience this satisfaction of desire aesthetically and vicariously. And as we shall see, the main figure in the fairy tale, Hyacinth, does become "immortal" in a curious sense of the word. However, he does so only by remaining consigned to a space of ontological impurity in which life and death no longer represent oppositional concepts, but rather, become compossibilities. There are a number of steps we must traverse before we can understand the implications of this special type of immortality.

Let us return to the novice and the novice's role in the narrative given the eighteenth-century associations with the institution of Sais. In the first part of the novel, before he has heard the fairy tale, the novice's desire to lift the veil gives him his identity as a "true" novice. The desire of the novice therefore distances the text as a whole from a tradition that had cast this very gesture in the light of grave transgression. For Schiller, for example, in the ballad "The Veiled Image at Sais" ("Das verschleierte Bild zu Sais"), the lifting of the veil of Isis is an act of violence. It is against this background that the radicality of Novalis's resignification of the novice's words—in which an act of disobedience and defilement is transformed into the promise of immortality and the fulfillment of desire—must be read.

Schiller's poem seeks to normatively enforce the boundary between the visible and the invisible, or that which reveals itself and that which ought to remain hidden, punishing those unable to sublimate their desire for sensuous revelation. The youth in Schiller's ballad, although supposedly engaged in the noble pursuit of extra-corporeal knowledge, is incapable of divesting himself of the instinctual urge for sensuous gratification in the attainment of this knowledge. The acquisition of knowledge becomes coextensive with existential illness, with a sinfulness of the spirit:

> A youth, whom the burning thirst for knowledge
> Drove to Sais in Egypt, to learn
> The priesthood's secret wisdom,
> Had hurried through many a grade with quick spirit,
> His desire to seek knowledge propelled him ever onward

> Ein Jüngling, den des Wissens heißer Durst
> Nach Sais in Ägypten trieb, der Priester
> Geheime Weisheit zu erlernen, hatte
> Schon manchen Grad mit schnellem Geist durcheilt,
> Stets riß ihn seine Forschbegierde weiter (*NA* 1:254)

As the youth lifts the veil of Isis, he is confronted with the reflection of his own desire:

> Whatever might lie behind it! I will lift it up.
> (He calls with a loud voice) I will behold it!
> Behold!
> A distant echo yells back in mockery.

> He says the word and has lifted the veil.
> "Now, you inquire, what revealed itself to him?"
> I don't know. Senseless and pale,

That's how the priests found him the following day
Prostrate before the pedestal of Isis.
Of what he saw and learned
Never did his tongue speak. But for eternity
The happiness of his life was gone,
Deep grieving propelled him to an early grave.
"Woe be to him," such was his word of warning,
When impetuous questioners forced themselves upon him,
"Woe be to him, whose path to truth goes through guilt,
Such truth will never be a source of joy."

Sey hinter ihm, was will! Ich heb ihn auf.
(Er rufts mit lauter Stimm) Ich will sie schauen.
Schauen!
Gellt ihm ein langes Echo spottend nach.

Er sprichts und hat den Schleier aufgedeckt.
"Nun fragt ihr, und was zeigte sich ihm hier?"
Ich weiß es nicht. Besinnungslos und bleich,
So fanden ihn am andern Tag die Priester
Am Fußgestell der Isis ausgestreckt.
Was er allda gesehen und erfahren,
Hat seine Zunge nie bekannt. Auf ewig
War seines Lebens Heiterkeit dahin,
Ihn riß ein teifer Gram zum frühen Grabe.
"Weh dem, dies war sein warnungsvolles Wort,
Wenn ungestüme Frager in ihn drangen,
"Weh dem, der zu der Wahrheit geht durch Schuld,
Sie wird ihm nimmermehr erfreulich seyn. " (*NA* 1:256)

It is tempting to read Schiller's poem as a simple Kantian allegory: the novice is guilty because he oversteps the limits that pure reason sets for itself, aiming to attain some form of noumenal truth beyond the boundaries of human cognition.[10] Or perhaps one might understand the veil of Isis as a representation of the power of the sublime, since Schiller himself sees the inscription of Isis as an example of how "everything that is *concealed* [*verhüllt*], everything *mysterious*, contributes to terror, and is therefore capable of sublimity" (*NA* 20:191). In this sense, the novice capitulates to the sublimity of the goddess.

However, the central problem of the ballad consists not in the sublimity of Isis, but precisely in the lack thereof. Schiller, in his treatise "On the Sublime" ("Vom Erhabenen"), which was written in 1793, two years before he wrote "The Veiled Image at Sais," distinguishes two forms of the sublime. One form he calls "theoretical" (roughly corresponding to the Kantian "mathematical" sublime), the other he calls "practical" (corresponding to the Kantian "dynamic" sublime). The theoretical sublime is the result of an object "whose representation challenges the adequacy of the imagination" (*NA* 20:173). The practical sublime is the result of an object that "brings with it the representation [*Vorstellung*] of a danger before which our physical power [*Kraft*] feels incapacitated" (*NA* 20:173).

Schiller prioritizes practical sublimity over theoretical sublimity because it is here that the human mind experiences its own freedom. It does so by elevating itself above instinctive and natural responses to states of danger, situations in which the physical survival of the self is at stake:

> Our *intelligible self*, that which is not nature in us, must differentiate itself from the sensuous part of our essence during the activation of the drive for self-preservation, and must become aware of its autonomy, its independence from everything that physical nature effects, in short, it must become aware of its freedom. (*NA* 20:184)

For Schiller, an encounter with the sublime is supposed to elevate the human being over its instinctual drive for self-preservation, releasing the self from its dependence on sensuous nature and from a reduction to mere action and reaction within a chain of causes and effects. The inscription of Isis may be easily assigned to the first form of the sublime (the theoretical sublime, or the sublime as transcending and challenging the limits of human cognition), but seems less pertinent as an instance of the second (the practical sublime, or the capacity of the human being to overcome the animal instinct for self-preservation). However, in spite of its primary appearance as representational problem, the goddess and the veil fuse both forms of the sublime, the theoretical and the practical.

The ballad becomes a case of a misrecognized sublime, since arguably the more important manifestation of the sublime in this context is that of the failure of the practical sublime, or the overwhelming presence of sensuous drives that bypass the freedom of the will. The goddess as practical sublime, as a challenge to sensuous drives and an incitation for human beings to reveal their freedom in the world of appearances, goes unnoticed by the novice; indeed, the practical sublimity of those who confront the goddess is covered up by the theoretical sublime of the goddess herself, which, as an object that eludes the imagination's capacity for representation, ironically becomes a temptation to submit to one's sensuous impulses. The ballad therefore stages these two forms of the sublime at cross-purposes with one another, in an agonistic state of tension rather than in a state of mutual reinforcement.

Schiller's poem is remarkable to the extent that it degrades the very emblem of theoretical sublimity—the incapacity of the human being to conceptualize omnipresence and omnipotence, above all as they are condensed in the symbol of the veil—to a mere object of desire. Indeed, the inscription *fails* to produce the desired effect—sublime terror—in the novice, and therefore can only be properly conceptualized as an aesthetic misfire. In his essay on the sublime, Schiller attributes a lack of receptivity to such sublime objects to an "imperfection of the subject" (*NA* 20:192), and it is this crime—an insensibility to the sublime and the novice's conversion of what should be fear into sensuous desire—that the novice must expiate. Indeed, if the novice did experience fear but nevertheless overcame this fear in order to lift the veil, then the transgressive moment of the poem would have succeeded as an instance of the practical sublime; as it stands, the novice subordinates the disembodied ideal of knowledge to the corporal and sensuous instinctuality of desire: "the burning desire for knowledge robs him / Of sleep" (*Ihm raubt des Wissens brennende Begier / Den Schlaf* [*NA* 1:255]). It is not a hubristic sin against the limits prescribed to human knowledge that the poem condemns as much as the contamination of the pursuit of knowledge itself with unbridled sensuality.

The "guilt" alluded to in the final line of the poem refers then, not merely to an act of disobedience, but to a fundamental failure of aesthetic cognition. The encounter with the sublime—which, in its practical form, ideally leads to a detachment of the subject from an overdependence on sensuous reality—here simply intensifies and aggravates the subject's drive toward the fulfillment of an almost corporeal desire. The freedom of the subject and the sanctity of the moral law are only revealed in the overcoming of sensuous desire, in a form of volition that distances itself from instinctual animality, and it is this failure that the poem makes visible. The punishment of the novice thus seeks to restore the order—including the aesthetic operation of the sublime—that had previously been transgressed. Above all, the "punishment" must restore the aura of sublimity to the symbolic space of the temple, and it is this that the poem aims to achieve. The echo supposedly emanating from the mysterious and sacred space—behold! (*Schau!*)—appears outside of the verse, an echo not merely in content, but also a formal echo, one that ultimately disrupts the integrity of the metrical line. The echo is a reflection of the speaker's own voice; and yet, it simultaneously merges with the voice of the goddess, the shrill and mocking imperative of an otherworldly authority that dares its subject to disobey. The promised "spiritual vision" (*Schau*), far from granting an intuition of plenitude, makes the novice into a degraded copy of his previous self, an echo just as hollow as the words that ring back to him from the halls of the temple.

The attempt to restore sublimity to the violated object nevertheless ends up once again generating its own temptation to transgress this reestablished order. The temptation falls on the shoulders of the readership of the poem itself, a readership that incidentally aligns itself more with the transgressive act than with the restoration of sacred authority. The readership itself becomes akin to the "impetuous questioners," reenacting the very pursuit of forbidden knowledge that characterizes the hubris of the youth. The youth's narrative, far from serving as a negative example, generates the desire for yet another transgression, this time in those who clamor to hear the youth's story.

This temptation is therefore to be found not merely in the parable itself, but in the structure of desire characteristic of the relation between text and reader. The reader is therefore called upon to take seriously the words spoken by the disillusioned youth: the renunciation of a desire that is overly sensuous in nature, even if this desire is for something as purportedly noble as truth. For Schiller, the restoration of sacred authority is coextensive with the aesthetic reinstatement of the sublime. The ballad effects something akin to a displacement of the sublime, whose power has been transferred from the statue to the story of the novice, indeed, to the poem itself. The poem seeks to produce the awe in its audience that the statue failed to inspire in the novice; poetry would thereby succeed where the image and the inscription fails.

As one can glean from Schiller's texts, the institution of Sais comes to exhibit at least two points of attraction in the imagination of late eighteenth-century German literature: on the one hand, it represents the birth of monotheism, an interpretation of the cosmos as organized around a singular, transcendent divinity. On the other hand, it sets in place a structure of obedience that consolidates the distinction between the known and the unknown, demands a renunciation of sensuous desire, and repurposes the aura of the sublime to discourage acts of boundary violation.

Everything aims at the restitution of the order of the moral and institutional law. In Novalis's text, the teacher appears as the embodiment of this law. He forms the middle point of lines of force simultaneously pushing people outside of the institution and drawing people toward this institution. In a text saturated with multiple points of view, the teacher might seem to foreclose on the simultaneous and equal—indeed, polyphonic—pull of the many voices to be heard in the narrative.[11] As the fragment stands in its current state, after all, the teacher has the final word. Here, as with Schiller's ballad, the problem of obedience is also inscribed into the relationship of the text and its readership. One is tempted to grant the teacher and the institution surrounding the teacher a monopoly over the capacity to assign meaning; however, it is *against* this urge that the text seeks to warn its readers. In this sense, Novalis's text is directly opposed to Schiller's respect for the sublime, refusing the terms set by any aesthetic object that demands a renunciation of desire as a precondition for the revelation of freedom, indeed, renouncing the very terms through which a subject comes to understand itself as self-legislating, as autonomous, as separate from the sensuous world.

The Tyranny of Order

In Schiller's ballad, the youth sees the embodied truth, regardless of how empty and damaged this truth leaves him. The poem's imaginative space violates the boundaries of pure reason, suspending the Kantian doctrine that there is an unknowable world of things in themselves, forever closed and inaccessible to human sentience. There is a truth to be known. However, if this truth is attained by improper means—"through guilt," or through the incapacity to renounce one's sensuous desires and make visible the realm of disembodied freedom which is, properly speaking, the very ground of morality—it is not reconcilable with human happiness.

In the fairy tale "Hyacinth and Rosenblüthchen" in *The Novices of Sais*, after Hyacinth comes to the end of his pilgrimage and lifts the veil of the goddess, he and his beloved seem to be rewarded rather than punished, blessed with generations of grandchildren. There is no law forbidding Hyacinth to lift the veil of Isis, nor is there any institution to regulate the boundaries between the sacred and the profane, the true and the false. And unlike the youth in Schiller's ballad, it is not the desire for knowledge that drives Hyacinth, nor is it knowledge that the confrontation with the goddess imparts. At first, Hyacinth appears in the fairy tale as an enigma, as incomprehensibility itself. It is simply stated that he is ill and in need of healing. But precisely what motivates him to seek out the goddess is unknown even to him. It is indeed perhaps the unknown itself, a feeling [*Gefühl*] that can be neither cognized nor recognized, that pushes him toward the goddess.

In the narrative economy of the novel, it is important to comprehend that the episode of the fairy tale represents an alternative to the institutional organization of the school at Sais. In the main narrative, within the walls of the institution, the teacher is emblematic of a certain relationship to the way the sensible world is ordered: he gathers and organizes, he reduces indeterminacy, and he assigns values to events that threaten the orientation of the mind. One may see the primacy of the teacher as an institutional figure at the very beginning of the novel. The narrative opens with the first-person perspective of the novice, who, after a short prologue, gravitates inexorably to a confirmation of the teacher's gathering function. He listens to voices, one of which says: "The holy scripture requires no exegesis. Whoever speaks truly is full of eternal life, and his scripture seems to us wondrous, related to true secrets, for it is a chord from the symphony of the cosmos" (*NS* 1:79). The novice attributes this idea, which articulates the essence of the logos, to the teacher: "The voice was doubtless speaking of our teacher, for he knows how to gather the traits that are dispersed everywhere" (*NS* 1:79). The teacher is endowed with the capability of binding disparate elements, as he forms the central point toward which the acts of discourse themselves gravitate. The utterances, which appear in the form of generalized statements, in fact are bound and gathered into the figure of the teacher, and it is above all language itself that circles around the teacher like planets around a star.

The teacher's philosophy consists in an extreme form of aesthetic askesis. According to the novice, "He often told us how, as a child, the drive to exercise, to occupy, and to fulfill his senses left him no peace. He used to watch the stars and copy their movements, their positions in the sand. . . . He gathered stones, flowers, insects of every sort, and put them in rows of many different kinds" (*NS* 1:80). The teacher has mastered the specific form of aesthetic exercise whose central injunction consists in attending to and imitating the order of nature. More importantly, nature opens itself as a field that enables the disciplinary movements of attentiveness; indeed, the description of natural objects, as a writing technology that exercises sense perception, was integrated into the pedagogical practices of the eighteenth century, for example, by Johann Georg Sulzer, in his *Preparatory-Exercises for the Stimulation of Attention* (*Vorübungen zur Erweckung der Aufmerksamkeit*, 1771–82).[12]

The teacher does not merely view nature as an object to be seen, but as its own paradigm of productive organization. His specific exercise consists in attempting to organize nature just as nature seems to organize itself, presupposing that nature is a well-ordered system. He therefore stands in a negative relation to the miraculous and the wondrous, to the disorganization of experience that the fantastic provokes and the aesthetics that would be adequate to this disruption of expectation. Already in the early eighteenth century, Breitinger had defined the wondrous as that which occurs when "a representation [*eine Vorstellung*] seems to stand opposed to the usual concepts that we have of the orderly course of things" (*CD* 136). The teacher coordinates the exercise of his senses with the organization of nature, even when this order does violence to nature itself, the supposed source of the mimetic model on which his own perceptual exercises are based. As we shall see, the teacher misreads the movements of this mimetic source. His misreading of nature as source—as that which can be made to fit a determinate spatiotemporal order—comes to exert an influence over almost all discursive utterances in the institution, thus seeming to bring order to a highly complex, polyphonic texture of linguistic acts. The organizing influence of the teacher is made manifest in the sequentiality of the narrative itself: although every "opinion" about nature in the opening pages of the novel is articulated from a different speaker and from a different point of view, every speech act nevertheless appears as part of a "row," with each taking its proper place.[13]

As the natural objects later reveal, there can be a disjunction between the self-organization of nature and the way human beings organize themselves. Human beings are not simply "identical with" or "part of" nature, at least not unproblematically so; there is no necessarily mimetic or isomorphic relation between the movements of nature in itself and how the human being perceives and responds to these movements. The teacher's approach to nature—organizing and placing natural objects in rows as exempla to be seen, observed, and constantly exhibited—ironically constitutes one example of a deviation from natural order rather than its successful imitation. He displaces nature from its own habitat, constructing a museum as a wonder cabinet, filled with natural objects whose display represents not the order of nature, but a traumatic violation of this order. After the fairy tale of Hyacinth and Rosenblüthchen, the narrative focus shifts suddenly, and the reader sees the story unfold from the perspective of the natural objects that the teacher himself had put into rows:

> The broad, echoing halls stood empty and bright, and the wondrous discussion continued on in innumerable languages among the thousandfold natures that had been brought together in these halls and exhibited in manifold orders. Their inner forces played against one another. They struggled to return to their freedom, to their former relations. Few stood in their actual place, and these calmly observed the varied activity happening around them. The others were complaining about horrifying agonies and pains, and they were lamenting the old, glorious life in the womb of nature, where a communal freedom united them, and each one received what it needed from itself. "O! if the human being," they said, "understood the inner music of nature and had a sense of exterior harmony. . . . He can't let anything be, tyrannically he separates us and clutches about him in sheer dissonances." (*NS* 1:95)

The shift in perspective of this scene is typical of *The Novices of Sais*, which alternates from the first-person perspective of the novice in the first half of the fragment to a third-person, seemingly omniscient narrator in the second. It is only through this narrative heterogeneity that the reader perceives the insufficiencies of the order of the institution. This passage, directly following the interlude of the fairy tale of Hyacinth and Rosenblüthchen, does more than cast a critical light on the school; it fundamentally problematizes the relation of the teacher to nature.[14] Indeed, the result of the teacher's own activity seems to contradict his purported identity as a gatherer of nature. His so-called gathering activity, from the point of view of nature, divides and disperses phenomena rather than unifies them.

Ultimately, it is nature itself that suffers from the order of pedagogical discipline. The structural analogies between school and prison cannot escape even the casual reader in the context of this representation of the natural objects. The displacement of these objects causes inner strife as they play *against* one another; they strive for "freedom," being contained against their will; most of them are displaced, as only a few exceptional ones stand "in their actual place" and are therefore able to look on in relative peace; most of these objects consider their captivity a form of torture that has torn them from the places in which they belong, where they enjoyed "communal freedom." These words correlate the teacher's principles of organization with a form of tyranny that has undermined the freedom of nature in itself.

The natural objects suggest that an overabundance of reflective thought is responsible for this tyrannical form of organization. The voices urge the reader to a different cognitive stance, namely that of feeling: "Will [the human being] ever learn to feel [*fühlen*]? He is still barely acquainted with this heavenly, this most natural of all senses" (*NS* 1:96). Feeling, however, never appears concretely in a symbolic or semiotic system; as we gleaned from the *Fichte Studies*, feeling is present only negatively as that which inverts reflective orders and pushes the imagination into movements of continual overcoming. To "learn" feeling would precisely initiate a process of an infinite inversion of orders. The natural objects have insight into this dynamic of feeling: "through feeling [*durch das Gefühl*]. . . . [the human being] would become master of an infinite game and he would forget all of his foolish endeavors in an eternal, self-sustaining and constantly expanding pleasure [*Genusse*]" (*NS* 1:96). The teacher's attempt to classify nature, bind and separate the world of phenomena through exercise, discourse, and logos, must be supplemented by a different sort of exercise, a play that results from the palpable, and yet ultimately absent, presence of feeling as a continual perturbation of schemas of organization, as an infinite game.

The very activity that the teacher performs with the natural objects, he performs with the novices themselves, deciding which novices have an aptitude for the study of nature and which do not. The novice says, "Several of us have left him. They returned to their parents and learned a trade" (*NS* 1:80). And even when the teacher appears to renounce his authority, he nevertheless exercises control over the state of exception, which is, as Carl Schmitt points out, the very definition of sovereignty.[15] Among the novices, a messianic figure makes a brief appearance: "one of them was still a child, no sooner had it arrived, and [the teacher] wanted to make him the teacher" (*NS* 1:80). The child disappears without any explanation, and it is presumably only in the later, unwritten sections of the novel (according to Novalis's sketches) that this child would return to announce his form of the gospel—a gospel only possible, incidentally, after the era of the teacher passes.

The voices of the natural objects frame the teacher as a false prophet. The teacher could be easily mistaken for a prefiguration of a messianic arrival, a John the Baptist who announces the divinity to come, or a preparatory figure in the grounding of a new church of nature. Such possibilities would correspond to his own self-interpretation, as he claims in his final monologue:

> He who is filled with an ardent desire for nature . . . will recognize as a teacher and as a friend of nature one who speaks with devotion and belief about nature, one whose speeches have the wondrous, inimitable penetration and inseparability [*Unzertrennlichkeit*] through which true gospels, true prophecies are announced. (*NS* 1:107–8)

He has called himself a teacher and has accepted the name; therefore he claims for himself the pronouncement of this "new" gospel, playing the role of a mediator that brings him closer to embodying the mouthpiece of God. The natural objects, however, denounce precisely this tendency: "[The human being's] desire to become God separated him from us" (*NS* 1:96), they say. The sophistication and complexity of the teacher's rhetorical elegance place the reader in danger of overlooking the problematic nature of the institutional structures within which such thought and behavior are controlled and organized by a charismatic individual. The voices of the natural objects open up a narrative space that loosens the rhetorical mechanisms whereby the teacher maintains and reproduces his authority.

The teacher's rhetorical performances secure the admiration of the novices, an admiration that ultimately bolsters his position as master. One child appears not to fit into the order of the institution: "He couldn't see into the distance, he didn't know how to lay colorful rows. He broke everything so easily. And yet, no child had such a desire and such pleasure in seeing and hearing" (*NS* 1:81). This child is pure sensuous drive, *physis* without *technē*. After having left the school one day in a state of depression, however, he returns transfigured, carrying an object, "an inconspicuous little stone of the most strange form" (*NS* 1:81). The teacher's reaction to this episode is to place this wonder of nature into one of his rows: he "lay this stone in an empty place, among other stones, at precisely the point where, like rays, many rows touched one another" (*NS* 1:81). The teacher takes the wondrous stone—which, according to the definition of the fantastic by Breitinger, encompasses that which precisely cannot be fit into an order—and places it into an order, thereby divesting the stone of the aesthetic glow of wonder. The moment is infused with an iconographical aura; the novice declares, "I will never forget these moments" (*NS* 1:81) during the laying of the stone.

From the later discussion between the natural objects, it becomes clear in retrospect that at this precise moment, the teacher is in the process of making "nature" into "natures," dividing up and ultimately denaturing that which he wishes to elevate as an ideal. What neither the reader nor the novice sees nor understands at this point is the pain, cruelty, and arbitrariness that are the ultimate effects of this act, which remain unknown to the first-person narrative perspective of the novice. Beauty itself, the self-organization of the world of phenomena, covers up the damage and trauma that the sovereign drive to order itself produces. For the rows that touch each other like rays of light—dispersed from some unified source—are later revealed as elements struggling for space and suffering under the yoke of oppression. Ultimately, the teacher's gesture—the very gesture used to iconographically bolster his own position as mediator—occupies an ambivalent space between, to recall Schiller's characterization of the religious relics at Sais, "an emblem of hidden wisdom" and "mystical posturing" (*NA* 17:384): an act whose very truth consists in the propagation of falsehood.

Chaotic Pedagogy

There is no core philosophy of nature in *The Novices of Sais*. All utterances are perspectival, and there is no one perspective that claims validity over the others. This holds just as true for the third-person narrator of the second half of the fragment as it does for the first-person narrator of the first half. Novalis, in one of the notes to the novel, asks "whether *one true unity* grounds the doctrine of nature" (*NS* 1:111), and in the fragment that exists, he seems to have answered this question in the negative.

Instead of a hegemonic doctrine of nature, the text establishes relations between discursive acts, producing an aura of aesthetic truth that wanders between orders of representation. And such is indeed Novalis's conception of philosophy, namely, as a practice that abolishes fixed points and makes the inert and static elements of a system into something that floats ("aus dem Ruhenden ein Schwebendes," *NS* 3:377–78). Philosophical relativism, as a set of relations between utterances and the proliferation of multiple, reflective acts, only becomes problematic if the goal of the speaker or the listener is to attain one absolute view that would supersede all others. Aside from the words uttered by the natural objects—which importantly take place outside of the realm of human eyes and ears, as if they were presenting the readers with a noumenal view of nature—there is one other narrative mode that does not cohere with the teacher's attempt to gather and order discursive and phenomenal appearances in the institutional setting at Sais: the fairy tale.[16]

A fellow student recounts the fairy tale of "Hyacinth and Rosenblüthchen" to the novice as a response to a moment of crisis and cognitive confusion, one provoked precisely by the plurality of voices and the lack of any one dominant voice:

> The novice hears with trepidation the voices crossing one another. Each seems to him to be right, and a strange confusion takes over his mind. Gradually the inner turmoil dissipates, and a spirit of peace [*Geist des Friedens*], whose arrival announces itself through new courage and a surveying serenity [*überschauende Heiterkeit*], seems to float up over the dark, crashing waves. (*NS* 1:91)

It is not merely the sheer number of voices that overwhelms the novice, but also the fact that each of them advances a claim to universal validity such that the novice cannot decide which is right.[17] It is the main speech genre of the institutional setting—discursive argumentation—that triggers the crisis of the novice. The voices, "crossing one another," create formal parallels to the natural objects placed against one other, each clamoring for their own space. However, these voices are motivated by the attempt to discover a unified, universal theory of nature: an attempt that, like all attempts to express identity, ends up multiplying difference.[18] The proliferation of differences in discursive multiplication triggers the despair of the novice, and it is the job of the fairy tale to resignify this multiplicity, to make it into something positive rather than a source of anxiety.

The organization of discourse as argumentation produces a pathological condition of excitation in the novice; the provocation of the crisis coincides with an overstimulation of the novice's cognitive capacities, an excess of information that the novice appears incapable of processing. The appearance of the "spirit of peace" coincides with the presence of a young companion who chides the novice for his loneliness and exhorts him to embrace love and the power of erotic being (which is, in fact, the power of the multiple, of the erotic *two* rather than that of the *one*). This is the voice that recounts the tale of Hyacinth and Rosenblüthchen.

The role of the "spirit of peace" that descends upon the novice is indicative of the differentiated mood of the fairy tale. Indeed, this spirit produces a temporal and a causal indeterminacy preventing any localization of the precise act that cures the novice; either the novice has already been cured before the fairy tale, or the fairy tale is instrumental in the cure itself. The fairy tale does not adhere to clear relations of cause and effect, seeming to arrive from beyond the physical-mechanical nexus of empirical phenomena. The spirit of peace as a point of transition between fairy tale and institution posits an indifference point whereby the two regions come into contact through the establishment of a permeable zone. This indifference point allows the fairy tale to function as an inversion of the order at the institution of Sais, a perturbation of the row of voices whose principle of operation is to put the world of phenomena—and language—into alignment. The fairy tale, which unfolds in accordance with the fantastic rather than the probable—according to an idea already present in Breitinger's *Critical Poetics*—represents precisely that which *disrupts* the row of voices, and indeed, overturns the act of setting something in a row, organizing and producing a coherent series.

Novalis remarks that a certain type of fairy tale can be useful: "There is a higher-order fairy tale that manifests itself when, without disavowing the spirit of the fairy tale, some *understanding* [Verstand]—(coherence, meaning—etc.) is applied. A fairy tale could perhaps even be *useful*" (*NS* 3:455). Novalis suggests that the fairy tale must have a meaning, at least interacting with the context that conditions its narration. In the case of Hyacinth and Rosenblüthchen, the coherence (*Zusammenhang*) or meaning (*Bedeutung*) emerges not just from the internal organization of the fairy tale itself, but in its relationship to the framing narrative. The fairy tale is constructed to fit the situation of the despairing novice, and thereby succeeds in creating a coherence, or hanging-together (*Zusammenhang*) between two different orders of narration. However, the relation between the two orders of narration, between the novice's experiences at Sais and the world of the fairy tale, is neither a parallelism nor an opposition. The two orders converge at some points and diverge at others.[19]

The narrative of Hyacinth and Rosenblüthchen nevertheless coincides with an act of regeneration, itself associated with alternative frameworks of temporal and spatial organization. Novalis remarks in a fragment linked to Hyacinth and Rosenblüthchen that the fairy tale makes reference to "the time of widespread anarchy—lawlessness—freedom—the *natural state of nature*—the time before the *world* (state)" (*NS* 3:280). If the teacher and the institution form the contours of a state in its most basic form—the organization of human life—then the narrative space of the fairy tale momentarily intrudes upon this order as the appearance of a space of pre-normative anarchy. The fairy tale makes reference to a time before the establishment of laws—ethical or moral laws, social contracts, or the laws separating phenomena from one another. And this time before laws or the drawing of boundaries—analogous to the cognitive act of feeling, which precedes and makes possible the order of reflection—announces itself in its differentiation *from* the given orders of the institution. The function of the fairy tale is therefore not simply to transport human beings back into the state of nature, but to draw on the anarchic reserve of the natural world in order to generate an alternative to the boundary-drawing, normalizing institutional order.

The fairy tale begins not with an idyllic vision of the human being at one with nature, but rather, with a space in which human life is already divided—cut off from others, not transparent to itself, within a world out of joint. The protagonist of the fairy tale, Hyacinth, is alienated from an already alien world, a figure both excessive and miraculous, "uncommonly wondrous [*über die Maaßen wunderlich*]" (*NS* 1:91). Those around him are happy, while he, miserable, thinks only of nothing; he appears first as an enigma, motivated by no reason at all, and indeed, stands under the sign of nothingness (*nichts*): "He was incessantly depressed for no reason at all [*um nichts und wieder nichts*]" (*NS* 1:91). His ironic incomprehension of his own situation, and indeed, his own being *as* incomprehensibility, or as the manifestation of a nothingness, already prefigures what he will eventually find, namely death or a zone of anarchic indifferentiation in the oneiric and phantasmagoric temple of Isis. This zone of indifferentiation is ultimately framed, however, not as an origin, but as a telos that affirms its own ontological instability (and hence, is not a "pure" telos). How Hyacinth ends unfolds the dynamic of how he is originally represented, as one who utters "sheer foolishness enough to make one laugh oneself to death [*zum Todtlachen*]" (*NS* 1:92).

Hyacinth is in love with Rosenblüthchen, who appears in her original state not as nature, but as artifice. Rosenblüthchen too seems to belong to the world of the dead, even causing those who look at her to wish to die: "[she] looked like wax, hair like gold silk, cherry-red lips, built like a little puppet, smoldering coal-black eyes. She was so lovely that whoever looked at her might have died" (*NS* 1:21). If everything around the two central figures appears animated and lively, these figures themselves nevertheless belong to a higher-order level of otherness, the others of a world that is already other, a latent death in the midst of life.

As Novalis suggests in his theoretical remarks on the fairy tale, the world of the fairy tale is, however, not wholly other. There exist points of contact between frame and interior, between the two fictional characters, Hyacinth and the novice. Hyacinth, like the novice, appears in a state of despair and melancholy; like the novice, he has taken leave of his family; like the novice, his ultimate desire is to seek out Isis. Hyacinth also becomes the audience of a fairy tale within the fairy tale, and ironically, the tale that purportedly has an effect on the novice is robbed of its healing power in the fairy tale itself: "The goose told fairy tales. . . . But [Hyacinth's] ill-humor and seriousness were stubborn" (*NS* 1:91–92). Only the erotic attraction to Rosenblüthchen and a poem told by a lizard eventually force him to laugh, giving him a brief respite from his unhealthy nothingness.

Yet another fall follows this brief regeneration: Hyacinth is drawn from his attachment to Rosenblüthchen by an old man who gives him "a little book . . . that no human being could read" (*NS* 1:93). Hyacinth, like the novice, who cannot decipher the validity of the voices that cross themselves before him, exists at this stage in a state of aporia, attracted to the book but unable to glean its sense. Although indecipherability is normally positively connotated by the Jena romantics, Hyacinth must burn the book before he can undertake his journey to Isis. The burning of the book both refuses and transfigures the logos, making possible an overcoming of one order of practice and its substitution for another.[20] It is the "strange woman" (*wunderliche Frau*) that convinces him to burn the book, and the "innumerable grandchildren" of Hyacinth and Rosenblüthchen at the end of the fairy tale owe their existence to this woman. The old woman, like the old man, initiates a turning point, a moment when one course of life turns to another: the overturning of the order of the book forms a point of entry into the order of eros, of Hyacinth's desire for Isis. The old woman clears the way that was blocked, and the fairy tale itself then moves forward by means of leaps, discontinuities, excitations, and perturbations.

In the fairy tale, Isis herself functions as a point of indifferentiation, a figure that unites Christian and pagan iconography, virginity and fertility; she is veiled virgin and mother of all things. The function of this figure of desire is to produce in Hyacinth an attraction to novelty and differentiation: a taking-leave of the law of the home, the *oiko-nomos*. The story he tells his parents is as follows:

> "I have to go away to foreign lands," he said, "the old, strange woman in the forest told me how I shall be healed, she threw the book in the fire and convinced me to go to you and ask for your blessings. Maybe I will come back soon, maybe never again. Give my greetings to Rosenblüthchen. I would have liked to speak to her, I have no idea what I'm doing, it's pushing me onward. . . . I would like to tell you

> where I'm going, but I myself do not know—to where the mother of things lives, the veiled virgin. It is for her that my mind burns [*Nach der ist mein Gemüt entzündet*]." (*NS* 1:93)

Hyacinth's desire is fueled by a condition in which his mind is inflamed, *entzündet*. His previous despondency, or a lack of stimulation that had as its core a gaping nothingness, has now been converted into an excess of stimulation. One may compare this state of mind with that of the person to whom the tale is directed, namely, the novice, whose mind is overexcited by a movement of dispersion, of multiple crossing voices. Hyacinth, on the other hand, undertakes a journey that, like the code of the beautiful itself, is a purposeless purposiveness; he is inflamed by a single object, by Isis, although this single object will also prove to be multiple and duplicitous when he lifts the veil of Isis only to discover his beloved Rosenblüthchen. His departure is therefore at the same time a return; he abandons his beloved object only to find her, almost accidentally, through this abandonment. The central narrative function of Isis is to produce an attraction away from the home and from the initial erotic object and toward that which is unfamiliar, indeterminate, and unknown. Isis, as mother of things, supplants Rosenblüthchen as the origin of desire. However, fidelity to the origin, to Isis, provokes an infidelity in the world of appearances that is unveiled *as* a higher-order fidelity; or rather, fidelity to the origin consists precisely in an affirmation of the duplicity of appearances, of the drive to differentiation.

In his journey to the goddess, Hyacinth organizes sense experience in ways that diverge from the practices of the institution at Sais.[21] Whereas the discursive space of the institution overwhelmingly focuses on *sound*, Hyacinth, before he reaches Isis, travels through every space of sense perception: on the journey, he enjoys "a fresh drink"; the dwelling of Isis lies among "palms and other exquisite plants"; he falls asleep "under heavenly scents"; he seeks Isis amidst rooms "full of strange objects with charming sounds [*reitzenden Klängen*] and in alternating chords"; after lifting the veil he hears "a distant music" (*NS* 1:95). When he enters the inner sanctum of the goddess and lifts the veil, however, what he sees is, at first, left unrepresented. The tale does not describe his *vision* of Rosenblüthchen, who has taken the place of the goddess Isis, but merely how upon lifting the veil, she "sank into his arms" (*NS* 1:95). In the fairy tale, every sensuous domain appears stimulated, and yet, when the moment of plenitude arrives, the narrator leaves the corresponding sensuous modality unfocalized; vision itself pauses, leaving in its place a lack or a gap. As in Schiller's ballad, the unrepresentable moment remains, to a certain extent, unrepresented. Some part of sense experience always remains unsatisfied, and must remain unsatisfied as a condition for generating and intensifying its own stimulation.

The fairy tale culminates not in an absolute vision, but in an indifferentiation of differences. The two possibilities that Hyacinth considers as possible end points of his journey—perhaps he will come back soon, perhaps never, as he says to his parents—are both true and false in the narrative of the tale. On one level, he is reunited with his family in the world of the dream. On another level—and this level remains unspoken and almost suppressed by the fairy tale itself—Hyacinth remains asleep in a desert oasis. He therefore both dies and lives immortally:

> His heart beat in infinite yearning, and the sweetest agitation permeated him in this dwelling of eternal seasons. Among the heavenly scents, he fell asleep, for only the dream can lead him into that which is most holy.
>
> . . . .
>
> He stood before the heavenly virgin, he then lifted the light, shining veil and Rosenblüthchen sank into his arms. Hyacinth lived afterwards for a long time with Rosenblüthchen among his happy parents and playmates, and innumerable grandchildren owed their lives to the old, strange woman for her advice and her fire; for at the time, people had as many children as they wanted. (*NS* 1:95)

Only the dream—as a cognitive state that invests the sensible world with its own unconscious logic—can lead Hyacinth to a sacred space where eternity and temporality unite in the "dwelling of the eternal seasons." The entry into this space produces a split in Hyacinth himself, a double narrative ontology of the fictional-real and the fictional-dream.[22] The fairy tale accomplishes the duality of destiny through denying—and yet, nevertheless maintaining as a possibility—the temporal and spatial logic of its own reality. If the dream has the final word in the realm of the fairy tale, it is only at the cost of suppressing the alternative operation of real space and time, which, lurking in the background, points not to the procreative excess of Hyacinth and Rosenblüthchen, but to the sleep of Hyacinth in an oasis far away from his loved ones, in all likelihood, a sleep that can only be conceived as death inasmuch as he never awakens. In the middle of the dream, the narrator hints at Hyacinth's death; immediately before he sees the goddess, "the final earthly flight vanished, as if consumed in the air" (*NS* 1:95). The ontology of the dream, however, both maintains and supersedes that of the real in the fairy tale, producing a chiasmatic effect: if both Hyacinth and Rosenblüthchen seem dead amidst the living, they remain alive in the state of death.[23]

The fairy tale produces a double ontology in another and perhaps more important sense inasmuch as it *duplicates* the very emblem of being, the fixed point of the institution and the central symbol of its authority, namely, the statue of Isis.[24] The statue itself—as Schiller notes, "I am all that is, that was, and that will be" (*NA* 17:385)—embodies the very fictionality of the absolute itself, a finite and physical presence that claims to represent the unrepresentable non-difference of being. At the moment in which the fairy tale announces the presence of Isis in its own dream space, the *real*—and yet fictive—statue, as sensuously manifest presence in Sais, must inhabit the same space as the speaking narrator and the listening student. The fairy tale makes from this *one* representation a double ontology, thereby revealing again the physiologically driven multiplication of difference as the product of a tautology. Indeed, the name of the goddess herself is nothing other than the law of duplicity, a mirroring of identical graphemes that produces a numeric and phonemic doubling: *Isis*.

Isis: the name of the goddess is a formula for the fictionality of identity. The fairy tale appears poetic—*Poësie ist Poësie*—inasmuch as it once again expands the space of the tautology, creating difference from those figures that seem to provide a point of entry into a zone of indifferentiation (or, in the language of the *Fichte Studies, Seyn*). Isis, through her (absent) inscription, represents precisely this discursive act: the *claim* to represent the absolute, everything that is, that was, and that will be. In the realm of philosophy, this claim ends in pathology, but in the world of fantasy, where such a claim produces differentiation, individuation, and expansion, it contributes to the health of the process of self-overcoming.

In the dream, in the fairy tale, Hyacinth succeeds in lifting the veil, and the goddess reveals herself not as *absolute Being*, but as a particular being: as Rosenblüthchen.[25] In a fragment, Novalis writes, "One person succeeded—he lifted the veil of the goddess at Saïs—/But what did he see? He saw—miracle of miracles—himself" (*NS* 1:110). In the fairy tale, this is indeed, in a rather remarkable sense, what happens. For although he sees Rosenblüthchen after lifting the veil, the erotic other or the "Not-I" in Fichtean terminology, in fact he sees her only in his own dream.[26] And yet, the dream does not thematize Rosenblüthchen as a mere reflection of Hyacinth. On the contrary, the veil reveals a self-produced differentiation at the core of being. This differentiation does not remain inarticulate, in a state of absolute or pure indifference, but is moved forward, or posited forth, by an erotic attraction culminating in substitution and reproduction: from Isis to Rosenblüthchen to grandchildren. The reproductive act, in a certain sense, remains merely imaginary; it misfires as *concrete* reproduction within the diegetic real of the fairy tale. Instead, reproduction, as the generation of uncountable grandchildren, becomes a property of the physiology of the imagination, a positing that undoes a previously posited order (taking leave of the law of the house) and one that celebrates a transgressive act that violates the symbol of power organizing the institution at Sais (lifting the veil of Isis). The lifting of the veil, and the logic of the dream—predicated, as it is, on taking leave of that which is one's own and entering into the domain of the foreign, which is in turn a domain of sensuous differentiation and indifferentiation—consists less in a positing of the I or even of the Not-I, but rather, in the bare activity of physiological being, a positing forth, a *Fortsetzen*, which is Novalis's definition of a drive.

Novalis's *The Novices of Sais* suggests that health requires an act of self-differentiation, the ability to generate narrative spaces that are *other* than those contained in the frame, or that which seeks to limit discursive acts to a circumscribed set of possibilities. The dream, far from becoming the apotheosis of the fairy tale or the space of "absolute union," performs an instance of narrative self-differentiation within the fairy tale. The fairy tale, as one might recall, is incapable of curing Hyacinth in the space of the fairy tale itself. Only another narrative form, one that differentiates itself from the space of the dominant discursive system from within this system, appears capable of curing the sick individual. What the fairy tale is to the novice, the dream is to Hyacinth.

Hence, what the "higher-order" fairy tale reveals is in fact the ability of language to produce self-differentiation from within seemingly coherent systems. The ability of discourse to interrupt the order of a framing narrative and differentiate itself from this frame is correlated to a movement deeper into imaginary ontologies, which in turn restore the sick individual to a state of health. Moreover, health is never *fully* restored, since Hyacinth partakes of a dual ontology that renders him both whole and fragmented, alive and dead. To be perfectly healthy would be to refuse the relativizing moment of individuation and differentiation that is the central function of illness. Indeed, the function of the fairy tale in the larger narrative heals or distracts the novice from his despair, but precisely by *differentiating* Hyacinth and the novice: Hyacinth lifts the veil of Isis, the novice only *desires* to do so. Even Isis, the emblem of being, appears differentiated and multiplied. Each narrative frame generates a disequilibrium with another narrative frame that both stimulates desire and yet denies ultimate fulfillment—in the form of a perfect synthesis between differentiated spheres—for its listener or its protagonist.

Unlike Schiller's novice, Hyacinth does not seek *truth* behind the veil; rather, it is the indeterminacy of desire itself—which is unfaithful and differential (shifting from Rosenblüthchen to Isis) as well as faithful and indifferential (shifting from Isis back to Rosenblüthchen)—that the fairy tale stages. Hyacinth's motivation remains unknown, as does his ultimate ontological status as living or dead. Concerning the drive to seek Isis, he knows only that "it" forces him somewhere (*es drängt mich fort, NS* 1:93), an impersonal construction denoting an unspecified power: an inarticulable feeling that pushes Hyacinth into continually differentiated spaces of narrative organization.

Hyacinth's turn away from the book—if anything the burning of the illegible book symbolizes if not a direct renunciation of knowledge, at the very least an overcoming or transformation of the desire to know—attunes him to difference, a mode of being that in turn contravenes the univocal authority of the discursive acts characteristic of the institutional life at Sais. The temple of Isis (like the fairy tale itself) makes possible the multiplication of differences by opening zones of indifferentiation, that is, permeable boundaries through which one particular identity can pass into another, or through which the fairy tale can mark itself as other to the institution of Sais while at the same time being a part of it. The fairy tale works not through placing particulars into distinct rows, but by facilitating passage between differences; at the end of the fairy tale, as part of Hyacinth's dream life, Hyacinth, Rosenblüthchen, and Isis are all "the same" figures at the end of the fairy tale, and yet, internally differentiated. One figure can embody both self and other at one and the same time.

Novalis remarks, "The world of the fairy tale is the thoroughly [opposed] world to the world of truth (history)—and precisely for this reason so *similar to it*—like the *chaos* of *consummated creation* [*das* Chaos *der* vollendeten Schöpfung]" (*NS* 3:280). The world of the fairy tale, by opposing itself to the fixed form of appearances of truth and of history, emerges nevertheless not as a space of pure difference, but participates in the dynamic that governs the sensible world. Only in this way can the fairy tale draw upon its own anarchic reserve, a matrix of possibilities, in order to provoke the world's own internal self-differentiation: a relativization of the normalizing forces of truth and history. The fairy tale represents an alternative model of relationality than that on display in the disciplinary contexts at Sais, which gravitates toward fixed points—the centripetal order of discourse that seeks a master—and the lockdown of differentiation in predetermined positions. Rather, the poetic dynamic of the fairy tale consists in following an indeterminate foreignness, a movement of departure outside of the house, a differentiation and disequilibrium in the attempt to find one's own identity—the duplicity of *a* = *a*—and seeing in this movement, from the first "a" to the second, the movement of life itself, a *Fortsetzen*.

We do not know if the Rosenblüthchen that falls into Hyacinth's arms is the same as or different from the one that he abandoned when he undertook his journey into foreign lands, to the veiled mother of all things, to Isis. This Rosenblüthchen is and is not identical with her representation, just like Hyacinth himself, as representation, oscillates in an ontological duplicity between the frame narrative in which he lies asleep and the dream narrative in which he fathers countless grandchildren. Hyacinth arrives in a zone situated between nothingness and plenitude; it is the space of poetry, *Poësie ist Poësie*, an operation wherein the disequilibrium of differences is seen as constitutive of life. Novalis calls the fairy tale "reasonable Chaos," "Chaos^2 or ∞" (*NS* 3:281)—not pure difference as such, but the drive to differentiation, which sees in the overcoming of imaginative and reflective orders the only infinity of which the human being is capable.

The End of Mastery

As a prelude to the fairy tale, the companion says to the despairing novice: "'You are sulking,' he called, 'you are on the wrong path. You won't make any great progress like that. The best thing everywhere is joyous mood [*Stimmung*]. . . . How can you sit there in solitude?'" (*NS* 1:91). After the fairy tale, we read the following: "The novices embraced and departed" (*NS* 1:95). The fairy tale produces a form of discourse other than the pedagogical rationality of the teacher and the agonistic discursivity of the institution. Its effect on the novice is therefore diametrically opposed to that of the discipline of the school. Whereas the teacher's institutional organization of nature is associated with pain and confusion, the confusion of the fairy tale is bound up with joy and erotic union. The act of telling the fairy tale itself produces a physical bond between the novices. It provides a stark contrast to the exercise of the senses preached by the teacher's strenuous askesis:

> The originally favorable disposition of such a natural mind must be supported and educated with incessant diligence from the beginning of youth, with solitude and silence—since talking is incompatible with the continual attentiveness demanded of such a person—with a childlike, humble nature and indefatigable patience. (*NS* 1:108)

Tireless diligence, loneliness, silence, exercise, attention, patience, and childish modesty—obedience—form the background of the teacher's pedagogical philosophy. The teacher is granted the final word in the fragment, adding to the deceptive aura of finality and authority accorded to his utterances. He finishes his discourse with a self-portrait as an instructor of nature:

> With the aid of these acquired insights [the person drawn to nature] will construct a system in order to use these means for every given individual, one based on experimentation, analysis and comparison, and will then begin his rewarding business. Only this sort of person can correctly be called a teacher of nature, since every other mere naturalist will only awaken the sense for nature arbitrarily and sympathetically, like an event of nature itself. (*NS* 1:108–9)

The teacher presents himself as the executive of a "rewarding business"—and the institution of Sais has established itself as such, bringing travelers to its doorsteps in search of the cult of knowledge. The system of experimentation, analysis, and comparison outlined by the teacher recalls the natural objects' complaints concerning humankind's arbitrary "division" of nature, thereby revealing itself as a practice that does not expose itself adequately to the overturning of its own order.

The teacher's characterization of his own gospel as a "rewarding business" (*belohnendes Geschäft*) similarly recalls Novalis's own criticism of *Wilhelm Meister*. In a letter to Tieck dated February 23, 1800, Novalis writes: "I see the great art with which poetry was destroyed through its own means in the *Meister* [*die Poësie durch sich selbst im Meister vernichtet wird*]—and while it fails in the background, the household order [*die Oeconomie*] amuses itself amicably with friends, standing safely on solid ground, and shrugs its shoulders while looking out to sea" (*NS* 4:323). The teacher never strays into such a crass dismissal of the attraction of art and nature, and many of his pronouncements cohere with statements that one can find in Novalis's notes and fragments. The teacher, like Goethe himself, is not a mere negative example. Such a view is simplistic and would invite refutation. However, he is problematic, in the sense of a figure that generates a task for thought: an incitement that demands its own overcoming. Novalis writes elsewhere, "One must exercise all of one's powers and regularly educate—the imagination—as well as the understanding [*Verstand*]—and the power of judgment, etc." (*NS* 2:257). The danger of the teacher's regime of aesthetic exercises lies in the prioritization of a specific way of training the senses and organizing the world that does not open itself to otherness, indeed, that does not *provoke* its own otherness. In this sense, one might very well say with Novalis—albeit with a different meaning: poetry annihilates itself in the Master (*die Poësie wird durch sich selbst im Meister vernichtet*).

In one of the paralipomena to *The Novices of Sais*, one may find the following note:

> Transformation of the Temple at Sais
> Appearance of Isis.
> Death of the teacher.
> Dreams in the temple.
> Workshop of *Archaeus*.
> Arrival of the Greek Gods.
> Induction into the secrets.
> Columns of Memnon.
> Journey to the Pyramid
> The child and his Johannes. The messiah of Nature. *New* Testament—and new nature—as *New Jerusalem*. (*NS* 1:111)

In this sketch, the fairy tale world bleeds into the frame narrative. Different ontologies and cultural spaces flow into one another, passing through zones of indifferentiation: Egypt and Greece, polytheism and monotheism, Old Testament and New Testament. After Isis appears in the temple, the teacher dies. Why or how this happens, one will never know. However, just as Hyacinth burns the book in the fairy tale, it seems that the novel produces its own movement of transcendence, one that requires overcoming the specific discipline of the senses represented by the teacher and his institution.

According to the natural objects, the problem of the institution appears in its refusal to let its own system of organization be perturbed by the inarticulable presence of feeling. It does not open itself to the negative of its own system; it does not allow itself to be touched by chaos. There is indeed a space for the disciplining and the exercise of the senses. The more important exercise, however, consists in a refusal of sovereignty and fixity: an openness to the disruption of any specific manner of organizing the world, above all one that posits itself as an absolute.

Conclusion to Part Two

✦

Incited Speech

Novalis, unlike Hölderlin, does not see poetry as an exercise that permits the human being to verify the order of nature and history, but rather, as the attempt to provoke disorder, to stimulate, and thereby to contribute to the process of continual overcoming governing the reproduction of life. Novalis's poetic works, however, cannot be reduced to this simple rule. They use their own formal organization and disorganization to carry the mind through different attractions and heterogeneous spaces, and one must follow the movements in order to enter into the dynamic transition between orders of reflection.

Novalis's *Fichte Studies* themselves follow and disrupt the path of Fichte's thought by summarizing, questioning, diverting, and contaminating philosophical movements with personal reflections, scientific discourses, and imaginative digressions. The operations described in the *Fichte Studies* enter into the texture of the aesthetic works, attracting language and consciousness to various orders of reflection and their perpetual inversion. The first movement of aesthetically inflected cognition for Novalis consists in the attempt to conceptualize absolute Being in its undifferentiated, perfect identity—an attempt that ends up generating a multiplicity of beings, signs, thoughts, and reflections. The central property of Being, as it appears within human thought and aesthetic action, is *generative*. The second movement consists in an inversion of orders, conceived initially as the attempt to approach *feeling*—an originary awareness before the self has been differentiated and has acquired the boundaries of subject and object—by inverting determinate reflective acts. The third movement displaces the concept of the absolute from one of undifferentiated Being to the absolute of a physiological drive. The drive-character of life propels the activity of the mind to perpetually invert its orders of representation and produce differences-in-identity and identities-through-difference that come into contact with one another across zones of indifferentiation. It is ultimately this absolute, whose central dynamic consists in the continual displacement of *figures*, *signs*, or *symbols* of the absolute itself, that stimulates and motivates aesthetic cognition to imaginative acts of self-overcoming.

In the works themselves, Novalis therefore does not attempt to *intuit* absolute Being, but rather, to make absolute Being appear as a void among the order of representations, as that which continually causes a shift in frameworks of organization. Being manifests itself as *perturbation*, and it manifests itself primarily through, as noted above, points of indifference. In the *Hymns to the Night*, death, the beloved, the womb constitute indifference points, points at which orders of organization are both inverted and remain in contact with the form of organization that they invert. In *The Novices of Sais*, the spirit of peace and the embrace of the students, each of which articulates transitions between frame and fairy tale, constitute such indifference points. The most important point of indifference in *The Novices of Sais* is Isis herself, the self-differentiating emblem of the indifferentiation of Being that permits the novice to move from institution to fairy tale to dream and back to the institution, establishing permeability between the realm of disciplinary authority and the disorganizing potentiality of fantasy.

The movements of the fairy tale produce, in contrast to the organization of the institution at Sais, *self-differentiation*; the univocity of reality is undermined by narrative consistencies and inconsistencies, shifting and relating ontological frames. The ontological destabilization of the fairy tale unfolds through exploring the cognitive possibilities (and impossibilities) of the dream. Readers are left in a state of oscillation, incapable of deciding between two incompatible narrative orders: whether the dream represents a mere imaginary space (and Hyacinth is, at the end of the fairy tale, asleep or dead) or a higher reality (and Hyacinth is, at the end of the fairy tale, immortal). The fictional status of the fairy tale perhaps allows the text to entertain both of these mutually exclusive possibilities at the same time.

If Hyacinth and Rosenblüthchen appear in one sense to attain the absolute, it never becomes manifest as an object for intuition, not even in the lifting of the veil of Sais. Rather, the absolute, as physiological stimulation, as movement and attraction, consists in a movement across indifference points between narrative frames—dream and fairy tale, fairy tale and Sais—and only in the penetration and interpenetration of these heterogeneous spheres does infinite imaginative reproducibility become possible: the "innumerable grandchildren" of the infinite mind (*NS* 1:95).

The ending of the fairy tale seems, when read in this light, to cohere with the generically similar happy ending characteristic of other fairy tales.[1] However, the ending of Hyacinth and Rosenblüthchen does not merely restore the order of bourgeois domesticity. Novalis takes this familiar topos, the generation of children and the sanctity of the domestic sphere, and transforms it into a sensuous manifestation of the physiological absolute, as an act of continual imaginative positing, of *Fortsetzen*. The very form of the ending coincides with a narrative bifurcation that ironizes the integrity of the idyllic familial setting. According to the logic of the fairy tale itself—and such is the act that Novalis calls "romanticizing the world"—the familiar topos is made unfamiliar, and the unfamiliar is made familiar. Hyacinth and Rosenblüthchen generate grandchildren that cannot be counted, that cannot therefore be brought into any determinate order—let alone into a stable or univocal ontology—and hence overturn any attempt to fit the particularity of the phenomenal world into predetermined formal schemas of organization.

The *Hymns to the Night* and *The Novices of Sais*, each in their own domain, generate unstable ontologies that permit the continual reversal of orders of reflection, a back-and-forth movement between life and death, dream and reality, self and other. Novalis induces a form of aesthetic cognition that produces a type of being whose very activity is to *not be a subject*, that is, not to fit into any prescribed or disciplinary patterns of thought, behavior, ways of associating and dissociating ideas and entities, or attempts to delineate the boundaries of the self. Being as perturbation, which multiplies differences and explores the possibility of their communion, constitutes the essential movement in poetic cognition. The movement within, between, and among mutually exclusive ontologies construes art as a mode of practice that eludes an ontology founded upon identity, transforming Being itself into configurations of motion and attraction.

Our concluding thoughts on Novalis will lead us to touch upon a work far too complex to have been considered in detail in this study, but one that nevertheless merits consideration. In *Heinrich von Ofterdingen*, the blue flower—like the "womb" in the *Hymns* or Isis in *The Novices of Sais*—appears on the scene of the novel as an *attractive* point of indifference that makes possible an inversion of different reflective orders. It originates not simply from the inner imagination of Heinrich, but "from the foreigner and his stories" (*NS* 1:195). The flower comes from outside the narrative before it has even become the core of the narrative; it comes into being through a figure whose first appearance is marked by an anterior exteriority; and moreover, the flower itself cannot even be localized in one narrative, but rather, moves among multiple narratives that appear in the story. The flower differentiates Heinrich but also links him to others through a counter-movement of indifferentiation. As a sensuous givenness, the absolute can never be present, and it only remains effective when it is absent, precisely when it comes from the outside, appearing to the world of the human as from an alien world. Its central metaphysical function is, if we return to a concept developed by Baumgarten, *heterocosmic*; it not only appears in worlds that are other, but makes possible individuals that do not precisely fit with the world into which they were born. Heinrich says, "I often feel an enchanting sense of well-being, and it is only when I don't have the flower present before me that I am overcome by a deep, inner drive: no one can, and no one will, understand this" (*NS* 1:195).

One cannot stress enough that art—the particular cognitive exercise that it performs—does not merely present its own absolute ideal as merely unrepresentable or incomprehensible. To reduce the romantic absolute to unrepresentable Being lures readers into divesting themselves of the need to interpret the work, to move in its rhythms and concepts, to produce something in its light, to cease to be wholly other to it: to *live* with the work, in the work. One might be misled to believe that interpreting a poem always *misses the point*, because after all, the meaning of the poem ultimately remains ineffable. However, in the world of poetry, it is quite the contrary: missing the point *is* the point. The ineffability of art cannot live in a world of silence. On the contrary, what Novalis shows is that this ineffability, if it is functioning correctly, *generates* fictions, *multiplies* differences, *produces* interpretations, *incites* speech. The sphere of art does not represent the unrepresentable as much as make present the unrepresentable as an intensity in the mind, a fever for thought, a contraction of the skin, a tension of the muscles, an organism in a state of maximum attraction.

Unrepresentability, if it plays a role at all in the aesthetic exercise, must, as perturbation, incite the desire for presentation and representation, it must bend itself to the play of points of indifference and inversions of orders. And for this process to function, one must be thoroughly inhabited *by* these orders—that is, there must be an *indifference point* between text and organism in the act of reading—so that the inversion of orders and the indifference points *in* the text are felt in experience itself. There is nothing so deadly for poetry than the idea that it represents the unrepresentable, and therefore, one no longer has to say anything about it. On the contrary: poetry intensifies the capacity of language to attract language to itself. It brings the body, the mind, the organism in its entirety along with it.

Part Three

✦

Pleasure, Immanence, Novelty

Chapter 7

✦

Pleasure, Utility, and Transcendental Saturation

The Contingent Coupling of Utility and Pleasure

The thought that a work of art might do nothing more than create pleasure, than add a quantum of energy to the amount of possible collective joy available to human experience, was a scandalous thought to a great number of philosophers, writers, and thinkers in the eighteenth century. The formula *prodesse et delectare*—to instruct and to delight—provided one of the central conceptual frameworks that permitted public intellectuals to construct, classify, comprehend, and justify the existence of the work of art. This paradigm of artistic productivity and receptivity, which coupled two heterogeneous codes to one another—the code of delight and the code of utility—arguably constituted the dominant aesthetic ideology before Karl Philipp Moritz and Immanuel Kant advocated the notion that artworks are autonomous, that they exhibit an inner purposiveness apart from any given social utility.

When Moritz, in 1785, wrote his "Essay on the Unity of the Fine Arts under the Concept of That Which Is Perfect in Itself" in the *Berlin Monthly* (*Berlinische Monatsschrift*), he was concerned to differentiate the notion of aesthetic autonomy—or works of art that exist only for their own sake and not for any other exterior purpose—from both pleasure and function.[1] If the work of art is still capable of generating pleasure, it does so only as a by-product of its own internal perfection: "When the artist says: if my work pleases or arouses pleasure, then I have reached my goal; then I say: it is exactly the opposite! Because you have attained your goal, that is why your work pleases."[2] A work that merely delights appears as an insufficient condition for any work's claim to being art.

The inadequacy of mere pleasure as an essential feature of the work of art is something that the aesthetics of autonomy shares with the doctrine of *prodesse et delectare* characteristic of Enlightenment poetics. According to the formula *prodesse et delectare*, supposedly derived from Horace, the work of art must delight *and* educate; the arousal of pleasure alone, without any other purpose, signals a deficit in any work of art. For Horace, *prodesse* and *delectare* ironically did not necessarily belong together as part of a normative poetic doctrine. In his words, "poets aim either to benefit, or to amuse, or to utter words at once both pleasing and helpful to life [*idonea vita*]."[3] Horace, who is here speaking more descriptively about what poets do and not normatively about what they ought to do, notes that they either want to educate, to delight, or to say both delightful and useful things at one and the same time. Even poets who seek only to produce pleasure in their readers still merit the name of poets. This possibility, although overwhelmingly in practice during the eighteenth century, was nevertheless the subject of a deep cultural divide, with philosophers and poets attempting to resignify the contingency of Horace's first either/or possibility (either delightful or useful or both at the same time) into the normatively necessary conjunction of utility and pleasure (delightful *and* useful).

When Horace speaks of poetry as a form of speech that may convey both pleasant things and things useful for life, or *idonea vitae*, he is in all likelihood referring to didactic poetry—such as Hesiod's *Works and Days* and Virgil's *Georgics*—that transmits practical knowledge. In other words, Horace's dictum may have had less to do with the moral improvement of the subject than with the use of poetic form to convey useful knowledge. Gottsched, in his *Critical Poetics*, to his credit, interprets Horace's *prodesse* from such a historical-generic point of view, saying "Only in the actual didactic poems [*Lehrgedichten*] must the issue be articulated so clearly to the reader, that the poet's intent was indeed actual instruction" (*VCD* 500). Although Gottsched approaches Horace's dictum as a legitimation of didactic poetry as a genre (*das Lehrgedicht*), his intellectual rival, Johann Georg Breitinger, magnifies and anthropologically expands the meanings of *prodesse* and *idonea vitae*.

Breitinger, in his *Critical Poetics* (1740), interprets the Horatian *prodesse* and *idonea vitae* as the attempt to harness pleasure in order to lead human beings to virtuous contentment. Aesthetic enjoyment becomes sublimated into the functionality of the work of art itself, namely, as the production of a normatively stable subject. After citing these lines from Horace's *De arte poetica*, Breitinger urges the reader to recall that "poetry, inasmuch as it is an art that consists in imitation [*Nachahmung*], necessarily must delight, and moreover, all arts and sciences that contribute to human happiness must be utilized [*müssen gebraucht werden*]" (*CD* 116–17). Breitinger, along with the vast majority of his contemporaries, inherits Aristotle's conception of poetry as an art of imitation. The act of reproducing the world—albeit, following Aristotle, as an art of probability (*Wahrscheinlichkeit*) rather than an immediate and direct representation of the real—produces various forms of delight: delight in the skill of the artist, delight in the probable verisimilitude between real and representation, and ultimately for Breitinger, delight in the wonder generated by the divergence of the work from one's given norms and forms of understanding.

Because imitation cannot be separated from pleasure, Breitinger sees a danger inherent in a form of poetic activity that does not mobilize the pleasure of imitation in order to direct it toward the useful:

> Nothing that is not at the same time useful cannot, in its correct and rational application [*in seinem rechten und vernünftigen Gebrauch*], cause delight. Therefore those people who separate the useful from the delightful open the gates to the most disgraceful abuse of the arts and make the arts into tools of base appetites. (*CD* 117)

The heart of Breitinger's argument unfolds in a self-referential structure that can be discerned within the tangled poetic codes of utility, pleasure, and mimesis. According to him, no "correct and rational application" of pleasure can be merely pleasurable; all such pleasure must always be useful. However, this repurposing of pleasure assumes its "correct and rational application," that is, by already subsuming pleasure to the law of utility. One may reformulate Breitinger's thought as a tautology: any correct and rational use of pleasure always produces a correct and rational use of pleasure.

The tautological structure of Breitinger's arguments obscures the inherent instability of the conjunction of pleasure and utility. Breitinger harmonizes pleasure in the receptive act with the norms governing the production of the work of art, that is, with rhetorical strategies of mimesis, thereby constructing an isomorphism between the act of production and reception: both normative spheres—the production of a work of art and its effect on the viewer—are organized according to how they represent possible worlds. Pleasure, conceptualized as the pleasure of mimesis, however, in no explicit way includes its "correct and rational application" as a logical or phenomenological prerequisite for its own actualization in the work of art. Locating pleasure in the process of representation even foregrounds the possibility of an incorrect and irrational application of pleasure, a possibility that Breitinger explicitly mentions. Those who separate the useful from the pleasurable (*welche das Nützliche von dem Ergetzlichen sondern*) abuse and pervert the formative dimension of the work of art.

Breitinger's poetics therefore reveal pleasure and utility as two heterogeneous codes, and it is precisely the contingent nature of these two codes' conjunction that sparks his anxiety about those who would seek to separate them. If mimesis and pleasure appear inextricably linked to one another, the only code capable of generating utility is the code of utility itself. Instead of proving an inherent link between pleasure and utility, Breitinger describes the operation of two parallel processes that may or may not coincide. The attempt to make pleasure productive—a project that justifies the existence of poetry according to Breitinger—appears, even in his own system, as a coupling of heterogeneous codes that can at any moment be uncoupled.

Utility for Breitinger describes that process by which the poet's own—supposedly stable and virtuous—character might be transferred onto that of his audience. Breitinger notes, "A poet is simultaneously human, citizen, and Christian [*ein Mensch, ein Bürger und Christ*]. . . . Therefore the delight that may be granted by poetic art must encourage the human being to the observation of natural, civic, and Christian duties" (*CD* 117). Breitinger reinterprets the Horatian *prodesse et delectare* as an anthropological imperative: poetry is used to create a certain type of subject rather than merely to convey information useful for life (*idonea vitae*). Nature, civil society, and Christianity become the three central codes around which the work of art orients itself as it seeks to fashion this ideal subject. In the work of art, pleasure—mimetic or otherwise—is anthropologically functionalized.

Breitinger links pleasure to what one may designate as transcendental organizing schemas. With the term "transcendental," I am referring not to the Kantian concept, namely, that by virtue of which knowledge is possible, but rather, to an *ontological* conception of the transcendental, as frameworks of intelligibility that lie outside of the work of art and its pleasure but nevertheless anchor this work of art in the norm-generating practices of its world, its creator, and its audience. Such schemas are "transcendental" not in the strictly philosophical sense of the word—as a priori conditions of possibility—but in the sense that these codes ground and make possible the work of art as a source of normativity for any given subject.

In the first half of the eighteenth century, the transcendental schemas of a work of art index the codes toward which the pleasure of the work must direct itself in order to produce a normatively ideal type of human being. As we have seen, utility and pleasure appear in fact as heterogeneous codes that may be coupled and uncoupled. For Breitinger, the conjunction of these codes in the work of art contributes to the project of producing an ideal human being, one whose ethical duties must be balanced between nature, civil society, and Christianity. Breitinger's poet—a human being, a civilian, and a Christian—repurposes the pleasure of the poetic instance to create an image in his own likeness: "a human, a citizen, and a Christian" (*CD* 117).

Breitinger's central philosophical maneuver, the binding of heterogeneous codes to one another in order to generate normatively stable human subjects, becomes an almost paradigmatic maneuver in eighteenth-century poetics and aesthetics. In Breitinger's case, the work of art, or rather, its imaginative space, is positioned at the edge of disorder or moral uncertainty, only to be pulled back from this edge by a second operational code (utility) that mitigates the risks of the first (mimetic pleasure).

The relation between pleasure and utility duplicates patterns of potential peril and concomitant stabilization visible in other aspects of Breitinger's conception of the work of art. In order to function, the work of art requires a charge of energy or an increase in attractive power that fascinates its viewers or readers and extracts them from the stultifying pull of habit. He attempts to harness this energy through his elevation of the fantastic, or *das Wunderbare*, to a generative poetic principle. At the same time, this energy is intensified by a tension in the relationship between the fantastic, *das Wunderbare*, and the probable, *das Wahrscheinliche*. It is the destabilizing dynamic of this relationship—which threatens to undermine the anchor of the work of art in mimesis—that he redresses by once again fusing these heterogeneous domains (*das Wunderbare* and *das Wahrscheinliche*) that he himself had set in a seeming opposition to one another.

The relation between the fantastic and the probable constructs a model of the work of art as a disjunctive synthesis of oppositional codes. One may see this model, one in which two contingent and heterogeneous codes enter into tension with one another only to ultimately be coupled together and brought into alignment with one another, in the relation both between pleasure and utility as well as between the fantastic and the probable. In these disjunctive syntheses, the moment of danger, the looming threat to the stability of the dynamic that undergirds the work of art and its proper reception, lies on the side of pleasure and the fantastic, respectively.

If pleasure is to utility what the fantastic is to the probable, one may draw upon Breitinger's poetics to reconceptualize pleasure as an expansive and disjunctive force that allows aesthetic patterns of existence to deviate from the organization of the world of appearances according to any given sociocultural transcendental schema of intelligibility.[4] The power of the work is maximized when it is simultaneously derivative and deviant, that is, when the inner tendencies of the work turn against themselves and become antagonistic principles, increasing the conflict between these principles until the work reaches a point of maximum tension and synthesizing this disjunction just before the mechanism breaks.

Novelty and the Possibility of Other Worlds

Breitinger's conception of the work of art owes many of its features to ideas developed by other thinkers of the eighteenth century, most notably Dubos, Addison, and even his rival in Leipzig, Johann Christoph Gottsched. Breitinger, along with his Swiss compatriot Johann Jakob Bodmer, articulate many of their ideas in polemics explicitly or implicitly directed against Gottsched, who had attempted to establish a center of literary activity in Leipzig and had crafted his system of normative poetics roughly in line with classical ideals and the French interpretation of these ideals. Bodmer and Breitinger's feud with Gottsched is perhaps most visible in their diametrically opposed evaluation of Milton's *Paradise Lost*. Whereas Bodmer and Breitinger defend and enthusiastically embrace Milton's epic, seeing in it a new form of religious poetry and imaginative stimulation, Gottsched, whose ideals were much more aligned with the French Enlightenment interpretation of the supernatural as mere superstition, finds Milton "much too tasteless for our times, and [he] could hardly be recited to children without their laughing" (*VCD* 238). Gottsched does not disavow the fantastic, but he construes it more as "uncommon" and "strange" than as that which is physically inconceivable: "Both good and evil can become fantastic [*wunderbar*], as long as it is not something common and quotidian, but rather something uncommon and strange" (*VCD* 244).

For Gottsched, the fantastic is most effective when it stimulates and provokes attentiveness in the representation of uncommon actions rather than in acts that contradict the apparent order of nature. He claims, "The fantastic [*Das Wunderbare*] must still always remain within the confines of nature and not climb too high" (*VCD* 246). It is precisely this hubris that Gottsched reproaches in Milton, who is, in a certain sense, the father of fantastic literature in the German tradition, whose "adventurous Song,/That with no middle flight intends to soar/Above th' *Aonian* Mount."[5] According to Gottsched, the fantastic, in order for it to be effective, must remain within the bounds of probability (*Wahrscheinlichkeit*). As such, he does not see anything inherent in the definition of the fantastic that necessarily enters into opposition with the probable.

For Bodmer and Breitinger, however, one can observe a tension in the attractive pulls of the opposing tendencies of the fantastic and the probable. Whereas Gottsched diminishes this potential conflict between the fantastic and the probable, Breitinger intensifies this conflict and seeks nevertheless to hold these two forces together in the same work of art. Although Breitinger also believes in the restraining counter-force of probability, his conception of poetry nevertheless calls upon the fantastic as a source of novelty characterized by its *difference* from one's own given normative frameworks of intelligibility. He defines novelty, *das Neue*, as follows:

> [Novelty] is everything that is considered rare, that because of time or place is much too distanced from our way of seeing, that does not cohere [*nicht übereinstimmet*] with our concepts, customs, and habits, and precisely through its foreign upward pull powerfully takes control over our senses, causing in us an attentive and pleasant admiration. (*CD* 124)

For Breitinger, novelty does not exist as a property of the work of art, but results from the interface between work and reader. There is no concern with the novelty of the work of art as such, no interest in that which differentiates the work from all those that came before it or that which makes it unique. Rather, novelty is located in the exercise of the mind. A repetitive and derivative work of art can, by the perceptual and mental generation of difference, achieve an intensification of novelty. Such a way of thinking requires that one detach oneself from the aesthetics of the genius and the corresponding reading technologies of the nineteenth century, where novelty will be displaced ontologically onto the artwork itself, and the main question will be: how is this work *unique* or how does this work *differentiate itself* from others in the same genre, rather than how does this work *introduce difference* into a horizon of experience as a perceptual given, as an imaginative process, as a form of practice?

Novelty as a value will similarly guide and underpin the rococo and Anacreontic poetry of the period, but not according to the definition of novelty as nineteenth-century critics would conceptualize it, that is, precisely not as novelty within art as an autonomous discourse. As objects capable of being differentiated from one another, as pure works of art, most Anacreontic and rococo poems are not novel. The vast majority of them are clearly repetitive and derivative. And yet, as works that introduce a gap between the poem's imaginative space and the cultural practices of intelligibility of its readership, each and every poem takes novelty as its goal, aiming to become a perpetual source of cognitive differentiation. Frauke Berndt characterizes the law of the Anacreontic poem as follows: "From one make two" (*Aus eins mach' zwei*).[6]

For Breitinger as well as for Gottsched, the enemy of the mind is *habit*, which constrains and deadens *aisthesis*: "The power of habit is so great, that it binds our senses, robs us of all sensation, and sinks us into an unthinking stupidity [*eine achtlose Dummheit*]" (*CD* 121). Following Dubos, Breitinger believes that the force of habit requires perturbation in order for new patterns to be generated. Poetry provides the model for a form of novelty that increases human attentiveness through difference.

The function of novelty in poetic beauty enters into an equally tense relationship with the other pillar of aesthetic pleasure, namely mimesis. The work of art therefore depends upon two seemingly oppositional but complementary sources of aesthetic value: the pleasure of difference and the pleasure of similarity. Breitinger nevertheless claims that novelty constitutes "the originary fount of all poetic beauty [*Urquelle aller poetischen Schönheit*]" (*CD* 136). He cites Longinus's dictum: that which is opposed to existing notions is nevertheless always wondrous (θαυμαστὸν δ' ὅμως ἀεὶ τὸ παράδοξον, *CD* 130). The work of art uses novelty in order to move outside its own epistemological and normative regularities, becoming, in the Greek sense of the word, paradoxical. The experience of novelty is measured by "different degrees and scales . . . according to the degree by which it diverges from our customs and distances itself [from us]" (*CD* 136). Although Breitinger never disavows the principle of mimetic pleasure as an integral feature of the work of art, its power derives not merely from a correspondence between what is represented and what is experienced, but also from the irreducible presence of difference in values and ways of organizing the world.

Novelty taken to the extreme turns into the fantastic, or *das Wunderbare*: "when the distance goes so far that a representation [*Vorstellung*] seems to stand opposed to the usual concepts [*Begriffen*] we have about the orderly course of things, it loses the name of the new, and receives in its stead the name of the fantastic" (*CD* 136). Breitinger's analysis of the fantastic, far from placing the work of art on a secure pedestal in which forms of representation and ethical norms that differ radically from those of its readers and viewers are suppressed, emphasizes the work of art's production of otherness. The fantastic work of art widens this region of differences, gradually diverging from the orders of organization in the normative structures implicit in any reading community. The manifest presence of other ways of organizing the world harnesses the energy generated in this process of differential perturbation in order to catapult the audience out of the clutches of a torpor-inducing habit.

For Breitinger, the work of art entails a cognitive process in which a representation (*Vorstellung*) may be detached from a concept (*Begriff*). Later in the eighteenth century, for both Baumgarten and Kant, one of the central features of aesthetic experience constitutes its inability to be exhausted by conceptual thought. In his attempt to grapple with the particularity of the experience of art, Breitinger, perhaps influenced by Leibniz, notes that art ultimately appears irreducible to any given conceptual schema. More importantly, he functionalizes this insight, seeing in the work of art a powerful form of mental representation (*Vorstellung*) in which a community may be productively alienated from its own normative frames of reference (*Begriffe*).[7]

The transition from the new to the fantastic does not mark a difference in degree, but in type. The fantastic work of art does not merely make visible a "different" way of organizing the world, but goes further, lingering in sensuous forms that are perceived not merely as different but as contradictory. The encounter with the self-evidence of an opposing reality principle exposes readers and viewers to the contingency of their own norms and frameworks of intelligibility. As opposed to the merely new (*das Neue*), the fantastic "divests itself of the appearance of truth and possibility [*Schein der Wahrheit und Möglichkeit*], and takes up the undeniable appearance of the false and the self-contradictory in itself. . . . In the new, the appearance of the true dominates over the false; in the fantastic, however, the appearance of the false takes precedence over the true" (*CD* 136). The work of art establishes a site in which conflicting tendencies and heterogeneous codes—the true and the false, the fantastic and the probable, the useful and the pleasurable—enter into agonistic relations with one another. Art makes visible and exaggerates the struggles that animate it and render it an object of attentiveness, although the ultimate victory of truth over falsehood, of plausibility over contradiction, of utility over pleasure, is never really called into question, even in the fantastic work: "The fantastic must always be grounded in real or possible truth" (*CD* 137). However, for the fantastic to be grounded in the probable merely intensifies the structure of opposition and conflict at the core of the work.

The mode of appearing [*Schein*] of the fantastic and the probable form two mutually exclusive paradigms of discursive organization, a tension that Breitinger foregrounds by framing one concept as the inversion of the other:

> I understand under the name of the fantastic everything that is of an image contradictory to others or excluded from a proposition assumed to be true; what appears to us at first glance to block the light of our usual concepts of the essence of things, of the forces, laws, and the course of nature, and all previously recognized truths, and seems to contest the validity of these things. (*CD* 136–37)

> I understand by the probable in poetry everything that is not an image contradictory to others nor excluded from a proposition supposed to be true, everything that seems to be arranged according to our concepts, everything that seems to cohere with our knowledge and the essence of things and the course of nature. (*CD* 139)

The fantastic forms an inverted mirror image of the probable; whereas the fantastic includes everything that is excluded from sentences held to be true, the probable consists in everything that is not excluded from propositions held to be true.[8] To claim that the fantastic is grounded in the probable is tantamount to claiming that works of art are only grounded upon the movement of a higher-order opposition between the fantastic and the probable: "the more the fantastic grows and increases in a representation [*Vorstellung*], the more the probable hides and diminishes itself" (*CD* 143). Breitinger establishes intensification as the central dynamic of the work of art: those works that increase the fantastic to a maximum while diminishing the probable to a minimum arouse and excite the greatest force of attraction.

The attractive potentiality of the work depends upon the continual maintenance of an oppositional relationship to the concepts that structure the experience of the audience. The work detaches itself from familiar modes of representation, but never completely: it must retain the thread of an attachment to the reader's frameworks of intelligibility in the form of *possible* worlds. The relation between the fantastic and the probable therefore takes the form of a disjunctive synthesis. At the same time, this disjunctive synthesis, by widening the gap between the fantastic and the probable, simultaneously expands the realm of the possible in order to permit the *appearance* of a complete negation of the laws that govern physical reality and ethical normativity.

In a move that duplicates the tenuous relation between utility and pleasure in works of art—where pleasure detached from utility opens up the possibility of works of art devoid of a moral center—Breitinger uses the concept of the fantastic in order to move the work of art closer to its dangerous other, namely, the nothingness of the bare lie. He says, "if ever the fantastic would be robbed of all truth, then the most crude liar would be the best poet, and poetry would be a pernicious art" (*CD* 137). The fantastic therefore only generates the appearance or the *Schein* of contradiction and falsehood, and it is the logic of appearances—which nevertheless consists in maintaining a zone of friction between truth and falsehood—that generates pleasure. *Schein* makes fantastic art possible, for it is only in the appearance of a seeming contradiction that the work of art can be endowed with a perturbational force that nevertheless does not merely remain within the horizon of the false as such. Poetic truth, *poetische Wahrheit*, as a particular form of the appearance of truth, therefore incorporates the appearance of falsehood into its own logic of presentation.[9] The fantastic, then, both makes possible and threatens this specific form of truth, *poetic* truth; the fantastic work that cannot be reintegrated into the world of plausibility produces a mere lie. The work of art's dynamic and oppositional structure only exists because it remains tethered to these two functions—mimesis and stimulation—each of which seems to move the tendencies of the work in opposed affective and interpretive directions. The pleasure generated from mimesis, which moves along the axis of resemblance, clashes with the pleasure generated from novelty, which moves along the axis of differentiation.

Another paradoxical consequence of Breitinger's conception of the work of art can be expressed as follows: perturbation, or the disruption of given schemas of organization, appears as one of the central mechanisms used to reproduce, stabilize, and maintain these very schemas. It is only through the stimulation of difference that the work of art generates a stable subject, or "a human, a citizen, and a Christian" (*CD* 117). For Breitinger, as for Baumgarten, the work of art ultimately consists in an askesis, that is, in a stimulation of attentiveness that produces certain types of human beings. However, the means of representation used by the work of art differ dramatically from its purported ends; according to Breitinger's understanding of the fantastic, works that *appear* inhuman, amoral, and non-Christian can nevertheless be used to generate human, moral, and Christian subjects. The fantastic mobilizes the irruption of the new and unexpected as a disruptive force in order to ultimately implement and stabilize the distinctions between true and false, right and wrong, noble and base. It is for this reason that Breitinger subordinates the disruption of the fantastic to the codes of the probable and the useful. The danger of a theory of art as a mere force of perturbation lies precisely in its inability to account for the supposed presence of truth in art or to explain how art could, without such a tethering to transcendental frameworks of intelligibility, remain even obliquely meaningful to those who experience it.

All works must therefore be intelligible according to the codes of the probable—which he defines as propositions capable of generating truth—and the useful, which he defines as a system of norms that produces a human being, a citizen, and a Christian. Breitinger's emphasis on the fantastic as a means of perturbation, one that both makes possible and threatens the production of poetic truth in certain works of art, overshadows the other enabling and threatening operational process in the work of art, namely the pleasure of the work itself. Just as the work of art holds two heterogeneous codes in a disjunctive synthesis in the movement of poetic truth, namely the fantastic and the probable, so too does the *ascetic* function of the work of art, its attempt to produce certain subjects, depend upon the synthesis of the potentially disjunctive codes of pleasure and utility. The relation between the fantastic and the probable is therefore analogous to that of the pleasurable and the useful. In both instances, the perturbation-value of the work must be harnessed by maintaining the integrity of both dyadic pairs (the fantastic/the probable and pleasure/utility). Breitinger says about the poet, "It is not enough that his representations be natural and fantastic, but they must also be honorable and useful" (*CD* 120). Just as the fantastic must be reintegrated into the probable, so too must the pleasurable—after tarrying with the prospect of its own uselessness—be ultimately redirected toward and reintegrated into the useful.

If the fantastic enters into tension with a reader's habitual concepts and produces a moment of seeming falsehood that in fact participates in the generation of truth, one might ask whether or not pleasure exhibits a similar structure: that of a conceptual perturbation and a restabilization. Earlier Breitinger had noted that those who separate the pleasurable and the useful in works of art make them into "tools of base desires" (*CD* 117). It would seem, then, that pleasure without utility is just as pernicious as fantasy without probability. The stimulation of pleasure generated in the play of mimetic similarity and difference (for it is indeed both difference from the real as well as the similarity to it that engenders pleasure) may, without an anchoring in the useful, produce an effect in the human being that perverts or diverges from the normative sphere of the *human*, the *citizen*, or the *Christian*.

Unlike Breitinger, Gottsched allows for the possibility of a morally unproductive poem, and his efforts at writing in the Anacreontic style may even represent examples of such didactic uselessness. However, he does not view this form of poetry as the highest sort of which the human being is capable: "Many [poems] are only made to jest and to amuse. . . . [The composers of such poems] receive only minor praise, because a very shallow mind and moderate wit is sufficient in order to realize a single poetic intention" (*VCD* 140). Despite his denigration of the mere joke or the minor amusement, he does not ontologize poetry in such a way as to deny such works the status of worthy poetic creations. In this critical difference between Gottsched and Breitinger, the ontological burden that Breitinger has placed on art and on poetry becomes apparent. For Breitinger, the fantastic opens up the potentiality for completely different ways of organizing the world. This understanding of poetry was not alien to Gottsched, but for Gottsched, the internal dynamics of poetry are not predicated upon the intensification of oppositional tension as they are for Breitinger.

If the fantastic constitutes the heart and soul of the poetic act for Breitinger, for Gottsched it is the fable that maximizes the potential of poetry as an imitation of nature: "The fable is principally the origin and soul of all of poetry" (*VCD* 202), he says. Gottsched uses the German *Fabel* as a translation of Aristotle's μυθοσ, or, in its most basic sense, the binding and unbinding of possible events. As for Breitinger, the fable is neither completely true nor completely false: "Indeed, every fable must have in itself something true and something false" (*VCD* 203). A fable is false inasmuch as it narrates a course of events that does not actually happen and does not belong to the world of actuality, and true inasmuch as it conveys "a moral lesson that certainly must be true" (*VCD* 203).

A fable, according to Gottsched, always remains in the modality of possibility and therefore never violates the order of nature; it is the "narrative of an event that did not really happen, but one that is under certain circumstances possible, in which a useful moral truth lies hidden. Philosophically, one might say, [the fable] is a piece from another world [*ein Stücke von einer andern Welt*]" (*VCD* 204). Gottsched's conception of the fable as a possible world, like the theory articulated by Breitinger, presupposes Leibniz's and Wolff's elaboration of the doctrine of possible worlds, and both agree with these thinkers that no possible world can violate the basic laws of reason or diverge from what Leibniz calls necessary truths. Breitinger differs from Gottsched inasmuch as he locates the power of poetry in a friction generated by an increasingly widening rift between the fantastic and the probable, in a disjunctive synthesis that is willfully held open. For Gottsched, the fable only functions when inscribed in the world of *plausibility*—in a *conjunctive* synthesis between the fantastic and the probable—whereas for Breitinger, the fantastic and the probable enter into direct conflict with one another, and it is only in this tension that poetic truth can exist alongside the increased intensity of imaginative stimulation.

If Gottsched believes that a poetic work, by its very definition, can never contradict the order of nature, the pleasure associated with poetic creation similarly never presents a threat to the given order. Breitinger's expansion of the capacity of the poem—indeed his very elaboration of the mechanism of poetic truth—presupposes the ability of the work of art to seem to contradict any given way of organizing phenomena. Just as the fantastic may enter into explicit contradiction with orders of probability, so too is the code of mimetic pleasure—as pure pleasure—in danger of undermining utility, or the particular didactic end of a specific work of art. However, Breitinger never develops a theory of the "pleasurable" as an increase in stimulation, as a disruptive force that would similarly shield cognition from the stultifying force of habit. To have developed such a theory of aesthetic pleasure—as opposed to the fantastic, for example—would have required thinking a form of pleasure that is not redirected to the normative structuring schemas (human, citizen, Christian) beyond its own plane of immanence.

The possibility of such a poetic act—using pleasure as perturbation and perturbation as pleasure—although left untheorized by Breitinger, operated as a latent dynamic of certain poetic practices in the eighteenth century. It is to these practices that we now turn, and we do so because these particular practices appear to be one of the most radical forms of an aesthetic *counter-askesis*. At the very point of emergence of aesthetic philosophy—when Baumgarten was developing the discipline of aesthetics in Halle—there appeared a form of poetry that, while exhibiting certain resonances with Baumgarten's positive reevaluation of sensuous cognition, developed an idiom whose exercise value implicitly challenges the normative subject of the aesthetic exercise in the eighteenth century.

From roughly 1740 to 1760, there emerged a popular way of writing and reading poetry that came to be known as the "Anacreontic" style, often considered a sub-genre of a larger cosmopolitan tradition that scholars call rococo poetry. It is nevertheless the case that not all examples of rococo poetry can be called Anacreontic, and not all Anacreontic poetry is written in the rococo style.[10] Poetry is considered "Anacreontic" inasmuch as it is self-consciously derived—whether through formal or thematic means—from what was, at the time, perceived to be the writings of the archaic Greek poet Anacreon. Most of the poems attributed to Anacreon at this time were in fact not written by Anacreon himself, but derived from an entire poetic tradition comprising the poems of Anacreon and his imitators, or the *Anacreontea*. Such poetry tends to gravitate toward lightness and pleasure, and it differentiates itself explicitly from epic or heroic poetry: it is poetry of love, wine, friendship, song, and playful irony.

Rococo and Anacreontic poems have been interpreted as coherent with certain strands of Enlightenment thought while entering into tension with other aspects of the Enlightenment (for example, moral improvement, normative universality, rational autonomy).[11] My purpose in this study is neither to examine this poetry in relationship to the early Enlightenment, to Pietism, or to any other intellectual movements or tendencies, nor to examine the stylistic features of rococo or Anacreontic poems and attempt to extract a unified "poetics" of the rococo and the Anacreontic. I presuppose the notion that the rococo, as with other literary styles, movements, and genres, cannot be reduced to rules that would unambiguously permit scholars to be able to decide which poems "belong" to the rococo style. And if one could articulate such rules, it is uncertain whether such a system of classification would add to or detract from the analysis and interpretation of individual poems and their attractive force.[12]

The interest of these poems for this study consists in the manner in which they imply an alternative poetics to those articulated by Breitinger or Gottsched, and along with this alternative poetics, an alternative exercise of sensuous cognition through the act of writing and reading poetry.[13] Rather than drawing on the fantastic as a source of tension generated by its contradiction with probable orders—or with order as such—rococo and Anacreontic eighteenth-century poetry draws on its own stylistic resources to perturb, undercut, and reorganize the anthropological, social, and religious-cultural codes intent upon producing virtuous human beings, citizens, and Christians.

Only a select number of poets and poems of this period adopt poetic practices that are not transcendentally saturated, that is, practices that do not attempt to form a human subject according to normalizing codes subtended by some metaphysical "beyond." To be "transcendentally saturated" in this sense means to direct the poetic utterance toward some particular norm or ideal that could be linked to a sociocultural, economic, or political imperative: be a human being, be a citizen, be morally virtuous, be an economically productive member of society. In opposition to such transcendentally saturated imperatives, one may see in certain Anacreontic and rococo poems a tendency toward de-transcendentalizing play, or a linguistic provocation that imaginatively detaches human beings from their own given conceptual patterns, perceptions, habits, and norms.[14] The latent poetics of these poems therefore function analogously to Breitinger's poetics of the fantastic.[15] Rather than entering into contradiction with orders of plausibility by pushing the limits of the imagination, however, they disorganize their own cultural patterns of normalization by submitting them to an unremitting aesthetics of play.

In one of his jocular songs, Gleim says: "Long live what exercises by joking!" (*Es lebe, was sich scherzend übt!, SL* 52). Although these poems rarely foreground the ascetic value of their own poetry—and Gleim's statement is thus the exception rather than the rule—they may nevertheless be read as a sort of aesthetic exercise, indeed, as a counter-model to the concept of the aesthetic exercise as articulated by Baumgarten. To read them as such entails an examination of the movements of the poems themselves: what are these poems asking the reader to perform cognitively, what sort of practice is the poem (as joke) seeking to instantiate in its particular imaginative and semiotic operations? Here, the exercise value of art does not produce a *happy aesthete*, or one whose acts of sensuous cognition facilitate an analogical relation between the perfection of the work and the perfection of the totality of existence. Instead of the happy aesthete, we encounter the Anacreontic poet, or one whose central practice consists in the systematic perturbation of precisely this metaphysical-analogical semiosis.

I do not claim that this exercise of disorganization constitutes an essential or defining characteristic of rococo poetry as such. It only exists as a potential attractor in some of its configurations. This poetic attractor is, however, strong enough and frequent enough to merit prolonged investigation. The two volumes of Gleim's *Attempt in Jocular Songs* (*Versuch in scherzhaften Liedern*)—here, "attempt" should be understood in the sense of the *essai*, that is, as exploration and experiment—stand as the apotheosis of Anacreontic aesthetics in this regard. The poems exhibiting this attraction to strategies of normative disorganization harness their own form of pleasure as a perturbational force—just as Breitinger drew upon the fantastic in order to disrupt the stultification and limitation of the mind through habit—but do not bend this form of pleasure to serve the formation of the civically virtuous, economically productive, or theologically pious human subject. At stake is more than a simple "divergence" from these norms or a poetic idiom that was infamously excoriated by cultural critics for being immoral. Rather, the precision and extent of this form of poetry's assault on a transcendentally saturated subject may be regarded as a systematic dismantling of normalizing structures of society rather than a simplistic immoralism.

At the same time, it must be stressed that Anacreontic poetry operates wholly on the level of the aesthetic imagination, making no pretension to *actually* producing an Anacreontic subject in reality. Gleim writes in the preface to the second volume of *Attempt in Jocular Songs*, "Never infer the moral principles of a poet from his writings. You will find yourself betrayed; because they only write in order to show their wit [*ihren Witz zu zeigen*], even if they should thereby cast suspicion on their virtue" (*SL* 71). The identity that Gleim adopts as an Anacreontic poet differs from his quotidian and everyday identity. However, if the poet writes merely to display his wit, his definition of wit (*Witz*) seems to admit, even embrace, the potential conflict with the dictates of virtue. This understanding of wit, as something that *might* operate according to laws other than those of virtue, constitutes neither a necessary nor a sufficient condition for Anacreontic poetry, but rather, is framed as a possibility for a particular aesthetic display. The imagined perturbation of social norms and codes of organization is not for that matter any less real. To effect change in the life of the mind nevertheless introduces novelty in the totality of contexts of being; thoughts, feelings, and affects, although invisible to the eye, do not exist in a domain outside of what may be considered reality.

As I briefly mentioned above, these particular poems were most popular at a moment in which aesthetics as a discipline was beginning to take hold of the poetic and philosophical imagination. Indeed, two of the most important Anacreontic poets, Gleim and Uz, were students of Baumgarten in Halle. Gleim pays ambivalent tribute to him—in a way that somewhat mitigates the ridicule and scorn normally reserved for the figure of the philosopher in this idiom—in the poem "To Herrn Professor A. G. Baumgarten in Frankfurth" in the second volume of *Attempt in Jocular Songs* (*SL* 94–95). Gleim, it seems, was continually misplacing, searching for, and finding Baumgarten's dissertation *Philosophical Meditations on Certain Matters Pertaining to Poems*, and at one point, after having relocated the text, he offered to send it to Uz.[16] Although in this treatise Baumgarten uses poetry to develop a science of sensuous knowledge, or "επιστημη αισθητικη,"[17] he nevertheless evaluates sensuous knowledge according to the Leibnizian notion of perfectibility, a paradigm of thought ultimately directed toward the affirmation of the divine origin of the world: "For just as we are part of the city of God, however many we happen to be, so are we obligated to attest to such things with songs that promote virtue and religion, just as has been done by all throughout the vicissitudes of the ages."[18]

Georg Friedrich Meier, who popularized Baumgarten's aesthetics and corresponded with the poets from Halle, writes in his treatise *On Jokes* (*Gedancken von Schertzen*), originally published in 1744 and revised in 1753 (it is this version, rewritten after the publication of Baumgarten's *Aesthetica*, to which this study refers), that "a joke is a form of sensuous knowledge and a display of this knowledge" (*GS* 24).[19] In this treatise, he approaches a subject matter notoriously resistant to philosophical thought through the discourse of philosophy, claiming that "the entire investigation of the rules of joking must be based on the principles of aesthetics" (*GS* 26). At the same time that Meier undertakes the—admittedly unamusing—attempt to uncover the "rules" of joking by using Baumgarten's aesthetics to analyze the joke as a literary genre, his attempt to take this genre as seriously as possible ends up endowing the joke with an aesthetic exercise value.

According to Meier, the perfect joke presupposes the coordination of sensuous cognitive capacities familiar from the rationalist tradition of thought, namely wit (*Witz*), or "the ability to recognize the coherence of things in a distinct manner" (*GS* 49), and acumen (*Scharfsinnigkeit*), or "the ability to recognize the distinctions or the differences of things" (*GS* 51). Jokes engage the capacity to differentiate and relate, thereby activating the sensuous faculties of readers. Although Meier submits the aesthetic exercise of the joke to the doctrine of perfectibility of the human senses, remaining ultimately a metaphysician and a rationalist, he nevertheless sees the joke as a form of infinite activity, an oscillation between identity and difference that never ends: "The joke must be a short embodiment of many movements of comparison [*ein kurtzer Inbegriff vieler Vergleichungsstücke*]. It must, so to speak, be similar to an abyss [*einem Abgrunde ähnlich*] in which one sees more and more the longer one peers into it" (*GS* 103).

The joke opens an abyss that initiates an endless play of similarities and differences. Meier does not seem to have lingered on the ramifications of his own insight, choosing instead to reintegrate the joke into the perfectibility of the human being, thereby nullifying its counter-ascetic attractivity. And for the most part, Anacreontic poets such as Gleim and Uz do not base their poetic practices on the doctrines of Meier or Baumgarten.[20]

And yet, Meier's interpretation of the joke as an aesthetic form that stimulates a cognitive interplay of identifications and differences does describe part of what constitutes the exercise value of Gleim's Anacreontic poems. Gleim's poetry does enact a play with sensuality, albeit one whose pleasure derives from the senses' capacity to confuse, subvert codes, and generate alterity rather than redirecting sensuous knowledge toward the hidden operation of a transcendent order—in other words, by intensifying and foregrounding the moment of *difference* or *novelty* between poetic acts and the way his own culture organizes phenomena and dictates norms. Steffen Martus, in his book on Friedrich von Hagedorn, notes: "The 'joke' exhibits many clear affinities to the category of the 'fantastic' by binding the sense of possibility in 'wit' [*Möglichkeitssinn des 'Witzes'*] with that of 'novelty.' "[21] This thought is of central importance in order to comprehend the primary aesthetic gesture motivating the Anacreontic poetry that will be the focus of this study.

It may appear in hindsight that German literature, even given the possible exception of Klopstock, did not develop aesthetic practices that would realize the potential of Breitinger's conception of the fantastic until later, namely in the works of romanticism (although, as we have seen, Novalis's poetic ontology cannot be reintegrated into any transcendent order based on the principle of sufficient reason).[22] And to be sure, Breitinger had intended to construe the fantastic as a practice underlying and generating great works of sublime grandeur, works such as Milton's *Paradise Lost*. At the precise time that Breitinger was writing, however, there existed poetic practices drawing upon the very power that lay at the origin of the fantastic, namely in the intensified disjunction between representations generated in art (*Vorstellungen*) and patterns of cultural intelligibility and normativity (*Begriffe*). Such works were there in plain sight, for everyone to see—not in the lofty products of the sublime imagination, but in the diminutive and seemingly insignificant form of the joke.

Chapter 8

The Depth of the Surface and Anacreontic Reflexivity

Unbounded Play

In order to bring to light the movement of transcendental de-saturation in rococo poetry in the eighteenth century, it is perhaps instructive to examine the contrast between works that imbue their own poetic acts with the residue of the world of the beyond and those that divest the world of its anchor in schemas of organization grounded in an implicit onto-theology. Perhaps nowhere can one better observe such a shift from transcendental resonance to semiotic immanence than in the attempt to conceptualize poetic activity through the category of play.[1]

The concept of play, in its everyday usage, implies a delimitation: here, one is playing; there, where play ends, the business of real life begins. Play, then, does not refer merely to unbridled imaginative or sensuous activity, the pleasure of freedom and the freedom of pleasure. The very category of play seems to produce something like an ontological difference: it would seem that play must be bounded, set apart from another realm that is *not* play, in order for it to exist *as* play. Since at least the seventeenth century, however, the notion of unbounded play, or a form of play that refuses to differentiate itself from other contexts of existence, appears as a possibility for thought.

In the mid-eighteenth century, a period in which one may observe the blossoming of the Anacreontic song as a poetic form in German-speaking lands, an unbounded form of play manifests itself that is adamant in its absolute refusal of seriousness and of transcendence. Although rococo and Anacreontic poetry was composed well into the nineteenth century and beyond, the development and popularity of this style as a culturally relevant form begins with Hagedorn and effectively ends with the Sturm und Drang movement. When Herder uses poetry as a genre to manifest and foment a specific national character and Goethe relegates Anacreon and Theocritus to lesser sources of inspiration by making Pindar the new muse of genius in "The Wanderer's Stormsong," the death knell of Anacreontic poetry and the rococo style has been sounded.

One might be tempted to regard the rococo form of aestheticizing activity—one that often seems to construe its own conceptions of poetic play as an integral part of life itself—as a precursor to philosophies of aesthetic autonomy and to the aesthetics of German romanticism. Both rococo and romanticism do share a common disdain of Enlightenment didacticism and a refusal to reduce poetry to its social-functional utility. However, rococo and Anacreontic play must be differentiated from the form of aesthetically autonomous play of romanticism. To be sure, like Schlegel's concept of "progressive universal poetry" (*KSA* 2:182), Anacreontic play foregrounds itself self-consciously *as* play, often universalizing itself across all contexts of life—at least from within its own poetic idiom—such that it does not seek to demarcate itself from a realm of non-play. The eighteenth-century Anacreontic style permits, even encourages, the erasure of an aesthetic ontological difference—the undoing of the demarcation: "here is play, there is life"—in its own poetic activity. However, unlike romanticism, this seeming totalization of aesthetic activity never becomes a total principle of life and remains unbound only within the bounds of its imaginative game; and more importantly, Anacreontic play never becomes tethered to some higher purpose or metaphysics, whether of Being or of Becoming.

Anacreontic or rococo play, as poetry written by mostly bourgeois authors for a mostly bourgeois audience, never manages to incorporate itself into a total practice of life such as the romantic poets intended to achieve. Schlegel's explicit goal was to "render life and society poetic" (*KSA* 2:182). The force of rococo and Anacreontic poetry lies less in its poeticization of life than in its perturbation and disruption of given patterns of life. It never attempts to become these very patterns, at least not in any other context than role-playing or self-stylization in epistolary correspondence.[2] The Anacreontic poets of Halle were functionaries and pastors, and their poetry is constantly at odds with the prose of their quotidian lives. Gleim writes in a letter to Uz, "I shall be a secretary once again, and indeed, for the old Prince of Dessau. I am supposed to leave tomorrow already to show myself before him and to see if he likes me. If I appear before him like an Anacreontic ode, I will certainly be sent away."[3] The Anacreontic ode is not held up as a universalizing form of activity, but rather, as one that distinguishes itself in its incompatibility with bureaucratic, economic, and bourgeois contexts of life. Gleim's Anacreontic poetry exists much more as a limited form of counter-practice, breathing vitality into the lives of those whose daily routines are incapable of generating a movement of joyous affirmation that itself would be at odds with the burdens of civic and economic duty: "The years of manhood bring cares and official duties, and age is lacking cheerfulness and fire. One must compose poems in youth, and sing them in old age."[4]

If Gleim posits a tension between bourgeois (or more accurately: bureaucratic) duties and Anacreontic play, romanticism would explore precisely this tension between the poetic and the prosaic life, albeit drawing on the counter-practical domain of the fantastic as the main source of oppositionality against the bourgeois world. E. T. A. Hoffmann, for example, explores the boundaries between these two realms in many of his narratives—for example in *The Golden Pot* and "The Sandman"—and hypothesizes about what an erasure or destabilization of such boundaries would entail. The Anacreontic code of pleasure, in a certain sense, represents an aesthetic modality that rivals the fantastic in its attempt to submit all areas of life to an imaginative overturning of zones of comfort. At the same time, essential differences remain in place. If Novalis seeks to continually overturn orders of representation and create permeability between the homogeneous domains of a heterogeneous cosmos, Gleim is more interested in maintaining the fundamental incompatibility of his own poetic activity and the world in which he lives, holding the disjunction between the real and the representation open rather than oscillating between shifting orders of representation.

In the later eighteenth century, at the cusp of romanticism, one may nevertheless observe an anxiety concerning the limits of play as an aesthetic and anthropological category that presupposes and demarcates its own boundaries. This anxiety is especially clear in the wake of Kantian aesthetics, or in the attempt to find some manner of constructing a human subject that would be fully capable of being both a moral agent and a sensuous being. In Schiller's *Letters on the Aesthetic Education of Man*, two central human drives, the sensuous drive and the form drive, which correspond respectively to the drive to be receptive to sensuously given matter and the drive to actively form this matter using the will, are unified in the play drive. Play reconciles the contingency and pleasure of sensuous perception with the necessity and morality of the autonomous human subject that gives itself the moral law. It is only through playing that the human being harmonizes the contradictory drives of duty and inclination, contingency and necessity, sensuality and rationality, thereby becoming a total human being: "the human being only plays when he or she is in the most full sense of the term a human being, and *a human being is only entirely human, when he or she plays*" (*NA* 20:359). Play, for Schiller, allows sensuous receptivity and moral activity to become cognitively compossible. Schiller moralizes aesthetic practices and aestheticizes moral practices, using play to make the given reality of appearances compatible with the universal and immutable laws of reason. The purpose of the play drive transcendentally saturates human cognition in the reconciliation of two contradictory modes of being: "to sublate time in time [*die Zeit in der Zeit aufzuheben*], to unify becoming with absolute being, change with identity" (*NA* 20:353). Play frames a project of transcendental askesis, a training of the human being that constructs this being in relation to an eternal and timeless realm. In play, one frees oneself from time in time and reconciles the world of changing appearances with the eternal moral law.

Schiller uses play not merely to harmonize inclination and duty through the freedom of imagination in aesthetic cognition, but also to demarcate the aesthetic realm from the ontology of everyday life. He notes, "the poet . . . steps outside of his bounds when he attributes existence to his work, and when he aims to achieve a certain existence with this work" (*NA* 20:401). For Schiller, play does not extend across all contexts of existence. Moreover, unlike rococo poetry, play does not appear *in* the aesthetic work itself as part of its formal structure, but merely as a drive that is excited in the reception of the work. The purely cognitive activation of the play drive, akin to an aesthetic *epochē*, does not apply itself to the external world; Schiller endows play with a preparatory function within projects of formation, making it into a power that attunes the human being to its own cognitive capacities and to the givenness of sensuous reality without actually claiming to constitute sensuous reality as such. Play must therefore always be distinguished from reality. For Schiller, the anxiety around play may be articulated as follows: the play drive must presuppose certain boundaries in the very act of suspending others.

Another author of the late eighteenth and early nineteenth century that calls into question the boundary between the imaginary and the real frames aesthetic play as a higher-order seriousness. In 1804, Jean Paul writes:

> Every play [*Spiel*] is an imitation of seriousness, every act of dreaming presupposes not only a past state of waking, but also a future one. The reason and the goal of a game is not a game; one plays not for play, but for seriousness. Every play is simply the gentle twilight that leads from one surmounted seriousness to a higher one [*von einem überwundenen Ernst zu seinem höhern führt*].[5]

Although one may question Jean Paul's own sincerity in this statement, it is nevertheless a legitimate and common maneuver in the early nineteenth century to direct play toward the fulfillment of a higher purpose. Jean Paul specifically underscores the state of waking after the dream as the telos of the dream itself; art then unfolds in a liminal or transitional state from one stage of life to a higher one. Even Schlegel, who regarded the aestheticization of life as an absolute postulate, mobilizes aesthetic play as the endless quest for an unattainable transcendence, which, although never fulfilled and never able to be fulfilled, sustains the creative production of new imaginative ventures. Such, indeed, is Schlegel's definition of Socratic irony: "In [Socratic irony], everything should be joke and everything serious, everything sincere, and everything deeply feigned. . . . [Irony] contains and excites a feeling of the inextinguishable conflict between the conditioned and the unconditioned [*Widerstreit des Bedingten und Unbedingten*]" (*KSA* 2:160). For Schlegel, irony is *transcendental*; it refers continually to some postulated concept of the absolute, even if this reference remains within the play of signifiers and never attains the status of any sort of transcendental signified. Irony nourishes itself from an oscillation between the positing of a higher purpose and the repeated annihilation of this higher purpose. It achieves its effect when language transfigures its own form and becomes infinite, triggering movements of continual progression and regression, creation and annihilation, tension and release.

Although one can find evidence for a concept of unbounded play in Anacreontic poetry, its signifying structure differs dramatically from the conceptions of unbounded play at work in romanticism as well as an unbounded conception of play, yet to be examined, that one may find in the seventeenth-century baroque mourning play (*Trauerspiel*). An important difference between the play of baroque tragedy and Anacreontic poetry may be articulated as follows: Anacreontic poetry displays a tendency toward *de-transcendentalizing* play. Anacreontic play differs from both early modern play and romantic play not merely in its explicit refusal of transcendence, but in its active struggle against regimes that attempt to bind immanence to transcendence. The world is flattened out, all anchoring or organizing discourses are stripped of their power: everything hovers (*alles schwebt*).[6] The very lightness of Anacreontic verse pushes it toward a radical transcendental detachment without ever lingering on the potentially nihilistic ramifications of a world unchained from its horizons that can be found, for example, in the works of Nietzsche.

That such a concept of play could be mobilized in order to relativize human existence and stress its inherent nothingness could already be seen in the seventeenth century. Daniel Caspar von Lohenstein, in the preface to *Sophonisbe*, articulates a conception of play that could be read as a manifesto of the baroque poetics of the mourning-play (*Trauerspiel*).[7] In the *Trauerspiel*, the play of the cosmos itself becomes a transcendental organizing structure that renders the human being a mere toy, degrading the human to a thing subject to forces beyond its control: "Whoever mixes joke and seriousness/And plays with wisdom/Has often attained the proper goal./Is not the work of nature itself a constant play?"[8] When Lohenstein speaks of the seriousness of play, it is from the perspective of one who experiences the play of nature as a necessary and inescapable process signaling the nullity of human agency. The seriousness of play should not be mistaken here with Jean Paul's "higher" seriousness or Schlegel's transcendental irony. Play, for the romantics, presupposes autonomy, both aesthetic autonomy as the independence of art from social utility and human autonomy as the imaginative capacity to produce one's own reality. For Lohenstein, the gravity of play signals precisely the heteronomy of the human subject, or the subject's continual capitulation to cosmological forces larger than itself.

In Lohenstein's *Sophonisbe*, play, as a natural force, culminates in the inevitability of mourning, and it is to this extent that his dedication appears to universalize the dynamics of the *Trauerspiel* as a mirror of the transcendent order of the world. In such a cosmos, everything plays with everything else, organizing the world of appearances, and yet guaranteeing the nothingness of these appearances. Play is infused with a relativizing force that applies itself mercilessly to all differentiated domains, both natural and historical, both in the order of creation and in the order of empire. Such play, while accounting for the differentiated nature of the cosmos, simultaneously collapses these differences within the framework of a transcendent schema that makes little distinction between the rise and fall of dynasties and the play of animals.[9] Indeed, in the preface, it is written: "The activity of wild animals is nothing but a play [*nichts nicht als ein Spiel*]."[10] The doubled negation, *nichts nicht als ein Spiel*, a formula that Lohenstein uses frequently, is no mere rhetorical flourish; the formula itself places a distinct emphasis on the nullity of appearances, a nullity that spreads across all forms of differentiation, from the lowest form of life to the dynastic claims of imperial powers.

The play of the play itself multiplies, organizes, and categorizes these appearances as forms of play, leading the differentiation of phenomena back to a schema of self-organization that does not leave room for meaningful human agency. Even reason, a seeming master faculty that is supposed to subdue the chaos of the affects and introduce order into the capriciousness of human action and political power, finds itself swallowed by and subordinated to the larger transcendence of play. Indeed, it is play itself that ultimately exercises the true power of sovereignty: as a cosmic principle, it continually changes form, dictating the rise and fall of states and empires, ultimately illuminating a power against which disobedience has no meaning. The air plays with the movement of the stars, the wind plays with waves that in turn play with ships, animals play with one another—even tragedy, or mourning in the form of a *Trauerspiel*, becomes part of the inevitable structure of play, displaying its power in the very form of the spectacle: "The first mourning-play [*Das erste Trauerspiel*]/That brings displeasure [to the child]/Is put on by the despised institution/Known as the school."[11] The mourning plays, which were used in schools as tools of education, become examples of the disciplinary structure inherent in the very play of nature from which it is impossible to escape. Performing the play and watching the play therefore confirm the domination of the order whose mastery it proclaims.

The wonder associated with the variegated world of appearances exhausts itself in the nothingness of the play of time: "Above all, the human being is a play of time [*Spiel der Zeit*]./Fortune plays with him, and he plays with everything."[12] Lohenstein uses his own play—the play of the play—to examine the macrocosmic domination of nature, which recursively governs the play's own aesthetic activity. The play launches the spectators into the transcendent operation of time, itself characterized as the mere play of nature, in turn imbuing human existence with the arbitrariness of its own whimsicality. Just as humans play with objects, so too does nature play with humans; all of nature becomes synonymous with play as the texture and fabric from which the human being is woven. The play of nature plunges the world of appearances into impermanence and reveals every culture as in some sense relative and in another sense necessary: just as the Roman empire rises and falls, so must every regime of worldly governance grow and decay, eternally supplanted by another regime that follows this same pattern. Time, as the force to which all appearances are ultimately subject, stands in for absolute power. To step out of time through death thus signals a capitulation to the laws of temporality rather than an escape from them. Martyrdom is a higher-order servitude that merely masquerades as freedom.

Although romantic play and baroque play, as expressed respectively in Schlegel's account of irony and Lohenstein's preface to *Sophonisbe*, appear diametrically opposed on one level, they cohere in what one might call their level of transcendental saturation. For both, play does not merely refer to the immanence of poetic activity, but refers to itself in order to point beyond itself: to the very structure of the logic governing appearances as such (Lohenstein) or to the structure of the human mind and its infinite attempt to imaginatively express the inexpressible (Schlegel). Lohenstein's play of transcendent nature, displaying and exercising its claim to universal domination, proclaims the ultimate nothingness of the sphere of the human. Schlegel uses the play of aesthetic experience in order to push the human being into an eternal process of self-overcoming. And although both develop unbounded concepts of play, they share with Schiller's aesthetic education the attempt to attach the very phenomenality of play to an operation indexing a beyond to the mere givenness of human sensuous experience.

Like both its baroque and romantic counterparts, and unlike Schiller's aesthetic education, Anacreontic play is unbounded. It makes its way through the totality of appearances from within its own rhetorical space. The singularity of Anacreontic play in its most radical manifestations consists in the fact that, unlike each of the other paradigms of play, it divests itself of every attraction to transcendence.

One may observe this process of transcendental de-saturation in a poem by Willamov entitled "The Life Story of the Human Being" ("Der menschliche Lebenslauf").[13] In this poem, play is universalized but not integrated into a higher-order structure of transcendence. The main movement of the poem is reductive rather than expansive, contracting the timeline of human existence to its most basic elements. Play appears not, as it was for Lohenstein, as the hidden mechanism of nature in which variegated and differentiated phenomena interact with and play with one another, a latent structure of self-organization, ultimately subjecting human activity to its impenetrable and capricious whims. The Anacreontic poem does not link the human being to the truth of its own nature; it does not push the human being toward an unattainable goal; and it does not push the human being toward a specific social calling or moral obligation. As a purely rhetorical gesture, Anacreontic play, as manifest in this poem, flattens out human experience, equating the actions of social figures associated with gravitas—the hero, the politician, and the poet—with the mere play of children:

The Life Story of the Human Being

The girl plays with dolls
And grooms and looks at her reflection;
The boy plays with drums
And chivalrously plays with sticks.

The youth plays with girls
And plays too with his book;
The beauty plays at her night-table
And plays with visitors.

With his beloved wife
The husband plays as well,
Whenever occasion decides
To grant him such a thing.

The hero plays with heads,
Entrusted to him by Mars;
The statesman with projects
That he founds upon hope.

The poet plays with rhymes,
And thus plays every man,
Until, interrupted by death,
He can play no more.

Der menschliche Lebenslauf

Das Mädchen spielt mit Puppen
Und putzt und spiegelt sich;
Der Knabe spielt mit Trommeln
Und Stöcken ritterlich.

Der Jüngling spielt mit Mädchen
Und spielt auch mit dem Buch;
Die Schöne spielt am Nachttisch
Und spielet mit Besuch.

Mit seiner lieben Gattin
Spielt auch der Ehemann,
Wenn anders das Geschicke
Es ihm gewähren kann.

Der Held spielt mit den Köpfen,
Die Mars ihm anvertraut;
Der Staatsmann mit Projekten
Die er auf Hoffnung baut.

Der Dichter spielt mit Reimen;
Und so spielt jedermann,
Bis er gestört vom Tode,
Nicht weiter spielen kann.[14]

The iambic trimeter with alternating feminine and masculine endings—which begins in the first strophe as a children's rhyme and culminates in the representation of its own poetic act in the last—provides the rhythmic framework in which an astonishing variety of human activities will be reduced to play. The socialization of the child, burgeoning adolescent sexuality, erotic life in marriage, the violent spoils of war, the administration of the state, and finally the composition of the poem itself are all drawn into a system of equivalences. The central linguistic operation at work in the poem consists in stripping these forms of existence of their weight and depth, thereby making human endeavor appear not futile, but merely inconsequential. The inconsequentiality of human activity is undertaken through the reduction of all spheres of life to the same basic notion of play. The central principle of the poem—as is the case with many rococo poems and Anacreontic odes—is repetition rather than forward motion. Play actualizes itself in this poem through a system of phonemic, semantic, and rhythmic equivalences that refuses to integrate violence, poetic achievement, or sociopolitical order into any teleological order greater than that of the child's game.

The structure of the poem establishes a reflexive isomorphism in the concept of play, the general emblem of which is the mirror with which the poem begins. The little girl looks in the mirror (*spiegelt sich*), and this gesture works its way into the organization of the poem itself. At every stage of life, the form of the girl or the boy will embody the mirror image of the previous stage. Moreover, this mirroring of stages of life is taken up in a resemblance at the level of the phoneme; the sonic concordance of "mirroring" and "playing" (*spiegeln* and *spielen*), mimesis and poiesis, is perhaps the central relation of the poem, the figure around which everything turns. Mirroring and playing become conjoined together as principles that structure the entire course of life.

The female and male figures exist as parts of a larger poetic game of mirroring inversions made manifest by alternating subjects from strophe to strophe. The feminine element, however, is gradually supplanted by masculinity, with the last figure in this chain of pas de deux appearing as death itself. This dance of life (which is also a dance of death) exhibits the following structure: "young girl/young boy," "boy/girl," "wife/husband" (this stanza technically only concerns the husband), "hero/politician," "poet/death." The image of the mirror, which is the image that pulls the poem together, gathers the stages of life as if they were caught up in a series of reflections. The instances of reflection in the rococo poem, however, points not to any reality beyond itself, but more intensively to its own rhetorical game. Words become caught in the play of mirrors, in their own patterns of appearing, with each image, each strophe reflecting the last, reproducing and repeating a previous pattern rather than creating a new reality or referring to another level of reality.

At the same time, repetition and reflection are enhanced by variation, the differentiation of which constitutes a necessary precondition for the aesthetic exercise of the joke: the play of similarities and differences that brings the mind to alternate between wit and acumen. The first two strophes mirror one another not by reproducing an identical structure, but by reversing this structure, by changing, as if in a row dance, the partners with which one plays.

The attraction of the rococo poem reproduces itself in a dynamic that could be properly termed autoerotic, although it is an eroticism that organizes the phenomenality of human life according to caricatures of gender roles. The young girl that begins the poem is fascinated by herself. However, the vanity of the little girl is not negatively inflected, as it conditions her own existence as an erotic object both for herself and for others. The girl who plays with dolls and mirrors will later play at sexual games at her "night-table," and the same woman will eventually play with her husband. The sexual game is connected to the act of reading as well; the "boy" plays with "girls" and "the book" (*Der Jüngling spielt mit Mädchen/Und spielt auch mit dem Buch*). Playing with books, especially for a boy who has just been playing with girls, perhaps references the eighteenth-century anxiety surrounding reading and masturbation.[15] The reader, too, after all, plays with a book in the act of reading, drawn into the mirror of the text as part of the human course of life (*der menschliche Lebenslauf*) that the text itself describes.

In this mirror of erotic attraction, the suppressed presence of death and violence nevertheless surfaces as an ineliminable part of human life. And yet, as the most profound and most potentially traumatizing elements of existence, they have become stripped of their consequentiality, of their trauma, by becoming a subject of play. The little boy who plays with sticks and drums as a child will later play with the morbid fruits of warfare: the human heads granted to him by the god of war. The poem describes the action of the hero, as a play with these macabre trophies, in much the same way that it describes the girl playing with her puppets. The poem desacralizes life itself, equating death not with pain or sin, but with an abrupt end to the game. In this idiom, play does not describe, as it did for Lohenstein, the process by which life becomes subject to a law beyond human control. In Lohenstein's *Sophonisbe*, death provides yet another piece of evidence for nature's indifferent game with humans, and as such indexes the transcendent nature of this differentiated indifference. In the context of the Anacreontic poem, however—because play is equated with life itself—death appears not as a part of the structure of play, but as its other and its disruption: *And thus plays every man,/Until, interrupted by death/He can play no more.* Death even breaks the pattern of the poem up until that point inasmuch as it is the only subject that appears as a passive agent. Indeed, death does not act at all. Instead of playing, it disrupts play; it indicates nothing but the cessation of the immanence of the game.

The semantic game also manifests itself in a play with a concept whose semantic field encompasses a multiplicity of meanings: *das Geschicke*, which, in this context, may be translated as chance, opportunity, or skill. In the eighteenth century, *das Geschicke* can also be invoked as a reference to fate, the overall plan of the cosmos that sends signals of its design to human beings as a reminder of their finitude and of their place in the transcendent order. In the case of "The Life Story of the Human Being," *das Geschicke* is downgraded to its "basic" definition, a definition summarized by Adelung as follows: "a continuous or repetitive sending, in everyday life; from the verb to send, *mittere*."[16] Here, it is quite simply the pretext for an erotic encounter, and that which potentially designates the order of the beyond is folded into the immanence of sexual desire: "With his beloved wife/The husband plays as well/Whenever occasion decides / To grant him such a thing."

Whereas thinkers in the middle of the eighteenth century such as Herder will tend to view the phenomenon of human life as a progressive unfolding and self-development, or what becomes codified later as *Bildung*, the Anacreontic poem revels in stasis, repetition, or even regression. The effectiveness of its rhetorical gesture depends upon a refusal of the very concept of maturation. The child in the rococo poem does not tend to symbolize anything beyond its own linguistic game: the child is neither the subject of an idealized dream, a lost world of innocence, nor an object of discipline that absorbs and validates the norms of the adult world. Let us examine a poem by Friedrich von Hagedorn:

The Child

When mama saw me
Kissing little Hans
She punished me.
And yet she laughed,
When papa today
Gave her a little peck.

Why does she always instruct me:
Girl! Do as I do?
Look what the others are like.
Now when I do such a thing,
She scolds me:
O me, poor child!

Sisters, tell me straight:
Because I'm small,
Am I not allowed a kiss?
You see: I'm already growing
Since the neighbor's son
Has started calling me his sweetheart.

Das Kind

Als mich die Mama
Hänschen küssen sah,
Strafte sie mich ab.
Doch sie lachte ja,
Als ihr der Papa
Heut' ein Mäulchen gab.

Warum lehrt sie mich:
Mädchen! mach's wie ich?
Sieh, was andre sind.
Nun ich solches thu'
Schmählt sie noch dazu:
Ach ich armes Kind!

Schwestern! sagt mir's fein:
Ist mir, weil ich klein,
Noch kein Kuß vergönnt?
Seht! Ich wachse schon,
Seit des Nachbars Sohn
Mich sein Schätzchen nennt.[17]

The title of the poem is "The Child" ("Das Kind"). Who is the subject of the poem? If it refers to the speaker, this "child" is (perhaps) already pregnant, telling her "sisters," a term often used to refer to female readership in the eighteenth century: "You see! I'm already growing/Since the neighbor's son/Has started calling me his sweetheart." "The child" refers therefore just as much to the child to come, the baby in the womb of the speaker, as it does to the speaker of the poem herself. This speaker is not as easily classifiable as it might seem, since she appears both as child and adult, as daughter and mother.

At the same time, the speaker does not understand the significance of the punishment that would signal her acceptance of the law of the family, the mark of her passage from childhood to maturity. The mother punishes the child for kissing Hänschen while at the same time demanding that the child take her, a woman who kisses the "father" of the family, as a model to be imitated. The speaker is punished precisely because she imitates her maternal model—and in more than one sense, because she herself ultimately becomes, perhaps unawares, a mother figure in the final lines of the poem. The poetic voice thereby implicitly calls into question mimesis as an anthropological or normalizing principle, since it is this very principle that she invokes in order to undermine the authority of the mother: if you kiss father, why can't I kiss Hänschen?

The lyrical voice, in a transitional state between childhood and adulthood, exists, if not in a utopian space, at least in a state of normative suspension: the mother has not yet imposed her law on the child, and the child has not yet internalized the codes of bourgeois morality. Her mimetic model unconsciously gravitates to the other function of motherhood, namely fertility and reproduction. When the child says she is "growing," she is in fact doing so literally rather than figuratively, physically rather than psychologically. The speaker of the poem places mind and body along separate tracks of development: the practice of the body belongs to that of an adult, whereas the practice of the mind—as it reveals itself in the poetic voice—belongs to that of a child.

The crux of the poem appears to lie in the problem of exemplarity: such is not merely the subject matter, but also the performance of the poem. The speaker appears either impossibly ignorant or cunningly naive: a subject who cannot be integrated into the codes governing household life and bourgeois morality, and hence, one who stubbornly refuses to become an example, either positive or negative. The reader does not even know if the "Hänschen" of the first strophe is identical to the "neighbor's son" of the last strophe, implying the possibility of a speaker with multiple erotic partners. The poem, however, inasmuch as it is focalized through a problematic subject, never makes an issue of the speaker's divergence from regimes of disciplinary normativity. The speaker's failure—or refusal—to submit reproductive and sexual instinct to the law of the mother generates a counter-model to the normative structure of the family.

So too in Willamov's poem does the language of the child overtake all exemplary forms of life, examining the heroism of the warrior and the skill of the politician from the perspective of pre-normative practices of life. Willamov's poem ends with a reflection on its own activity, presenting the reader with an act of poetry in which play becomes declared as its own law: "The poet plays with rhymes." The poet as subject or creator plays and writes that the poet plays and writes. All of the verses are grounded in this moment of self-reflexive folding in which mirroring and play become ontologically identical: to reflect on oneself (*sich spiegeln*) becomes to play oneself (*sich spielen*). Although the poem exhibits a *mise-en-abyme* structure typical for comic and ironic self-reflexivity, the poetic activity does not remain in a state of containment by referring only to its own activity, but spreads into other domains of life, most notably, the two roles that were seen as responsible for the fate of the nation: the national hero and the political administrator.

When the poem nears its end, it nevertheless gestures at a domain that eludes its own form of sensuous play: death. Whereas death was reintegrated into the cosmological order of appearances in Lohenstein's concept of play, death here appears as a perturbation coming from outside the system of play. Although death appears in the poem as rupture—a moment of transcendence that threatens to explode the game as a game—the poem itself nevertheless robs death of its power to relativize the poet's own aesthetic activity. Indeed, the poem performs and confirms its own metapoetic perspective (whereby life and play are collapsed into one another through the poetic act) by verifying that its own act of speech belongs to the realm of life: *the poet plays with rhymes*. The poetic voice has not yet been "disturbed" by death. Even poetry, to a certain extent, overcomes death as an intrusion of the beyond into human affairs—but not through a gesture of immortalization, but simply by reproducing the forms of its own sensuous activity. It succeeds in playing with the very phenomenon that would otherwise put an end to its own game.

It would nevertheless be too hasty to regard the poem as the expression of an ontology of play. Indeed, play refashions the narrative of the human life (*den menschlichen Lebenslauf*) not by locating play as the ground of being, but by reflecting on the very absurdity of the reduction of life to play. The *Lebenslauf* in the eighteenth century was a written story of one's life. The emphasis on play cannot therefore be taken literally as a normative injunction to bring one's life into line with the narrative of the poem. Rather, the normative content of the poem disappears and is supplanted by a perturbation of the imagination of the reader: the universalization of play jostles against the everyday notion of the way life *ought* to be (*der menschliche Lebenslauf*), thereby emptying out its own utility as a source of normative legitimacy or as an accurate description of life. Such forms of verse do not cease to demean—in the sense of making something less, and not more, meaningful—the human condition, and it is through the act of demeaning that their attractive power is consolidated.

Transcendentalizing the Senses: Brockes's *Earthly Delight in God*

I have been referring thus far to the "Anacreontic poem" and the "rococo poem" in a general sense. This designation is purely heuristic, and to a certain extent problematic. The poets of the eighteenth century were not necessarily conscious of writing in a style that later epochs designated—in a pejorative sense, no less—as "rococo." Furthermore, poets who at certain times wrote in the rococo style, at other times composed dithyrambs, moralistic songs, religious poetry, or war poetry. One should not expect from the rococo style a coherent program such as one finds in the Sturm und Drang or romanticism, but rather, attractions and tendencies that operate within specific generic forms. And yet, as I stated previously, it is not my intention to attempt to demarcate the characteristics of the rococo or Anacreontic style, and even less to evaluate whether or not it coheres with the tenets of the Enlightenment or anticipates forms of aesthetic autonomy in the later eighteenth century.

I am attempting to sketch the contours of a phenomenon that emerges contemporaneously with the development of aesthetics as a discipline. Aesthetics, as inaugurated by Baumgarten, does not merely reevaluate the importance of sensuous knowledge for the domain of epistemology, but suggests how art, as a set of practices, can produce a certain type of human being by engaging specific cognitive acts. The aesthetic sphere itself introduces a certain degree of uncertainty and indeterminacy in how the aesthete—as a type of subject—is formed; aesthetics is directed toward finite and fallible cognitive functions rather than to geometrical and mathematical certainty. The ability to stimulate sensuous cognition, to alter methods of associating phenomena, of binding and loosening, remembering and forgetting, opens up the possibility of an aesthetic refusal to cohere with a culture's predominant patterns of subject formation—as manifest in schools, religious institutions, political and administrative structures, the economic imperatives of civil society, and household and familial norms, to name a few such contexts.

The specific form of art that I am examining, a form that appears predominantly in rococo and Anacreontic texts, I have called de-transcendentalizing art. The aesthete confronted with the contingency of sense experience stands at a crossroads: does the aesthete lead the world of sensuous experience and its contingent forms into the fold of divine order or the comfort of geometrical and mathematical certainty, leading it upwards, so to speak, toward the realm of ideas, ideals, and perfectible forms—or does the aesthete tarry with the world of the senses, negate its potential sublimation into some higher realm of ideality, or refuse to make it cohere with the dictates of utility? In the eighteenth century, certain poets and poems make the movement in one direction, others in the other, and hybrid forms are everywhere visible. Aesthetic activity that advances a claim to art and yet refuses to let its own activity be integrated into a higher purpose other than the reproduction of its own pleasure—such is the phenomenon that is under investigation in the Anacreontic poetry presented here. Even the claim of aesthetic autonomy as advocated by Moritz and Kant fails this criterion, since autonomy itself *becomes* the higher purpose.

Outside of the rococo or Anacreontic modes in the mid-eighteenth century, however, language and sensuality lend themselves to operations of transcendentalization (for example, in the didactic or religious works of Brockes, Ramler, or Klopstock): the formal organization of sensuous matter is used as a sounding device for the presence—or absence—of that which operates beyond the immanence of sensuality as such. The aesthetic technique binding the sensuous and the transcendent through poetic language was refined in the early eighteenth century and arguably constituted the dominant aesthetic ideology in lyric poetry for centuries thereafter, uniting poets as disparate as Hölderlin, Novalis, Rilke, Benn, and Celan, among others.

As one of the first coherent and systematic attempts to transcendentalize the domain of pure sense experience stands Barthold Heinrich Brockes's *Earthly Delight in God*. The nineteenth-century critic Gervinus claimed that "Brockes *emancipated the senses*; this is his great service, without which there could never have been poesy in Germany."[18] In a relative sense, this verdict may be true. However, Brockes did not so much *emancipate* the senses as much as *bind* them to the operations of a mind seeking the immanence of the transcendent. His vast collection of poems, appearing in multiple volumes from 1721 to 1748, uses poetry to link perception, empirical inquiry, and immediate affect to a metaphysical realm beyond human experience. The very title of the collection indicates the synthesis of two potentially disparate domains—at least disparate according to a certain strand of Christian thought since Saint Augustine—namely that of the earthly and that of the divine. Brockes's text establishes a paradigm of poetic activity that, just as Baumgarten was attempting to rethink the possibilities of human experience in relationship to knowledge generated by the senses, links this aesthetic realm to the presence of the divine realm operating beyond the senses. The linking of the sensuous to the transcendent infuses the immanence of human experience with the redemptive presence of the beyond, tethering microcosm to macrocosm, sensuous contingency to rational order, poetic form to cosmic coherence.

Brockes's poetry aims to rehabilitate the earthly and the sensuous by translating the religious concept of epiphany into physiological and aesthetic terms. Pleasure becomes channeled into an awareness of divine presence, which in turn produces a poetics of stimulation. One of his poems is entitled "The Pleasure of Hearing in Spring That Stimulates Us to Devotion, in a Song-Poem" ("Die uns zur Andacht reitzende Vergnügung des Gehörs im Frühlinge, in einem Sing-Gedichte").[19] The poem begins as follows: "Everything speaks and sings/Everything tones and sounds/God, of your miraculous power!" (*Alles redet itzt und singet,/Alles tönet und erklinget,/Gott von Deiner Wunder-Macht!*).[20] Within the "everything" that speaks and sings is included its own utterance. The poem—much like Willamov's self-verification of rococo play in the act of writing—functions as an example that proves the rule of its own proposed ontology. Not only do these lines link the world of appearances to the divine order, but they embed poetry itself in the world of appearances to be examined, thus establishing and performing a binding procedure—from microscopic poetic utterance to the macrocosmic view of all things, from the world of earthly appearances to the presence of a transcendent (albeit not wholly transcendent) divine order.

The "Introduction" to Brockes's fourth volume of *Earthly Delight in God* (*Irdisches Vergnügen in Gott*, 1732) understands the poetic stimulation and training of the senses as a gateway into the mysterious operations of latent order.[21] It may be read as a poetic predecessor to Baumgarten's *Aesthetica*, a poetological and programmatic attempt to evaluate the specific claims and functions of sense perception. Brockes, like Baumgarten, endows the immersion in the world of the senses with a heightened exercise value. The senses bring the human subject outside of its limited environment and provide compelling experiential and rhetorical evidence that the world is indeed of divine origin.

For Brockes, human perception constitutes the surest route to an affirmation of existence as a whole. This pantheistically inflected empiricism differentiates Brockes from Baumgarten, whose system functions through an operation of analogy that construes sensuous knowledge in a state of formal equivalence with the rational ground of being.[22] Brockes's theodicy is neither guaranteed through reason alone nor through the structure of the human mind, neither through a doctrine of possible worlds nor through the principle of sufficient reason, as Leibniz would claim. The justification of existence must be undertaken through the bare evidence of the phenomenal world. Brockes's poetry constructs a cathedral of poems whose most lofty goal aims at an elaborate, empiricist theodicy.

If, as Plato says, philosophy begins in wonder, so too does poetry for Brockes. Poetic wonder designates not a state of intuitive attunement to ideality, but rather—in a conscious inversion of Plato—by a turn to the givenness of sense perception itself. The overturning of Plato is evident in Brockes's introductory poem to *Earthly Delight in God*, which returns to the primordial scene of the cave. Coming out of the cave entails not a movement into the realm of ideas, but a return to perception; as the human being steps into the light of day, he experiences the wonder of the world through a systematically organized and sensually overwhelming influx of perceptual experience:

> If someone somewhere in a cave,
> Where his mind and soul,
> Free of all fellow creatures and of reproach,
> Were raised in constant twilight;
> And if he were to enter suddenly into the world,
> Especially at the lovely time of Spring
> And were he to see then the splendor of the sun,
> Were he to see a green field full of flowers,
> . . .
> And were he to hear a twittering turmoil,
> . . .
> And were he to taste a thousand sweet fruits,
> . . .
> And were he to smell all sorts of flowers,
> . . .

And were he to feel the mild lukewarm airs,
And feel the wondrously sweet impulses
Of a love that has been sanctioned,
. . .
In what sort of strange way
Would he not be delighted by this!
Would he not count himself half blessed?
He would certainly remain with the impression
That he be, at the very least in paradise,
If not already in heaven.

And we, who have all of these gifts
Indisputably around us and in us,
We sense it less than a stone;
Indeed, for us these things instead
Make paradise almost into hell.
What could be the cause of this?

Wenn iemand irgendswo in einer Höhle,
Allwo desselben Sinn und Seele
Von aller Creatur und allem Vorwurff leer,
In steter Dämmerung erzogen wär;
Und trät' auf einmahl in die Welt,
Zumahl zur holden Frühlings-Zeit
Und sähe dann der Sonnen Herrlichkeit,
Und säh' ein grün beblühmtes Feld,
. . .
Und hört' ein zwitscherndes Getümmel,
. . .
Und schmeckte tausend süsse Früchte,
. . .
Und röche Bluhmen mancher Arten,
. . .
Und fühlte sanfte laue Lüfte,
Und fühlte Wunder-süsse Triebe
Von einer zugelaßnen Liebe
. . .
Auf welche sonderbare Weise
Würd' er sich nicht darob ergetzen!
Würd' er sich nicht halb selig schätzen?
Er bliebe gantz gewiß dabey,
Daß er, aufs mindst' im Paradeise,
Wo nicht schon gar im Himmel sey.

Und wir, die alle diese Gaben
Unstreitig um und an uns haben,
Empfindens minder als ein Stein;
Ja machen uns, an deren Stelle,
Das Paradeis fast selbst zur Hölle.
Was mag daran wohl Ursach seyn?[23]

The poem begins with a thought experiment, a hypothetical subject, anonymous, in a sensory deprivation chamber, who, much like the denizens of Plato's cave, lives in perpetual twilight. This twilight existence is put to an end by being born into the world of appearances. The poem in fact describes an autochthonous birth, a movement from womb to world, from senselessness to sensuality, and may be read as a poetic and epistemological meditation on the process of coming into being. The person in the cave, fetus-like, a blank slate free of sin and sociability—"Free of all fellow creatures and of reproach" (*Von aller Creatur und allem Vorwurf leer*)—leaves the womb and is confronted with the world of perception. All those who are thus born approach the world of sense experience with wonder. Brockes's poetry therefore does not sing the glory of the creation as much as the glory of perceiving the creation, reflecting on it, organizing it, generating knowledge about it.

Poetry represents a form of language that links the world of the appearances to the sacred origin of sensuous order through a long, immense, and systematic organization of the senses. Brockes's poetry, which predates Baumgarten's *Aesthetica*, nevertheless constitutes one of the first and most extensive attempts to use poetic language as an aesthetic exercise, a particular semiotic-pragmatic model that will have a long and rich history subject to numerous variations and inversions. In the nineteenth century, for example, Rimbaud, whose ostensible goal is to arrive at "the unknown" (*l'inconnu*), and whose poetic persona departs from the eighteenth-century idea of the poet as "a human, a citizen, a Christian," instead becoming "among all people the great invalid, the great criminal, the great accursed man" (*le grand malade, le grand criminel, le grand maudit*),[24] conceives of poetry as an inverted aesthetic exercise: "The poet makes himself into a *visionary* by means of a long, immense, and systematic *disorganization of all the senses*" (*Le poète se fait* voyant *par un long, immense et raisonné* dérèglement de tous les sens).[25] Rimbaud's disorganization of all the senses in order to approach the transcendent unknown appears precisely as an inverted image of Brockes's attempt to approach the divine *through* the senses.

After being born into perception, the human being confronts each specific sensory input as a circumscribed domain: seeing, hearing, tasting, smelling, feeling—each sensory realm appears discrete, grouped together, with the rare poetic enjambment. As the senses organize themselves poetically, they reveal their own visible-invisible order to those who in turn make their sensuous apparatus into a poetic and perceptual divining rod. Poetic form thereby not only mirrors, but *makes visible* the inherent organization of sensory experience. For Brockes, the central problem of the human being lies in the stubborn refusal to perceive the world; as subjects insensitive to the miracles around them, they pass rapidly into the realm of the inorganic, as if they were stones and hence frozen and dead: "And we, who have all these gifts/Indisputably around us and in us/Sense it less than a stone." Not to exercise oneself in the perception of the world—something that Brockes believes can be achieved through poetic taxonomy, or a revelation of the laws that constitute divine and natural order in poetry—turns the world into the opposite of what it in fact seems to be, namely, hell. The human being who refuses the call to train perception becomes an unwitting demonic agent and, perhaps inadvertently, inverts the order of the creation.

Brockes seeks to restore the primordial wonder of experience by returning human beings to their own perceptual and reflective capacities, thereby initiating a second birth. The paradigm of rebirth—the transformative conversion experience that gives a subject a new identity (a topos that is above all present in the Christian tradition)—is realized not through relating a subject to the figure of the mediator or the savior, but through establishing a more intensive relation to sense experience. For Brockes, the sacrality of mediation, as concentrated in a relation to a human-divine figure (e.g., Christ), has been sublimated into an attentiveness to sense experience as such, in turn grounded on a poetic phenomenology, a specific form of attunement that emerges from the act of poiesis.[26]

Such poetry initiates several steps in part of a poetic process of bringing human beings to a full experience of the immanence of the divine, one whose telos culminates in a transformation of perception through perception itself. Attention is concentrated and focalized on the givenness of experience. The manifold world of things appears at first highly differentiated, but each of these differences is led back to a divine source in which all things are unified, in which they all belong to the same world. However, the ground through which all things belong to the same world is largely invisible, although it is nevertheless to be sought in the logic of visible appearances. The divine origin therefore reveals itself—and hides itself—in a zone that is both latent and manifest, visible and invisible. In the poem "Play of Nature in the Different Movements of Different Animals" ("Spiel der Natur, in verschiedener Thiere verschiedener Bewegung"), the poet notes, "This miracle-work, as it unfortunately usually happens,/Everyone sees and does not see" (*Dieß Wunder-Werck, wie leider meist geschicht,/Sieht jedermann, und sieht es nicht*).[27]

In this poetic phenomenology, empirical knowledge is not simply a mere discursive form, but part of the process of mediation between the sensuous and the transcendent. The scientific experiment reshapes the unfolding of experience, or the way in which the order of appearances makes itself manifest to the senses; experimentation is not reducible to a positivistic discursive form, but becomes a conduit for the order of the sensible world: a phenomenology. Brockes invokes Boyle's air pump to show how air is necessary for fire and sound, thus using the scientific experiment to poetically bind the elemental and the sensuous:

> 7.
> . . .
> No fire at all could burn,
> Nothing at all could one hear,
> If the tender flow of our air
> Did not nourish both sound and blaze.
> 8.
> As one clearly sees,
> When one sucks out the air
> Through the air-pump,
> That the flames immediately
> Extinguish, disappear, and die.

> 7.
> . . .
> Gar kein Feuer könnte brennen,
> Nichts würd' einer hören können,
> Nährte nicht so Ton als Gluth
> Unsrer Lüfte zarte Fluth.
> 8.
> Wie man solches klärlich siehet,
> Wenn man sie von einem Ort
> Durch die Luft-Pump' auswärts ziehet
> Daß die Flammen alsofort
> Löschen, schwinden und vergehen.[28]

Brockes's invocation of Boyle's air pump in his aesthetic affirmation of divine order places his poetic utterance along an epistemological divide, crossing a fault line drawn in the seventeenth century between apodictic knowledge generated by natural philosophy and empirical, provisional experimentation.[29] The poet does not fetishize direct or immediate sense experience as the only pathway into transcendence, but admits artificially produced experiences through experimentation as part of his empirical theodicy. At the same time, his appreciation of air initiates a logical-transcendental feedback loop: air makes possible sense experience, which in turn makes possible the human being's affirmation of air as a revelatory medium. The mediation of the experiment in the production of experience harmonizes with the wonder of the poetic gaze, fusing two supposedly divergent epistemologies: onto-theological natural philosophy, and inductive empirical experimentation.

Brockes embraces an aesthetic, non-apodictic presentation of divine order as part of poiesis, admitting technologies of knowledge-production in the attempt to make the latent and invisible cosmic regularities available to human reason. The affirmation of experience as well as all forms of experiential mediation (through tools such as the microscope or the telescope) presupposes a universalism of scope that invokes a poetic as well as an empirical challenge. All technological advances can be converted into an overarching naturalism; as in Baumgarten's aesthetic exercise, the boundary between *technē* and *physis* is rendered permeable.

Brockes is an aesthete in the most totalizing sense of the term: no domain of sensuous experience is off limits, and everything must be perceptually aestheticized. In Brockes's poetic universe, no perception is prosaic, and nothing is resistant to becoming a poetic object: even the air pump, extracted from its knowledge-producing and discursive context—no longer in the domain of mere *technē*—can provoke the aesthetic experience of wonder.

In the process of tracing the manifold world of appearances back to a primordial divine origin, the poet develops a perceptual anthropology that separates the human from the animal and inorganic nature. Only the human being is capable of perceiving the order of the world, and hence only the human being can poetically organize, enumerate, and catalogue the works of the creation. In "Play of Nature in the Different Movements of Different Animals," the act of noticing forms both the privilege and the imperative of human consciousness:

> But if you want, o human being! to be human, and not a stone,
> During this miracle-play of creatures;
> Then let your heart, through the power of sight,
> Notice with devotion and pleasure
> The creator's wise power and order in his works.
> This is the duty of human beings;
> This alone it is that differentiates them from animals.

> Willst aber du, o Mensch! ein Mensch, und nicht ein Stein,
> Bey diesem Wunder-Spiel der Creaturen, seyn;
> So laß dein Hertz, durch das Gesicht,
> Des Schöpfers weise Macht und Ordnung in den Wercken,
> Mit Andacht und mit Lust, bemercken!
> Dieß ist der Menschen Pflicht;
> Dieß ist es bloß, was sie von Thieren unterscheidet.[30]

The vision of the play of the world is perceived through the capacity of sight (*das Gesicht*), a form of perception that functions as a conduit to human affect through its ability to *notice* (*bemercken*). Such noticing, which will become one of the faculties to be trained in Baumgarten's *exercitia aesthetica*, fuses pleasure with duty (*der Menschen Pflicht*), and ultimately leads the human being back to the inexplicable divine origin of all things. Vision gives rise to a poetic exercise designed to reveal to the human being its own position in the creation and its participation in an ever-changing world of creaturely movement. The poetic movement provokes a condensation of ancient and Christian spiritual exercises, producing equanimity in the soul amidst the turmoil of the world:

> And yet, he who rejoices in God, attends to his miracles,
> Observes in everything his favor and wise power,
> Sees in all places God all-present,
> Will, with tranquil soul and cheerful mind,
> When others are displeased, grumbling about everything,
>   complaining,
> He, in peaceful equanimity,
> Will bear whatever happens to him.

> Doch wer sich Gottes freut, auf Seine Wunder achtet,
> In allem Seine Huld und weise Macht betrachtet,
> An allen Orten Gott allgegenwärtig sieht!
> Wird, mit gelass'ner Seel' und fröhlichem Gemüth,
> Wenn andre mißvergnügt, um alles murrend, klagen,
> In friedlicher Gelassenheit,
> Was ihm begegnet, tragen.[31]

Brockes does not understand miracles as exceptions to the natural order; rather, the entire natural order itself becomes miraculous. This miracle, however, must be continually made present to the human mind. Pleasure, admiration, and attentiveness form the central cognitive capacities exercised by poetry that train the human being to act in the world with joy and composure. The discontent of the world is relegated to a single dissonant line, referring to other human beings who "displeased, grumbling about everything, complaining" (*Wenn andre mißvergnügt, um alles murrend, klagen*)—a thought that itself is suppressed and submerged by the aesthetic exercise that surrounds and contains it.

For Brockes, the immanence of the poetic word is transcendentally saturated—not in the sense that it refers to a god "outside" appearances, but rather, inasmuch as the sensuousness of the poetic word bears the traces of a divine power that, while triggered by the sheer materiality of sound, nevertheless exceeds this materiality:

Even the name alone seems
To be the epitome of springtime pleasure.
If someone says for example: the nightingale sang;
The mere sound of the words can almost
Have such an effect,
That in most listeners' eyes
A secret pleasure shows itself.

Es scheint so gar der Nam' allein
Ein Inbegriff des Frühlings-Lust zu seyn.
Wenn etwa jemand spricht: es sang die Nachtigall;
Kann fast des blossen Wortes Schall
So viel zu wircken taugen,
Daß in der meisten Hörer Augen
Sich ein geheim Vergnügen zeiget.[32]

The transcendentally saturated poetic word functions metonymically. Every singular noun not only embodies the whole cosmos of which it forms a part—leading to an order of particulars that somewhat resembles a sensuous, rather than a disembodied, monadology—but reveals this very metonymic contiguity as part of the coherence of divine totality. The "name alone," that is, the signifier as signifier, conjures the "epitome of springtime pleasure," bearing the phenomenon and the affect in its very immediacy. The "arbitrary" sign that is chosen freely by an intelligent being becomes simultaneously a "natural" sign, or one that, in the words of David Wellbery, expresses "the order and perfection of the natural world and make[s] this order transparent and knowable to man."[33] However, unlike monads, words are not windowless, for each provides a view onto something else, grounded as they are in the world of the senses and processes of perception. The word fuses cognitive channels of vision and sound—*in most listeners' eyes*—and this impetus gives rise to the secret pleasure, *ein geheim Vergnügen*, of the poetic word. At the same time, Brockes leaves open the possibility that some ("in der *meisten* Hörer Augen") will be excluded from this ultimately incommunicable pleasure, a pleasure that Brockes nevertheless makes public despite its hermetic nature. Even this aesthetic exercise cannot guarantee the shared perceptual affect of *all* listeners.

Inasmuch as poetry belongs to language, it produces a secret pleasure of the word, one whose mere sound excites a synesthetic imaginary process. The pleasure of the word, after all, appears before the *eyes* of most listeners (*der meisten Hörer Augen*), and hence not in the sound alone. The phrase that Brockes chooses to convey this message—"the nightingale sang" (*es sang die Nachtigall*)—appears striking both for its poetic and non-poetic qualities. On the syntactical level, the phrase appears ordinary. It belongs to an almost banal order of prosody. And yet, as with the air pump, every phrase, even the most clichéd and trite, can be amplified by poetic concentration. If the mere sound of the phrase, "es sang die Nachtigall," suffices to excite the imaginary processes of the listener, it is because this phrase in particular is functioning metonymically for the act of poetry itself, for the secret pleasure that the phrase itself supposedly realizes, not only in the act of its enunciation, but in the history of poetic language that conditions the act as a literary topos. Walther von der Vogelweide's poetic representation of the sound of the nightingale, *tandaradei*, represents only one of the many imitations of birdsong that have been invoked as secret pleasure. Whereas Walther invents a new poetic sound to conjure the nightingale, Brockes believes that pleasure can also be generated by mere designation, by the simple apparition of the signifier itself. And yet, he too uses the sonic properties of the signifier, rhyming *Nachtigall* with the precise word that leads auditory experience back to its most basic form, *Schall*. It is as if the poem desperately wants to prove that even the most prosodic and banal of phrases can be transformed into the epitome of poetic language through attentive pleasure to the secret and invisible harmony of the world made visible through sound. In a certain sense, Brockes's poetry, by claiming for poetry the capacity to aestheticize everything that appears, unintentionally undermines the very difference that makes possible his own discourse, namely, the distinction between poetic and non-poetic language.

Although the telos of Brockes's poetry consists in an aesthetically constructed theodicy, the fact that this theodicy occurs through the senses and is then endowed with an exercise value for the human subject reveals the second-order tenuousness and fragility that accompany any attempt to aesthetically or poetically justify existence. The "Introduction" to *Earthly Delight in God* ends not in an assertion but a question: if attentiveness to the phenomenal world gives us access to divine order, how does one explain the fact of suffering, or the fact that the world appears more aligned with hell than with heaven to some of those who live in it?

In Brockes's poetry, divine order is both presupposed and confirmed through the senses. The intensification of sensuous experience through poetry constitutes something like a poetic imperative, an injunction to continually make present the latent order within the givenness of phenomenality. Without the evidence of the senses and the poetically intensified concentration on this evidence and the pleasure that it brings, the human being encounters the possibility of its own nothingness. This fundamental doubt and the desire for order weave themselves into the texture of the poetry itself, into its formal organization and the order of its signification. For Brockes, the phenomenal world does not function merely allegorically, nor even symbolically; for it is not that light symbolizes God, but rather, light *is* God: "For without the shine and ray of this very light of the sun,/We are not only not beautiful; we are a real nothingness [*wir sind ein wircklich Nichts*]."[34] On the surface the poem makes a claim that sounds Augustinian: without divine mediation, human beings are dust and sin, a "real nothingness." However, more radically, the true nothingness appears in literal darkness: a space without the light of the sun, that is, without the evidence of the senses. To be mere mind, or a windowless monad, would plunge the human being into a form of unbearable insubstantiality. The supposedly allegorical sign, the shine and ray of the sun, is diverted away from its customary allegorical referent, God, and directed back toward its own phenomenality: light itself.

To gaze at and meditate upon the world of appearances through the evidence of the senses may ultimately lead to the conclusion that existence cannot be affirmed, that all ends in meaninglessness and futility. Schopenhauer would later make this idea into the cornerstone of an inversion of Baumgarten's metaphysics of aesthetics. If Brockes is to be believed, however, redemption—not in the world of the beyond, but in this world, as the possibility of concrete human happiness, of a heaven on earth—lies hidden in plain sight, invisibly hidden in the visibility of the world itself. He turns the poetic gaze to the processes of perception themselves, but this inward turn also rebounds onto the world of appearances, onto that which appears to the senses.

It may be instructive to compare Brockes's poetry with that of Hölderlin, for both conceptualize sensuous poetic form as a medium for a latent or hidden divine order. It is not merely that the divine has become problematic for Hölderlin—a question of the confounding relation between the multiple and the one, the Greeks and the Germans, polytheism and monotheism, law and eros, violence and order—whereas for Brockes, the link between the immanent and the transcendent was never called into question, neither theologically nor poetologically. There is indeed a chasm separating as well as a bridge linking Brockes's *Earthly Delight in God* to Hölderlin's later reflections on poetry as a specific form of mental and sensuous activity that provides human beings with the redemptive evidence of its own connection to the divine. For both poets, poetry appears as evidence, as the ground upon which an affirmation of life can succeed or fail. If the ground gives way beneath Hölderlin's feet, it is partially because poetic language has at this point been saddled with more than it can bear: with the entire weight of cosmic order and with the suffering of a world in a state of perpetual revolution, a world that is continually seeking, but never finding, its own ideal form.

Ultimately, Brockes and Hölderlin understand language and the poetic medium in ways that diverge dramatically; poetry thus possesses an utterly different exercise value for each of them. For Brockes, the word opens an immediate channel to divine order; indeed, the word is part of this order. The poet merely directs the attention of consciousness, through a movement of imaginative intensification, from the transparency of the sign to the organization of that which appears to the senses. For Hölderlin, language is anything but transparent. The form of poetic language does not open directly onto the divine, but stimulates practices of interpretation and cognition that would be adequate to the challenge of securing coherence in a world that seems to belie this very possibility. The poetic spirit can only grasp the divine, which is continually receding from the confusing realm of phenomena, when language proves capable of holding contradictory and multiple intensities and modalities in one and the same mental space: necessity, possibility, and reality; the Greek and the Christian gods (polytheism, monotheism, pantheism); or subject, object, and absolute identity of both. One need only compare Brockes's "The nightingale sang," which manifests directly and immediately the thing itself and the divine order that undergirds it, with Hölderlin's poem "Half of Life." In this poem, the world as it appears to the senses does not suffice to conjure up the redemptive presence of the divine—it is only in the movements activated by the poem in the mind of the reader, who may or may not provide the other half of life, that the divine may or may not become present:

> But oh, where shall I find
> When winter comes, the flowers, and where
> The sunshine
> And shade of the earth?
> The walls stand
> Speechless and cold, in the wind
> Weathercocks clatter.

> Weh mir, wo nehm' ich, wenn
> Es Winter ist, die Blumen, und wo
> Den Sonnenschein
> Und Schatten der Erde?
> Die Mauern stehn
> Sprachlos und kalt, im Winde
> Klirren die Fahnen. (*MA* 1:445)

In Hölderlin's later works, the poetic mind grappling with the sensory world—which does not always provide flowers, sunshine, shadows of the earth—appears incapable of guaranteeing the redemption that Brockes seems to think it can deliver. At the very least, Hölderlin's poetic act is held in a space of tension between necessity, possibility, and reality. Inasmuch as the poetic word directs its own exercise to the conditions of possibility of the appearance of the divine, Hölderlin's poetry, like that of Brockes, could be said to exist in a state of transcendental saturation; unlike Brockes's form of poetry, transcendental saturation does not *manifest* itself simply and immanently, but must be made present and unraveled in the density of poetic reception. In Hölderlin's case, especially in the later odes, the poet stumbles *because* of the evidence of the sensory world. For Hölderlin, the historical, factical, sensuous world is simultaneously a site of beauty and violence, and the contamination of the one domain with its other cannot be clearly disentangled. For Brockes, one need only open one's eyes and attend to that which is given. In Brockes's world, only a mind confined to its own twilight reality—cut off from the colors of the sky, the sounds of animals, the smells of spring, the sweet taste of fruit, and the feeling of love both spurned and reciprocated—exists truly in a state of nothingness.

The Alignment of Pleasure and Virtue

Brockes's turn toward the senses, toward poetry as an exercise that trains human beings to perceive the divine in earthly givenness, construes concentrated sensuous cognition as a sacred medium of revelation. Poetry turns its own language to the invisible anchor of all things, becoming a "secret" pleasure, *geheim Vergnügen*, or a pleasure that then is justified and elevated both by its own place in the divine order as well as by its ability to make this order manifest to the mind. Although Brockes's poetry has seemingly few affinities with the rococo style—characterized by smallness, irony, erotic delicacy, friendship, wine, and women—it nevertheless shares with this style a turn to the sensuous world.[35] From the perspective of the relationship of poetry to the dual codes of pleasure and utility, however, certain forms of rococo poetry function in ways diametrically opposed to the attempt to link the world of appearances to the invisible sphere that organizes these appearances.

If these examples of rococo poetry produce pleasure more from disorganization than from order, more from perturbation than from harmony, in de-transcendentalizing and de-sacralizing codes—religious, moral, political, and anthropological—that organize and make intelligible human life, not all such poems function in such a manner. On the contrary, the disorganizing and perturbational force of pleasure appears as a potentiality of this poetic idiom rather than a fixed or necessary structure of the rococo as a style. Moreover, differences and nuances in poetic tendencies emerge—even within the scope of the rococo's poetics of immanence—that vary between geographical locales, individual poets, and even individual poems within an anthology or by the same poet. The character of any given poem emerges from the specificity of the game being played rather than from any form of coherence with overarching principles of style.

One may therefore find numerous examples of poets who write in a recognizably "rococo" or Anacreontic style and yet align their poetic work with points of normative anchoring. The code of virtue, or *Tugend*, whether of heart or of mind, forms one such point of transcendental organization (transcendental not in the Kantian sense, but in the sense that the function of virtue as signifier affectively refers to a form of communal normativity in which each particular invocation of the concept exerts a claim to validity over practices of life, regardless of how vague and indeterminate this concept may ultimately be). The concept of virtue appears not only overwhelmingly in pan-European sentimental literature of the period—Richardson, Gellert, and then later, Rousseau, to name but a few authors—but also in pedagogical contexts in order to designate those values and practices that enable and facilitate integration into bourgeois society. Rousseau's *Emile* describes the careful control and discipline required to produce the sort of subject that could become a virtuous citizen in a republic. For women, both in Rousseau's *La nouvelle Heloïse* and Richardson's *Pamela*, virtue was often equated with the renunciation of sensual or self-interested desires for the sake of a higher value. The ideology of virtue in the eighteenth century often requires a distance from physical gratification, gravitating instead toward the glorification of acts of renunciation.

Johann Nikolaus Götz, although integrated in the Halle circle of poets along with Gleim and Uz, refers continually to the concept of virtue in his poems, thereby reconciling the Anacreontic form with the content of virtue familiar from other speech genres of his time, and above all from sentimental literature. His poetry repurposes Anacreontic pleasure to reinforce the standards of reason, the order of nature, and the ethics of virtue, and may therefore be considered more transcendentally saturated. In the *Attempt of a Citizen of Worms in Poems* (*Versuch eines Wormsers in Gedichten*, 1745), Götz describes his ideal poetic type as follows: "O how I would like to be like you, beloved bees!/Grand in inner spirit, although in body, small" (*O möcht ich, so wie ihr, geliebten Bienen, seyn!/An innerm Geiste gros, obwohl von Cörper klein*).[36] Götz invokes a standard topos of rococo poetry, namely the disproportionate amount of energy contained in the small form, here embodied by the bee, whose traditionally industrious nature has become transformed into a poetological figure for the rococo poem itself, which in turn has been folded into a relation between mind and body. The poet associates grandeur of mind (*an innerm Geiste gros*) with the smallness of the body, linking magnanimity of the soul to the diminutive character of the Anacreontic song (*von Cörper klein*).

His verse, "rich in art and order" (*an Kunst und Ordnung reich*),[37] fuses delight with utility. His poetic imperative thus aligns itself with the eighteenth-century coupling of *prodesse et delectare*: "Strive to delight the true friend through utility [*durch Nutzen zu ergötzen*]."[38] And finally, just as the poet wishes to be both small in body and large in spirit at the same time, so too do his poems intend to nourish both mind and body: "As nourishing for the spirit as they are sweet for the senses" (*So nahrhaft für den Geist, wie für die Sinnen süsse*).[39] In Götz's extended metaphor, bees produce honey through diligence, and the structure of the poem nourishes the spirit through the sweetness of aesthetic experience. The bourgeois order of productivity and the productivity of the poet are bound together, both being anchored in the diligence of the *homo faber*.

From Götz's poetry, it becomes apparent that the art of perturbation—that is, the association of artifice with the disorganization of shared normative codes—is not a universal characteristic of the rococo style. Götz's bee, perennial symbol of the small verse form, does not sting; rather, it becomes the emblem of bourgeois productivity. In contrast, one may find a different poetological model derived from the bee in a poem by Lessing:

The Bee

When Amor once, in the golden ages,
Ran across fields of flowers
Enamored with pastoral amusements,
A little bee all of a sudden,
Which was sleeping
On rose petals where it normally gathered honey,
Stung the tiny god of the gods.

Amor was made wiser by this sting.
The inexhaustible deceiver
Devised a new stratagem.
He eavesdropped among carnations and roses;
A girl came along to caress them;
He flew out as a bee, and stung.

Die Biene

Als Amor in den güldnen Zeiten
In schäferliche Lustbarkeiten
Verliebt, auf Blumenfeldern lief,
Da stach den kleinen Gott der Götter,
Ein Bienchen, das auf Rosenblätter,
Wo es sonst Honig holte, schlief.

Durch diesen Stich ward Amor klüger.
Der unerschöpfliche Betrüger
Sann einer neuen Kriegslist nach.
Er lauschte unter Nelk und Rosen;
Ein Mägdchen kam, sie liebzukosen;
Er floh als Bien heraus, und stach.[40]

The poem describes the genesis of its own rhetorical enunciation. Amor, the god of love, appears at first to embody a specific literary topos; he directs his erotic energy not to any specific object, but, as one "enamored with pastoral amusements," is immersed in his own generic figuration. The god is in love with the idyll as a genre. The bee, which otherwise produces honey, in this instance stings the god, producing a decisive alteration in Amor. Lessing's poem, unlike that of Götz, uses the bee to illustrate and activate a process of poetic perturbation and transference. The sting provokes a transformative shift in identity, and it is as if the very genre of the poem changes from the first strophe to the second, from naive pastoral idyll to strategic rococo deception. Amor, previously directed toward "pastoral amusements," becomes a seducer, one who hides and awaits his prey. Behind the idyll lurks the threat and the danger of the sting.

By the end of the poem, Amor adopts a new identity, flying and stinging "as a bee." What it means to "sting" for Amor—whether he stings the girl in order to make her fall in love with another or for his own pleasure—is left unsaid. However, the sting of the bee gives Amor a paradigm of action. An unexpected event catapults him from the open pastoral field (where everything is supposedly visible) to the rococo garden (where the threat of danger lies hidden). The bee is endowed with a specific poetic function: it lays bare the mechanism through which one identity is supplanted by another. The poem of the title, "The Bee," indicates this transference of identity: the first bee stings Amor, and Amor himself becomes a second bee. The title thus refers less to a concrete entity, and more to the process of becoming something different than what one once was, to the role that the Anacreontic poet himself adopts: the "as" (*floh als Bien*) makes Amor not merely *like* a bee, but poetically, functionally, and ontologically identical to a bee.

The poem implies that the girl will find herself similarly altered; for Amor, being stung initiates the transition from innocence to experience, from the pleasure of the shepherd to the strategy of the seducer, from bucolic transparency to Anacreontic dissimulation. Nature becomes artifice. And for those on the receiving end of the sting, the transformation will be similar. The poem itself, which describes the sting, becomes the sting, a deception whose purpose is to clothe itself in beauty, in roses and violets, and to exact a transformational and transferable alteration of erotic identity. The poem aims at a reproducible series of stings, from one bee and one sting to multiple bees with multiple stings. One bee generates a second, which then generates a third, and so on. Each of these transformations can then be subsumed under the category: "the bee." The title of the poem refers both to instigator and effect, origin and product: to the bee that stings, but also to the person that then becomes a bee, thereby embodying the metaphorical figuration of its own textual mechanism. In Lessing's hands, the rococo poem becomes catastrophic: a tiny and hidden disruption produces a disproportionately large and visible systemic change.

For Götz, on the other hand, the bee represents a paradigm of social integration and collective action, a worker producing honey for the spirit through industriousness. Bourgeois identity appears confirmed rather than overturned. It is here that one may locate decisive differences between different poets and isolate idiosyncratic forms of rococo productivity. Although both Götz and Gleim write Anacreontic verse in a rococo style, for example, a close examination of their respective rhetorical and aesthetic strategies reveal critical points of divergence. Gleim, in his *Attempt in Jocular Songs*, rarely speaks of virtue, and if virtue occasionally appears in the poems, it is almost immediately undercut. A poem that proposes to "build huts/So that virtue will live secure" (*SL* 7) ends with an address to his friend: "Go! You fetch your blond girl/I will go get the brown-haired Doris" (*Geh! Hole du dein blondes Mädchen,/Ich will die braune Doris holen, SL* 7).

This difference may be brought into relief in the poem "To Herrn Professor A. G. Baumgarten in Frankfurth." Here, Gleim's Anacreontic poet addresses the professor of philosophy, noting his ability to excite the love of virtue in those who listen to him:

> Behold, how that man who loves virtue,
> That man, when you [Baumgarten] were condemning vices,
> Suddenly swore: I will hate them.
> Through the powers of your doctrines,
> You forced him to the love of virtue.
> O how does one grant one's teachings
> Such powers, such blessings?
> Teacher, if you teach me this,
> O then I will force girls,
> So that they will suddenly have to swear
> To love me, if I love them.

> Sieh, wie der die Tugend liebet,
> Der, als du die Laster schaltest,
> Plötzlich schwur: ich will sie hassen.
> Durch die Kräfte deiner Lehren,
> Zwangst du ihn zur Tugendliebe.
> O wie schaft man seinen Lehren
> Solche Kräfte, solchen Seegen?
> Lehrer, wenn du mich es lehrest,
> O so will ich Mädchen zwingen,
> Daß sie plötzlich schweren müssen,
> Mich zu lieben, wenn ich liebe. (*SL* 95)

The Anacreontic poet finishes his poem not in admiration of the content of Baumgarten's doctrines, whether aesthetics or ethics, both of which supposedly contribute to virtue (*die Tugend*), but rather, Baumgarten's rhetorical and productive power, his ability to intensify the affective engagement of those who listen to him. The Anacreontic poet imitates the rhetorical gesture of the philosopher—and, through imitation (which is, in typical Anacreontic fashion, in fact a distortion rather than an imitation)—channels the power of speech toward seduction rather than virtue. If philosophy, since Plato, has attempted to subdue and sublimate erotic desire, turning it toward the abstract forms of the Idea, the Anacreontic poet redirects this sublimated energy back into his own poetic idiom. The Anacreontic poet *de-sublimates*, reappropriating the energy directed toward the Idea (or for Baumgarten: toward understanding sensuous cognition as an analogy of reason) in order to turn it back toward a purely sensuous object of desire.

One may also express the point of Gleim's poem as follows: the form of the aesthetic exercise (in Baumgarten's sense) remains, but its goals are inverted. Götz, on the other hand—and Uz would later join him in this regard with the publication of his "Essay on the Art of Always Being Happy" ("Versuch über die Kunst stets fröhlich zu seyn," 1760)—harmonizes the exercise value of the rococo poem with the claims of virtue. Let no one be seduced by the similarity of their poetic forms or the seeming intimacy of their correspondence: a deep cleft divides Götz from Gleim, a line of demarcation that on one side aligns poetry with aesthetic utility, and on the other, deploys poetry as aesthetic perturbation.

Götz's fixation on virtue appears as one move in a larger tendency to aggrandize the Anacreontic form through transcendental saturation. In 1746, Götz and Uz translate Anacreon's poetry, or rather, the *Anacreontea*, which most scholars falsely regarded as the work of Anacreon (although debate had already begun to cast doubt on the authenticity of this corpus). In a poem that serves as an introduction to the translation of Anacreon's works, Götz writes the following words set apart in bold and emphasized in quotation marks:

> "What the graces wrote,
> What Venus herself improved,
> Outlives all times
> And remains eternally worthy of being loved."

> "Was die Gratien geschrieben,
> Was Cythere selbst verbessert,
> Ueberlebet alle Zeiten,
> Und bleibt ewig liebenswürdig."[41]

For Götz, Anacreontic poetry establishes a link to a classical tradition in which the words of the poet are still divinely inspired, meriting a claim to immortality that would seem inappropriate for a cultural object posing as a bagatelle. Götz gives to his translation of Anacreon a divine origin story: he is merely mediating that which the Graces themselves have written and Aphrodite has improved.

Anacreontic poetry becomes an act of reception, a cultural translation, and, if Götz is to be believed, may be regarded as one of the most significant European classicisms of the eighteenth century. Contrary to the claims that would later be advanced by the aesthetics of originality and genius, the derivative nature of Anacreontic verse assures its immortality: it is not the unique and individualized cultural object itself that remains eternal, but rather, the values at the core of this object, the grace and beauty forever worthy of admiration. Götz (in contrast to Hagedorn, as we shall see) explicitly states that all poetic objects strive for a realm of existence beyond themselves, for an immortality of tradition that is assured by a universality of values across cultural contexts. The poetic object is not an idiosyncratic event, but the sedimentation of a tradition that transcends its own individual sensuous manifestation while modifying itself to fit its particular sociocultural moment.[42]

Götz's attempt to use Anacreontic poetry as a mode of harmonizing pleasure with virtue appears in its most concentrated form in his 1774 poem "Pleasure" ("Das Vergnügen"). Approximately thirty years after the initial fervor for Anacreontic poetry in Halle, Götz continues to saturate the small, derivative form with the presence of disembodied forces that organize nature and human society. For Götz, the Anacreontic poem renders visible a cosmic pleasure principle, transplanting rhetorical strategies familiar from Brockes's *Earthly Delight in God* into the more diminutive rococo form. The poem begins with the following lines:

That which moves the whole world,
And also moves in little worms;
That alone which, good and mild,
Fills our whole soul:
Pleasure alone follows
Gentle drives of nature.

Das die weite Welt bewegt,
Und sich auch in Würmgen regt;
Das alleine gut und mild
Unsre ganze Seele füllt:
Das Vergnügen folget nur
Sanften Trieben der Natur.[43]

Much like Lohenstein's concept of play, pleasure universalizes itself as an expansive drive permeating nature; it manifests itself even in the lowliest of creatures, the worms (*Würmgen*), rendered doubly small through the invocation of the diminutive form. Pleasure can equally be found in the most lofty and elevated of cosmic appearances, in the human soul (*Das . . . unsre ganze Seele füllt*), in turn linking the worm to the soul, and all human beings to one another.

The connection between the worm and the human—which links the two without establishing a necessary hierarchy of beings—does not reveal any fear of degradation on the part of the human being. Unlike Lohenstein's concept of play, pleasure as a cosmic principle is devoid of any nihilistic or relativizing implications. Its essence is, however, dynamic, stimulative, in perpetual motion. In this capacity, it might seem to share certain features with Dante's conception of divine love—albeit devoid of Dante's hierarchizing and moralizing topography—whose great poem ends with divine love as a principle of motion: "Already my desire and my *will* was turning,/Just like a wheel that is equally being moved,/The love that moves the sun and the other stars [*l'amor che move il sole e l'altre stelle*]" (*Paradiso* 33:143–45).[44]

If Dante's vision of divine love moves as a concentric rotating force, regulating both human appetitive desire and the conscious operation of the will, for Götz, pleasure appears incapable of being localized. It is a diffuse and vague presence that evades the human being's attempt to demarcate its boundaries and fix its position. Already in the first line of the poem, the presence of pleasure announces itself as something that is temporally extended and deferred (following the structure: "That which . . . /that which . . .") and therefore belies direct and immediate gratification. Pleasure cannot be satisfied if it is to remain a cosmic principle of perpetual motion. It is indeed this deferred nature of pleasure, marked by the initial absence of a substantive referent, that binds the tiny worm with the lofty soul. When this power finally becomes concretized, endowed with a signifier that provisionally stabilizes the referent—in the fourth line, the poet finally labels the force that moves through all things as *das Vergnügen*—pleasure moves away from the world of individual beings and becomes a function of the organization of nature as a whole ("Pleasure alone follows/Gentle drives of nature"). It is given a sign, but this sign refers to a spatially and temporally extended process rather than a specific thing or an intentional object.

Although pleasure characterizes the organization of nature—or perhaps *because* it characterizes the organization of nature—it raises the problem of its own representability. It functions precisely as a sign that attracts, but that can never be fully captured or localized:

> No one who wants to describe it
> Hits the mark; for it doesn't hold still.
> To pursue it means to flee from it;
> To feel it, is to call it into being.

> Keiner, der es schildern will,
> Trifft es: dann es hält nicht still.
> Es verfolgen heißt es fliehn;
> Es empfinden, nach sich ziehn.[45]

Pleasure continually evades and simultaneously produces the moment of poetic articulation itself. The poem, entitled "Pleasure," produces pleasure by describing how the attempt to describe pleasure fails. The poet locates the mechanism of pleasure in novelty rather than in beauty: "the novelty of the buds/Pleases more than beauty" (*der Knospen Neuigkeit/Mehr, als Schönheit, es erfreut*).[46] Presumably the poem is presenting its own meta-theory of pleasure: the pleasure in novelty that the poem describes corresponds to the pleasure produced by the poem itself. In the search for the universal force that pervades all things, the poem points outward only to be directed back to its own sensuous form.

At first, the characterization of aesthetic pleasure as a combination of indeterminacy and novelty appears unsurprising in the intellectual context of the time. For Baumgarten, the aesthetic consists of the domain of "confused" sense impressions, perceptual instances that cannot be broken down into their constitutive elements. For Breitinger, novelty constitutes the very source of the poetic imagination, which operates not through mimetic beauty alone, but by a divergence from plausibility. Götz's poem, however, disarms and defuses the potentially explosive pleasure of novelty. The pleasure of novelty is made harmless.

Instead of framing novelty as an instance of difference that foregrounds a possible world organized in a manner other than our own—as Breitinger does—novelty is reinscribed in an economy of pleasure caught circulating between the poles of morality and rationality:

> Friends, do you know where I found [pleasure]?
> Where I bound it with flowers?
> Between virtue and reason.
>
> Freunde, wiß't ihr, wo ichs fand?
> Wo ich es mit Blumen band?—
> Zwischen Tugend und Verstand.[47]

If the earlier half of the poem stresses the unlocalizability of pleasure, the final *pointe* in fact limits its potentially chaotic distribution by reining it in and establishing its boundaries. The *pointe* in fact undoes the initial tendencies of the poem by moving the mechanism of pleasure from ineffability and novelty toward the domain of its counterpart: the universality of rationality and the moral law. For if, in other iterations of Anacreontic pleasure, one encounters a concept of pleasure that is *unbound*—nothing appears off limits, and that which is sacred may always be exposed to mockery—in this later example, published in 1774 after the sentimentalization and the transcendental turn of sacred poetry (popularized above all by Klopstock) had made their marks on literary history, one finds the attempt to bind and limit the scope of pleasure itself. Where pleasure was previously incapable of being localized, it is now "found"; where it was previously movement and stimulation, it is now "bound"; where it previously sought novelty, it now is held between the twin poles of virtue and reason, *zwischen Tugend und Verstand*.

The poem does not quite reverse its previous characterization of pleasure, as it does not hold pleasure in its place, but merely delimits its sphere of activity. Ultimately, some part of pleasure retains its indeterminacy, moving *between* virtue and reason. Neither virtue nor reason will ever be able to fully govern pleasure, since it operates autonomously from these two capacities, although bound by them. Finally, the *pointe* itself corresponds to a linguistic excess, a triple rhyme (rather than a couplet), which both coheres with and deviates from the pattern of rhyming couplets established in the rest of the poem. Götz, who has foregrounded the role played by novelty in pleasure, acknowledges the importance of difference and perturbation in any given schema of expectations. And yet, when it comes to the final (formal) instantiation of novelty and difference—the triple rhyme, *fand, band, Verstand*—this difference is in fact nothing but a multiplication of sonic equivalences. It is a difference that is in fact more of the same. The novelty of pleasure is thereby relocated within the constraints of reason and morality, effectively nullifying any potentially radical perturbation in the reception of its own poetic act.

Hagedorn and the Origin of De-Transcendentalizing Art

It would be inaccurate, then, to suppose that all examples of rococo poetry are concerned primarily with unbinding the bourgeois subject from the practices conditioning the production of this subject. If one may discover among rococo and Anacreontic poets consistent attempts to disown and disorganize ways of being in the world, detaching readers from their values and normalizing practices, it must nevertheless be emphasized that such a style does not articulate a *total* way of being. Rococo poetry plays with roles, identities, and perspectives, which, like masks, can be taken on and off. One must never lose sight of the fact that this poetic idiom exists alongside other forms of poetry—didactic, moralistic, and religious, among others.

As one may see from Götz's translation of Anacreontic odes, this sort of poetry does not merely begin in the eighteenth century ex nihilo, but draws upon a poetic tradition whose works were interpreted as harmonizing particularly well with the turn toward immanence and away from something "beyond" the life of the senses and its pleasures. And despite Götz's attempt to reinscribe the Anacreontic idiom back into a divinely sanctioned poetic tradition, examples of this poetic style were able to draw upon this very tradition in order to release their own utterances from an indebtedness to the realm of the gods. The turn to poetic immanence—for which Catullus as well as Anacreon furnished the central models—may already be found in examples of rococo poems that predate the rage for Anacreontic verse driving poetic production in the wake of Gleim's *Attempt in Jocular Songs* (1744–45). One may describe the general tendencies exhibited by this turn to immanence in certain forms of rococo verse: the rococo poet cannot be called a seer or a prophet; the poet's domain makes no claim to a special knowledge that would single him or her out from the lot of fellow mortals; and the rococo poem—unlike the Pindaric ode, for example—refuses the mythology of the divinely inspired poet-genius and affirms its own derivative nature.

No poem, however, inasmuch as it is a linguistic artifact—since language itself bears the traces of a history that points to an existence beyond its own utterances—could possibly attain a state wherein the attraction to transcendence reaches a zero point. One may recall Nietzsche's oft-repeated insight that our belief in grammar seems to imply a realm of transcendent Being, some real existence outside our experience that grounds our experience: "I fear we will not get rid of God because we still believe in grammar."[48] Rococo poems, however, muster their rhetorical force—which may nevertheless be bolstered by various alternative discourses such as those of happiness, of health, of the poetic tradition of classical antiquity, and so on—to undermine the claims of other, more transcendentally saturated discourses.[49] Such poems are not radically new. They do not attempt to isolate themselves from tradition or make a break with the past. Rather, they draw upon their poetic predecessors and their predecessors' rhetorical strategies to effect a movement away from the attempt to ground human beings in metaphysics, in virtue, in the history of the nation, or in other codes that would exercise a monopoly about how human beings ought to be formed or how the world of appearances ought to be organized.

Such an attempt may be found in the works of Friedrich von Hagedorn, a contemporary of Brockes and the best known of the earlier generation of poets in the eighteenth century. He casts the rococo idiom as a form of poetic writing focused entirely on immanence:

> Too vain is the praise of friends:
> Enemies threaten us in posterity,
> They think our greatness small.
> To these times, rich in songs,
> I commend these trivialities:
> They do not wish to be immortal.

> Zu eitel ist das Lob der Freunde:
> Uns drohen in der Nachwelt Feinde,
> Die finden unsre Größe klein.
> Den jetzt an Liedern reichen Zeiten
> Empfehl' ich diese Kleinigkeiten:
> Sie wollen nicht unsterblich sein.[50]

It is easy to read Hagedorn's metapoetic interpretation of his own work as a rhetorical flourish, a mere topos of modesty, or as a disingenuous downplaying of his own achievement. To read Hagedorn's words in such a way, however, suppresses the novelty of the poetic gesture: Hagedorn's songs, which are small both in form and in claim to greatness, are written explicitly for this world, renouncing—at least on an ironic and playful level—the desire to endure which had been one of the main characteristics of the poetic tradition since antiquity. Catullus had already both ironized and confirmed the notion of lyric poetry as an extension—rather than an overcoming—of the limits of human life, as he says of his little book (*libellum*), "which, o patron virgin,/May it remain enduring, for more than one generation" (*quod, o patrona virgo,/plus uno maneat perenne saeclo*).[51] Catullus, who wishes that his little book, *libellum*, would last more than one generation, does not *preclude* the claim to eternity. After all, a work that is celebrated eternally satisfies the condition of lasting more than one generation. And yet, Catullus relativizes the temporality of eternity that undergirds fantasies of poetic duration: merely one generation would suffice.

Hagedorn goes one step further than Catullus by going one step fewer. His poems do not desire to subsist even more than one generation. In fact, they explicitly negate this desire—"they don't want to be immortal" (*sie wollen nicht unsterblich sein*)—by exhausting themselves in their own specific time and place. They also renounce their claim to uniqueness, as part of an age "rich in songs." The rococo poem, as Hagedorn understands it, distinguishes itself by being indistinguishable, by refusing its individuality and idiosyncrasy (which is, perhaps ironically, a mark of its individuality and idiosyncrasy). For the arbiters of culture—the "enemies" of minor poems who see greatness only in the fantastic or the sublime—such poems barely qualify as works of art. In Hagedorn's case, the poem only asserts itself and justifies its existence by making itself meaningless.

The refusal of immortality, uniqueness, and transcendence, the retreat into insignificance, meaninglessness, and pure immanence—each of these strategies invests the poetic word with the ability to diverge from eighteenth-century patterns of subject formation and value systems. The short lyric form popularized by Hagedorn, far from exhausting itself in a mere poetic game, elaborates a consistent and powerful model of poetics whose very claim of insignificance—songs that "do not want to be immortal"—facilitates novel forms of aesthetic activity and expands the realm of what can be said.[52]

A concrete example of such an expansion of possibilities for speech may be seen in the poems of Johanna Charlotte Unzer. As a woman writing Anacreontic poetry, she feels the need to justify her poetic persona in her *Attempt in Joke Poems* (*Versuch in Scherzgedichten*, 1751–53):

> And yet, one could think that it is unnatural when a woman sings about wine; because there are no drinkers among us, or because it

> would be improper for a woman to want to carouse; and moreover it won't do to have a woman extol love because it goes against the reclusiveness of our sex to even give the appearance of making much ado about love. And yet, an Anacreontic drinker and an Anacreontic lover praises and advises only loving and drinking in order to make a joke and to excite laughter.

> Doch man könnte denken, es wäre unnatürlich, wenn ein Frauenzimmer vom Weine singt; weil es unter uns keine Trinker giebt, oder weil es eine Unartigkeit seyn würde, wenn ein Frauenzimmer zechen wollte; und eben so könne es nicht wohl angehen, daß sie die Liebe erhebt, weil es wider die Eingezogenheit unsers Geschlechtes ist, auch nur den Schein von sich zu geben, als wenn man viel Werk aus der Liebe machte. Allein ein anakreontischer Trinker, und ein anakreontischer Liebhaber, rühmt und räth bloß das Lieben und das Trinken, um einen Scherz zu machen, und ein Lachen zu erregen.[53]

Unzer's poems were popular enough to be released in a second edition. Her preface addresses the difficulty of imagining a female poet that adopts the persona of a lover or a drinker. The joke, by framing itself as non-serious speech—a gesture familiar from the figure of the fool and the particular speech acts associated with this figure in early modern literature—allows something to be spoken that otherwise could not be spoken, or at least not without grave repercussions and the threat of ostracism. The force of Unzer's writing is directed not toward a negative critique of society, but toward a positive expansion of the capacities for speech among the subjects of society. In her introductory remarks, her specific mode of speech is made more complex inasmuch as the delineation between "joke" and "not-joke" is never transparently articulated. Her characterization of women as inherently "reclusive," as subjects who never make a fuss about love, may, on the one hand, easily fit within the strategic conventions that legitimize female writing, and on the other hand, it ironizes these very conventions and strategies, making them appear in the light of an absurdity. The language construed potentially as a "non-joke"—as a strategy of legitimation characteristic of women's writing that elucidates precisely what sort of being the woman is—is thereby contaminated by the speech act of the joke and makes the definition of "woman" into something that is suddenly open to other possibilities. Using Meier's terminology, Unzer opens the definition of her own identity to the differential abyss of the joke.

The attempt to frame her work as a "mere joke" reveals to what extent rococo and Anacreontic poetry both diverge from "reality" and simultaneously attempt to modify this reality by expanding possibilities for speech.[54] In the "Notice to the Second Edition" Unzer compares her own poetic activity to that of Hagedorn, ironically duplicating his presumed gesture of modesty while trying explicitly to differentiate herself from her predecessor:

> For the pieces that have been newly added [to this edition], I have nothing to add other than what I have to say about all of them in general, and what I can say about my works with thousandfold more justification than *Herr von Hagedorn* has said about his—these works, because of this modesty that makes us other poets blush with shame, upon which I have nevertheless thrown a small poetic furor: To these times, rich in songs,/I commend these trivialities:/They do not wish to be immortal.

> Wegen der neuhinzugekommenen Stücke habe ich weiter nichts zu erinnern, als was ich von allen überhaupt zu sagen habe, und was ich mit tausendmal mehr Rechte, als der *Herr von Hagedorn* von den seinigen sagen kann, auf den ich, dieser Bescheidenheit wegen, die uns andere Dichter alle schamroth macht, in der That einen kleinen poetischen Zorn geworfen habe: Den itzt an Liedern reichen Zeiten/Empfehl ich diese Kleinigkeiten,/Sie wollen nicht unsterblich seyn.[55]

Unzer uses Hagedorn's denigration of his *Songs* in order to justify her own poetic project. And although she reads Hagedorn's poetry as a topos of modesty, herself appealing explicitly to this topos in order to excuse her own writing in view of her femininity, this claim to nothingness nevertheless permits the introduction of novelty in the horizon of the imagination.

However, one ought not to exaggerate this gesture: Unzer purchases the right to speak differently by capitulating to her age's dominant understanding of what a woman ought to say. Her poems thus encourage the reproduction and proliferation of feminine speech acts only by stepping back from the precipice of a fully liberated sexual desire and from the threat of all-out conflict with the dictates of virtue. She addresses her fellow "sisters" (e.g., female readership) as follows:

> Compose beautiful songs;
> Sing about love!
> But if you love men;
> O! then love only one,
> Love him ever so tenderly,
> Joke with your friend:
> And then you will be ever so happy!

> Dichtet schöne Lieder;
> Singet von der Liebe!
> Liebt ihr aber Männer;
> O! so liebt nur einen,

Liebet ihn recht zärtlich,
Scherzt mit eurem Freunde:
So seyd ihr recht glücklich![56]

Unlike some of her male Anacreontic counterparts, Unzer reinforces normative eighteenth-century conceptions of erotic activity and reproduces the acceptable rhetorical and behavioral codes of love: *liebt nur einen*, love only one man. However, although she does not transgress the norms of virtue in poetry, she nevertheless adopts the role of the Anacreontic poet. While the content of the text appears normatively stable, the *gesture* of the text introduces an important difference: the text itself and its play allow Unzer to alienate herself from her habitual role, if only imaginatively and if only in language. If her poem proclaims happiness as the love of one man, she nevertheless includes in this notion of happiness the imperative of song: *Compose beautiful songs! Sing about love!* The coupling of a poetic imperative along with a hetero-normative affirmation of monogamous love confirms the validity of her own rhetorical game and her identity as a poet.

Unzer's need to defend herself and downplay her poetic achievements—which is not merely a gender issue, but a genre issue as well, since Gleim felt compelled to make a similar remark differentiating his poetic persona from his "real" identity in his *Attempt in Jocular Songs*—reveals to what extent Anacreontic poetry entered into conflict with socially normalizing patterns of behavior. Unzer's poetic model, Hagedorn, had in fact already drawn upon the potential divergence of poetic speech from codes of social organization in his songs. In one of his poems, the "insignificance" of the song is used as a cover in order to counter one of the most supposedly cohesive domains organizing eighteenth-century life, namely the bourgeois family and its household order. He describes "the orderly household" as one in which the man of the house remains inebriated all day while his wife plays with the neighbor:

Hardly has Crispin run to the new banquet
And gotten wind of pleasant wine:
Than his little woman sneaks out of the house
And leads the neighbor inside.
All of their household and business affairs
Are well-ordered and exquisite.

Kaum rennt Crispin zum neuen Schmause
Und wittert angenehmen Wein:
So schleicht sein Weibchen aus dem Hause
Und führt den Nachbar selbst hinein.
Ihr ganzes Haus= und Wirthschafts=Wesen
Ist ordentlich und auserlesen.[57]

Pleasure—the pleasure in the poem and the pleasure of the poem—aligns itself with the overturning of household order, of the domain of the *oikos*, both in an erotic and in an economic sense, for neither the man nor the woman fills roles that contribute to the reproduction of life. Lest one would think wine or adultery appears as the "theme" of the poem—both of which indeed account for a great number of rococo and Anacreontic jokes—the poet makes explicit that the pleasure of the poem consists less in the inebriation of the man or in the erotic exploits of the woman than in the negation of economic logic as such. "All of their household and business affairs/Are orderly and exquisite" is the refrain that keeps repeating itself as the *pointe* of the poem. The refrain serves as an ironic commentary or *explicatio* of the representation, the terms of which alter from strophe to strophe. In this structure, however, the very concept of order is overturned. This inversion is registered on the semantic level by the ironic dissimulation that results from the dissonance between representation (what Crispin does) and explication (their economic and domestic space is well-ordered).

Hagedorn's poem does not violate any specific injunction as much as allow the poet to play with and invert schemas of order and disorder. Whereas Hagedorn does not hesitate to moralize in his odes (gathered in a collection entitled *Moral Odes*), in his shorter songs, the insignificance of the small form creates a space into which the functionality of bourgeois society cannot penetrate and in which its claims to universality falter. Such poetry becomes invested with the capacity to make contingent the patterns of behavior necessary for the reproduction of bourgeois society: the organization of the household, the laws of economic productivity, and the sustenance and reproduction of existence. If such spheres represent one way in which the utility of any cultural product can be measured, the rococo poem is granted the freedom to construct its version of pleasure in direct contrast to such utility.

Hagedorn's rococo poems, which he gathers under the name of songs (*Lieder*), initiate a gesture of perturbation and disorganization that will continue to reverberate in the poets of later generations based in Halle, most notably Gleim and Uz. This perturbation, which transforms ways of organizing the world that tend to be seen as necessary into contingent appearances, becomes correlated with pleasure and delight, with humor and with irony rather than with the fantastic and the expansion of the imagination. In "Existence" ("Das Daseyn"), Hagedorn attacks not merely the rules of bourgeois society, but the Cartesian conception of the world, philosophical practices that attempt to reduce language to the operation of logic and generate a coherent style of life from such an operation:

Existence

A dark enemy of exhilarating drinks,
A philosopher, recently came up

And spoke: Gentlemen, know: I am.
Believe me, I am. Yes, yes! Why? Because I think.

A drunk came and staggered over to him
And swore by his pubkeeper and his wine:
I drink, o therefore must I be.
Believe me, I drink; I am. Who can refute me?

Das Daseyn

Ein dunkler Feind erheiternder Getränke,
Ein Philosoph, trat neulich hin
Und sprach: Ihr Herren, wisst; ich bin.
Glaubt mir, ich bin. Ja, ja! Warum? Weil ich gedenke.

Ein Säufer kam und taumelt ihm entgegen,
Und schwur bei seinem Wirth und Wein:
Ich trink, o darum muß ich seyn.
Glaubt mir, ich trink; ich bin. Wer kann mich widerlegen?[58]

Few readers of Hagedorn's poetry would suspect that a poem entitled "Existence" would undertake an analysis of Being or take as its central thematic horizon the ontological ground of human existence. In rococo poetry, the philosopher almost always appears ridiculous, a figure who speaks in foreign tongues and organizes the world around ideas that are patently incompatible with everyday life. Just as Voltaire's *Candide* sought to refute Leibnizian ontology with absurdity, so too does Hagedorn attack Descartes with Shaftesbury's "test of ridicule"—a test that the philosopher inevitably fails.

The failure of philosophy in the poem is above all a failure of speech. The philosopher's utterance in the poem—*Gentlemen, know: I am*—shifts the context of Cartesian ontology from meditation or thought, the dialogue of the self with the self, to a dialogue with others in a public space. It is in life with others that the philosopher appears doomed to ridicule. The drunk, whose statements are no less ridiculous than the philosopher's, throws himself into absurdity rather than attempting to adopt a form of language that excludes the absurd from its horizon. Ontology itself, or the attempt to metaphysically ground existence (*Das Daseyn*), dissolves into a play of words. The drunk makes drinking, or one particular act, into the ground of being—as counterpoint to the philosopher's "I think." The poem thereby exposes the very grounding or anchoring of the world in a universal or logical form of speech to the barbs of ridicule. The drunk's victory over the philosopher is a poetic victory: a victory of language over thought. Not only does the drunk imitate the philosopher in rhyme and meter, mastering his iambs and feminine endings, but he becomes the better poet: the drunk's rhyme pair (*entgegen/widerlegen*) trumps the more clumsy pair of the philosopher (*Getränke/gedenke*).

If there is one seemingly inviolable property that the rococo poem holds up as its very reason for being, the element around which it turns and in which it exults, it is most certainly the health of the organism and the belief that sensual pleasure focuses, sharpens, and intensifies the vital power of the human being.[59] The correlation of aesthetic form with the health of the organism, however, practically nullifies the opposing claims of virtue, social status, or economic productivity as master codes dictating legitimate practices of life. In Hagedorn's "Rural Pleasure" ("Die Land-Lust"), the poet fuses mental and bodily health with a rococo aesthetic manifesto incarnated in the body of the idealized peasant girl, one who makes visible and embodies the attractive power of the song itself:

> [The girl], as many a fresh maiden
> Makes herself pretty from that brook;
> And in breast and brow is not inferior
> To the most beautiful girls.
> Health and pleasure
> Animate her eye and heart,
> Exude charm in her features,
> And laugh in her joke.

> Wie manche frische Dirne
> Schminkt sich aus jenem Bach;
> Und gibt an Brust und Stirne
> Doch nicht den Schönsten nach.
> Gesundheit und Vergnügen
> Belebt ihr Aug' und Herz,
> Und reizt in ihren Zügen
> Und lacht in ihrem Scherz.[60]

The poetic stylization of pastoral life, in a tradition that extends back to Theocritus's *Idylls* and Virgil's *Eclogues*, constructs identities that differ radically from those associated with the violence and chaos of heroic poetry or urban space.[61] The bucolic subject reconciles the claims of eros and the toils of labor. It thus functions as a proxy for poetic activity as a mode of speech both naturally given and artificially constructed. Hagedorn's peasant girl, the "fresh maiden," incarnates the rococo idiom by translating style into flesh. If ever there were any hint that such a style aims to imitate or appeal to aristocratic sensibilities, the very existence of the peasant girl drives a wedge between Hagedorn's vision of the rococo and the gallant literature of the court. The peasant girl, far from being merely raw or purely natural, however, becomes an ornament: "she makes herself pretty [*schminkt sich*] from that brook." The poem inserts its own product and reason for being, pleasure, into a poetic physiological circulatory system, whereby it traverses sense and mind, surface and depth, exterior and interior. Health and pleasure manifest themselves in an act of vivification: they travel along sense experience, attain the heart (*Health and pleasure/Animate her eye and heart*), re-exteriorize themselves in the traits of the face (*Exude charm in her features*), and become the very emblem of an Anacreontic joke (*And laugh in her joke*).

The final stanza of the poem constructs its ideal of wisdom as an aesthetic exercise, an exercise that negates subject formation as disciplinary binding:

> Nothing is permitted to bind the wise man,
> Who exercises all his senses,
> In order to experience the charm
> That surrounds land and field.
> The broad meadow shines for him
> And the bedewed pasture:
> For him pleasure and joy grows green,
> For him nature paints.

> Nichts darf den Weisen binden,
> Der alle Sinnen übt,
> Die Anmuth zu empfinden,
> Die Land und Feld umgibt.
> Ihm prangt die fette Weide
> Und die bethaute Flur:
> Ihm grünet Lust und Freude,
> Ihm mahlet die Natur.[62]

The exercise of the senses, one directed toward the gracefulness that manifests itself in all of nature, renders the act of reception and the act of creation indistinguishable. In the twentieth century, Merleau-Ponty, in "Cézanne's Doubt," will describe how the landscape thinks itself in Cézanne, noting that in the act of painting, the most supposedly interiorized desires, intentions, perceptions, become so inextricably enmeshed with the givenness of the outside world that it no longer makes sense to distinguish between interior and exterior, subject and object.[63] Although Hagedorn is not concerned at all with the boundaries between subject and object, his poem articulates a form of practice in which the conception of the human being as an autonomous, closed individual already appears implausible—even if this way of being is ultimately made manifest in a genre that hovers between idyll and joke. In the domain of the aesthetic exercise (*the wise man/Who exercises all his senses*), discipline as self-mastery or subject formation is replaced by an attentiveness that opens perception, allowing it to experience physical reality: *to experience the charm* [*Anmuth*]/*That surrounds land and field*. The senses become the world that is at one and the same time interior and exterior to human experience. Strictly speaking, in such a world there can be no transcendence.

The poem claims that nature paints for the ascetic aesthete (*Ihm malet die Natur*). To paint signifies at the beginning of the eighteenth century precisely to imitate appearances. The imitation of nature, the cornerstone of artifice and poetic creation, thus becomes located in nature itself. The poem naturalizes itself through artifice, and the drive to imitate nature becomes a property of the landscape, which is responsible for its own poetic reproduction. The exercise of the senses allows nature to show itself as an artist, infusing perception with the delight of representation. Nature and artifice, perception and landscape coalesce. Such an exercise releases the human being from its constraints: *Nothing is permitted to bind the wise man*. In Hagedorn's song, the aesthetic exercise does not discipline. It unbinds.

Goethe's *Annette* and the Opposing Attractions of Rococo Poetry

Goethe may have become a pan-European celebrity upon the publication of *The Sorrows of Young Werther* (1774), but he began his literary career as a composer of poems written in the rococo style. Examples of these poems, written in the midst of the "culture of wit" in Leipzig, may be found in the collection *Annette* (1767), which remained unpublished during his lifetime. For a long time, these poems were considered to be merely derivative examples of an inherently superficial style, and hence unworthy of attention.[64]

Let us turn briefly to some of the texts in this collection. With remarkable precision, certain key poems of *Annette* direct their energy to the task of disclosing the presuppositions of their own poetic function. Like a poetic X-ray, these texts provide a window onto a conflict between opposing attractors and tendencies inherent in the rococo style itself: one tending toward transcendental schemas of organization, the other toward pure immanence; one toward immortality and duration, the other toward presence and transience; one toward virtue and the ethical, the other toward sensuality and aesthetic immorality.

The potential tension between the ethical and the daemonic that characterizes Goethe's later work already appears, albeit in a different form and with different stakes, as a latent dynamic of his rococo poems. Here, opposing tendencies manifest themselves in the configuration of the texts themselves—as a metapoetics—rather than as a theory of the cosmos, although these oppositions do pose the question of the sort of subject that is called into being and attracted to rococo textuality. Through attention to this agonistic struggle that underlies the world of *Annette*, one may gain an insight into Goethe's evaluation of the function of poetic form: does *Annette* exist in a tense state of relative equilibrium between these two attractions, between the pull toward sensuality, immanence, transience, and the pull toward the ethical, transcendence, immortality—or does it feel drawn more toward one point of attraction than toward the other?

The opposing poles of attraction travel through the collection of poems along the axes of two pairs of two narratives, each explicitly labeled as narratives (*Erzählungen*). Their status as narratives differentiates them from the other poems in *Annette*. One pair of narratives is entitled "The Art of Catching Prudes" ("Kunst, die Spröden zu fangen"), the other, "Triumph of Virtue" ("Triumph der Tugend"). The works are intended as parallel and oppositional representations of one another. The first part of "The Art of Catching Prudes" ends with the victory of the seducer over the prude and implies the sought-after pleasure of sexual consummation in the second narrative: "The cheeks burned and the bosom heaved. I then called: Victory! Victory, Amor, victory!"[65] In this instance, eros conquers ethics. However, they are traversed by an opposing aesthetic and ethical axis, marked by narratives entitled "Triumph of Virtue." In these works, virtue conquers desire. The would-be seducer ends in defeat and resigned acceptance: "My arm sank, and from its grasp, [the beloved sank] to the earth,/I prayed, cried, tore myself away and fled" (*Es sank mein Arm, aus ihm zur Erd' [die Geliebte] nieder,/Ich betet', weint', und riß mich los, und floh*).[66] The seducer relinquishes his victim, she falls to the earth, and he is integrated into the ethical through the movements of prayer, shame, and renunciation. The following day, he meets with the beloved again: "Down,/Looking to the ground/I stood there" (*Nieder/Zur Erde blikkend stand/Ich da*).[67] The last act of the poet draws the gaze to the very place where he let the beloved fall: toward the earth—and the gesture of defeat, looking to the ground, fuses eros, shame, renunciation, and ultimately, comfort in the solidity of the ethical.

These two pairs of narratives, one leading to erotic consummation and the other to virtue, dramatize the potentiality of the rococo style *as* a potentiality, namely, as an idiom that tends toward licentiousness but then may be repurposed to fit the demands of virtue. *Annette* provides an inside glimpse into the attractive pulls of rococo lyric, freezing the conflicting tendencies of the rococo and holding them open in a state of disjunction, placing the reader at the unstable bifurcation point between these opposing vectors.

And yet, one ought to ask the question: does Goethe's *Annette* merely situate rococo poetry in a space of indeterminate potentiality, poised between the ethical and its suspension, or does it feel more pulled to one operation over the other? Although the poetry seems to conclude with the "Triumph of Virtue," which in turn alienates the poetic voice from his persona as a seducer, it nevertheless maintains the line of attraction along the axis of immanence, perhaps, as the stronger pull.

The prioritization of the sensual over the ethical, pleasure over virtue, appears concentrated in the figure of Annette herself, who acts almost as a magnetic node that draws readerly intentionality into her orbit and casts a field of attraction over the entirety of the collection. What matters is not whether this relationship "actually" happens or whether it is invested with a referential authenticity outside the text, but rather, how the text itself construes the status of the game between lyric persona and erotic object. In the second narrative, "The Art of Catching Prudes," the lyric persona gives his account of the seduction of Charlotte. He claims that Charlotte was "always reticent, always severe with me, just like my Annette is now when her mother is looking."[68] The narrator establishes an explicit link between Charlotte and Annette, suggesting that this particular narrative form, in which sensuality trumps ethics, has maintained a stronger resonance with the primary game of the first-person lyric persona, that is, the relation between the lyrical subject and Annette herself. Moreover, the first-person lyric persona only mentions Annette by name in this particular narrative. Hence, the "Triumph of Virtue," although it follows "Art of Catching Prudes" in the sequence of the collection, can only be read ironically when considering the first-person lyric persona's affirmation of sensualism via the representation of his own relationship to Annette. He makes certain that the readers are privy to the nature of this relationship by animating speech from Annette to himself:

Annette to Her Beloved

I saw how Doris stood with Damot,
He took her tenderly by the hand;
Long they gazed at one another,
And looked around to see if the parents were awake,
And since they saw no one,
Quickly—in short, they did it the way we do it.

Annette an ihren Geliebten

Ich sah wie Doris bey Damöten stand,
Er nahm sie zärtlich bey der Hand;
Lang sahen sie einander an,
Und sahn sich um, ob nicht die Aeltern wachen,
Und da sie niemand sahn,
Geschwind—Genug sie machtens, wie wirs machen.[69]

In the logic of the game, these words belong not to the poetic persona, but to Annette herself. These words are then transmitted from Annette to the poetic persona to the reader. In this structure of double transmission, the poem doubles the voyeuristic act: Annette watches a couple in the act of love, and conveys to the poetic persona the similarity between this act and her own erotic activities with the poetic persona.

The parallels between these two acts of immediate desire are not confined to this poem alone, but resonate with the other texts in the collections (suggesting the collection should be read not as a series of isolated poems, but as a gathering of multiple poems that forms a larger whole). Doris and Dämot look around to see whether or not their parents are awake; and in the "Art of Catching Prudes," Annette must always be "strict" (*streng*) with her lover, but only when her mother is looking. When unobserved, they indulge in the very same erotic pleasure as Doris and Dämot. And just as Annette conveys her own illicit act of voyeurism to her beloved, so too does her beloved then convey their own intimate posture to the readers of this poem, making the readers complicit as second-order voyeurs, while the author himself becomes—an exhibitionist.[70]

Annette's victory, as a persona and as a name, announces itself in the first poem of the collection, a dedication that constructs Annette as a synecdoche, a mere part of the book that can nevertheless stand in for the whole:

> Why should I, Annette,
> You who are to me divinity, muse,
> And friend, and everything,
> Not also name this book
> After your beloved name?

> Warum sollt' ich, Annette,
> Die Du mir Gottheit, Muse
> Und Freund mir bist, und alles,
> Dieß Buch nicht auch nach deinem
> Geliebten Nahmen nennen?[71]

The identity of Annette, who unites transcendence (*Gottheit*), the mediation of transcendence (*Muse*), and immanence (*Freund*), therefore takes priority over the other poetic personae that appear in the same collection. Annette, as a persona in the collection, flaunts her sexuality in the face of the opposing forces of virtue—thereby assuring the victory of Anacreontic sensual immanence over the moralization of the rococo style in the struggle between these two tendencies that this collection so vividly dramatizes.

Goethe's *Annette* embodies the latent tensions of the rococo style itself, poised between the purely immanent affirmation of desire and the contradictory pull toward the sphere of the ethical. The poetic persona, however, reveals himself—and perhaps his readers as well, since they read Annette's letter out of the same voyeuristic impulses with which she watches Doris and Dämot—as one pulled more to the attraction of immanence than to the ethical. As mentioned previously, in Goethe's later works, this very attraction to an extra-moral power would metamorphose and reconfigure itself as the pull of the daemonic: "a power that, where not directly opposed to the moral order of the world, nevertheless traverses it, so that one could take the one [e.g., the moral order] for the warp and the other for the woof" (*GMA* 16:821–22). The daemonic, however, as a transcendental-cosmological principle, departs from the pull of rococo pleasure as the celebration of pure immanence: a ripple of stimulation that comes from no specific point in the cosmos and remains caught in the pleasure of its own game.

Chapter 9

✦

Anacreontic Play and the Disorganization of Transcendental Orders

Johann Ludwig Gleim's *Attempt in Jocular Songs*

Is there a secret history, a concordance or discordance of purposes, at work in the contemporaneous emergence of aesthetics as a discourse and in the flourishing of Anacreontic poetry in Halle in the 1740s? The question is a difficult one to answer. As mentioned earlier, Gleim and Uz, two of the most important Anacreontic poets, were students of Baumgarten and attended his lectures. Gleim's poem addressed to Baumgarten grants to the philosopher the dubious honor of functioning as origin and as rhetorical model for the Anacreontic poet's language games. In the process, the linguistic power of the ethical is redirected to the affirmation of immanent sensuality, to the play of erotic seduction. In this poem lies a clue to the relation between the Anacreontic poet and the philosophical discourses of the time: they are drawn upon only to be redirected to a different object, and in the process, their central operations are inverted and resignified.

For Baumgarten, any poetic work could become the subject of an aesthetic exercise and could be used to produce the specific personality type of the aesthete. The aesthete modifies his or her own sensuous dispositions in order to render the sensuous perfection of the self analogous to a metaphysical and rational coherence of multiples. In Gleim's case, his specific poetic idiom stages and reproduces an utterly different personality type: the Anacreontic poet. Although Gleim never frames his own poetic activity as such, the function of the Anacreontic poet may nevertheless be regarded as an inverted aesthetic exercise. The central function of his or her linguistic and rhetorical exercise is not to reveal a deep coherence between the sensuous modification of the self and metaphysical truth as the *ordo plurium in uno*, but on the contrary, to radically—*and systematically*—detach this self from the structures of intelligibility that seemingly articulate the truth of its own being.

The potentiality of Anacreontic play to function as a perturbation or displacement of social and transcendental symbolic codes of organization reaches an apex in Gleim's *Attempt in Jocular Songs*. The songs, widely read and imitated in the eighteenth century in German-speaking countries, appeared in two volumes in 1744 and 1745. Gleim replaces transcendental functions—which I have defined as culturally informed ways of ordering phenomena, normalizing behavioral patterns, or linking the world of appearances to organizing principles operating beyond appearances—with the immanence of a universalized erotic desire and poetic pleasure.[1] The *Jocular Songs* may draw upon a set of poetic topoi specific to their genre and tradition—many of which can already be found in the corpus of *Anacreontea*—but they direct themselves to forms of intelligibility specific to eighteenth-century culture, forms whose afterlife extends far beyond their specific time and place. Especially in the first volume, these songs take as their subject what might seem like a catalogue of eighteenth-century spheres of organization that are of decisive importance for the constitution of the modern subject. These songs aim at a systematic poetic disorganization of the codes that order existence.

Each section of this chapter will take as its focus one of these spheres of organization and examine how the Anacreontic poem proceeds to dismantle the mechanisms of its power. The pleasure of Anacreontic poetry loosens the hold of transcendental codes in a similar manner to Breitinger's use of the fantastic, *das Wunderbare*, which harnesses the energy of the poetic act by confronting readers with differences from their own received cultural norms. The fantastic was explicitly framed as an assault against the deadening empire of habit over imaginative life. The Anacreontic joke, however, is simultaneously more superficial and deeper than the fantastic, for it takes aim not at physiological inertia, but at the forces that govern the coherence of the social as such.

The Anacreontic Question and the Implosion of the Public Sphere

In "Answer to the Question: What Is Enlightenment" (1784), Kant describes the necessary preconditions for Enlightenment as follows: "Nothing is necessary for this form of enlightenment other than freedom; and indeed, the least harmful among all things that could be called freedom, namely this: the freedom to make *public use* of one's freedom in all matters" (*AA* 8:36). According to Kant, the public use of reason consists in the dissemination of one's opinions as a scholar in journals and books for an audience of readers: "By the public use of one's reason I understand the following: the use that someone makes as a *scholar* before the entire *reading public*" (*AA* 8:37). Kant articulates what had long been part of the culture of eighteenth-century life, namely, the circulation of ideas through publications, written disputes, and public correspondence.[2]

Gottsched's disagreement with Bodmer and Breitinger concerning the aesthetic value of fantastic literature became one of the most famous literary debates of the eighteenth century, a debate that operated within the scope of what Kant would later construe as the public use of reason. For the Anacreontic poets in Halle, this particular use of reason fell prey to the pitfalls of philosophical thinking: if it had been subjected to Shaftesbury's famous test of ridicule, the entire debate would have failed. Gleim writes to Uz: "I know that your opinion of the conflict between Gottsched and the Swiss [Bodmer and Breitinger] is the same as mine. Both camps make themselves look ridiculous to reasonable people."[3] In his correspondence, Gleim appeals to reason in order to underscore the absurdity of the debate between Gottsched and the Swiss critics. In his poetry, however, it is not the public use of reason that demarcates the line between the ridiculous and the valid; rather, the public use of reason is itself made ridiculous. Gleim's Anacreontic poet takes up a poetic identity marked by a refusal to integrate itself or position itself in the debates of the scholarly world:

The Scholar

Should I learn from the journalists
How to write my name?
Should I make visible new worlds
In the vault of stars?
Should I help Wolff or Knutzen
Undo knots of doubt?
Should I steal material and ethical doctrines
For the pamphleteers?
Should I learn from the book critics
How to scold or criticize?
Should I search the history of the world
For the trials of courageous fools?
Should I ask my spirit:
What it is, and where it lives?
. . .
Should I melt lead into gold?
Should I teach advisors how to advise?
Should I criticize Milton's devil?
Should I compose works of wonder?
Or should I explicate them?

Der Gelehrte

Soll ich von den Zeitungsschreibern
Meinen Namen schreiben lernen?
Soll ich in dem Sterngewölbe
Neue Welten sichtbar machen?

> Soll ich Wolfen oder Knutzen
> Zweifelsknoten lösen helfen?
> Soll ich Stoff und Sittenlehren
> Für die Blätterschreiber stehlen?
> Soll ich von den Bücherrichtern
> Schimpfen oder tadeln lernen?
> Soll ich in der Weltgeschichte
> Proben tapfrer Narren suchen?
> Soll ich meinen Geist befragen:
> Was er sei, und wo er wohne?
> . . .
> Soll ich Blei zu Golde schmelzen?
> Soll ich Räthe rathen lehren?
> Soll ich Miltons Teufel schelten?
> Soll ich Wunderwerke dichten?
> Oder soll ich sie erklären? (*SL* 28)

The poem, in its disdain of discourses associated with public rationality, reveals its own awareness of these discourses. The use of the list, itself a form of bringing order to discursive multiplicity, becomes associated with a horizon of repeated and expected behavior—*ought I?* (*soll ich?*)—that the Anacreontic poet explicitly rejects: "No. My relative should do this" (*Nein. Das soll mein Anverwandter, SL* 28). The "relative" in this case—who is therefore not completely different from the Anacreontic poet—is the scholar. The Anacreontic poet is not simply a negation of the scholar; rather, he uses the codes of the scholar in order to institute a differential relation: an alternative rather than an opposition.

In another poem, entitled "Duties of Life" ("Lebenspflichten"), the poet makes a counter-list, an enumeration of acts of sensuous pleasure. The Anacreontic poet portrays these acts as duties for life in a manner that differs radically from future attempts, such as those undertaken by Schiller, to fuse ethics and inclination:

> Should I drink? Should I love?
> Should I dance? Should I laugh?
> . . .
> Yes I should, and my father
> Teaches all this to me with his grey hair.
> He calls them: duties of life.

> Soll ich trinken? Soll ich lieben?
> Soll ich tanzen? Soll ich lachen?
> . . .

> Ja, dis soll ich, und mein Vater
> Lehrt es mich bei grauen Haaren,
> Und er nennt es: Lebenspflichten. (*SL* 27)

The list of the duties of life of the Anacreontic poet inverts the list of the scholar. The figure of the father, or the paterfamilias, has been contaminated in this instance with the poetic father: Anacreon himself, whose poetic figuration is invoked in order to recast the law of the father as the law of desire.

To return to "The Scholar": the poet refuses to engage precisely those discourses that establish normativity through a dialogue between equals in the public sphere. The poem composes a discursive list of language games aimed at the perfectibility of human knowledge: the public use of reason (lines 1–2), the Copernican revolution in astronomy (3–4), metaphysical inquiries about doubt (5–6), the exercise of virtue (7–8), the judgment of literary criticism (9–10), the historiography of nationalism, heroism, and world history (11–12), disputations on the nature of the mind (13–14), the legitimacy of religious practices (15–16), alchemical experimentation (19), and principles of governance (20). The poem mocks its own procedure of enumeration, flaunting its superficiality with regard to the most pressing issues of the day. It is indifferent to all claims of epistemological advancement or validity.

The list concludes with a compressed representation of the debate between Gottsched—"Should I criticize Milton's devil?"—and Bodmer and Breitinger, "Should I compose works of wonder?" (*SL* 28). The Anacreontic poet positions himself on neither side of the debate: he refuses to take a stand. His is an act of non-judgment. The non-oppositionality of the Anacreontic poet's stance is critical, for a "no" within the debate has a different epistemic value than a "no" to the very terms of the debate in the first place. This refusal nevertheless may also be read poetologically: as a practice of writing and reading, Anacreontic poetry coheres neither with Gottsched's didacticism nor with Bodmer and Breitinger's defense of the fantastic. The Anacreontic poet does not ignore the public sphere—the mere compilation of the list of public discourses suggests as much—but undercuts its attempt to universalize itself and impose its patterns of behavior and thought over all written forms of discourse. The joke is a form that both gathers discourses and frames itself as an alternative to these discourses; it engages a mode of speech against all forms of discourse that legitimize themselves through conditions of publicity.

The scholar, as the gathering figure of Enlightenment reason, is both relative to and archenemy of the Anacreontic poet. The Anacreontic poet thus replaces the public sphere characterized by validity claims with the immanent desire that circulates among a circle of friends. The poet offers Anacreontic friendship as an intersubjective alternative to public reason, thus construing his own aesthetic activity as substitute for the particular reading practices associated with the scholar:

He, the archenemy of my friends,
Should read himself pale and miserable.
And then I'll ask him:
Does my girl make me miserable as well?

Er, der Erbfeind meiner Freude,
Soll sich blaß und elend lesen.
Und dann will ich ihn befragen:
Macht mich auch mein Mädchen elend? (*SL* 28)

The scholar's reading practices, which demand that one read until one is pale and miserable, contrast with the reading practices triggered by the poem itself, which excite, stimulate, and invigorate according to its own rhetorical maneuvers. Ultimately, the poet beats the scholar at his own game. The final rhetorical gesture addresses the scholar directly with a question, ironically generating the public debate that at first was disdained. However, the question is not one that the scholar could take seriously. The question is designed only to reveal the superiority of the poet's form of life, the value of his eroticized and fetishized girl (*Mädchen*)—and his own culture of reading and writing—over a culture of reading and writing that attempts to judge, evaluate, analyze, understand.

The poem ends with a question: "Does my girl make me miserable as well?" This question has a double audience. It is addressed both to the scholar in the poem and to the reader of the poem. The question ultimately invokes the term around which Anacreontic poetry revolves: the figure of the girl, *das Mädchen.*

Although the point may seem obvious, it is worth emphasizing: the *Mädchen* of the Anacreontic poem is never actually a girl. The *Mädchen* of the Anacreontic poem designates more a semiotic function than a referent. She may have qualities—brown hair or shining eyes—but is almost always devoid of flesh: a sign approaching a purely formal operation. The flattening out of the *Mädchen* concentrates all of the energy of the sign into its specific strategic gesture. To be sure, as a signifier, it is designed to concentrate, channel, and redirect desire, and therefore cannot be wholly abstracted from the sexual object that it supposedly invokes. But the *Mädchen* of Gleim's Anacreontic texts almost always functions as a point of attack, as a parasite in a system that, by binding the Anacreontic poet to this essentially empty sign, throws a wrench into the gears of dominant discursive systems (truth, religion, nation)—systems in which the girl functions as a non-entity, as a matter of indifference or an *adiaphoron.*

In "The Scholar," the *Mädchen* refers precisely to the poetological function of its own sign character rather than to any fleshly female entity. The final question of the poem may therefore be rephrased as follows: has the *Mädchen* of the Anacreontic text made the writer or reader of the text miserable—not the *Mädchen* as a real girl, but the *Mädchen* in its immanent presence as word, intensity, signifier, poetic topos, rhetorical game? The affect generated *by* the text confirms (or denies) the implicit claim that Anacreontic reading generates a form of pleasure that differs radically from the travails of scholarly reading. The *Mädchen* stands in for an entire manner of producing and receiving texts, an alternative mediated form that calls into being its own specific ideal audience and aims at its own discursive reproduction. The Anacreontic community is not predicated on judgment or consensus, but on an affective harmonization. The *Mädchen* forms a conduit through which the desire that binds together this community of readers and writers may travel. The eighteenth century would call this affective harmonization: sociability (*Geselligkeit*).[4] And although such a practice may seem to in fact undertake a "binding" function, it does so only by detaching its own reading and writing community from the normalizing schemata of organization that permeate the spheres of the social. This community is constituted not by reference to any order beyond its own game, but by the immanent circulation of its own system of signs, of which *das Mädchen* is both an element and a central point of concentration.

For the poet, the question—*does my girl make me miserable too?*—does not need to be answered. In this question that is not a real question, one may find a parasitic form that strikes against the dominion of public debate as a rational form of discourse that occurs among equal participants, a form of discourse that submits all speech acts to the claims of logical and universal validity.[5] The Anacreontic question, in this instance at least, is not dialectical. It does not provoke a *yes* or a *no*. The question itself makes the alternative discourse—the public exchange of scholarly opinion—appear even more devoid of flesh than its own rhetorical game. More important than the question itself is perhaps the final alliterative flourish, the delight of the letter *m* and its copulation with hard and soft iterations of *ch*: *Macht mich auch mein Mädchen elend?* To listen to the final line and its specific alternation of sounds uncovers its own game as an expansion of the sonic possibilities of the signifier as signifier: *Mädchen*.

Finally, what is this poem other than an extension and reproduction of insincere questions, questions that are not intended to be answered? This form of the question operates along a wholly different plane of activity than the question of the scholar, and it disavows the Socratic tradition of the question as a pathway into knowledge. There is no interrogation. Such a form of questioning is, in the deepest and most superficial sense, rhetorical.

Anacreontic Impiety

In Gleim's "The Creator" ("Der Schöpfer"), the poet asks the gods: "Let me create something too," saying, "I promise you, most dear gods,/To create nothing but girls" (*Ich verspreche Euch, liebste Götter,/Nichts als Mädchen zu erschaffen*, *SL* 104). The invocation of the *Mädchen* gives a clue to readers that the poet's parody of theological creation may also be read as a poetological statement. The Anacreontic poet does not seek to create novelty or even beauty, but merely to reproduce and multiply objects of desire. Novelty is generated not *in* the poem, but by the exercise of the poem, by the difference that it introduces between its own de-transcendentalizing poetics and the cultural framework of intelligibility of its readership.

The poet does not produce anything new; rather, he claims for his idiom a *reproductive* poetics—more so even than Novalis—in the literal sense of the term: "So that space itself, up unto heaven,/Is everywhere swarming with girls" (*Daß der Raum, bis an den Himmel,/Überall von Mädchen wimmelt*, *SL* 104). His tower of Babel, reaching to the sky, fills the entirety of space, and it is composed of the poet's own erotic desire projected onto the ethers and up to the heavens. The poet's unbounded desire undoes the vertically differentiating, hierarchizing logic of the Creation. There is nothing more foreign to the Anacreontic poet than the sort of cosmos portrayed by Dante, which rotates circularly and is organized vertically. Here there is a simple saturation of space as such with signs that multiply themselves. Gleim's own poetry—which itself "swarms with girls"—replaces the space of the divine.

The transcendence of the Creation, typically manifested by a vertical upwards journey to God or to the Idea, here becomes subject to a homogeneous flattening, just as the density of immanent desire is maintained and multiplied. If Hölderlin's poetry desires to move the vertical axis of the divine onto the horizontal axis of the sensuous world, Gleim moves the horizontal onto the vertical, in essence eliminating all verticality through the expansive spread of reproductive immanence.[6] Anacreontic eros leads not to higher realms of ideality, but rather, to the repetition, multiplication, and diffusion of a self-sustaining desire.

In "The Rainbow" ("Der Regenbogen"), the Anacreontic poet captures the color of the cheeks of a woman during her first erotic encounter with her groom and fills the heavens with this color, preferring this imagined projection to a natural rainbow:

The Rainbow

The pale cheeks of timid beauties
Redden quickly with shame,
When a desired groom
Appears before the dear mother;
When she, by the command of her mother,
Receives his first kiss:
The tender red is heightened,
And then it is like young roses.
But when they—without the mother—

Kiss and are kissed,
Then the red of the cheeks puts
All roses, all purple to shame.
Let me put a thousand such cheeks
Around half the firmament
And arrange them all into rounded order
Under this rainbow here.
Suddenly it should disappear,
For it will yield to the cheek-bow [*Wangenbogen*]
As the moon does to the sun.

Der Regenbogen

Blöder Schönen blasse Wangen
Werden schnell vor Scham erröthet,
Wenn sich bei der lieben Mutter
Ein erwünschter Bräut'gam meldet;
Wenn sie auf Befehl der Mutter
Seinen ersten Kuß empfinden:
Wird das holde Roth erhöhet,
Und dann gleicht es jungen Rosen.
Aber wenn sie, ohne Mutter,
Küssen und sich küssen lassen,
Dann beschämt das Roth der Wangen
Alle Rosen, allen Purpur.
Laßt mir tausend solche Wangen
Um den halben Himmel setzen
Setzt sie mir in runder Ordnung
Unter diesen Regenbogen.
Plötzlich soll er sich verlieren,
Denn er soll dem Wangenbogen,
Wie der Mond, der Sonnen weichen. (*SL* 49)

The beauty of nature and its own forms of self-multiplication and diffusion in the rainbow must yield to the "cheek-bow" (as opposed to the *rainbow*; the word *Wangenbogen*, the curve of the cheeks, is clunky in translation). The artificial creation of a poetic imagination, heightened by a voyeuristic view onto a moment that alludes to a scene of deflowering (the red of the cheeks trumps the red of the rose), is greater than the order of nature. Brockes's imperative to attend to the perception of natural appearances is replaced with the imperative to imagine a scene of intimacy. Intensity is more important than variation. The multiplicity of the colors of the rainbow is trumped by the univocity of sexual desire: red becomes the only color.

The glorification of artifice over nature in the Anacreontic poem posits itself as an alternative to onto-theological thinking, and above all, to the forms of religiousness that were dominant in Halle. [7] Gleim believed that Pietism was a sect, and he sets the Anacreontic poem in opposition to it. After citing two lines from an anti-Pietistic poem in a letter to Uz, he notes: "If you have a friend that you would like to disabuse of this sect, then I'll just send this poem over to you."[8]

In the poems themselves, the poetic persona distances itself not only from Pietistic forms of spirituality and inwardness, but from any form of religiousness that posits a law exterior to the operation of desire. In "The Atheist" ("Der Atheist"), the poet threatens to deny God—or rather, the god of love—if he does not aid the poet in the seduction of a prude:

> If you haven't subdued
> This prude in three minutes:
> O! then in the fourth,
> I will renounce you and your mother.

> Hast du mir nach drei Minuten
> Diese Spröde nicht gebändigt:
> O! so will ich in der vierten
> Dich und deine Mutter läugnen. (*SL* 36)

The prude (*die Spröde*)—who is a sort of counterpoint to the *Mädchen*—is an important signifier for the Anacreontic poet: functionally, she impedes desire, and is therefore one of the most threatening figures of this particular poetic idiom. Where the *Mädchen* often facilitates the flow of desire, the *Spröde* will block this flow.

And yet, the prude functions like the girl inasmuch as she permits the Anacreontic poet to organize the world differently and thereby extract the subject from the confines of onto-theological religiousness. In this case, the Anacreontic poet contaminates mythological and Christian forms of transcendence with his own poetic desire; or more precisely, he displaces Christian forms of thought with his own mythological vocabulary. "The Atheist" does not merely deny the mythological god of love, but the divine as such. While this refusal is never made explicit, it nevertheless constitutes the main thrust of the *pointe*. The denial of Eros and Aphrodite is performed as a proxy for the denial of Christ and Mary: *if you haven't subdued/This prude in three minutes/ . . . /I will renounce you and your mother*. The sentiment places the Anacreontic poet in the position of the wayward apostle. He *challenges* the divine, invoking heresy—precisely that which the divine order attempts to marginalize—as a form of power over the transcendent. The Anacreontic poet reinstates a covenant through the power of his devotion: if you help me,

I will not renounce you. In this covenant, however, the believer has usurped divine power.

The mediation of the divine and the human, the very crux of Christian thought—a figure that Hölderlin would make the central theme of his poetry—becomes downgraded to the facilitation of an erotic encounter, willfully confusing Christian iconography and the rococo iconography of Cupid. In a poem entitled "The Mediator" ("Der Vermittler"), the miraculous appearance of the god of love permits both poet and god to play the role of the intermediary: the otherwise despised figure of the coupler (*Kuppler*), whose central function is to facilitate erotic encounters. Mediation here, or the poet as mediator (*Vermittler*), refers simply to an operation in which two earthly bodies are erotically bound with one another. It is one of the few poems in the *Jocular Songs* that explicitly foregrounds its own violation of the laws of probability, even referring to the fantastic, or *das Wunderbare*, in order to describe the appearance of the god from a rosebud: "What a miracle!/Amor came springing out" (*welch ein Wunder!/Amor kam herausgesprungen*, *SL* 9). Amor's miraculous appearance is framed as a redemption, first in the economic sense: he comes out of the rose in order to facilitate the repayment of a debt (*Schulden*, *SL* 7) of kisses that an Anacreontic *Mädchen*, Doris, owes to her lover as the result of his winning a game.

Rather than linking the realm of the divine and the human, Amor mediates between worldly lovers: "Swaying he flew, like an angel,/Between me and my beautiful girl" (*Schwebend flog er, wie ein Engel,/Zwischen mir und meiner Schöne*, *SL* 9). At the same time, his presence, like Lessing's bee, converts both the poet and his erotic object themselves into figures of mediation. He commands the poet to shoot the resistant erotic object with his own rose blossoms, thereby drawing the poet into the game of mediation. After Amor has finished his task—by inflicting wounds upon the girl and then healing them to guarantee the girl's submission, not only to the desire of the poet, but also to her own misrecognized desire—he entrusts to his "Sylphs" the task of gathering tears of joy in order to keep the lovers' kisses continually moist, "until he goes once again to heaven/To the beautiful mother" (*bis er zu der schönen Mutter/Wieder in den Himmel käme*, *SL* 12). The poet vocalizes the desire to make the appearance of the god manifest in the flesh: "If I could just make visible/The apparition [of Amor] to these timid beauties!" (*Könnt ich doch den blöden Schönen/Die Erscheinung sichtbar machen!*, *SL* 12). The poem takes as its central task the attempt to convert others into believers concerning an improbable event: the god, who shows himself to redeem a debt, makes himself visible by virtue of a miracle before rejoining his mother in heaven. The poem thereby reproduces the rhetoric of conversion and mediation that animates Christian theology. In this case, it is not Christ, but the god of love who is called upon to unite two lovers and provoke a rhetorical game that seeks to compensate for the lack of visible evidence of divine existence.

The poet finally tells his readership to assure themselves of the existence of the god by looking at the miraculous rosebuds that blossom on the bosom of Doris:

> Three minutes after the miracle
> Both of the miracle-roses bloomed
> In the most beautiful rose blossom
> On the bosom of my Doris.
> Brothers, you don't want to believe it?
> Just go and take a look at the roses.

> Drei Minuten nach dem Wunder
> Blühten beide Wunder-Rosen,
> In der schönsten Rosenblüte,
> Auf den Busen meiner Doris.
> Brüder, wollt ihr es nicht glauben?
> Geht nur hin, und seht die Rosen. (*SL* 12)

The roses are presented as a miracle that will secure the belief in the existence of the god of love. The proximity of the rose blossoms to Doris's breasts produces a metonymic transference: the object of desire becomes the proof of the power of the god. The miracle roses that function as a gateway between the realm of the gods and the sensuous world of mortals direct the gaze of the skeptic to its proper place: not to the roses, not to the miracle of divine mediation, but to the immediacy of the erotic object, the breasts of the girl. In the injunction to verify the existence of the divine, the very symbol of divine mediation is rendered superfluous by the presence of the flesh that is the actual target of the Anacreontic joke. If there is an Anacreontic faith—which remains a dubious proposition—it is a faith not in the guarantee of the beyond, but in the immanence of desire that circulates in its own poetic play.

The Copernican Revolution and the Anacreontic Eye

The movements of the stars have perennially pointed beyond themselves for those bound to the earth. At different times and in different places, the stars have evoked widely varying interpretive activities: they may be repositories of immortal deeds; signs upon which destinies are inscribed; the evidence of a divine love animating and pervading all things; the source of astrological knowledge guiding the power of prophecy; the incomprehensible mystery of God; or the order of nature operating according to observable and mathematically comprehensible universal laws.[9]

Gleim consecrates two of his *Jocular Songs* to the figure of the stargazer. In the wake of the Copernican Revolution, the stargazer in the eighteenth century is caught between different paradigms of knowledge and different reading practices. To examine the change in status of the stargazer in the eighteenth century reveals a shift from the astrological hermeneutics of the early modern period to the technological and progressive positivism of what would become modern scientific astronomy. Gazing at the stars was therefore not merely one form of human activity among others. The refutation of the geocentric world altered the very conception of God, the human being, and the cosmos, while simultaneously defining the methods and modes of generating evidence for that which qualified as empirical knowledge.[10]

In Gleim's poem "The Stargazer" ("Der Sternseher"), the eponymous figure—one who looks up to the sky rather than to the world as manifest before the senses—is a miserable human being: "Without jest and love,/Every night [he] remains awake" (*Ohne Scherz und Liebe,/Durch alle Nächte wachet*, *SL* 33). The Anacreontic poet, who has been invited by the stargazer to partake in his nightly activities, appears at first uninterested in these new technologies of perception that, as Hannah Arendt would note, alienate the senses from their attachment to the earth.[11] Indeed, he rejects the practices governing the production of empirical knowledge. When the stargazer asks him to look at the moon, the poet does not approach the moon as a scientific object. He personifies it, portraying it metaphorically as a tyrant who ought to graciously permit the other stars to shine. The moon is transformed from an object of knowledge to an object of apostrophe: "Then suffer, tyrant,/By your high gleam,/The small lights of the heavens!" (*SL* 33). The stargazer does not understand this mode of address:

> Alas the stargazer
> Sighed at my idiocy,
> And called out at the last sigh:
> You idiot, be silent!
> I stood up; he said: stand still!
> And he lays upon my shoulder
> A rod, as if he wanted to shoot.
> I begged for my life,
> But now I have to laugh—
> He didn't have a barrel or gunpowder,
> As the supposed musket,
> The rod on my shoulder,
> Was only a long eye
> With which he pulled down the moon.

Allein der Sternbeseher
Beseufzte meine Dummheit,
Und rief beim letzten Seufzer:
Du Dummer, steh doch stille!
Ich stand; er rief: Steh veste!
Und legt auf meine Schulter
Ein Rohr, als wollt er schiessen.
Ich bat ihn um mein Leben,
Allein ich muß ietzt lachen,
Es fehlt ihm Rohr und Pulver,
Denn die vermeinte Flinte,
Das Rohr auf meiner Schulter,
War nur ein langes Auge,
Womit er durch die Lüfte
Den Mond herunter holte. (*SL* 33)

The Anacreontic poet operates outside of the epistemological paradigm of scientific knowledge. He misrecognizes not only the physical characteristics of the moon—converting a supposed object of knowledge into a poetic figure—but also misreads the technological symbol of the modern scientific revolution: the telescope.

The poet's manner of seeing subordinates the form of the telescope to the law of resemblances, perceiving the telescope first as a weapon rather than as a tool that mediates perception. He thereby alienates the telescope from its use-value, drawing upon a willful reserve of ignorance in order to distance himself from the practices and technologies that produce knowledge. Finally, when he does grasp the function of the device, he calls it "only a long eye." In accordance with the Anacreontic blurring of artifice and nature, the technological device, metal and glass, becomes an extension of an organ of perception.

The Anacreontic poet's position is not uncontroversial or banal. Indeed, the telescope was not always considered an adequate artificial expansion of natural sense perception. As Blumenberg notes, "Copernicanism tore asunder the fit (which was already loosened, anthropologically) between the world and man's organs: the congruence between reality and visibility."[12] When the Anacreontic poet calls the telescope "a long eye," he closes or overlooks the divide between the world and the human senses, a divide that was partially occasioned by the telescope and the subsequent insufficiency of the naked human eye to attain the truth of the world. For the Anacreontic poet, in this case, technology merely extends the sensuous capacities of the human being. And yet, the Anacreontic poet does not seem concerned about the *fit* between the senses and the exterior world.

The poet has a different concern. For him, the artificial eye imposes a way of seeing that depoeticizes the world and subordinates it to physical laws. The split between the poet and the stargazer is therefore a conflict between a poetic manner of reading and producing signs—a way of reading that submits the sensuous world to a play of resemblances and differences—and scientific rationality, or the reading of signs as the revelation of immutable physical and geometric laws operating behind phenomenal appearances. The poem portrays the clash of these two ways of reading in order to show which system ultimately triumphs.

The empirical scientist, at first, only seems to be driven by knowledge, the desire to classify and measure, to use the laws of mathematics and geometry to bring the world of the beyond down to the realm of the human and fetch the moon from its place in the heavens. Empirical knowledge, in this instance, seeks to move aside the veil that nature uses to hide herself, even if, behind this veil, there appears only another veil.[13] However, scientific knowledge does not merely bracket the world beyond the senses. An ontological transcendence—which posits a "reality" beyond or behind appearances—no longer belongs merely to the domain of metaphysicians and theologians, but also to that of scientists and philosophers attempting to ascertain the secrets of nature in the form of universal physical and geometric laws. The stargazer places himself in proximity to this ontology inasmuch as he acts according to epistemological imperatives that aim to integrate physical reality into a categorical system. His first impulse is to measure and classify the moon, to make it an object of knowledge: "I want to count the moon's / Valleys full of pine trees / And all the forests; / I want to measure the mountains" (*Ich will im Monde / Die Thäler voller Tannen, / Und alle Wälder zälen; / Ich will die Berge messen*, *SL* 33). The stargazer sees the telescope as a tool that allows him to deploy *ratio*, to measure and count, a process that would seem at first merely aimed toward generating series of numbers.

Even for the stargazer, however, the attractions of erotic desire constitute a more primordial motivational force than the drive to knowledge or the desire to classify. He unexpectedly follows his praise of numbers with the exclamation: "Girls are living on the moon!" (*Im Monde wohnen Mädchens!*, *SL* 34). Once again, the power of the *Mädchen*—as a sign that interrupts dominant ideological systems of interpretation—makes itself felt. The empirical, technologically mediated gaze, which at first takes as its object a landscape that is to be categorized, measured, and subordinated to the claims of knowledge, is channeled back into the domain of fantasy.

Empirical technologies of vision become contaminated by the erotic imagination, fusing sensual desire and epistemological desire, the visibility of dancing girls and the visibility of forms of Euclidean geometry.[14] The stargazer looks through the telescope and describes what he sees:

> I see little girls;
> They are dancing among little boys,
> They are dancing in figures,
> In angles and squares,

In spheres and cylinders,
In circles and ovals,
And play with the circle,
And stand on high summits,
And see with eyes longer
Than those of Newton or Copernicus.

Ich sehe kleine Mädchens;
Sie tanzen unter Knaben,
Sie tanzen nach Figuren,
Nach Winklen und Quadraten,
Nach Kegeln und Cilindern,
Nach Zirkeln und Ovalen,
Und spielen mit dem Zirkel,
Und stehn auf hohen Gipfeln,
Und sehn mit längern Augen,
Als Neuton und Kopernik. (*SL* 34)

The claims, techniques, and methods of Newtonian and Copernican science, even in the case of the stargazer, are subordinated to the more fundamental operations of desire. The "long eye" that astronomers use to probe the secrets of the universe is finally replaced by the even longer eyes of the girls dancing on the moon—dancing with angles and squares, cylinders and spheres. The theoretical sciences, whose exercise depends on sensuous knowledge just as much as theoretical rationality, geometry, and mathematics, are eventually overcome by the dynamics of the aesthetic itself, by the irreducible presence of the senses in all forms of empirical knowledge. If Baumgarten seeks to harness sensory cognition in the development of an epistemological theory, the Anacreontic poet reclaims the senses from their epistemological sublimation, bringing them back into the irrepressible economy of physical desire.

The Anacreontic poet regains interest after the stargazer conveys to him this geometrical and scientific sexual fantasy, succumbing for a short while to the temptation to see with the "eye" of the scientist:

Oh let me see the girls
With my eye.
He immediately grabbed at my eye,
And spoke, like magicians speak:
May this eye become longer.
While saying this,
A jolly girl,
Who was observing me and him,
Who was ridiculing me and him,

Let her black eyes sparkle.
Quickly I called out: Begone from my eye!
My eye should not grow.
You observe your girls,
I'm going to play with these.

Ach laß mir doch die Mädchen
Mit meinem Auge sehen.
Gleich grif er an mein Auge,
Und sprach, wie Zaub'rer sprechen:
Dis Auge werde länger.
Indem er dieses sagte,
Ließ ein vergnügtes Mädchen,
Das mich und ihn beschau'te,
Das mich und ihn verlachte,
Die schwarzen Augen funkeln.
Schnell rief ich: Weg vom Auge!
Mein Auge soll nicht wachsen.
Besieh' du deine Mädchens.
Ich will mit diesen spielen. (*SL* 34)

The poem locates the imaginary impulse driving the physical sciences not in a complete description of the cosmos or a theory of the universe, but rather, in the desire for a perpetual lengthening of the eye. Unsatisfied by the reality offered up by the visible world, incapable of pulling aside the veil that would reveal the secret essence of matter, the scientist attains satisfaction only by producing vision with an ever-expanding artificial organ, a fetishistic object that gathers and embodies the scientist's power. The Anacreontic poet rejects the transformation of the eye into an enormous phallus: a tool that continually grows, penetrating deeper into the unknown reaches of cosmic reality.

The stargazer's vision is contaminated by sensuous tendencies that are incompatible with the purely theoretical gaze. The true identity of the stargazer betrays itself in the intrusion of sexual desire into his pretension to knowledge: he is motivated by the same impulses as those that drive the Anacreontic poet. Unlike the poet, the erotic intentionality of the scientist is displaced onto a realm that can only be attained with an artificially lengthened, perpetually growing eye. At last, he betrays his own scientific identity when he speaks with the language of the counter-epistemological model of the empirical sciences themselves: magic. When the stargazer speaks as a magician—*wie Zaub'rer*—in order to "lengthen" the eye of the poet, he becomes the very figure from which the modern empirical scientist sought to distinguish himself. The homoerotic posture in which the two men find one another compounds the shame of this scene when they appear not as the subjects of their own sovereign gaze, but as objects of the gaze of another, of a girl whose eyes register the homo/heteroerotic game unfolding between the poet and the stargazer.

The unconscious desire of the Anacreontic poet, all along, was to see with his own eye, *mit meinem Auge*, that is, with an eye opposed to the hyper-phallic and fetishistic eye of the stargazer. The poet's epiphany arrives, however, when he ceases to be the subject that sees, but himself becomes the object being seen by the "jolly girl/Who was observing me and him,/Who was ridiculing me and him." Becoming the object of another's gaze catapults the poet out of his own voyeuristic fantasy, disabusing him of whatever it is that attracts him to an invisible realm operating beyond the world of appearances and inaccessible to naked sensory perception. He thereby becomes subject—or object—of a test of ridicule that, as an Anacreontic poet, ought to be his privileged domain. The female gaze tears the poet's eye from the orbital pull of the stars. More importantly, this gaze blocks the attempt to locate meaning in the beyond or heal the rift between the realm of the senses and the hidden mechanisms of nature. For the poet, the model of vision that takes priority over all other models is neither microscopic nor telescopic. It is the look that travels from one human being to another, performed with eyes that excite shame, scorn, pleasure, or desire. Such eyes bring human beings back into this world instead of projecting them into the world above or attempting to bring the world above down to earth.

The Discipline of the Family and the Law of the *Muß*

The most obvious and most effective production of bourgeois subjects in the mid-eighteenth century—of citizens, Christians, and human beings, as Breitinger would put it—crystallized around the organization of family life and depended upon the authority of the law of the father. Rococo poetry often addresses itself to fathers, to mothers, to sisters, to children—to all members of the family and therefore to the family structure as such—in ways that draw attention to the exercise of discipline in its particular organization of life. At times, the Anacreontic poet simply bypasses the family structure entirely. Gleim's Anacreontic poet, in the poem "Free Love" ("Die freie Liebe"), prefers erotic freedom to marriage. In this instance, he comes dangerously close to the figure of the French libertine—a proximity that one can hear in the association of erotic activity with freedom, *la liberté*. Unlike Götz, Gleim is not concerned with resolving the conflict between pleasure and virtue. On the contrary, he seeks to hold them apart, separating the codes of enjoyment and virtue, aesthetic pleasure and ethical utility: "The most worthy of all pleasures,/A sweet and secret kiss/Is made bitter through the little word: must" (*Der allerwürdigste Genuß/Ein süsser und verschwiegner Kuß/Wird bitter durch das Wörtlein: Muß*, *SL* 51). Throughout the poem, the poet celebrates the freedom to choose an erotic object outside of the institutional confines of marriage.

The true freedom of "Free Love," however, consists not in the free choice of an erotic object, but in unfettered poetic activity. Poetic practice produces its own form of disciplinarity: an aesthetic exercise. The exercise itself does not imply the full cognitive range of acts demanded by Baumgarten's version of the aesthetic exercise. Indeed, the Anacreontic definition of freedom is characterized by its liberation from the strenuous reintegration of the poetic exercise into contexts of significance that surpass the poem's purely sensuous claims over its readership:

> Long live that which exercises by joking!
> Long live that which surrenders itself to me!
> And yet that which in this act loves freedom,
> Freedom, my darling on earth.

> Es lebe, was sich scherzend übt!
> Es lebe, was sich mir ergiebt!
> Und doch dabei die Freiheit liebt,
> Die Freiheit, meinen Schatz auf Erden. (*SL* 52)

Freedom, a concept that would later become inextricably associated with autonomy, giving one's self the law, and the dignity or worth of the human being conveyed by this specific form of agency—in short, the moment of transcendence at the core of the human—itself becomes the ultimate erotic object. The Anacreontic poet calls freedom his "treasure," or *Schatz*—itself a term of endearment for a beloved—which initiates a double movement: just as the poet degrades freedom to the terms set by an erotic game, the erotic game itself becomes raised to one of the utmost potentialities of human agency. Freedom doubles back on itself, but only inasmuch as it constitutes both the subject and the object of Anacreontic love. The poet is in love with the freedom of his own love, and this freedom only manifests itself in the exercise of the poem itself. Freedom for the Anacreontic poet is a treasure *on earth* and *in the poem*, and it takes the form of a language that operates outside the ethical law. According to Anacreontic freedom, socially sanctioned erotic attachments violate the pleasure principle, and it is this principle that reigns supreme in the play of Anacreontic lyrics. Freedom in this instance consists in the validation of an alternative order to that of the necessary, an order that contravenes the "must" (*Muß*). Moreover, this freedom is not compatible with the freedom of "all others," since Anacreontic freedom demands the submission of all erotic objects (*Long live that which surrenders itself to me*). These submissive objects include not only the "girl" within the poem, but the readers of the poem themselves, or those who enter into the poetic game being played.

In the age of spiritual practices inflected by Pietism, marriage does not merely function as a guarantor of economic or familial stability, but mediates between the worldly and the divine.[15] The divine order, the economic order, and the ethical order intertwine and become fused in the marriage contract. And yet, at the basis of this contract there lies an irreducible sensuality—a circulation of desire that threatens the hold of the ethical over this relation—that cannot simply be expunged from the terms of the agreement. In Gleim's poem, the metonymic relationship between marriage and the ethical—later, figures such as Mittler in Goethe's *Elective Affinities* and Judge Vilhelm in Kierkegaard's *Either/Or* would continue to draw upon the relation between the two, a relation in which marriage "stands in" for the ethical as such—dissipates into poetic libertinism. Such is indeed the target at which the poet takes aim: the ethical sphere as a whole, the *Muß*.

The libertinism of the Anacreontic poem, however, could not possibly be confused with its aristocratic and courtly literary and philosophical counterparts. The seventeenth- and eighteenth-century libertinisms of France and England, although notoriously complex in their heterogeneity of practices and textual forms, are clearly distinct from that which one finds in the Anacreontic poem: here, there is no "reality effect," no aristocratic intrigue, no explicit scene of sexual transgression. The libertine engages the real; the Anacreontic poet loosens the pull of the real over imaginative life. The poem thus attacks the ethical not directly, but makes the ethical lose its hold over all discursive domains, and above all, over its own acts of speech, by stripping the ethical of its transcendental contexts of meaning. The ethical, in this instance, belongs neither to ontology nor to metaphysics, and is not part of the structure of the world: it is simply a move in a poetic language game. The joke (as opposed to the "wit" of the libertine) is a necessary part of this strategic deployment of signs: as a form of speech that cannot be read literally, it is an exercise for the imaginative fantasy, for aesthetic procedures of binding and separating that are caught in a play of identities and differences. And it is in fact the joke—"Long live that which exercises by joking!" (*SL* 52)—rather than sexual liberty that provides the condition of possibility of Anacreontic freedom.

Marriage stabilizes and reproduces the ethics of bourgeois society by reproducing the structure of the family. In the Anacreontic poem, however, the family, as a gathering space of norms and practices designed to reproduce its own structural stability—as the central set of relations that define, anchor, and propagate the functional roles of man, woman, and child—loses control of its own ability to generate such stabilized subjects. In the poem, "To My Parents" ("An die Eltern"), the poet relates what can only be described as a failure of discipline in the attempt to transfer subject-formation from the law of the father to the institutions of Church and State. The eighteenth century is said to have discovered the individuality of the child, or more specifically, the child as a problem for discourse and thought, demanding specific techniques of formation in all areas of life, in families, schools, and churches.[16] Rousseau's *Emile* (1762), which, although written twenty years after Gleim's poems, responds to the problems posed by the subjectivity of the child that were already being discussed in the early eighteenth century, portrays the child as a being that demands constant attention and control; the slightest false input can disrupt the formation of the virtuous citizen. Family life becomes organized according to the unrealizable ideal of total organization, an ideal that Rousseau expresses paradoxically as a free and autonomous subject that can only come into being through the omnipresence of control. All areas of life in which children are present become structured according to the potential effects they have on the formative narrative of development.

Rousseau's thematization of childhood as a phenomenon demanding an intensified disciplinary attention was preceded by the emergence of institutions that had constructed the child as a problem. Indeed, some of Gleim's Anacreontic poems direct themselves against attempts to organize and normalize the life of the child that were characteristic of pedagogical innovations originating specifically in Halle. A. H. Francke (1663–1727) had established a famous school and orphanage at Halle dedicated to raising children in accordance with Pietist spirituality. And it was precisely Francke's Pietism that—albeit indirectly—contributed to a "pedagogical realism" eventually leading to the establishment of *Realschulen*, or schools that trained children from early stages to take up a practical profession and serve the reproduction of civil society.[17] Some years before the *Attempt in Jocular Songs* was published, Christoph Semler had founded the first *Realschule* in Halle in 1738.[18]

Gleim's Anacreontic poet intervenes in this institutional and ideological landscape. In a poem entitled "The School," the poet tells children: "take pleasure in learning" (*SL* 13). The children ought to learn not from books, but from observing the animals of nature, initiating a series that culminates in the injunction: "Also learn something from the rabbit" (*lernt auch etwas vom Kaninchen*, *SL* 13). The sexuality of nature is then transposed onto an alternative disciplinary space constituted by pleasure: pleasure becomes the law, and the relationship between poet and the beautiful girl replaces the institution of the school: "Learn from me and my beautiful girl/To play well, to kiss well:/Just look, school is open" (*Lernt von mir und meiner Schöne/Gut zu spielen, gut zu küssen:/Seht nur her, wir halten Schule*, *SL* 13).

The poet takes aim not merely at pedagogical institutionality, but at the structure of the family that often functioned as the origin of an induction into civil society, directing himself against the rules of the paterfamilias and the *oikos*. In "To My Parents" ("An die Eltern"), the poet usurps the will of the father, inverting the hierarchization of the father-child relationship:

Fathers! Never force your children
To learn those arts
That they do not wish to learn!

Väter! Nöthight eure Kinder,
Nie zum Lernen solcher Künste,
Die sie nicht erlernen wollen. (*SL* 22)

The poet's injunction to "listen to the child" does not, at this point, entail an anti-disciplinary stance. On the contrary, such an ideology signals the intensified anxiety surrounding the importance of producing a stable identity for the child. Nevertheless, a significant number of Anacreontic poems are drawn to the abnormality of child development, foregrounding pedagogical patterns that diverge widely from the normalizing practices of the time.[19]

This poem, however, represents a failed education, one in which the poetic persona fashions itself as a bad subject: a subject incapable of being disciplined and formed in precisely those social roles whose central function is to guarantee the reproduction of disciplinary institutions. The poet speaks:

I, his son, was also forced,
But did it yield anything?
First I was supposed to take up the black cloth
To learn to care for souls
Because my mother so desired it.
But my father saved me
From such difficult cares;
And then I was supposed to, against my will,
Learn to care for bodies;
But my father found out,
That I would rather learn nothing at all.
Finally he took me by the arm,
Led me to the lawyer's office,
And exhorted him so that I heard it:
Cousin, teach this one to practice law.
Be strict with him, and give him work.
Briskly my cousin gave it to me.
Beheading, hanging, whipping, the breaking wheel—
I was supposed to learn this all from the papers.

Ich, sein Sohn, ward auch gezwungen,
Aber hat es was gefruchtet?

> Erst sollt ich im schwarzen Kleide,
> Sorgen vor die Geister lernen,
> Weil es meine Mutter wollte;
> Doch es rettete mein Vater
> Mich von solchen schweren Sorgen;
> Und da sollt ich, wider Willen,
> Sorgen vor die Körper lernen;
> Aber es erfuhr mein Vater,
> Daß ich lieber gar nichts lernte.
> Endlich nahm er mich beim Arme,
> Führte mich zum Advokaten,
> Und ermahnt ihn, daß ichs hörte:
> Vetter lehre diesen rechten,
> Halt ihn scharf, und gieb ihm Arbeit.
> Hurtig gab sie mir der Vetter.
> Köpfen, Hangen, Peitschen, Rädern
> Sollt ich aus den Blättern lernen. (*SL* 22)

The poem describes in its basic form a struggle for power over the formation of identity, a wandering disciplinarity that is transferred from domain to domain: from the mother to the father to the school system. This transfer corresponds to a movement from care for the soul, to care for the body, to care for social order as a whole: the mother wants the child to become a priest; the father wants him to become a doctor; and the child is ultimately forced to become a representative of the law. In each case, the child is to be made responsible for the reproduction and maintenance of institutions of discipline: the church, the hospital, the legal system. In each case, he either fails or deviates from the norms of disciplinary institutions whose very function is to guarantee the production of functional subjects.

The Anacreontic poet, when faced with the inevitability of a social role that appears fundamentally incompatible with his own inclinations and drives, explodes the disciplinary space by amplifying the marginal elements of normalizing practices:

> But he gave me trials
> That had to do with lost love letters,
> Welcome night apparitions,
> And relatives caught red-handed.
> . . .
> Immediately head and pen became diligent
> And my teacher could see
> That I would not learn any trade
> Other than the commerce of those in love.

Aber gab er mir Prozesse
Von verlornen Liebesbriefen,
Von willkommnen Nachtgespenstern,
Von ertappten Anverwandten;
. . .
Gleich war Kopf und Feder fleißig
Und mein Lehrer konnt es merken,
Daß ich nichts erlernen würde,
Als die Händel der Verliebten. . . . (*SL* 23)

Ultimately, the poet is forced to take up a legal apprenticeship, although his concentration on the "business of lovers" essentially renders him useless from the social-functional perspective of the law. In the normalizing practices that regulate the economy of crime and punishment, the poet makes himself marginal. From within the space of the institutions that dictate the valid forms of bourgeois life, he alienates himself from the practices that ground the reproduction of these institutions.[20] Reproduction is de-socialized: only "the commerce of those in love" counts as that which permits a reproductive flow to circulate between subjects, readers, and words.

The Non-Melancholic Sign: The Attraction to Death Approaches Zero

Max Weber, in his study of the Protestant work ethic, describes the bourgeois subject as one who views its own economic activity as a *calling* (*Beruf*).[21] Economic expansion and the continual growth of capital respond to the call of a higher order, thereby suffusing the most quotidian of daily activities and economic responsibilities with the sanction of transcendent grace. However, just as the conception of a calling refers to a sphere of activity in life, so too does it govern death. For death—its manner, time, and circumstance—also is a calling: an inevitable exit that comes for a specific person when the time of life has run its course. Death too has an economy: it demands the repayment of the loan of life that had been granted at the moment of birth. Upon dying, Socrates says that he owes Asclepius a cock. The economy of life and death is conceptualized upon a model of exchange (although, according to Nietzsche, Socrates's singular response seems to overturn this logic, interpreting death as the gift rather than life).[22]

Death, in its literary-historical manifestations, has appeared as a calling, as a figure that demands payment, and as a relativizing and individualizing force (princes and paupers are both subject to it; and when death calls, as Heidegger would emphasize, it calls for a particular individual, a call that cannot be deferred or transferred to another).[23] There have been numerous literary representations of the power governing the movement between life and death, between this world and the next—one thinks, for example, of the many positions on this issue in *The Ploughman from Bohemia* (*Der Ackermann aus Böhmen*, 1401)—that stabilize and make intelligible this boundary by reflecting upon it, functionalizing it, and naturalizing it.

The attempt to approach death from the perspective of intelligibility, either making sense of death or making sense out of how such a thing could possibly make sense, involves human beings in a set of paradoxes for thought. Heidegger's attempt to locate death as a structure of intelligibility of *Dasein* can only understand death as an "impossibility" vis-à-vis the realm of intelligibility. As part of the way human beings make sense of the world, death makes possible the realm of possibility itself *as* an impossibility, awakening an *Unmöglichkeitssinn* (sense of impossibility) that loosens any particular culture's supposedly sovereign hold over the practices of every individual. Death, as structure of intelligibility (here, the intelligibility of something unintelligible), thus introduces the necessary gap that allows *Dasein* to both be inevitably part of and yet free from its own culture's practices.[24]

Even for Heidegger, then, death appears coextensive with freedom. Although his reinterpretation of death in *Being and Time* inverts the everyday understanding of death as an end to life, in essence making possible *novelty* and the opening of new worlds, he nevertheless conceptualizes death as a structure of intelligibility. For Heidegger, death as a structure of intelligibility re-modalizes that which appears given or actual as one form of being among many other possibilities, making that which is intelligible suddenly appear meaningless or contingent; this particular form of intelligibility, as the precondition for a certain type of sentient freedom (the freedom of thinking the real as contingent possibility), marks a difference between authentic and inauthentic *Dasein*.

In the context of a history of cultural forms that approach the phenomenon of death, the Anacreontic tradition appears singular in its refusal to regard death as a matter of ontological importance.[25] In a poem entitled "The Choice" ("Die Wahl"), the Anacreontic poet begins by reflecting on his own art, and specifically, what forms of life he would call into being if he could paint and sing. The reflection darkens as the poet grants himself a poetic sovereignty, an absolute power over life and death:

The Choice

If I could paint like Apelles
Then I would paint all sorts of girls;
If I could play like Orpheus,
All sorts of girls should dance;
If I could bring the dead back to life,
All sorts of girls would live;
But if I could, as I would wish

Let many die again;
Many again would die,
Many I would wish to paint over
So that they would remain unpainted,
And tired from the first dance,
Many should dance never again.

Die Wahl

Könnt ich malen, wie Apelles,
Lauter Mädchens wollt ich malen;
Könnt ich nur wie Orpheus spielen,
Lauter Mädchens sollten tanzen;
Könnt ich Todte lebend machen,
Lauter Mädchens wollten leben;
Aber könnt ich, wie ich wollte,
Viele wieder sterben lassen,
Viele sollten wieder sterben,
Viele wollt ich überstreichen,
Daß die ungemalet blieben,
Und vom ersten Tanz ermüdet
Sollten viele nicht mehr tanzen. (*SL* 19)

The line between life and death provides nothing more than the pretext to play with art. This play is nevertheless carefully structured, and it may be instructive to examine this structure. The poem has thirteen lines. The numerological significance embedded in the poem's own structure shifts the light Anacreontic mode into a darker imaginative and rhetorical space. A split in the center of the poem, occurring around line 7, marks the transition from life to death, or more precisely, from the power of imagined representational practices that give life to those that give death.

In addition to moving from eros to thanatos, from the life drive to the death drive, the poem also marks a gender split, one in which life is associated with the feminine and death is without gender distinction: the poet calls into life only "girls" (lines 1–6), but then wishes death upon a genderless multiplicity, "many" (*viele*). Life is also associated with a poetic vivification transferred between media: the poet moves through various forms of *ekphrasis*, the representations of representations: from painting (lines 1–2), to music (3–4), to life (5–6), from death (8–9), back to painting (10–11), and then to music (12–13). Line 7, the central line around which the structural inversion turns, expresses the limitless desire of the imagination of the Anacreontic poet, a fantasy about the omnipotence of the poetic will: *But if I could [do], as I would wish* (*Aber könnt ich, wie ich wollte*). The poem's carefully crafted thematic counterpoint substitutes for its lack of a rhyming structure: A (life in painting), B (life in music/dance), C (death to life), C (life to death), A (death in painting), B (death in music/dance). The structure of the poem as a whole is compressed in lines 5–9: from death to life, from life to death.

In the second half of the poem, the poet explores the other side of an interpretation of art that had previously only emphasized its life-giving and reproductive properties; in the inverted world, art becomes an act of de-creation, a death wish coextensive with murder. It unleashes a rage that would seem inappropriate for the Anacreontic poem were it not for the aestheticized witticism: "Many I would wish to paint over" (*viele wollt ich überstreichen*). The orphic dance, which animates inanimate objects, becomes a dance of death. The "choice" (*die Wahl*) that the poet mentions in the title of the poem is a choice not merely about aesthetic representation, but a fantasy about the power over life and death. Or so it would seem. In fact, the following poem in *Jocular Songs* is also entitled "The Choice," and it reworks the content of the previous one—only with rhymes rather than with unrhymed rhythm. The content of the second poem entitled "The Choice" is not arranged according to the same structural stringency as the first: the death-giving properties of art are introduced in line 18 out of a total of 24 lines.[26] The proportional—almost classical—structure of the first poem is therefore contrasted with the looseness of the second. The first version is Anacreontic in its structure, the second, in its thematic coherence.

If, according to Meier, the joke opens an abyss of differences and similarities, the abyss of these poems lies not in crossing the line between life and death, but rather, in a more important choice: to rhyme, or not to rhyme. "The Choice" refers primarily not to the choice between life and death, demarcating the line between Being and Non-Being, but rather, to the poetic choice between rhymed and non-rhymed speech, between a French-inspired song to be sung, or the unrhymed rhythms of Anacreon himself. The poet notes in the introductory dedication, a fictional letter to his lover: "When Frau Dacier wanted to make the jokes of the most jocular Greek poet appealing to ladies, she had to teach them in her *native tongue*. If your sisters want to sing songs in your honor, then you have to translate them into rhymed verse, as I have done with 'The Choice' " (*SL* 4). The choice, *die Wahl*, occurs in sound, in a poetic form that situates the poem on opposing sides of a cultural divide: classicist or populist, past or present, Greek or French. Rhyme is not a matter of life and death; life and death are a matter of rhyme.

This poetic form, supposedly centered on pleasure, on immanence and life, nevertheless does not exclude death from its horizon of inquiry.[27] As a matter of poetic importance, as a pretext for the play of life, death remains paramount. The central task of Gleim's Anacreontic poet, when faced with death, may be formulated as such: how can one deflect the inevitable calling of death, one that calls us away from this world, pushing our spirit and our earthly deeds into the space of eternity?

It is not the *denial* of death that motivates the Anacreontic poet, but the transformation of its sign character. The Anacreontic poet is locked in a struggle with death, not to evade it—which would be impossible—but to loosen its attraction to mourning, melancholy, finitude, vanity, any frame of reference that would inevitably link death to transcendence.

The poet fantasizes about making death more economically pliable: perhaps death can be bribed, or perhaps the debt can be transferred to another person. When death comes for the poet, he seeks to transfer the calling of death for the poet to the calling of his neighbor for death: "Do you not hear the neighbor calling? / Go fetch him, he will thank you for it. / Death, you are making a mistake!" (*Hörst du nicht den Nachbar rufen? / Hol ihn nur, er wird dirs danken. / Tod du irrst dich!, SL* 16). After attempting to settle his debt to death by exchanging his life for the life of another, the poet shifts codes from the currency of life and death to actual money: "Take the gold, and let me live" (*Nimm das Gold, und laß mich leben, SL* 16). In each case, lives can be exchanged, individuals are interchangeable, and the poet manipulates death as an economic agent. Life itself becomes as exchangeable, fluid, and insubstantial as money.

In "To Death" ("An den Tod"), the poet fantasizes about transferring the debt of life that leads to death not from himself to another, but between other people—specifically between his mother and his *Mädchen*—this time acting as an intermediary:

> Death, can you also fall in love?
> Why then are you taking my girl?
> Can't you take my mother instead?
> For she rather looks like you.
> Fresh rose-red cheeks
> That colored so prettily my desire
> Do not bloom for pale bones,
> Do not bloom for your lips.
> Death! What do you want with this girl?
> With your teeth without lips
> You can't even kiss her.

> Tod, kannst du dich auch verlieben?
> Warum holst du denn mein Mädchen?
> Kannst du nicht die Mutter holen?
> Denn die sieht dir doch noch ähnlich.
> Frische rosenrote Wangen,
> Die mein Wunsch so schön gefärbet,

Blühen nicht für blasse Knochen,
Blühen nicht für deine Lippen.
Tod! Was willst du mit dem Mädchen?
Mit den Zähnen ohne Lippen
Kannst du es ia doch nicht küssen. (*SL* 27)

The poet uses death to underscore the priority of the erotic attachment over the claims of the family structure. Death, no longer a symbol of transience or the nothingness of human existence, itself is addressed as an Anacreontic seducer. The emblem of the death's head, the visual iconography of death itself, makes the *pointe* of the poem possible: death, whose mouth consists in bones and teeth rather than lips (*Zähnen ohne Lippen*), cannot even properly play the role of lover. This does not stop the Anacreontic poet from making death into a reflection of his own identity: one who seeks an embrace with another to satisfy an erotic drive. The similarity in appearance between the skeletal mother and fleshless death—death and the maiden becomes death and the mother, *For she rather looks like you*—makes the mother a more appropriate erotic object for death. The poet, who tries to subdue death by projecting his own identity onto it, uses this projected identity to break the ties to his mother and nullify the laws of familial piety.

Even the death of the hero, one who dies the beautiful death in sacrifice for the *patria* or fatherland, king or nation, is stripped of its significance. The tradition of Anacreontic poetry manifest in the *Anacreontea* tends to differentiate itself from the epic, whose primary function is to immortalize and disseminate the glory of the hero. The poems of the *Jocular Songs*—although the final poems of the second volume refer explicitly to the events of the Second Silesian War between Prussia and Austria and exhibit a certain streak of patriotic propaganda—do not approach the ideological conceit that will later undergird Gleim's other most imitated work, the *Prussian War Songs* (*Preußische Kriegslieder*). In the *War Songs*, the events of the Seven Years' War are told from the perspective of a grenadier, who, as a simple foot soldier rather than an Achilles, nevertheless does not fully cohere with the usual figure of the mythical-nationalist hero. The war songs, which fuse literary play with a burgeoning nationalistic consciousness, anchor their own idiom in transcendental points: God, Fatherland, and Frederick II.[28] The Anacreontic poet of the *Jocular Songs*, however, seeks an alternative to such organizing discourses (the divine, the nation, the sovereign)—albeit without actively undermining them:

Am I then like a lazy man
In my prince's camp?
No: know my deeds,
No, know this, god of warriors:
My prince conquers countries,
And I conquer girls.

Bin ich denn wie ein Fauler,
Im Lager meines Prinzen?
Nein, wisse meine Thaten,
Nein, wiß es, Gott der Krieger:
Mein Prinz erobert Länder,
Und ich erobre Mädchen. (*SL* 116)

If the form of the joke exercises the ability to analyze and respond affectively to similarities and differences, in this case, the subversive *pointe* consists not in a direct negation of the prince, but in the comparison between the prince and the figure of the Anacreontic poet. The "and" of the final line ("My prince conquers countries,/And I conquer girls") simultaneously recognizes the legitimacy of the prince's endeavors while at the same time relativizing these endeavors by constructing an analogy between prince and poet. This analogy, however, sets in motion a play of similarities and differences. The poet exploits the high and low registers in the notion of "conquest" (erotic vs. imperialistic), all the while refusing to hierarchize these registers or to evaluate one as more worthy than the other. The poet does not question the violence of war as such, but foregrounds its contingency, emphasizing the futility of the immortalization of the hero in the very banality of his own representations of wartime death. In a poem "To the Warriors" ("An die Krieger"), the poet makes the sacrifice of warriors appear meaningless, asking them: "Why do you want to bleed to death?" (*Warum wollt ihr euch verbluten?*, *SL* 117).

As in Willamov's "Life Story of the Human Being," the Anacreontic poet often describes death—traditionally linked to the realm of the beyond—as the sudden disruption of life. Gleim's poem "On the Death of a Nightingale" ("Auf den Tod einer Nachtigall")—in which the nightingale seems to stand for the idealized Anacreontic poet—exemplifies one of the predominant modes of poetic practice in the Anacreontic attitude to death.

The nightingale's attitude to death may be described as singularly non-philosophical: it does not make the end of life an object for thought. The nightingale shows no signs of the impending death that will overtake it, instead singing and warbling until, as the sudden and unexpected end of life, the end simply comes. What appears astonishing about the nightingale for the Anacreontic poet is precisely the *lack* of death as a signifier, its failure to announce itself or to manifest itself as a calling in the world of appearances: "Did he have to fade so quickly?/Just yesterday he sang so cheerfully" (*Must er denn so schnell erblassen?/Gestern sang er noch so munter*, *SL* 43). The nightingale refuses to allow death not merely to become the ontological ground of its being, but to exert its sway over any form of signifying activity:

Among his bright tones
Not one sounded like tones of mourning.

Why then did he not sing sadly?
Did he perhaps, as a wise man,
Wish to jest unto his death?

Unter seinen hellen Tönen
Klang kein Ton, wie Trauertöne.
Warum sang er denn nicht traurig?
Wollt er etwa, wie ein Weiser,
Seinem Tod entgegen scherzen? (*SL* 43)

For the Anacreontic poet, facing death without the slightest manifestation of melancholy or trauma occasions at first incomprehensibility, and then yields to wonder and admiration. That which designates the actions of a "wise man," undoubtedly a reference to Anacreon, consists less in control over death than control over how to integrate death into human signifying practices.

Language itself does not, as it does in Benjamin's account of the baroque mourning-play in his *Origin of German Tragic Drama*, bear the traces of the fallen creature, registering the transcendental weight of the beyond in its own system of signs.[29] On the contrary, Anacreontic language signals the possibility for the human being to deny its fallen condition, to refuse the fall into melancholy, trauma, and mourning. The Anacreontic poet therefore offers a counter-semiotic model to Benjamin's understanding of baroque allegory. The language of the Anacreontic poet does not point beyond itself to any transcendental code that secures its meaning. When faced with mortality, the goal of the Anacreontic poet is to make death a nullity, a sign at a zero state. This goal does not amount to ignoring death. The ability to make death a nullity, to joke when faced with the imminence of demise—although it appears natural to the nightingale—for the human being, demands the control and exercise that only one who is wise can muster.

One may therefore perceive an important difference between the nightingale's song and the song of the Anacreontic poet: unlike the Anacreontic poet, the nightingale does not register mortality—not even negatively—in its trilling expressivity. Ultimately, it is not the similarity between the Anacreontic poet and the nightingale that comes to the fore in the poem as much as their difference, a difference that emerges between the act of enunciation (the Anacreontic poet who approaches death as a perturbation, as a question or problem) and the ideal of wisdom represented (the nightingale that does not even register death; it is a being for whom death is not a problem, not even an entity). The poet does not render this difference in the attitude toward death an anthropological one, claiming that only the human being has consciousness of mortality, and that the lack of consciousness on the part of the animal signals its exclusion from the order of sentience. Rather, the animal still functions as the model for a wise man, *ein Weiser*, albeit suggesting a way of being that the poet himself cannot quite achieve.

The nightingale's refusal to recognize the power of the transcendent, its total absorption in the immanence of life, does not occasion a recognition of the impossibility of this ideal for the poet. Instead, the nightingale becomes a positive model for the poet—not because it sings so sweetly, but because, even at the moment of its departure from the world of sensuous forms, there is no trace of death in its song. Even at its most allegorical—for the poem "On the Death of a Nightingale" activates allegorical modes of reading, suggesting that what is really being discussed is not the death of a bird, but the death of another poet—the language of Anacreon does not fall into the clutches of the eternal. The temporality of Anacreontic poetry refuses to make the moment anything more than a moment.

The Anacreontic poet therefore cannot sing a song of consolation for the survivors. Mourning only appears as that which is excluded from the set of possibilities of his own idiom: a song of mourning cannot be realized within a system of signs that seeks to rob death of its annihilating, determinative power.

The poet of immanence therefore refuses even the gesture of consolation. The poetry of consolation is poetry of the grave, a *Grablied*. The movement of consolation makes death meaningful; it bestows upon death a signifying value that confirms its attractive pull rather than seeking to reduce it to a zero state—an ideal that, at any rate, cannot be achieved, a fact to which the Anacreontic poet's practice itself testifies.

The *Grablied* seeks to overcome the eternity of death through its own counter-movement of eternalization, something that the Anacreontic poet cannot—or will not—provide. The Anacreontic poet refuses to mourn the nightingale, thereby coming closer to the ideal that the nightingale represents: a being for whom its own death is meaningless. It is a fallacy to claim that the life of a being for whom death is not an issue is equally meaningless; on the contrary, such a being represents immanent life in its purest state. What sort of poet could sing a song of mourning for this miraculous creature, and thereby misrecognize and do violence to the central virtue of the nightingale, namely, to extract life from its dependence on death as a source of meaning? In the final lines of Gleim's poem, we learn who could sing this song, the song of mourning. Such a task is reserved for the poet of aesthetic transcendence, one who links the world of the senses to the world of the beyond:

> O! A better poet than myself
> Must immortalize this bird.
> One who consoles better than I
> Must banish the grief of my friend.
> Broks, the herald of his brothers,
> Broks should sing him a funeral song.

O! es muß ein beßrer Dichter
Diesen Vogel ewig machen.
O! es muß ein beßrer Tröster
Meines Freundes Trauer tilgen.
Broks, der Herold seiner Brüder,
Broks soll ihm ein Grablied singen. (*SL* 45)

Absolute Poetry

In the first of the *Jocular Songs*, the poet describes himself as the "true disciple" (*treuer Schüler*, *SL* 5) of Anacreon, establishing a transmission of poetic knowledge and practice that travels from antiquity to his time and place. In this first poem, the poet does more than merely link his own practice to antiquity: he gives himself an identity, a poetic persona modeled on Anacreon. The second song takes up the poet's Anacreontic identity, transposing it onto the formative logic of the bourgeois family. The disciple, or *Schüler* of Anacreon, then becomes a *Rechenschüler*, or an accounting student: "My father is teaching me to calculate/He counts pounds and thalers;/But me, I count girls" (*Mein Vater lehrt mich rechnen/Er zälet Pfund und Taler;/Ich aber zäle Mädchens*, *SL* 6). Both the first and the second poems describe the process of a transmission of knowledge. The poetic identity, however, both trumps and contaminates his bourgeois identity and the instrumental logic pervading civil society. When the disciple of Anacreon becomes an accounting student, he interprets this activity through his primary poetic identity. Anacreon, if he does not quite overcome the law of the father, infiltrates its main symbolic system: the economic system and circulation of money. Gleim's tenure as an accounting student is taken over by fantasies of social-sexual reproduction:

. . . He asks me
How much is the sum?
And when he asks me like this
Then I think about the reproduction
Of the sisters and brothers
And laugh, when I calculate.

. . . Er fragt mich
Wie viel beträgt die Summe?
Und wenn er mich so fräget
So denk ich ans Vermehren
Der Schwestern und der Brüder
Und lache, wenn ich rechne. (*SL* 6)

The universalization of Anacreontic play does not subvert the logic of bourgeois reproduction and render vain the domain of human activity; rather, the poet repurposes instrumental rationality, replacing the code of money with that of biological reproduction.

The universalization of play as a generalized cognitive state can be observed in the poem "Business" ("Geschäfte"). This poem turns on itself, construing its own activity as a repeated form of bureaucratic uniformity, where every act reproduces the same patterns and generates the same attractive sign, the *Mädchen*, which functions as a poetic generator of reproduction:

Business

It seems to me, whenever I sleep,
I sleep among so many girls;
And always whenever I dream,
I dream of nothing but girls;
And when I wake up,
I think about nothing other than girls;
In sleep, in dream, while awake,
I play with so many girls.

Geschäfte

Mir deucht, so oft ich schlafe,
Schlaf ich bei lauter Mädchen;
Und immer, wenn ich träume,
Träum' ich von nichts als Mädchen;
Und wenn ich wieder wache,
Denk ich an nichts als Mädchen;
Im Schlaf, im Traum, im Wachen
Spiel ich mit lauter Mädchen. (*SL* 14)

The relation between work and play is unclear in this poem: is play becoming tedious, or is the tedium of life becoming play? At first, the poem functions in an exemplary sense for the Anacreontic exercise of unbounded play. The poem iterates and differentiates physical and cognitive modalities—sleeping, dreaming, waking—all the while stressing their permeability with one another as well as their ultimate reduction to the realm of play. The opening line declares the primacy of an imagined eroticism, a mental impression expressed in terms of its probability or improbability: *Mir deucht*, it seems to me, "whenever I sleep,/I sleep among so many girls." Already the poet moves in the logic of appearances, not of realities. The logic of appearing, however, refers not to the *Mädchen* themselves, but rather, to the poet's own bodily and mental activity; the "it seems to me" (*mir deucht*) applies to each of the temporal phrases, each of which in turn thematizes a corporeal or cognitive modality.

Here, in a highly compressed form, appears the Anacreontic cogito: the imagined reality of seeming overtakes every order of being, projecting itself across syntactical structures just as it permeates all instances of cognition. The logic of appearances, "seeming," subsumes every moment of sleep, every moment of dreaming, every moment of waking. Similarly, the "I play" of the final line applies itself across these very corporeal-cognitive states; in essence, then, the poem expresses an identity between the "it seems to me" and the "I play," the *mir deucht* and the *ich spiele*, both of which have priority over unconscious and conscious corporeal and cognitive acts. Self-observation leads to a differentiation between various cognitive states according to their ontological vividness (sleeping, dreaming, waking), modes of cognitive attunement that condition the appearance of all beings, only to collapse these differentiations in the higher-order activity of play.

The structure of the poem reveals a tension between its own production of cognitive differentiation and the effacing of this differentiation by a universalizing, homogenizing principle of play. The operation of play appears nowhere more clearly than in the poem's own formal organization, in the structure of its poetic enunciation. Three different realms with different ontologies and relations to consciousness and cognition—sleeping, dreaming, waking—occur in roughly parallel syntactical structures, perturbed by minor differences that are obscured by resemblances and parallelisms. These cognitive realms enter into an identity with themselves, again linguistically perturbed by a slight differentiation in the elision of the "e" at the beginning of the even lines in order to fit the meter: *schlafe/schlaf', träume/träum', wache/denk*. Each of these pairs is identical except for the final one. The difference between lines 5 and 6, *wache/denk* (I am awake/I think), creates not a dissonance, but a variation that is conspicuous compared to the previous lines. The poem creates the difference only to elide it through the repeated syntactical pattern as well as the semantic equation of waking with thoughts about *Mädchen*: "I think about nothing other than girls."

In this poem, then, the principle of play on a formal level reveals itself as the action of non-differentiation following a differentiation, following Meier's understanding of the joke as an abyss of resemblances and differences. Moreover, if Gregory Bateson describes an element in a system as a difference that makes a difference, this form of play introduces differences that then do not end up making a difference.[30] These differences matter only inasmuch as they perpetuate the activity of play itself.

Differences that are in other contexts decisive become stripped of consequence. In the Anacreontic cogito, as it appears in this poem, play does not differentiate between cognitive states and ontologies typically hierarchized according to their relation to reality, transcendent or otherwise. Jean Paul's later claim that "every act of dreaming presupposes not only a past state of waking, but also a future one"[31] implodes under the indifference—the "non-differentiation"—of Anacreontic play. In Gleim's version, the same activity of play permeates both dream and reality: "In sleep, in dream, while awake/I play with so many girls." This non-differentiation is quite different than Novalis's use of points of indifferentiation, which is bolstered by its own particular metaphysics—or more precisely, the exteriority of absolute identity that nevertheless moves through all differences and makes them able to drift into one another—that can in turn be traced back to Being as an event excluded by representation. Here, non-differentiation is neither primordial nor ontological, but the simple product of a specific configuration of signs.

Gleim calls this poem "Geschäfte." *Geschäfte*, or business transactions, appear as those activities against which play must define itself and that, by definition, exclude the presence of play: here, one is playing, there, where play ceases, the business of real life begins. In this poem, all work appears to be play and vice versa; business and play collapse into one and the same principle, into an *indifference*, even though this very opposition (work/play) conditions the existence of the two domains as discrete spheres of practice.

As we have seen in the correspondence between the Anacreontic poets, Gleim seems perfectly aware that his own poetic activity is a game that must ultimately yield to the claims of reality; for him, Anacreontic poetry is fundamentally incompatible with bourgeois identity. Anacreontic poets create realms of absolute play that have ultimately no place in their everyday lives, dominated as they are by rules, bureaucracy, the pursuit of money, the administration of life. The split between play and business for them is only too palpable, whence their desire to create poetry in which this main difference, the differentiation of play itself from its lifeless other, holds no validity.

Anacreontic play radicalizes itself by defining its other—*Geschäfte* or business transactions—as the logic of its own appearance. The *Mädchen* dominate the poet with just as powerful a voice as the call to economic affairs; they will not leave him alone. They work their way into every nook of the poet's conscious and unconscious life, infiltrating and saturating the very space of his imagination. And yet, it is not mere business that appears on the page. It is the essence of the joke, that abyss of similarities and differences that does not permit one to differentiate whether business has become eros, or eros has become business. Perhaps here, *Geschäfte* must be resignified and bent toward its original meaning, toward its root, that is: "schaffen," to create, or in Greek, poiesis. No longer does *Geschäfte* refer to the business of everyday life, but rather, to that which one has created in poetry.

Conclusion to Part Three

The Death of Anacreon

It did not take long for rococo and Anacreontic poetry to fall out of fashion as a culturally relevant poetic form, despite the fact that it continued to be written well into the nineteenth century. Being "fashionable" as a purely immanent mode of being, as the renunciation of any claim to immortality and an affirmation of the present as present, is in fact what this poetry seeks. When this poetry ceases to be fashionable, according to its own self-understanding, it dies.

At the same time, however, Anacreontic poetry is part of a tradition that immortalizes poetic acts almost in spite of themselves. It is Goethe who most clearly perceives this performative contradiction.

Following the fashionable rise of Anacreontic verse, which in any case was always contemporaneous with genres and styles (didactic, religious, sentimental) that did not exhibit any de-transcendentalization of poetic language, the dominant literary movements—which are characterized by a heterogeneity to whose complexity I am unfortunately unable to do justice here—explore alternative semantics of transcendental investment. The messianic and sentimental poetry of Klopstock fuses linguistic form, overwhelming affect, and metaphysical sacrality. Goethe's early Sturm und Drang lyrics, which turn explicitly to Pindar as a model, definitively mark a shift in poetic function from surface to depth, from derivation to primordiality, from convention to genius, and from linguistic immanence to transcendental poetics.[1]

This representation of the course of literary history is naturally too schematic. One may find exceptions to the supposedly monolithic effort to transcendentalize poetic form, above all, in Goethe's work. Although Goethe disavows Anacreon and Theocritus and turns to Pindar in the "Wanderer's Stormsong" ("Wanderers Sturmlied"), he is always capable of making a gesture, if in a rather unsystematic way, toward de-transcendentalized poetry (above all in *Faust II*). If Anacreontic poetry ceased to exist as a culturally relevant form, certain works nevertheless preserved this form and maintained it in the twilight of a poetic afterlife.

In 1785, Goethe composed the poem "Anacreon's Grave":

Anacreon's Grave

Where the rose here blossoms, where vine curls about the laurel
Where the turtledove beckons, where the little cricket delights
What sort of grave is this here, which all the gods beautifully
Planted and adorned with life? It is Anacreon's resting place.
Spring, summer and fall the happy poet enjoyed.
And in the end, the mound has protected him from winter.

Anakreons Grab

Wo die Rose hier blüht, wo Reben um Lorbeer sich schlingen,
Wo das Turtelchen lockt, wo sich das Grillchen ergötzt
Welch ein Grab ist hier das alle Götter mit Leben
Schön bepflanzt und geziert? Es ist Anakreons Ruh.
Frühling, Sommer und Herbst genoß der glückliche Dichter
Vor dem Winter hat ihn endlich der Hügel geschützt. (*GMA* 2:1:101)

The poem sings the grave of Anacreon. It is one of the first poems that Goethe undertakes in the form of the elegy, and it is written in clearly marked distichs. In this poem, the life and death of Anacreon stand not only for the poet, but also for Anacreontic poetry as a way of writing and as a way of looking at the world. Goethe's poem is thus both poetological and historiographical; it tells the history of both ancient and modern poetic practices and paves the way for a classicism that will ultimately supplant Anacreontic classicism.

The poem cannot be called Anacreontic, although it integrates elements of Anacreontic poetry into its own manner of speech, most notably in the diminutive forms *Turtelchen* (turtledove) and *Grillchen* (cricket) and in the final *pointe* of the poem, in which the mound of the grave protects Anacreon from the winter. The mood of the poem, however, diverges significantly from that of Anacreontic verse. The *locus amoenus*, with its roses and grapevines intertwining, marks not a space of erotic play, but of soft and wistful remembrance. The elegiac form already marks a difference from the Anacreontic ode, although characteristics of the ode surface as vestigial remnants of a bygone era. The happy poet has enjoyed only spring, summer, and fall, and although the winter inevitably arrives in death, his own grave protects him from the harshness of the elements. The elegiac couplets are therefore both dissonant and consonant with the Anacreontic content that they are representing. They are dissonant inasmuch as they posit themselves as other to the Anacreontic elements that they both contain and whose passing they document; but they are consonant with this style inasmuch as they preserve, in a subterranean manner, the hidden body of Anacreon: Anacreon's corpus.

Does the Anacreontic corpus truly and irrevocably die? Let us examine more closely how the poem works. There are three distichs. Each corresponds respectively to the following domains: life, death, afterlife. The first distich of the poem is immersed in what might otherwise appear a typical Anacreontic or idyllic environment. The language is unabashedly hypotactic, piling up instances of the deictic "where." Each instance of "whereness" aligns itself with the beginning of a line or with caesurae. The space itself binds together poetologically charged flowers: the laurel (Apollo) and the grape vine (Dionysus). In Anacreontic poetry, Apollo and Dionysus are not oppositional figures. Dionysus, god of wine, is a humorist, and Apollo, god of music, is a poet. Anacreon unites both Dionysus and Apollo. Such is the poetry of Anacreon, one in which Apollo and Dionysus do not refer to a poetic or metaphysical antagonism (for example, rational order vs. irrational dissolution), but coalesce in intertwining strands of sensuous binding.

The second distich interrupts this excess of hypotactic linkage with the paratactic intrusion of the grave: *what sort of grave* (*welch ein Grab*) is this? The series of questions takes a melancholic turn. Here the fall of the caesura in the fourth line aligns itself precisely with death (and specifically with a movement from life to death): *What sort of grave is this here . . . / . . . planted and adorned with life? It is Anacreon's resting place* (*Es ist Anakreons Ruh*).

The third distich then resuscitates the Anacreontic idiom—not only by ending with the *pointe* (the typical end of an Anacreontic poem) that Anacreon is protected from winter by his grave mound—but also by showing how Anacreon becomes preserved in the poetic tradition itself, indeed, in this very poetic object. The third distich transforms the natural categories of the seasons into cultural or figural historiographic categories. Spring, summer, and autumn, the poet enjoyed: the birth of Anacreontic verse, its attainment of a cultural high point, and its final waning. But Anacreon has been protected from winter, that is, from complete cultural death, in a paradoxical sense by his own grave mound. It is death, or the earthly index of death, that ironically preserves the Anacreontic legacy: its cultural irrelevance anchors this mode of speech to a specific temporality whose moment has already passed. When Anacreontic speech resurfaces, an entire historical tradition—albeit detached from its living contexts of significance—makes its own life present as a form of death. It exists in an afterlife.

Goethe, for whom the question of *Bildung* and organic organization would become of paramount importance, was sensitized to the sedimented history of poetic speech: poetic progress does not always imply a revolutionary overturning or a pure negation, but perhaps bears some part of the "other" that it seeks to overcome in its own path of development. Goethe's poem holds its Anacreontic corpus in a state of unrealizable presence-absence, in a poetic space suffused with melancholy and sensuality. The poem itself is caught between the competing claims of an elegiac, transcendentalizing classicism, and an Anacreontic, immanent classicism. Something like a "pure joke" that robs death and mortality of its power over the imagination is no longer possible in Goethe's poetic speech. Death itself, the grave mound, has become coextensive with the Anacreontic poetics of immanence: death is the *pointe* that preserves the Anacreontic body of work. This gesture puts the Anacreontic tradition into relation with some sort of a beyond—even if this beyond consists in the belief in a conditional immortality through a poetic-historical preservation. In Goethe's poem, pure immanence, or an idiom that dedicates itself only to pleasure, has finally succumbed to death. But this death makes possible an afterlife. Underneath the mound lies the body of Anacreon, just as beneath the melancholic distichs, there lies the hidden promise of a poetic form unexposed to the winter of total annihilation.

Some forms of poetry, like all organic beings and all ways of life, die. They become incorporated into a tradition, absorbed like the decaying body that enters back into the earth. There is always the possibility that they will point only to their own past and never to a future. Whether or not they might one day, Lazarus-like, rise again into the light of day and give birth once more to a world of significance is a matter not of necessity or even of probability. Some ways of being die out, and like Anacreon, there they lie: all sensuous signs that remain are then marked by finitude, and they become present only as cultural memory. Perhaps they lie in wait for someone to come, to make them an object for thought once more, or even more radically, to make them a part of living poetic practices.

Even when resurrected, though, the singularity of the moment—a particular sensuous manifestation that allows a tradition to resonate with the imaginative life of others—is gone. In the early eighteenth century, this singularity flared up like a bright light and faded into extinction. Poets such as Goethe and Novalis, both of whom continued to experiment with this idiom even in their later works, nevertheless continued to feel the power of this particular form of signification. The Anacreontic exercise of unbounded play created an imaginary space that permitted, if only for a brief amount of time, not only respite from the forces that were attempting to organize the world according to the dictates of truth, morality, God, productivity—but, as if in an aesthetic state of perennial carnival, the pleasure of seeing these forces imaginatively overturned.

Afterword

✦

World Regeneration

Not a picture of the world, but how we envision ourselves moving toward it and away from it; not a clearly articulated set of systemic or functional relations, but states toward which processes tend over time; not the relatively static body of statements that can be brought under the rubric of knowledge, but the evolving, fluid, organizing and disorganizing, progressive and regressive flow at the intersection of mind and world, permeating mood, affect, and thought—such are the domains proper to the movements governed by attraction.

In the *Ideas toward a Philosophy of Nature* (1797), following Newton and Kant, Schelling describes the powers of attraction and repulsion as the transcendental conditions of possibility of any natural system: "The general forces of attraction and repulsion, inasmuch as they are conditions of possibility of matter at all, lie beyond all experience."[1] All matter, continually in motion, requires the powers of attraction and repulsion in order to appear at all. Because these forces belong to a transcendental realm, they are themselves inaccessible to empirical inquiry. Attraction and repulsion are nowhere and everywhere. For Schelling, these forces do not merely constitute the conditions of possibility of matter, but of mind as well. They announce their presence in the observation of the physical world interacting with itself and in the feeling of the mind as it strives to achieve its purposes and wishes: the mind pushes itself in one direction only to find itself pulled in another as it encounters both resistance and success in its drive to self-actualization.

Although Schelling's *Ideas toward a Philosophy of Nature* undertakes an epistemological and nature-philosophical inquiry, he draws upon one of the most powerful patterns of aesthetic askesis in the eighteenth century, namely the provocation of moments of non-identity or otherness (what he calls "restrictedness") in order to describe how the mind transcends its own capacities and inclinations in a confrontation with sensuous reality. The philosophy of nature uncovers a grammar of appearances that invests sensuous reality and its subjective intuition with the structure of an exercise. In Schelling's words, the examination of nature reveals "a *striving* [*Bestreben*] of matter to step outside of its equilibrium and to give itself over to the free play of its forces."[2]

By linking mind and matter in the originary disequilibrium of forces, Schelling articulates a latent aesthetic theory that differs from his later attempt to make art into an "intellectual intuition" of the absolute. This aesthetic theory contains as its central imperative not to lead back appearances to some realm of primordial identity, but to sensuously and discursively follow the organization and disorganization of mind, matter, and discourse. If one were to read Schelling's *Naturphilosophie* as an aesthetics, transposing its insights onto the order of language, music, and the plastic arts, signs would be redefined as points of attraction and repulsion, pulling the mind and the body into spaces that are both strange and familiar, provocative and comforting. The form of the aesthetic exercise as I have been elaborating it in this study is predicated on something like this logic, one in which a disequilibrium in appearances, driven by the production of differences, pushes the mind to a continual readjustment of its situation and a reinterpretation of its own capacities. This basic dynamic can be found in Novalis's poetics of autostimulation, in Hölderlin's alternation of tones (*Wechsel der Töne*), and in the aesthetics of the Anacreontic joke. If one were to take a broader look at the eighteenth century, and indeed, at the history of literature and art as a whole, one would undoubtedly find more examples (e.g., Wieland's philosophy of the graces, Goethe's theory of morphology, Schiller's aesthetic education) that would corroborate this pattern.

Let us turn briefly to Schelling. Schelling's own analysis of the internal dynamic of mind and nature, which owes a great debt to Fichte, describes the process underlying cognition as movement toward infinite unrestrictedness (*Unbeschränktheit*). It describes a point of attraction to which the human mind tends in its drive to actively shape its reality that is then limited by a "restrictedness" (*Beschränktheit*) pulling the human being back into the world of appearances through receptivity, a necessary yielding to the physical world, the laws of ethics, the presence of others.[3] These "two opposing activities" appear "as necessary conditions of possibility of an intuition [*Bedingungen der Möglichkeit einer Anschauung*]."[4] Intuition, the ability to perceive both external and internal phenomena, is only made possible by the active and productive movement of the mind in tension with a necessary structural moment of resistance and receptivity.

The mind is therefore always impeded in its desire for mastery over itself and over the world. Schelling describes the resistance that makes possible the motion of mind as that which pushes the human being toward an "infinite approximation" of its own unlimited activity:

> For this is the secret of the activity of our mind [*Geist*]: we necessarily and infinitely approach a point that infinitely escapes every determination. . . . If we ever should reach this point, then the entire system of our spirit—this world that only finds duration in the conflict of opposing tendencies—would sink back into nothingness, and the final consciousness of our existence would lose itself in its own infinity.[5]

The mind can never be perfectly identical with itself, and it is in fact this moment of non-coincidence with its own activity that makes identity possible as something that can be felt and integrated into practices of life. Perfect equilibrium would not only result in stasis, it would make identity as the presence of a self to itself impossible. Consciousness would in fact be excluded from appearing at all and remain in a non-state, in primordial nothingness. For Schelling, as for Fichte, self-relation consists not in a limitation, but in a continual *process*. As with the movement of attraction and repulsion, the mind's attempt to determine its reality only becomes meaningful when it encounters resistance and otherness, when its motion is produced not by a divine harmony, but by an initial disequilibrium that always disrupts the attempt to achieve perfect identity with itself, total self-actualization.

In the works of Novalis and Hölderlin, language itself activates attractions and repulsions, harmonies and oppositions, and these patterns form the conditions of the particular exercise that their works evoke. Words are not discrete signifiers as much as markers of a system larger than their own particular form of representation, reference, or signification.[6] Novalis sees signification itself, a system of differences that attempts but fails to represent identity, as analogous to the structure of cognition: as a series of reflections that attempt but fail to express an originary feeling of absolute identity. Being—and feeling—therefore constitute negative voids, intimations of exteriority within the system of representations and reflections itself that push this system to internally self-differentiate. Self-differentiating systems are nevertheless made permeable with one another (e.g., the real world and the dream, the frame narrative and the fairy tale, self and other, life and death) through points of indifferentiation, and are therefore prevented from falling into a simple co-presence of discrete and incoherent multiples. Points of indifference permit a movement between differential spheres: a passage between worlds.

Being (*Seyn*), as a void in the symbolic system that produces difference and as a plane of indifference that facilitates movement between seemingly mutually exclusive domains and singular entities, secures the possibility of a continual intensification in a process of semiotic and cognitive autostimulation. If the mind is in danger of stasis or equilibrium, Being (as void) perturbs the reflective and representational system. If the mind is in danger of being overwhelmed by the proliferation of difference (overstimulation), a release valve is opened through spheres of indifference, thereby enabling an energetic flow or oscillation (one thinks of the goddess Isis or the womb [*Schooß*] of the *Hymns*). Novalis configures aesthetic cognition so as to reproduce tension from any momentary release, thereby pushing language and mind further into the adventure of their own possibilities. For a system characterized by continual disequilibrium, stimulation can be the only absolute.

For the Anacreontic poets, the aesthetic exercise is also conditioned by a state of disequilibrium, or more precisely, by a divergence between poetic language and sociocultural forms of intelligibility and normativity. The Anacreontic sign—the *Mädchen*, for example—functions like an existential flip switch, a set of linguistic strategies used to strip the world of transcendental and metaphysical depth. It provides a counterweight to poetry explicitly thematizing trauma and melancholy, which, in "working through" trauma, often calls it into being and fortifies the stranglehold of its power. Anacreontic poetry, on the contrary, does not linger in loss.

The aesthetic exercise of pleasure in the joke generates a never-ending series of movements oscillating between resemblance and difference. As Meier states in his *On Jokes*, "the joke must be a short embodiment of many movements of comparison [*ein kurtzer Inbegriff vieler Vergleichungsstücke*]. It must so to speak be similar to an abyss [*einem Abgrunde ähnlich*], in which one sees more and more the longer one peers into it" (*GS* 103). For Meier, the joke produces a sustained process of cognitive activity, a process that he himself designates as *aesthetic*.

Caught up in a play of differences and similarities, the joke never progresses beyond itself into any realm of transcendental organization. The condition of its effectiveness as a form of play nevertheless consists in both an identification with and a divergence from that which is given to the senses. It therefore introduces novelty, or *das Neue*, into the exercise of aesthetic cognition, something that Breitinger wanted to claim exclusively for the domain of the fantastic. The Anacreontic poem produces novelty not through the alien experience of possible fictional worlds, but by producing difference in the imagination from patterns of intelligibility and processes of normalization in the *given* world, by loosening the pull—in the imagination, in the *aesthetic* exercise—of values in the public sphere, political administration, pedagogical formation, familial authority, religious piety, scientific and epistemological progress, nationalistic propaganda, economic productivity, and orders of life and death.

If the aesthetic exercise exerts its power by *producing* a state of disequilibrium for Novalis and the Anacreontics, the world itself already exists in a state of disequilibrium for Hölderlin. This state of dissonance is the primordial wound from which poetic activity issues. For Hölderlin, the cognitive act associated with poetic language exercises the mind in navigating, processing, and reinterpreting what appears to the subject as a world out of joint. Poetry can restore neither equilibrium nor unity to the damaged world. It can only *reveal*—make present as evidence for oneself and others—a latent order that no longer appears self-evident.

Poetry activates a sustained cognitive process that attempts to digest the inedible world, a world that appears at first to manifest only signs of disharmony and violence, emptied out of possible redemptive content. The decapitated head of John the Baptist lies on its platter, "like inedible writing" (*uneßbarer Schrift gleich*, *MA* 1:465). The poetic mind begins with figures such as these: problematic appearances that push us to interpret the world, to make it intelligible, and to supply the connective tissue in what appears as a chain of discontinuous ruptures.

The surprising gesture in Hölderlin's poetry, given its purported wish and desire for intelligibility and coherence, consists in deepening and intensifying the experience of contingency instead of attempting to poetically reduce or eliminate this experience. The intensification of possibility, fragmentation, and bifurcation fortifies the mind in its task to resignify contingency as necessity, to give order to chaos, to put the world of the senses in touch with the power of the divine. To make present the divine entails holding freedom, perception, and determination—potentiality, reality, and necessity—in one and the same aesthetic-cognitive space. The world of appearances must appear both contingent *and* necessary if freedom is to be reconciled with divine order.[7]

In the "Remarks on Oedipus," Hölderlin notes that the language of tragedy must find its way in a world characterized by historical catastrophe, political disorder, and cognitive disorientation, "among plague and the confusion of the senses and a universally inflamed spirit of prophecy" (*MA* 2:315). In the midst of sensuous derangement, when signs cannot properly be read and the yearning for prophecy inflames the spirit of the age, only tragedy can guarantee the order that none can perceive, "so that the course of the world has no gaps and *the memory of the heavenly ones does not disappear*" (*MA* 2:315–16). For Hölderlin, the tragic speech act aims to close the gaps of history, to verify the organization of a higher-order harmony that is not directly accessible to human experience, but one that potentially manifests itself *through* human experience. It is not that poetry makes this order visible—precisely because it cannot ever be made visible—but rather, that it stimulates forms of cognition that aid in the intimation of order as such. Memory, the ability to perceive unity amidst difference, acts of binding and holding (*festhalten*)—such are the poetic and cognitive techniques that work their way into the very form of Hölderlin's poetry. The willful intermingling of Christianity and antiquity, which reflects more than a mere concern with figures of mediation, fuses different and contradictory forms of the divine in the same poetic space. The figure of bifurcation, whose oscillation between different modalities ("by day/ . . . or also/by night," *PF* 511) does not impede the perception of the divine in "The Rhine," becomes a problem in "The Ister," a poem in which all phenomena—even the most seemingly "necessary"—can unexpectedly be returned to their initial state of contingency. The mind ceases to be able to hold heterogeneous spaces in one and the same cognitive act, the order of history succumbs to the confusion of the senses, language falls into disarray, coherence fails, and finally: the exercise breaks the spirit whose integrity it was meant to uphold.

In 1806 the raving Hölderlin is taken to Authenrieth's clinic. In 1807 he is transferred to the care of Ernst Zimmer in Tübingen. He lives in a tower overlooking the Neckar, is visited numerous times by later generations of poets, plays the piano, and writes poetry until his death in 1843.

The poetry that he writes during this time speaks in a voice that is both different from and similar to the poetry composed before 1806. Over time, Hölderlin's poetry detaches itself from those anchoring points that, in his earlier poems, were to function as guarantors of order: the divine disappears, the I disappears, history disappears. In place of these tenuous signs appear seasons, the human being (*der Mensch*), friendship, vistas, shifting temporal frames, and the name Scardanelli: a poet who always signs with subservience, *mit Unterthänigkeit*.

Hölderlin's final poetic creations, like those of the rococo and Anacreontic poets, are poems of immanence.[8] Unlike the Anacreontic poets, his poems do not delight in unraveling schemas of organization as such; they are neither ironic nor overtly self-referential, and they do not willfully resist the order of their own world. They may still, however, be considered aesthetic exercises, and, in some sense, they bear the name more appropriately than any of the other poems that have been examined in this study.

Baumgarten considered aesthetics as a science of sensuous cognition. Sensuous cognition refers both to the immediate givenness of intuition and to acts of the imagination, or the act of making present in the mind something that is absent to the senses. Although imagination always functions as part of human cognition, as Kant would later demonstrate, there is a qualitative difference between aesthetic exercises that conjure a new reality *for* the senses (exercises of the imagination) and aesthetic exercises that focus on that which is given to the senses (exercises of perception). The former, exercises of the imagination, attempt to bring the invisible as such into the world of the visible, and they are always accompanied by a constant, energetic vibration between the imagined and the given. The latter, exercises of perception, describe, rework, investigate, intensify, and transfigure the immediate presence of experience. The poets we have examined thus far have been primarily concerned with the former type of aesthetic exercise, the exercise of the imagination.

And yet, to make perceptual givenness the source of its own aesthetic exercise produces a different form of attentiveness to the world: new points of focus are brought into relief, and the act itself illuminates the irreducible presence of invisibility—something that is unseen—as part of the visible world, as part of sense perception. Merleau-Ponty defines depth as "the dimension in which the thing is presented not as spread out before us but as an inexhaustible reality full of reserves."[9] The aesthetic exercise of immediate perception—which one may discover in Goethe's morphology and theory of colors as well as in Faust's opening monologue in *Faust II*—aims to transform experience starting from the givenness of the world to the senses. Such works do not insist on a strict distinction between perception and imagination. Indeed, they draw upon that which evades direct perception in the act of sensuous intuition in order to fashion a different sort of imaginary exercise.

In the *Ideas toward a Philosophy of Nature*, Schelling claims that perception expands into domains that exceed the immediate horizon of that which is given to the senses. Perception, as an opening onto a spatial and temporal organization of experience that transcends experience—since the limits between what can and cannot be perceived are marked from within the horizon of perception—transports the human being into the heart of this very transcendence. He describes this process as the "bliss of sight," *die Wonne des Sehens*, a sensation derived from the interaction between light and eye:

> With the more abundant light of the springtime sun, the ever-changing play appears anew and variegated, in colors on the surface of our earth that flow into one another—a surface that just a short while ago bore the monotonous cloak of winter—and the rise and fall, the emergence, alternation, and disappearance of these colors are the measure of a counting of time that, everywhere present, accompanies us straight into the middle of nature itself. From a vast distance the youthful light of the stars shines and binds our being to the existence of a world that is unreachable to the imagination—and yet, is not entirely closed to our eyes.

> Mit dem reichlichern Licht der Frühlingssonne erscheint auch aufs neue das immer wechselnde Spiel vielfach in einander fließender Farben auf der Oberfläche unserer Erde, die kaum vorher noch das einförmige Gewand des Winters getragen hatte, und das Steigen und Sinken, das Entstehen, Wechseln, und Vergehen dieser Farben, ist das Maaß einer Zeitrechnung, die, überall gegenwärtig, uns in die Mitte der Natur selbst begleitet. Aus weiter Ferne erscheint uns das jugendliche Licht der Gestirne, und knüpft unser Daseyn an die Existenz einer Welt an, die für die Einbildungskraft unerreichbar, doch dem Auge nicht ganz verschlossen ist.[10]

The human being experiences the bliss of sight when the visible world reveals difference, becoming, absence, and a contiguous unfolding as part of its own presence to perception. For Schelling, the bliss of the eye does not result from an atemporal snapshot of the present moment, but foregrounds the temporality of space, a temporality that *accompanies us straight into the middle of nature itself* (*uns in die Mitte der Natur selbst begleitet*). If Hölderlin's poetological goal was to discover "becoming in dissolution," *das Werden im Vergehen*, Schelling sees this very project less as a task for the poetic imagination, and more as part of the immanent visibility of the world itself, or the world as it appears in the act of perception. The visible world *includes* temporality in its visibility. It does not graft time onto space like butter over bread, but reveals itself as a nexus of visible-invisible space-time *only* in the process of sense perception.

The bliss of sight is not accessible to the imagination, which makes the absent present rather than seeing absence as part of presence. Schelling describes, in effect, another type of artist: one for whom every perceptual moment can disclose a work of art; one who continually attends to the absence that lines the givenness of the phenomenal world; and one who sees in this aesthetic absence a mode of transport into other worlds of intensity. For this artist, perception itself, *aisthesis*, carries its own otherness within it, and hence can put the human being in contact with this otherness at the heart of nature. The existence of temporal and spatial difference—the horizon on the eye that recedes and reveals some other part of the world to be seen (but cannot be seen)—never becomes fully transparent to the eye. And yet, it is not completely closed to the eye either, or in Schelling's words, *nicht ganz verschlossen*.

Schelling describes, in his rhapsody to the bliss of sight, a poetics of the *vista*, something that is both beyond and inside sense perception. Hölderlin has a word for this phenomenon in his later poetry: *die Aussicht*. The following poem is regarded as Hölderlin's final poem, written days before his death:

The Outlook

When into the distance the life of men goes dwelling,
Where into the distance the time of the vines shines unto itself
There is at the same time the summer's empty field,
The forest appears with its dark image;

That nature completes the image of the times,
That it lingers, that they glide quickly by,
This is from perfection, the hight of heaven shines
To human beings, like the blossom crowns trees.

Your humble servant,
May 24th 1748.
Scardanelli

Die Aussicht

Wenn in die Ferne geht der Menschen wohnend Leben,
Wo in die Ferne sich erglänzt die Zeit der Reben
Ist auch dabei des Sommers leer Gefilde,
Der Wald erscheint mit seinem dunklen Bilde;

Daß die Natur ergänzt das Bild der Zeiten,
Daß die verweilt, sie schnell vorübergleiten,

Ist aus Vollkommenheit, des Himmels Höhe glänzet
Den Menschen dann, wie Bäume Blüth umkränzet.

mit Unterthänigkeit
d. 24 Mai 1748.
Scardanelli (*MA* 1:938)

The first impression of this poem is one of immediacy, or a description of that which appears directly to the eye: the transmission of pure perception.[11] However, the second strophe does not merely describe what has been seen, but pronounces a judgment upon it. The judgment is positive. It embraces not merely what is visible, but more specifically, that which has been made visible in the first strophe. The second strophe thus affirms the implicit organization of the senses in the first strophe.

The first strophe mixes temporal and spatial frames; it spatializes time and temporalizes space. The poem begins with a temporal clause that has as its subject the life of men, a life that itself is spatialized inasmuch as it "dwells": *When into the distance the life of men goes dwelling* (*Wenn in die Ferne geht der Menschen wohnend Leben*). The second line begins with a spatial clause, *Where into the distance* (*Wo in die Ferne*), but has as its subject an expanse of time, *the time of the vines* (*die Zeit der Reben*). The title of the poem, "The Outlook" ("Die Aussicht"), refers both to a spatial vista as well as to a temporal prospect: a possibility in the future. To look at the visible world is also to experience the temporality of the visible world, a temporality that places it in a movement toward disappearance, at a vanishing point on the horizon. Even if the image of nature disappears into the distance, there nevertheless remains *summer's empty field* and *the forest . . . with its dark image* (*des Sommers leer Gefilde* and *der Wald . . . mit seinem dunklen Bilde*) in the line of sight. At the end of the first strophe, the phenomena that show themselves in proximity to the poetic voice (the field and the forest)—not in recessive disappearance beyond the horizon—nevertheless appear in their own right as empty or obscure.

And yet, the second half of the poem says *yes*. It says *yes* to nature, to perception, and more specifically, to its own poetic description of nature.

What, precisely, is being affirmed?

It is the dynamic of time that Hölderlin in his earlier poems felt to be so problematic, namely, that human perception contains negativities, that there appear to be gaps and absences, *Lücken* in the organization of time and space.[12] In the earlier poetological writings, the dissonance of the world must be repaired with an "idealistic memory," a reconstruction of a course of events that resignifies discontinuities as the birth of a new order. In the process of poetic cognition, what is at first perceived as discontinuous and dissonant is integrated into a higher-order harmony that only becomes visible to the mind that has been trained by the poem's particular exercise of language. Such, we might recall, is the general operation of idealistic memory.

In this later poem as well, there are gaps in space and time, blind spots that touch the world of things (*leer Gefilde*), the remnant of a distance, time that travels either fast or slow (*nature . . . that . . . lingers*, or *the image of the times . . . that glide quickly by* [*die Natur . . . die verweilt* or *das Bild der Zeiten . . . die schnell vorübergleiten*]). Poetry foregrounds the ineluctable presence of something unseen, of blindness inherent to perception itself. These gaps, both temporal and spatial, are felt in the organization of sound and syntax. In the second strophe, time splits into two different, but parallel, temporal orders. There is nature, *die Natur*, which lingers, *die verweilt*. And there is the image of the times, *das Bild der Zeiten*, and these glide quickly by, *schnell vorübergleiten*. The differentiation of time occurs in a syntactical structure that lifts each temporal modality out of its harmonization, creating a bifurcation in the flow of the poem that one can feel in the mind:

> That nature completes the image of the times,
> That it lingers, that they glide quickly by

> Daß die Natur ergänzt das Bild der Zeiten,
> Daß die verweilt, sie schnell vorübergleiten

The difference between alternative temporal frames—"nature" and "the image of the times"—is introduced not merely through a semantic distinction, one lingering and the other flowing by, nor merely in syntactical separation, but in the alteration of the pronoun forms *die* and *sie*. These forms could be grammatically identical (the feminine singular and plural definite pronouns share the same form), but in this instance, they split into singular and plural, *nature* and *times*, *die* and *sie*, introducing a deictic difference between two temporal orders. And precisely this bifurcation—in effect, a double bifurcation, since it is a split within a line of a line that is already doubled in the form "That . . . /That . . ."—occurs "from perfection," *aus Vollkommenheit*:

> That nature completes the image of the times,
> That it lingers, that they glide quickly by,
> This is from perfection, the hight of heaven shines
> To human beings, like the blossom crowns trees.

> Daß die Natur ergänzt das Bild der Zeiten,
> Daß die verweilt, sie schnell vorübergleiten,
> Ist aus Vollkommenheit, des Himmels Höhe glänzet
> Den Menschen dann, wie Bäume Blüth umkränzet.

What begins as an act of receding into distance in the first line of the poem (*Wenn in die Ferne geht der Menschen wohnend leben*) ends in the coming of fullness, in perfection. And yet, although the poem speaks with the language of presence, it is precisely the present moment in all of its plenitude that appears *absent* in the poem's vision of perfection.[13]

This detail, the absence that dwells and moves at the limit points of the presence of perception, suggests that Hölderlin's later poems do not operate according to the same poetological goals that motivate his earlier hymnic production, nor are they poems of total presence or pure immanence.[14] To analyze the later poems as continuations of his earlier poetological goals may seem to restore to these latest poems a sort of poetic dignity and sophistication, but such a gesture obscures the particularity of their sensuous phenomenality; this poetry can speak on its own terms. It is true that the poem is highly structured and organized, as Roman Jakobson has demonstrated.[15] More importantly, there is a latent metaphysics that inhabits the poem, one whose structure and organization consist in the production of harmonious bifurcations—of shifting temporal and spatial frameworks—that foreground absences and lacunae as part of the perfection of nature itself.

The poem produces two different points of attraction, two gestures, in the interface between the language of the poem and the movements of mind that it presupposes and institutes: one gesture splits phenomena, bifurcates time semantically and syntactically, creates and maintains distances, intensifies gaps and inversions, places the visible world in relation to the void (*des Sommers leer Gefilde*) and the darkness (*der Wald erscheint mit seinem dunklen Bilde*). The other gesture connects and intertwines phenomena, generates communication and resonance between spaces and signs, makes images, sounds, meanings embrace: *Leben* is *wohnend*, *wenn in die Ferne* becomes *wo in die Ferne*, *die Zeit der Reben* is taken up in *das Bild der Zeiten*, *der Wald* is composed of *Bäume*, blossom crowns these trees, *Bäume Blüth umkränzet*, the soft alliteration of *Himmels Höhe*, whose heights hold the hope of resplendence, comes back down to earth, becoming *Bäume Blüth*, a blossom that blooms in sound, and from the initial disappearance of life receding, *Wenn in die Ferne geht*, there emerges the perfection to come, *Es ist aus Vollkommenheit*.

There is no higher order, no process of idealistic memory that fills in the gaps of time. The gaps remain as part of the perfect order of nature. It is as if the world of the senses—at times difficult, dark, sorrowful, at times joyous, blissful, ecstatic—were no longer demanding that everything be clear, distinct, without death and without pain, as if the poem were suggesting to us that the consonance of things can only appear in dissonance.

NOTES

Introduction

1. Edmund Husserl, *Wahrnehmung und Aufmerksamkeit: Texte aus dem Nachlass (1893–1912)*, in *Husserliana*, ed. Thomas Vongehr and Regula Giulani, vol. 38 (Dordrecht: Springer, 2004), 108.

2. Ibid., 107.

3. I am drawing upon Stanley Fish's understanding of the "interpretive community" as mentioned in Stanley Fish, *Is There a Text in This Class: The Authority of Interpretive Communities* (Cambridge, Mass.: Harvard University Press, 1980).

4. Pierre Macherey, *A Theory of Literary Production*, trans. Geoffrey Wall (London: Routledge, 1992), 7.

5. Peter Sloterdijk, *Du mußt dein Leben ändern* (Frankfurt am Main: Suhrkamp, 2008), 14.

6. Ibid., 47.

7. Michel Foucault, *The Use of Pleasure*, vol. 2 of *The History of Sexuality*, trans. Robert Hurley (New York: Vintage, 1985), 8. For an excellent analysis of Foucault's concept of *askēsis*, and an analysis of this quote in particular, see Edward F. McGushin, *Foucault's Askēsis* (Evanston, Ill.: Northwestern University Press, 2007). McGushin discusses philosophy not merely as an exercise, but as a poiesis, as an "artistic transformation of life" (286).

8. Judith Butler, *Excitable Speech: A Politics of the Performative* (New York: Routledge, 1997), 153.

9. Stephen Greenblatt describes self-fashioning as "the cultural system of meanings that creates specific individuals by governing the passage from abstract potential to concrete historical embodiment," and notes that literature aids this process by functioning "as a manifestation of the concrete behavior of its particular author, as itself the expression of the codes by which behavior is shaped, and as a reflection upon these codes." Stephen Greenblatt, *Renaissance Self-Fashioning: From More to Shakespeare* (Chicago: University of Chicago Press, 1980), 3–4.

10. Foucault, *The Use of Pleasure*, 9.

11. See Fish, *Is There a Text in This Class.*

12. Martin Heidegger, "Der Ursprung des Kunstwerkes," in *Holzwege*, vol. 5 of *Gesamtausgabe*, ed. Friedrich-Wilhelm von Herrmann (Frankfurt am Main: Vittorio Klostermann, 1977), 29. For a clear account of Heidegger's ontology of art that has shaped my thinking about the subject, see Hubert L. Dreyfus, "Heidegger's Ontology of Art," in *A Companion to Heidegger*, ed. Hubert L. Dreyfus and Mark A. Wrathall (Oxford: Blackwell, 2005), 407–19. I do not share Heidegger's belief that a work of art only "works" in relation to a culture's understanding of being. In my view, this requirement for the work excludes from consideration what could otherwise be called works of art—works that may not

be working for an entire culture, but do manage to work for individuals as attractions for thought.

13. Horace, *Opera*, ed. D. R. Shackleton Baily (Stuttgart: Teubner, 1985), 127.

14. Wolfram von Eschenbach, *Parzival*, ed. Karl Lachmann (Berlin: de Gruyter, 1998), 287.

15. See Richard Brilliant, *My Laocoön: Alternative Claims in the Interpretation of Artworks* (Berkeley: University of California Press, 2000). For an analysis of the way in which the Laocoon functioned as a focal point for the aesthetic and semiotic discourses of the eighteenth century, see David Wellbery, *Lessing's Laocoon* (Cambridge, Eng.: Cambridge University Press, 1984).

16. See Jennifer Milam, *Fragonard's Playful Paintings* (Manchester: Manchester University Press, 2006).

17. Baumgarten sees poetry as only one form of art among many; he himself conceives of aesthetics as a science of sensory knowledge encompassing music, dance, and the plastic arts. See Frederick Beiser, *Diotima's Children: German Aesthetic Rationalism from Leibniz to Lessing* (Oxford: Oxford University Press, 2009), 122.

18. "El estilo arcaizante de Menard—extranjero al fin—adolece de alguna afectación. No así el del precursor, que maneja con desenfado el español corriente de su época." Jorge Luis Borges, "Pierre Menard, Autor del Quijote," in *Obras Completas*, vol. 1, ed. Carlos V. Frías (Barcelona: María Kodama y Emecé Editores, 1989), 449.

19. Sophie von la Roche, *Geschichte des Fräuleins von Sternheim* (Stuttgart: Reclam, 1983), 349.

20. Such is Lessing's definition of the fable: "Wenn wir einen allgemeinen moralischen Satz auf einen besonderen Fall zurückführen, diesem besondern Falle die Wirklichkeit erteilen, und eine Geschichte daraus dichten, in welcher man den allgemeinen Satz anschauend erkennt: so heißt diese Erdichtung eine Fabel." Gotthold Ephraim Lessing, "Abhandlung über die Fabel," in *Werke: 1758–1759*, vol. 4 of *Werke und Briefe*, ed. Wilfried Barner et al. (Frankfurt am Main: Suhrkamp, 1997), 376.

21. Søren Kierkegaard, *Fear and Trembling*, trans. Alastair Hannay (London: Penguin, 2003), 72.

Chapter 1

1. Pierre Hadot, *Philosophy as a Way of Life*, trans. Michael Chase, ed. Arnold Davidson (Oxford: Blackwell, 1995), 82.

2. Paul Rabbow, in his groundbreaking work *Seelenführung*, explores the connection between textual practices (mainly reading and writing) and their "psychagogic" function. Paul Rabbow, *Seelenführung: Methodik der Exerzitien in der Antike* (Munich: Kösel, 1954), 218–22. The act of reading and writing trains and forms the soul and institutes new patterns for the mind. He goes on to link this form of linguistic exercise with psychoanalysis, and specifically with forms of "suggestive" therapy (284–89).

3. The formative interaction between language and affect is almost self-evident, as Rabbow notes: "Es ist bekannt und augenscheinlich—die einfache Selbstbeobachtung lehrt es—daß man sich durch das Aussprechen des Gedankens, des Gefühls stark in der Richtung des Gedanken- und Gefühlsinhalts beeinflussen kann." Rabbow, *Seelenführung*, 202.

4. Although Baumgarten is considered the "father" of aesthetics, Beiser puts forth convincing reasons to see Christian Wolff as equally important in the founding stages of aesthetics as a discipline. See Beiser, *Diotima's Children*, 48.

5. See Kai Hammermeister, *The German Aesthetic Tradition* (Cambridge, Eng.: Cambridge University Press, 2002), 6.

6. Gottfried Wilhelm Leibniz, *Discours de métaphysique*, in vol. 4 of *Die philosophischen Schriften*, ed. C. I. Gerhardt (Berlin: Weidmannsche Buchhandlung, 1880), 449.

7. The ambivalence of beauty as an "ontological" predicate of Being and as "functional" input into systems of sensuous perfectibility has been discussed by numerous scholars. See, for example, Friedhelm Solms, *Disciplina aesthetica: Zur Frühgeschichte der ästhetischen Theorie bei Baumgarten und Herder* (Stuttgart: Klett, 1990), 58–60. See also Frauke Berndt, *Poema/Gedicht: Die epistemische Konfiguration der Literatur um 1750* (Berlin: de Gruyter, 2011), 84.

8. Baumgarten describes different forms of beauty as "pulcritudo rerum et cogitationum," "pulcritudo ordinis," and "pulcritudo significationis" (*BA* 22).

9. According to Frauke Berndt, beauty as striving toward perfection appears not only as the property of a subject, but also of a poem: "In diesem Paragraphen [§14] macht Baumgarten auf die Mangelstruktur aufmerksam, durch die das Gedicht nicht als ein (Bruch-)Teil des Ganzen, sondern als eine Tätigkeit ausgewiesen wird. Diese Tätigkeit übersetzt die Funktion des Strebens . . . die zielstrebige Bewegung—in eine metaphysische: in jene nämlich, das Ziel der Vollkommenheit zu begehren" (Berndt, *Poema/Gedicht*, 83).

10. Frauke Berndt draws attention to the implications of Baumgarten's conception of aesthetics as a metaphysics of beauty when she says, "Der schöne Geist ist nichts Geringeres als ein Agent in metaphysischer Mission, die bei der Exzentrik der symbolischen Mangelstruktur beginnt" (Berndt, *Poema/Gedicht*, 117).

11. See Petra Bahr's discussion of an "anthropologische Revision der Rhetorik," or the way in which rhetorical categories become part of a new definition of the human being. Petra Bahr, *Darstellung des Undarstellbaren: Religionstheoretische Studien zum Darstellungsbegriff bei A.G. Baumgarten und I. Kant* (Tübingen: Siebeck, 2004), 47–61.

12. Steffen Groß notes, the *felix aestheticus* is "der in sich ruhende, sich seiner gewisse, ganze Mensch, der—so paradox es klingen mag—niemals zur Ruhe kommen kann." Groß, *Felix Aestheticus: Die Ästhetik als Lehre vom Menschen.* (Würzburg: Königshausen & Neumann 2001), 174.

13. Michel Foucault, *Discipline and Punish*, trans. Alan Sheridan (New York: Vintage, 1977), 139.

14. Hannah Arendt excoriates Epictetus's conception of philosophy as a training of the will, a philosophy that seems to culminate in the fantasy of willing reality itself. If the will were reducible to a desire for omnipotence—a desire that would ultimately end with its own impotence—"man in that case would have been given a 'monstrous' faculty (Augustine), compelled by its nature to demand a power it is able to exercise only in the illusion-ridden region of sheer phantasy—the inwardness of a mind that has successfully separated itself from all outward appearance in its relentless quest for absolute tranquility." Arendt, *The Life of the Mind: Willing*, vol. 2 (New York: Harcourt, 1978), 84. For Arendt, spiritual exercises constitute one more form of alienation from the world. Contrary to Arendt,

Pierre Hadot shows how Epictetus's and Marcus Aurelius's spiritual exercises contribute to a form of action: "il s'agit d'engager sa responsabilité et non plus de consentir, il s'agit d'entrer en relation avec des êtres, nos semblables, qui provoquent d'autant plus nos passions qu'ils sont nos semblables, des êtres qu'il nous faudra aimer, bien qu'ils soient souvent haïssables." Hadot, *La citadelle intérieure: Introduction aux "Pensées" de Marc Aurèle* (Paris: Fayard, 1992), 199. Hadot sees stoic spiritual exercises precisely not as world alienation, but as an impetus for action with others. Whatever the case may be, the type of exercise we will be exploring in this study, the aesthetic exercise, is qualitatively different from the form of exercises articulated in Roman and Hellenistic philosophy. The aesthetic exercise, characterized as it is by formal indeterminacy, shapes the human precisely by liberating it from any attempt to "mold" the mind as if it were the raw material given to poetic language for the purpose of cohering with a philosophical doctrine.

15. Beiser notes that from the perspective of the history of aesthetics, Christian Wolff was in many ways more important than Baumgarten in establishing the philosophical engagement with art. However, he notes, "Baumgarten gives a much greater value than Wolff or Gottsched to the distinctive qualities of sensible cognition. His fundamental achievement in the rationalist tradition was that he gave a clear conceptual status and firm systematic place to these unique qualities." Beiser, *Diotima's Children*, 122.

16. Beiser singles out this aspect of Baumgarten's thought as well: "The beautiful spirit will not only be a poet by vocation, but a fully developed and all-rounded human being, someone who has the sensitivity and refinement to write verse as well as the acuity and subtlety to write philosophy. The program of aesthetic education developed by Schiller in his *Aesthetische Briefe* already lies *in nuce* in Baumgarten's *Aesthetica*." Beiser, *Diotima's Children*, 121.

17. For an interpretation of the "felix aestheticus" as a new type of human being, see Groß, *Felix Aestheticus*, 163–74. He does not focus, however, on the aesthetic as a form of exercise, but rather, as the articulation of a new conception of the human being. He claims, and rightly so, that "[Baumgarten's] *felix aestheticus* ist nicht der Künstler oder der Dichter in der engeren Bedeutung des jeweiligen Terminus, sondern der ganze Mensch in der höchst widersprüchlichen Ganzheit seiner Anlagen, Vermögen, und Möglichkeiten" (17). One might add that Baumgarten uncovers not merely new potentialities of the human from an aesthetic perspective, but also suggests new practices that would develop the specifically aesthetic, and hence malleable, tendencies of perception itself.

18. "Objectorum sensibilium absentium ideas mens reproducere valet, seu, quod perinde est, Si qua sensu percepit anima, eorum perceptiones reproducere potest, objectis licet absentibus" (*Psychologia Empirica* §91). See Christian Wolff, *Pyschologia Empirica*, in vol. 5 of *Gesammelte Werke: Part 2: Lateinische Schriften*, ed. Jean Ecole (Hildesheim: Georg Olms, 1968), 53.

19. "Dispositio naturalis ad imaginandum . . . quia 1) saepe praeterita pulcre cogitanda sunt, 2) praesentia saepe praetereunt ante, quam absolvatur pulcra eorundem cogitatio, 3) non ex solis praesentibus, sed et praeteritis, futura cognoscuntur" (*BA* 28).

20. Gotthold Wilhelm Leibniz, *Confessio Philosophi: Papers Concerning the Problem of Evil, 1671–1678*, ed. and trans. Robert C. Sleigh, Jr. (New Haven, Conn.: Yale University Press, 2005), 43.

21. "Neque tamen ipsa recognoscendi facultate supersedere potest pulcre e.g. narraturus, immo fingentem, ne antecedentia turpiter sequentibus repugnent, oportet esse memorem" (*BA* 30).

22. "Hinc veritas singularis de contingentibus aut ea sistit, ut possibilia et partes huius universe . . . ut possibilia alterius universi, eiusque partes, cognitioni hominum mediae, VERITAS HETEROCOSMICA" (*BA* 418).

23. One may already find a departure from a conception of transparent subjectivity in Leibniz with his doctrine of "petites perceptions," although far from undermining the order of reason, the *petites perceptions* show the bypassing of conscious self-awareness to be coherent with, and even constitutive of this order. However, this opacity is in turn linked to the notion of the *fundus animae*. See Bahr, *Darstellung des Undarstellbaren*, 84.

24. See Groß, *Felix Aestheticus*, 269.

25. The aesthete therefore cannot allow his or her own dispositions to be fully heteronomous, nor can the futurity of the work be fully guided by the dictates of potentially problematic public opinion: "Der wird selten gefallen, der sich die ganze Welt vorsellet, wann er schreibt, und seine Schrift an das sogennante Publikum richtet" (*AGB* 182).

26. See Berndt, *Poema/Gedicht*, 37.

27. Frauke Berndt notes that Baumgarten's theory of signs culminates in a "konzeptualisierte Performativität." Berndt, *Poema/Gedicht*, 41.

28. "Facultas characteristica minima esset, quae unicum minimum signum cum unico minimo signato, maxime debiles inter praevias perceptiones et socias heterogeneas remississime coniungeret. Ergo quo plura, quo maiora signa com quo pluribus, quo maioribus signatis, quo fortiores inter socias et praevias perceptiones, hoc maior est" (*Metaphysica* §662). Alexander Gottlieb Baumgarten, *Metaphysica*, part 1, vol. 2 of *Historisch-kritische Ausgabe*, ed. Günter Gawlick and Lothar Kreimendahl (Stuttgart: Frommann-Holzboog, 2011), 328.

29. Although one might tend to regard this notion as a result of the condescension and chauvinism characteristic of early eighteenth-century Germany, it nevertheless remains interesting that the *felix aestheticus* appears gender-neutral, since Baumgarten includes women—even if in a derogatory and frankly insulting manner, especially considering that there were quite a few popular female poets in Germany at the time—as possible subjects of the aesthetic exercise.

30. To this drive corresponds the symbolic structure of poetic "striving" as recently elaborated by Frauke Berndt; see Berndt, *Poema/Gedicht*, 83–4.

31. Aristotle, *Poetics*, trans. and ed. Stephen Halliwell (Cambridge, Mass.: Harvard University Press, 1995), 38–39.

32. Edgar Landgraf has recently shown how improvisation was devalued in the Enlightenment but became more important with the advent of the aesthetics of autonomy. One may therefore see Baumgarten as a figure who, within the heart of the Enlightenment tradition, nevertheless holds open a space for improvisation. See Edgar Landgraf, *Improvisation as Art* (New York: Continuum, 2011).

33. Anthony Krupp notes that there is an educational process at work in Baumgarten's account of the development from childhood to adulthood: from the boy, who spontaneously plays games, to the youth, who reads irregularly, to the man, who can formulate rules. "All that precedes the man is (now) marked by imperfection or deficiency." Krupp, "Cultivation as Maturation: Infants, Children,

and Adults in Alexander Gottlieb Baumgarten's *Aesthetica*," *Monatshefte* 98, no. 4 (2006): 533. However, it is worth noting that this "deficiency" of childish improvisation is necessary for the adult who is carried away by aesthetic inspiration; as a prerequisite for inspiration, the adult needs "Excitatior natura, iam in ipsis αὐτοσχεδιάσμασι" (*BA* 62), which is then refined by means of the *ars erudita*. In other words, the spontaneity of play prepares the adult for the spontaneity of inspiration, which, it is true, is qualitatively different than the spontaneity of children, but is nevertheless incapable of being reduced to rule-driven behavior.

34. "*Excitatior natura . . . iam in ipsis* αὐτοσχεδιάσμασι" (*BA* 62).

35. Ernst Cassirer heralded Baumgarten's aesthetics as a shift in "philosophical anthropology." See Cassirer, *Philosophie der Aufklärung* (Tübingen: J. C. B. Mohr, 1932), 472. According to Friedrich Solms, Baumgarten's philosophy paved the way for anthropology as a new discipline. See Solms, *Disciplina aesthetica*. See also Carsten Zelle, "Sinnlichkeit und Therapie: Zur Gleichursprünglichkeit von Ästhetik und Anthropologie um 1750," in *Vernünftige Ärzte: Hallesche Psychomediziner und die Anfänge der Anthropologie in der deutschsprachigen Frühaufklärung*, ed. Carsten Zelle (Tübingen: de Gruyter, 2001), 5–24.

36. Rüdiger Campe has traced this shift in the conception of probability in his exhaustive study of this concept, underscoring its centrality for eighteenth-century aesthetics. See Campe, *Spiel der Wahrscheinlichkeit: Literatur und Berechnung zwischen Pascal und Kleist* (Göttingen: Wallstein 2002), 344–418.

37. Frauke Berndt draws attention to the implications of Baumgarten's conception of aesthetics as a metaphysics of beauty when she says, "Der schöne Geist ist nichts Geringeres als ein Agent in metaphysischer Mission, die bei der Exzentrik der symbolischen Mangelstruktur beginnt." Berndt, *Poema/Gedicht*, 117.

Chapter 2

1. In a letter to Schiller, Hölderlin does claim to seek an "intellectual intuition" that reveals the unification of subject and object in aesthetic reception, but only in a way that makes semiosis a never-ending process: an "infinite approximation" that itself remains a logical impossibility akin to the "squaring of a circle" (*MA* 2:595–96).

2. Many have written about the relation between Kant and Hölderlin. For a recent example of a work investigating the relation between Kant's conception of religion and Hölderlin's own religious thought, see Ian Cooper, *The Near and Distant God: Poetry, Idealism, and Religious Thought from Hölderlin to Eliot* (London: Modern Humanities Research Association and Maney Publishing, 2008).

3. William Fitzgerald gives a sensitive reading of Hölderlin's "Patmos" from the perspective of the agonistic relation between horizontal (human) time and vertical (divine) mediation. See William Fitzgerald, *Agonistic Poetry: The Pindaric Mode in Pindar, Horace, Hölderlin, and the English Ode* (Berkeley: University of California Press, 1987), 72.

4. Norbert von Hellingrath linked Hölderlin's "harte Fügung" to Pindaric poetic modes, whereas Adorno's "Parataxis" ascribes to Hölderlin's use of formal disjunction a refusal to submit the particular to the violence of identity. See Norbert von Hellingrath, *Pindarübertragungen von Hölderlin: Prolegomena zu einer Erstausgabe* (Leipzig: Breitkopf, 1910); and Theodor Adorno, "Parataxis," in *Noten zur Literatur* (Frankfurt am Main: Suhrkamp, 1997), 447–91.

5. Bart Philipsen remarks, "Das 'Subjekt' von H.s geschichtsallegorischer Geographie aber ist kein reflexionslogischer Erkenntnisakt, sondern ein Sprachwerdungsprozeß. In den späteren Gesängen und erst recht den Entwürfen und späten Überarbeitungen nach 1803/04 wird es sich immer mehr in die oft apodiktische Zeichenhaftigkeit materieller Markierungen und Spuren zurückziehen, die als "Ausdruck, Zeichen, Darstellung" den verborgenen, prozessualen Zusammenhang des Ganzen zu bezeichnen und zu bewahren versuchen." Philipsen, "Gesänge," in *Hölderlin-Handbuch*, ed. Johann Kreuzer (Stuttgart: Metzler, 2002), 352.

6. For this element of Hölderlin's poetics in relation to "Patmos," see Jochen Schmidt, *Hölderlins geschichtsphilosophische Hymnen: "Friedensfeier," "Der Einzige," "Patmos"* (Darmstadt: Wissenschaftliche Buchgesellschaft, 1990), 185–288.

7. See Paul Guyer, "Kant's Ambitions in the Third *Critique*," in *Kant and Modern Philosophy*, ed. Paul Guyer (Cambridge, Eng.: Cambridge University Press, 2006), 538–87.

8. See Hannah Arendt, *Lectures on Kant's Political Philosophy*, ed. Ronald Beiner (Chicago: University of Chicago Press, 1992), 44–51.

9. Compare Bertaux's interpretation of Hölderlin as a "Jakobiner." Pierre Bertaux, *Hölderlin und die Französische Revolution* (Frankfurt am Main: Suhrkamp, 1974).

10. Ulrich Gaier notes the importance of systems-theoretical concepts for Hölderlin's conception of organization. He emphasizes the critical point that since Descartes, philosophers and natural scientists have used the concept of organization to link order *within* elements of a system to order *between* systems. See Ulrich Gaier, "Hölderlin und die Theorie der Organisation," *Text + Kritik* 7, no. 96 (1996): 51–61. Hölderlin conceives poetic language as participating in each of these layers of organization. For an exhaustive account of Hölderlin's conception of the self-organization of nature, see Michael Luhnen, *Organisation der Natur* (Heidelberg: Winter, 2007). Luhnen also understands poetry as an "experimental" procedure that justifies a posteriori the self-organization of nature as an ontological given (792).

11. Hölderlin attempts to make this organization "fühlbar" in the harmonic alternation of tones (*Wechsel der Töne*), suggesting that if it were not felt, it would remain merely "ein leeres leichtes Schattenspiel" (*MA* 2:78).

12. Ralf Knübel discusses Hölderlin's suffering from a psychological perspective, and, based on an interpretation of some lines from the *Homburger Folioheft*, suggests that Hölderlin's poetry constructs a "house" that must continually be supported through song: "[Das Haus] scheint einzustürzen, wenn die Wände, die nur durch die Bilder des Gesangs erzeugt werden, nicht ständig erneuert werden." Ralf Knübel, "Hölderlins Leiden: Der poetische Prozess als Versuch der Selbstverständigung," *Hölderlin-Jahrbuch* 36 (2009): 162.

13. *Metaphysica* §89. Baumgarten, *Metaphysica*, 87.

14. Dieter Henrich claims that Hölderlin's conception of *Urtheil* draws just as much from Fichte's philosophy of the subject as from Kantian a priori synthetic judgments. See Henrich, *Der Grund im Bewußtsein: Untersuchungen zu Hölderlins Denken (1794–1795)* (Stuttgart: Klett-Cotta, 1992), 47.

15. For a short discussion of the history of this concept from Kant to Schelling, see Annette Hornbacher, "'Eines zu seyn mit Allem, was lebt . . .': Hölderlins

'intellectuale Anschauung,'" in *Hölderlin: Philosophie und Dichtung*, vol. 5 of *Turm-Vorträge*, ed. Valérie Lawitschka (Tübingen: Hölderlin-Gesellschaft, 2001), 24–47.

16. Thomas Pfau notes that inasmuch as man is "bound up with a symbolic order and its attendant temporality, he can only have a more or less developed awareness of the impossibility of recuperating the withdrawn God without, once again, shattering his creation." Prau, critical introduction to *Essays and Letters on Theory*, by Friedrich Hölderlin, ed. Thomas Pfau (Albany: State University of New York Press, 1988), 25.

17. Dieter Henrich claims that some conception of "intellectual intuition" informs the totality of Hölderlin's poetic praxis. See Henrich, *Der Grund im Bewußtsein* 262. However, Annette Hornbacher makes a convincing case that Hölderlin changes his conception of intellectual intuition toward an "aesthetic" interpretation of this concept, that is, as an intuition of beauty. However, she collapses "memory" and "intellectual intuition" into one and the same process: "'Erinnerung' hat darum als Bewußtseinsform der poetischen Sprachfindung den gleichen Inhalt wie die 'intellectuale Anschauung' und kulminiert in Hölderlins Begriff der Freiheit." Hornbacher, "'Eines zu seyn mit Allem, was lebt . . . ,'" 43. However, as I hope to show, Hölderlin uses memory to represent a thread that holds together the alternation of intellectual intuition and subject-object separation in aesthetic perception—and is therefore not equivalent to intellectual intuition as such.

18. In Hölderlin's later doctrine of the *Wechsel der Töne*, intellectual intuition takes on a different function; as Annette Hornbacher notes, it becomes "ein Moment *innerhalb* des Tönewechsels. . . . [Die intellektuale Anschauung] ist jetzt der 'Grundton' des tragischen Gedichts." Hornbacher, "'Eines zu seyn mit Allem, was lebt . . . ,'" 43.

19. As Jamme and Völkel note: "Die Crux des Doppelblattes beseht eben darin, daß es von *beiden* Seiten gelesen und daß es *gewendet* werden kann." Christophe Jamme and Frank Völkel, eds., *Hölderlin und der deutsche Idealismus*, vol. 3.2 (Stuttgart: Frommann-Holzboog, 2003), 356. Special thanks to Jeremy Brett for drawing my attention to the materiality of this work.

20. The function of memory has been much discussed in the secondary literature. See, for example, Helmut Hühn, *Mnemosyne: Zeit und Erinnerung in Hölderlins Denken* (Stuttgart: Metzler, 1997).

21. For an exhaustive analysis of Hölderlin's *Wechsel der Töne*, see Lawrence J. Ryan, *Hölderlins Lehre vom Wechsel der Töne* (Stuttgart: Kohlhammer, 1960). Szondi claims that the *Wechsel der Töne* solves a poetic dilemma, allowing Hölderlin to turn to "Hesperian" material and conceptualize history within his poetic production. Peter Szondi, *Einführung in die literarische Hermeneutik* (Frankfurt am Main: Suhrkamp, 1975), 105–46.

22. Johann Kreuzer has shown that memory constitutes the central binding feature of Hölderlin's poetology. See Johann Kreuzer, *Erinnerung: Zum Zusammenhang von Hölderlins theoretischen Fragmenten "Das untergehende Vaterland . . ." und "Wenn der Dicther einmal des Geistes mächtig ist . . ."* (Königstein: Anton Hain, 1985). Viewing memory not only as the cultural or historical memory of a past—as archive—but also as an act of cognitive "retention" establishes a link between Hölderlin's poetic form and its connection to reading or listening, as I hope to show in my interpretation of "The Rhine."

23. See Johann Kreuzer, "Logik von Zeit und Erinnerung—Was unterscheidet die Wirklichkeit des Gesangs von der Form des Begriffs?" in *"Es bleibet aber eine Spur / Doch eines Wortes": Zur späten Hymnik und Tragödientheorie Friedrich Hölderlins*, ed. Christoph Jamme and Anja Lemke (Munich: Fink, 2004), 465–83.

24. See Johann Christoph Adelung, *Grammatisch-kritisches Wörterbuch der hochdeutschen Mundart*, vol. 1 (Vienna: Bauer, 1811), 1888.

25. This thesis is articulated in Rainer Nägele, *Literatur und Utopie: Versuche zu Hölderlin* (Heidelberg: Lothar Stiehm, 1978), 105–50. See also Helmut Hühn, *Mnemosyne* 24–67; Marion Hiller, *"Harmonisch Entgegengesetzt": Zur Darstellung und Darstellbarkeit in Hölderlins Poetik um 1800* (Tübingen: Max Niemeyer, 2008), 43–45 .

26. See Hiller, *"Harmonisch Entgegengesetzt,"* 17–22.

27. Lawrence Ryan notes, "Der Roman stellt demnach im Spiegel des Erinnerungsberichts einen Reflexionsprozeß dar, so daß der Erzähler gerade beim Erzählen und durch das Erzählen ein anderes Verhältnis zu den dargestellten Vorgängen und daher ein anderes Selbstverständnis gewinnt." Ryan, "Hyperion oder Der Eremit in Griechenland," in *Hölderlin-Handbuch*, ed. Johann Kreuzer (Stuttgart: Metzler, 2002), 177.

28. See Ryan, "Hyperion oder Der Eremit in Griechenland," 195.

29. Adorno, "Parataxis," 476.

30. Johann Georg Sulzer, *Allgemeine Theorie der schönen Künste in einzeln, nach alphabetischer Ordnung der Kunstworter aufeinanderfolgenden, Artikeln abgehandelt*, vol. 3 (Hildesheim: G. Olms, 1994), 664–65.

31. For "The Rhine" as a critique of autonomy, see Jochen Schmidt, commentary on "The Rhine" in Friedrich Hölderlin, *Sämtliche Gedichte*, ed. Jochen Schmidt (Frankfurt am Main: Deutscher Taschenbuch Verlag, 2005), 858; as a critique of proximity to the gods, see Bernhard Böschenstein, *Hölderlin's Rheinhymne* (Zürich: Atlantis, 1968), 10; as a figure of mediation, see ibid., 123–24; as a document that reveals the "priority of consciousness over the sensuous object," see Paul de Man, *The Rhetoric of Romanticism* (New York: Columbia University Press, 1984), 45; for the poem as illustration of its own linguistic metaphoricity (which is essentially "erotic" in a Platonic sense), see Rainer Nägele, *Text, Geschichte und Subjektivität in Hölderlins Dichtung: "Uneßbarer Schrift gleich"* (Stuttgart: Metzler, 1985), 209.

32. Hölderlin began composing this hymn in 1801 in Hauptwil; he first dedicated it to Heinse, although he later changed the dedication to Isaak von Sinclair, perhaps underscoring the importance of their common intellectual and political point of view, as will be discussed in the following interpretation. His later addition of Rousseau to the *Reinschrift* also suggests a more explicit politicization of the aesthetic and cognitive movements of "The Rhine." See Jochen Schmidt, commentary on "The Rhine," 854–55.

33. Rainer Nägele claims that this law constitutes "eine Folge von chiastischen Entgegensetzungen und Entsprechungen." Nägele, *Hölderlins Kritik der poetischen Vernunft* (Basel: Engeler, 2007), 71. This "law" therefore links up the formal structure of the poem with the movement of consciousness as described within the poem.

34. This reading of Hölderlin also assumes a similarity between Hölderlin's attempt to hermeneutically fill out the "gaps" in poetry (and hence in nature and

in history) and Wolfgang Iser's concept of "Leerstellen." See *The Act of Reading: A Theory of Aesthetic Response* (Baltimore: Johns Hopkins University Press, 1978), 180–231.

35. Plato, *Symposium*, in *Lysis, Symposium, Gorgias*, trans. W. R. M. Lamb (Cambridge, Mass.: Harvard University Press, 1925), 205–6.

36. For an extensive analysis of Hölderlin's concept of "Maas," see Elena Polledri, "*. . . immer bestehet ein Maas*": *Der Begriff des Maßes in Hölderlins Werk* (Würzburg: Königshausen & Neumann, 2002).

37. Martin Heidegger, *Hölderlins Hymnen "Germanien" und "Der Rhein,"* vol. 39 of *Gesamtausgabe*, ed. Susanne Ziegle (Frankfurt am Main: Klostermann, 1980), 287.

38. Isaak von Sinclair, "Philosophische Raisonnements," in *Isaak von Sinclair zwischen Fichte, Hölderlin und Hegel: Ein Beitrag zur Entstehungsgeschichte der idealistischen Philosophie*, by Hannelore Hegel (Frankfurt am Main: Klostermann, 1980), 268.

39. Isaak von Sinclair, "Philosophische Raisonnements," 254. Manfred Frank translates A Εις (εαυτον) Θεσιν as "fortwährende Setzung, fortwährendes Sichselbst-Setzen," a translation that presents an alternative reading of the Greek. Manfred Frank, *Unendliche Annäherung* (Frankfurt am Main: Suhrkamp, 1997), 765. He reads ἀεί (continual, always) in Sinclair's formulation of *aeisthesis*, whereas the accusative Θεσιν in Hannelore Hegel's edition (which Frank mysteriously cites as Θεσισ) suggests that the Εις designates "in, toward," and the alpha is an alpha privative. In other words, whereas Frank translates Sinclair's concept as "continual positing," an alternative reading would be "not-into-itself positing."

40. Sinclair, "Philosophische Raisonnements," 276.

41. Ibid., 269.

42. Ibid. Manfred Frank notes that in this passage, two seemingly contradictory connotations in the concept of *aeisthesis* come to the fore: "Man beobachtet . . . den Umschlag der zweiten (negativen) Bedeutung von 'Ästhetik' in die erste (positive), in der Ästhetik zu einem Verstandes-Ideal wird: zur Utopie sinnlich dargestellter Einigkeit." Frank, *Unendliche Annäherung*, 765. However, Sinclair does not oppose two different conceptions of the aesthetic, but rather, attempts to integrate lower *aeisthesis*, as well as reflection, into a process leading to an ideal, unifying form of *aeisthesis*. In Manuscript A of Sinclair's philosophical papers, Sinclair uses a similar formulation, but without any semantic inversion in the concept of the aesthetic; indeed, in this variation, there is no discussion of "aesthesis," but rather, only pure practical or non-posited, athetic activity: "Das Wissen ist immer unvollkommen für das Praktische (Athetische), denn insofern es Produkt der Reflektion ist, sezt es immer die Urtheilung voraus, die es ihm unmöglich macht die Einigkeit als bestehend zu denken." Sinclair, "Philosophische Raisonnements," 246. In this passage, Sinclair opposes knowledge to practical and non-differentiated immediacy (*athetic*), not to the aesthetic.

43. Gilles Deleuze, *Logic of Sense*, trans. Mark Lester, ed. Constantin V. Boundas (New York: Columbia University Press, 1990), 174–76.

44. As Günther Mieth notes, "wie immer bei Hölderlin, bei dem wie bei kaum einem anderen Dichter dieser Periode das Politische mit dem Philosophisch-Ästhetischen und dem Dichterischen eine untrennbare Einheit bildet, ist diese

Krise des politischen Bewußtseins auf das engste mit seinem ästhetischen Denken und Tun verbunden." Mieth, *Friedrich Hölderlin: Dichter der bürgerlich-demokratischen Revolution* (Berlin: Rütten & Loening, 1978), 47.

45. In a letter to Hegel in January 1795, Hölderlin writes: "Den Begriff der Vorsehung behandelst Du wohl ganz parallel mit Kants Teleologie; die Art, wie er den Mechanismus der Natur (also auch des Schiksaals) mit ihrer Zwekmäsigkeit vereiniget, scheint mir eigentlich den ganzen Geist seines Systems zu enthalthen" (*MA* 2:569). Hölderlin's concept of "fate" signifies a historical and political teleology that operates in a manner similar to Kant's account of natural purposiveness. This interpretation of Kant—and the centrality of Kant's teleological conception of nature and political organization—continues to resonate throughout Hölderlin's poetic oeuvre. In another letter to Niethammer in March 1796, Hölderlin discusses the possibility of an intellectual intuition explicitly *without* the help of practical reason; he wants to find a principle in which the separation between subject and object disappears "ohne daß unsere praktische Vernunft zu Hilfe kommen müßte" (*MA* 2:615). The capability to intuit this originary inseparability of subject and object requires the formation of an "aesthetic sense"—and it is this sense that Hölderlin's poetry intends to develop and train.

46. Hölderlin writes to Isaak von Sinclair that the organization of natural phenomena in principle constitutes an anti-monarchical activity, since all elements depend on other elements: "die erste Bedingung alles Lebens und aller Organisation [ist], daß keine Kraft monarchisch ist im Himmel und auf Erden. Die absolute Monarchie hebt sich überall selbst auf, denn sie ist objectlos; es hat auch im strengen Sinne niemals eine gegeben" (*MA* 2:723). Even a monarch is, to a certain extent, dependent on others; inasmuch as a monarch must organize himself or herself in a world with others, an "absolute" monarchy is an impossibility, just as is an absolute subject. Hölderlin's letter to Sinclair reveals explicitly the extent to which he politicizes his ontology and ontologizes his political philosophy.

47. Gerhard Kurz makes a convincing case for a link between Hölderlin's poetological statements and his revolutionary ambitions in Gerhard Kurz, *Mittelbarkeit und Vereinigung: Zum Verhältnis von Poesie, Reflexion und Revolution bei Hölderlin* (Stuttgart: Metzler, 1975). My reading views Hölderlin's poetology less as an attempt to institute the republican order, but more to hermeneutically self-reflect on its historical viability, on its legitimacy in the face of violence.

48. For more about Hölderlin's relation to the French Revolution and the supposed attempt to assassinate the Kurfürst of Württemburg, see the debate between Bertaux and Szondi in Bertaux, *Hölderlin und die Französische Revolution*, and Szondi, *Einführung in die literarische Hermeneutik*. When Hölderlin was taken away to be interrogated concerning this incident, one document notes, "[er] schimpft beständig auf Sinclair und die Jakobiner und ruft in einem fort: *ich will kein Jakobiner bleiben, Vive le roi!*" Adolf Beck, *Hölderlin: Chronik seines Lebens* (Frankfurt am Main: Insel, 1975), 98. With Bertaux, one might be inclined to claim that Hölderlin's words comprise a mere ruse undertaken for self-preservation; regardless of the reliability of the statement, the words show that he did consider himself to be a Jacobin. They may also potentially reveal disillusionment with the goals and strategies of the Jacobins. To compound the issue, the document itself may not be reliable; at best one is left with speculation and ambiguity.

49. As Anke Bennholdt-Thomsen and Alfredo Guzzoni note, the possibility of the failure of historical self-organization only becomes an explicit part of Hölderlin's poetological thought in his "Anmerkungen zur Antigonä." See Anke Bennholdt-Thomsen and Alfredo Guzzoni, *Analecta Hölderliniana II: Die Aufgabe des Vaterlands* (Würzburg: Königshausen & Neumann, 2004), 39.

Chapter 3

1. The caesura has been the subject of numerous interpretations. Many of these interpretations see in the caesura a figure of interruption, of perturbation, and hence, of melancholic inevitability. For example, Lacoue-Labarthe claims, "man forgets himself and forgets the God, 'because he exists entirely within the moment'; the God forgets 'because he is nothing other than time' (*Essays*, 1–7), and that is to say, the law of irreversibility: the 'this is irretrievable' of tragic destiny." Philippe Lacoue-Labarthe, "Hölderlin's Theatre," in *Philosophy and Tragedy*, ed. Miguel de Beistegui and Simon Sparks (London: Routledge, 2000), 134. Karin Dahlke, for example, claims, "Dieser Ort in der Mitte zwischen den beiden Hälften ist, wie schon in den vorherigen poetologischen Texten, der Ort des Todes und der Leere, ist der Ort einer Abwesenheit, der unter der Zäsur markiert wird von dem reinen Wort, das das Leiden ausspricht." Dahlke, *Äußerste Freiheit: Wahnsinn/Sublimierung/Poetik des Tragischen der Moderne* (Würzburg: Königshausen & Neumann, 2008), 488. In my reading, the caesura renders the historical moment, if not transparent, then capable of being made intelligible.

2. Jochen Schmidt, for example, calls the poem "wohl unvollendet," in Hölderlin, *Sämtliche Gedichte*, 1026.

3. Rainer Nägele discusses how problematic the "knees" have been for interpreters of the poem; see Nägele, *Hölderlins Kritik der poetischen Vernunft*, 103. He says, "Eine Bedingung ist gesetzt: wenn einer, ein Einzelner, die Prüfung bestanden hat, dann mag dieser Eine *spüren das Waldgeschrei*" (102). It seems to me, however, difficult to equate "wenn die Prüfung durch die Knie gegangen ist" with the successful completion of the test.

4. Beissner notes in his explication of "Waldgeschrei": "Von den in Grimms deutschen Wörterbuch 13,1136 f. unterschiedenen drei Bedeutungen (Jagdrufe, Vogelsang, kunstloser Gesang) trifft am ehesten die zweite zu," in Friedrich Hölderlin, *Sämtliche Werke*, ed. Friedrich Beissner, vol. 2.2 (Stuttgart: Kohlhammer, 1951), 813.

5. Michael Hamburger translates "Ist der zufrieden" with "if he is contented" (*PF* 585). I do not believe that this translation makes sense, and so I have replaced it with my own alternative translation. Hamburger thinks "zufrieden" (content) applies to the Rhine. This is incongruous with the images of the Rhine that immediately precede this line, where the river is "grinding the bit [*In den Zaum knirscht er*]." Rather, I believe that the pronoun "der" is being used demonstratively to refer to the Ister: where "the other one" (e.g., the Rhine) is chomping at the bit, "this one" (e.g., the Ister) is flowing peacefully. This is precisely the aberration to be explained, and in a rare case of (in my view) a faulty translation, this meaning remains obscured in Hamburger's version.

6. Lawrence Ryan discusses the resonance between a politically infused *Bildung*, one that would lead to a functioning republican-democratic order, and Hölderlin's poetics: "Die selbständigen und durch und durch individualisierten, aber innig

verbundenen Teile eines lebendigen Ganzen sind im politischen Zusammenhang sicherlich auch die Staatsbürger—die Ausbalancierung des Einzelnen und der Allgemeinheit im Staatsgefüge entspricht der Verteilung der poetisch evozierten Ganzheit und des stofflich Individualisierten in der poetischen Verfahrensweise. Fast könnte man sagen, ein republikanisch-demokratisch gebildeter Staat hätte nach Hölderlins Vorstellung eine 'poetische' Verfassung." Ryan, "'Was bildet aber, stiften die Dichter': Zu Hölderlins Konzeption von 'Bildung,'" *Hölderlin-Jahrbuch* 36 (2009): 49. If Ryan is correct, then "Der Ister" casts further doubt on the education of a subject that could function in a republican order; in the poem, there is only the dysfunctional Ister or the Rhine, full of potential, and yet, the river has not yet been "tamed" as in "The Rhine."

7. Johann Christoph Adelung, *Grammatisch-kritisches Wörterbuch der hochdeutschen Mundart*, vol. 3 (Vienna: Bauer, 1811), 1510.

8. Other critics do not see a disconnection between "das Zeichen" and the rivers themselves. Böschenstein, for example, claims, "[es] ist darauf hinzuweisen, daß der Strom zum 'Zeichen' wird . . . welches das Wesen eines Stromes transzendiert." Bernhard Böschenstein, "Oden-Flüsse—Hymnen-Ströme," *Hölderlin-Jahrbuch* 35 (2007): 201. One might add, precisely this "transcendence" of the sign does not appear to function in the poem.

9. Rainer Nägele notes that "Nicht einmal, von welchem Strom hier die Rede ist, ist wissbar. Ist jener der Rhein oder der Ister?" Nägele, *Hölderlins Kritik der poetischen Vernunft*, 128.

10. Rainer Nägele has beautiful words to say about Hölderlin's invocation of Hertha: "Die Sprachlichkeit des Namens Hertha wird im 'Ister' syllabisch sibyllinisch überdeterminiertes Echo in der Silbe *Her*. Hertha antwortet als Echo dem den Vers eröffnenden ***Herunter*** und im weiterhin tönenden Echo dem Namen dessen, der zum Ister als Gast geladen ist: ***Herkules***. Und sie alle sind Echo des elidierten *her* der Fernangekommenen. Und wird auch die Silbe noch verkürzt auf den Buchstaben, von dem sie ausgeht, dem gehauchten H, so treten Hertha und Himmel im Pneuma dieses Hauches, der auch den herunterkommenden Höchsten haucht, aufs zärtlichste zusammen." Ibid., 127. Even in the sound *her*, which designates motion from somewhere, the poem rests in a potentiality, not in a telos, one that also appears bifurcated between the Germanic and the Greek *Hertha* and *Herkules*.

11. Hölderlin scholarship has belabored his fascination with cultural difference and displacement, the famed "Kulturwanderung" from east to west, from the Greek to the Hesperian. See Hansjörg Bay, "'Die eigene Rede des andern': Hölderlins Poetik des Fremden," in *Die Ordnung der Kulturen: Zur Konstruktion ethnischer, nationaler und zivilisatorischer Differenzen 1750–1850*, ed. Hansjörg Bay and Kai Merten (Würzburg: Königshausen & Neumann, 2006), 333–56.

12. Between the Rhine and the Danube, one may therefore perceive different paradigms of textual fluidity and corporeal fluidity. Albrecht Koschorke notes in reference to the literary culture of *Empfindsamkeit* that textual fluidity sublimates the model of humoral-pathological streams: "So bieten die Empfindsamen nicht nur das Weinen, die literarisch beförderte Rührung, sondern auch die Vorgänge des Lesens und Schreibens als solche eine Sublimierungsstufe des älteren Modells der physiologischen Ströme." Koschorke, *Körperströme und Schriftverkehr* (Munich: Fink, 2003), 215.

13. Joseph Vogl speaks of a "Zauderfunktion" that returns events to states of potentiality. In a certain sense, one may speak of "Der Ister" as a poem that—like the river—itself performs a sort of *Zauderfunktion*. In other words, it is not that the river is "betrübt," but that it hesitates between being "betrübt" and "zufrieden." Vogl notes: "Im Unterschied zu verwandten Spielarten wie Unentschlossenheit, Trägheit, Ratlosigkeit, Willensschwäche oder bloßem Nichtstun, es hat vielmehr einen meta-stabilen Charakter und lässt gegenstrebige Impulse immer von Neuem einander initiieren, entfesseln und hemmen zugleich." Vogl, *Über das Zaudern* (Zürich: Diaphanes, 2007), 23. The Rhine and the Danube seem to inhabit precisely such a system of hesitation and equilibrium, regression and struggle.

14. Jochen Schmidt calls this poem "hermeneutische Dichtung," drawing attention to the way in which the poem integrates biblical passages into its own form of textuality, which in turn provides the model for a way of reading history that is itself infused with divine presence. See Jochen Schmidt, *Hölderlins geschichtsphilosophische Hymnen* (Darmstadt: Wissenschaftliche Buchgesellschaft, 1990), 185–288.

15. Angela Esterhammer discusses poetry as performative intersubjective speech acts, especially in relation to "Patmos." See Esterhammer, *The Romantic Performative* (Stanford, Calif.: Stanford University Press, 2000), 233–39.

16. See Schmidt, *Hölderlins geschichtsphilosophische Hymnen*, 185–197.

17. See Schmidt's commentary in Hölderlin, *Sämtliche Gedichte*, 1006.

18. See Alice Kuzniar, *Delayed Endings: Nonclosure in Novalis and Hölderlin* (Athens: University of Georgia Press, 1987), 170–90.

19. Hölderlin would have come into direct contact with the visible traces of the French Revolution in Bordeaux. Günther Mieth notes, "Die Place Dauphine, wo die Guillotine gestanden hatte, war wegen des blutigen Andenkens kaum noch bewohnt. . . . Vor allem aber war das allgemeine Bewußtsein der Bordeleser Einwohner noch derart stark von der revolutionären Zeit geprägt, daß sie von ihr—ohne gefragt zu werden—berichteten." Mieth, *Friedrich Hölderlin: Dichter der bürgerlich-demokratischen Revolution*, 140.

20. Recent scholarship has called into question the extent to which these poems can rightly be called "Christian"; the poet thematizes Christ as the brethren of pagan gods, in certain cases descending from Zeus himself. Anke Bennholdt-Thomsen and Alfredo Guzzoni argue that Christianity becomes absorbed into a polytheism that shares more characteristics with pagan antiquity than with Christian orthodoxy. See Anke Bennholdt-Thomsen and Alfredo Guzzoni, *Analecta Hölderliana: Zur Hermetik des Spätwerks* (Würzburg: Königshausen & Neumann, 1999), 126.

21. Boris Previšić points out that the first version of "Patmos" utilizes a hexameter verse that is spread out over multiple lines. The subsequent versions of "Patmos" similarly break up the rhythmic integrity of the hexameter. See *Hölderlins Rhythmus* (Frankfurt am Main: Stroemfeld, 2008), 202.

22. The work of Jochen Schmidt reveals to what extent the problem of theodicy was central for Hölderlin: "Die Theodizee und ihre kosmologische und geschichtsphilosophische Dimensionierung ist in Hölderlins Werk von grundlegender Bedeutung." Schmidt, *Hölderlins geschichtsphilosophische Hymnen*, 226.

23. For Hölderlin's relationship to Heraclitus, see Bennholdt-Thomsen and Guzzoni, *Analecta Hölderliana: Zur Hermetik des Spätwerks*, 120.

24. After trying to imitate the divine, the poet sees this anger visibly: "Im Zorne sichtbar sah' ich einmal / Des Himmels Herrn, nicht, daß ich seyn sollt etwas, sondern / Zu lernen" (*MA* 1:452). Jochen Schmidt interprets the notion that some things may go lost not as a false path, but as the reformulation of a more modest and rational interpretation of theodicy. See *Hölderlins geschichtsphilosophische Hymnen*, 288. To read this phrase in such a manner tears it out of context, for in the poem, precisely this thought begins the process through which the lyrical voice draws the ire of the gods.

25. See Bennholdt-Thomsen and Guzzoni, *Analecta Hölderliana: Zur Hermetik des Spätwerks*, 98.

26. This is my translation drawing on Hamburger's translation of a different fragment (*PF* 571).

27. Rainer Nägele interprets the *uneßbare Schrift* of John the Baptist's head as the indigestible "excess" of the hermeneutic project. This suggestion is fruitful, but does not mention the importance of the religious context. Nägele, *Text, Geschichte und Subjektivität*, 2. Charles de Roche goes one step further and interprets this "writing" as a parody of the Eucharist: "Die Eucharistie ist in der Szene schon vom biblischen Text her gegenwärtig, der sie vor dem Hintergrund eines 'Abendmahls' spielen lässt und in der Darbietung des Hauptes auf der Schüssel die Parodie und Kontrafaktur des später geschilderten stellt." De Roche, *Friedrich Hölderlin: Patmos: Das scheidende Erscheinen des Gedichts* (Munich: Fink, 1999), 198. I am claiming this passage is more than just a parody; it is a negative representation of the rites of the Eucharist.

28. Georg Wilhelm Friedrich Hegel, *The Phenomenology of Spirit* (Oxford: Oxford University Press, 1977), 360.

29. This is my translation that uses some formulations from Hamburger's translation of another fragment (*PF* 573).

30. The famous *Gang nach Canossa* acquired a heavy nationalistic significance in 1872 when Bismarck claimed that Prussia would not grovel before the pope in order to resolve the *Kulturkampf* between the Catholic Church and the Prussian state. It goes without saying that this ideological significance is not present in the eighteenth century, let alone in Hölderlin's verses. Rather, the lines referring to Henry IV are much more to be understood as the desire to sing of one who has "returned" to the church and suffered for it—an act toward which the poet seems to have a certain ambivalence.

31. Compare De Roche, *Friedrich Hölderlin: Patmos*, 213–15.

32. De Roche also mentions the proximity of the "Schlüssel" to the "Schlüssen," but does not place this shift in relation to the doctrine of the solid letter. See ibid., 212.

33. In Isaak von Sinclair's copying of the manuscript and in the printed version in the *Musenalmanach für das Jahr 1808*, for example, one reads "Der feste Buchstab," not Hölderlin's formulation as "Der veste Buchstab," a difference that Sattler emphasizes in his historical critical edition (*FA* 8:69).

34. This is my translation that uses some formulations from Hamburger's translation of another fragment (*PF* 573–75).

35. Ovid, *Metamorphoses*, vol. 1, trans. Frank Justus Miller (Cambridge, Mass: Harvard University Press, 1951), 132–33.

Conclusion to Part One

1. It seems that Hölderlin intended to develop a counter-theory to Schelling's theory of modality written in 1794, a theory that conceptualized the absoluteness of the I as pure possibility; for a more detailed history of Hölderlin's modal thinking in "Urtheil, Seyn," see Dieter Henrich, *Der Grund im Bewußtsein*, 707–26.

2. In this sense, one might tend to see necessity aligned with Being. However, Dieter Henrich claims, "'Seyn schlechthin' ist als solches nicht einmal unter dem Gedanken der Notwendigkeit zu denken, der, wie die anderen Modalbegriffe, nur innerhalb des Wissens seinen Ort und seine Funktion hat." Henrich, *Der Grund im Bewußtsein*, 712. I do not believe Hölderlin's text actually allows this conclusion; rather it seems that Hölderlin implicitly constructs a space for "necessity" only in the realm of *Seyn*, whereas this modality appears explicitly banished from *Urtheil*.

Chapter 4

1. Gerhard Schulz claims about these oft-cited poetological remarks that they seem to bolster the "irrationalist" interpretation of romanticism: "Irritierende Gedanken bleiben sie, denn schließlich ist ein aporetischer Satz wie 'Poësie ist Poësie' im Grunde nichts anderes als die Abdankung aller Versuche, ihr mit Hilfe jenes begrifflichen Denkens näherzukommen, auf das nun einmal die Wissenschaft angewiesen ist." Schulz, "Poesie als Poetik oder Poetik als Poesie?" in *Novalis: Poesie und Poetik*, ed. Herbert Uerlings (Tübingen: Niemeyer, 2004), 102. However, as I hope to show, *Poësie ist Poësie* actually condenses the poetic act to its most basic form: the tautology.

2. Such, for example, has been, the usual understanding of the meaning of poetry for Novalis. His conception of poetry is usually assimilated to Schelling's notion of poetry as another form of intellectual intuition, or an intuition of the unrepresentable ground of being. René Wellek, for example, notes, "[Novalis] gives a more mystical twist to Schelling's theory and connects it more clearly with the special conception of poetry as dream and fairy tale. Poetry in Novalis is virtually identified with religion and philosophy, and the poet is exalted beyond any other human being. A sense of poetry, he recognizes, has much in common with a taste for mysticism." Wellek, *A History of Modern Criticism 1750–1950: The Romantic Age*, vol. 2 (Cambridge, Eng.: Cambridge University Press, 1981), 82. He proceeds to cite the above quote as evidence for his claim, and as I hope to show, by making poetry "indefinable" he does not make it the subject of an *Unsagbarkeitstopos* or permit an "intellectual intuition" of absolute being, but rather, sees poetry as a continual perturbation and overturning of reflective orders, of ways of organizing the world. Poetry therefore functions more as stimulus than as mystical intuition. Or rather, mystic writing itself *performs* this production of difference; as Novalis says in *Glauben und Liebe*, "The mystical expression is one more stimulation of thought [*Der mystische Ausdruck ist ein Gedankenreiz mehr*]" (*NS* 2:485).

3. Ludwig Wittgenstein, *Tractatus Logico-Philosophicus*, trans. C. K. Ogden (New York: Barnes & Noble, 1992), 157.

4. Manfred Frank, for example, claims, "Nur die unausdeutbare Sinnfülle des Kunstwerks kann positiv zeigen, was sich nicht definitiv in Wissen auflösen läßt.

So wird das Kunstwerk zur einzig möglichen 'Darstellung des Undarstellbaren' (NS III 685/6, Nr. 671)." Frank, *Einführung in die frühromantische Ästhetik* (Frankfurt am Main: Suhrkamp, 1989), 255. He provides much evidence to support this point of view. However, he neglects the apparent performative contradiction at the core of Novalis's fragments: Novalis keeps *representing* the unrepresentability of art. Therefore, when Novalis speaks of art as "representing the unrepresentable," he is not necessarily claiming that art accesses a reality that is unavailable to reflective thought, but rather, that art sees this unrepresentability as a *generator* of representations, as part of the drive toward multiplicity. Frank's proposition appears questionable from the perspective of the aesthetic exercise: if he is correct, and art represents what is unrepresentable, then we no longer need to bother with interpreting the work of art, since its essence lies in making visible a non-articulable *feeling*, and any one interpretation necessarily misses this unrepresentable essence. However, Novalis explicitly ties this unrepresentability to the idea of an infinite poem, something to which we must keep returning, something that keeps working and keeps generating reflective orders of fictionality. And in this sense, the critic's imperative consists in generating as many different interpretive orders as possible, in drawing upon the representation of the unrepresentable as a *Fortsetzen*, the drive to language itself.

5. See above all Frank, *Einführung in die frühromantische Ästhetik*; and Winfried Menninghaus, *Unendliche Verdopplung* (Frankfurt am Main: Suhrkamp, 1987).

6. See Frank, *Unendliche Annäherung*, 809.

7. See Manfred Frank's comparison of early romantic theories of poetry with Heidegger's concept of the work of art in *Einführung in die frühromantische Ästhetik*, 22–24.

8. The duplicity of identity leads Winfried Menninghaus to speak of romantic aesthetics as "unendliche Verdopplung." He notes that "in Novalis 'Wechsel' . . . die Differenz 'das übergreifende Allgemeine' [ist] und die Identität nur ein gleitender Effekt ihres Spiels." Menninghaus, *Unendliche Verdopplung* (Frankfurt am Main: Suhrkamp, 1987), 97. However, as Manfred Frank would assert, difference cannot be thought without identity, and, as it so happens, Being (*Seyn*) is also just as necessary to the functioning of what I will call the *physiological* absolute, as it functions as a source of stimulation (the "negative" as such) that, by announcing its presence *as* an absence, increases and intensifies differentiation in a system.

9. Form, for Novalis, expresses "was man in Beziehung denken muß," whereas content or *Stoff* designates "was man allein denken kann" (*NS* 2:172). Form is relational, whereas content admits of no relationality, and hence can only be conceived as an independent ground. Novalis's central problem consists in how this relationless substance, the realm of pure Being, nevertheless comes into contact with the realm of determinate beings, and hence with the realm of mortals.

10. As Menninghaus notes, "In diakritischer Reflexion entdeckt also Novalis schon im scheinbar unverdächtigsten Ausdruck der Identität mit sich (a = a) eine Differenz, die diese Identität, qua Verdopplung in sich selbst, spaltet." Menninghaus, *Unendliche Verdopplung*, 91.

11. Alexander Schlutz, in his reading of Novalis's philosophy, emphasizes this point when he says, "As a mode of representation ("Darstellung"), in

which the subject always appears as *both* philosophical reflection and poetical construction—both truth and illusion are the products of imagination—the work of art will always indicate that the unity of transcendental poetics can only be realized in the realm of the *ordo inversus* and hence *as a fiction*." Alexander M. Schlutz, *Mind's World* (Seattle: University of Washington Press, 2009), 178.

12. Menninghaus concentrates on Novalis's "Schöpfung aus Nichts" in *Unendliche Verdopplung*, 142–46.

13. Ingrid Strohschneider-Kohrs claims that Novalis's "Monologue" exhibits the classical patterns of romantic irony: "Was hier geschieht: das Sich-Durchsetzen und Wirklichwerden des Sinnes, des in diesem Text von der Sprache und ihrem Geheimnis Gemeinten, *kann und darf nicht Aussage werden* . . . . Nur *in actu negationis* kann der Sinnvollzug liegen, niemals in einer neuen Aussage." Ingrid Strohschneider-Kohrs, *Die romantische Ironie in Theorie und Gestaltung* (Tübingen: Niemeyer, 1977), 264. One ought to add that irony can only be produced *in* and *from* these utterances, and therefore requires language in order to come into being. Romantic irony is therefore not merely the appearance of a negative, but the production of a positive, that is, a paradoxical generator of language.

14. For a detailed account of this process, see Manfred Frank and Gerhard Kurz, "Ordo Inversus: Zu einer Reflexionsfigur bei Novalis, Hölderlin, Kleist, und Kafka," in *Geist und Zeichen: Festschrift für Arthur Henkel*, ed. Bernhard Gajek, Herbert Anton, and Peter Pfaff (Heidelberg: Winter, 1977), 77–97; see also Menninghaus, *Unendliche Verdopplung*, 72–131.

15. See Frank, *Einführung in die frühromantische Ästhetik*, 248–61.

16. Jocelyn Holland has convincingly articulated a central feature of Novalis's poetry as a poetics of procreation. She notes, "Countless children bless the union of Hyacinth and Rosenblütchen. Like the geometric series which ended with mankind as generation 'infinity,' the apprentice's narrative (also an 'account' or *Erzählung*) can never be told to its very end, and has only symbolic completeness." Holland, *German Romanticism and Science: The Procreative Poetics of Goethe, Novalis, and Ritter* (London: Routledge, 2009),103–4.

17. See Jürgen Daibler, *Experimentalphysik des Geistes* (Göttingen: Vandenhoeck & Ruprecht, 2001).

18. Richard Hannah discusses the importance of art as *Gemüthserregungskunst*; see *The Fichtean Dynamics of Novalis' Poetics* (Berlin: Peter Lang, 1981), 159–60. Also, for a study of Novalis's philosophy of language as stimulation, see Verena Anna Lukas, *Der Dialog im Dialog: Das Inzitament bei Friedrich von Hardenberg* (Bern: Peter Lang, 2000).

19. Badiou's ontology is almost diametrically opposed to Novalis's reflections on Being, although they both value the disruptive power of the Event. Being for Novalis signifies the fictional imagination of a non-differentiated absolute identity. Being, for Badiou, consists in indifferent multiplicities; he starts from the multiple rather than the one. Because Novalis begins from the positing of the *one*, he perceives multiplicity as outside the domain of pure Being. It is this drive to multiplicity that allows Novalis to see the realm of phenomena as such as a realm of fiction or deception that is itself coextensive with truth. Badiou, on the other hand, claims "Ontology, axiom system of the particular inconsistency of multiplicities, seizes the in-itself of the multiple by forming into consistency all inconsistency and forming into inconsistency all consistency." Badiou, *Being*

and Event (London: Continuum, 2005), 30. Because Being organizes inconsistency from an originary givenness of multiplicity, consistency and organization as procedures are themselves "normalized," whereas the absolute inconsistency or rupture with this very process of generating consistency can only appear outside of Being as the Event. Novalis, on the other hand, sees Being as a negative for the imagination that attracts the imagination to it. It therefore establishes a different logic than the mere inconsistency of multiplicities, focusing rather on the *attractive* value of Being and its role in the generation of specific differences and points of indifference. However, Novalis's poetic practice suggests that a disruptive force need not refer to anything global that reconfigures procedures for generating consistency, but rather, it may also manifest itself on a microscopic level in the configuration of language, cognition, and sensible appearances. Being, for Novalis, functions as an imaginary Event that can be conjured up at will in imaginative aesthetic exercises.

20. Sigmund Freud, *Neue Folge der Vorlesungen zur Einführung in die Psychoanalyse*, in *Gesammelte Werke*, ed. Anna Freud, vol. 15 (London: Imago, 1946), 86.

21. See Frank, *Einführung in die frühromantische Ästhetik*, 255.

22. Herbert Uerlings notes, "Was Novalis . . . aber ganz besonders auszeichnet, ihn bereits von den allermeisten Zeitgenossen und wohl erst recht von uns Nachgeborenen unterscheidet, das ist das unbegrenzte Vertrauen auf die Fähigkeit des Menschen, sich *selbst* zu entwerfen." Uerlings, "Einbildungskraft und Poesie bei Novalis," in *Novalis: Poesie und Poetik*, ed. Herbert Uerlings (Tübingen: Niemeyer, 2004), 62.

23. For an analysis of the importance of Leibniz for Novalis, see Daniel Lancereau, "Novalis und Leibniz," in *Novalis und die Wissenschaften*, ed. Herbert Uerlings (Tübingen: Niemeyer, 1997), 188.

24. Menninghaus, *Unendliche Verdopplung*, 77.

25. Holland discusses at length the importance of *Indifferenz* for representations of gender difference. See *German Romanticism and Science*, 136–41.

26. Brugmans describes the points of indifference as follows: "In jedem Stabe, er sey von Eisen oder Stahl, AC giebt es zwey Punkte M und N, die so beschaffen sind, daß, wenn man bey ihnen mit dem Streichen eines starken Magnets, womit man an einem Ende, wie in A, angefangen hat, aufhört, bald in A, bald in C keine magnetische Kraft hervorgebracht wird. Wenn man nämlich nur bis M gestrichen hat, so wird in A kein Magnetismus erscheinen; streicht man aber bis N, so wird er am andern Ende C mangeln; ob man schon, wenn man dies = oder jenseits der Punkte M und N mit Streichen aufhört, einen bermerkbaren Magnetismus an beyden Enden hervorbringt.

"Da diese Punkte M und N von Niemand, so viel ich weiß, bemerkt worden sind, so will ich sie, wie es mir scheint, nicht ganz unschicklich, die *Punkte* der *Indifferenz* nennen, weil die Enden der Stäbe, die bis dahin gestrichen worden, auf die Pole einer Magnetnadel ohne Unterschied (indifferent) wirken, und beyde mit gleicher Leichtigkeit anziehen." Brugmans, *Philosophische Versuche über die magnetische Materie* (Leipzig: Crusius, 1784), 69–70.

27. Friedrich Schelling, *Erster Entwurf eines Systems der Naturphilosophie*, in vol. 3 of *Sämmtliche Werke*, ed. Karl Friedrich August Schelling (Stuttgart: Cotta, 1858), 260.

Chapter 5

1. The theses that understand the *Sophien-Erlebnis* as central to the interpretation of *Hymnen an die Nacht* have fallen out of scholarly favor. Heinz Ritter defends the thesis of an "Urhymne" concerning Sophie von Kühn in *Der unbekannte Novalis: Friedrich von Hardenberg im Spiegel seiner Dichtung* (Göttingen: Sachse und Pohl, 1967). Uerlings gives many reasons why this thesis seems untenable. See Uerlings, *Friedrich von Hardenberg, genannt Novalis* (Stuttgart: Metzler, 1991), 280–82. However, Dirk von Petersdorff has rearticulated the importance of the religious gesture in the identification of Christ with Sophie von Kühn. See Dirk von Petersdorff, "Die Auferstehung Sophie von Kühns in den 'Hymnen an die Nacht,' " in *Novalis: Poesie und Poetik*, ed. Herbert Uerlings (Tübingen: Niemeyer, 2004).

2. See, for example, Sibylle Schönborn, *Das Buch der Seele* (Tübingen: Niemeyer, 1999). C. F. Weisse, in 1771, explicitly mentions the use of the journal as a pedagogical technology in order to generate increased self-reflection: "[Die Kinder] lernen dadurch genau auf ihre Handlungen acht geben." C. F Weisse, "Das Tagebuch als Erziehungsmittel," in *Schwarze Pädagogik: Quellen zur Naturgeschichte der bürgerlichen Erziehung*, ed. Katharina Rutschky (Berlin: Ullstein, 1977), 185.

3. Uerlings describes the "Hin und her Direktion" characteristic of Novalis's poetics as "Narrative Konstruktion immanenter Transzendenz." See Uerlings, *Friedrich von Hardenberg*, 229–32.

4. Friedrich Schelling, *Vom Ich als Prinzip der Philosophie oder über das Unbedingte im menschlichen Wissen*, in vol. 1 of *Sämmtliche Werke*, ed. Karl Friedrich August Schelling (Stuttgart: Cotta, 1856), 166.

5. See Fritz Stemme, "Die Säkularisation des Pietismus zur Erfahrungsseelenkunde," *Zeitschrift für deutsche Philologie* 72 (1953).

6. Karl Philipp Moritz, "Zur Seelendiätetik," in *Dichtungen und Schriften zur Erfahrungseelenkunde*, ed. Heide Hollmer and Albert Meier (Franfkurt am Main: Deutscher Klassiker, 1999), 837.

7. Ignatius of Loyola, in his *Spiritual Exercises*, says, "Here it is to be noted that, in a visible contemplation or meditation—as for instance, when one contemplates Christ our Lord, Who is visible—the composition will be to see with the sight of the imagination the corporeal place where the thing is found which I want to contemplate." Ignatius of Loyola, *The Spiritual Exercises of St. Ignatius of Loyola*, trans. Father Elden Muller (New York: Cosimo, 2007), 35.

8. In Haller's *De partibus corporis humani sensilibus et irritabilibus* (1732), irritability and sensibility form the central powers of life. The irritable parts of the human body contract when touched by a foreign body, whereas the sensible parts of the body transmit an impression upon being touched.

9. See John Neubauer, "Dr. John Brown (1735–88) and Early German Romanticism," *Journal of the History of Ideas* 28, no. 3 (1967): 20.

10. For a thorough account of John Brown's importance for Novalis's poetics, see John Neubauer, *Bifocal Vision* (Chapel Hill: University of North Carolina Press, 1971).

11. John Brown, *The Elements of Medicine*, vol. 1 (London: Johnson, 1788), 3.

12. Ibid., 5.

13. For a clear and succinct discussion of the importance of Brown's physiology for German romanticism, see Neubauer, "Dr. John Brown (1735–88) and Early German Romanticism."

14. William Hogarth, *The Analysis of Beauty*, ed. Joseph Burke (Oxford: Oxford University Press, 1953), 24–25.

15. Gotthold Ephraim Lessing, *Laokoon*, in vol. 5.2 of *Werke und Briefe*, ed. Wilfried Barner (Frankfurt am Main: Deutscher Klassiker, 1985), 224.

16. Simon Richter draws attention to the early discursive resonance between physiology and aesthetics through the notion of stimulus, or *Reiz*: "Mylius übersetzte das Werk [*The Analysis of Beauty*] ins Deutsche und gab ihm den Titel *Die Zergliederung der Schönheit*, der die im englischen 'analysis' latente Mehrdeutigkeit hervorkommen läßt. Damit wird bereits im Titel der Verfahrensweise Hogarths völlig entsprochen, der sich wie ein Physiologe ausschließlich auf die materiellen Eigenschaften des Kunstwerks konzentriert, und sich strikt distanziert von 'je ne sais quoi' oder Schönheitsmetaphysik. Von besonderem Interesse ist für die oben formulierte Untersuchungsthese die Übersetzung des grundlegenden ästhetischen Prinzips des Kupferstechers Hogarth von englisch 'line of grace' als 'Reizeslinie.' " Richter, "Medizinischer und ästhetischer Diskurs im 18. Jahrhundert: Herder und Haller über Reiz," *Lessing Yearbook* 25 (1993): 85.

17. Johann Georg Sulzer, *Allgemeine Theorie der schönen Künste in einzeln, nach alphabetischer Ordnung der Kunstworter aufeinanderfolgenden, Artikeln abgehandelt*, vol. 2 (Hildesheim: G. Olms, 1994), 88.

18. Ibid.

19. Johann Joachim Winckelmann, "Von der Grazie in Werken der Kunst," in *Kleine Schriften, Vorreden, Entwürfe*, ed. Walther Rehm (Berlin: de Gruyter, 2002), 157.

20. For an interpretation of Winckelmann's concept of grace that emphasizes its specific forms of embodiment—a sort of sensuous askesis—see Eckart Goebel, *Charis und Charisma* (Berlin: Kadmos, 2006).

21. Brown, *Elements of Medicine*, 135.

22. Ibid., 127.

23. See Neubauer, "Dr. John Brown (1735–88) and Early German Romanticism," 377.

24. Daniel Lancereau notes: "Was ist der Wille zur Nacht anderes als eine Operation der Differenzierung? Im Gegensatz dazu ist der Wille zur Aufklärung ein Versuch der Integration." Lancereau, "Novalis und Leibniz," 188. This nuanced reading of Novalis's "Wille zur Nacht" coheres with my reading of the final hymn as an exercise in an oscillation between differentiation and integration.

25. This passage is often abstracted from its context as a response to problematic physiological paradigms. See, for example, Theodor Haering, *Novalis als Philosoph* (Stuttgart: Kohlhammer, 1954).

26. Uerlings notes that this thought "liest sich wie eine medizinische Interpretation des Ordo inversus." Uerlings, *Friedrich von Hardenberg, genannt Novalis*, 177.

27. For an alternative account of Novalis's "anthropology of the senses," one that emphasizes a dynamic but revisable normative ethics in Novalis's conception of poetry (whereas I tend to emphasize the disruption of normativity), see Chad Wellmon, *Becoming Human: Romantic Anthropology and the Embodiment of Freedom* (University Park: Pennsylvania State University Press, 2011), 213–35.

28. Frank, on the other hand, sees the magical idealist as a manifestation of "pathologische Philosophie": "Absolute Magie als Forderung an ein Individuum wäre der erste Grundsatz einer kranken Philosophie." Manfred Frank, "Die

Philosophie des sogenannten 'Magischen Idealismus,'" *Euphorion* 63 (1969): 109. Frank understands the sickness of magical idealism as a form of limitation, or as pathological philosophy. However, as an exercise, one could imagine a more positive role for the sickness of magical idealism, especially in oscillation with magical realism. The switching of frames from the fairy tale of Hyacinth and Rosenblüthchen to the speech of the "natural objects" might represent precisely such an operation.

29. Before Novalis, Herder had articulated the notion that sickness could be used as a "Werckzeug" for the development of human capabilities: "denn wenn das Organ aus seiner Proportion mit andern gesetzt und also für den gewöhnlichen Kreis des Erdelebens unbrauchbar worden ist, so scheint's natürlich, daß die innere rastlose Kraft sich nach andern Seiten des Weltalls kehre und vielleicht Eindrücke empfange, deren eine ungestörte Organisation nicht fähig war, deren sie aber auch nicht bedorfte." Johann Gottfried Herder, *Ideen zur Philosophie der Menschheit*, in vol. 6 of *Werke in zehn Bänden*, ed. Martin Bollacher (Frankfurt am Main: Deutscher Klassiker, 1985), 197.

30. Géza von Molnár emphasizes the importance of the "via negativa" as a point that distinguishes Novalis from Fichte. See Géza von Molnár, *Novalis' Fichte Studies: The Foundations of His Aesthetics* (The Hague: Mouton, 1970), 26.

31. Schlutz notes, "the work of art will always indicate that the unity of transcendental poetics can only be realized in the realm of the *ordo inversus* and hence *as a fiction*." Schlutz, *Mind's World*, 178.

32. Novalis does speak of the "Kunst allmächtig zu werden—Kunst unsern Willen total zu realisiren" (*NS* 2:587). However, the art of totalizing the will becomes subordinated to the project of shaping the world, using the body as "Werckzeug zur Bildung und Modification der Welt" (*NS* 2:587). The attempt to totalize the will functions as stimulus not only by virtue of its unrealizability, but because there is a performative contradiction at the heart of the utterance. If "modification of the world" constitutes the telos of the attempt to totalize the will, Novalis nullifies even the desire for such a realization, since its completion would render the goal of modifying the world impossible and meaningless. The art of realizing the totality of the will only becomes meaningful—that is, only functions in its capacity to *modify* the given world—if it is never achieved.

33. William Arctander O'Brien notes, "The regal praise of the first hymn signals a revolution in the works, an undermining of the Light as sufficient ground of 'appearance.'" William Arctander O'Brien, *Novalis: Signs of Revolution* (Durham, N.C.: Duke University Press, 1995), 259.

34. The copy of the manuscript can be found in Henry Kamla, *Novalis' Hymnen an die Nacht: Zur Deutung und Datierung* (Copenhagen: Munksgaard, 1945).

35. Neubauer discusses the importance of "indifference" for health. See *Bifocal Vision*, 101.

36. This historical-mythological narrative was popular in the eighteenth century, its main predecessor being Schiller's "Die Götter Griechenlands." For the details surrounding the controversy generated by Schiller's poem when it was published in 1788 in Wieland's *Teutsche Merkur*, see Mario Zanucchi, *Novalis—Poesie und Geschichtlichkeit* (Paderborn: Schöningh, 2006), 52.

37. Mario Zanucchi offers a nuanced and complex reading of the fifth hymn, one that shows the overturning of orders as well as points of indifference between historical moments—or in his terms, shared characteristics by Christianity and antiquity—as part of the historical-philosophical movement in the text. He notes, importantly, that Christianity offers "die Möglichkeit, diese sinnliche Lust in gesteigerter Form wieder zu erfahren." Zanucchi, *Novalis—Poesie und Geschichtlichkeit*, 60. His analysis suggests that the interaction between overturned orders and points of indifference increases stimulation.

38. Henry Kamla claims, "Der Kerngehalt der Hymne 5 ist somit der Nachweis, dass die christliche Weltansicht die einzig haltbare ist." Kamla, *Novalis' Hymnen an die Nacht: Zur Deutung und Datierung*, 75. If this statement is true, then the sixth hymn once again disrupts the boundaries between pagan and Christian; the poet who desires to sink into the father's womb still *desires* the "Vorwelt" of pagan antiquity, and thereby does not merely interpret the Christian worldview as "die einzig haltbare."

39. Schelling, *Erster Entwurf*, 260.

40. Ibid., 223

41. Novalis was familiar with Ritter's galvanic experiments. See Holland, *German Romanticism and Science*, 147.

42. William Arctander O'Brien notes, "The German word for 'lap,' *Schooß*, has already been used seven times in the *Hymns*—including the first line of the sixth—with its other meaning, 'womb.' An unspeakable difference between the 'lap' and the 'womb' of the father thus concludes the *Hymns* with a figure of the Absolute that remains impossibly poised between genders, a figure of a divine wholeness that cannot be expressed as such, but only in contradiction, at odds with language, positively unspeakable." Arctander O'Brien, *Novalis: Signs of Revolution*, 270. He also notes, "The *Hymns to the Night* succeed at presenting 'the unrepresentable' (*das Undarstellbare*) because they 'present' it *as* the unrepresentable. Or more exactly: the *Hymns* present the unpresentability of the unpresentable." Ibid., 271.

43. Winfried Kudszus underscores the importance of this movement back into the space of the third hymn, since the linguistic operations in the third hymn disrupt the teleological-historical narrative as well as any form of historicality that seeks to root the present in an originary moment. See Winfried Kudszus, "Geschichtsverlust und Sprachproblematik in den *Hymnen an die Nacht*," *Euphorion* 65 (1971).

44. The "Wechselbestimmung" has been long identified as a central aspect of Novalis's poetics. See for example, Bernward Loheide, *Fichte und Novalis: Transzendentalphilosophisches Denken im romantisierenen Diskurs* (Amsterdam: Rodopi, 2000), 114.

Chapter 6

1. For an incisive analysis of the influence of Rousseau on German conceptions of *Bildung*, see Richard Velkley, "The Tension in the Beautiful: On Culture and Civilization in Rousseau and German Philosophy," in *The Legacy of Rousseau*, ed. Clifford Orwin and Nathan Tarcov (Chicago: University of Chicago Press, 1997).

2. See Jerrold Seigel, *The Idea of the Self: Thought and Experience in Western Europe Since the Seventeenth Century* (Cambridge, Eng.: Cambridge University Press, 2005), 332.

3. See Rolf-Peter Janz, "Bildungsroman," in *Deutsche Literatur: Eine Sozialgeschichte*, ed. Horst Albert Glaser, vol. 5 (Reinbek: Rowohlt, 1980).

4. For a presentation of the various attempts to read these two novels in relation to one another, see Uerlings, *Friedrich von Hardenberg*, 444–58.

5. Kant understands *Bildung* as part of *Erziehung*. He says, "Die Erziehung schließt *Versorgung* und *Bildung* in sich" (*AA* 9:452). He says in the same essay, "Der Mensch braucht Wartung und Bildung. Bildung begreift unter sich Zucht und Unterweisung" (*AA* 9:443).

6. For a description of the eighteenth century as a "pedagogical century," see Notker Hammerstein and Ulrich Herrmann, eds., *Handbuch der deutschen Bildungsgeschichte*, vol. 2 (Munich: Beck, 2005).

7. J. B. Basedow and J. H. Campe, "Von der eigentlichen Absicht eines Philanthropens," in *Schwarze Pädagogik*, ed. Katharina Rutschky (Munich: Ullstein, 1977), 64.

8. J. H. Pestalozzi, "Wie der Erzieher die Wirklichkeit repräsentieren kann," in *Schwarze Pädagogik*, ed. Katharina Rutschky (Munich: Ullstein, 1977), 395.

9. See Pierre Hadot, *The Veil of Isis: An Essay on the History of the Idea of Nature*, trans. Michael Chase (Cambridge, Mass.: Harvard University Press, 2006), 237–43.

10. Jeanne Riou, for example, claims that the poem "warns of the attempt to commune directly with the truth, to view the naked virgin 'unveiled' in her temple." Riou, *Imagination in German Romanticism: Rethinking the Self and Its Environment* (Bern: Peter Lang, 2004), 105.

11. The novel may be polyphonic in the same way that Bakhtin interpreted Dostoevsky's novels to be polyphonic; his description of Dostoevsky's aesthetic sounds as if it were derived from *Die Lehrlinge zu Saïs*: "In contrast to Goethe, Dostoevsky attempted to perceive the very stages themselves in their *simultaneity*, to *juxtapose* and *counterpose* them dramatically, and not stretch them out into an evolving sequence. For him, to get one's bearings on the world meant to conceive all its contents as simultaneous, and *to guess at the interrelationships in the cross-section of a single moment*." Mikhail Bakhtin, *Problems of Dostoevsky's Poetics*, trans. Caryl Emerson (Minneapolis: University of Minnesota Press, 1984), 28.

12. Wolfgang Schmale gives an example of "Schulbuchempfehlungen der Verordnung von 1782 für die protestantischen Schulen (Gymnasien und Lateinschulen) in Cleve-Mark," and in this recommendation, one may find Sulzer's *Vorübungen zur Erweckung der Aufmerksamkeit*. Wolfgang Schmale, "Die Schule in Deutschland im 18. und frühen 19. Jahrhundert: Konjunkturen, Horizonte, Mentalitäten, Probleme, Ergebnisse," in *Revolution des Wissens? Europa und seine Schulen im Zeitalter der Aufklärung (1750–1825)*, ed. Wolfgang Schmale and Nan L. Dodde (Bochum: Dieter Winkler, 1991), 723. In addition to "Beyspiele" and didactic fables, one may find a highly detailed description of "Merkwürdigkeiten der Natur" that organize and describe nature as an exercise in attentiveness in Johann Georg Sulzer, *Vorübungen zur Erweckung der Aufmerksamkeit und des Nachdenkens*, vol. 3 (St Petersburg: Kayserliche Akademie der Wissenschaften, 1814), 1–99.

13. Jürgen Daibler understands the "Reihe" as a positive poetic principle: "Die Reihe ist jene Figur, mit der die nicht herstellbare Synthesis von Mensch und

Natur sichtbar gemacht werden soll." Daibler, *Experimentalphysik des Geistes*, 199. It seems, if one associates the "row" with the organization of discourse in the space of the institution, that the critical feature of a *row* is that it can be disordered, perturbed, broken.

14. Some critics are in agreement with this interpretation of the teacher; see Schlutz, *Mind's World*, 294. Jocelyn Holland notes, "Collectively, these voices express a dissatisfaction which threatens to undermine the pedagogical project of the temple." Holland, *German Romanticism and Science*, 105.

15. See Carl Schmitt, *Political Theology*, trans. G. Schwab (Chicago: University of Chicago Press, 2005).

16. Jürgen Daibler reads the fairy tale not as standing in tension with the "crossing voices," but rather as *part* of the "row" of these discursive utterances: "der Märchenerzähler [bildet] nur eine unter den vielen Stimmen des unendlichen Gesprächs. Das Märchen wäre also lediglich ein Glied im Netzwerk der Stimmenreihen der Reisenden, des Lehrers, der Lehrlinge, etc. Ihm käme damit keine Schlüsselfunktion im Sinne des unendlichen Gesprächs zu." Daibler, *Experimentalphysik des Geistes*, 202.

17. Daibler claims, "Wichtig ist, daß diese Stimmen nicht in einem dialogischen Verhältnis zueinander stehen und einander nicht vom Wahrheitsgehalt des jeweils Gesagten zu überzeugen scheinen." Daibler, *Experimentalphysik des Geistes*, 192. However, if these voices are not claiming universal validity explicitly, it is nevertheless the attempt to extract a truth, a "Wahrheitsgehalt," that instigates the crisis in the novice.

18. Petersdorff discusses the text as an "unendliches Gespräch in seiner immanenten Pluralität, in seiner Negation materieller Finalität, seinem Verzicht auf wissenschaftstheoretische und strukturelle Hierarchien und seiner Selbstreflexivität." Dirk von Petersdorff, *Mysterienrede: Zum Selbstverständnis romantischer Intellektueller* (Tübingen: de Gruyter, 1996), 182.

19. For an excellent analysis of the relation between the fairy tale and the school at Sais, see Ulrich Gaier, *Krumme Regel: Novalis Konstruktionslehre des schaffenden Geistes und ihre Tradition* (Tübingen: Niemeyer, 1970).

20. For the varying interpretations of the burning of the books, see Uerlings, *Friedrich von Hardenberg*, 362.

21. Ingrid Kreuzer discusses these voices as moving in a different acoustic-aesthetic space than the other discursive spaces in the novel. For her, the voices constitute a "Schallraum, dessen Grenze die Dimension des Hörens bildet." Kreuzer, "Novalis' *Die Lehrlinge zu Sais*: Fragen zur Struktur, Gattung und immanenten Ästhetik," *Jahrbuch der deutschen Schillergesellschaft* 23 (1979): 288.

22. See Volker Klotz, *Das europäische Kunstmärchen* (Stuttgart: Metzler, 1985), 142. Alexander Schlutz also emphasizes this point: "[The fairy tale] takes place, after all, within a dream that is part of a fairy tale, which in turn is narrated by one of the many narrators within the complex texture of Hardenberg's Romantic novel." Schlutz, *Mind's World*, 188. Schlutz focuses more on the *ordo inversus* as a narrative technique signaling the continual movement within an imagined space rather than an inversion of different frameworks of intelligibility, or ways of relating phenomena.

23. Ulrich Gaier notes, "Geschieht der Fund und Vereinigung im Traum, so muß der Traum zugleich Wirklichkeit haben, dann wäre der Traum irreal, so

hätte Hyazinth Rosenblüthchen gar nicht gefunden und nicht mit ihr leben und Kinder haben können." Gaier, *Krumme Regel*, 23.

24. Gaier notes, "Der Ort, an dem Hyazinth Rosenblüthchen findet, ist als Behausung der Isis aller Wahrscheinlichkeit nach Sais; zugleich muß es auch der Ort 'weit gegen Abend' sein, an dem Rosenblüthchen mit den Eltern und Gespielen wohnt. Auch die Zeit tritt in eine schwebende Verbindung; die Wohnung der Isis ist 'die Behausung der ewigen Jahreszeiten'; die Zeit schwebt hier zwischen Zeitlichkeit und Ewigkeit, Wechsel und Ruhe. Insofern kann auch der Ort der Isis nicht bloß jenes Sais sein, an dem die Lehrlinge sich das Märchen erzählen, sondern muß zugleich ein transzendenter Ort sein, eine Wohnung mit unendlichen Gemächern." Ibid., 24. Gaier explains the duplicitous ontology by making the fairy tale into a "transcendent" space. The act of narration appears to me philosophical in Novalis's sense of the term: "[es] hebt wie das Copernikanische System die *festen* Puncte auf—und macht aus dem Ruhenden ein Schwebendes" (*NS* 3:377–78), making the very centripetal power of the institution a similarly floating system of points.

25. Johannes Endres sees the veil itself as a "liminal" point; in his sensitive reading he notes: "Der Schleier, der solchen Vorgängen voranschwebt, wird zum Relais, zur 'Schwelle,' die 'reziproke Übergänge' vermittelt. 'Permeabel' geworden, organisiert der 'Schleier' Bezüge, die um vieles komplexer sind, als es die Formeln vom 'Sozialisationstheater' oder vom 'sozialen Drama' suggerieren, Kulturmuster, die im wesentlichen auf linearen Prozessen basieren. . . . Worauf Novalis' Liminalitätskonzept abzielt, ist nicht Situierung, sondern 'Wechsel' um des Wechsels willen, der seinerseits zur Regel erhoben und auf Dauer gestellt wird." Johannes Endres, "Der Schleier des Novalis," in *Novalis: Poesie und Poetik*, ed. Herbert Uerlings (Tübingen: Niemeyer, 2004), 121–22.

26. Arctander O'Brien says about Novalis's idea that the novice who lifts the veil finds only himself: "Such a resolution would be simple Fichteanism, and similar to the self-absorption of the novice: one would find that the 'Not-I' is merely a mask for the 'I,' or everything would lead back to 'oneself.' Instead, Hardenberg insists that one finds the 'beloved' outside oneself." Arctander O'Brien, *Novalis: Signs of Revolution*, 212. However, to what extent is Rosenblüthchen really "outside" Hyacinth, since this reunion takes place in his dream?

Conclusion to Part Two

1. Daibler disregards the ontological instability provoked by the ending, instead making the fairy tale *conform* to the organization of the institution, "Als biedere Prosa [!], welche die angestrebte Harmonie von Natur und Geist zur unendlichen Aufgabe macht und die Reihe der suchenden Stimmen nicht abbrechen läßt." Daibler, *Experimentalphysik des Geistes*, 212.

Chapter 7

1. For a description of the relation between the Horatian *prodesse et delectare* and Moritz's articulation of aesthetic autonomy, see Jonathan Hess, *Reconstituting the Body Politic: Enlightenment, Public Culture, and the Invention of Aesthetic Autonomy* (Detroit, Mich.: Wayne State University Press, 1999), 49–57.

2. Karl Philipp Moritz, "Versuch einer Vereinigung aller schönen Künste und Wissenschaften unter dem Begriff des in sich selbst Vollendeten," in *Schriften zur Ästhetik und Poetik*, ed. Hans Joachim Schrimpf (Tübingen: Niemeyer, 1962), 7.

3. The original Latin is as follows: "Aut prodesse volunt aut delectare poetae/aut simul et iucunda et idonea dicere vitae." Horace, *Satires, Epistles and Ars Poetica*, trans. H. Rushton Fairclough (Cambridge, Mass.: Harvard University Press, 1991), 478.

4. My thesis harmonizes in many points with arguments made by Heinz Schlaffer: "Das poetische Bild verdankt seine Existenz gerade seiner Nicht-Wirklichkeit und damit der bestehenden Wirklichkeit, die jene utopische Wirklichkeit jetzt noch im Zustand der Nicht-Wirklichkeit hält. Unter dieser generellen Bedingung von Poesie lebt auch der Scherz doppeldeutig als Negation des Bestehenden vom Zugeständnis an dieses Bestehende, dessen Anderes er ist." Heinz Schlaffer, *Musa iocosa: Gattungspoetik und Gattungsgeschichte der erotischen Dichtung in Deutschland* (Stuttgart: Metzler, 1971), 142. The goal of this study is to show how Anacreontic poetry functions as an aesthetic exercise, which in turn introduces elements of contingency into its own culture's values and normalizing discourses on the level of poetic form. I intend to follow some of these poems in their manner of perturbing these structures of intelligibility.

5. John Milton, *Paradise Lost*, in vol. 1 of *The Poetical Works of John Milton*, ed. Helen Darbishire (Oxford: Oxford University Press, 1992), 6.

6. Frauke Berndt, *Poema/Gedicht*, 186. For Berndt, Baumgarten represents a central figure that reconceptualizes the poetic artifact as a locus of discursive condensations in the mid-eighteenth century, a reconfiguration that first manifests itself in Klopstock's poetry but is central for an epistemic understanding of the poem in the later eighteenth century as well. Berndt provides an alternative account of the relation between Baumgarten and the Anacreontic poets, linking more concretely the language of Anacreontic poetry to the cognitive operations and aesthetic categories of Baumgarten's *Aesthetica*.

7. Jill Anne Kowalik claims that Breitinger's definition of the fantastic "connects his poetics with Leibniz's system," arguing that "the wondrous in Breitinger's system comprises not those things we reject, but those things we may have never noticed but then eventually assimilate." Kowalik, *The Poetics of Historical Perspectivism: Breitinger's Critische Dichtkunst and the Neoclassic Tradition* (Chapel Hill: University of North Carolina Press, 1992), 84. According to her reading, the fantastic does not "alienate" a reader from his or her own framework of organization. However, this interpretation of Breitinger tames the subversive elements of his theory. It also does not seem to take Breitinger at his word, seeing his intellectual sources (i.e., Leibniz) as more critical to his theory than that which he explicitly claims in terms that expand beyond their technical philosophical usage. When Breitinger says that the fantastic consists in "was uns, dem ersten Anscheine nach, unsren gewöhnlichen Begriffen von dem Wesen der Dinge, von den Kräften, Gesetzen und dem Laufe der Natur, und allen vormahls erkannten Wahrheiten in dem Licht zu stehen, und dieselben zu bestreiten düncket" (*CD* 131), he does not seem to be discussing something that we at first do not notice, but rather, narrative elements that really contradict "our usual concepts" of the way the world makes sense.

8. Jill Anne Kowalik claims that Breitinger is describing a Leibnizian "rejection of perception," which "means that 'petites perceptions' never 'rise' to that level of activity where they represent themselves in perception." Kowalik, *The Poetics of Historical Perspectivism*, 84. This proposition seems aimed at those who would

make Breitinger into a predecessor of romanticism or of the Brechtian *Verfremdungseffekt*. Nevertheless, it does not seem to me that Breitinger is referring to a Leibnizian rejection of perception; it is not the "petites perceptions" that make Milton's *Paradise Lost* a work of the fantastic, but rather, the fact that the work does not seem structured according to the laws of physical reality as we typically know them.

9. Hans Peter Herrmann notes, "Die Spannung zwischen Naturnachahmung und Imagination als die der Poesie eigentümliche Spannung zwischen Wahrheit und Schein wird in Breitingers 'Critischer Dichtkunst' zum ersten Mal in einter deutschen Poetik bennant. Allerdings: diese Spannung als Einheit zu begriefen und adaequat zu formulieren, mußten Bodmer und Breitinger Späteren überlassen." Herrmann, *Naturnachahmung und Einbildungskraft* (Bad Homburg: Max Gehlen, 1970), 275. In my view, the fact that they do *not* formulate this tension as a unity makes possible the power of the fantastic, namely, as mobilizing the figure of *disjunction*.

10. For this distinction, see Alfred Anger, *Literarisches Rokoko* (Stuttgart: Mezler, 1962), 52–56.

11. To be sure, it is easy to integrate rococo into a certain strand of Enlightenment poetics: the liberation of the senses, the loosening of religious dogmas, an anthropological conception of the human as a sexual being, and the diatetic stimulation of health through excitement, pleasure, and laughter. See Manfred Beetz, "Anakreontik und Rokoko im Bezugsfeld der Aufklärung—Eine Forschungsbilanz," in *Anakreontische Aufklärung*, ed. Manfred Beetz and Hans-Joachim Kertscher (Tübingen: Niemeyer, 2005), 1–17.

12. I use the terms "rococo" and "Anacreontic" as heuristic concepts and I hope that their flexibility and relative cohesiveness enables rather than weakens this study. I will examine individual poems that have been interpreted as commensurate with what has become known as the rococo style, and while I acknowledge the potential methodological and terminological problems that such a decision invokes, I will not dwell on these problems so that I can turn to the poems themselves. I will be focusing on rococo poems that exhibit affinities to the Anacreontic style.

13. For an excellent introduction to rococo and Anacreontic poetry, see Alfred Anger, *Literarisches Rokoko*.

14. This interpretation of Rococo poetry has been articulated in various guises in the critical literature. Heinz Schlaffer notes, "Die Erotik, von den anderen Lebensäußerungen als amor bestialis abgetrennt und verurteilt, behauptet dagegen zuerst ihr Eigensinn, dann ihren Wert und schließlich ihre Überlegenheit, indem sie ihrerseits alle anderen Tätigkeiten—Krieg, Handel, Tugend und Denken—negiert, ihnen zur metaphorischen Verwendung in der erotischen Welt ironisch stattgibt . . . um sie durch den herabstimmenden Wechsel der Stilhöhe lächerlich zu machen und damit das Erotische so zu erhöhen, daß es sich als befriedigender Ersatz für die anderen scheinbar so wichtigen Bereiche des menschlichen Lebens ausweist." Schlaffer, *Musa iocosa*, 97. The goal of this study is to locate the operation of this movement—a movement that Schlaffer attributes more to the erotic, but one that is equally present in the joke—on the level of poetic form. Moreover, I do not see love as *Ersatz* for the other important areas of life; rather, the Anacreontic ode seems to derive pleasure from the undermining of the very concept

of importance as such, without any need for an *Ersatz* or some other source of importance. While I agree with much of Schlaffer's analysis, his disdain for Gleim as an "editor" of others' works does not preclude his work from the very movement that Schlaffer reserves for the omnipotent power of the erotic. Schlaffer says, "Vor allem Gleim, Haupt und Organisator der anakreontischen Schule im 18. Jahrhundert, spielte dabei die Rolle eines Vor-Zensors, der seine moralisch-bürgerlichen Vorurteile als literarische Maßstäbe ausgeben konnte." Ibid., 229.

15. Steffen Martus foregrounds the *Möglichkeitssinn* of the joke. Martus frames this insight according to the joke's activation of resemblances and differences: "Der 'Scherz' hat deutliche Affinitäten zum 'Wunderbaren,' indem er den Möglichkeitssinn des 'Witzes' mit der 'Neuheit' verbindet. Damit rückt der 'Scherz' die zu vergliechenden Gegenstände zwar weiter auseinander als der 'Witz,' aber ihre Ähnlichkeit muß gewahrt bleiben—auch das 'Wunderbare' ist ein Mögliches." Martus, *Friedrich von Hagedorn—Konstellationen der Aufklärung* (Berlin: de Gruyter, 1999), 73.

16. On May 1, 1745, Gleim writes to Uz: "Ich habe unter den von Halle erhaltenen Sachen die Baumgart.[ensche] Disp.[utation] de nonnullis ad poema pertin.[entibus] mit s.[eligen?] Rudnicks Anmerckungen, wie auch einige von den Briefen, so sie mit ihm gewechselt, wiedergefunden. Soll ich sie überschicken?" Johann Wilhelm Ludwig Gleim, and Johan Peter Uz, *Briefwechsel zwischen Gleim und Uz*, ed. Carl Schüddekopf (Tübingen: Lauff, 1899), 75–76. One year later, in June 1746, Gleim writes: "A propos habe ich ihnen Baumgart.[ens] Disp.[utation] de nonnullis ad poema pertinentibus schon geschickt? Ich weiß wahrhaftig nicht, wie ich daran bin. Sie hat sich gefunden, aber ich weiß nicht, ob sie sie schon wieder haben. Wenn sie es mir nicht schreiben, so muß ich alle meine Papiere durchsuchen." Ibid., 120–21. Gleim and Uz clearly developed ideas in reference to this text, although I have found little evidence that would make explicit the precise relation between Baumgarten and their poetic production at the time.

17. Alexander Baumgarten, *Meditationes philosophicae de nunnullis ad poema pertinentibus*, ed. Heinz Paetzold (Hamburg: Meiner, 1983), 86.

18. Ibid., 46.

19. For the relation between Meier, Baumgarten, and the "Zweiter Hallescher Dichterkreis," see H.-J. Kertscher, *Anakreontik: Zweiter Hallescher Dichterkreis: Gleim, Götz, Rudnick, Uz* (Halle: Hallescher, 1993), 8–9.

20. For a more thorough analysis of the relation between "Witz" and "Scherz," as well as a discussion of Meier's relation to the *Anakreontiker* from Halle, see Christoph Perels, *Studien zur Aufnahme und Kritik der Rokokolyrik zwischen 1740 und 1760* (Göttingen: Vandenhoeck & Rubrecht, 1974), 169–72.

21. Martus, *Friedrich von Hagedorn*, 73.

22. See, for example, Herrmann, *Naturnachahmung und Einbildungskraft*, 275.

Chapter 8

1. Jörg Neuenfeld has written a cultural history of play since Kant, although he does not examine the Anacreontic conception of play. Unlike culturally productive forms of play or forms of play that become subordinated to a framework of philosophical intelligibilty, Anacreontic play does not claim to "produce" or reproduce the values of the society or forms of human life considered as

normatively binding in the eighteenth century. Compare Jörg Neuenfeld, *Alles ist Spiel: Zur Geschichte der Auseinandersetzung mit einer Utopie der Moderne* (Würzburg: Königshausen & Neumann, 2005).

2. There has been increased critical interest in the cross-dressing and role-playing in the *Gleimkreis*; see, for example, Simon Richter, "The Ins and Outs of Intimacy: Gender, Epistolary Culture, and the Public Sphere," *German Quarterly* 69 (1996). However, W. Daniel Wilson has recently cautioned against seeing in the epistolary correspondence anything but an elaborate imaginative game; see Daniel W. Wilson, "But Is It Gay? Kissing, Friendship, and 'Pre-Homosexual' Discourses in Eighteenth-Century Germany," *Modern Language Review* 103, no. 3 (2008).

3. Gleim, *Briefwechsel zwischen Gleim und Uz*, 74.

4. Ibid., 134.

5. Jean Paul Richter, *Vorschule der Ästhetik*, in vol. 5 of *Werke*, ed. Norbert Miller (Munich: Hanser, 1987), 444.

6. The saying has been attributed to Anton Webern; see Philippe Lacoue-Labarthe, *Typography: Mimesis, Philosophy, Politics* (Stanford, Calif.: Stanford University Press, 1998), 208.

7. I would like to thank Niklaus Largier for drawing my attention to the importance of this preface as a poetological document.

8. Daniel Caspar von Lohenstein, *Sophonisbe*, in *Afrikanische Trauerspiele*, ed. Klaus Günther Just (Stuttgart: Anton Hiersemann, 1957), 245.

9. Eric Downing, in an e-mail exchange about *Sophonisbe* on February 21, 2013, saw the presence of "indifference" at work in the play that "negates every operant binary meant to suggest difference."

10. Lohenstein, *Sophonisbe*, 246.

11. Ibid., 247.

12. Ibid., 246.

13. Johann Gottfried Willamov (1736–1777) was known in his time as the "German Pindar" because of his renewal of the ode. See Rudolf Schreck, *Johann Gottlieb Willamov* (Heidelberg: C. Winter, 1913).

14. Johann Gottlieb Willamov, *Sämmtliche poetische Schriften*, vol. 2 (Vienna: Schraemel, 1794), 100–101.

15. In one report by J. Oest and J. H. Campe, "Vollständiges System zur Verhütung der Selbstschwächung" (1787), reading becomes a temptation to masturbation. The authors suggest carefully choosing which books children should read: "Man wähle mit äußerster Sorgfalt die wenigen Bücher, welche Kindern in die Hände gegeben werden dürfen." J. Oest and J. H. Campe Oest, "Vollständiges System zur Verhütung der Selbstschwächung," in *Schwarze Pädagogik*, ed. Katharina Rutschky (Frankfurt am Main: Ullstein, 1977), 314. Some of the most dangerous literature in this respect comprises: "Alle Poesien und prosaische Schriften, deren Gegenstand Liebe ist. " Ibid.

16. Johann Christoph Adelung, *Grammatisch-kritisches Wörterbuch der hochdeutschen Mundart*, vol. 2 (Vienna: Bauer, 1811), 607.

17. Friedrich von Hagedorn, *Oden und Lieder in fünf Büchern* (Hamburg: Johann Carl Bohn, 1747), 91.

18. Georg Gottfried Gervinus, *Geschichte der deutschen Dichtung*, vol. 3 (Leipzig: Wilhelm Engelmann, 1848), 529. Wolfram Mauser writes, "Gervinus

wurde nie widersprochen, es gilt aber zu klären, was es bedeutete, um 1700 die Sinne zu emanzipieren und in welchem sozialen und geistigen Raum dies geschehen konnte." Mauser, *Konzepte aufgeklärter Lebensführung: Literarische Kultur im frühmodernen Deutschland* (Würzburg: Königshausen & Neumann, 2000), 50.

19. Barthold Heinrich Brockes, *Irdisches Vergnügen in Gott*, vol. 1 (Hamburg: Christian Herold, 1744), 21.

20. Ibid.

21. Barbara Thums (in my view, correctly) sees Brockes's poetry as part of "[einer] asketischen Technik der Wahrnehmungsstrukturierung." Thums, *Aufmerksamkeit: Wahrnehmung und Selbstbegründung von Brockes bis Nietzsche* (Munich: Fink, 2008), 40.

22. It is difficult to say whether or not a conceptually coherent theology exists in Brockes's works, and this has been a subject of much scholarly debate. See Hans-Georg Kemper, *Deutsche Lyrik in der frühen Neuzeit* (Tübingen: Niemeyer, 1991), 6–7. For Brockes's "pantheism" and his other possible theological tendencies (above all, deism), see ibid., 47–75.

23. Barthold Heinrich Brockes, *Irdisches Vergnügen in Gott*, vol. 4 (Hamburg: Conrad König, 1745), 2–5.

24. Arthur Rimbaud, *Oeuvres complètes*, ed. André Guyaux (Gallimard: Paris, 2009), 344.

25. Ibid.

26. See Thums, *Aufmerksamkeit*, 33–44.

27. Brockes, *Irdisches Vergnügen in Gott*, vol. 1, 158.

28. Barthold Heinrich Brockes, *Irdisches Vergnügen in Gott*, vol. 2 (Hamburg: Christian Herold, 1734), 274.

29. The air pump became the focal point of contention in a debate between Hobbes and Boyle concerning the appropriate means for generating or securing knowledge, with Hobbes arguing that only natural philosophy can guarantee knowledge, and Boyle using experimental methodology to produce "matters of fact." See Steven Shapin and Simon Schaffer, *Leviathan and the Air-Pump* (Princeton, N.J.: Princeton University Press, 1985). Interestingly, Shapin and Schaffer claim that Hobbes denied the validity of the experiments with the air pump partially because the epistemological practices underlying these experiments did not cohere with his conception of divine order. Here, Brockes uses the air pump to *link* physical reality and the divine order.

30. Brockes, *Irdisches Vergnügen in Gott*, vol. 1, 158.

31. Ibid., 159

32. Ibid., 63.

33. See David Wellbery, *Lessing's Laocoon* (Cambridge, Eng.: Cambridge University Press, 1984), 28. Wellbery makes the cogent point that for the early Enlightenment, artificial and natural signs "are not esentially different from one another" (28).

34. Brockes, *Irdisches Vergnügen in Gott*, vol. 4, 14.

35. For a presentation of the main themes and motifs of rococo poetry, see Alfred Anger, *Literarisches Rokoko*.

36. Johann Nikolaus Götz, *Gedichte aus den Jahren 1745–1765*, ed. Carl Schüddekopf (Stuttgart: Göschen'sche Verlagshandlung, 1893), 5.

37. Ibid.

38. Ibid.
39. Ibid.
40. Gotthold Ephraim Lessing, *Frühe Schriften 1751–1753*, in vol. 2 of *Werke und Briefe*, ed. Jürgen Stenzel (Frankfurt am Main: Deutscher Klassiker, 1998), 77.
41. Johann Nikolaus Götz and Johann Peter Uz, *Die Gedichte Anakreons und der Sappho Oden* (Karlsruhe: Michael Macklot, 1760), 51.
42. Boris Maslov has written about the centrality of this concept in the theory of historical poetics developed by Alexander Veselovsky. See Maslov, "Comparative Literature and Revolution, or the Many Arts of (Mis)reading Alexander Veselovsky," *Compar(a)ison* 2008/2 (2013): 101–29.
43. Johann Nikolaus Götz, "Das Vergnügen," in *Lyrische Bluhmenlese*, vol. 1 (Leipzig: Weidmanns Erben und Reich, 1774), 52.
44. Dante Alighiere, *Paradiso*, vol. 4 of *La commedia secondo l'antica vulgata*, ed. Giorgio Petrocchi (Florence: Casa Editrice le Lettere, 1994), 558.
45. Götz, "Das Vergnügen," 52.
46. Ibid., 53.
47. Ibid.
48. Friedrich Nietzsche, *Götzendämmerung*, in *Werke*, ed. Giorgio Colli and Mazzino Montinari, vol. 6.3 (Berlin: de Gruyter, 1969), 72.
49. Wolfram Mauser continually emphasizes the "diatetic" function of Anacreontic lyrics. See Wolfram Mauser, "Anakreon als Therapie? Zur medizinisch-dietätischen Begründung der Rokoko-Dichtung," *Lessing Yearbook* 20 (1988).
50. Hagedorn, *Oden und Lieder*, 4.
51. Catullus, *Catullus, Tibullus, Pervigilium Veneris*, trans. Francis Warre Cornish, ed. G. P. Goold (Cambridge, Mass.: Harvard University Press, 1988), 2.
52. According to Steffen Martus, "Hagedorn war sich darüber im klaren, daß der 'Scherz' die aufklärerische Ordnung gefährdet." Martus, *Friedrich von Hagedorn*, 73.
53. Johanna Charlotte Unzer, *Versuch in Scherzgedichten* (Halle: Carl Herman Hemmerde, 1753), 4–5.
54. The novel as a genre allowing for possible spaces of transgression, or in Helga Meise's words, a "Raum der Übertretung," has been well documented. Helga Meise, *Die Unschuld und die Schrift: Deutsche Frauenromane im 18. Jahrhundert* (Frankfurt am Main: Helmer, 1992), 204. However, whether the poetic exercise translated into *real* liberation is difficult to say; see, for example, Susanne Kord on Anna Louise Karsch. Kord shows that Karsch's stylization as a "natural genius" did not necessarily work to her advantage; Susanne Kord, *Women Peasant Poets in Eighteenth-Century England, Scotland, and Germany: Milkmaids on Parnassus* (New York: Camden House, 2003), 87–89. However, it seems to me that rococo poetry's explicit adopting of *roles* and an emphasis on its inherent *meaninglessness* expanded the possibilities for what could and could not be said and by what sort of person, or so Unzer seems to suggest in her preface.
55. Unzer, *Versuch in Scherzgedichten*, 11–12.
56. Ibid., 5.
57. Hagedorn, *Oden und Lieder*, 52.
58. Ibid., 50.

59. Wolfram Mauser notes, "Die deutsche Rokokodichtung ist—vor allem in ihren besonders gelungenen Leistungen—nicht Nachahmung höfisch-spielerischer Formen und Gedanken im Kreis eines wohlhabend und gebildet gewordenen Bürgertums, sondern der Versuch, im Zusammenhang vielfältiger diätetischer Anstrengungen der Zeit, 'sinnliches Vergnügen' nicht nur zu fordern und theoretisch zu begründen, sondern in poetischen Inszenierungen auch vorzustellen." Mauser, *Konzepte aufgeklärter Lebensführung*, 324. Mauser's observation is rich in consquences for an understanding of this type of poetry. In the eighteenth century, it seems that the diatetic effect of poetry was coherent with a thorough disorganization of sociocultural normativity. In Anacreontic poetry, health and the inversion of norms and values were able to be deeply intertwined.

60. Hagedorn, *Oden und Lieder*, 90.

61. Theocritus's *Idylls* invoke and thematize the problematic differentiation of pastoral poetry from heroic poetry; see Judith Haber, *Pastoral and the Poetics of Self-Contradiction: Theocritus to Marvell* (Cambridge, Eng.: Cambridge University Press, 1994).

62. Hagedorn, *Oden und Lieder*, 90.

63. "'The landscape thinks itself in me,'" he said, 'and I am its consciousness.' " Maurice Merleau-Ponty, *Sense and Non-Sense*, trans. Hubert L. Dreyfus and Patricia Allen Dreyfus (Evanston, Ill.: Northwestern University Press, 1991), 17.

64. Alfred Anger's unflagging efforts sparked a reevaluation of the rococo as a style and of Goethe's early poems in particular. See his "'Annette an ihren Geliebten': Ein Gedicht Goethes aus der Leipziger Zeit," *Deutsche Vierteljahrsschrift für Literaturwissenschaft und Geistesgeschichte* 37, no. 3 (1963): 439–62.

65. Johann Wolfgang von Goethe, *Annette*, in vol. 1 of *Der junge Goethe*, ed. Hannah Fischer-Lamberg (Berlin: de Gruyter, 1999), 175.

66. Ibid., 179.

67. Ibid.

68. Ibid., 173.

69. Ibid., 187.

70. Alfred Anger notes the *pointe* of the poem: "indem [der Leser] den Fortgang der Doris-Dämot-Episode errät, verrät er unfreiwillig sich selbst. Der eine Sünder ertappt den anderen; er hebt den Schleier und entlarvt—sich selbst." Anger, "'Annette an ihren Geliebten,'" 461.

71. Goethe, *Annette*, 167.

Chapter 9

1. I am aware that technically, the proper term is *transcendent* and not *transcendental* when referring to a conception of the world beyond appearances. However, I am not using the term "transcendental" in its Kantian sense, but rather I use this term to refer to social and cultural processes of normalization that generate order, intelligibility, judgments, norms in certain spheres of life—not all of which are "transcendent" (for example, the norms of familial piety are not "transcendent," beyond experience, but they are, in my sense, *transcendental*, because they organize behavioral patterns in a way that grounds or legitimizes the activity within their own sphere).

2. See Jürgen Habermas, *Strukturwandel der Öffentlichkeit* (Frankfurt am Main: Suhrkamp, 1990).

3. Gleim, *Briefwechsel zwischen Gleim und Uz*, 53.

4. Such a bond would seem to integrate the Anacreontic lyric back into a certain tendency of the Enlightenment. For the "positive" interpretations of the utility of rococo poetry in discourses of the time, see Perels, *Studien zur Aufnahme und Kritik der Rokokolyrik*, 138–55.

5. See Habermas, *Strukturwandel der Öffentlichkeit*.

6. Fitzgerald's interpretation of "Patmos" stresses how Hölderlin attempts to move the divine from the vertical to the horizontal axis of language, thereby increasing the agonistic properties of the poem. See Fitzgerald, *Agonistic Poetry*, 48–72.

7. For a summary of the tension between religious institutions and Anacreontic poetry, see Perels, *Studien zur Aufnahme und Kritik der Rokokolyrik*, 123–37.

8. Gleim, *Briefwechsel zwischen Gleim und Uz*, 55.

9. For an excellent representation of this history, see Hans Blumenberg, *The Genesis of the Copernican World*, trans. Robert M. Wallace (Cambridge, Mass.: MIT Press, 1987).

10. Karl S. Guthke describes how the new technology of the telescope functioned as a crystallization point around which the fantasy of "new worlds" came into being, and it is perhaps against this form of practice that Gleim directs this particular Anacreontic song. See Karl S. Guthke, *Der Mythos der Neuzeit: Das Thema der Mehrheit der Welten in der Literatur- und Geistesgeschichte von der kopernikanischen Wende bis zur Science Fiction* (Bern: Francke, 1983), 217–50.

11. See Hannah Arendt, *The Human Condition* (Chicago: University of Chicago Press, 1998), 262–63.

12. Blumenberg, *The Genesis of the Copernican World*, 642.

13. Blumenberg notes that in the seventeenth century, "the new 'world-optics' still enter the service of the Baroque metaphors for the world: The human eye penetrates through one new backcloth and stage set after another, into backgrounds that in their turn are also backcloths and sets." Ibid., 641. The Anacreontic poet's understanding of optics does not enter into the space of this bad infinity; indeed, he does not even turn his gaze to the stage behind the stage, but tears his eye away from the text of the heavens and toward the gaze that has been observing *him*.

14. Blumenberg describes how "Berkeley had asserted for the first time in 1709 that geometry does not have to do with the structure of optical space. . . . It is not without rational charm to see that a line leads from the ramifying consequences of Copernicanism for optical self-consciousness into the history of the origins of non-Euclidean geometries." Ibid., 642.

15. Ulrike Gleixner describes marriage in Pietistic bourgeois life as "Zwischen göttlicher und weltlicher Ordnung"; see Ulrike Gleixner, *Pietismus und Bürgertum* (Göttingen: Vandenhoeck & Ruprecht, 2005), 209–70.

16. See Ulrich Herrmann, "Pädagogisches Denken," in *Handbuch der deutschen Bildungsgeschichte*, ed. Notker Hammerstein und Ulrich Herrmann, vol. 2 (Munich: C. H. Beck, 2005).

17. For a brief introduction to A. H. Francke, see Herrmann, "Pädagogisches Denken," 101–2.

18. For a history of the development of the *Realschule* in Halle, see Wolfgang Neugebauer, "Niedere Schulen und Realschulen," in *Handbuch der deutschen*

Bildungsgeschichte, ed. Notker Hammerstein und Ulrich Herrmann, vol. 2 (Munich: C. H. Beck, 2005), 245–47.

19. However, there were also movements that ascribed to Anacreontic poetry a social-pedagogical function and attempted to bring these poetic practices in line with Enlightenment functionality. See Perels, *Studien zur Aufnahme und Kritik der Rokokolyrik*, 138–55. The exercise values of the poems themselves, however, often stand in tension with the attempt to align them with certain values of the Enlightenment.

20. Jean Weisberger suggests that the process of self-alienation forms a central component of the role-playing of rococo poetry, although he then reintegrates this alienation into the code of self-knowledge: "Le 'rôle' permet à l'acteur de se distancier de lui-même, peut-être donc de se mieux connaître." Jean Weisberger, *Les masques fragiles* (Lausanne: L'Age d'Homme, 1991), 76.

21. Max Weber notes, "Nun ist unverkennbar, daß schon in dem deutschen *Worte* 'Beruf' ebenso wie in vielleicht noch deutlicherer Weise in dem englischen 'calling,' eine religiöse Vorstellung—die einer von *Gott* gestellten *Aufgabe*—wenigstens *mit*klingt und, je nachdrücklicher wir auf das Wort im konkreten Fall den Ton legen, desto fühlbarer wird." Weber, *Die protestantische Ethik und der "Geist" des Kapitalismus* (Tübingen: J. C. B. Mohr, 1905), 35–36. His description of this word is followed by a lengthy excursus in a footnote about Luther's translation of the Bible and the tranlsation of κλησις, or divine sanction, as *Beruf*.

22. See Nietzsche, *Götzen-Dämmerung*, 67, as well as Jacques Derrida, *The Gift of Death*, trans. David Wills (Chicago: University of Chicago Press, 1995), 11.

23. See Martin Heidegger, *Sein und Zeit* (Tübingen: Niemeyer, 1967), 240.

24. For Heidegger, death, as a structure of Dasein (*Sein zum Tode*), makes possible the possible as such and renders the shared world of intelligibility contingent, allowing *Dasein* to see the possibility of the impossibility of *das Man* and preventing *Dasein* from a form of intelligibility that derives solely from the dictates of publicly shared norms: "*Die nächste Nähe des Seins zum Tode als Möglichkeit ist einem Wirklichen so fern als möglich*. Je unverhüllter diese Möglichkeit verstanden wird, um so reiner dringt das Verstehen vor in die Möglichkeit *als die der Unmöglichkeit der Existenz überhaupt* . . . . Im Vorlaufen in diese Möglichkeit wird sie 'immer größer,' das heißt sie enthüllt sich als solche, die überhaupt kein Maß, kein mehr oder minder kennt, sondern die Möglichkeit der maßlosen Unmöglichkeit der Existenz bedeutet." Ibid., 262.

25. Death was a favorite subject of Anacreontic poets; see Perels, *Studien zur Aufnahme und Kritik der Rokokolyrik*, 81.

26. One could also argue that the second version is not as dark as the first version, perhaps because it would have been "sung" by his "Mädchen," as he notes in the preface. Nevertheless, it is noteworthy that precisely the poem he mentions in the preface treats thematic material that represents the poet's own capacity—even in other media—to give life *or* death.

27. Gleim's approach to death has been explored in a beautiful and insightful paper by Karl S. Guthke. Guthke sees Gleim's lyric as part of the turn to this world, and hence, as part of a strand of Enlightenment thought: "die anakreontische Lyrik als Dokument der aufgeklärten Zuwendung zu dieser Welt ist nicht nur im allgemeinen lebenssteigernd, sondern a fortiori in ihrer Behandlung des

Todes. Solche Begegnung mit dem Tode wie in Gleims Scherzgedicht (so dürfen wir, nur halb in Scherz, die Lektion der Anekdote formulieren) fördert das Leben in 'dieser Welt,' ja bewahrt es allererst." Guthke, "Der Tod und die Mädchens—und Gleim: Behagen und Unbehagen in der Aufklärung," *Euphorion* 98, no. 1 (2004): 25. He goes on to analyze the relation of Gleim's Anacreontic poetry to his later lyrics, including his patriotic songs. In the later lyrics, he nevertheless remains attached to "this life," but death becomes more traditional, regaining some of its power over the imagination; later Gleim will write: "Der Tod, der stärkre Tod, der alles überwindet/ . . . /Der wirft nun bald auch mich ins Grab./Ach! Diesen Feind bewegt nicht Bitten und nicht Flehen,/Nicht List und nicht Betrug." Johann Wilhelm Ludwig Gleim, *Ausgewählte Werke*, ed. Leonhard Lier (Leipzig: Reclam, 1885), 194.

28. See Hans Peter Herrmann, "Krieg, Medien und Nation: Zum Nationalismus in Kriegsliedern des 16. und 18. Jahrhunderts," in *"Krieg ist mein Lied": Der Siebenjährige Krieg in den zeitgenössischen Medien*, ed. Wolfgang Adam and Holger Dainat (Göttingen: Wallstein, 2007), 31.

29. The rococo and Anacreontic signifying systems stand in diametric opposition to Benjamin's conception of baroque allegory: "Das ist der Kern der allegorischen Betrachtung, der barocken, weltlichen Exposition der Geschichte als Leidensgeschichte der Welt; bedeutend ist sie nur in den Stationen ihres Verfalls. Soviel Bedeutung, soviel Todverfallenheit, weil am tiefsten der Tod die zackige Demarkationslinie zwischen Physis und Bedeutung eingräbt." Walter Benjamin, *Ursprung des deutschen Trauerspiels* (Frankfurt am Main: Suhrkamp, 1969), 183. The rococo and Anacreontic stand in not merely stylistic opposition to baroque allegory, but also in the manner in which signs carry the traces of the beyond; they are opposed in their very semiotic function. The Anacreontic sign empties itself out of the beyond, it approaches the state in which transcendence = 0.

30. See Gregory Bateson, *Steps to an Ecology of Mind* (Chicago: University of Chicago Press, 1972), 315.

31. Jean Paul Richter, *Werke*, vol. 5, 444.

Conclusion to Part Three

1. For the complexity of this shift, see Wellbery's groundbreaking work on Goethe's early lyrics: David Wellbery, *The Specular Moment* (Stanford, Calif.: Stanford University Press, 1996).

Afterword

1. Friedrich Schelling, *Ideen zu einer Philosophie der Natur* (Leipzig: Breitkopf und Härtel, 1797), 104.

2. Ibid.

3. Schelling notes, "Allem Denken und Vorstellen in uns geht also nothwendig voran eine *ursprüngliche Thätigkeit*, die, *weil* sie allem Denken *vorangeht*, in so fern schlechthin—*unbestimmt*, und unbeschränkt ist. Erst nachdem ein Entgegengesetztes da ist, wird sie beschränkte, und eben deswegen *bestimmte* (denkbare) Thätigkeit. Wäre diese Thätigkeit unseres Geistes *ursprünglich* beschränkt, (so wie es die Philosophen sich einbilden, die alles auf Denken und Vorstellen zurückführen), so könnte der Geist niemals sich *beschränkt fühlen*. Er

fühlt seine *Beschränktheit* nur, in so fern er zugleich seine *ursprüngliche Unbeschränktheit* fühlt." Schelling, *Ideen*, 134–35.

4. Ibid., 135.

5. Ibid., 135–36.

6. Thomas Pfau notes, "Novalis conceives of aesthetic form as ceaselessly evolving, progressing, and imbued with a magical aura. In its syntagmatic organization as 'text,' the aesthetic emulates life itself." Thomas Pfau, *Romantic Moods: Paranoia, Trauma, and Melancholy, 1790–1840* (Baltimore: Johns Hopkins University Press, 2005), 57.

7. Scotus is the first philosopher who understands that freedom of the will and contingency mutually imply one another: "at the same moment the will has an act of willing, at the same and for the same moment it can also have an opposite act of willing." John Duns Scotus, *Contingency and Freedom: Lectura I 39*, ed. A. Vos Jaczn et al. (Dordrecht: Kluwer, 1994), 116. However, for Scotus, God has a foreknowledge of what he has willed (which, as a single act of will, must be contingent in order to allow for the freedom of the divine will), whereas for Hölderlin, human beings must be trained to perceive the necessity of contingent things and to hold contradictory and mutually exclusive modalities in one and the same cognitive space.

8. An excellent study by Christian Oestersandfort examines Hölderlin's *Turmdichtung* from this perspective, revealing considerable connections between Hölderlin's latest poems and the tradition of "diatetic" poetry. He elaborates his thesis, following Winfried Kudszus, as follows: "Die Turmdichtung wird nicht als Produkt gestörter Psyche begriffen, sondern als ein Textkorpus, der den Motivbereich der Psyche einschließt." Oestersandfort, *Immanente Poetik und Poetische Diätetik in Hölderlins Turmdichtung* (Tübingen: Niemeyer, 2006), 27. See also Winfried Kudszus, "Versuch einer Heilung: Hölderlins spätere Lyrik," in *Hölderlin ohne Mythos*, ed. Ingrid Riedel (Göttingen: Vandenhoeck & Ruprecht, 1973).

9. Merleau-Ponty, *Sense and Non-Sense*, 15.

10. Schelling, *Ideen*, 85.

11. This poem has been extensively analyzed by Roman Jakobson. He shows, without any doubt, that the latest poems of Hölderlin are not unstructured acts of speech, but highly complex textures of thematic, syntactic, and semantic patterns. However, he tends to assimilate Hölderlin's later work to the poetological reflections of his earlier work. See Jakobson, "Ein Blick auf *Die Aussicht* von Hölderlin," in vol. 3 of *Selected Writings: Poetry of Grammar and Grammar of Poetry*, ed. Stephen Rudy (The Hague: Mouton, 1981), 417. While I agree that one can read the later work in light of the earlier poetological reflections, I do not believe that the later works address the same concerns that Hölderlin was expressing earlier in his life. More specifically, I do not believe the later poems cohere with Hölderlin's earlier conception of "Ein lebendiges Ganze," nor are they "durch und durch individualisirt" (417). Instead, they see the totality of nature as inherently *not* a whole given up to human perception, and the very lack of wholeness—a very different concept of plenitude—*constitutes* the perfection, *Vollkommenheit*, of the given world.

12. Oestersandfort deemphasizes the gaps, obscurities, and dissonances in these poems. He claims, for example, "Das dunkle Bild (4) wird durch die Ergänzung zum hellen: 'des Himmel [*sic*] Höhe glänzet/ . . . dann' (7/8)." Oestersandfort,

Immanente Poetik und Poetische Diätetik in Hölderlins Turmdichtung, 143. However, it is not "das dunkle Bild" of the forest that is completed by nature, but "das Bild der Zeiten." Moreover, the second strophe, with its repetition of "Daß . . . /Daß . . ." constitutes an expansion of the first; they are linked by a semicolon. The darkness of the forest remains, and it is *this* darkness that represents perfection. It is not merely the harmony of the late poems, but the *dissonances* that cannot be taken as signs of mental disturbance—they too form part of the aesthetic affirmation of life.

13. Bernhard Böschenstein interprets Hölderlin's latest poems as a celebration of the transparency of nature, "Die winterliche Szene aber betritt [der Dichter] kaum, da in ihr der Geist selber sich in seiner Transparenz kundtut." Böschenstein, "Hölderlins Späteste Gedichte," *Hölderlin-Jahrbuch* 14 (1965/66): 47. And yet, he emphasizes the partial and incomplete nature of these poems: "Zu solcher Totalität gehört, daß sie auch die Epochen einbezieht, die außerhalb ihrer selbst liegen. Was schon bei den Sommergedichten angedeutet werden konnte, jenes Drängen über den eigenen Moment hinweg, gilt in erhöhtem Maße von den Wintergedichten." Ibid., 48. This observation suggests that Hölderlin can only approach immanence as something that bears its otherness within itself, something that will therefore never be capable of being totalized. However, it is this precise feature of the visible world, the fact that it opens *vistas* and does not present itself to the senses all at once, that Hölderlin sees as a mark of its perfection.

14. Oestersandfort describes this difference as follows: "Das consolatorische, erbauliche und therapeutische Konzept der Turmdichtung ensteht aus einer nach 1806 gegenüber dem Spätwerk modifizierten Ausrichtung der Kunst." Oestersandfort, *Immanente Poetik und Poetische Diätetik in Hölderlins Turmdichtung*, 347. However, he sees the basic tendency of these poems as the illumination of everything, as clarity, peace, comfort: "Wenn es in der Turmdichtung heißt, daß der 'ganze Sinn des hellen Bildes lebet,' sind in diesem Vers die Grundprinzipien des diätetischen Konzepts enthalten. Der 'helle Sinn' wird dem 'dunklen' entgegengestellt und zum 'hellen' Geist, in dem das 'Bild' entsteht. Diese Erhellung des 'lebendigen Sinns' läßt auch die Turmdichtung zu einem diätetischen 'Kunstwerk des Lebens' werden." Ibid., 346. In this last of Hölderlin's poems, however, one may observe light and dark in a simultaneous chiaroscuro of experience, and it is precisely this mixture that describes the affirmative content and formal movement of the poem.

15. See Jakobson, "Ein Blick auf *Die Aussicht* von Hölderlin."

WORKS CITED

Adelung, Johann Christoph. *Grammatisch-kritisches Wörterbuch der hochdeutschen Mundart.* 4 vols. Vienna: Bauer, 1811.

Adorno, Theodor. "Parataxis: Zur späten Lyrik Hölderlins." In *Noten zur Literatur*, 447–91. Frankfurt am Main: Suhrkamp, 1997.

Anger, Alfred. "'Annette an ihren Geliebten': Ein Gedicht Goethes aus der Leipziger Zeit." *Deutsche Vierteljahrsschrift für Literaturwissenschaft und Geistesgeschichte* 37, no. 3 (1963): 439–62.

———. *Literarisches Rokoko.* Stuttgart: Metzler, 1962.

Arctander O'Brien, William. *Novalis: Signs of Revolution.* Durham, N.C.: Duke University Press, 1995.

Arendt, Hannah. *The Human Condition.* Chicago: University of Chicago Press, 1998.

———. *Lectures on Kant's Political Philosophy.* Edited by Ronald Beiner. Chicago: University of Chicago Press, 1992.

———. *Willing: The Life of the Mind.* Vol. 2. New York: Harcourt, 1978.

Aristotle. *Poetics.* In *Poetics*, with *On the Sublime* and *On Style.* Edited and translated by Stephen Halliwell. Cambridge, Mass.: Harvard University Press, 1995.

Badiou, Alain. *Being and Event.* Translated by Oliver Feltham. London: Continuum, 2005.

Bakhtin, Mikhail. *Problems of Dostoevsky's Poetics.* Translated by Caryl Emerson. Minneapolis: University of Minnesota Press, 1984.

Basedow, J. B., and J. H. Campe. "Von der eigentlichen Absicht eines Philanthropens." In *Schwarze Pädagogik*, edited by Katharina Rutschky, 61–65. Munich: Ullstein, 1977.

Bateson, Gregory. *Steps to an Ecology of Mind.* Chicago: University of Chicago Press, 1972.

Baumgarten, Alexander. *Ästhetik.* Translated by Dagmar Mirbach. Hamburg: Meiner, 2007.

———. *Handschrift der Ästhetik.* In *Alexander Gottlieb Baumgarten: Seine Bedeutung und Stellung in der Leibniz-Wolffischen Philosophie und seine Beziehungen zu Kant: Nebst Veröffentlichung einer bisher unbekannten Handschrift der Ästhetik Baumgartens*, edited by Bernhard Poppe. Leipzig: Robert Noske, 1907.

———. *Meditationes philosophicae de nunnullis ad poema pertinentibus.* Edited by Heinz Paetzold. Hamburg: Meiner, 1983.

———. *Metaphysica: Historisch-kritische Ausgabe.* Edited by Günter Gawlick and Lothar Kreimendahl. Stuttgart: Frommann–Holtzboog, 2011.

Bay, Hansjörg. "'Die eigene Rede des andern': Hölderlins Poetik des Fremden." In *Die Ordnung der Kulturen: Zur Konstruktion ethnischer, nationaler und zivilisatorischer Differenzen 1750–1850*, edited by Hansjörg Bay and Kai Merten, 333–56. Würzburg: Königshausen & Neumann, 2006.

Beck, Adolf. *Hölderlin: Chronik seines Lebens*. Frankfurt am Main: Insel, 1975.

Beetz, Manfred. "Anakreontik und Rokoko im Bezugsfeld der Aufklärung—Eine Forschungsbilanz." In *Anakreontische Aufklärung*, edited by Manfred Beetz and Hans-Joachim Kertscher, 1–17. Tübingen: Niemeyer, 2005.

Beiser, Frederick. *Diotima's Children: German Aesthetic Rationalism from Leibniz to Lessing*. Oxford: Oxford University Press, 2009.

Bender, Wolfgang. "Rhetorische Tradition und Ästhetik im 18. Jahrhundert: Baumgarten, Meier und Breitinger." *Zeitschrift für deutsche Philologie* 99 (1980): 481–506.

Benjamin, Walter. *Ursprung des deutschen Trauerspiels*. Frankfurt am Main: Suhrkamp, 1969.

Bennholdt-Thomsen, Anke, and Alfredo Guzzoni. *Analecta Hölderliana: Zur Hermetik des Spätwerks*. Würzburg: Königshausen & Neumann, 1999.

———. *Analecta Hölderliniana II: Die Aufgabe des Vaterlands*. Würzburg: Königshausen & Neumann, 2004.

Berndt, Frauke. *Poema/Gedicht: Die epistemische Konfiguration der Literatur um 1750*. Berlin: de Gruyter, 2011.

Bertaux, Pierre. *Hölderlin und die Französische Revolution*. Frankfurt am Main: Suhrkamp, 1974.

Blumenberg, Hans. *The Genesis of the Copernican World*. Translated by Robert M. Wallace. Cambridge, Mass.: MIT Press, 1987.

Borges, Jorge Luis. "Pierre Menard, Autor del Quijote." In vol. 3 of *Obras completas*, edited by Carlos V. Frías, 444–50. Barcelona: María Kodama y Emecé Editores, 1989.

Böschenstein, Bernhard. *Hölderlins Rheinhymne*. Zurich: Atlantis, 1968.

———. "Hölderlins Späteste Gedichte." *Hölderlin-Jahrbuch* 14 (1965/66): 35–56.

———. "Oden-Flüsse—Hymnen-Ströme." *Hölderlin-Jahrbuch* 35 (2007): 197–201.

Breitinger, Johann Jakob. *Critische Dichtkunst: Schriften zur Literatur*. Edited by Volker Meid. Stuttgart: Reclam, 1980.

Brilliant, Richard. *My Laocoön: Alternative Claims in the Interpretation of Artworks*. Berkeley: University of California Press, 2000.

Brockes, Barthold Heinrich. *Irdisches Vergnügen in Gott*. Vol. 1. 7th ed. Hamburg: Christian Herold, 1744.

———. *Irdisches Vergnügen in Gott*. Vol. 2. Hamburg: Christian Herold, 1734.

———. *Irdisches Vergnügen in Gott*. Vol. 4. 3rd ed. Hamburg: Conrad König, 1745.

Brown, John. *The Elements of Medicine*. Vol. 1. London: Johnson, 1788.

Brugmans, Anton. *Philosophische Versuche über die magnetische Materie*. Leipzig: Crusius, 1784.

Butler, Judith. *Excitable Speech: A Politics of the Performative*. New York: Routledge, 1997.

Campe, Rüdiger. *Spiel der Wahrscheinlichkeit: Literatur und Berechnung zwischen Pascal und Kleist*. Göttingen: Wallstein, 2002.

Cassirer, Ernst. *Philosophie der Aufklärung*. Tübingen: J. C. B. Mohr, 1932.

Catullus. *Catullus, Tibullus, Pervigilium Veneris.* Edited by G. P. Goold. Translated by Francis Warre Cornish. 2nd ed. Cambridge, Mass.: Harvard University Press, 1988.

Cooper, Ian. *The Near and Distant God: Poetry, Idealism, and Religious Thought from Hölderlin to Eliot.* London: Modern Humanities Research Association and Maney Publishing, 2008.

Dahlke, Karin. *Äußerste Freiheit: Wahnsinn/Sublimierung/Poetik des Tragischen der Moderne.* Würzburg: Königshausen & Neumann, 2008.

Daibler, Jürgen. *Experimentalphysik des Geistes.* Göttingen: Vandenhoeck & Ruprecht, 2001.

Dante Alighieri. *Paradiso.* Vol. 4 of *La commedia secondo l'antica vulgata*, edited by Giorgio Petrocchi. Florence: Casa Editrice le Lettere, 1994.

De Man, Paul. *The Rhetoric of Romanticism.* New York: Columbia University Press, 1984.

De Roche, Charles. *Friedrich Hölderlin: Patmos: Das scheidende Erscheinen des Gedichts.* Munich: Fink, 1999.

Deleuze, Gilles. *Logic of Sense.* Translated by Mark Lester, edited by Constantin V. Boundas. New York: Columbia University Press, 1990.

Derrida, Jacques. *The Gift of Death.* Translated by David Wills. Chicago: University of Chicago Press, 1995.

Dreyfus, Hubert L. "Heidegger's Ontology of Art." In *A Companion to Heidegger*, edited by Hubert L. Dreyfus and Mark A. Wrathall, 407–19. Oxford: Blackwell, 2005.

Endres, Johannes. "Der Schleier des Novalis." In *Novalis: Poesie und Poetik*, edited by Herbert Uerlings, 109–23. Tübingen: Niemeyer, 2004.

Esterhammer, Angela. *The Romantic Performative: Language and Action in British and German Romanticism.* Stanford, Calif.: Stanford University Press, 2000.

Fish, Stanley. *Is There a Text in This Class: The Authority of Interpretive Communities.* Cambridge, Mass.: Harvard University Press, 1980.

Fitzgerald, William. *Agonistic Poetry: The Pindaric Mode in Pindar, Horace, Hölderlin, and the English Ode.* Berkeley: University of California Press, 1987.

Foucault, Michel. *The Use of Pleasure.* Vol. 2 of *The History of Sexuality.* Translated by Robert Hurley. New York: Vintage, 1985.

Frank, Manfred. "Die Philosophie des sogenannten 'Magischen Idealismus.'" *Euphorion* 63 (1969): 88–116.

———. *Einführung in die frühromantische Ästhetik.* Frankfurt am Main: Suhrkamp, 1989.

———. *Unendliche Annäherung.* Frankfurt am Main: Suhrkamp, 1997.

Frank, Manfred, and Gerhard Kurz. "Ordo Inversus: Zu einer Reflexionsfigur bei Novalis, Hölderlin, Kleist, und Kafka." In *Geist und Zeichen: Festschrift für Arthur Henkel*, edited by Herbert Anton, Bernhard Gajek, and Peter Pfaff, 77–97. Heidelberg: Winter, 1977.

Freud, Sigmund. *Neue Folge der Vorlesungen zur Einführung in die Psychoanalyse.* Vol. 15 of *Gesammelte Werke*, edited by Anna Freud. London: Imago, 1946.

Gaier, Ulrich. "Hölderlin und die Theorie der Organisation." *Text + Kritik* 7, no. 96 (1996): 51–61.

———. *Krumme Regel: Novalis' "Konstruktionslehre des schaffenden Geistes" und ihre Tradition*. Tübingen: Niemeyer, 1970.

Gervinus, Georg Gottfried. *Geschichte der deutschen Dichtung*. Vol. 3. 3rd ed. Leipzig: Wilhelm Engelmann, 1848.

Gleim, Johann Wilhelm Ludwig. *Ausgewählte Werke*. Edited by Leonhard Lier. Leipzig: Reclam, 1885.

———. *Versuch in Scherzhaften Liedern und Lieder*. Edited by Alfred Anger. Tübingen: Niemeyer, 1964.

Gleim, Johann Wilhelm Ludwig, and Johan Peter Uz. *Briefwechsel zwischen Gleim und Uz*. Edited by Carl Schüddekopf. Tübingen: Lauff, 1899.

Gleixner, Ulrike. *Pietismus und Bürgertum*. Göttingen: Vandenhoeck & Ruprecht, 2005.

Goebel, Eckart. *Charis und Charisma*. Berlin: Kadmos, 2006.

Goethe, Johann Wolfgang von. *Annette*. In vol. 1 of *Der junge Goethe*, edited by Hannah Fischer-Lamberg, 167–88. Berlin: de Gruyter, 1999.

———. *Sämtliche Werke nach Epochen seines Schaffens*. 21 vols. Edited by Karl Richter et al. Munich: Hanser, 1985–98.

Gottsched, Johann Christian. *Versuch einer Critischen Dichtkunst*. Vols. 6.1 and 6.2 of *Ausgewählte Werke*. Edited by Joachim Birke and Brigitte Birke. Berlin: de Gruyter, 1973.

Götz, Johann Nikolaus. "Das Vergnügen." In vol. 1 of *Lyrische Bluhmenlese*, edited by Karl Wilhelm Ramler, 35–36. Leipzig: Weidmanns Erben und Reich, 1774.

———. *Gedichte aus den Jahren 1745–1765*. Edited by Carl Schüddekopf. Stuttgart: Göschen'sche Verlagshandlung, 1893.

Götz, Johann Nikolaus, and Johann Peter Uz. *Die Gedichte Anakreons und der Sappho Oden*. Karlsruhe: Michael Macklot, 1760.

Gross, Steffen. *Felix Aestheticus: Die Ästhetik als Lehre vom Menschen: Zum 250. Jahrestag des Erscheinens von Alexander Gottlieb Baumgartens "Aesthetica."* Würzburg: Königshausen & Neumann, 2001.

Guthke, Karl S. *Der Mythos der Neuzeit: Das Thema der Mehrheit der Welten in der Literatur- und Geistesgeschichte von der kopernikanischen Wende bis zur Science Fiction*. Bern: Francke, 1983.

———. "Der Tod und die Mädchens—und Gleim: Behagen und Unbehagen in der Aufklärung." *Euphorion* 98, no. 1 (2004): 1–38.

Guyer, Paul. "Kant's Ambitions in the Third *Critique*." In *Kant and Modern Philosophy*, edited by Paul Guyer, 538–87. Cambridge, Eng.: Cambridge University Press, 2006.

Haber, Judith. *Pastoral and the Poetics of Self-Contradiction: Theocritus to Marvell*. Cambridge, Eng.: Cambridge University Press, 1994.

Habermas, Jürgen. *Strukturwandel der Öffentlichkeit*. Frankfurt am Main: Suhrkamp, 1990.

Hadot, Pierre. *La citadelle intérieure: Introduction aux Pensées de Marc Aurèle*. Paris: Fayard, 1992.

———. *Philosophy as a Way of Life*. Translated by Michael Chase, edited by Arnold Davidson. Oxford: Blackwell, 1995.

———. *The Veil of Isis: An Essay on the History of the Idea of Nature*. Translated by Michael Chase. Cambridge, Mass.: Harvard University Press, 2006.

Haering, Theodor. *Novalis als Philosoph*. Stuttgart: Kohlhammer, 1954.

Hagedorn, Friedrich von. *Oden und Lieder in fünf Büchern*. Hamburg: Johann Carl Bohn, 1747.

Hammermeister, Kai. *The German Aesthetic Tradition*. Cambridge, Eng.: Cambridge University Press, 2002.

Hannah, Richard. *The Fichtean Dynamics of Novalis' Poetics*. Berlin: Peter Lang, 1981.

Hegel, Georg Wilhelm Friedrich. *The Phenomenology of Spirit*. Translated by A. V. Miller. Oxford: Oxford University Press, 1977.

Heidegger, Martin. "Der Ursprung des Kunstwerkes." In *Holzwege*, vol. 5 of *Gesamtausgabe*, edited by Friedrich-Wilhelm von Herrmann, 1–74. Frankfurt am Main: Vittorio Klostermann, 1977.

———. *Hölderlins Hymnen "Germanien" und "Der Rhein."* Vol. 39 of *Gesamtausgabe*, edited by Susanne Ziegler. Frankfurt am Main: Klostermann, 1980.

———. *Sein und Zeit*. Tübingen: Niemeyer, 1967.

Hellingrath, Norbert von. *Pindarübertragungen von Hölderlin: Prolegomena zu einer Erstausgabe*. Leipzig: Breitkopf, 1910.

Henrich, Dieter. *Der Grund im Bewußtsein: Untersuchungen zu Hölderlins Denken (1794–1795)*. Stuttgart: Klett-Cotta, 1992.

Herder, Johann Gottfried. *Ideen zur Philosophie der Menschheit*. Vol. 6 of *Werke in zehn Bänden*, edited by Martin Bollacher. Frankfurt am Main: Deutscher Klassiker, 1985.

Herrmann, Hans Peter. "Krieg, Medien und Nation: Zum Nationalismus in Kriegsliedern des 16. und 18. Jahrhunderts." In *"Krieg ist mein Lied": Der Siebenjährige Krieg in den zeitgenössischen Medien*, edited by Wolfgang Adam and Holger Dainat, 27–64. Göttingen: Wallstein, 2007.

———. *Naturnachahmung und Einbildungskraft*. Bad Homburg: Max Gehlen, 1970.

Herrmann, Ulrich. "Pädagogisches Denken." In vol. 2 of *Handbuch der deutschen Bildungsgeschichte*, edited by Ulrich Herrmann and Notker Hammerstein, 97–133. Munich: C. H. Beck, 2005.

Herrmann, Ulrich, and Notker Hammerstein. *Handbuch der deutschen Bildungsgeschichte: 18. Jahrhundert*. Vol. 2. Munich: Beck, 2005.

Hess, Jonathan. *Reconstituting the Body Politic: Enlightenment, Public Culture, and the Invention of Aesthetic Autonomy*. Detroit, Mich.: Wayne State University Press, 1999.

Hiller, Marion. *"Harmonisch Entgegengesetzt": Zur Darstellung und Darstellbarkeit in Hölderlins Poetik um 1800*. Tübingen: Max Niemeyer, 2008.

Hogarth, William. *The Analysis of Beauty*. Edited by Joseph Burke. Oxford: Oxford University Press, 1953.

Hölderlin, Friedrich. *Poems and Fragments*. Translated by Michael Hamburger. London: Anvil, 2004.

———. *Sämtliche Gedichte*. Edited by Jochen Schmidt. 3 vols. Frankfurt am Main: Deutscher Taschenbuch Verlag, 2005.

———. *Sämtliche Werke*. Edited by Friedrich Beissner. Vol. 2.2. Stuttgart: Kohlhammer, 1951.

———. *Sämtliche Werke*. Edited by D. E. Sattler. 20 vols. Frankfurt am Main: Stroemfeld, 2000.

———. *Sämtliche Werke und Briefe*. Edited by Michael Knaupp. 3 vols. Munich: Hanser, 1992.

Holland, Jocelyn. *German Romanticism and Science: The Procreative Poetics of Goethe, Novalis, and Ritter*. London: Routledge, 2009.

Horace. *Opera*. Edited by D. R. Shackleton Baily. Stuttgart: Teubner, 1985.

———. *Satires, Epistles and Ars Poetica*. Translated by H. Rushton Fairclough. Cambridge, Mass.: Harvard University Press, 1991.

Hornbacher, Annette. "'Eines zu seyn mit Allem, was lebt . . .': Hölderlins 'intellectuale Anschauung.'" In *Hölderlin: Philosophie und Dichtung*, vol. 5 of *Turm-Vorträge*, edited by Valérie Lawitschka, 24–47. Tübingen: Hölderlin-Gesellschaft, 2001.

Husserl, Edmund. *Wahrnehmung und Aufmerksamkeit: Texte aus dem Nachlass (1893–1912)*. Vol. 38 of *Husserliana*, edited by Thomas Vongehr and Regula Giulani. Dordrecht: Springer, 2004.

Iser, Wolfgang. *The Act of Reading: A Theory of Aesthetic Response*. Baltimore: Johns Hopkins University Press, 1978.

Jakobson, Roman, and G. Lübbe-Grothues. "Ein Blick auf *Die Aussicht* von Hölderlin." In vol. 3 of *Selected Writings*, edited by Stephen Rudy, 388–446. The Hague: Mouton, 1981.

Jamme, Christophe, and Frank Völkel, eds. *Hölderlin und der deutsche Idealismus*. Vol. 3.2. Stuttgart: Frommann-Holzboog, 2003.

Janz, Rolf-Peter. "Bildungsroman." In vol. 5 of *Deutsche Literatur: Eine Sozialgeschichte*, edited by Horst Albert Glaser, 144–63. Reinbek: Rowohlt, 1980.

Kamla, Henry. *Novalis' Hymnen an die Nacht: Zur Deutung und Datierung*. Copenhagen: Munksgaard, 1945.

Kant, Immanuel. *Kant's Gesammelte Schriften*. Edited by the Königlich Preussische Akademie der Wissenschaften. Berlin: de Gruyter, 1922—.

Kemper, Hans-Georg. *Deutsche Lyrik in der frühen Neuzeit*. Tübingen: Niemeyer, 1991.

Kertscher, H.-J. *Anakreontik: Zweiter Hallescher Dichterkreis: Gleim, Götz, Rudnick, Uz*. Halle: Hallescher Verlag, 1993.

Kierkegaard, Søren. *Fear and Trembling*. Translated by Alastair Hannay. London: Penguin, 2003.

Klotz, Volker. *Das europäische Kunstmärchen*. Stuttgart: Metzler, 1985.

Knübel, Ralf. "Hölderlins Leiden: Der poetische Prozess als Versuch der Selbstverständigung." *Hölderlin-Jahrbuch* 36 (2009): 151–68.

Kord, Susanne. *Women Peasant Poets in Eighteenth-Century England, Scotland, and Germany: Milkmaids on Parnassus*. New York: Camden House, 2003.

Koschorke, Albrecht. *Körperströme und Schriftverkehr: Mediologie des 18. Jahrhunderts*. Munich: Fink, 2003.

Kowalik, Jill Anne. *The Poetics of Historical Perspectivism: Breitinger's Critische Dichtkunst and the Neoclassic Tradition*. Chapel Hill: University of North Carolina Press, 1992.

Kreuzer, Ingrid. "Novalis' *Die Lehrlinge zu Saïs*: Fragen zur Struktur, Gattung und immanenten Ästhetik." *Jahrbuch der deutschen Schillergesellschaft* 23 (1979): 276–308.

Kreuzer, Johann. *Erinnerung: Zum Zusammenhang von Hölderlins theoretischen Fragmenten "Das untergehende Vaterland . . ." und "Wenn der Dicther einmal des Geistes mächtig ist . . . ."* Königstein: Anton Hain, 1985.

———. "Logik von Zeit und Erinnerung—Was unterscheidet die Wirklichkeit des Gesangs von der Form des Begriffs?" In *"Es bleibet aber eine Spur/Doch eines Wortes": Zur späten Hymnik und Tragödientheorie Friedrich Hölderlins*, edited by Christoph Jamme and Anja Lemke, 465–83. Munich: Fink, 2004.

Krupp, Anthony. "Cultivation as Maturation: Infants, Children, and Adults in Alexander Gottlieb Baumgarten's *Aesthetica*." *Monatshefte* 98, no. 4 (2006): 524–38.

Kudszus, Winfried. "Geschichtsverlust und Sprachproblematik in den *Hymnen an die Nacht*." *Euphorion* 65 (1971): 299–311.

———. "Versuch einer Heilung: Hölderlins spätere Lyrik." In *Hölderlin ohne Mythos*, edited by Ingrid Riedel, 18–33. Göttingen: Vandenhoeck & Ruprecht, 1973.

Kurz, Gerhard. *Mittelbarkeit und Vereinigung: Zum Verhältnis von Poesie, Reflexion und Revolution bei Hölderlin*. Stuttgart: Metzler, 1975.

Kuzniar, Alice. *Delayed Endings: Nonclosure in Novalis and Hölderlin*. Athens: University of Georgia Press, 1987.

Lacoue-Labarthe, Philippe. "Hölderlin's Theatre." In *Philosophy and Tragedy*, edited by Miguel de Beistegui and Simon Sparks, 115–35. London: Routledge.

———. *Typography: Mimesis, Philosophy, Politics*. Stanford, Calif.: Stanford University Press, 1998.

Lancereau, Daniel. "Novalis und Leibniz." In *Novalis und die Wissenschaften*, edited by Herbert Uerlings, 169–91. Tübingen: Niemeyer, 1997.

Landgraf, Edgar. *Improvisation as Art: Conceptual Challenges, Historical Perspectives*. New York: Continuum, 2011.

Leibniz, Gottfried Wilhelm. *Discours de métaphysique*. In vol. 4 of *Die philosophischen Schriften*, edited by C. I. Gerhardt. Berlin: Weidmannsche Buchhandlung, 1880.

Lessing, Gotthold Ephraim. "Abhandlungen zur Fabel." In *Werke 1758–1759*, edited by Gunter E. Grimm, vol. 4 of *Werke und Briefe*, edited by Wilfried Barner et al., 345–411. Frankfurt am Main: Deutscher Klassiker, 1998.

———. *Laokoon*. In *Werke 1766–1769*, edited by Wilfried Barner. Vol. 5.2 of *Werke und Briefe*, edited by Wilfried Barner et al. Frankfurt am Main: Deutscher Klassiker, 1985.

Loheide, Bernward. *Fichte und Novalis: Transzendentalphilosophisches Denken im romantisierenen Diskurs*. Amsterdam: Rodopi, 2000.

Lohenstein, Daniel Caspar von. *Sophonisbe*. In *Afrikanische Trauerspiele*, edited by Klaus Günther Just. Stuttgart: Anton Hiersemann, 1957.

Loyola, Ignatius of. *The Spiritual Exercises of St. Ignatius of Loyola*. Translated by Elden Muller. New York: Cosimo, 2007.

Luhnen, Michael. *Organisation der Natur*. Heidelberg: Winter, 2007.

Lukacs, Georg. "Hölderlins Hyperion." In *Deutsche Literatur in Zwei Jahrhunderten*. Vol. 7 of *Werke*, 164–84. Neuwied: Luchterhand, 1964.

Lukas, Verena Anna. *Der Dialog im Dialog: Das Inzitament bei Friedrich von Hardenberg*. Berlin: Peter Lang, 2000.

Macherey, Pierre. *A Theory of Literary Production*. Translated by Geoffrey Wall. London: Routledge, 1992.

Martus, Steffen. *Friedrich von Hagedorn—Konstellationen der Aufklärung*. Berlin: de Gruyter, 1999.

Maslov, Boris. "Comparative Literature and Revolution, or the Many Arts of (Mis)reading Alexander Veselovsky." *Compar(a)ison* 2008/2 (2013): 101–29.

Mauser, Wolfram. "Anakreon als Therapie? Zur medizinisch-dietätischen Begründung der Rokoko-Dichtung." *Lessing Yearbook* 20 (1988): 87–120.

———. *Konzepte aufgeklärter Lebensführung: Literarische Kultur in frühmodernen Deutschland.* Würzburg: Königshausen & Neumann, 2000.

McGushin, Edward F. *Foucault's Askēsis.* Evanston, Ill.: Northwestern University Press, 2007.

Meier, Georg Friedrich. *Gedancken von Schertzen.* Halle: Carl Hermann Hemmerde, 1754.

Meise, Helga. *Die Unschuld und die Schrift: Deutsche Frauenromane im 18. Jahrhundert.* Frankfurt am Main: Helmer, 1992.

Menninghaus, Winfried. *Unendliche Verdopplung.* Frankfurt am Main: Suhrkamp, 1987.

Merleau-Ponty, Maurice. *Sense and Non-Sense.* Translated by Hubert L. Dreyfus and Patricia Allen Dreyfus. Evanston, Ill.: Northwestern University Press, 1991.

Mieth, Günter. *Friedrich Hölderlin: Dichter der bürgerlich-demokratischen Revolution.* Berlin: Rütten & Loening, 1978.

Milam, Jennifer. *Fragonard's Playful Paintings.* Manchester: Manchester University Press, 2006.

Milton, John. *Paradise Lost.* Vol. 1 of *The Poetical Works of John Milton*, edited by Helen Darbishire. Oxford: Oxford University Press, 1992.

Molnár, Géza von. *Novalis' Fichte Studies: The Foundations of his Aesthetics.* The Hague: Mouton, 1970.

Moritz, Karl Philipp. "Versuch einer Vereinigung aller schönen Künste und Wissenschaften unter dem Begriff des in sich selbst Vollendeten." In *Schriften zur Ästhetik und Poetik*, edited by Hans Joachim Schrimpf, 3–9. Tübingen: Niemeyer, 1962.

———. "Zur Seelendiätetik." In *Dichtungen und Schriften zur Erfahrungseelenkunde*, vol. 1 of *Werke*, edited by Heide Hollmer and Albert Meier, 836–38. Frankfurt am Main: Deutscher Klassiker, 1999.

Nägele, Rainer. *Hölderlins Kritik der poetischen Vernunft.* Basel: Engeler, 2007.

———. *Text, Geschichte und Subjektivität in Hölderlins Dichtung: "Uneßbarer Schrift gleich."* Stuttgart: Metzler, 1985.

Neubauer, John. *Bifocal Vision.* Chapel Hill: University of North Carolina Press, 1971.

———. "Dr. John Brown (1735–88) and Early German Romanticism." *Journal of the History of Ideas* 28, no. 3 (1967): 367–82.

Neuenfeld, Jörg. *Alles ist Spiel: Zur Geschichte der Auseinandersetzung mit einer Utopie der Moderne.* Würzburg: Königshausen & Neumann, 2005.

Neugebauer, Wolfgang. "Niedere Schulen und Realschulen." In vol. 2 of *Handbuch der deutschen Bildungsgeschichte*, edited by Notker Hammerstein and Ulrich Herrmann, 262–77. Munich: C. H. Beck, 2005.

Newton, Isaac. *Philosophical Writings.* Edited by Andrew Janiak. Cambridge, Eng.: Cambridge University Press, 2004.

Nietzsche, Friedrich. *Götzen-Dämmerung.* In vol. 6.3 of *Werke*, edited by Giorgio Colli and Mazzino Montinari. Berlin: de Gruyter, 1969.

Novalis [Friedrich von Hardenberg]. *Novalis Schriften: Historisch-kritische Ausgabe in vier Bänden, einem Materialienband und einem Ergänzungsband in Vier Teilbänden.* 6.2 vols. Edited by Hans-Joachim Mähl and Gerhard Schulz. Stuttgart: Kohlhammer, 1960.

Oest, J., and J. H. Campe. "Vollständiges System zur Verhütung der Selbstschwächung." In *Schwarze Pädagogik*, edited by Katharina Rutschky, 304–315. Frankfurt am Main: Ullstein, 1977.

Oestersandfort, Christian. *Immanente Poetik und Poetische Diätetik in Hölderlins Turmdichtung.* Tübingen: Niemeyer, 2006.

Ovid. *Metamorphoses.* Vol. 3 of *Ovid in Six Volumes.* Translated by Frank Justus Miller, edited and revised by G. P. Goold. 3rd ed. Cambridge, Mass.: Harvard University Press, 1984.

Perels, Christoph. *Studien zur Aufnahme und Kritik der Rokokolyrik zwischen 1740 und 1760.* Göttingen: Vandenhoeck & Ruprecht, 1974.

Pestalozzi, J. H. "Wie der Erzieher die Wirklichkeit repräsentieren kann." In *Schwarze Pädagogik*, edited by Katharina Rutschky, 395. Munich: Ullstein, 1977.

Petersdorff, Dirk von. "Die Auferstehung Sophie von Kühns in den 'Hymnen an die Nacht.'" In *Novalis: Poesie und Poetik*, edited by Herbert Uerlings, 125–39. Niemeyer: Tübingen, 2004.

———. *Mysterienrede: Zum Selbstverständnis romantischer Intellektueller.* Tübingen: de Gruyter, 1996.

Pfau, Thomas. Critical introduction to *Essays and Letters on Theory*, by Friedrich Hölderlin, 1–29. Edited by Thomas Pfau. Albany: State University of New York Press, 1988.

———. *Romantic Moods: Paranoia, Trauma, and Melancholy, 1790–1840.* Baltimore: Johns Hopkins University Press, 2005.

Philipsen, Bart. "Gesänge." In *Hölderlin-Handbuch*, edited by Johann Kreuzer, 347–78. Stuttgart: Metzler, 2002.

Plato. *Symposium.* In *Lysis, Symposium, Gorgias*, translated by W. R. M. Lamb. Cambridge, Mass.: Harvard University Press, 1925.

Polledri, Elena. "*. . . immer bestehet ein Maas*": *Der Begriff des Maßes in Hölderlins Werk.* Würzburg: Königshausen & Neumann, 2002.

Poppe, Bernhard. *Alexander Gottlieb Baumgarten: Seine Bedeutung und Stellung in der Leibniz-Wolffischen Philosophie und seine Beziehungen zu Kant: Nebst Veröffentlichung einer bisher unbekannten Handschrift der Ästhetik Baumgartens.* Leipzig: Robert Noske, 1907.

Previšić, Boris. *Hölderlins Rhythmus.* Frankfurt am Main: Stroemfeld, 2008.

Rabbow, Paul. *Seelenführung: Methodik der Exerzitien in der Antike.* Munich: Kösel, 1954.

Richter, Jean Paul. *Vorschule der Ästhetik.* In vol. 5 of *Werke*, edited by Norbert Miller. Munich: Hanser, 1987.

Richter, Simon. "The Ins and Outs of Intimacy: Gender, Epistolary Culture, and the Public Sphere." *German Quarterly* 69 (1996): 111–24.

———. "Medizinischer und ästhetischer Diskurs im 18. Jahrhundert: Herder und Haller über Reiz." *Lessing Yearbook* 25 (1993): 83–95.

Rimbaud, Arthur. *Oeuvres complètes.* Edited by André Guyaux. Gallimard: Paris, 2009.

Riou, Jeanne. *Imagination in German Romanticism: Rethinking the Self and Its Environment*. Bern: Peter Lang, 2004.

Ritter, Heinz. *Der unbekannte Novalis: Friedrich von Hardenberg im Spiegel seiner Dichtung*. Göttingen: Sachse und Pohl, 1967.

Ryan, Lawrence J. *Hölderlins Lehre vom Wechsel der Töne*. Stuttgart: Kohlhammer, 1960.

———. "Hyperion oder Der Eremit in Griechenland." In *Hölderlin-Handbuch*, edited by Johan Kreuzer, 176–97. Stuttgart: Metzler, 2002.

———. "'Was bildet aber, stiften die Dichter': Zu Hölderlins Konzeption von 'Bildung.'" *Hölderlin-Jahrbuch* 36 (2009): 30–52.

Schelling, Friedrich. *Erster Entwurf eines Systems der Naturphilosophie*. In vol. 3 of *Sämmtliche Werke*, edited by Karl Friedrich August Schelling. Stuttgart: Cotta, 1858.

———. *Ideen zu einer Philosophie der Natur*. Leipzig: Breitkopf und Härtel, 1797.

———. *Vom Ich als Prinzip der Philosophie oder über das Unbedingte im menschlichen Wissen*. In vol. 1 of *Sämmtliche Werke*, edited by Karl Friedrich August Schelling. Stuttgart: Cotta, 1856.

Schiller, Friedrich. *Schillers Werke: Nationalausgabe*. 41 vols. to date. Edited by Julius Petersen et al. Weimar: Hermann Böhlaus Nachfolger, 1943–.

Schlaffer, Heinz. *Musa iocosa: Gattungspoetik und Gattungsgeschichte der erotischen Dichtung in Deutschland*. Stuttgart: Metzler, 1971.

Schlegel, Friedrich. *Kritische Friedrich-Schlegel-Ausgabe*. 28 vols. to date. Edited by Ernst Behler et al. Paderborn: Schöningh, 1958–.

Schlutz, Alexander M. *Mind's World*. Seattle: University of Washington Press, 2009.

Schmale, Wolfgang. "Die Schule in Deutschland im 18. und frühen 19. Jahrhundert: Konjunkturen, Horizonte, Mentalitäten, Probleme, Ergebnisse." In *Revolution des Wissens? Europa und seine Schulen im Zeitalter der Aufklärung (1750–1825)*, edited by Wolfgang Schmale and Nan L. Dodde, 627–767. Bochum: Dieter Winkler, 1991.

Schmidt, Jochen. *Hölderlins geschichtsphilosophische Hymnen: "Friedensfeier," "Der Einzige," "Patmos."* Darmstadt: Wissenschaftliche Buchgesellschaft, 1990.

Schmitt, Carl. *Political Theology: Four Chapters on the Concept of Sovereignty*. Translated by G. Schwab. Chicago: University of Chicago Press, 2005.

Schönborn, Sibylle. *Das Buch der Seele*. Tübingen: Niemeyer, 1999.

Schulz, Gerhard. "Poesie als Poetik oder Poetik als Poesie?" In *Novalis: Poesie und Poetik*, edited by Herbert Uerlings, 93–107. Tübingen: Niemeyer, 2004.

Scotus, John Duns. *Contingency and Freedom: Lectura I 39*. Edited by A. Vos Jaczn et al. Dordrecht: Kluwer, 1994.

Seigel, Jerrold. *The Idea of the Self: Thought and Experience in Western Europe Since the Seventeenth Century*. Cambridge, Eng.: Cambridge University Press, 2005.

Shaftesbury, Anthony Ashley Cooper, Earl of. *Characteristicks of Men, Manners, Opinions, Times*. 2 vols. Edited by Philip Ayres. Oxford: Clarendon, 1999.

Shapin, Steven, and Simon Schaffer. *Leviathan and the Air-Pump*. Princeton, N.J.: Princeton University Press, 1985.

Sinclair, Isaak von. "Philosophische Raisonnements." In *Isaak von Sinclair zwischen Fichte, Hölderlin und Hegel: Ein Beitrag zur Entstehungsgeschichte der idealistischen Philosophie*, edited by Hannelore Hegel, 243–83. Frankfurt am Main: Klostermann, 1980.

Sloterdijk, Peter. *Du mußt dein Leben ändern*. Frankfurt am Main: Suhrkamp, 2008.

Solms, Friedrich. *Disciplina Aesthetica*. Stuttgart: Klett, 1990.

Stemme, Fritz. "Die Säkularisation des Pietismus zur Erfahrungsseelenkunde." *Zeitschrift für deutsche Philologie* 72 (1953): 144–58.

Strohschneider-Kohrs. *Die romantische Ironie in Theorie und Gestaltung*. Tübingen: Niemeyer, 1977.

Sulzer, Johann Georg. *Allgemeine Theorie der schönen Künste in einzeln, nach alphabetischer Ordnung der Kunstworter aufeinanderfolgenden, Artikeln abgehandelt*. 5 vols. Hildesheim: G. Olms, 1994.

———. *Vorübungen zur Erweckung der Aufmerksamkeit und des Nachdenkens*. Vol. 3. St. Petersburg: Kayserliche Akademie der Wissenschaften, 1814.

Szondi, Peter. *Einführung in die literarische Hermeneutik*. Frankfurt am Main: Suhrkamp, 1975.

Thums, Barbara. *Aufmerksamkeit: Wahrnehmung und Selbstbegründung von Brockes bis Nietzsche*. Munich: Fink, 2008.

Trapp, E. "Erklärung des pädagogischen Totalitarismus." In *Schwarze Pädagogik: Quellen zur Naturgeschichte der bürgerlichen Erziehung*, edited by Katharina Rutschky, 150–58. Berlin: Ullstein, 1977.

Uerlings, Herbert. "Einbildungskraft und Poesie bei Novalis." In *Novalis: Poesie und Poetik*, edited by Herbert Uerlings, 21–62. Tübingen: Niemeyer, 2004.

———. *Friedrich von Hardenberg, genannt Novalis*. Stuttgart: Metzler, 1991.

Unzer, Johanna Charlotte. *Versuch in Scherzgedichten*. Halle: Carl Hermann Hemmerde, 1753.

Velkley, Richard. "The Tension in the Beautiful: On Culture and Civilization in Rousseau and German Philosophy." In *The Legacy of Rousseau*, edited by Clifford Orwin and Nathan Tarcov, 65–86. Chicago: University of Chicago Press, 1997.

Vogl, Joseph. *Über das Zaudern*. Zürich: Diaphanes, 2007.

Weber, Max. *Die protestantische Ethik und der "Geist" des Kapitalismus*. Tübingen: J. C. B. Mohr, 1905.

Weisberger, Jean. *Les masques fragiles*. Lausanne: L'Age d'Homme, 1991.

Weisse, C. F. "Das Tagebuch als Erziehungsmittel." In *Schwarze Pädagogik: Quellen zur Naturgeschichte der bürgerlichen Erziehung*, edited by Katharina Rutschky, 185–88. Berlin: Ullstein, 1977.

Wellbery, David E. *Lessing's Laocoon: Semiotics and Aesthetics in the Age of Reason*. Cambridge, Eng.: Cambridge University Press, 1984.

———. *The Specular Moment: Goethe's Early Lyric and the Beginnings of Romanticism*. Stanford, Calif.: Stanford University Press, 1996.

Wellek, René. *A History of Modern Criticism 1750–1950: The Romantic Age*. Vol. 2. Cambridge, Eng.: Cambridge University Press, 1981.

Wellmon, Chad. *Becoming Human: Romantic Anthropology and the Embodiment of Freedom*. University Park: Pennsylvania State University Press, 2011.

Willamov, Johann Gottlieb. *Sämmtliche poetische Schriften.* Vol. 2. Vienna: Schraemel, 1794.

Wilson, Daniel W. "But Is It Gay? Kissing, Friendship, and 'Pre-Homosexual' Discourses in Eighteenth-Century Germany." *Modern Language Review* 103, no. 3 (2008): 767–83.

Winckelmann, Johann Joachim. "Von der Grazie in Werken der Kunst." In *Kleine Schriften, Vorreden, Entwürfe*, edited by Walther Rehm, 157–62. 2nd ed. Berlin: de Gruyter, 2002.

Wittgenstein, Ludwig. *Tractatus Logico-Philosophicus.* Translated by C. K. Ogden. New York: Barnes & Noble, 1992.

Wolfram von Eschenbach. *Parzival.* Edited by Karl Lachmann. 6th ed. Berlin: de Gruyter, 1998.

Zanucchi, Mario. *Novalis—Poesie und Geschichtlichkeit.* Paderborn: Schöningh, 2006.

Zelle, Carsten. "Sinnlichkeit und Therapie: Zur Gleichursprünglichkeit von Ästhetik und Anthropologie um 1750." In *Vernünftige Ärzte: Hallesche Psychomediziner und die Anfänge der Anthropologie in der deutschsprachigen Frühaufklärung*, edited by Carsten Zelle, 5–24. Tübingen: de Gruyter, 2001.

INDEX